BY STUDY AND
ALSO BY FAITH
VOLUME 2

Hugh W. Nibley
(Photograph courtesy of Mark A. Philbrick.)

Essays in Honor of Hugh W. Nibley
on the Occasion of His Eightieth Birthday
27 March 1990

BY STUDY AND
ALSO BY FAITH
VOLUME 2

Edited by
John M. Lundquist
Stephen D. Ricks

Deseret Book Company
Salt Lake City, Utah
and
Foundation for Ancient Research and Mormon Studies
Provo, Utah

Library of Congress Cataloging-in-Publication Data

By study and also by faith : essays in honor of Hugh W. Nibley on the
    occasion of his eightieth birthday, 27 March 1990 / edited by John
    M. Lundquist and Stephen D. Ricks.
        p.   cm.
    Includes bibliographical references.
    ISBN 0-87579-340-1
    1. Book of Mormon—Criticism, interpretation, etc.   2. Bible—
Criticism, interpretation, etc.   3. Kingdom of God—History of
doctrines.   4. Church history—Primitive and early church, ca.
30–600.   5. Mormon Church.   6. Church of Jesus Christ of Latter-day
Saints.   7. Nibley, Hugh, 1910–   . I. Nibley, Hugh, 1910–   .
II. Lundquist, John M.   III. Ricks, Stephen D.
BX8627.B9   1990
291—dc20   89-77960
                                                                   CIP

Printed in the United States of America

10   9   8   7   6   5   4   3   2   1

Contents

Modern Themes: Religion, Literature, and Society

1

Religious Validity:
The Sacrament Covenant
in Third Nephi

Richard Lloyd Anderson
Brigham Young University, Provo, Utah

I have just finished another reading of the Book of Mormon, and what a wonderful rejuvenation this has been as vistas of doctrine open up. The spirit is a complex thing. It comes as it will, as Jesus said to Nicodemus (John 3:8). Sometimes you feel a burning and a warmth, and sometimes you feel a peace and clarity of thought. The latter is my experience in reading the Book of Mormon this time. In the first reading I felt the warmth intensely. I can remember my impressions of specific chapters—for instance, Alma 42, where I could not put the book down for the intensity of the feeling of its truth.

Years later I look back on a lifetime of historical study and writing. I now have experience with how history was written in many different periods. History is a record of both spectacular and commonplace events. So an authentic historical document may be dull, and the Book of Mormon has places like that. Having analyzed methods of ancient historians, I recognize the accuracy of the steps described by Nephi, Mormon, and Moroni in putting their documents together. Without any question, the Book of Mormon is a historically sophisticated book. A young person like Joseph Smith did not write it. When you add the spiritual clarity of the doctrine to that archival framework, the validity of the Book of Mormon is to me unquestion-

able. Full proof of the depth of the Book of Mormon and
the Pearl of Great Price is that these books have held the
attention of Hugh Nibley for a lifetime, with rich historical
yields throughout five decades of intense scholarship. He
is personally unsurpassed at any university in range of
reading, languages mastered and utilized, facts retained,
day and night hours given to his field, and spontaneous
honesty.[1]

My topic of religious validity includes correctness of
doctrine and also spiritual values in applying it. Because
of the statement of Joseph Smith stressed by our current
Prophet, we are aware of the correctness of the Book of
Mormon.[2] Surprisingly, that book does not contain the full
range of teachings revealed in the Doctrine and Covenants.
However, the Book of Mormon is a guidebook for our age
because it collects foundational doctrines, and these are
bound together in the central practice of partaking of the
sacrament. As will be seen, Joseph Smith singled out "precepts" or teachings in his "closer to God" statement about
the Book of Mormon. And the concept of covenant is one
of the essential doctrines of salvation. Indeed, the Book of
Mormon makes the change of "many covenants" a sure
mark of Christian apostasy (1 Nephi 13:26). The result of
this study should be a far broader understanding of Nephi's prophecy and of how completely it is justified by
ancient and recent history of worship.

"Covenant" in the Bible and the Book of Mormon

Joseph Smith's well-known evaluation of the Book of
Mormon will lead us to personal covenants as the heart of
the religious message of the Book of Mormon. Yet the
original source of the Prophet's tribute to the Nephite scripture is little known. One reads the following in his official
history under the date of November 28, 1841: "I told the
brethren that the Book of Mormon was the most correct

of any book on earth, and the keystone of our religion, and a man would get nearer to God by abiding by its precepts, than by any other book."[3] But these words to the Twelve do not really come from the Prophet's own journal. Like the Nauvoo Temple, the Prophet's history was planned by him but was completed according to his format after his death. His clerks assigned to draft the history felt authorized to impose first-person style on appropriate documents after the martyrdom took place. When Joseph Smith died, the history had been basically compiled through the Missouri period. Wilford Woodruff, who recorded so much of Joseph Smith's public and private discourse, wrote down the Prophet's "most correct" comment. In the Woodruff journal of the above date, he outlines the Prophet's visit with the Twelve, and adds: "Joseph said the Book of Mormon was the most correct of any book on earth and the keystone of our religion. And a man would get nearer to God by abiding by its precepts than any other book." So the quotation in the official history is exact, with the addition of one clarifying preposition, though shifted to the first person to reproduce as nearly as possible Joseph Smith's original words.

Will the reader get "nearer to God" in every Book of Mormon chapter? About half of the Book of Mormon is political and military history. As in the Old Testament or classical chronicles, the reader is often shocked by bloodshed, one of the unfortunate realities in records of mankind. Another segment of the Book of Mormon consists of occasional long quotations from Old World prophets, about ten percent. But the remainder of this book—about forty percent—contains the teachings of New World prophets. Obviously these are the sections of the Book of Mormon that Joseph Smith referred to in saying that we would get "nearer to God by abiding its *precepts*."[4]

There are tighter circles of significance in the Book of Mormon. Within the "teachings" category of this record, main topics and terms appear. The dominating subject here is Jesus Christ. Reviewing the Book of Mormon after years of New Testament teaching, I am struck with the difference in audience on each side of the world. Christ often had to be subtle in teaching the Jews and used carefully wrought parables in his earlier ministry. Yet how plain he could be with the Nephites, a people educated by their own mighty exodus tradition. Scholars' vested interests were a huge barrier when the Savior sought to cut through Jewish ceremonialism and stand as a Messiah without earthly credentials. But his very direct American message is providentially preserved to correct our own false sophistication in the latter days. Here is a simple book, for simple and faithful people, then and now.

Within the Book of Mormon doctrinal circle, there is the tighter circle of teachings about Christ and from Christ. And within this is a precious core of what the Master expects of his disciples—his gospel as he very carefully outlined it in 3 Nephi 11 and 3 Nephi 27. A central principle of gospel relationships is "covenant," a main term of God's revelation on both hemispheres. That word appears in the Old Testament around 250 times, and scholarly literature on the subject is seemingly endless because of the importance of "covenant" in all of God's dealings with Israel.[5] So it is a test of religious authenticity that "covenant" is woven into the Book of Mormon with patterns remarkably parallel to the Bible.

The word "covenant" appears in the Book of Mormon about a hundred times, so it is as historically prominent there as it is in the Bible. Both books have oaths and covenants made between private parties. Indeed, the human agreements of the Old Testament are extremely useful in assessing the kind of covenant God made with Israel's patriarchs. They made the same type of covenant with God that they made in private situations. There were obligations and conditions on both sides. In pre-Christian sections of the Bible and Book of Mormon, the most frequent use of "covenant" is the promise that God will honor the house of Israel, on the condition that Israel will faithfully serve God. Despite many theological assertions to the contrary, God's consistent covenant relationship with Israel is that of a two-party covenant.

The English derivation of *covenant* is literally a "coming together," a contract involving mutual obligations. Various Christian theologies struggle with applying such a concept to God. If he is the all-powerful sovereign, can his plans fail because mankind fails? If he is all-loving, does he not distribute his blessings without any condition? Controversial terms are not far below the surface: predestination, unconditional election, salvation by grace alone. Here we cannot directly discuss these issues, though they are doctrinally related to God's covenant. Protestant explanations tend to emphasize a one-sided covenant—the sovereign giver and the unworthy receiver. But in only a very general sense do God's promises appear without reciprocal obligations. Of course, Jesus acknowledged that the Father showers sun and rain "on the just and on the unjust" (Matthew 5:45). Ancient and modern scriptures also teach the unconditional and universal gift of the resurrection, while at the same time indicating qualitative distinctions, for there is a higher "resurrection of life" (John 5:29), and there is the "first resurrection" of the faithful before all the rest are called up (Revelation 20:5). God reserves his greatest blessings not for those professing, but for those obeying (Matthew 7:21-23).

But much Christian literature rejects such personal responsibility by treating Moses' revelations as a covenant of works and the New Testament as a covenant of grace. However, Paul argued that the Gentiles had strict obligations of faithfulness to maintain a covenant relationship with God (Romans 11:17-21). That Apostle characteristically quoted Jeremiah's prophecy. Because Israel broke the covenant of Exodus (Jeremiah 31:32), God would give a "new covenant" (Jeremiah 31:31). Israel would be forgiven, and Israel would truly "know the Lord" (Jeremiah 31:34). Although Jesus blessed bread and wine as symbols of newness, there is more than a free promise of grace as the "new covenant." Jeremiah really promised no change in a reciprocal relationship, but saw the day when Israel would live up to its obligations. They would accept "my law" in their hearts (Jeremiah 31:33), actually meaning that the covenant relationship would not change, but that Israel would finally keep God's requirements. And this conditional covenant is as religiously central in the New Testament as it is in the Old. "Covenant" appears about thirty times in the New Testament. The word summarizes God's relationship with the Church, but "covenant" also is prominent in connection with the most frequent early Christian public ordinance, the sacrament of the Lord's Supper. Although there are other sacraments, or sacred ceremonies, Mormons follow a Christian trend to use "sacrament" alone to refer to receiving the symbols of Christ's body and blood. And "sacrament" here will refer to that particular ceremony.

The New Testament Sacrament Covenant

Christ clearly established the sacrament. Three of the four Gospels plus Paul's letter, 1 Corinthians, contain concise reports. First Corinthians preceded the Gospels. Its date is about A.D. 57, some twenty-five years after the upper room. Paul repeats what he has reliably learned, introducing the account with these words: "For I have received *of the Lord* that which also I delivered unto you" (1 Corinthians 11:23, emphasis added). Not claiming a vision, Paul has reports of what came from the Lord.[6] Luke also says that his own information is from "eyewitnesses" (Luke 1:1-4). And Matthew and Mark are similarly based.[7] Each of these four accounts has individuality, showing that none simply copied another. Yet all agree on the basics. Significantly, each quotes Jesus as saying that the cup represents "the new testament."

Today "testament" suggests "a solemn declaration" or "a formal witness." However, the technical meaning of Christ's "new testament" is "new covenant." In Acts and in Paul's epistles, Old Testament verses about the Hebrew "covenant" (bərît) are translated by the Greek diathēkē, which in secular Greek denoted a formal will, a legal bequest. Thus the Gospels, Acts, and epistles are reapplying the Old Testament "covenant," with its strong background of reciprocal promises. Yet many Protestant commentators discuss the Greek "will" in the abstract, stating that New Testament writers considered the new covenant as God's unilateral gift. But the Greek diathēkē developed an expanded biblical usage, for it was consistently used to translate "covenant" in the Septuagint version long before Christ. So New Testament authors definitely use an Old Testament covenant concept, with its regular contexts of mutuality. Moreover, we shall see that Christ spoke of strict conditions on which the new covenant is offered.

Evidence from the Gospels suggests that Jesus privately spoke Aramaic, a language closely related to Hebrew. Thus, as Jesus held up the cup, he spoke the word "covenant," calling up ancient images of continuity in the minds of the Apostles. Early Christian literature suggests no change in the idea of covenant — newness consisted in the change of the sacrifice that put the covenant into effect. In other words, the two-party promises between God and his people did not change. But the bloody sacrifices of Abraham and of Moses were modified — they prefigured the ultimate sacrifice of the Son of God. Here we are summarizing the argument of the last part of Paul's letter to the Hebrews, where half of the New Testament usages of the Greek word for "covenant" appear. The Apostle there speaks of a "better testament" (Hebrews 7:22) or a "better covenant" (Hebrews 8:6) because Jesus is superior to all former sacrifices.

This continuity is shown in the opening scenes of each Gospel in the New Testament, according to which John the Baptist comes to renew the relationship of God with individuals who would meet God's conditions. In the prophetic context this is nothing less than the renewal of the covenant, as John's father said in blessing his son. John was sent to announce the Messiah's mission, which was to reinstate God's compact with the patriarchs: "To perform the mercy promised to our fathers, and to remember his holy covenant; The oath which he sware to our father Abraham, That he would grant unto us, that we . . . might serve him without fear, In holiness and righteousness before him, all the days of our life" (Luke 1:72-75). John's father saw "holiness and righteousness" as Israel's responsibility under the covenant, and his son single-mindedly preached that Israel must repent individually to have a relationship with God restored.

Christ reapplied the language of the Mosaic covenant in instituting the sacrament, a reality noted by most Bible commentaries on the Gospels. At the beginning of Exodus, Moses was called to remember the covenant of Abraham and lead Israel out of bondage. At Sinai, Jehovah's law was given only after Israel had promised to meet prerequisites. They would be "a peculiar treasure unto me above all people," with a major condition: "if ye will obey my voice indeed, and keep my covenant" (Exodus 19:5). Here are mutual promises, and it is irrelevant that this is not an agreement between equals. Of course God's majesty and glory are on one side, and Israel's fallible abilities on the other. Nevertheless, the covenant is contingent. Eternal blessings will only come as the children of Abraham commit themselves to obedience and follow the commitment.

God gave the core Ten Commandments accompanied

by considerable expansion of their meaning. Soon after this, the covenant was reiterated and consummated after another agreement of the people. Moses "told the people all the words of the Lord, and all the judgments," and they unanimously agreed to follow them (Exodus 24:3). Moses then wrote these laws, clarifying what was required: "And he took the book of the covenant and read in the audience of the people. And they said, All that the Lord hath said will we do, and be obedient. And Moses took the blood, and sprinkled it on the people, and said, Behold the blood of the covenant, which the Lord hath made with you concerning all these words" (Exodus 24:7-8).

These events were the Jewish constitution. And in giving the sacrament, Jesus quoted or closely paraphrased Moses' words in renewing the ancient covenant. Although this is obscured in the King James translation of "testament," the Savior surely did not use Greek then. Thus modern translations are correct in having Jesus offer the cup as a sign of the "new covenant." His words come in two closely related forms. The early converts — Paul and Luke — use the same phrase of offering the cup: "the new covenant in my blood" (Luke 22:20; 1 Corinthians 11:25). Matthew and Mark, Gospels based on apostolic testimony, use Moses' words adapted by Jesus in offering the cup: "This is my blood of the new covenant" (Matthew 26:28; Mark 14:24).[8]

Jesus' sacramental words are too often quoted in a vacuum. But here he had an audience skilled in scripture. The Lord was never outclassed in discussion with trained priests because he was steeped in Jewish tradition. So were the Apostles. If Jesus presented a form of covenant that departed from the divine format to Moses, he would not have used the words of Exodus. Repeating Moses meant repeating or renewing the covenant, with its mutuality. Full grace was offered to ancient Israel conditionally. In reiterating the ancient words, Jesus asserted that much was expected to receive his grace. Jesus did not revoke the ancient covenant—he restored it.

Artificial walls are built by the existence of four different Gospels. Scholars intensify the problem by labeling John theological and not historical, as if one reporting Jesus could not be both. Indeed, Matthew, Mark, and Luke similarly present the public ministry, whereas John emphasizes intimate conversations among Christ and the Twelve. It came down to church historian Eusebius that John wrote last, that he looked over the other Gospels with approval but realized that a fuller story could be told. Thus John really wrote an appendix to the other Gospels.[9] This fits our records, because John's letters are preoccupied with what Jesus taught "from the beginning," a phrase that introduces many major references to the Last Supper discourse. Thus we know that John paid special attention to Jesus' teachings during and after the Christian sacrament. With such concern, he obviously took special care to preserve these teachings. To have the full picture of Christ's first sacrament, one must take the words of its establishment from the Synoptic Gospels and 1 Corinthians, adding the beginning of the Last Supper discourse, which appears only in John.

John's story of the Last Supper blends well with those of Matthew and Mark, but Luke's account does not as easily fit. Apparently he first surveys the meal, then portrays the sacrament as the main event of the Last Supper, and finally drops back to mention the accusation of Judas. This seems clear because the consecrated cup is described as "the cup after supper" (Luke 22:20). In any event, Matthew and Mark agree that Jesus accused Judas during the meal and before the sacrament. This is significant because John says that the betrayer left while others ate, which brings us nearly to the end of John 13. Next John reports four short segments of teaching by Jesus toward the end of the meal itself: the prophecy that Jesus will now be taken and his disciples left (John 13:33-34); Peter's offer to die to prevent Christ's death (John 13:36-38); Christ's assurance that by leaving he will prepare for the coming of the Twelve into the Father's kingdom; and a question and answer about the Father (John 14:1-12). After this point Jesus speaks without interruption. The above topics would naturally arise from Jesus' introduction of the sacrament as the symbol of his atoning death.

Indeed, John's words of leaving and reuniting closely fit Matthew's report of Jesus' words immediately after distributing the bread and wine—that he would not drink again with them until all would reunite "in my Father's kingdom" (Matthew 26:29). This correlates with John's "my Father's house" (John 14:2). So a comparison of the two Gospels shows that the first part of the Last Supper discourse came right after blessing the bread and wine. Jesus' continuous comments begin in the middle of John 14, but John soon interrupts the flow of Christ's message before twenty verses have been given: "Arise, let us go hence" (John 14:31). While more of Jesus' farewell instructions follow, John sharply terminates the words of the upper room. The Apostle clearly intended the second half of chapter 14 to be Jesus' explanations right after distributing the bread and cup.

What insight do Christ's retrospective comments give on the sacrament? In the name of the Father, Jesus makes specific promises. On earth his followers will have the special relationship that insures answers to their deepest prayers (John 14:13-14). On earth they will have the peace and instruction of the Holy Ghost (John 14:16-17, 26-27). On earth they might have visions of the Father and Son, and their presence in the hereafter (John 14:19-23). Is all this given by totally unmerited grace? To the contrary, God required the identical condition of the covenant at Sinai: "All that the Lord hath said will we do, and be obedient" (Exodus 24:7). That same commitment was required by the

Lord to validate the sacrament. "If ye love me, keep my commandments" (John 14:15); "He that hath my commandments, and keepeth them, he it is that loveth me" (John 14:21); "If a man love me, he will keep my words" (John 14:23). Jesus not only paralleled Moses' words in speaking of the "blood of the new covenant" — he required the same obedience of the ancient covenant. Jesus gave the sacrament and then outlined its obligations and promises. Because Jesus gave the bread and cup with mutual commitments, the sacrament itself is a covenant.

Changing the Baptismal Covenant

The Book of Mormon provides a clearer picture of Christ, and the sacrament covenant is more completely explained there as well. President Benson reminds us that this American record was compiled for future readers — and for the conversion of unbelievers.[10] On the other hand, except for the Gospels, the New Testament is the product of believers speaking to believers. The Book of Mormon records Hebraic treaty-covenants, but its overarching covenant is that of God with his people, tenuous because of the constant threat that these transplanted Israelites will forget their heritage and the miracles of their New World exodus. As John the Baptist reminded Judah, a national relationship can continue only to the extent of valid individual relationships with God — these add up to the general divine covenant. The Book of Mormon brings us closer to God because no scripture more specifically ties the Christian ordinances of baptism and the sacrament to the covenant concept. No book does more to bring the national covenant down to individual responsibility.

The sacrament renews the baptismal covenant in the Book of Mormon. American prophets taught the religious necessity of baptism and the clear doctrinal purposes for it. The most striking teaching is that baptism was required even for the Savior. The visionary Nephi saw the future mission of Jesus, including Christ's baptism (1 Nephi 11:27). Speaking by inspiration afterward, Nephi explained the Savior's insistence on baptism at John's hands: "For thus it becometh us to fulfil all righteousness" (Matthew 3:15). Since Nephi had a vision of this baptism, he evidently heard these words. He explains that Jesus' immersion was an act that "witnesseth unto the Father that he would be obedient unto him in keeping his commandments" (2 Nephi 31:7). Here Nephi's language indicates more than the humility required to keep the commandment of baptism. He heard Christ's voice declaring immersion as a covenant for believers, who by that act "witnessed unto the Father that ye are willing to keep my commandments" (2 Nephi 31:14). As quoted above, Nephi applies similar phraseology to Christ's immersion, really teaching that the Savior set the example by baptism as a promise of future virtue.

Thus Nephi presents a complete parallelism between the baptisms of Christ and of the believer. In this sermon, Christ was immersed to prove his obedience through baptism, but also as a pledge of future loyalty "that he would be obedient." The believer's baptism also indicates "that ye are willing to keep my commandments." "To be willing" is mainly future: it is the language of personal covenant in Book of Mormon religious contexts. Indeed, Nephi's sermon stresses the lifetime commitment to righteousness one makes through baptism (2 Nephi 31:15-21). Nephi's overall point is that the believer should follow Christ both in baptism and also in keeping the personal promises made then. Immersion is a means of forgiveness, but covenant baptism is also preventive medicine. It is a solemn promise not to sin—a promise even shared by Christ. He entered that baptismal covenant and lived up to it perfectly, so Nephi finally calls on everyone baptized to "endure to the end, in following the example of the Son of the living God" (2 Nephi 31:16).

In the Book of Mormon, the baptismal contract is best

outlined when Alma reestablished the Church near the wilderness waters. He explained baptism as a "testimony that ye have entered into a covenant to serve him" throughout life (Mosiah 18:13). These inspired doctrines were well known when Jesus later came to the New World. He gave baptismal messages at the beginning and end of his Nephite ministry. Christ taught the interrelationship of repentance and baptism; the formalism of immersion without a subsequent change of life is empty in the Lord's sight. In summarizing his gospel, he identified baptism as a conditional promise of forgiveness: "whoso repenteth and is baptized in my name shall be filled; and if he endureth to the end, behold, him will I hold guiltless before my Father at that day when I shall stand to judge the world" (3 Nephi 27:16).

In the Book of Mormon purification by baptism always depends on righteousness. Does the New Testament support this doctrine? Each Gospel stresses Jesus' own baptism, and in each Gospel John the Baptist challenges his Jewish generation to obtain forgiveness of past sins through baptism and retain that forgiveness by changing their lives. John's baptism was for "remission of sins" (Mark 1:4), and the Apostles' baptism had the same purpose (Acts 2:38). Based on this baptismal foundation, apostolic sermons and letters urge believers to retain a relationship with God through righteous living. Thus the New Testament follows the covenant-righteousness patterns of the patriarchal, Mosaic, and prophetic dispensations. In the fullest letter of free grace, Paul emphasizes baptism as the burial of old sins, and the resurrection to a new moral life, which comes by the exercise of prayerful self-control (Romans 6:3-13). Sometime later the Apostle repeats the baptismal-burial metaphor (Colossians 2:12), and insists on the baptismal commitment to live specific moral standards (Colossians 3:1-10).

Thus Paul holds out full salvation to those who effect

moral reform through their faith and baptism, and he denies entrance into the kingdom to Christians who will not
conform to its laws (1 Corinthians 6:9-11). Many Protestant
scholars talk meaningfully of God's general covenant with
his people but lack full understanding of baptism and the
sacrament as specific promises to live the commandments.
Protestantism in practice supports baptism, but in theory
has difficulty explaining it. For instance, we are told that
God promises eternal life in the "covenant of grace," but
man's obligation is "faith in Jesus Christ as the only 'work'
required of the believer (John 6:29)."[11] By Book of Mormon
standards, such thinking is foggy. Peter did not invent
baptism for the "remission of sins" (Acts 2:38). This interpretation went back to Christ, for Peter taught it on the
day of Pentecost, a month after Jesus commanded "the
eleven disciples" to go to the world and baptize believers
(Matthew 28:16-20).

An infant cannot sin, nor know enough to promise not
to sin. Yet the major Christian churches—Protestant and
Catholic—divorce individual responsibility from baptism
in the practice of baptizing infants. Adults must be proxy
for infants who cannot personally take upon themselves
the name of Christ. This thinking is reflected in the traditional Church of England ritual. The baby is presented,
and the priest asks the sponsors: "Dost thou therefore, in
the name of this child, renounce the devil and all his works,
the vain pomp and glory of the world and the sinful desires
of the flesh, so that thou wilt not follow, nor be led by
them?" The answer is: "I renounce them all, and by God's
help will not endeavor to follow nor be led by them." The
priest asks again: "Having now, in the name of this child
made these promises, wilt thou also on thy part take heed
that this child learn the Creed, the Lord's Prayer, and the
Ten Commandments, and any other things which a Christian ought to know and believe to his soul's health?" Sponsors answer: "I will by God's help."[12]

Such a ceremony has religious value in committing the godparent or parent to teaching the child. Yet the sponsor, not the child, makes the baptismal covenant. This is not the Lord's way, for there is no example of infant baptism in the Bible, and the Book of Mormon prophets denounce such practice by revelation. Since baptism is a covenant, infant baptism usurps the agency of a child not yet ready to make the promise for himself. Thus it is Catholic and Protestant practice to bring the child to the church for instruction and confirmation when old enough to be accountable. In this case, the baptismal covenant is shifted to a later confirmation covenant. So the unauthorized change in one ordinance has forced an unauthorized change in the purpose of another.

Christ's Words and the Nephite Sacrament Prayer

The baptismal commitment is the companion covenant to the sacrament in the Book of Mormon. This is vivid in the Nephite manual of ordinances, found at the beginning of Moroni, the final book in the Book of Mormon. It compiles documents of Nephite practices authorized by the Lord. Here Moroni summarizes the baptismal covenant as taking upon them "the name of Christ, having a determination to serve him to the end" (Moroni 6:3). And the accompanying sacrament prayer carries the same phraseology of personally taking the name of Christ. The baptismal commitment of serving Christ to the end is paralleled in the sacrament promise to "always remember him." Those baptismal vows more closely follow the sacrament prayer over the bread, which will be studied here because the prayer over the cup is a compressed restatement. In summary, the Book of Mormon presents the overall covenant of God with his people, with individualized promises made in baptism, to be renewed in the sacrament.

The Nephite sacrament prayer incorporates the "words of institution" when Christ gave the sacrament in America.

Background chapters are the Savior's explanation of baptism in 3 Nephi 11, followed by his discourse on the sacrament in 3 Nephi 18, the climaxing event of his first appearance to them. Jesus clearly unfolded the meaning of the bread and wine that should be administered "unto all those who shall believe and be baptized in my name" (3 Nephi 18:5). New World disciples were to witness through the symbols of his body and blood that "ye do always remember me." But their thoughts were to rise to plans for righteous acts, for the mutual covenant relationship was valid only "if ye shall keep my commandments"; only then would they "have my Spirit to be with you" (3 Nephi 18:11-14).

All these commitments combine in the Nephite sacrament covenant, the prayer consecrating the bread. Although Moroni gives it some centuries later, he leaves no doubt as to its source: "and they administered it according to the commandments of Christ" (Moroni 4:1). This probably means that the Savior gave the prayer. Each of its promises follow Jesus' Nephite sacrament sermon. As Mormon finished his selection of Christ's teachings, he mentioned the fuller record "of the things which Jesus did truly teach unto the people" (3 Nephi 26:6-8). Indeed, his son Moroni shows a special interest in rounding out the record with additional sayings of the Savior (Mormon 9:22-25), so perhaps Moroni took the sacrament prayers from a fuller account of Christ's teachings. This method parallels the manner in which Christ's teachings were kept in the New Testament and earliest Christian literature. Core collections were later supplemented by additional sources and recollections. Here is another of the many stylistic and structural patterns where the Book of Mormon has the marks of an ancient history. As stated, each phrase of the Nephite sacrament prayer has an exact equivalent in Christ's words of institution in 3 Nephi 18. And Moroni insists that "the

manner," or form, of the prayer is "true," meaning specifically that it was authorized by Christ (Moroni 4:1).[13]

Since the Savior established the sacrament on both
hemispheres, the American consecration prayer can be
tested by the Gospels. The above discussion has correlated
the covenant doctrine, but there are also specific parallels
in the Nephite pledges. Comparison suffers because the
New Testament—and early Christian literature—is more
fragmentary than the Book of Mormon. As we have seen,
combining John with the three earlier Gospels enriches the
record. To do this requires synthesis—blending corresponding Gospel details. Most New Testament scholars
are untrained in this approach. Scholarly literature favors
a dissecting method that sorts out and separates. But one
can see the need of synthesis by reading newspapers and
news magazines. In major stories, no single reporter will
have the whole, but all responsible journalists will have
pieces that finally combine well enough to re-create the
original event. Such an analogy is essential in handling the
first Christian literature, for the earliest stratum contains
apostolic letters responding to specific problems, and the
second stratum is the historical literature (the Gospels and
Acts) outlining the general story of Christ and the rise of
the Church. Nothing like Moroni's manual of ordinances
has survived in the New Testament itself.

Nevertheless, the biblical sources intricately supplement each other for Christ's institution of the sacrament.
In a like manner, in Mormon journal work I regularly find
that several accounts of the same event agree on the basics,
but each recorder selects differing details. I have come to
recognize general agreement plus unique individual insights as sure marks of validity of independent accounts.
The same is true with the four primary accounts of Christ's
words about bread and wine, in the Synoptic Gospels and
in Paul's review in 1 Corinthians 11. As noted by the *Catholic Encyclopedia*, "Their fundamental harmony amid dif-

ference of detail is a precious sign that they have faithfully
transmitted the thought of Jesus in His institution of the
Eucharist."[14] Though fragmentary, these accounts and
John's support the phrases of the Nephite consecration
prayer on the bread: "That they may eat in remembrance
of the body of thy Son, and witness unto thee, O God,
the Eternal Father, that they are willing to take upon
them the name of thy Son, and always remember him,
and keep his commandments which he hath given them,
that they may always have his Spirit to be with them"
(Moroni 4:3).

Remembering Christ is the first purpose of the Nephite
prayer and is also a characteristic of the biblical accounts
of Luke and Paul, both of which give slightly fuller detail
than Matthew and Mark. To repeat, Paul's first Corinthian
letter was written before the Gospels, and specifically bases
the information on what the first Christians had told him
(1 Corinthians 11:23). Indeed, the letter suggests its
sources. Paul mentions the Jerusalem Apostles and gives
their personal testimonies of the resurrection as coming
down to him (1 Corinthians 15:3-7). Since he knew the
detailed history of the resurrection from them, his information on the Last Supper no doubt came from them
also.

The American prayer follows "remembrance" by a recommitment "that they are willing to take upon them the
name of thy Son." That fundamental acceptance is made
through baptism, whether in the Bible or Book of Mormon.
For instance, Paul talks of more than verbal confession:
"For as many of you as have been baptized into Christ
have put on Christ" (Galatians 3:27). In fact, the most
powerful insight into "putting on Christ" was given to the
faithful Eleven immediately after Christ handed them the
bread and cup. As discussed earlier, John supplemented
the Synoptic Gospels, beginning Jesus' postsacrament discourse in the middle of chapter 14. The theme there is

intimacy with Jesus Christ. Theologians can mysticize the remarks, but Jesus' words fit the concepts of fellowship or communion. Right after ingesting the symbols of Christ's person, Christ explained that relationship. As Christ is in the Father, so are "ye in me, and I in you" (John 14:20). Neither here nor in the subsequent prayer of John 17 is the individuality of any believer compromised. As in John 6, the act of eating signified total acceptance of the Lord. Likewise, the Nephite prayer underlines the meaning of the act of eating—as the elements are within the believer's body, the name of the Lord is upon and within the believer's soul.[15]

In the American consecration prayer, "remembering" and taking "the name" are followed by commitment to action. Imitating Christ follows meditating on him. This purpose is hardly seen in scholarly commentary, which focuses on Christ's "words of institution" preceding the bread and wine. But as discussed above, John gives the phrase "keep my commandments" (John 14:15) immediately following the bread and wine. Surprisingly, that is the exact sequence of the American ministry. After eating and drinking, Nephite Christians were told by the Savior that their act was a commitment "that ye are willing to do that which I have commanded you" (3 Nephi 18:10). In both situations the Savior commented on the meaning of their act as they digested the elements. And there is another intricate parallel. John, present at the Last Supper, gives the challenge to love and keep the commandments just before the promise of the Holy Spirit. Commitment to "keep my commandments" (John 14:15) is immediately followed by the assurance of the Comforter, "that he may abide with you for ever" (John 14:16). In the Nephite sacrament prayer the sequence is the same: revered remembrance, commandment keeping, with the reward "that they may always have his Spirit" (Moroni 4:3; cf. 3 Nephi 18:10-11).

These Bible-Book of Mormon correlations are more impressive because they are not superficially obvious. They come with the slight opacity that one would expect in moving through language and culture barriers. Close verbal parallels might suggest surface copying, but profound conceptual parallels show that Jesus' thinking is found in every element of the Book of Mormon sacrament prayer. Each petition is mirrored in Jesus' first instructions in the upper room. In the American prayer of consecration, we indeed hear Christ's voice.

The Early Christian Sacrament Covenant

Does the Book of Mormon sacrament prayer fit the ceremony of the first generations of Mediterranean Christians? The answer is impressive, even though first-century worship is thinly documented. Yet the regularity of the sacrament appears in the first postapostolic sources. Early in the second century a guard escorted the bishop of Antioch across Asia Minor to martyrdom in Rome. Midway in this journey, Ignatius wrote seven letters exposing the strong apostate sects. Four letters mention the bread or wine of the sacrament, showing that it was a basic part of meetings. Since the Church was threatened by Christian seceders, Ignatius emphasized that true administration of the sacrament required authority: "Let that be considered a valid Eucharist which is celebrated by the bishop, or by one whom he appoints."[16] With other contemporaries, Ignatius uses "sacrifice" and "altar" in connection with the sacrament, but these are Mosaic metaphors rather than New Testament doctrines. Ignatius calls the broken bread "the medicine of immortality," a phrase alluding to eternal life with God, as used by Jesus in his bread of life sermon that foreshadowed the sacrament (John 6:48-51).[17] Thus the sacrament is associated with eternal salvation; this doctrine fits the thrust of every letter from this martyr bishop — honor Christ's name by living his teachings. In these letters, that result comes through faithfulness to scripture, to true church and priesthood, to baptism and the sacrament.

Through Paul's correction of the Corinthians, we can actually part the curtain on a first-century "sacrament meeting." Their selfish feasting merged with the sacred symbols and was offensive to the Apostle. We have already seen that he reminded these Greco-Romans of Jesus' words inaugurating the first sacrament. Then Paul concisely discussed what the Christian ceremony should accomplish (1 Corinthians 11:26-32). What did the Apostle mean by warning careless Corinthians not to eat and drink "unworthily"? Many commentators are mechanical, suggesting that Paul only commented on the abuse of feasting before the sacred memorial. But his repeated phraseology is that of inner resolve.

In immediate connection with eating and drinking, Paul warns: "let a man examine himself." Paul adds that the thoughtless will eat, "not *discerning* the Lord's body." I emphasize *"discerning"* because the same verb (*diakrinō*) soon introduces the culminating purpose of the sacrament: "For if *we would judge* ourselves, we should not be judged." English translations scarcely disclose that the two italicized words are the same. Paul uses a verb of intense evaluation. He elsewhere applies the noun form to the "discerning of spirits" (1 Corinthians 12:10) or discerning of "good and evil" (Hebrews 5:14). In 1 Corinthians 11, Paul first asserts that the unworthy do not *discern* the Lord's body, and then he repeats the verb to indicate that the faithful should *discern* themselves. Thus these are parallel processes that occur while taking the sacred symbols — as one thinks on the Lord, he evaluates himself in relation to the Lord. For this personal response to Christ, Paul uses three matching ideas: eating worthily, self-examination, and self-discernment. True, Paul is condemning a particular practice of gluttony, but the correction goes beyond narrow rebuke to explain and teach why Christians took the bread and wine.

Similarly, in 1 Corinthians 15, Paul starts with narrow errors concerning the resurrection and then broadens his discussion to encompass the entire range of that doctrine. And in 1 Corinthians 11, Paul corrects the malpractice and then outlines the true practice. In Paul's personal preaching, "he reasoned about righteousness, self-control, and the judgment to come" (Acts 24:25, New King James Version). This is precisely his logic at the end of the Greek sacrament correction: "For if we would judge ourselves, we should not be judged. But when we are judged, we are chastened of the Lord, that we should not be condemned with the world" (1 Corinthians 11:31-32). Thus the criticism closes by indicating that self-judgment in the sacrament prepares the Christian for the final judgment. The worldly Corinthians would be condemned with the world unless true repentance would come through remembering Christ in the sacrament. So Paul presents a double purpose—remembrance and resolve to live a righteous life.

With slight subtlety, Paul gave the same perspective in the previous chapter. Most visible in 1 Corinthians 10 is the inconsistency of social eating in pagan temples, and the most obvious sacrament teaching is that one cannot "be partakers of the Lord's table, and of the table of devils" (1 Corinthians 10:21). But again, many commentators see only the narrow correction and miss the larger scope of the sacrament that Paul stressed. This oversight comes mainly from underplaying the parallel that begins chapter 10. Paul's examples come from ancient Israel, but he is really warning volatile Greek converts. The Apostle was trained under Jewish scholars to use patterns and types. In this case Paul loosely compares Christian baptism to Israel's figurative immersion in the sea and under the cloud of God's presence in the Exodus (1 Corinthians 10:1-2).

Then Paul adds the symbolic "spiritual food" of the manna and the "spiritual drink" that Jehovah-Christ gave miraculously to "quench their thirst" (1 Corinthians 10:3-4; 1 Nephi 17:28-29). But the point is really what Christians commit to by taking the "cup" and the "bread" (1 Corinthians 10:16), and so Paul develops an intricate allegory, not only of Israel's general unfaithfulness, but of Israel's unfaithfulness after immersion and eating and drinking. Several recognize that this is simply Paul's parable of Christian ceremonies: "The point of these illustrations is clear. The reception of sacraments will not by itself save anyone. Paul emphasizes the fact that all of the Israelites had these benefits, yet *most of them* were destroyed. Despite their sacraments at the present time, the Corinthians may likewise be destroyed."[18]

When Paul names Israelite sins in the next seven verses, he is historically matching Corinthian sins. The idolatry of the Exodus is now eating at the idol's feast (cf. 1 Corinthians 8 and 10); the adultery of the Exodus is the immorality that Paul corrects (cf. 1 Corinthians 5 and 6); the murmuring against Moses is the criticism of the Apostle (cf. 1 Corinthians 4 and 9). As in Christ's "new covenant" at the Last Supper, we are again reminded of the relevance of the Old Testament to the Christian sacrament. The Jews of the Exodus had made a solemn covenant to obey and then rebelled through the above sins. Paul begins his warning with ancient types of baptism and the sacrament, showing clearly that Christian converts were obligated to avoid idolatry, immorality, and speaking against church leaders. Baptism and the sacrament had raised specific obligations of righteousness. Thus Paul treated these ordinances as Christian covenants.

A Roman governor confirmed this picture after investigating whether Christian assemblies were subversive. He reported to the Emperor concerning his province of Bithynia-Pontus, in the north of present Turkey. It bordered on the province of Asia, where John spent his final known days. It was approximately A.D. 110, and Pliny's letter to the Emperor Trajan is used here because the Apostle John was historically known just before this. That generation of Christian leaders had been in touch with the last Apostle. Pliny's long letter to Rome describes how pagan worship had fallen off, blaming the vigorous Christian movement. Rome was suspicious of private associations, and the governor had power to forbid assemblies — he could also interrogate by torture and order death.

Pliny was a capable administrator who was puzzled by the resolution of Christians who preferred martyrdom to denying their faith. Although persecution details are intensely interesting, Pliny's report on Christian meetings is significant here. He asked Trajan to rule on punishing good citizens who were technically disloyal to the state because they would not offer pagan sacrifice. Pliny found a highly moral people behind this rebellious conduct. Trajan answered that the law required a penalty, unless the accused renounced Christ's name. The correspondence shows an Emperor and governor who are troubled. Pliny had carefully questioned former Christians and learned of their meetings:

> They had met regularly before dawn on a fixed day to chant verses alternately among themselves in honor of Christ as if to a god, and also to bind themselves by oath, not for any criminal purpose, but to abstain from theft, robbery, and adultery, to commit no breach of trust and not to deny a deposit when called upon to restore it. After this ceremony it had been their custom to disperse and reassemble later to take food of an ordinary, harmless kind. But they had in fact given up this practice since my edict, issued on your instructions, which banned all political societies.[19]

From this source some envision prayer and reading in the morning, plus a later gathering to eat and partake of the sacrament. But that does not fit Pliny's description. The reassembly did not take sacred food, but "food of an ordinary, harmless kind." Paul's Corinthian corrections suggest that the sacrament should be separated from the fellowship meal. Pliny's Christians easily gave up eating together, though they would not have renounced core worship without a struggle. In their early meeting, an "oath" was taken to avoid all evil. No weekly Christian practice fits such language except the sacrament, and this was while they gave "honor to Christ." So the Book of Mormon is historically on target to say that Christ gave the sacrament as both remembrance and commitment to live his commandments. Some second-century evidence also supports this, such as Justin Martyr's profile of Christian worship. But other second-century documents, including the miscellaneous collection known as the Didache ("Teaching"), give a more generalized worship. This suggests a loss of the concise sacrament covenant soon after the disappearance of directing Apostles. Even so, the Didache collects Christian practices of the midsecond century, many of which have earlier roots, and John W. Welch has pointed out half a dozen striking parallels between this work and the Savior's American instructions in connection with the sacrament. This is all the more impressive because the Didache was not discovered until half a century after the publication of the Book of Mormon.[20]

About a decade before Pliny's investigation, the Apostle John wrote his letters, and his Gospel not long before that. All of John's writings were composed in Asia Minor a little before Ignatius wrote to the same area about similar difficulties.[21] The surviving Apostle addressed the problem of how Christians could be faithful in the midst of worldly evils and major Christian apostasy (1 John 2:18-19; 4:1-3). These issues are more obvious in John's letters, where the relevance of the Christian sacrament is suggested by upperroom teachings. The Apostle asks for loyalty to what was taught "from the beginning." And John repeatedly uses this phrase to underline two specific doctrines of Christ's Last Supper discourse. One is the command to love one another, given by Christ at the meal and afterward (1 John 3:11; 2 John 1:5). The other "beginning" doctrine is Jesus' postsacrament challenge to keep the commandments. John says it is really an "old commandment" after repeating Christ's challenge in the upper room (John 14:15): "And hereby we do know that we know him, if we keep his commandments" (1 John 2:3). John paraphrases other teachings of Christ given right after the sacrament, such as the mutual indwelling, making the same point: "And he that keepeth his commandments dwelleth in him, and he in him" (1 John 3:24). The key to understanding John's message is to realize that "from the beginning" is a Christian code for the Savior's teachings in connection with the first sacrament. In reality the Apostle is saying that Christians can only be true to Christ by honoring covenants of obedience made through the ordinance of baptism and the sacrament.[22]

The problems disclosed in John's letters already existed when John wrote his Gospel, no doubt in the same area and evidently but a few years before. His memory and probably his own records reached beyond half a century, when he had walked with the Lord. From his personal experiences John added teachings of Christ not yet recorded in any public Gospel. Since he could not write everything (John 21:25), he obviously chose what would help the Church in the war against evil and desertion. This new material included Jesus' Last Supper discourse and also Jesus' imagery of the bread and cup in the discourse after the feeding of the five thousand. In the case of the first sacrament, the three earlier Gospels had narrated the event but had not given Jesus' explanations afterward. John, on the other hand, did provide Jesus' teachings given both after the sacrament and after Jesus fed the multitude and returned to the Capernaum synagogue to challenge the Galilee audience to accept him fully.

In the synagogue the Lord used the vivid comparison of eating and drinking his flesh and blood. Jesus regularly communicated to the Jewish culture in their striking metaphors, witness his illustration of straining at a gnat and swallowing a camel (Matthew 23:24). Jews applied language of eating and drinking to digesting or accepting great teachers and teachings. Indeed, Jesus had declined food from the Apostles in Samaria, saying that his real nourishment was spiritual: "My meat is to do the will of him that sent me, and to finish his work" (John 4:34). This eating-obeying equation was probably John's deliberate foreshadowing to help the reader understand Jesus' introduction of imagery of the sacrament two chapters later.

John relates how Capernaum Jews came back from across the lake, where they had eaten loaves and fishes miraculously supplied. In the synagogue Jesus began by offering eternal nourishment, not mere earthly food (John 6:27). Then he outlined that he would be their food, for he would give his flesh and blood "for the life of the world" (John 6:51). Those who took his flesh and blood to themselves would have intimate fellowship with him (John 6:56). These statements make a double prophecy — that Jesus would give his life, and that its significance would be commemorated by eating and drinking. In Capernaum Christ predicted not only the sacrament symbols, but the full meaning of the future ceremony: "As the living Father hath sent me, and I live by the Father: so he that eateth me, even he shall live by me" (John 6:57). That is, the total obedience that Jesus gave the Father would be the commitment of the believer in eating and drinking in the future. At the end of the first century, John recorded Jesus' sacrament prophecy to teach the Church its duty. Jesus himself had insisted that the fellowship of the sacrament was based on resolve to obey Christ as he had obeyed his Father.

The Sacrament in Christian History

How do contemporary Christians view the sacrament? Most agree that it is an acceptance and memorial of Christ's atonement for sin. Luke and 1 Corinthians 11 say that Christ gave the elements as a remembrance of his blood shed for mankind. And Paul also insisted that eating and drinking are public affirmations of the atoning death. Through eating and drinking, "ye do shew the Lord's death till he come" (1 Corinthians 11:26). Here the LDS edition of the Bible notes that "shew" is not strong enough. The Greek verb (katangéllō), as the footnote says, means "proclaim, announce," a term consistently used in Acts and the letters for preaching. Thus major translations say that the believer "proclaims" Christ's death in partaking of the sacrament. To whom? Obviously other human beings see this witness, but Paul's context of inner resolution highlights an act done in the presence of God. Thus the commitment clause of the Book of Mormon prayer closely fits Paul's context: "and witness unto thee, O God, the Eternal Father, that they are willing to take upon them the name of thy Son."

Christians share several sacrament titles generated from the Bible. Many faiths use the term Eucharist, adapting the Greek word for giving thanks, which Jesus used in the accounts of the institution of the sacrament. But Jesus also gave thanks in blessing the food at the feedings of the four thousand and of the five thousand. Thus his characteristic appreciation to the Father at the Last Supper was evidently not intended to be a continuing part of the sacrament ceremony itself. Prayers of thanksgiving over the bread and wine are found in the second century, but they seem creative adaptations of the Gospels rather than common practices of the early church. Another regular Christian term derived from the New Testament is *Communion*, coming from Paul's introductory remark to the Corinthians on the sacredness of the sacrament: "The cup of blessing which we bless, is it not the communion of the blood of Christ? The bread which we break, is it not the communion of the body of Christ?" (1 Corinthians 10:16).

"Communion" here is the simple Greek word "sharing," often translated "fellowship." There is a fellowship of the Saints throughout the letters of Paul and John, but there is also a fellowship with God, Christ, and the Holy Ghost. This divine fellowship is the main object of the sacrament in 1 Corinthians. Today's Christians increasingly emphasize brotherhood in their sacrament ceremony. Concern for others of the faith is a valid aspect of holy commitments to God, as indicated in the first sacrament services after the Gospels: "And they continued stedfastly in the apostles' doctrine and fellowship, and in breaking of bread, and in prayers" (Acts 2:42). Yet 1 Corinthians 10:16 states a communion relationship primarily with body and blood, the symbolic sharing of Christ's person, which in application means the adoption of all that he stands for. Thus Paul's "communion" is deeply harmonious with the Nephite sacrament prayer—taking on the name of Christ and promising to keep his commandments. "Communion" in thought without comparable conduct is not a full one, since the argument of 1 Corinthians 10 is that Christians must not partake of baptism and sacrament and thereafter violate their covenants.

Roman Catholics go beyond taking Christ's name in the sacrament to sharing the very presence. The historical doctrine of transubstantiation asserts that the elements' appearance is not changed but the substance or reality becomes Christ at the words in the Mass: "this is my body . . . this is my blood." Yet Jews spoke in vivid personal metaphors. Jesus' command that Peter "feed my lambs" (John 21:15) simply linked lambs to followers in a concise leadership parable. Since Jesus so regularly used metaphors as illustrations, one should not argue change of substance in the sacrament without Christ explaining such a strange doctrine. Through symbols of body and blood, Jesus gives an object lesson that we take him to our spirits as we take the elements into our bodies. The accounts must be read as a whole to get the entire meaning — the Lord's full instruction to partake "in remembrance" is found in Luke, Paul, and 3 Nephi.

What do Christian churches stress in their sacrament memorials? The answer is complex, yet it can be outlined through handbooks of worship, explanations of religious leaders, or grass-roots understandings of the worshipper. Catholic traditions are more mystical. Many know through television at Christmas time that the Roman Mass is high drama. There is a place for some of this, as Mormons would agree in accepting the restored temple endowment. But there are major questions. Is traditional complexity man-made? Does it obscure the personal commitment to live Christ's commands that the Master stressed while yet in the upper room?

Historians of every Christian persuasion document the radical changes from the primitive sacrament ceremony, though their judgments on the meaning of these changes are quite different. This paper can only name main modifications of the sacrament in the nineteen centuries after Christ established it. Since there is little disagreement on the highlights, one Catholic theologian's summary will give a checklist of changes:

> After 312 A.D., when Christianity became the official religion of the Roman Empire, the size of the communities increased rapidly and the celebration of the Eucharist took on a more official character. . . . More ceremonies and rituals were added to these eucharistic celebrations, which more and more came to resemble official Roman ceremonies. . . . As the celebration of the

Eucharist became enlarged and more official, it lost some of the intimacy experienced in this sacrament in earlier times. . . . The celebration of the Mass, however, became locked into the Latin language for many centuries. . . . This sense of all the people participating in the celebration of the Lord's Supper began to be lost in the sixth century, when priests started saying Masses by themselves. Their original intention was to pray for special needs, but this practice detracted greatly from the original purpose of the Eucharist. . . . During the Dark Ages (eighth through eleventh centuries) the private character of the Mass began influencing community Eucharists. We see in the old missals the Mass prayers change from the use of "we" to "I," and gradually almost all the prayers were said silently by the priest alone. . . . The architecture of the churches reflected this understanding by setting the action of the priest farther and farther from the people. Since the people in the community were no longer actively participating in the eucharistic celebration, their main action became worshiping the sacred objects of the Mass. . . . This led to . . . less frequent reception of communion. Communion began to be received on the tongue while kneeling. Drinking from the cup was eliminated altogether. . . . The bread and wine once shared as a symbol of unity, sacrifice and commitment gradually became objects too "sacred" for the community to receive. With these developments the sacrament of the Eucharist lost much of its original meaning. We can also see in these developments the origins [of] the Benediction and processions with the sacred bread. The main action of the people had become adoration rather than communal sharing.[23]

As the above quotation vividly shows, Roman Catholics have led out in self-criticism of the older Mass. How Catholic worship could better conform to Christ's concerns has been debated—and papacy, priesthood, and scholars have united in the past decades to effect radical reforms in the name of "liturgical renewal."[24] Catholicism in the twentieth century inherited the patterns of the medieval church. Consecration of the elements was then a transcendent sacrifice in which the priest was central and the people peripheral. How far the pendulum has reversed is too complicated for assessment here, but the basic trend is to restore personal involvement in the sacrament. New principles were adopted by the Second Vatican Council, meeting 1962 to 1965. Papal implementation afterward modified the Mass: "The general objectives were to make the liturgy more *simple*, more *participatory*, more *intelligible* and more *dynamic*."[25] Specific changes included "celebrating the liturgy in the language of the people, moving the altar to a more central place, giving more emphasis to the reading of scripture, encouraging more frequent reception of Communion, eliminating the many unnecessary signs and gestures that accumulated during the Middle Ages, and restoring the action of drinking from the cup."[26]

Note that the Mass early shifted to mystical sacrifice instead of the personal pledge documented in the Book of Mormon and early Christian literature. Such significant reversals are a red flag. The covenant function of the sacrament was obscured for over fifteen hundred years. Specialists agree on the trends. Until the current century, innovation moved from the simple to the complex in the ceremony, from personal participation to spectator status in the worshipper. For instance, in the pre-Vatican American Mass, the altar boy regularly spoke to the priest for the silent congregation, in the pattern of the baptismal sponsor making promises for the baby incapable of speaking for himself.[27] Catholic theologians would not dispute these patterns, but they would emphasize a theory of sacred presence and evaluate personal participation as desirable but not basic for continuous divine approval. But if Christ intended the sacrament as a personal covenant, moving the worshipper to the fringes changed its central meaning.

Catholic spokesmen maintain that essentials were not lost but that unauthorized modifications were corrected: "The liturgical reforms mandated by Vatican II restored the Eucharist to its original purpose and structure."[28] Yet after reading and pondering the new English Missal, I still ask what is considered central. I sense great devotion to Christ, reverence for his incomprehensible sacrifice, recommitment to love and understand him, periodic promises to do his will. But measured by the Last Supper and first-century worship, the intricacies are confusing. What are the main purposes? Current Catholic literature says essentially that the church has preserved the mystery of the sacred presence while reemphasizing divine and brotherly communion and a responsive offering of the believer's life. This is a major move to restore essentials, but lengthy rituals wander. This is not seen as a weakness in current Catholic analysis: "At its present stage of development, therefore, the eucharistic liturgy is a multivalent religious ritual, that is, it is a complex sacramental sign which can express and reveal a variety of Christian values and meanings. . . . It is as though the eucharist today is not a single door to the sacred but a multiple door to sacred truth and mysterious reality."[29]

If current Roman rites do not highlight the primary self-examination of earliest Christianity, how successful was Protestantism in reestablishing the personal sacrament? The answer contains a paradox, for the traditional Reformation mainly stands for renewing the individual's relationship with God, a reaction against the authoritarian Medieval Church. Yet major Protestant churches of the sixteenth century were surprisingly conservative in modifying worship, whether from lack of knowledge of ancient models or doubts about authority for striking out in new directions. So the structure of the Mass was adapted by the main Protestant groups. This inherited ceremonialism was typically mixed with the simple promises to remember Christ by being loyal to him, the underlying theme in formal Protestant worship services. These promises to serve and obey are traditionally sprinkled through devotional sections that broadly correspond to medieval categories. Some informal names for the main stages are: introduction, invitation, group confession, consecration, distribution, and thanksgiving.

The real issue of the sacrament covenant is how to remember Christ. Protestant services invariably incorporate Paul's or Luke's remembrance summary. But since reformers stressed justification through faith alone, even ceremonial words of loyalty to Christ may not be understood as an obligation to keep his commandments. The theology of grace is of course reflected in the traditional Lutheran service. The distribution closed with the admonition: "May this strengthen and preserve you in the true faith unto life everlasting." Then the thanksgiving closed with the prayer: "rule our hearts and minds by Thy Holy Spirit that we may be enabled constantly to serve thee."[30] This phraseology names the active work of God and adds a certain passive acceptance of it. To the degree that a worshipper takes active responsibility, he is committed to obey God. Indeed, in the whole range of formal and informal Protestant sacrament services, the duty is implicit to live a Christian life in gratitude for Christ's sacrifice. But does a Communion service emphasize only meditation? What explicit commitment is there to keep Christ's commandments?

The traditional Episcopal service invited those to the sacrament table who intend "to lead a new life, following the commandments of God, and walking from henceforth in his holy ways." This commitment was repeated in the closing thanksgiving—a prayer to be sustained to "do all such good works as Thou hast prepared for us to walk in."[31] In the derivative Methodist worship, the opening call to a new life was retained, but salvation through grace was stressed in the final thanksgiving. There the worshipper offered himself to the Lord, but prayed not for good works but to "be filled with thy grace and heavenly benediction."[32] Presbyterian worship was also influenced by the Episcopal ceremony. One invitation was extended to partake if one was willing to commit to a new life, in the same words as quoted above. And a closing thanksgiving was similar but verbally more passive: "So enrich us by Thy continual grace that . . . thy kingdom be furthered through all such good works as Thou hast prepared for us to walk in."[33]

The above churches represent the most structured Protestant groups. At the other end of the spectrum are decentralized communions represented by Baptists and Congregationalists. The latter inherited covenant concepts from their common Calvinistic heritage with the Presbyterians. But the present worship service is principally praise and gratitude for forgiveness, with general personal commitment in the thanksgiving section at the end of the service — a prayer "to strengthen our faith in thee and to increase our love toward one another."[34] Today's Protestant tendency is toward this less structured worship. The dilemma of the Reformation is how to end reform. Roman Catholic "liturgical renewal" finds a current parallel in Protestant revisionism in worship. Since traditional ceremonies are not biblical, modernizing creativity is an active force, as demonstrated by the recent papal statement asking for control of "outlandish innovations" in the Mass.[35]

Thus a Protestant historian projected a future of change: "The second half of the 20th century should produce a new and exciting chapter in the history of liturgies."[36] But the danger is variety for the sake of variety. Protestant reforms tended to bring back personal promises into the Communion service, but recent revision tends to delete specific commitments of personal righteousness and obedience and make the believer's response to Christ very general. For instance, private handbooks give ceremonial options for less formal Protestant churches. A recent one presents well-written "traditional and contemporary approaches."[37] A dozen invitations to Communion are given, and just half suggest obligations of Christian obedience. Eight consecration prayers are given, and half include any commitment to keep the commandments. The essence of one is the request: "hear us as each in his own way seeks personal communion with Thee through Jesus Christ."[38]

Formal Protestant worship has generally been rewritten in recent decades. Besides simplified Christian loyalty, typically there is increased social awareness but less definite language on commandment-keeping and personal moral standards. An example of this interfaith trend is the revised Presbyterian service, printed in 1972, to "serve a new age in the church."[39] The old invitation to the table was for those "who do truly and earnestly repent of your sins, and are in love and charity with your neighbors, and intend to lead a new life, following the commandments of God, and walking from henceforth in His holy ways."[40] In the new summons, the Savior simply "invites those who trust him."[41] The old group confession was for "sins . . . by thought, word, and deed."[42] The current revision stresses human failings in selfishness and indifference — basically a failure to show love.[43] The older offering of self before blessing the elements is retained; the current language is: "we give ourselves to you."[44] But the older standard of biblical commandments is heavily shifted to community ethics. Thus the sacrament services reflect humanistic trends: "Among United Methodists, for example, the proportion of laity who regarded individual salvation as the chief goal for the church to pursue dropped from 63 percent in 1958 to 55 percent in 1975 to 31 percent in 1983."[45] Social action is not irrelevant to biblical covenants, but they included much more. Christ founded the sacrament above all as a commitment of living for eternal exaltation.

Loss, Restoration, and the Book of Mormon

Recent developments in Christian worship are one more validation of the Book of Mormon. Liturgical reform has concerned all major faiths since midcentury. Tradition-oriented churches have tried to correct unauthorized additions to the ceremony that Christ intended. Such formal worship has been simplified, and a deeper personal commitment has been sought through the sacrament. On the other hand, less formal groups have reduced the sacrament ceremony to little more than remembrance and human fellowship. In America the Savior twice identified the twin dangers of either more or less than he intended (3 Nephi 11 and 27) — and historic Communion services continually illustrate both trends. The Book of Mormon gives blunt prophetic criticisms that churches will add ritual without authority and produce ceremony that does not promote Christlike lives. The many Book of Mormon prophecies concerning worship continue to be dramatically fulfilled.

Christ spoke of Satan sowing tares to spoil the wheat after his ministry, and Nephi saw that process in vision as the spoiling of the sacred biblical revelations. Nephi foresaw a Jewish record which contained the Old and New Testaments, since he saw that book carried to the New World by Gentile immigrants. That book contained "the covenants of the Lord" from the prophets and Christ's Apostles (1 Nephi 13:23-24). Next the book passed through the hands of a "church," which in context would include western and eastern churches. Indeed, Eastern Christianity breaks down into many national churches. The plainness of the Bible was lost after it passed through this worldly "church," and afterward that book went to "all the nations of the Gentiles," including those "across the many waters." This sequence reaches the time period of Western Catholicism, Eastern Catholicism, and major Protestant groups, since New World nations and major Bible distribution are post-Reformation developments.

At first glance it seems that scribes mutilated the book, since "many plain and precious things" were "taken away from the book, which is the book of the Lamb of God" (1 Nephi 13:28). Yet a second process is at work. For decades I have included New Testament manuscripts in my studies. Though they contain thousands of minor changes in spelling, synonyms, transpositions, and accidental omissions, major additions or deletions are more rarely in evidence. Known lost letters of Apostles might well have been suppressed, but what survives is generally authenticated by a broad range of manuscripts, many of them relatively early. This picture exactly fits what Nephi saw, for the "records of the twelve apostles of the Lamb" would stand side by side with other revealed records in latter days (1 Nephi 13:41). These "last records" — which include the Book of Mormon — would "establish the truth of the first, which are of the twelve apostles of the Lamb." Clearly the latter-day Bible would have a great degree of historical accuracy, though doctrinal confusion would still reign.

We have much to learn about Nephi's prophecy, if Book of Mormon commentaries are any indication. These generally focus on the two times that the Book of Mormon prophet indicated subtractions from the Bible (1 Nephi 13:28-29). But in many more verses in this chapter Nephi notes subtractions from the "gospel of the Lamb." In recent centuries, rationalism has subtracted Christ's divinity from the Bible by selective interpretation, not physical destruction of manuscripts. Various Christian theologies have regularly ignored major parts of the scriptures. Nephi's prophecy contains broader concepts of change than biblical text alone. Lost writings are overshadowed by lost principles — those overlooked or explained away, though still mentioned in the biblical records. Nephi's prophecy really emphasizes deletions of doctrine, and there is a special component: "They have taken away from the gospel of the Lamb many parts which are plain and most precious; and also many covenants of the Lord have they taken away" (1 Nephi 13:26). So there were changes in documents, in the gospel itself, and in ceremonies; for removing "many covenants" includes changing essential church ordinances. And this prophecy is impressive because history so clearly reveals constant modifications of Christian rites. Since ceremonies teach lessons by physical actions, their survival is virtually assured by repetition and imitation. But their meanings are far more fragile.

We have examined two changed covenants. One is the baptismal commitment to Christ for those old enough to have faith, repent, and make the promise to keep the commandments. This has been radically modified by the legal fiction of a stand-in for an unaware baby. Catholics and most major Protestant churches have perpetuated infant baptism by rationalizing it instead of correcting it. In addition, the sacrament covenant of remembrance and recommitment was expanded with elaborate practices that tended to produce awed onlookers, forcing individual repentance into nonscriptural channels like scheduled penance and the last rites. Here the biblical accounts were a standard for Protestant reemphasis on the personal promises of the sacrament stressed by Christ and by Paul.

But the Bible gives general principles and only incidental details about early Christian ordinances. Thus the full sacrament covenant could not be restored until the ancient American consecration prayer came to light through the Book of Mormon. The Latter-day Saint sacrament prayer is in the founding revelation on Church government, Section 20 of the Doctrine and Covenants. Why is that full blessing (D&C 20:77) identical to the Nephite blessing (Moroni 4:3)? The apparent answer is suggested in a manuscript in the LDS Historical Department in the handwriting of Oliver Cowdery, dated June 1829, which copies the basic Book of Mormon ceremonies for the benefit of the first members of the Restored Church. He labeled his inspired compilation "The Articles of the Church of Christ," a title then commonly used for a list of formal church beliefs.[46] In his old age David Whitmer remembered either this or a similar collection, reviewing the year 1829: "The Book of Mormon was still in the hands of the printer, but my brother, Christian Whitmer, had copied from the manuscript the teachings and doctrine of Christ, being the things which we were commanded to preach."[47]

Here is a parallel process to the early history of the Doctrine and Covenants. Important revelations through Joseph Smith circulated in manuscript form to instruct the Church before the tedious process of collection and printing was completed. Similarly, as soon as the Book of Mormon appeared in manuscript, key portions were hand copied to aid the first baptisms and meetings of late 1829 and early 1830. Oliver's copy might precede or even incorporate Book of Mormon passages that David Whitmer said his brother transcribed. But clearly the Cowdery document was seen as modern instruction, for its preface indicates a divine direction to "write the words which I shall command you concerning my Church, my gospel, my rock, and my salvation."[48] This first known priesthood "handbook" fulfills the promise to the Second Elder of using his "gift" to bring to light "those parts of my scriptures which have been hidden because of iniquity" (D&C 6:27). His document included Christ's instructions on baptism and the sacrament from 3 Nephi 11 and 18, the sacrament prayers from Moroni 4 and 5, and many quotation-paraphrases about the Church from Christ's instructions to the Nephites and from the great doctrinal revelations of June 1829 (D&C 17 and 18).

The Cowdery version was apparently used during 1829 but was superseded by the fuller revelation on doctrine that Joseph Smith described writing in his *History* at a point just before the organization of the Church. Now known as Section 20, it followed the model of the inspired Cowdery summary of Nephite ordinances for the use of the Restored Church. Thus the Nephite sacrament prayer went from Moroni's compilation of ancient Church ordinances, to the Book of Mormon manuscript, to the Cowdery ceremony summary, to Joseph Smith's fuller statement of doctrine and practice in the Doctrine and Covenants. The conditions for baptism there have the same genealogy. Thus the Book of Mormon was instrumental in restoring the ancient covenant forms of gospel ordinances. It is "Another Testament of Christ," both in the intended sense of a second witness—and in the biblical sense of containing Christ's personal covenants in their original forms.[49]

The sacrament prayer was restored as given "according to the commandments of Christ" in ancient America (Moroni 4:1). Although derived independently of the Bible, every purpose stated in it corresponds to Christ's words in instituting the sacrament or to Christ's commentary immediately afterward. Two New Testament accounts stress Jesus' command of remembrance in establishing the sacrament, but the full record is broader than the summaries in the Synoptics. "Remembrance" and "communion" are common denominators of Christian rites, and traditional Christian ceremonies have well over nine parts appreciation to one part determination to live the gospel. Yet Christ evenly balanced these purposes. After the first sacrament he fully explained communion or fellowship with him. The Apostles' relationship of branch to stem of the vine would be maintained "if ye keep my commandments" (John

15:10). Their divine friendship had a firm condition: "if ye do whatsoever I command you" (John 15:14). These words were spoken right after the invitation to leave the upper room, and they repeat the same challenges reiterated right after the sacrament (John 14:15, 21, 23). Thus the Book of Mormon prayer contains Christ's full purposes in that founding hour. He gave bread and cup while commanding remembrance, but while the taste lingered he explained that loyalty must be coupled with righteous living. This is the same ratio of Christ's fullest biblical statement of discipleship, the Sermon on the Mount. There he unfolded the meaning of righteousness, closing with the challenge that hearing must be followed by doing (Matthew 7:24, 26). The Savior also closed his ministry with this double thrust in the sacrament covenant. While still in the upper room (John 14:31), he explained mutual promises: "If ye love me, keep my commandments. And I will pray the Father, and he shall give you another Comforter, that he may abide with you for ever" (John 14:15-16).

The sacrament prayer of the Book of Mormon has religious validity because it repeats the above essentials given by Jesus: "always remember him, and keep his commandments . . . that they may always have his Spirit to be with them" (Moroni 4:3). Human eloquence and devotional creativity cannot add significantly to these basics. They are stated in balance. "Much speaking" (Matthew 6:7) will muddy these central promises. Christ's own principles establish historical validity, so the correlation of the Book of Mormon prayer with the full Last Supper teachings shows its divinity. The American prayer states the Lord's views simply; it contains no more. A current slogan insists that the person with more than three goals has no goals. The Son of God never overexplained, and the Book of Mormon sacrament prayers bear his stamp. The baptized believer, in partaking of the sacrament, retakes the Lord's name with the double purpose of remembrance and resolve—of loving the Lord and living his teachings. Thus Christ's words on both hemispheres illuminate each other. With all my soul I know that both the Bible and Book of Mormon are true, that both contain the Savior's ancient words. And I know that as I live in my heart and in my life the covenant of the sacrament—to remember Christ and be faithful—the sweet spirit of the Lord attends me, a companionship that is beyond all price and beyond all purchase. That is the ultimate religious validity.

Notes

1. This paper is a revised presentation, originally given as the First Annual Book of Mormon Lecture, sponsored by the Foundation for Ancient Research and Mormon Studies, March 2, 1988. Since Hugh Nibley was patient enough to listen to the spontaneous version, I am pleased to present more coherent arguments in honor of my first teacher of Classical Greek, who from that time (1949) has been an impressive source of information and a consistent example of academic and religious integrity.

2. Ezra Taft Benson, *A Witness and a Warning* (Salt Lake City: Deseret Book, 1988), vii.

3. Joseph Smith, *History of The Church of Jesus Christ of Latter-day Saints* (Salt Lake City: Deseret Book, 1978), 4:461.

4. Emphasis added. The statistics are furnished by research assistant Deborah Browning Dixon, based on classifying chapters and half chapters in one of the listed categories. For a convenient transcription of the Woodruff quote, see Scott G. Kenney, ed., *Wilford Woodruff's Journal*, 9 vols. (Midvale, UT: Signature Books, 1983), 2:139.

5. A survey of the complex covenant literature is accessible in bibliographies in the major Jewish, Catholic, and Bible encyclopedias.

6. Compare Paul's knowledge of both the upper room and the resurrection events from others, who appear to be his associates in the apostleship (1 Corinthians 11:23; 15:3-7). For the dating of 1 Corinthians, see Richard L. Anderson, *Understanding Paul* (Salt Lake City: Deseret Book, 1983), 95, 395.

7. For Matthew originally collecting Christ's words, and Mark reporting Peter's experiences, see Eusebius, *Ecclesiastical History* III, 39, 14-16.

8. For the apostolic basis of Matthew and Mark, see ibid. Mod-

ern translations eliminate "new," making the Savior's words correspond exactly to Moses' phrase of the first covenant. This is done by following the favored manuscripts of the currently influential textual critics. These manuscripts are the oldest known, but date only from the fourth century. Critics assume that scribes added "new" from the accounts of Luke and 1 Corinthians. See Bruce Metzger, *A Textual Commentary on the Greek New Testament*, corr. ed. (New York: United Bible Societies, 1975), 64, 113. However, the above manuscripts tend to be the most literary and also of an Egyptian character, so they may perpetuate "corrections" of ancient scholars. "The new covenant" appears in the majority of manuscripts, and statistically some of these are likely copied from a period before the surviving manuscripts. It is just as probable that ancient revisers would seek to conform exactly to the words of Exodus as to borrow language from another Gospel. Moreover, in Greek the three words of "the new covenant" all have the same "*-ēs*" ending, making a possible accidental omission of "new." Joseph Smith's translation tends to re-create the whole event in each source; yet his readings may be inspired narration of meaning rather than a restoration of the original language of any one Gospel.

9. This reason for John's writing was in Eusebius's sources, *Ecclesiastical History* III, 24, 7-13. This approach of integrating John with the Synoptics is largely resisted by scholars, but the argument for blending has both literary and historical considerations, whereas skepticism about blending mainly rests on literary arguments. All four Gospels obviously describe the same event in narratives of the Last Supper—witness details of the place, announcement of betrayal, the sop given to Judas, etc. Many argue that John intended an earlier day for the occasion, though John's correlation with the Synoptics on this point has strong evidence. See A. T. Robertson, *A Harmony of the Gospels, for Students of the Life of Christ* (New York: Harper & Row, 1950), 279-84.

10. Benson, *A Witness and a Warning*, 9-10, 19-20.

11. George N. M. Collins, "Covenant Theology," in Everett F. Harrison, ed., *Baker's Dictionary of Theology* (Grand Rapids, MI: Baker Book House, 1960), 144. The Covenant of Grace in Reformed theology is generally the post-Fall covenant of God with the patriarchs, Israelites, and Christians. Salvation through God's pre-Christian decree makes baptism all the more dispensable, in this theory. While Protestantism upholds baptism as a command, there is a good deal of ambiguity on its necessity. For instance, see Herschel H. Hobbs, *The Baptist Faith and Message* (Nashville, TN: Convention Press, 1971),

which has the following positions. Baptism "should be observed" because it is a commandment of Christ: "Failure to do so is to be disobedient to the Lord's will" (p. 91). Yet, "the New Testament abundantly teaches salvation apart from baptism" (p. 85). Thus the ordinance appears to have a function more practical than eternal: "Baptism is not necessary for being in the kingdom of God or the church in general. But it is necessary for fellowship in the local church." Similar viewpoints are expressed in some other Protestant faiths.

12. *The Book of Common Prayer* (Church Pension Fund, 1940), 276-77. This earlier service states the theory of representation plainly and is typical of traditional Catholic and Protestant forms of infant baptism. A somewhat modernized Episcopal version is now in the *Book of Common Prayer* (Seabury Press, 1979), 301-3. A proxy baptismal covenant is superficially similar to the proxy baptism for the dead in The Church of Jesus Christ of Latter-day Saints, but there exist certain essential differences. Foremost, baptism for the dead is authorized by both the Bible (1 Corinthians 15:29) and modern revelation (D&C 127-128), whereas tradition, not revelation, is asserted as the basis for infant baptism, with the New Testament giving no positive authority on the subject. Moreover, the New Testament clearly makes personal repentance a condition of baptism. Whereas the physical act of immersion can be received by another, it violates divine free agency to delegate resolve to change to another. The New Testament parallels proxy baptism with preaching in the spirit world to prepare the dead for judgment (1 Peter 3:16-20; 4:5-6). And in restoring baptism for the dead, Joseph Smith insisted that vicarious ordinances are valid only when accepted personally. See Anderson, *Understanding Paul*, 406-7, 410-11. Joseph F. Smith's panoramic revelation on preaching to the spirits indicated that only "the dead who repent will be redeemed" (D&C 138:58). This brings up the final logical point that proxy promises are unnecessary for the infant, for he can wait until the age of discretion to be baptized and make them for himself. However, proxy baptism is necessary for those who failed to have the opportunity, for this is a physical, earthly ordinance. In summary, infant baptism is wrong because it cannot be a true covenant (Moroni 8:8-26), but baptism for the dead is valid when the covenant is personally accepted in the spirit world.

13. For a convenient line-by-line comparison of Christ's sacrament sermon (3 Nephi 18) and the sacrament prayers (Moroni 4-5), see John W. Welch, *The Nephite Sacrament Prayers: From King Ben-*

jamin's Speech to Moroni 4-5 (Provo, UT: F.A.R.M.S., 1986), 12. This "Preliminary Report" stresses the covenant language of King Benjamin as possibly handed down in the Nephite religious heritage. The concept should be extended, however, inasmuch as most of the Benjamin-prayer parallels are found in Nephi's covenant discussion of baptism in 2 Nephi 31 (cf. 1 Nephi 15:25: "give heed to the word of God and remember to keep his commandments always in all things"). The format of "remember—keep commandments" goes back to ancient Israel, witness the constant theme of remembering the hand of God in the books of Exodus and Deuteronomy. The commitment of obedience of Exodus 24 was repeated in language similar to King Benjamin's covenant renewal. See Deuteronomy 5:29: "that they would fear me, and keep all my commandments always"; see also Deuteronomy 11:1: "Therefore thou shalt love the Lord thy God, and keep . . . his commandments, alway." Thus the Nephite sacrament prayer continues the basic obligations of the Old Testament covenant, though its language almost totally reflects Christ's words in America. See the similar pattern with regard to the divine name in Welch, *The Nephite Sacrament Prayers,* 25.

14. C. Bernas, "Eucharist (Biblical Data)," *New Catholic Encyclopedia,* 15 vols. (New York: McGraw-Hill, 1967), 5:595. Compare the judgment of William Barclay, *The Lord's Supper* (Naperville, IL: SCM Book Club, 1967), 104: "In our view we have in the New Testament records of the Last Supper, accounts, and reliable accounts, of an actual historical happening. . . . It seems to us that the very divergence in the accounts of the Last Supper are the best proof of that. If this had been a deliberately constructed cult legend, then we would have expected a stereotyped form—which is exactly what we do not get. The divergences are the proof that the roots of this are in history and not in liturgy."

15. A complete Bible concordance will show how taking "the name" of Christ was the result of conversions and baptisms throughout the book of Acts and Paul's letters. Since this doctrine fully appears right after Christ's resurrection, it is no doubt part of Christ's teachings to the young Church.

16. Ignatius, *To the Church at Smyrna* VIII, 1. And "it is not lawful . . . to baptize . . . without the bishop" (ibid., VIII, 2). Translations of Ignatius here are from Kirsopp Lake, *The Apostolic Fathers* (Cambridge, MA: Harvard University Press, 1949).

17. Ignatius, *To the Church at Ephesus* XX, 2.

18. Clarence T. Craig, in *The Interpreter's Bible,* 12 vols. (New York: Abingdon-Cokesbury Press, 1953), 10:109.

19. Pliny, *Letters* X, 96-97, tr. by Betty Radice, *Pliny, Letters and Panegyricus* (Cambridge, MA: Harvard University Press, 1969).

20. See Welch, *The Nephite Sacrament Prayers*, 28-32. Though fragments of this early document were previously identified, a full text was not located until the late nineteenth century. See Johannes Quasten, *Patrology 1* (Westminster, MD: Newman Press, 1962), 30: "Until the year 1883 it was quite unknown." This was the year of publication of the recently discovered Greek manuscript. Cf. ibid., 38-39, for a listing of editions and translations, all of which postdate the above year.

21. An outline of sources on John's later life is in Richard L. Anderson, "What Do We Know of the Life of John the Apostle after the Day of Pentecost?" *Ensign* 14 (January 1984): 50-51. Irenaeus, second-century bishop of Lyons, details his early contact with Polycarp, earlier bishop of Smyrna, who had known John the apostle (cf. Eusebius, *Ecclesiastical History* V, 20, 4-8, and Irenaeus, *Against Heresies* III, 3, 4.). Irenaeus says that John wrote his Revelation "towards the end of Domitian's reign" (*Against Heresies* V, 30, 3). Then in several statements, Irenaeus says that John was known as an aged apostle up to Trajan's reign (beginning A.D. 98). Irenaeus also puts John's letters and John's Gospel in the context of opposing the early apostate Cerinthus, whom he dates in the period after John had been on Patmos. For instance, John wrote his Gospel "during his residence at Ephesus in Asia" (*Against Heresies* III, 1, 1) to refute Cerinthus, who perpetuated the errors of the previous Nicolaitans, mentioned in the Revelation of A.D. 96 (*Against Heresies* III, 11, 1). Many scholars recognize that John's letters assume that the readers are familiar with his Gospel, and Irenaeus speaks of the letters in this same period. Although these insights are only historical glimpses, they come through a known channel of information. Alternative theories are more speculatively based. The above considerations would give the sequence of Revelation, then Gospel, then John's letters, in the period of about a decade after A.D. 96. The letters of Ignatius of Antioch were written about A.D. 108 in this same area and give no hint that John was still known. The above translations are from Alexander Roberts and James Donaldson, eds., *The Ante-Nicene Fathers* (Grand Rapids, MI: Eerdmans, 1956), vol. 1.

22. "If ye love me, keep my commandments" (John 14:15) is the theme that John returns to at the end of his first letter. He says that Christians know they are truly born again "when we love God, and keep his commandments" (1 John 5:1-2). This is, of course, the New

Testament baptismal rebirth metaphor (John 3:3-7, 22-23; Titus 3:5), followed by the Savior's comment immediately after the sacrament. John's physical imagery afterward is understood by knowing something of his opponents. Right after John's letters, Ignatius is sarcastic on how dissenters explain away Christ's physical reality on the cross and in the resurrection, saying that they "abstain from Eucharist . . . because they do not confess that the Eucharist is the flesh of our Savior" (*To the Church at Smyrna* VII, 1). John makes the similar criticism that they confess "not that Jesus Christ is come in the flesh" (1 John 4:3). From many sources it is known that these mystical dissenters sought to separate divinity from any contamination with the physical. Thus John bears his testimony that Christ did come in the flesh (John 1:14; 1 John 1:1), and "not by water only, but by water and blood" (1 John 5:6). Clearly he is saying that Christ himself entered the physical world so far as to be baptized and pour out his blood on the cross. Then when John follows by admonishing the believer to accept the witness of "the Spirit, and the water, and the blood" (1 John 5:8), the connection with the ordinance of baptism is plain, which suggests that the "blood" is the symbolic cup of accepting Christ's atonement in the sacrament, and through faithfulness to these double ordinances, gaining the spirit.

23. Rev. Paul A. Feider, *The Sacraments: Encountering the Risen Lord* (Notre Dame, IN: Ave Maria Press, 1986), 40-43. For outlines of these developments, see the major Roman Catholic encyclopedias under titles of "Eucharist," "Mass," "Liturgy," and "Worship." For the Latter-day Saint evaluation of such changes as evidence of apostasy, see James E. Talmage, *The Great Apostasy* (Salt Lake City: Deseret Book, 1965), 119-22, 127-28.

24. For a survey of twentieth-century developments, see F. R. McManus, "Liturgical Reform," in *New Catholic Encyclopedia*, 1:908-10.

25. Thomas Bokenkotter, *Essential Catholicism* (Garden City, NJ: Image Books, 1986), 168.

26. Feider, *The Sacraments*, 45.

27. For a convenient summary of the words and actions of the traditional Mass, see James Coniff, *The Story of the Mass* (New York: Dauntless Books, 1954). See the representative view of John A. Hardon, *The Catholic Catechism* (Garden City, NY: Doubleday, 1975), 470-71: "Although implicit in this concept of participation by the faithful, one feature that has been specially clarified since Vatican II is the community character of the people's involvement in the

liturgy. . . . In any case, when the liturgy is being enacted, the end in view is that all those who participate have a sense of sharing what is being done and not only feel they are watching what someone else is saying to them or doing in their stead. This represents a major development in the Church's contemporary understanding of sacramental (especially Eucharistic) worship."

28. Richard P. McBrien, *Catholicism* (San Francisco: Harper & Row, 1981), 773.

29. Joseph Martos, *Doors to the Sacred* (Garden City, NY: Image Books, 1982), 303.

30. Evangelical Lutheran Synodical Conference of North America, *The Lutheran Hymnal* (St. Louis: Concordia Publishing House, 1941), 29, 31. For Lutheran background, I acknowledge the help of Gary Gillum, former theological student and current Religion and History Librarian at Brigham Young University.

31. *Book of Common Prayer* (1940), 75, 83.

32. *The Methodist Hymnal* (Baltimore: Methodist Publishing House, 1939), 528, 531.

33. General Assembly of the Presbyterian Church in the USA, *The Book of Common Worship* (Philadelphia: Board of Christian Education of the Presbyterian Church in the USA, 1964), 156, 174. For Reformed background, I acknowledge the help of Roger Keller, former Presbyterian minister and now fellow-teacher of religion at Brigham Young University.

34. *Pilgrim Hymnal* (Philadelphia: Pilgrim Press, 1972), 496.

35. "Pope Urges Deeper Grasp of Liturgy, End to Abuses," *Intermountain Catholic*, 19 May 1989, 5.

36. Jerald C. Brauer, *The Westminster Dictionary of Church History* (Philadelphia: Westminster Press, 1971), 506.

37. James L. Christensen, *The Complete Handbook for Ministers* (Old Tappan, NJ: Fleming H. Revell, 1985), 13.

38. Ibid., 61.

39. Joint Committee on Worship, *The Worship Book* (Philadelphia: Westminster Press, 1972), 9.

40. *Book of Common Worship*, 156.

41. *Worship Book*, 34.

42. *Book of Common Worship*, 156.

43. *Worship Book*, 26.

44. Ibid., 36.

45. Robert Wuthnow, *The Restructuring of American Religion* (Princeton, NJ: Princeton University Press, 1988), 172.

46. See Robert J. Woodford, *The Historical Development of the Doc-*

trine and Covenants, 3 vols., Ph.D. diss., Brigham Young University, 1974, 1:288-89.

47. David Whitmer, *An Address to All Believers in Christ* (Richmond, MO: David Whitmer, 1887), 32.

48. Woodford, *The Historical Development of the Doctrine and Covenants,* 1:288 (spelling and punctuation modernized).

49. President Benson suggests that both meanings of "testament" apply to the Book of Mormon (see *A Witness and a Warning,* 17).

2

The Lamanite View
of Book of Mormon History

Richard L. Bushman
Columbia University, New York, New York

History is one of the spoils of war. In great conflicts, the victors almost always write the history; the losers' story is forgotten. We remember the patriots' version of the American Revolution, not the loyalists'; the Northern account of the Civil War, not the Southern story of the War between the States. Ordinarily the winners' account of events commands our memories as completely as their armies controlled the battlefield. The reverse is true of the Book of Mormon. The Lamanites vanquished the Nephites and survived; yet by virtue of a record that went into the earth with them, the Nephites' version of the history is the one we now read. We think of the Nephites as the superior nation because they wrote the history, even though in the end the Lamanites won on the battlefield. How would the story go if the Lamanites had kept the records, and their view were in our hands today? We cannot say in any detail of course, but there are enough clues scattered through the Nephite record to offer a few conjectures about a Lamanite history of Lehi's descendants. Since the way we write history is tied closely to fundamental cultural values, in recovering the Lamanite perspective, we obtain a clearer view of the two cultures, and, as it turns out, a deeper understanding of Nephite religion.

One fact would surely figure as prominently in the Lamanite record as the Nephite: the frequent wars between the two peoples. Especially in their first six hundred years, the Lamanites or those leading them exerted relentless pressure on the Nephites, driving or causing them to move farther and farther north, to the lands of Nephi, Zarahemla, and Bountiful, and at last the land northward. That being true for both nations, in order to write a Lamanite account of these events, we must know why the Lamanites fought. Though the Lamanites ultimately triumphed (for other reasons), more often than not in the first six hundred years of their stormy relationship, they lost the wars with the Nephites. They sent vast armies into Nephite territory, won a battle or two, and then were defeated with a huge loss of life and driven back to their own lands. For hundreds of years these attacks and defeats succeeded one another with no apparent gain. What brought the Lamanites back during this time year after year to be outmaneuvered and outfought by the Nephites?

The Nephite record says little more than "they delighted in wars and bloodshed, and they had an eternal hatred against us, their brethren" (Jacob 7:24). Without questioning the essential truth of that judgment, as moderns we wish to know more. Were not the Lamanites seeking more substantive gains for themselves than mere vengeance? We could understand the wars if the Lamanites suffered from a land shortage and wished to capture new territory. While that was possibly the case, there is no mention of a land shortage, and there is evidence of a plentitude of land. The Lamanite king welcomed the people of Zeniff when they migrated into Lamanite territory as if there were enough land to go around. Why would a Lamanite king clear out his people from a broad valley to make room for Nephites if he lacked land? The king did benefit from Zeniff's presence in one respect: he exacted tribute. Traditionally that has been a powerful motive for imperial expansion, and whenever a Nephite people came under Lamanite control the Nephites paid heavy tribute.

But the Lamanite armies failed so consistently for eight hundred years, never actually conquering a Nephite people for more than a few years at any one time so far as can be known, that it is difficult to believe that the expectation of tribute sustained the Lamanites through all their losses.

The Nephite record gives a further explanation for those wars, in words directly quoted from Lamanite documents. In 63 B.C., Ammoron the Lamanite king wrote to Moroni about a prisoner exchange and explained why they fought: "For behold, your fathers did wrong their brethren, insomuch that they did rob them of their right to the government when it rightly belonged unto them" (Alma 54:17). The war would stop, Ammoron said to Moroni, if you "lay down your arms, and subject yourselves to be governed by those to whom the government doth rightly belong" (Alma 54:18). Ammoron referred, of course, to Laman's complaint that Nephi "thinks to rule over us," when Laman himself claimed the right of rulership. "We will not have him to be our ruler; for it belongs unto us, who are the elder brethren, to rule over this people" (2 Nephi 5:3). Ammoron represents the war as a continuation of an ancient feud between the two sets of brothers in Lehi's family. That hardly makes sense to us. Would countless thousands of men hundreds of years later throw themselves into battle simply to reclaim an ancient right? It is all the more puzzling because after the landing in America, Nephi and his descendants made no claims that we know of to rule the Lamanites. Quite to the contrary, Nephi withdrew from the site of the first landing by command of the Lord, leaving the area to his brothers (2 Nephi 5:5-7). The first King Mosiah also withdrew by command of the Lord (cf. Omni 1:12-13), pulling back from the Lamanites and not forcing his rule on them. Until near the end, the Nephites never fought aggressive wars. The Lamanites were the ones to attack, not the Nephites. How could such an abstraction as this ancient hurt motivate people over so many centuries? We have to credit the Book of Mormon explanation for the wars, coming as it does from both sides, but the source of its power remains a puzzle. Why should Nephi's one-time claim to rule arouse the wrath of the Lamanites generation after generation for hundreds of years?

In attacking this puzzle, we are best advised, I believe, to begin where the evidence points, with the story of the brothers in the opening pages. In summing up Lamanite animus against the Nephites, Ammoron attributed it to the original contest between Laman and Nephi, and that is probably reason enough for recognizing its primal importance to Lamanite culture. But there is another reason for taking these stories seriously. The Book of Mormon, like other ancient narratives, blends family history and national history. The story of a whole people grows out of the story of a single family, as the history of Israel begins with the family of Abraham. Israel thought of itself as the descendants of Abraham, Isaac, and Jacob, and what the patriarchs did to a large extent determined what Israel was for thousands of years. In our day, a revolution and the work of a convention in the Philadelphia state house determine our national identity. In ancient times, family events founded nations and determined their character ever after. That is why the story of the competing brothers requires close analysis.

The most powerful impression we get from the family story is of Laman's and Lemuel's complaining natures. They were forever raising objections to Lehi or Nephi, becoming first sullen, then angry, and finally violent. We have to allow for Nephi's stern, exacting estimation of his brothers, but there is no reason to question the reality of their complaints. We too may have objected to the sacrifice of a comfortable life in Jerusalem for an arduous trek in the desert toward an unknown destination. Nor is there ason to question Laman's and Lemuel's resort to violence. At least five times they physically punished Nephi or threatened his life. After the second visit to Laban, when they left all their property behind as they fled, Laman and Lemuel took out their anger on their younger brothers, smiting them with a rod (1 Nephi 3:29). A little later, on the way back from Jerusalem with Ishmael's family, Laman and Lemuel and a few of Ishmael's children grew so angry with Nephi's preaching that they bound him with cords and planned to kill him (1 Nephi 7:16). After the broken bow incident and Ishmael's death, Laman and Lemuel planned to kill both Lehi and Nephi (1 Nephi 16:37). When they arrived at the sea and Nephi proposed to build a ship, his brothers' patience wore thin again, and they tried to throw him "into the depths of the sea" (1 Nephi 17:48). Finally, aboard ship on the way to the promised land, Nephi reproached them for their merrymaking, and Laman and Lemuel bound him with cords and treated him with "much harshness" (1 Nephi 18:11). By that time, Nephi's reproaches, the brothers' murmuring, and the violence had fallen into a pattern that characterized their relationship, establishing the recurring subplot of First Nephi.

On the other hand, a frequent result of the brothers' assaults on Nephi was a rebuke from the Lord. Once an angel appeared to chastise them, and on another occasion they heard the voice of the Lord. They gave way in the face of these rebukes, but on one occasion they did more than relent. When Nephi was about to construct a ship and the brothers in anger tried to throw him into the sea, Nephi was given the power to shock them physically with a touch. This show of power so overwhelmed Laman and Lemuel that they swung to the opposite extreme. Nephi says they "fell down before me, and were about to worship me," and he had to reassure them he was still only their brother (1 Nephi 17:53-55). This reaction, combined with the brothers' repeated violent assaults on Nephi, suggests that force was their characteristic reaction to crisis, the only language they understood in such situations. It seemed to be a matter of smite or be smitten.

There is another element in the founding story along with the complaints and the violence, namely deprivation. That theme is most evident on the ship. Laman and Lemuel, the sons of Ishmael, and their wives made themselves merry—dancing, singing, and speaking with much rudeness. Nephi, ever fearing the Lord would be displeased, spoke to them soberly, and they grew angry. Immediately his brothers came forth with the classic complaint: "We will not that our younger brother shall be a ruler over us," and bound him with cords (1 Nephi 18:9-10). In this case it seems that the denial of pleasure and the objections to Nephi's rule are closely linked. The attempt to stop the merrymaking aroused the thought of his unfounded claims to govern. The connection is most clear on the ship, but it has a place throughout the narrative. The brothers' complaint from the beginning is that Lehi and Nephi cause them needless physical suffering. Laman and Lemuel did not want to leave their home and leave behind "their gold, and their silver, and their precious things, to perish in the wilderness" (1 Nephi 2:11). That basic deprivation underlay their truculence throughout. Then it was the loss of their precious things to Laban that set off the first physical attack—they beat Nephi with a rod (1 Nephi 3:24-28). Once on their way in the desert, suffering and deprivation become their common lot. The loss of the steel bow brought the problem to a head when "they did suffer much for the want of food," causing the brothers to "murmur exceedingly" (1 Nephi 16:19-20). The death of Ishmael made things worse, his daughters complaining that "we have suffered much affliction, hunger, thirst, and fatigue; and after all these sufferings we must perish in the wilderness with hunger" (1 Nephi 16:35). Even amidst the abundance of Bountiful by the sea, the brothers held a grudge against Nephi for the eight years of wandering with their ofttimes pregnant wives, suffering in the desert when all along they might "have enjoyed [their] possessions and the land of [their] inheritance" (1 Nephi 17:20-21). Nephi's intervention to stop the shipboard merrymaking was the straw that broke the camel's back. They had undergone untold afflictions in the wilderness—hunger, thirst, raw food—and now when they sought a little pleasure for themselves, he wanted to prevent them once more. To Laman and Lemuel, all the deprivations they suffered could be blamed on Nephi. It was not merely that he claimed rulership unjustly. His governance became unbearable when it was driven home that he used his power to cause them suffering. Nephi was the cause of their deprivation. Deep down they may have believed Nephi sought his own pleasure at their expense. They said once that they suspected him of leading them away to make himself king "that he may do with us according to his will and pleasure" (1 Nephi 16:38).

Combining these clues, then, we can reconstruct events as the Lamanites probably understood them. Initially they were living a pleasurable life amidst their treasures and precious things in the land of Jerusalem. Their father's vision and subsequently Nephi's God-given claim to rule and teach them, tore them away from these pleasures and subjected them to danger, affliction, and hunger. They grew angry time after time whenever events brought their fundamental grievance to the surface: that they were made to suffer deprivations because of Nephi's attempts to rule them. It is noticeable in this reconstructed plot that force plays a large part. The brothers feel that Nephi and Lehi are compelling them; they use force to stop their intervention; and it is divine force that breaks their will and compels submission. The Freudians would say that Laman and Lemuel had archaic superegos—that is, the internal monitors that controlled their egos used terror rather than persuasion.

With this plot before us, we can begin to understand the dilemma of existence as Laman and Lemuel understood the world. They felt compelled to choose between two unfortunate alternatives. On the one hand, they could enjoy pleasure and comfort by refusing submission to their father and brother, and since these two spoke for the Lord, refusing submission to God, too. Or on the other hand, they could yield abjectly to the superior power of the two prophets and their God, giving up all claims to pleasure and even to honor. Judging from the stories, Laman and Lemuel felt driven by events to choose between rebellious pleasure and fearful self-denial and submission. They could not envision a middle ground where obedience was joined with love and pleasure, and where a flourishing of their egos was in a happy harmony with God's will.

Nephi tried to cope with Laman's and Lemuel's legitimate complaints. There is no reason to believe that he was dedicated to a puritanical repression of the desire for pleasure. He was the one, when the steel bow broke, to make another from a straight stick and slay game for the group. He came into the camp with the beasts, and "when they beheld that I had obtained food, how great was their joy!" That was an understandable reaction, of course, but Nephi goes on to say, "they did humble themselves before the Lord, and did give thanks unto him" (1 Nephi 16:32). One catches a brief, pitiful glimpse of boys deprived of simple pleasure and eager to be compliant when for the moment they felt provided for. But the humility did not last. At the next trouble, their hearts hardened again and they were plotting once more to slay Nephi. They acted as if force alone could be relied on. When Nephi said the party must leave Bountiful, the mysterious haven by the sea with its "much fruit and also wild honey" (1 Nephi 17:5), the brothers were at his throat immediately. With every call for a sacrifice they fell into the familiar pattern of murmuring and violence. Hovering in the distance was the promised land, enough to sustain Nephi and the faithful members of the party through the afflictions of the journey, but this was thin gruel for the suspicious and perhaps constitutionally deprived brothers.

Nephi's and Lehi's theology offered more enduring sustenance to Laman and Lemuel as a way to resolve the conflict between submission and pleasure. In the brothers' characteristic plot, submission meant deprivation, and pleasures came only through rebellion and violence. In their view of events, God's superior power forced them to submit and drove them into the sufferings of the wilderness. The family's theology and faith in Christ, by contrast, offered supreme pleasure and happiness, not through rebellion but through submission to God. Lehi's vision made the point most graphically with the tree "whose fruit was desirable to make one happy." When Lehi partook, he "beheld that it was most sweet, above all that I ever before tasted" (1 Nephi 8:10-11). Christ was presented as the resolution of the troubling conflict. The image of divine love in the form of luscious fruit should have appealed directly to Laman's and Lemuel's most fundamental need. But an understanding of Christ's love was beyond them. They were too firmly fixed in another pattern. Lehi regretfully reported that in the dream Laman and Lemuel did not take the fruit (1 Nephi 8:35).

In the ensuing centuries, the saga of the founding family formed the framework for the descendants of Laman and Lemuel to interpret events. Judging from the Lamanites' frequent references to the story, it remained as vivid in their national memory as the Revolution and Declaration of Independence do in ours. The relationship between the two peoples paralleled the relationship between Nephi and his brothers. Nephites were accused of unjust rule and suspected of schemes to deprive the Lamanites of their possessions just as Laman and Lemuel believed Nephi deprived them of their rightful pleasures. Zeniff's people, who came into bondage to the Lamanites around 160 B.C., learned that the Lamanites still taught their children that Nephi robbed their fathers, that all Lamanites should hate the Nephites, "and that they should murder them, and that they should rob and plunder them" (Mosiah 10:16-17). The immediate reaction of the father of Lamoni when he discovered his son fraternizing with Nephites was to suspect them of robbery. They are sons of a liar, he charged, who "robbed our fathers; and now his children are also come amongst us that they may, by their cunning and their lyings, deceive us, that they again may rob us of our property" (Alma 20:13). The Lamanites seemed to believe that the old story of deprivation would be played out whenever Nephites appeared on the scene.

And by the same token, the Lamanite response followed the line of the ancient story. How were the Nephites to be stopped from their habitual robbery of their brethren? Bind them, smite them, kill them. The father of Lamoni turned on Ammon with a sword, and that was always the way. Nephi said his brothers' hearts were like flint, and the most common Nephite characterization of the Lamanites described them as ferocious. They were a "wild and a hardened and a ferocious people; a people who delighted in murdering the Nephites, and robbing and plundering them" (Alma 17:14). It was nearly impossible for many of the Nephites to see anything gentle or loving in Lamanite life, because the boundary between the two peoples was defined by the founding saga as one of perpetual war. To his credit, Jacob recognized that national traditions distorted the Nephite view. He told the Nephites in his sermon on chastity that Lamanite "husbands love their wives, and their wives love their husbands; and their husbands and their wives love their children." They were not implacably ferocious in every relationship. Lamanite violence toward the Nephites grew out of tradition, not innate viciousness. "Their hatred towards you is because of the iniquity of their fathers," Jacob said (Jacob 3:7). And yet that hatred was so unrelenting, and the resulting violence so intense, that Jacob himself could only think that Lamanites "delighted in wars and bloodshed, and they had an eternal hatred against us, their brethren" (Jacob 7:24).

One of the most troubling occurrences in the Book of Mormon, for some modern readers, is the cursing of the Lamanites. It took place after the separation of the peoples when the cultural divide widened. Nephi apparently ruled over all the brothers when they first landed in America, but, chafing under his government, the Lamanites made an attempt on his life, forcing Nephi to flee with his people into the wilderness. The Lord explained that, in consequence of the brothers' refusal to follow Nephi, they would be cut off. The curse of blackness came because the Lamanites "hardened their hearts against him, that they had become like unto a flint" (2 Nephi 5:21). The purpose of the sign accompanying the curse, the dark skin, was to prevent the Nephites from mixing with the Lamanites; under the curse they would not be enticing. That idea troubles us because it makes skin color divisive in a way that we today dislike. But in a later incident, we learn more about the inner meaning of the curse. In the time of Alma a group of dissident Nephites called Amlicites joined the Lamanites in an attack on the Nephites. The Amlicites marked their foreheads with red paint to distinguish friends from enemies in battle. The marking led Mormon (presumably the editor of Alma's records) to comment on the curse. Mormon explained the reason why the Lord did not wish the Lamanites and Nephites to mix. It was not because of their contrasting skin colors. The curse was pronounced "that they might not mix and believe in incorrect traditions which would prove their destruction" (Alma 3:8). At issue was the story of their founding, deeply embedded as it was in Lamanite culture. The danger was not a mixture of races or skin colors but a mixture of false traditions with true ones. Mormon said the very identity of the Nephites lay in their acceptance of the true history of origins.

> Whosoever would not believe in the tradition of the Lamanites, but believed those records which were brought out of the land of Jerusalem, and also in the tradition of their fathers, which were correct, who believed in the commandments of God and kept them, were called the Nephites (Alma 3:11).

The two peoples were defined by their contrasting explanations of the enmity between Nephi and Laman, and the crucial issue was how to keep the true version intact. We may object to the selection of skin color as a means of separating the people and call these passages racist, but we should understand that in God's mind, and in the minds of his people, correct traditions, not skins, were the issue. The people of God would have objected just as heartily to a Nephite marriage with an Amlicite as to one with a Lamanite, when the only Amlicite mark was a painted forehead. The important thing was the Amlicite false belief and enmity to the Nephites. By accepting the false tradition, the curse fell on them as surely as upon the Lamanites. Mormon says the Amlicites fulfilled the wish of Providence in painting their foreheads, for in rebelling against God "it was expedient that the curse should fall upon them" (Alma 3:18). They were cursed, without receiving a dark skin, because they rebelled against God and embraced a false tradition. Presumably a dark skin on a person who embraced the true tradition would have no significance. Skin color was only skin deep; what mattered was the history one believed, and the hatred or love that went with each version.

It may be that the hatred against the Nephites polluted

Lamanite society more than they desired themselves. The Nephites thought the Lamanites were idle. Instead of working for riches, "they sought to obtain these things by murdering and plundering, that they might not labor for them with their own hands" (Alma 17:14-15). The customary violence against the Nephites spilled over into the treatment of each other; they fought for goods rather than working for them. We have to treat the charge of indolence with a little skepticism, considering that the Nephites mainly saw the Lamanites from a distance or up close in a murdering and plundering mode. But it is also true that King Lamoni suffered from a band of rustlers who drove off the king's herds from the watering place. These were not a hostile group of outsiders, but some of his own subjects. Rather than work to assemble their herds, they used force (Alma 17:26-27). The use of violence against the Nephites may have legitimized plundering within Lamanite society, just as veterans returning from wars in some instances settle personal quarrels with guns. National myths and practices can affect the limits of personal behavior, and, in Lamanite history, force was made a virtue.

However much the founding saga influenced individual Lamanites, there is no question that it definitively established Lamanite policy toward the Nephites. "Their hatred was fixed," Enos said (Enos 1:20). Even when circumstances acted to moderate the hatred, it only subsided; it was never wholly extinguished. In a sense it was a great national resource, a source of energy and resolve that malicious rulers could call upon to serve their selfish interests. One of the common phrases in the Book of Mormon is "stir up to anger." With mostly primitive governmental mechanisms at their disposal, Lamanite rulers commonly relied on oratory to govern. The people had to be aroused in order to mobilize them for the massive war efforts against the Nephites. In such instances, the tradition of the fathers was a resource like money or food. Zerahem-nah, an especially vicious king, made a special effort among his people "to preserve their hatred towards the Nephites, that he might bring them into subjection to the accom-plishment of his designs" (Alma 43:7). A national heritage, whether benign or malign, can fade from time to time, and must be revived if leaders are to use it to their advantage. After an especially disastrous defeat, a large group of La-manites refused to go into battle again, exhausted and fearful for their lives (Alma 47:2). The response of the king was to undertake a campaign to "inspire the hearts of the Lamanites against the people of Nephi." And how did he accomplish that? "He did appoint men to speak unto the Lamanites from their towers, against the Nephites" (Alma 48:1). We can easily guess at the message spoken from the towers, and the results were predictable. He "hardened the hearts of the Lamanites and blinded their minds, and stirred them up to anger" (Alma 48:3).

Lamanite resolve presented the Nephites with a nearly insoluble problem. There was seemingly no way to stop the Lamanite attacks permanently. If the problem had been a land shortage or the imbalance of wealth in the two societies, an agreement might have been worked out. But Lamanite hatred of the Nephites was far more profound than that. It was ingrained in their national identity. Their founding story depicted them as a people who had been robbed and therefore whose destiny it was to destroy those who had wronged them. Wars against the Nephites were to the Lamanites like fighting for freedom and equality is to us. Fighting wars maintained fundamental values of the society that were rooted in the mythic account of their national beginnings and were essential to their identity as a people. One could not expect them to stop the wars any more than we can be expected to renounce the idea of equality enunciated in the Declaration of Independence.

They would not be Lamanites, nor we Americans, if this occurred.[1]

Because war was part of the Lamanite identity, there was no resolution of the conflict—unless the Lamanites could be persuaded to forgo their own tradition. It seemed like a hopeless undertaking, like persuading the United States to return to monarchy and its attendant arbitrariness. But one valiant attempt was made. We think of the sons of Mosiah as giving up statecraft when they unitedly yielded their rights to the throne. Their abdication in advance of Mosiah's death compelled the king to introduce a major constitutional change in Nephite government, altering it from a monarchy to a rule by judges. We admire the young men for giving up the throne to preach the gospel, but we may question their judgment. Was it not irresponsible to refuse the duty that always falls on the sons of the king? Could not one of them have stayed behind to occupy the throne? But our doubts are quieted when we look closely at the reasons for the mission, for it appears that they went to the Lamanites for reasons of state as well as to right themselves with the Lord. The sons of Mosiah had been converted along with Alma and desired to "impart the word of God to their brethren, the Lamanites." But besides bringing them to a knowledge of God, they wished to "convince them of the iniquity of their fathers." It was not enough to teach Christ. They also had to attack the story of Laman and Lemuel as the Lamanites understood it—in other words, the tradition of their fathers. The reason for doing that was simple. The missionaries hoped that "perhaps they might cure them of their hatred towards the Nephites." That would permit them all to rejoice in the Lord their God, that they too "might become friendly to one another, and that there should be no more contentions in all the land" (Mosiah 28:1-2). It was a long shot, but by 92 B.C., after five hundred years of warfare, it may have been apparent to the king's sons that Lamanite warfare could only be halted by attacking its foundation, the tradition of their fathers.

The marvel is that they succeeded as well as they did. Traveling in the wilderness toward Lamanite lands, the missionaries prepared themselves by much fasting and prayer, beseeching the Lord to enable them to bring the Lamanites "to the knowledge of the truth, to the knowledge of the baseness of the traditions of their fathers, which were not correct" (Alma 17:9). And their prayers were answered. The method by which they achieved their purpose is inspiring as well as interesting. They did it by simple acts of love and generosity. The ease with which the Lamanites gave way before the missionaries belies the Nephite images of flinty and ferocious Lamanites. Instead, some of the Lamanites appear remarkably vulnerable. Lamoni's men bound Ammon when he entered their land, as they always did with Nephite intruders, but when he announced his wish to live with them, perhaps until the day he died, Lamoni was so touched he offered Ammon a daughter for a wife (Alma 17:20-24). Lamoni's tender heart was deeply moved by Ammon's faithful service, which prepared the king to be converted soon thereafter.

Lamoni's father reacted like Laman of old in drawing his sword against his son and then Ammon, and when Ammon overpowered him, the old king cowered before the missionary's greater power, again as Laman did before Nephi (Alma 16:20-24). But it was not Ammon's physical superiority that impressed the king; it was the love for the king's son that astonished him exceedingly (Alma 20:26). When another set of missionaries offered to serve Lamoni's father, he remembered this love and wanted to listen. Ammon's generosity, as well as his words, troubled the king, and he was ready to hear more (Alma 22:3). The willing service and acts of generosity and love, so contrary to the

Lamanite stereotypes of the Nephites, got through the armor and touched the hearts of the two kings.

These stories remind us of the time when Laman and Lemuel pulled back from their plan to slay Nephi as they returned from Jerusalem with Ishmael and his family. Instead of a show of force halting the attempt, one of Ishmael's daughters, along with her mother and a son, pleaded for Nephi. We see in the incident the beginning of a romance, but what may be far more significant is that a womanly appeal, from a mother as well as a daughter, softened the flinty hearts of the brothers. They responded as fully to this appeal as to the later shock of power from Nephi. The record says "they were sorrowful, because of their wickedness, insomuch that they did bow down before me, and did plead with me that I would forgive them of the thing that they had done against me" (1 Nephi 7:19-20). At the outset, gentleness succeeded where harsh rebukes failed, and in later history kindness and love again exercised influence where the Nephites' militant resistance bred only more warfare. Force may not have been the only language some of the Lamanites understood.

The conversions fulfilled the missionaries' hopes far more completely than they had any reason to expect. The two kings and many of the people believed. And it was not just the gospel they accepted. They were convinced that "the traditions of [their] wicked fathers" were wrong (Alma 24:7). That meant Laman and Lemuel were wrong and Nephi was right, a deep and profound reversal of their whole identity as a people that required an upending of old values. Their acceptance of this new tradition went hand in hand with their acceptance of the gospel. When the old king conferred the kingdom on his son, he gave him a new name, Anti-Nephi-Lehi, as if to recognize that a new set of founding fathers had to be embraced. The word sounds to us like opposition to Nephi and Lehi, but Hugh Nibley has told us it probably means the opposite, which the story itself of course strongly suggests. Anti-Nephi-Lehi and his brother Lamoni seemed to understand that some heroic effort would be required to root out the old tradition and set their people on a new course. They accomplished this reorientation by asking of their people an incredible sacrifice that directly attacked the besetting sin of Lamanite culture. The kings asked the people to give up violence. They agreed to bury their swords in the belief that Christ had removed the blood of many killings; for to fight again might leave a stain that could not be cleansed. That was the only way, they believed, to repent sincerely of their "many sins and murders." When the king had offered this covenant to the people, "they took their swords, and all the weapons which were used for the shedding of man's blood, and they did bury them up deep in the earth" (Alma 24:9-17). An attack of their unbelieving brethren did not cause them to waver. They knelt before the oncoming warriors and submitted to the slaughter. The reversal of old values was sealed with the converts' blood.

The missionary effort thus accomplished all that the sons of Mosiah had hoped for. Lamanites were converted to Christ, they gave up the tradition of their fathers, the spirit softened their hearts, and they "opened a correspondence with [their] brethren, the Nephites" (Alma 24:8). Having relinquished violence and plundering as the way to riches, the converts changed their living habits. "Rather than spend their days in idleness they would labor abundantly with their hands" (Alma 24:18). Peace with this transformed people was now perfectly natural. The Nephites welcomed the converts into their midst and gave them a land of their own.

These conversions did not permanently end the Lamanite wars by any means. The unconverted, still enmeshed in the tradition of their fathers, came up against the Nephites year after year bent on their destruction. But the sons of Mosiah showed how peace was to be achieved—by conversion to Christ and to the *correct* story of the nation's founding (see Alma 25:6). Their work set the pattern for later conversions by Nephi and Lehi, the sons of Helaman. The converts from this later proselyting effort also "did lay down their weapons of war, and also their hatred and the tradition of their fathers" (Helaman 5:51). With the false tradition out of the way, once more peace came to the two nations, commerce opened between them, and they enjoyed greater prosperity than at any time in their history to that point. This second missionary episode strengthens the implication that conversion to the gospel and repudiation of false traditions was the only workable basis for permanent peace.

Having reviewed this evidence, are we now in a position to rewrite the Book of Mormon from the Lamanite perspective? Perhaps we could sketch in some basic themes and a bare outline. But even in skeletal form, the history we might piece together would not be all we would like it to be. Our first impulse would be, perhaps, to vindicate the Lamanites, to lift them up and justify them. We may think that Nephi in all his grandeur is so hard on his brothers, so pitiless in his reproaches, and so sure of his mission that we should right the balance and find good in his rebellious brothers and their descendants, making a place for weaker souls in the annals of God's people. We cannot go as far in that direction as we would like. Lamanite history would be a bitter story, of a people obsessed with a perpetual sense of deprivation, wronged at the beginning, so they thought, and wronged ever after, living for vengeance, with blood on their swords. Lamanite history would honor valor and resolution in the face of repeated defeats but in a cause we can hardly admire.

On the other hand, we would gravely err to consider the Lamanites hopelessly benighted and persistently ferocious, hardened, and indolent in nature. Jacob warned against that error when he told his own people, speaking of the Lamanites, to "revile no more against them because of the darkness of their skins; neither shall ye revile against them because of their filthiness" (Jacob 3:9). The Lamanites who turned to Christ are among the most faithful and self-sacrificing in the Book of Mormon, giving themselves to be slaughtered rather than return to their sins. Even before conversion, they were faithful to each other in their families, at a time when the Nephites had taken up concubinage. Building on that foundation, the first Lamanite converts raised a generation of righteous offspring unmatched in the Book of Mormon. The source of Lamanite failings was not their natures but their tradition. Alma said it was "the traditions of their fathers that caused them to remain in their state of ignorance" (Alma 9:16). The Lamanites understood their national past erroneously, and so misconstrued their national purpose. Their history taught them that they had been wronged and that it was their destiny to right that wrong through relentless war on the Nephites. The incorrect tradition of their fathers was the cause of the misspent effort, the untold suffering, and the rivers of blood. The moral of the Lamanite story has nothing to do with their depravity but with the terrible consequences of misunderstanding the past.

There may be a moral for later generations of Book of Mormon readers, too. The story speaks to all who face implacable enemies, ones who are committed to aggressive incursions on peaceful peoples. The Book of Mormon tells us we may indeed have to defend ourselves with force in the face of an enemy onslaught, but it just as clearly states that militant defense will not ultimately end wars. Aggressive people, when meeting resistance, will come back generation after generation, century after century, even though soundly defeated time after time. Force, however benevolently intended, will not stop force permanently. As Christ said, he who lives by the sword dies by the sword; violence begets violence. In national as in personal affairs, kindness, truth, and service are the only avenues to lasting peace.

Note

1. For a similar perspective on Lamanite traditions, see Noel B. Reynolds, "The Political Dimensions in Nephi's Small Plates," *BYU Studies* 27 (1984): 15-37.

3

External Evidences of the Book of Mormon

Paul R. Cheesman
Brigham Young University, Provo, Utah

According to some scholars,[1] Palenque and the northern part of Guatemala were the cradle of the great Mayan culture (A.D. 250-850). The ancestors of the Maya, the Olmecs (1200-100 B.C.), built an impressive civilization even before the time of Christ. In Central and South America, we find the remains of this early Mayan culture which in some respects was equal to that of ancient Rome. The Mayan civilization persisted, under various ruling peoples[2] until 1500, when it and the neighboring Aztecs (A.D. 1400-1500)[3] were conquered by the Spanish.

Research has shown that all these people—Olmecs, Maya, and Aztecs—were deeply religious, and among their most persistent beliefs was one concerning the Great Spirit called Quetzalcoatl, represented in numerous paintings and carvings. A great leader, he is believed to have once visited the American continent, teaching them about religion, agriculture, and government.

As we try to visualize these ancient people, we are intrigued by a comparison with their descendants—the simple, unspoiled, friendly people who still make their homes nearby. One striking similarity is that the knowledge of Quetzalcoatl, handed down through centuries, persists even today.

The legend of the Bearded White God appears almost everywhere in this hemisphere. And though he is given

73

various names,[4] the allusion is always the same — a fair, bearded person with brown hair, blue eyes, and wearing a light robe.[5] He counseled the people, taught them, and left with the promise that he would someday return.[6]

In letters that Columbus sent back to Spain, he vividly described his reception upon arrival in the New World.

> The people of this land believed very firmly that I, with these ships and crew, came from the sky; and in such opinion, they received me at every place where I landed, after they had lost their terror.
>
> And to this day many of them are still of the opinion that I came from heaven. And they were the first to proclaim it wherever I arrived; and the others went running from house to house . . . with loud cries of 'Come! Come to see the people from heaven!'[7]

When they landed in Mexico, Cortez and his conquerors also experienced a lavish welcome from the great Montezuma and his people, the Aztecs.[8]

To the simple natives, both Columbus and Cortez represented the promised return of Quetzalcoatl, and they were received with great joy. The crafty Cortez, taking advantage of the legend, told the chiefs he was indeed sent by Quetzalcoatl, and their belief in the Great White God was so strong it is recorded that with this news they "wept so that for a long space of time they could make no reply."[9] The persistent belief in this white god is harmonious with the appearance of Christ in 3 Nephi 11-26.[10] On the other hand, Ruth and Hyatt Verrill argue for a merely legendary source for the white god myth from early Sumer.[11] This, too, in its way, supports the Book of Mormon in pre-Columbian Old-New World contact.

Other evidence also argues for Old-New World communication. Cortez wrote back to Spain describing an advanced civilization with forts so large that a city of fifteen thousand inhabitants could live within its walls. He mentioned forts containing forty or more towers of heavy con-

struction built better, in fact, than the cathedrals in Spain.[12]
He described aqueducts and water systems of great size
and efficiency.[13] King Montezuma indicated to Cortez that
his ancestors were not native to the New World.[14] Some
scholars believe these seafarers brought with them a culture comparable to that of the Phoenicians, Egyptians, and
Greeks.[15] Teotihuacan, the ruin just outside Mexico City,
exemplifies the high degree of civilization attained by these
ancient peoples. Traveling further south, there are the pyramids of Tikal in Guatemala which served a vast population
dating back before the time of Christ. In Copan, Honduras,
is found what is thought to have been a great seat of
learning. All of these great cities stretching from Mexico
on the north down through the Yucatan Peninsula to Copan give mute evidence to the fact that an extremely high
culture existed centuries before Columbus.

Francisco Pizarro, a later explorer, made conquests still
farther south. He landed in Peru, and was amazed to find
millions of people scattered from Ecuador to Chile. He
discovered complex irrigation systems, including sluice-
ways and reservoirs,[16] which suggest influence from already advanced cultures. The coastal plains thus watered
by mountain streams produced many staple products, including cotton of such unique content that botanists conclude it to be a hybrid combination of the Old and the New
World, and was likely brought to the Americas by ship or
raft.[17]

The craftsmanship in New World pottery-making was
high in quality. Some styles of pottery were Mediterranean,
while others resembled the ceramics of the Orient.[18] In
Cuzco, Peru, an ancient capital, Pizarro found the city
surrounded by a massive wall built centuries before. The
enormous, beautifully cut and fitted stones were assembled without the aid of mortar. In fact, they are so perfectly
fitted and laid that a knife blade cannot be forced into the
joints. Some of these gigantic stones weigh more than a

hundred tons. Placing them atop one another was a remarkable engineering feat in itself.[19] The only analogous
structures in the world are the Egyptian pyramids.

Another astonishing engineering wonder is Machu Pic-
chu, situated high in the Peruvian Andes, atop a peak with
a sheer precipice on one side and a high peak on the other.
It is believed to be a fortress city built in pre-Incan times
to protect its citizens from invasion. The advanced tech-
nological expertise in this city's construction seems to have
sprung up in Peru with no archaeological evidence of de-
velopmental or intermediate stages.[20] This may suggest
infusion from already advanced cultures.

Furthermore, a number of ancient American skills were
noteworthy, such as metal working and medicine. That
the ancients on the American continent were exceptional
goldsmiths is well known. Pizarro records that it took
"sixty Incan goldsmiths working steadily day and night
for one month" to reduce all of the stolen artifacts down
into bullion for transportation to Spain.[21] Gold was so common, in fact, that some gold objects were painted other
colors to break the monotony. Gold alloy was formed into
breastplates, and even flat, thin plates have been found
much like the aluminum foil in use today. The ancients
also worked with copper, silver, and some bronze in a way
similar to their Near Eastern counterparts.

In addition to being outstanding metalsmiths, artisans,
and builders, these ancient Americans were skilled in other
areas as well. They were gifted in the art of medicine to
an astonishing degree. They were familiar with the use of
narcotics, treated abnormal pregnancies, and even performed successful skull operations.[22] They were also accomplished musicians with a musical scale similar to that
found in the Mediterranean area. They were highly skilled
in astronomy and mathematics, using the zero even before
the Old World.[23] And over a thousand years before the
Old World had today's calendar, New World mathema-

ticians were using a more accurate system. The Aztec calendar, while not as accurate as the Mayan, is still quite
efficient.[24]

This people also showed a great interest in religion.
According to many interesting discoveries that have been
made, religion was the center of their lives. Some of these
early Americans possessed a story of the creation of the
world, of a great flood, a closed ark, the building of a high
tower, and a confusion of languages. Scholars obtained
this knowledge from the works of a royal Indian prince,
Ixtlilxochitl, who was taught the Spanish language by
padres, who followed the conquistadors. This prince inherited ancient Aztec records from his royal grandfather
and translated them into Spanish, working all his life on
the project. This history tells of how the Toltecs came to
this continent many years after the flood, and their dating
begins with the time "when Christ suffered."[25]

Later, some early Spanish scholars learned the native
language and translated the ancient histories and traditions
into Spanish. These translations are very interesting, and
one of these Spanish scholars, Sahagun, wrote of pre-
Christian and Christian Aztec beliefs, among which were
similarities to such basic Christian doctrines as the afterlife
and the kingdom of heaven, fasting, repentance, and a
kind of eucharist in which an imitation body of the god
was made of Amaranth dough and eaten.[26] There is some
evidence that the natives practiced circumcision and some
form of baptism.[27] These suggest that there may have been
pre-Columbian influences from the Old World.

The use of incense[28] in the ceremonies of the Indians
is another tie to the Old World. The marriage covenant
was sacred, indicating a high degree of morality among
these people.[29] In fact, the Spanish padres were surprised
at the great number of parallels between the religion and
practices of the ancient Indians and those of the Catholics
of the Old World—such things as sacrificial altars,[30] the

burying of honored deceased individuals inside the temples or pyramids,[31] and the manner of burial that indicated belief in immortality.[32] The Aztec Pyramid of the Sun at Teotihuacan bears great similarity in size and structure to those found in Egypt.[33] Most scholars today believe that the American Indian is a mixture of many races and blood types.[34] Recent studies and discoveries also link the Americas with Mediterranean cultures.[35]

So, there are a number of possible links between the Americas and the ancient world: belief in a white god, advanced building and engineering feats, metallurgy, and artisanship. An additional link with the Book of Mormon is the practice in the ancient world of writing on metal plates and their burying them in stone boxes.

In 1830, some ancient writing on plates was found in Palmyra, New York, by a young man named Joseph Smith, who described them as follows:

> These records were engraven on plates which had the appearance of gold, each plate was six inches wide and eight inches long, and not quite so thick as common tin. They were filled with engravings, in Egyptian characters, and bound together in a volume as the leaves of a book, with three rings running through the whole. The volume was something near six inches in thickness, a part of which was sealed.[36]

At that time, in 1830, Joseph Smith's discovery was new. But was it unique? Was writing on metal plates completely unknown? The answer is no.

In the 1400s in the medieval city of Gubbio, Italy, seven large bronze tablets, called the Iguvine Tablets,[37] which contained instructions for religious ceremonies, were discovered. Since then, lead plates containing commercial records of Italian families have been found in Bologna and Venice[38]—a common practice until the sixteenth century. Early Greek and Latin writings tell of metal plates used for treaty tablets and temple prayers.[39] These writings were

translated and read widely in Europe and America. Therefore, anyone familiar with these texts in 1830 would not
have been surprised at the idea of writing on metal.

Writing on metal took a variety of forms. When Sir
Francis Drake sailed into San Francisco Bay in the 1500s,
he claimed the territory and erected a bronze plaque to
document his claim.[40] The Tookabatcha Indians of Missis-
sippi and Alabama refer to five copper plates and two brass
plates that their tribe has preserved for generations. The
plates contain symbols resembling those of early Rome and
Greece. Several authors, including James Adair, described
these plates.[41]

All of these examples of writing on metal were found
before Moroni's first visit to Joseph Smith in 1823. Nevertheless, his discovery created much excitement—and some
skepticism—because it involved *gold* plates. Ancient writing on *gold* plates was not thought in 1823 to have been
as historically commonplace, but many have been found
worldwide since that time.

In Korea in 1965, nineteen gold plates dating back to
the tenth century A.D. were found buried in a bronze box
at the base of a pagoda. They were hinged together in
accordion style and measured 14 x 15 inches.[42] In the Rocke-
feller Museum in Jerusalem there is a plaque of thin gold
foil from the Roman period. On this plate, used to cover
the lips of the dead, is inscribed, "Take Courage Gos-
mos."[43] In 1920, at the headwaters of the Tigris River,
explorers found a gold tablet of King Shalmaneser in the
land now known as Iraq. Though the tablet is undated,
we know Shalmaneser lived about eight hundred years
before Christ.[44]

In 1938, while excavating the palace of King Darius I,
who reigned over Persia in the sixth century before Christ,
a team from the University of Chicago discovered the closest and most spectacular parallel to the Book of Mormon
plates: King Darius, in commemoration of the completion

of his palace at Persepolis, placed eight metal tablets (four gold and four silver) in four stone boxes[45] at the corners of the structure. Translations of the tablets reveal that they gave thanks to God and asked for protection of the royal household.

One of the oldest examples of writing on gold plates is found in the Louvre in Paris. It is the gold plate of Djokha Umma, and was discovered in the foundation of a sacred building in Iraq.[46] It measures less than 2 x 3 inches. Also in the Louvre are the six plates of Sargon II from King Khorsabad's palace in Assyria (ca. 700 B.C.).[47] Encased in a box were several plates, one of which was gold. The others were silver, lead, tin, and copper.

In Rome, prominently displayed in a famous archaeological museum, are three magnificent gold plates of Pyrgi (ca. 500 B.C.),[48] written in the language of the Phoenicians and Etruscans. The plates are about 5 x 7 inches. You can still see the holes where they were originally fastened with nails to the door of the temple of the goddess, Astarte. These plates were very nearly the size of those described by Joseph Smith.[49] In the British Museum in London are found two beautiful Maunggun gold plates, each measuring 1 x 14 inches, containing Buddhist scriptures[50] and dating back to the first century A.D. They each have three lines of writing in the Pali language.

Writing on gold plates was indeed a common practice anciently. When gold was not plentiful, other metals were used. Lead and bronze plates were found with inscriptions; an inscribed bronze scoop dating back to 2000 B.C., along with writing on mirrors and even on metal moulded animals were found; also, bronze statue pedestals bearing inscriptions have been found. An outstanding example of writing on silver comes from Bethany. This scroll, dated A.D. 400, was found rolled up in a copper tube. It can be seen at the Information Center on Temple Square in Salt Lake City, Utah.[51] It is very small (7-1/4 x 2-1/8 inches) and had to be photographed and magnified in order for the ancient Greek writing to be read. It lists religious beings who could ward off evil influences. A scroll similar to the Bethany scroll is on display in the archaeological museum in Jerusalem.

One of the famous Dead Sea copper scrolls from the Qumran community near Jerusalem, which existed before Christ, is proudly displayed in the National Archaeological Museum in Jordan.[52] This scroll, written in Hebrew, told of a buried treasure which has never been found. It told of tithing and temple receipts from the Qumran community.

In Rome, in addition to the gold plates of Pyrgi and the bronze tablets of Gubbio, there are two ancient books from America called codices. They were written on the pounded bark of trees and folded like an accordion. They contain beautiful colorful drawings and hieroglyphs which were made A.D. 1400 and are now being translated. These Mayan books are renowned for their perfect preservation and are housed in the Vatican Library.[53] Not only did ancient peoples write on metal plates, but they also wrote on metal columns,[54] such as the giant pillar from the Near East dating back to 1100 B.C., now housed in the Louvre.

When Joseph Smith reported that his ancient gold plates were bound with metal rings, once again the idea seemed novel. Actually, though, the ancient Sanskrit and Tamil plates from India dating to A.D. 769 are bound together with a copper ring. They are in the British Museum along with other copper, silver, bronze, and gold plates from India written in ancient Pali.[55] Some of these plates were a base metal covered with gold, with enameled black writing.

Joseph Smith is no longer alone in declaring that ancient American inhabitants in the New World could not only write, but that they preserved their writings in much the same manner as was previously done in the Old World.

Archaeologist Rivero and historian Tschudi mention possible instances of the ancient Peruvians writing on metal.[56] The well-known Hugo Cohen Museum in Lima, Peru, houses an intriguing gold plate found in a Peruvian area called Lambayeque.[57] It measures 4 x 8 inches and contains possible writing symbols. Several plates of copper, bronze, and gold have been found by modern natives digging in the ruins of Cuenca, Ecuador. Scientists are now studying the plates to determine their authenticity and relationship to the ancient languages of the Old World.

One of the best-known examples of ancient writing on metal in the New World comes from the sacrificial well, or *cenote*, in Chichen Itza on the Yucatan Peninsula in Mexico. When the Peabody Museum crew from Harvard University began dredging this well, they found embossed gold discs, among which was one with Mayan inscriptions.[58] This well predates Columbus, and the gold disc is now in the Peabody Museum. J. Eric S. Thompson, the Maya hieroglyph expert, says that inscriptions have been found (though rarely) on metal in postclassic Mesoamerica.[59] Juan de Torquemada, in discussing the ancient Toltec of Mexico, noted that they wrote in two columns — one of metal, and the other of stone.[60] A native Mexican writer of Colonial times wrote: "It is certain that there were this kind of Artisans in Oaxaca, . . . for [probably before 1880] the Mixtecs sold to some European antiquarians some very thin gold plates, evidently worked by hammering that their ancestors had been able to preserve, and which were engraved with ancient hieroglyphs."[61]

Six bell-shaped brass plates were found in Kinderhook, Illinois, in 1843, in a mound with a skeleton.[62] The date and origin are questionable and unknown. The writing is being studied, but no translation has been made. The Museum of the American Indian in New York City displays a gold disc thought to be a calendar. Inscriptions may have been placed on this metal about 800 B.C. somewhere in the Chavin area of Peru.[63]

Scholars and adventurers have been in awe as they have viewed the magnificent temples and carvings of ancient American cultures. They have marveled at their advanced society which revealed a knowledge of engineering, architecture, highway construction, astronomy, mathematics, religion, government, and art — evidences on every hand of a highly civilized people. Is it unreasonable to expect, then, that some of these ancient peoples were skilled communicators in the manner of their ancestors? I think not.

When Joseph Smith reported that he had found inscribed gold plates buried in a stone box, the idea seemed novel. Yet, prominently on display in the Louvre is a stone box[64] containing copper plates with writing from the foundation of the temple of Dagan at Mari.[65] These date back to 3000 B.C. The British Museum also houses two ancient boxes — one is from Balawat and contains two stone tablets;[66] the other is of clay and was found in Babylonia, dated 600 B.C.

Joseph Smith said that the history written on his gold plates was of a people whose roots began in the Middle East and who brought with them to the New World the traditions and customs of their land. These customs included writing on metal plates and burying them in stone boxes. Although stone boxes were used commonly in the Old World to bury and preserve histories and other treasures, only recently have ancient stone boxes been discovered in America in significant numbers. Many of these are now on display in the archaeological museum in Mexico.

Stone boxes have been found in the Old World as well as the New. These boxes usually contained gold, jewelry, tools, or other valuables. A stone box found in Persepolis, Iran, contained two thin metal plates — one of gold and the other of silver—upon which was an engraved record of King Darius.[67] Several hundred different histories engraved on gold, silver, and copper plates have been discovered in the Old World. In the year 1823, a stone box, much like those discovered later in Latin America, was shown to Joseph Smith in the side of a hill near Palmyra, New York. The stone box contained ancient golden plates with strange engravings upon them much like those found in Iran.

This record, when translated, was found to be God's dealings with some of the early inhabitants of the American continent, and was destined to change the course of history. It told of three groups of people migrating here by ship from the Old World. It described the rise and fall of two glorious civilizations that prospered under the hands of the Lord when they kept his commandments and were destroyed when they did not.

Eleven reputable men besides Joseph Smith were privileged to see these gold records. Eight of them signed the following statement:

> Be it known unto all nations, kindred, tongues, and people unto whom this work shall come: That Joseph Smith, Jun., the translator of this work, has shown unto us the plates of which hath been spoken, which have the appearance of gold; and as many of the leaves as the said Smith has translated we did handle with our hands; and we also saw the engravings thereon, all of which has the appearance of ancient work, and of curious workmanship. And this we bear record with words of soberness, that the said Smith has shown unto us, for we have seen and hefted, and know of a surety that the said Smith has got the plates of which we have spoken. And we give our names unto the world, to witness unto the world that which we have seen. And we lie not, God bearing witness of it.[68]

Running throughout the Book of Mormon narrative is

the story of two groups of people — one light-skinned and the other dark. We see possible evidence of this in murals at Bonampak, Mexico, as well as in murals at Chichen Itza. Legends still exist among these Indians about a dark people and a light people who lived there anciently.

The Book of Mormon also speaks of frequent warfare in this civilization. The actuality of this is borne out by the numerous fortifications and weapons found in Mexico and in Central and South America — weapons similar to those used in the Old World.

One of the most unforgettable stories in the Book of Mormon is Lehi's "tree of life" vision. References to the tree of life continue to crop up in such diverse places as Egypt, Mesoamerica, and in Paracas, Peru. Carved centuries ago in a mountain in Paracas, a representation is still called the tree of life by local natives. And in Izapa, Mexico, is one of the most detailed tree of life carvings to be found anywhere. One modern scholar who has made a thorough study of this stela has suggested 110 similarities between this sculpture and the dream of Lehi and Nephi in the Book of Mormon.[69]

Perhaps the most beautiful and memorable segment of the Book of Mormon is the portion that tells of the story of a visit of Jesus Christ. He taught the people, blessed the children, and, upon leaving, promised to return someday. His teachings were very similar to those of the Bearded White God who taught all goodness and virtue, and then promised to return. So great was the impact of Christ's visit to this continent that his story was repeated and handed down by word of mouth for centuries. Is it any wonder that the natives bowed down and worshiped Columbus, Cortez, and Pizarro upon their arrival here?

And this brings us full circle to the question of the Bearded White God, the most widely held legend in this part of the world. The story of the Bearded White God in these great civilizations of the past is no longer a complete mystery. We still have much to learn about them, but we have many clues.

There are the history of Ixtlilxochitl, the Mayan prince; the translated histories of the Spanish chronicles; and the Book of Mormon, which contains the most lengthy and detailed history of these people and emerges as the most valuable record known concerning this pre-Columbian civilization.

The Book of Mormon was not intended to be read as an archaeological document. Certain mundane activities were only mentioned to provide cohesion to the narrative. Discussing these factors, however, can raise, for some people, interest in the record itself. Evidence of their mathematics, astronomy, agricultural practices, mastery of weaving textiles, and so forth, helps document their greatness. The main purpose of the Book of Mormon is spiritual. The book contains God's dealings with three groups of immigrants to the American continent and is a second witness and testament of the mission and plan of Jesus Christ.

After the age of forty-two, I attended Brigham Young University for graduate studies and became a student of Hugh Nibley, admiring him as a scholar and friend. Dr. Nibley accompanied Dr. LaMar Garrard and me on a trip through the Navajo and Hopi Indian country, and later he and I accompanied a group on a tour through the Mexican pre-Columbian ruins. These experiences, along with the inspiration I have received from reading his many works, have endeared him to me immeasurably.

Notes

1. Constance Irwin, *Fair Gods and Stone Faces* (New York: St. Martin's, 1963), 102, 166; J. Eric S. Thompson, *Maya History and Religion* (Norman, OK: University of Oklahoma Press, 1970), 106; A. Hyatt Verrill, *Old Civilizations of the New World* (New York: Tudor, 1938), 100.

2. Cf. the Toltecs, for example, who ruled A.D. 950-1200.

3. The Aztec chieftain was the now famous Montezuma (ca. A.D. 1480-1520).

4. He was known by various names. To the Toltecs and Aztecs of Mexico, he was Quetzalcoatl; to the Incas, Viracocha; to the Maya, Kukulcan; to the Chibchas, Bochica; to the Peruvian Aymara, Hyustus. Cf. Pierre Honoré, *In Quest of the White God*, trs. Oliver Coburn and Ursula Lehrburger (New York: Putnam, 1964), 16. This god Quetzalcoatl should not be confused with an eighth-century hero who took upon himself the name of Quetzalcoatl.

5. Verrill, *Old Civilizations*, 182; see also A. Hyatt Verrill, *Great Conquerors of South and Central America* (New York: Appleton, 1929), 53-55; and A. Hyatt Verrill and Ruth Verrill, *America's Ancient Civilizations* (New York: Putnam, 1953), 67.

6. See Honoré, *In Quest of the White God*, 16, 98, 108; cf. Thompson, *Maya History and Religion*, 44.

7. John B. Thacher, *Christopher Columbus*, 3 vols. (New York: AMS Press/Kraus Reprint, 1967), 2:22-23.

8. Verrill, *Great Conquerors of South and Central America*, 61-62.

9. Hernando Cortez, *Five Letters 1519-1526*, tr. J. Bayard Morris (London: Routledge, 1928), 82.

10. Cf. Bruce Warren and Thomas S. Ferguson, *The Messiah in Ancient America* (Provo, UT: Book of Mormon Research Foundation, 1987), esp. 29-50.

11. Verrill and Verrill, *America's Ancient Civilizations*, 109, 293.

12. Cortez, *Five Letters*, 78, 90.

13. Ibid., 92-93.

14. Verrill, *Great Conquerors*, 51; Honoré, *In Quest of the White God*, 26-27.

15. Verrill and Verrill, *America's Ancient Civilizations*, 293; Honoré, *In Quest of the White God*, 22, 200-208.

16. Verrill and Verrill, *America's Ancient Civilizations*, 256, on the complex irrigation and reservoir system.

17. Cf. George Carter, "Before Columbus" in Paul R. Cheesman, ed., *The Book of Mormon: The Keystone Scripture* (Provo, UT: BYU Religious Studies Center, 1988), 164-86; cf. J. B. Hutchinson, R. A. Silow, and S. G. Stephens, *Evolution of Gossypium* (London: Oxford University Press, 1947).

18. Cf. Verrill and Verrill, *America's Ancient Civilizations*, 173.

19. Ibid., 235-38, 243-45, 247.

20. Ibid., 196-97, 246.

21. Verrill, *Great Conquerors of South and Central America*, 20-21.

22. Verrill and Verrill, *Ancient American Civilizations*, 153-54, 309.

23. For a reference on mathematics, see Donald Ediger, *The Well of Sacrifice* (Garden City, NY: Doubleday, 1971), 16; cf. Irwin, *Fair Gods and Stone Faces*, 107, 110-11, 115, 273; for astronomy, see Ediger, *The Well of Sacrifice*, 142, and Verrill and Verrill, *Ancient American Civilizations*, 195.

24. Verrill and Verrill, *America's Ancient Civilizations*, 260.

25. For the *Works of Ixtlilxochitl* compared with the Book of Mormon, see Milton R. Hunter and Thomas S. Ferguson, *Ancient America and the Book of Mormon* (Oakland, CA: Kolob, 1950), esp. 189-94, for the chronological correspondence between Christ's death and the Toltec calendrical dating, and cf. 89-90 for Toltec knowledge of the creation and flood. Cf. E. Wyllys Andrews, "Chronology and Astronomy in the Maya Area" in Clarence L. Hay et al., eds., *The Maya and Their Neighbors* (New York: Appleton Century, 1940), 150-61.

26. Fray Bernardino Sahagun, *General History of the Things of New Spain: Florentine Codex*, tr. Charles E. Dibble and Arthur J. O. Anderson, 13 vols. (Salt Lake City, UT: School of American Research and the University of Utah, 1950-70), 1: prologue to the argument against idolatry, chaps. 1, 12, 14, 19, 24; 2:chaps. 4 and 6; 3: chap. 1.

27. Ibid. Baptism as immersion is uncertain, but some form of ceremonial washing (1: chaps. 1 and 19), including washing of the feet (1: chap. 19) was performed. In addition, circumcision is also unclear since the term "man's skin" (2: chap. 21) might merely refer to the skin of the entire body, as in "wearing human skins" (1: chap. 18). Reference is elsewhere made to the wearing of "woman's skin" after a female sacrificial victim had been skinned (2: chap. 11; 1: chap. 8).

28. Thomas Gann, *Glories of the Maya* (New York: Scribners, 1939), 20-21, 84, 209-10.

29. Adultery was violently punished. See Oliver La Farge, "Maya Ethnology: The Sequence of Cultures," in Hay et al., *The Maya and Their Neighbors*, 284.

30. C. Bruce Hunter, *A Guide to Ancient Maya Ruins* (Norman, OK: University of Oklahoma Press, 1974), 16, 49-52, 55, 66, 77, 121-22.

31. Patrick Culbert, "Early Maya Development at Tikal, Guatemala" in Richard E. W. Adams, ed., *The Origins of Maya Civilization* (Albuquerque: University of New Mexico Press, 1977), 40-41; cf. Gann, *Glories of the Maya*, 113, 154, 172-77, 197, 206, 210, 264.

32. Cf. Gann, *Glories of the Maya*, 71, 145, 206, who claims that many ancient beliefs still persist.

33. Ediger, *The Well of Sacrifice*, 19, 142.

34. W. W. Howells, "The Origins of American Indian Race Types" in Hay et al., *The Maya and Their Neighbors*, 7.

35. Ibid.

36. HC 4:537.

37. See Irene Rosenzweig, *Ritual and Cults of Pre-Roman Iguvium* (London: Christophers, 1937); cf. Ambros J. Pfiffig, *Religio Etrusca* (Graz: Akademische Druck, 1975); cf. Paul R. Cheesman, *Ancient Writings on Metal Plates* (Bountiful, UT: Horizon, 1985), 57-59.

38. Cheesman, *Ancient Writings*, 63.

39. For example, on the bronze treaty tablets in the Athens Archaeological Museum, see Cheesman, *Ancient Writings*, 47-48; on the nine gold Orphic plates buried in Greece and now in museums in England, Naples, and Athens, see Cheesman, *Ancient Writings*, 55-56, 63.

40. *Drake's Plate of Brass: Evidence of His Visit to California in 1579* (San Francisco: California Historical Society, 1937), 1.

41. James Adair, *The History of the American Indians* (New York: Johnson Reprint, 1968), 178-79; cf. Albert J. Pickett, *The History of Alabama* (Birmingham, AL: Birmingham, 1962), 81-83.

42. National Museum, Seoul. Examined by the author in Korea, 1979.

43. Cf. Cheesman, *Ancient Writings*, 69.

44. Peabody Museum, Boston, Massachusetts.

45. Cheesman, *Ancient Writings*, 59-60; cf. H. Curtis Wright, "Ancient Burials of Metal Documents in Stone Boxes," in this volume.

46. Cheesman, *Ancient Writings*, 64.

47. Ibid., 61-62.

48. Ibid., 63.

49. National Museum of Villa Giulia in the Piazza de Villa Giulia 9.

50. Cheesman, *Ancient Writings*, 72, 75.

51. Ibid., 65.

52. Ibid., 59, 61.

53. Verrill and Verrill, *America's Ancient Civilizations*, 78.

54. Cheesman, *Ancient Writings*, 63.

55. Etruscan gold sheets with holes and rivets in a book format have also been found, ibid., 56-57.

56. Mariano Eduardo de Rivero y Ustariz and Dr. Juan Diego de Tschudi, *Antiguedades Peruanas* (Arequipa, Peru: Primer Festival de Libro Arequipeno, 1958; repr. of an 1851 ed.) However, the Spanish word for metal used here, "materia," can also mean subject matter or topic, so the reference to writing in metal is not clear.

57. Cheesman, *Ancient Writings*, 50.

58. Richard E. W. Adams, *Prehistoric Mesoamerica* (Boston: Little, Brown, 1977), 244-45.

59. J. Eric S. Thompson, "Maya Hieroglyphic Writing," in Gordon R. Willey, ed., *Handbook of Middle American Indians*, 16 vols. and suppl., Robert Wauchope, general ed. (Austin: University of Texas Press, 1965), 3:634.

60. Juan de Torquemada, *Monarquia Indiana*, 3 vols. (Mexico: Editorial Porrua, 1969; first ed. Seville, 1615), 1:chap. 14.

61. José A. Gay, *Historia de Oaxaca Mexico*, 2 vols. (Oaxaca: Tall-Tip. del Gobierno Oaxaca, 1933), 1:62 .

62. *HC* 5:372-79.

63. Verrill and Verrill, *America's Ancient Civilizations*, 304.

64. Cf. Wright, "Ancient Burials of Metal Documents in Stone Boxes," in this volume.

65. Cheesman, *Ancient Writings*, 77-78.

66. Ibid., 78-79.

67. Ibid., 59-60.

68. Introductory pages, "The Testimony of Eight Witnesses," in the Book of Mormon (Salt Lake City: The Church of Jesus Christ of Latter-day Saints, 1984).

69. M. Wells Jakeman, *The Complex "Tree of Life" Carving on Izapa Stela 5: A Reanalysis and Partial Interpretation* (Provo, UT: Brigham Young University, 1958).

4

A Second Witness for the *Logos:*
The Book of Mormon and Contemporary Literary Criticism

Eugene England
Brigham Young University, Provo, Utah

Until recently, attempts to vindicate the central claim of the Book of Mormon about itself — that it is a divinely inspired book based on the history of an ancient culture — have focused mainly on external evidences. Such attempts examine parallels in the geographies, cultures, and literatures of the Middle East and ancient America (especially parallels to knowledge that have become available only since Joseph Smith's time). These parallels are used to prove that the Book of Mormon is consistent with ancient knowledge and forms which Joseph Smith could have known only through an ancient manuscript and revelation. This essay takes a different approach, based essentially on internal evidence provided by the book itself. My reflections, stimulated by the work of Mormon scholars such as John Welch, Noel Reynolds, and Bruce Jorgensen, examine techniques developed by non-Mormon literary critics Northrop Frye and René Girard in their work on the Bible.

An earlier version of this essay appeared in Dialogue: A Journal of Mormon Thought *22/3 (Fall 1989): 32-51, as "Why Nephi Killed Laban: Reflections on the Truth of the Book of Mormon."*

91

Frye, by analyzing the Bible's unique typological literary structure and its kinds and qualities of language, and Girard, by examining its uniquely revealing and healing response to human violence, have each concluded that the Bible not only has literary qualities superior to those in all other books but is also uniquely divine. I concur with Frye and Girard — except in their claim for the Bible's uniqueness. One other book, the Book of Mormon, attains similar qualities of form and content and thus stands as a second witness not only for Christ, but for the *Logos*, the redeeming Word.

In 1985, while on tour in France with Brigham Young University students, I listened to Malcolm Miller "read" the windows at Chartres Cathedral. For nearly thirty years he has been learning to read the "book," actually the library, miraculously preserved in the stained glass of one — and only one — of the medieval cathedrals and now available to a nearly uncomprehending modern world. His one-hour lecture could only open the first few pages of the first book there at Chartres, but what a fascinating, strange, yet satisfying vision unfolded. He read the third window from the right along the north wall of the transept — the story of Joseph, projecting him as a "type," a pattern for the future Christ. Then he read the three great western windows, quite recently cleaned, whose brilliance and clarity suggest how the whole cathedral looked inside when it was young (and might again when funds for cleaning the other windows can be found). The central window on the west gives the greatest story in human history: God becoming like us in order to save us. On the right is the pattern of preparation for that event, Christ's descent through the loins of Jesse, and on the left are the details of Christ's life and death after the incarnation.

We went to the nave to read the great rose windows — the north one part of the pattern of Old Testament preparations; the south one focused on Mary, continuing the story of patterns in Christ's life that corresponded to the typological preparations. Everywhere I saw an obsession with order, pattern, types, parallels, prophecies, and ful- fillments in literal but meaningfully similar structures: the "soldiers" coming before Christ—the Old Testament prophets who foretold him—marshaled on the north; Christ and his "soldiers" that followed him, the martyrs and confessors, along the south; the four major prophets of the Old Testament with the New Testament evangelists literally standing on their shoulders; the Garden of Eden as Old Salem, the "lost peace," to be completed in the New Jerusalem; and, giving a shock of recognition to care- ful readers of the Book of Mormon, a deep green cross for Christ, based on the medieval legend that the "tree" he was hung upon was made from Eden's tree of life.

The Book of Mormon? Yes, because that most typo- logically structured book—the only one that uses biblical patterns with even greater frequency and consistency and ultimate significance than the Bible—has as its central pat- tern what Bruce Jorgensen has called "The Dark Way to the Tree," an archetypal journey to a tree which is multiple in form. With that image the Book of Mormon unites, to create greater understanding and power, four patterns of the human pilgrimage: (1) Adam and Eve as Everyman and Everywoman find their dark but necessary way to the tree of life through partaking of the tree of knowledge. (2) Christ provides the essential means for all men and women from Adam and Eve onward to make that dark journey, by personally taking his life's journey and ending upon a tree—death on a cross that makes possible eternal life. (3) Lehi's dream of personal search establishes the pattern in our souls through the powerful, patterning drama of the journey through darkness to partake of the fruit of a tree that represents God's love through Christ (1 Nephi 8 and 11). This dream begins the Book of Mormon narrative and, as Jorgensen has shown, becomes the type for its main stories. For instance, the conversions of Enos and Alma the Younger are told in ways that highlight their similarities to Lehi's dream pilgrimage, and even the overall structure of the book appears to be shaped as a version of such a journey for humankind. This typological structuring invites us all to participate in an individual journey of salvation, even as God is leading the whole earth (and human history) through such a journey in order to make our own journeys possible.[1] (4) Alma gives universal intellectual power to the pattern with his explication, uniquely appropriate for modern, science-oriented skeptics, of the central crux of the pilgrimage—how to know the truth and act upon it, which is best symbolized as planting a seed, growing a tree, and partaking of the fruit (Alma 32:28-43).

Patterns, and the process of patterning, are clearly central to both the Bible and the Book of Mormon. They seem to be central to basic human interests and needs. But mere pattern is not enough. We seem to yearn not only for pattern, but for meaningful, saving patterns, involving what Lehi in the Book of Mormon (2 Nephi 2:13) called "things . . . to act"—living agents, mortals and gods—rather than things "to be acted upon." Patterns obsess us because they emphasize what is most fundamental in the universe, what is repeated, necessary, irresistible, final. But there is a deep-set pattern, the source and goal of all our searching for pattern, what Northrop Frye in his book of the same title calls "The Great Code." It is the great scriptural pattern which, beyond what the universe is and has been, also images for us what the life of acting agents *can be* at its most satisfying, fulfilling, and enduring. That is the pattern Frye finds uniquely in the Bible. He traces the way that pattern has ultimately shaped our mythology, our metaphoric patterns, and our rhetoric itself—in other words, *all* our literature, not just that which directly alludes to the Bible. I believe that Frye's most important claims for the Bible can also be demonstrated for the Book of Mormon.

Actually, the Book of Mormon seems to me even more amenable than the Bible to Frye's analysis. It is mainly patterned by a single mind, that of Mormon, and the resulting unity is remarkably similar to the patterns only now being explicated in the Bible by critics such as Frye. Mormon and the other Book of Mormon writers had a remarkably full understanding of the role of Christ in human salvation and thus in history, perhaps fuller than that of biblical writers and thus more responsive to typological patterns in Israelite history as well as their own history. I believe that, given adequate attention by sympathetic critics, the Book of Mormon will provide an even deeper, more intellectually consistent, and powerful witness than the Bible for the *Logos*—both for Jesus Christ as our divine and only Savior and also for the Word, for language imbued with divine power.

Frye has long been intrigued by the Bible's unusual potential for "polysemous" interpretation; that is, for being understood and having enormous influence not only at the literal, historical level but even more so at various metaphorical levels. He has examined particularly the typological level, which connects events and people throughout history in a cohesive pattern of images and imitations of the process of salvation through Christ. He has also pointed to the success of medieval and subsequent commentators with the "moral" and "anagogical" levels of interpretation (at the moral level each passage is understood as teaching us, in addition to the literal story, how to imitate Christ's life in the practical world, at the anagogical level how to see our lives in the context of life in eternity with him).

Frye has finally concluded, and sets out in *The Great Code* to demonstrate, that "polysemous meaning is a feature of all deeply serious writing, and the Bible is the model for serious writing."[2] He argues that the biblical achievement with language is unique and its influence so powerful on all other uses of language that it alone has guaranteed the very possibility of retaining polysemous meaning in our modern culture, despite powerful influences to the contrary.

Such claims, of course, imply a particular history of language, which Frye provides. First he makes a crucial distinction, not provided in the single English word "language," between the structures of sound that make up a language, which of course cannot be adequately translated, and the essential sense and typological patterns of the language, which can. This latter is the French *langage,* as opposed to *langue. Langage* is "a sequence of modes of more or less translatable structures in words, cutting across the variety of *langues* employed, affected and conditioned but not wholly determined by them."[3] This is a valuable distinction; it turns us from exclusive attention to the formal elements of literature, such relationships of sound, multiple meanings, prose rhythms, concision, texture, and puns, that have preoccupied much literary criticism in this century. Such preoccupation has diverted us from other, perhaps weightier, matters, such as the large *patterns* of stories and repeated events that reveal the nature of sin and salvation. In the process we have been kept from full appreciation of the literary merit of the Bible — and almost *any* appreciation of the literary merit of the Book of Mormon. With few exceptions, such as Steven Walker's defense of the quality of language in the Book of Mormon,[4] its writing has been criticized as dull, flat, even awkward (overuse of phrases such as "And it came to pass"), and the extraordinary beauty of its concepts has been neglected (the remarkable philosophical sophistication of 2 Nephi 2 and Alma 32, the uniquely full and moving understanding of the atonement in Mosiah 3-5 and Alma 7, 34, and 42). Thus we have focused on *langue* (which might have been extraordinarily beautiful in the original but which—except for chiasmus, which we are learning to appreciate more fully—is untranslatable), rather than Frye's *langage*, the meanings that survive translation, such as the typologies of the tree of life.

According to Frye, the Bible is unique in its consistent power to preserve and to re-create in each new reader the reality of metaphorical language and typological patterns, because of the force with which it brings those two elements of *langage* into the modern world. It does this because, surprisingly, myth and metaphor provide the answer to the question: What is the "literal" meaning of the Bible? Frye also argues that the Bible invokes "a historical presence 'behind' [its language], as [French literary critic Jacques] Derrida would say, and that the background presence gradually shifts to a foreground, the re-creation of that reality in the reader's mind."[5] That historical reality is, of course, the typological keystone—Christ's involvement with the world, and it is a reality that I think Frye senses, though he never quite admits, is uniquely saving.

Frye is essentially right about the nature and importance of the Bible's contribution, by sustaining into the modern world the power of metaphorical language for *all* our literature. He is certainly wrong in his claim for the uniqueness of the Bible.[6] For there is one other book that preserves the full power of metaphorical language, typological structure, and Christ-centered moral and eschatological meaning for our secular, literalistic world. There is a second witness to Christ not only as the Savior of each individual and all the world but also to him as the *Logos*, the Word. Like the Bible, it witnesses that Christ is the one who used language, both as God and as a man, in ways that provide the most important clues to our nature and potential as his children, and it reminds us that we are inheritors of that same crucial gift of language. That second witness is the Book of Mormon.

Bruce Jorgensen has already cut a deep swath into the rich harvest of typological interpretation awaiting us in the Book of Mormon. In "The Dark Way to the Tree," he has demonstrated the book's potential with definitive examples and a persuasive overall typological reading and at the same time has developed a theory of the value of such a reading. The following passages give an example, summarize the theory, and suggest the quality of Jorgensen's contributions and the value of reading his entire essay:

> The narratives of the two Almas replicate a second movement of Lehi's dream that prefigures a large proportion of the Book of Mormon narrative. Having eaten the fruit and rejoiced, Lehi immediately "began to be desirous that [his] family should partake of it also" (1 Nephi 8:12); similarly, the forgiven Enos immediately "began to feel a desire for the welfare of [his estranged] brethren, the Lamanites" (Enos 1:9-11). As later with the two Almas, the converted man is moved centrifugally outward from private partaking of grace to communal sharing—from conversion to covenant or, if you will, from the sacrament of baptism to the sacrament of the Lord's supper. What drives the larger and more inclusive narrative of the Book of Mormon is a hunger for sanctified community. . . .

> For [the Book of Mormon prophets], typing or figuring or likening, guided by revelation, is simply the one way to make sense of the universe, time, and all the dimensions of individual and communal human experience. [Their work] may suggest a theology of the Word, which in turn might suggest a philosophy of history and of language.

> History may well be . . . a sequence without story. Yet to write history is to compose it, . . . to figure it, to order it by concept and metaphor. The minds that made the Book of Mormon clearly believed that this was not only possible but essential, even crucial, if humanity was to continue. Further, those minds believed that the mas-

ter-figures [in the typology] were both immanent and transcendent: that God could and would reveal them to human minds, and that once received, [they] would be seen (and could be used) to order all experience. . . . Likening, then, . . . might be seen as the root-act of language itself, logically prior to the utterance of any word even if temporally simultaneous with it. . . . The dynamics of the Word in the Book of Mormon entail a view of language deeply at variance with the post-modernist view that we dwell amid infinitely self-referential and nontranscendent signs. . . . The Book of Mormon seems . . . to say that signs point beyond themselves not finally to other signs but ultimately toward God. Our trouble . . . is to read them.[7]

Besides Jorgensen, Richard Rust and George Tate[8] made important initial contributions to the typological analysis of the Book of Mormon.[9] Steven Sondrup and Noel Reynolds[10] have built on John Welch's discovery of the use of the Hebraic poetic pattern, chiasmus, in the Book of Mormon.[11] What is needed is for one of these perceptive analysts to explore the relation between chiasmus and typology.[12] Chiasmus is the small-scale use of repetition, with inversion, of words, concepts, and other language units, focused on a central turning point (such as abc-cba); typology, however, is the large-scale repetition of events, persons, images, etc., all focused on the central event of Christ's mortal life, such as Lehi's dream and the Enos and Alma conversions or the tree-of-life images. Both these formal devices seem to have developed as natural expressions of a way of thinking and experiencing that we need to understand and recover in order to approach the formal beauty and powerful message of the Book of Mormon and to understand and experience how the beauty and message are integrated.

I hope that both scholars and ordinary readers will follow Jorgensen's lead into typological analysis and will

also explore the Book of Mormon text more fully on the
basis of other leads by Frye. One of the most intriguing
avenues, I think, might be an examination, using the Book
of Mormon, of some of the cruxes and problems Frye finds
in his analysis of the Bible. Because the Book of Mormon
is more unified and has had fewer problems of transmis-
sion and translation, it might provide better answers to
some questions than the Bible.

In addition, I am convinced from my own study and
teaching that a typological focus on the Book of Mormon
can help us to understand the Bible itself in new ways.
Such analysis and reflection will help us to see, much better
than we do now, I believe, that both books provide, in
their unique *langage*, the most powerful way to do the most
important thing words can do — that is, in the Book of
Mormon prophet Jacob's words, to "persuade all men not
to rebel against God, . . . but that all men would believe
in Christ, and view his death, and suffer his cross and bear
the shame of the world" (Jacob 1:8). That possibility for
language, as a direct access to both the meaning and the
saving personal experience of Christ's atoning sacrifice,
brings us directly to René Girard.

Frye's work on the Bible has provided us with new
insights to help us appreciate the *formal* elements of the
Book of Mormon, its metaphorical language and typological structure that are of a force and quality to rival that
of the Bible. Girard, another ground-breaking and influential contemporary literary critic, has given us new theoretical tools by which we can explore the unique power
of the Christ-centered *content* of the Book of Mormon, content which I believe is comparable, even in some ways
superior, to that of the Bible. Girard did not begin with
the Bible, but his work in anthropology led him to appreciate the close similarities between various mythologies
and the Bible that have led modern scholars and many
others into a dogmatic religious relativism — but that study

also helped him see crucial differences that powerfully "make manifest the uniqueness and truthfulness of biblical perspective."[13]

In *Deceit, Desire, and the Novel* and in *Violence and the Sacred*, Girard first presented convincing evidence, from his thorough study of anthropology and of classical mythology and literature, as well as more modern writers like Shakespeare and Dostoevski, that a mechanism we all recognize from common experience is indeed the central mechanism of human conflict.[14] We are motivated largely by desire. Like most human activity and feeling, desire tends to be imitative; that is, we often desire the things others desire, especially the things desired by those we admire, our models, largely because they desire them. Such competing desires, focused on the same objects, inevitably lead to envy, rivalry, to blaming others and making them scapegoats even as we imitate them, and to various forms of cruelty and violence. Girard has demonstrated with numerous examples from mythology and literature that societies develop a particular mechanism in order to survive this terrible process of imitative desire and violence, which tends to spread like a plague as people naturally respond to hurt by hurting others and to opposition to their desires with revenge: Groups of people, sensing the threat of expanding imitative violence, collectively choose scapegoats on which to focus blame and violence rather than acknowledging that their own imitative desire and revenge are the true sources of the plague. Masking the scapegoating process in ritual and rationalization, even using their religious and literary forms to authenticate this mechanism, people justify their violence against the innocent scapegoats.

In Girard's most recent book, *Things Hidden since the Foundation of the World*,[15] he argues that there is one effective alternative to the plague of imitative desire and violence that spiritually destroys both individuals and nations, despite their elaborate mechanism for controlling the plague through scapegoating and then hiding it through self-deception and ritual. Imitative desire and violence always break out in new cycles until they are faced and overcome, and Girard claims that the ideas and power necessary to do that are found uniquely in the central Judeo-Christian theology and ethics recorded in the Bible and epitomized and given ultimate, divine sanction and victory in the life and death of Christ. He reads Hebrew history and scriptures as a progressive effort to reveal the violence mechanism and to renounce its basis in scapegoating by taking the side of the victim. He finds in Christ's clear and persistent identification of the violence mechanism and his clear refusal to participate in it or to allow others to conscript him into it the superhuman victory over violence that creates the potential redemption of all humans and all human history.

Christ's unique answer is to renounce false desires and to eliminate the category of enemy—thus removing rivalry, blame, jealousy, revenge, and scapegoating. For Girard, the Bible is our greatest and truest book because it refuses to participate in the illusory suppression of violence through scapegoating. Instead it reveals the innocence of the scapegoat victims and offers examples, notably in the stories of Joseph in Egypt and Christ, of how to stop the cycle of imitative and self-perpetuating violence permanently by totally refusing to participate in it. The Bible, particularly in the Gospels, offers forgiveness and love—in imitation of, and empowered by, Christ's pure love expressed in the atonement—as the only solutions to hatred, scapegoating, and violence and thus the only source of ultimate human salvation.

A growing body of impressive evidence demonstrates the power of Girard's ideas to stimulate new thinking about the great myths, classic literature, and the scriptures. For instance, a Girardian reading of *Oedipus Rex* by Sandor

Goodhart offers good internal evidence that Sophocles does not, as most have assumed, simply agree with the traditional Oedipus myth's tendency to obscure the mechanism by which scapegoats are selected and unjustly victimized. Rather, Sophocles provides powerful hints that the Theban community conspires, and gets Oedipus himself to submit, in a kind of ritual sacrifice—thus scapegoating a man who had in fact not been guilty of parricide.[16] Gordon Thomasson has done a detailed reading of the Genesis account of Joseph and his brothers, building on Girard's insights, that reveals in even more detail the processes of scapegoating and mimetic violence there; he relates that story to the version of Joseph's story recalled in the Book of Mormon and to the striking parallel there between the stories of Joseph and of Nephi and *his* brothers. Thomasson traces the ways commentaries on the Joseph story from ancient rabbinic to post-Holocaust times display "an amazing willingness to explain away or modify crucial details" so that Joseph "becomes less admirable, less of a threat to our own consciences, and consequently a more justifiable victim." In particular, the commentaries "neuter the Joseph story as it might apply to us, and undermine the significance of his refusing to retaliate against his truly guilty brothers."[17]

In much modern Mormon commentary (including, I regret, some of my own teaching), there has been a similar tendency to see Nephi, like Joseph, as a favored son who somewhat insensitively and self-righteously intrudes upon his brothers' feelings. I have often heard people say of Nephi, as they do of Joseph, "With a younger brother like that, no wonder the older ones got mad." We thus conspire in the process Girard has illuminated as common in most mythology and much literature—that of justifying victimization and even the violence of the older brothers and clouding the ethical issues of sacrificial violence versus self-sacrificing reconciliation. Girard's perspective thus can help us better appreciate Nephi's remarkable efforts to stay out of the cycle of rivalry, reciprocal violence, and victimization with his brothers. But Girard can also perhaps help us penetrate one of the most troubling cruxes in Nephi's account, his killing of Laban.

Thomasson reminds us of the interesting parallels between events in 1 Nephi and details of the scapegoat tradition from Leviticus 16. Girard claims that the Leviticus account is a *product* of the violence mechanism operating in Hebrew society as well as a description of a religious ritual. Part of that ethically questionable Hebrew tradition was the choosing of *two* scapegoats by lot—one to be sent away and one to be killed. In the Book of Mormon, precisely as predicted by the age-old violence mechanism Girard describes, Lehi and his family are made scapegoats for Jerusalem's troubles, which Lehi has prophetically warned them about. Rather than face those troubles and repent, the community focuses its growing anger on Lehi, "even as with the prophets of old, whom they had cast out, and stoned, and slain" (1 Nephi 1:20). They thus force Lehi, who has been warned by the Lord, to take his family and flee for their lives. When Lehi's sons return for the brass plates, Laman, chosen by lot to approach Laban, the plates' keeper, is scapegoated by Laban in classic Girardian terms (that is, accused of a crime, robbery, to justify Laban in his envious desire to obtain his treasure) and is cast out and nearly killed. But then Laban himself is made into a second scapegoat, and the punishment of death he had decreed for Laman is meted out to him by Nephi.

The *problem* with this interesting parallel to the Leviticus tradition of two scapegoats lies in the justification offered for killing Laban, "It is better that one man should perish than that a nation should dwindle and perish in unbelief" (1 Nephi 4:13). This is a classic statement of the scapegoating rationale, and Girard claims that that rationale is the foundation of human violence and is absolutely repudiated by Christ — a repudiation Girard argues is the chief evidence that the Gospels and Christ are divine.[18] But Nephi tells us that that rationale is here expressed by the Spirit of the Lord — and he claims that Spirit also makes the ethically troubling claim that God not only uses his divine ends to justify violence by himself but also as the rationale for a demand that one of his children, Nephi, also use such violent means: "The Lord slayeth the wicked to bring forth his righteous purposes" (1 Nephi 4:13).

Girard goes to great lengths to show that the Old Testament passages seeming to implicate God himself in violence are records of a people gradually working their way beyond an inferior understanding of God that all other cultures retained: Though "in the Old Testament we never arrive at a conception of the deity that is entirely foreign to violence," in the later prophetic books, Girard claims, God is "increasingly divested of the violence characteristic of primitive deities."[19] Girard's analysis is persuasive, focused on a close look at the "suffering servant" passages of Isaiah, where we humans, not God himself, are clearly identified as the ones who (wrongly) ascribe responsibility for violence to God (Isaiah 53:4). Girard also points out explicit rejections of violence of any kind (even God's "righteous" vengeance) that emerge in the Old Testament: "I have no pleasure in the death of the wicked; but that the wicked turn from his way and live" (Ezekiel 33:11). Girard claims that such rejections become completely clear in the Gospels, where Christ explicitly describes the change from the Old Testament patience for "justified" violence to absolute New Testament rejection of *all* hatred and violence: "Ye have heard that it hath been said, Thou shalt love thy neighbour, and hate thine enemy. But I say unto you, Love your enemies, . . . and pray for them which despitefully use you, and persecute you; That ye may be the children of your Father which is in heaven: for he maketh his sun to rise on the evil and on the good" (Matthew 5:43-45).

Girard does not ignore the few passages in the New Testament that seem to contradict this demand by Christ, such as the cleansing of the temple and Christ's claim that he came not to send peace but a sword (Matthew 10:34). As with the similarly troubling passages in the Old Testament, he deals with each in detail, persuasively showing that some passages can be seen best as not prescriptive but merely *descriptive* of what was then still a violence-prone culture (rather than an expression of what Christ himself wants) and some as interpretations we impose from our own still violence-prone culture. In a few cases Girard claims a passage or its translation must simply be rejected as inconsistent with Christ's overwhelmingly central and oft-repeated nonviolence.

It is important to recognize that Nephi, probably recounting the killing of Laban many years after it happened, quotes the Spirit as using almost exactly the same words as the Jewish priest Caiaphas used in an ends-justifies-means argument to the Sanhedrin to condemn Christ: "It is expedient for us, that one man should die for the people, and that the whole nation perish not" (John 11:50). John, the recording evangelist, shows the dramatic shift from the Old Testament to the Gospel perspective when he writes that Caiaphas thus accurately, though unknowingly, "prophesied that Jesus should die for that nation" and also for all "the children of God" (John 11:51-52)—but would not be sacrificed or scapegoated in the usual manner. This raises the interesting, but rather troubling, image of Laban as a type for Christ, since the deaths of both figures are described as bringing the salvation of whole nations: Laban's death made possible the obtaining of the brass plates, the literal "word" that brought salvation to the Nephites, and Christ's death fulfilled his full mission as *Logos*, the "Word" that saves all peoples, including the Jews.

But even more troubling is the evidence, not only from

the Bible but from the Book of Mormon itself, that Nephi's account directly contradicts the full revelation of God's nature as the One revealed in Christ who utterly rejects violence—and who demands that we do the same. Fred Essig and Dan Fuller have written an exhaustive but inconclusive study of the legal status, in the religious and moral code of the Israelites, of Nephi's rationalizations for killing the unconscious, drunk Laban with his own sword. They remind us, "Few passages of the Book of Mormon have inspired more criticism. . . . Many point to this episode as evidence against the Book of Mormon being an inspired document."[20] Though Essig and Fuller clearly wish to counter that criticism and offer several reasons for legally exonerating Nephi, they finally admit, "Until we more thoroughly understand the role of Deity in the daily affairs of ancient Israel and how that role was perceived by the Israelites, we may neither condemn nor extol the acts of Nephi."[21] It is very difficult to wait for such understanding, which may be completely beyond scholarship, when this passage from the Book of Mormon is used by anti-Mormons to attack the book and by investigators to reject it. Some Mormons themselves continue to use the passage to justify troubling, violent rhetoric and even violent action—by assuming that the Spirit does indeed teach that the end justifies the means. (The fundamentalist Laffertys even used the passage in court to defend their "inspired" slaying of their sister-in-law and her baby in American Fork, Utah, in 1984.) For those of us terribly troubled by such rhetoric and actions, no other passage has seemed more contradictory to New Testament, as well as other Book of Mormon, teachings about the impartiality and absolute goodness of the Lord—and about the central role the rejection of violence plays in Christ's mission.

This is not the place for a full analysis of the Laban story, but I offer some questions and reflections, based on Girard's insights, to illustrate how his work can help us approach the Book of Mormon: First, is it possible that Nephi's decision—or at least his rationalization—was simply wrong and that he had deluded himself about God's approval? This very young man, already a victim of scapegoating and life-threatening violence by his own brothers, knew of Laban's murderous scapegoating of Laman. He had now found Laban temporarily vulnerable but still a threat to himself and his goals, which he was convinced were divinely inspired. He may have very naturally been tempted into revenge. Then, years of reflection may have genuinely convinced him that the Lord would have directed him to kill Laban to obtain the plates in this extreme circumstance—and thus had made possible the preservation of his people, which he had subsequently witnessed.

The text lends some support to this possibility: Nephi is still, much later, quite troubled by the experience and its moral meaning. His account contains a remarkable combination of unsparing completeness and honesty with what seems like rationalization, even obsessive focusing on what might be unnecessary but psychologically revealing details (see 1 Nephi 4, especially verse 9, where Nephi notices the sword before anything else and examines its hilt and blade in detail, and verse 18, where, after lengthy rationalization, he confesses, in what seem to be unneeded specifics, "[I] took Laban by the hair of the head, and I smote off his head with his own sword"). It seems, as one might expect of a highly religious and moral young man, that he had frequently reflected on his killing of Laban and with some ambivalence. Perhaps as a result of Nephi's obsessive reflection, the sword of Laban took on a powerful symbolic importance in the racial memory of the Nephites. It became a prominent heirloom, used literally to preserve the people and also preserved with sacred objects into modern times. Nephi used it as a model for the first swords his people made in America (2 Nephi 5:14) and himself "wielded" it in his people's defense (Jacob 1:10). Four hundred years later, King Benjamin also used the sword of Laban in battle (Words of Mormon 1:13, 17) and formally passed it on to his son with the sacred plates of Nephi and Lehi's spiritual compass, the Liahona (Mosiah 1:16). It was preserved in such company to our own day, when it was among the sacred artifacts that were to be shown to the Three Witnesses (D&C 17:1) and was present in the room full of ancient records and relics shown to Joseph Smith.[22]

Bruce Jorgensen, English professor at BYU, in a paper given at the Rocky Mountain Modern Language Association meetings in October 1988 on "Violence in the Book of Mormon," points out that the sword of Laban, archetype of all Nephite swords, hangs over all Nephite history to its violent conclusion. And Richard D. Rust, professor of English at the University of North Carolina, who has written a book on "The Book of Mormon as Literature," which is being considered for publication, examines the Nephites' fixation on the sword of Laban and their continual connection of sword imagery to word imagery: The power to divide asunder of the sword is transferred to the word, and the persuasive force of the word is continually able to have "more powerful effect upon the minds of the people than the sword, or anything else" (Alma 31:5; see also Christ's witness in 3 Nephi 12, his version of the Sermon on the Mount to the Nephites, that they must love their enemies because "old things are done away, and all things have become new," 3 Nephi 12:47).

Both of these developments from Nephi's killing of Laban can be explored with Girardian paradigms: the imitative violence and masking of violence descending directly, even ritualistically, from Laban's sword, and also the concerted efforts to transform the malign cycle under the sword into a benign cycle through the redemptive *Logos* or word of Christ.

To return to a strictly personal level, there is some indication that throughout his life Nephi continued to be

deeply troubled by something that may have consisted of —
or included — this killing of Laban: In his remarkable psalm
of self-reflection, Nephi asks, in obvious continuing pain,
"Why should I give way to temptations, that the evil one
have place in my heart to destroy my peace and afflict my
soul? Why am I angry because of mine enemy?" (2 Nephi
4:27). There is no explicit evidence that he was that angry
with Laman and Lemuel or even the Lamanites as a whole.
Was he angry enough with Laban to kill him and then feel
continuing remorse, which led to eventual self-justification?

On the other hand, Nephi's psalm speaks of his enemies "quaking" (2 Nephi 4:22), which seems to refer to
Laman and Lemuel quaking before him in 1 Nephi 17. In
addition, the very details Nephi is careful to include,
though to us they seem strangely irrelevant — such as that
he entered the city not knowing where he would go and
his insistence that the Lord delivered Laban into his hand —
are the details that would establish that the killing was not
premeditated and thus not murder (these conditions are
stated in Exodus 21:12-14 and Numbers 35:22).

Any reading that sees Nephi as making a mistake certainly challenges our conventional ideas. We think that a
prophet of God, even before he is called, should be above
such self-delusion and that the word of God is generally
above merely describing, without explicit condemnation,
such human mistakes. We tend to assume unconsciously
that the Book of Mormon tells us only what is best to do
rather than what actually was done. We do this despite
the book's own warning on its title page that "if there are
faults they are the mistakes of men." Whatever the case,
even an interpretation such as I have postulated, one that
finds a fault in Nephi or a mistake in his account, actually
increases my own conviction that the account has a psychological richness and sophistication, particularly given
Girard's insights, that is extremely hard to imagine Joseph

Smith — or anyone else — concocting. Even a reading that blames Nephi provides interesting and unusual evidence that the Book of Mormon is what it claims to be, an account of real experiences by a real person from the Israelite world.

However, there is another possible reading of this event that I believe is the best. Yet, though it avoids the problems I have just reviewed, it raises what I find to be even more profoundly troubling questions, questions that Girard has also been troubled by in his work with the Bible and has clearly not yet resolved. What if God truly did command Nephi to slay Laban, but not for the very questionable reasons most often offered by Latter-day Saints — reasons that God himself has denied often in other scriptures? What if it was an Abrahamic test, like the command to Abraham to kill Isaac? What if it was designed to push Nephi to the limits of the human dilemma of obedience versus integrity and to teach him and all readers of the Book of Mormon something very troubling but still very true about the universe and the natural requirements of establishing a saving relationship with God? What if it is to teach us that genuine faith ultimately requires us to go beyond the rationally moral — even as it has been defined by God, when God himself requires it directly of us?

This was the position taken by Elder Jeffrey R. Holland of the First Quorum of the Seventy, then president of BYU, in his devotional address to the BYU student body, 17 January 1989, "The Will of the Father in All Things." He suggests that the story of Nephi killing Laban is given so prominently and in such personal detail at the very beginning of the Book of Mormon to force all readers to deal with it and to focus "on the absolutely fundamental gospel issue of obedience and submission to the communicated will of the Lord. If Nephi cannot yield to this terribly painful command, if he cannot bring himself to obey, then it is entirely probable that he can never succeed *or* survive in the tasks that lie just ahead."[23] I think Elder Holland is right, but most of us need a little more help with the implied question: Why does God test our obedience, not only by asking us to give up our inferior desires and habits and holdings, not even by demanding at most our lives, but by asking us to turn directly against our greatest *values*, the very commands *he* has given us?

Here is the paradox: Nephi is asked by God to violate directly Christ's demand that we reject all violence, even against those who "deserve" it, and also his insistence that we never again try to justify our violence by projecting it onto God ("If ye do good to them which do good to you, what thank have ye? for sinners also do even the same. . . . But love ye your enemies, and do good, . . . and ye shall be the children of the Highest: for he is kind unto the unthankful and to the evil," Luke 6:33, 35).

Girard recognizes, with seeming anguish, that much of the Bible, especially the Old Testament, describes a natural order in human affairs with which God seems to have to compromise in order to bring about ultimate change. Perhaps we can come to Girard's aid a bit here. The evidence of Joseph Smith's inspired revision of the Bible, and the clear statement in Doctrine and Covenants 1:24 that God's revelations are given to prophets "in their weakness, after the manner of their language" (which must include their worldview), indicate that the Bible and the Book of Mormon are at least partly limited to the perspectives of the writers, not simply to that of God himself. It is natural that those writers, though prophets, would be limited in their perceptions of reciprocal violence and scapegoating in some of the ways Girard has documented as occurring in the mythology and literature of all societies. They could also be inspired to describe real human dilemmas of the kind Nephi experienced in ways that open up, with rich and educational moral complexity, the challenge of human violence.

Girardian analysis of Shakespeare helps us see how

the great dramatist pushes the scapegoat mechanism to tragic extremes — not because he accepts it but in order to reveal it more fully and make us abhor it. Thus Shakespeare becomes a kind of therapist, creating fictive dramas that imitate and thus reveal the mechanisms of violence and the ways we try to hide them. Shakespeare's plays also demonstrate how such therapy must sometimes be achieved through dramatic shock — even the telling of half-truths, as used by such healing figures as Prospero and Cordelia. Could it be that God, having similarly to deal with the limitations placed upon him by human agency, could create a dramatic action for Nephi, as both a test and a therapy, that reveals to him *in extremis* — and also to us — that *anyone* can become a scapegoater capable of imitative violence? Or could it be (and this is what, finally, I believe myself) that, as Holland and others have suggested, God was both teaching and helping Nephi to develop, through this Abrahamic test, into a servant and leader who could be obedient — but that God was also teaching Nephi (and us) the costs and limits of such obedience? Transgression of God's commandments against violence is only excusable in the extreme case of certain knowledge that God is directly commanding the transgression. Even then it will properly exact a toll of reluctance and continuing anguish in the true servant of God, such as Nephi, and it must never be used as a general rule to excuse anyone else's violence.

Certainly the experience with Laban taught Nephi something he never forgot, as is evidenced, perhaps, by his psalm of repentance — and is certainly shown in his harrowing, complex memory of the event many years later. The experience, of course, profoundly changed him and prepared him — perhaps through the softening of deep moral reflections — for additional teachings from God: soon afterwards he had the privilege to be the first among the Nephites to receive a full vision of the life and mission of the still far-future Christ and to understand Christ's atonement, symbolized in the tree of Lehi's dream ("It is the love of God, which sheddeth itself abroad in the hearts of the children of men," 1 Nephi 11:22). Based on that understanding, he later states unequivocally the true nature of God as revealed in Christ, the absolute opponent of all imitative desire, all violence, all scapegoating, in a way that seems to contradict directly his own earlier report of what an angel had told him about God:

> The Lord God hath commanded that men should not murder; that they should not lie; . . . that they should not envy; that they should not have malice; that they should not contend one with another; . . . and that they should do none of these things; for whoso doeth them shall perish. For none of these iniquities come of the Lord; for he doeth that which is good among the children of men . . . and all are alike unto God (2 Nephi 26:32-33).

While in London five years ago, just before the trip to Chartres, I saw, at the National Theatre, a version (based on the York cycle) of the medieval "Mystery Plays." These are the cycles of connected dramatic stories, generally taken from the Bible, that were performed annually at the feast of Corpus Christi (the main celebration of Christ's atonement), each segment performed by one of the town's guilds of workers. Much like the great cathedral windows, the plays taught the scriptural story of salvation to a mainly illiterate populace. In addition, much like the Mormon temple endowment ceremony, they served remarkably well to involve actors and audience in a reconfirming understanding of their own literal place in the ongoing divine drama, in patterns of grace that would save each of them, as well as Adam and Eve; Noah; Mary and Joseph; and Peter, James, and John.

The somewhat modernized script enacted by sympathetic and skilled actors in this production involved many in the audience in a surprisingly moving reconfirmation of our own faith in and understanding of salvation through Christ. One of the most powerful scenes was the sacrifice of Isaac, prolonged by an imagined dialogue between the son on the altar and his father with his knife, that stretched out our pain, shared with them, at this potential violence by God upon his own children and upon his own teachings. This, of course, heightened both our relief at God's saving intervention and our awareness of the medieval authors' genius (which has been confirmed by Frye and Girard) in cutting immediately from this scene to the annunciation of the birth of the Savior, Jesus Christ. The significance and force of this connection is intensified in the text by Abraham's cry as he sees Isaac's increasing anguish and knows he must now act: "Jesu, on me thou have pity / That I have most in mind." This anguish is echoed in God's words to Abraham, after his intervention, that make the connection to Christ explicit:

> Like thine Isaac, my loved lad
> Shall do full heartily his Father's will,
> But *not* be spared strokes sore and sad,
> But done to death upon a hill.[24]

In the London production, the effect was heightened even more when a group of actors representing the butchers' guild, traditionally assigned (with macabre appropriateness) to play the sacrifice of Isaac, came forward. After a complex, ritual dance of controlled violence at the completion of the scene, they ended by interweaving their long sword-like butcher knives into a Star of David and carried it up to the balcony, where it became the star of annunciation of Christ's birth.

The typology is certainly clear and has been recognized by many, including, of course, Jacob in the Book of Mormon (Jacob 4:5), but the connections between God's apparent endorsements of violence, such as in various Abrahamic tests, and the violent victimization of his own Son, which saves us, have not been very adequately explored. I think the Book of Mormon can help here, mainly because it provides the basis for an understanding of the at-one-ment of Christ that can complement, but also go beyond, Girard's fruitful ideas. The Book of Mormon provides as yet unexplored hints, suggesting connections between such things as Nephi's killing of Laban and his remarkable visions soon after of Christ as the "condescension of God" (the one who does not look down in judgment upon us from a physical and moral distance but who literally descends with us into mortal pain and suffering and sickness; 1 Nephi 11:26). Many subsequent Book of Mormon scriptures explore the idea that God accomplishes the atonement by transcending the paradox of justice and mercy, and in doing so these scriptures use the same image of condescension, of descending with us: He is the "Lord Omnipotent" who gives us the law and will ultimately judge us, but he is also the suffering servant who will "come down from heaven . . . and shall dwell in a tabernacle of clay" (Mosiah 3:5) and thus will learn how to save us by literally taking upon himself our "pains and . . . sicknesses" and "infirmities, that his bowels may be filled with mercy" (Alma 7:11-12).

The Book of Mormon is quite consistent, I believe, with Girard's very helpful focus on the atonement as achieved through love rather than through traditional sacrifice, through reconciliation rather than through payment. It makes much clearer than the surviving New Testament account that the center of Christ's at-one-ment was in the Garden of Gethsemane, not on the cross. As King Benjamin teaches and as Doctrine and Covenants 19 powerfully reconfirms in Christ's own words, it was in the Garden, when Christ momentarily shrank from what he knew was necessary and then fully joined all humankind as he experienced the worst sense of alienation and pain we can know — in fact, descended below all and the worst of our experience in order to raise us to accept our acceptance by him — it was there that "blood [came] from every pore, so great [was] his anguish for . . . his people" (Mosiah 3:7; D&C 19:18).

Perhaps most startling is the unique Book of Mormon witness that many people, such as King Benjamin's audience, who lived 125 years before Christ, were able to experience the atonement fully and were saved and completely changed into new creatures long before the atonement actually occurred in history. According to this witness, the atonement was not a sacrificial event that saved people from that moment on but an expression of unconditional love from God that freed them to repent and become like God simply by *knowing about it*, by hearing the prophetic witness, whether expressed *before* Christ lived or after.

In addition, the Book of Mormon gives perhaps the most direct affirmation in scripture of Girard's claim that Christ's atonement put an end to all claims for the legitimacy of sacrifice and scapegoating:

> [Christ's atonement will not be] a sacrifice of man, neither of beast, neither of any manner of fowl; for it shall not be a human sacrifice. . . . [But] then shall there be, or it is expedient there should be, a stop to the shedding of blood; then shall the law of Moses be fulfilled. . . . And thus he shall bring salvation to all those who shall believe on his name; this being the intent of this last sacrifice, to bring about the bowels of mercy, which overpowereth justice, and bringeth about means unto men that they may have faith unto repentance (Alma 34:10, 13, 15).

Besides confirming some of Girard's insights, the Book of Mormon also can help us go beyond Girardian analysis to see the proper role of justice, of punishment, even of God's own participation in processes that involve or threaten violence. Amulek's discourse on the atonement in Alma 34 and Alma's in Alma 42 make much clearer than anything available to Girard in the Bible the crucial part justice plays in God's plan for our redemption.

The Bible's well-known accounts of what seems like divinely directed or justified violence and its tendency, especially in the Old Testament, to obscure the violence mechanism Girard identifies, may result from imperfect attempts to express the principle of God's justice. The Book of Mormon more clearly shows why God must use the ideal of justice to establish conscience in us before his forgiving love, which ends the cycle of violence, can effectively operate. For instance, Alma teaches his son Corianton that God affixed laws and punishments, "which brought remorse of conscience unto man"; if he had not done so, "men would not be afraid to sin . . . [and] the works of justice would be destroyed, and God would cease to be God" (Alma 42:18, 20, 22). He also teaches Corianton that such a necessary condition brings the inevitable, unfortunate result of placing man "in the grasp of justice." It is therefore necessary, in order to counter that result, that "God himself [atone] for the sins of the world, to bring about the plan of mercy, to appease the demands of justice, that God might be a perfect, just God, and a merciful God also" (Alma 42:14-15).

A major problem for many of Girard's readers is his explanation of how original violence lies at the foundation of society and religion and then how that original violence is continually obscured over time, even in God-directed biblical cultures. The Book of Mormon may be able to help us understand how the constraints of human nature and agency require God, in working out a possible plan of salvation for us, to cooperate in—or at least allow—that natural obscuring process. Perhaps it is only in such a way, in which the processes of quid-pro-quo justice and thus imitative violence work with full force for a while, that our consciences can be adequately formed by justice. Then, as the Book of Mormon uniquely explains, such demands of justice in our own minds can be appeased by our knowing certainly, through prophetic witness, the plan of God's mercy (Alma 42:15). Thus our consciences, which remain too self-critical to accept Christ's forgiveness and accept-ance of us, can be overpowered by the bowels of his mercy (Alma 34:15). Our difficulty with apparently contradictory scriptures may be a matter of understanding how God's justice and his mercy work *together* to bring us to self-knowledge and guilt, but also to self-acceptance and re-pentance.[25]

In addition to all this, the Book of Mormon provides the only example I can find anywhere of a group actually *practicing* Girard's implied unique solution to imitative vio-lence—and with precisely the results he predicts. The people of Anti-Nephi-Lehi, a group of Lamanites con-verted to the Christian gospel, whose ancestors had con-tinually used the Nephites as scapegoats for their own troubles, make a covenant with God "that rather than shed the blood of their brethren they would give up their own lives" (Alma 24:18). In keeping with that covenant, they ritually bury their weapons. When attacked by vengeful Lamanites, they respond with astonishing and effective courage but in a way directly contrary to the universal tendency to reciprocal violence Girard has revealed: They "would not flee from the sword, neither would they turn aside to the right hand or to the left, but . . . would lie down and perish, and praised God even in the very act of perishing under the sword" (Alma 24:23). When the La-manites see this, the reverse pattern, what Girard calls the "benign reciprocity of love," takes over: "There were many whose hearts had swollen in them for those of their breth-ren who had fallen," and they too "threw down their weapons of war, and they would not take them again" (Alma 24:24-25). According to Mormon, the recording prophet, over a thousand were killed, but they were saved in the kingdom of God—and a greater number than that were converted. Most important, the violence was stopped in a way that actually *ended* it, rather than setting up continuing cycles of revenge—as the winning of battles, no matter how justified, always does. Speaking from the perspective of four hundred years later in Nephite history, Mormon draws a pointed lesson for his modern-day readers:

> And thus we see that, when these Lamanites were brought to believe and to know the truth, they were firm, and would suffer even unto death rather than commit sin. . . . They had rather sacrifice their lives than even to take the life of their enemy; and they have buried their weapons of war deep in the earth, because of their love towards their brethren. And now behold I say unto you, has there been so great love in all the land? Behold, I say unto you, Nay, there has not, even among the Nephites (Alma 24:19; 26:32-33).

It would be hard to imagine a better complement to Girard's analysis of the end of the Joseph story. In that episode Judah is being tested by Joseph, who has had an incriminating cup placed in Benjamin's sack and threatens to keep him in Egypt as a thief and let the others go. But Judah, archetypal head of the Jews, the race most made a scapegoat in our world—and the race which produced Jesus—this Judah, in an exact reversal of what had occurred when Joseph was originally scapegoated by his brothers, now offers to take Benjamin's place, to sacrifice self rather than make another a scapegoat. He thus moves Joseph to tears and to the forgiveness that ends the cycle of violence and reconciles him with his brothers. As Girard writes, "This dedication of Judah stands in symmetrical opposition to the original deed of collective violence which it cancels out and reveals."[26] In exactly the same way, the dedication of the people of Anti-Nephi-Lehi stands in symmetrical opposition to the original deeds of collective violence by Laman and Lemuel and their descendants, which produced the ongoing spiral of reciprocal scapegoating central to the Book of Mormon narrative — and for a time it cancels out, as well as reveals, that cycle of violence.

But I find in the Book of Mormon an even more powerful support for, and extension of, Girard's work. The central question still remains how to cope with the *desire* that leads to envy and rivalry and sets in motion all the problems that produce violence and our consciences' demands for reciprocal justice. For Christians, including Girard, the question is how Christ's atonement makes it possible for us to stop the cycle even before it starts — or at least to make repentance and forgiveness possible so it can end.

The Book of Mormon provides the best answer. King Benjamin teaches precisely how the redemptive process works and can be maintained. First he proclaims the essential and primary reality of the atonement, by which Christ extends unconditional love to us, even in our sins. Consistent with Amulek and Alma, he teaches that we can be moved by Christ's unconditional love to overcome the demands within ourselves, placed there by our God-given consciences, to punish ourselves and others. This breaking the bands of justice, he claims, enables us to accept Christ's mercy and forgiveness and become new creatures. Intensely moved by learning of Christ's love, the group of Nephites being taught by King Benjamin actually go through that saving process and begin to rejoice that they are indeed changed, that they "have no more disposition to do evil, but to do good continually" (Mosiah 5:2). King Benjamin also reveals the only way to *maintain* change, to retain "a remission of your sins from day to day" (Mosiah 4:26). The key is humility, the abdication of imitative desire through recognizing that we are "all beggars" (Mosiah 4:19). Just as God does not reject us for our sins, does not refuse to love us or to extend his healing grace and continual blessings because we sin, so we must respond to those who beg help from us though they do not "deserve" it. We must never judge their desires or condition; we must never think that "the man has brought upon himself his misery; therefore . . . his punishments are just" (Mosiah 4:17). If we do so we have "great cause to repent," and if we fail to repent we have "no interest in the kingdom of God" (Mosiah 4:18). Instead, we must constantly recognize our own weakness and our own position of dependence on God, judging no one else but engaging constantly in specific acts of sacrificial love: "feeding the hungry, clothing the naked, visiting the sick and administering to their relief, both spiritually and temporally, according to their wants" (Mosiah 4:26).

The point the Book of Mormon makes much more clearly than I find made in the Bible is this: To continue experiencing the atonement of Christ after we have received his grace, we must extend grace to others. Christ makes us into new creatures, into persons strong enough not to act contrary to what we know — that is, not to sin — if we will merely accept Christ's merciful, undeserved love; he gives us power to repent, the "means" by which we can "have faith unto repentance" (Alma 34:15). But if we then continue judging others, we will unconsciously judge ourselves. We must constantly give mercy to be able to accept it. We must never exact revenge, even in the name of perfect justice. We must not take vengeance, even upon ourselves, the sinners whom we inwardly know most certainly deserve it.

These two passages from the Book of Mormon, the account of he people of Anti-Nephi-Lehi and King Benjamin's address, provide a basis for meeting one of the main criticisms made of Girard's work. Even those who find that his hypotheses fit the available facts better than any others are troubled that despite the claim that his work can help us cope with violence in our lives and in relations between nations, neither he nor his disciples have offered concrete, practical steps toward that goal.[27] Active, self-sacrificing love, even of our enemies, and nonjudgmental, merciful feeding of the hungry are seldom recommended and even less seldom practiced in our world. The Book of Mormon provides powerful evidence, in theory and example, that they could work—and in fact are essential for our salvation.[28]

What do these reflections on some exciting recent literary criticism—and a reconsideration of Nephi's killing of Laban—suggest about the truth and value of the Book of Mormon? That none of us can dismiss it. No one has mastered or explained or exhausted it. It not only stands up to the most sophisticated modern thought about literature, but it continues to challenge our most sophisticated ethical, theological, and political concepts. I am encouraged by my study so far to find that what Frye and Girard have claimed for the Bible can also be claimed, point by point and often more clearly and usefully, for the Book of Mormon. But more important, their insights deepen my understanding and appreciation of a book I already believe is both as historically true and as spiritually valuable as the Bible. As I approach difficult parts of the book, such as the Laban story, with these new tools, I find the book responding with truth and richness.

Girard has focused on content, Frye on form. Girard has reminded us of the central ethic to look for at the heart of the *Logos*, mercy transcending justice; Frye has reminded us of the best way to get to that heart, pattern transcending reason. The Book of Mormon, if we will work—and open ourselves—to find it so, is a restored second witness to both the ethic and the pattern, to Christ as Redeemer and to Christ as the *Logos*.

Notes

1. Bruce W. Jorgensen, "The Dark Way to the Tree," in Neal A. Lambert, ed., *The Literature of Belief* (Salt Lake City: Bookcraft and BYU Religious Studies Center, 1979), 218-30.

2. Northrop Frye, *The Great Code: The Bible and Literature* (London: Routledge and Kegan Paul, 1982), 221.

3. Ibid., 5.

4. Steven C. Walker, "More Than Meets the Eye: Concentration of the Book of Mormon," *BYU Studies* 20 (Winter 1980): 199-205.

5. Frye, *The Great Code*, xx.

6. Ibid., 80.

7. Jorgensen, "The Dark Way to the Tree," 222-29.

8. Richard D. Rust, "All Things Which Have Been Given of God . . . Are the Typifying of Him: Typology in the Book of Mormon," 233-44, and George S. Tate, "The Typology of the Exodus Pattern in the Book of Mormon," 245-62, in Lambert, ed., *The Literature of Belief*.

9. More recently, Avraham Gileadi and Alan Goff have built on that pioneering work with detailed book-length studies of passages and themes, including explicit connections to biblical typology. Avraham Gileadi, *The Last Days: Types and Shadows from the Bible and the Book of Mormon* (Salt Lake City: Deseret Book, forthcoming 1990), and Alan Goff, "A Hermeneutic of Sacred Texts: Revisionism and Positivism, and the Bible and the Book of Mormon," Master's thesis, Brigham Young University, 1989.

10. Steven Sondrup, "The Psalm of Nephi: A Lyric Reading," *BYU Studies* 21 (Summer 1981): 357-72; Noel B. Reynolds, "Nephi's Outline," in Noel B. Reynolds, *Book of Mormon Authorship* (Salt Lake City: Bookcraft and BYU Religious Studies Center, 1982), 53-74.

11. John W. Welch, "Chiasmus in the Book of Mormon" in Reynolds, ed., *Book of Mormon Authorship*, 33-52.

12. An initial step in this direction has been taken by John W. Welch in his "Chiasmus in Biblical Law: An Approach to the Structure of Legal Texts in the Hebrew Bible," *Jewish Law Association Studies* 4 (Boston Conference volume, forthcoming 1990), connecting the balancing features of chiasmus with the reciprocal and proportional typologies of talionic justice.

13. René Girard, "The Bible Is Not a Myth," *Literature and Belief* 4 (1984): 8.

14. René Girard, *Deceit, Desire, and the Novel* (Baltimore: Johns Hopkins University Press, 1965), and Girard, *Violence and the Sacred* (Baltimore: Johns Hopkins University Press, 1977).

15. René Girard, *Things Hidden since the Foundation of the World* (Stanford, CA: Stanford University Press, 1987).

16. Sandor Goodhart, *"Leskas Ephaske*: Oedipus and Laius' Many Murderers," *Diacritics* 8 (Spring 1978): 55-71.

17. Gordon Thomasson, "Madness, Differentiation, and Sacrifice, or Reconciliation: Humanity's Options as Seen in 2 Maccabees and Genesis," unpublished paper presented 15 November 1984 at the Eighth Annual BYU College of Humanities Symposium, "Myth, Literature, and the Bible," 17. Copy in my possession.

18. Girard, *Things Hidden*, 141-79.

19. Ibid., 157.

20. Fred Essig and Dan Fuller, "Nephi's Slaying of Laban: A Legal Perspective," F.A.R.M.S. paper, 1982, 1.

21. Ibid., 25.

22. *JD* 19:38.

23. Jeffrey R. Holland, "The Will of the Father in All Things," pamphlet printing of devotional address, 17 January 1989 (Provo, UT: Brigham Young University, 1989), 6.

24. Tony Harrison, ed. and tr., *The Mysteries* (London: Faber and Faber, 1985), 48.

25. For additional exploration of this idea, see my "That They Might Not Suffer: The Gift of Atonement," in *Dialogues with Myself* (Midvale, UT: Orion Books, 1984), 77-92.

26. Girard, "The Bible Is Not a Myth," 15.

27. Robert North, "Violence and the Bible: The Girard Connection," *Catholic Biblical Quarterly* 47/1 (1985): 10.

28. For additional exploration of this idea, see my "Fasting and Food, Not Weapons: A Mormon Response to Conflict," *BYU Studies* 25/1 (Winter 1985): 141-55, and "Can Nations Love Their Enemies," in *Dialogues with Myself*, 135-52.

5

An Introduction to the Relevance of and a Methodology for a Study of the Proper Names of the Book of Mormon

Paul Y. Hoskisson
Brigham Young University, Provo, Utah

Since the appearance of the Book of Mormon in 1830, its proper names have been discussed in diverse articles and books.[1] Most of the statements proffer etymologies, while a few suggest the significance of various names. Because of the uneven quality of these statements this paper proposes an apposite methodology. First, though, a few words need to be said about the relevance of name studies to our understanding of the Book of Mormon.

Relevance

With the exception of a few modern proper names coined for their composite sounds,[2] all names have meanings in their language of origin. People are often not aware of these meanings because the name has a private interpretation, or the name has been borrowed into a language in which the original meaning is no longer evident, or the name is very old and the meaning has not been transmitted. For example, the English personal name *Wayne* is an old form of the more modern English word *wain*, meaning a "wagon" or "cart," hence the surname *Wainwright*, "builder/repairer of wagons."[3] However, to our contem-

126

porary ears *Wayne* no longer has a meaning; it is simply a personal name.

With training and experience, it is often possible to define the language of origin, the meaning, and, when applicable, the grammatical form of a name. Names like *Karen, Tony,* and *Sasha* (also written *Sacha* from the French spelling) have been borrowed into English from Danish,[4] Italian,[5] and Russian[6] respectively. The latter is particularly instructive because it represents a rather complicated transference of names. *Sasha* is a Russian diminutive (nickname) for *Aleksandr* (English *Alexander*), which in turn was borrowed from Greek *alexandros*, "defending men(?)." To most speakers of English, *Sasha* conveys neither the diminutive nature of the Russian nor any trace of the Russian form it was derived from, let alone the Greek origin and meaning of the name.

Names can preserve phonemes and lexemes of the language of origin. Thus, English *Alexander* retains a semblance of the original phonemes plus the initial and final lexemes *alex* and *andr*, but not the case ending *-os* of the Greek. In English the name "Wayne" was frozen in a state of the English language when *y* represented the sound later spelled *i*.[7] When we realize that the phonemes represented by *y*, *i*, and *g* can under certain conditions represent each other at different stages and in various dialects of written English, it is easy to see that wayne = wain = wagon.[8]

Even when the source language has been lost to memory, i.e., has become a nonspoken language, names often retain in their adopted language many of the sounds and therefore phonemes of the original, despite several transmigrations involving intermediate languages. For example, the English name *Esther* can be traced ultimately to the Babylonian name for the goddess of love and war, *Ištar*. However, the English form of the name is derived undoubtedly from the English Bible translations that go back to the Greek form in the Septuagint or to the Hebrew, *Esther*, both of which ultimately derive from the Babylonian *Ištar*.

For the above two reasons,[9] the onomasticon[10] of the Book of Mormon can preserve lexemes of the languages used to compose the book. Through a careful study of these names we can draw conclusions about their possible language origin and meaning. In this respect, the proper names in the Book of Mormon form a unique and useful tool for the study of the languages of the peoples of that book and make possible new insights for understanding the cultures of the Book of Mormon.

Such conclusions are valuable for two reasons. First, names can be employed to convey content. Giving a name in antiquity usually involved more than supplying a label. Names had meanings, and though not all names necessarily were consciously based on meaning,[11] some were. For instance, Isaiah gave his two sons long and, for most English speakers, unpronounceable names. These names were not given for any intrinsic quality of the two children but as a testimony to Isaiah's contemporaries. The names contained a message, and understanding that message gives insight into the literary work of a great prophet.[12]

Second, names can supply information about the milieu of the author or redactor. Names in the ancient world were subject to literary treatment or mistreatment. For example, one of Saul's sons must have been less than appreciated by his contemporaries. This is reflected not only in the biblical information concerning him (he was murdered), but also in the treatment of his name. His proper name, *Eshbaal*, which means "man of the lord,"[13] is preserved in the late account found in 1 Chronicles 8:33 and 1 Chronicles 9:39. However, in the earlier, more contemporary account found in 2 Samuel 2-4, his name was changed by the compilers of the book to *Ishbosheth*, meaning "man of shame." Changing a respectable word to a disreputable word is called a *dysphemism*, the opposite of a euphemism. This play on the name of Saul's son probably expresses an opinion of the author of 2 Samuel about that person. The redactor or author of 1 Chronicles used the original name, perhaps out of respect for the person since Saul's son was removed temporally and personally from the time of the composition of 1 Chronicles, or perhaps because any name containing *Baal* in those days was by itself sufficient shame.

A careful scrutiny of names can also lead to information about the times in which a work was composed. The relatively unknown play on words between the names of a famous Babylonian king, *Nebuchadnezzar,* in Kings (e.g., 2 Kings 24:1) and *Nebuchadrezzar* in Jeremiah (e.g., Jeremiah 37:1), could only have been made by someone familiar with the times these passages portray. The latter can be translated from Babylonian as "Nabu, protect the crown prince," while the former means "Nabu, protect the mule."[14] Only someone writing from an anti-Babylonian perspective would have used the dysphemism. The correct form of the name would have been used by pro-Babylonian, neutral, or politically removed writers. This corroborates the general anti-Babylonian tenor of Kings and the pro-Babylonian stance of Jeremiah. However, unlike *Ishbosheth* mentioned above, this dysphemism cannot be Hebrew in origin, but must have been borrowed from a current Mesopotamian wordplay on the Babylonian king's name.[15]

If a Semitic *Vorlage* is posited for the Book of Mormon, then the Semitic propensity to play with names should be evident in it, and it is. For instance, in the book of Alma the people of Ammon are given a land called Jershon. The etymology of this toponym can be traced to a Hebrew root meaning "to inherit."[16] Alma 27:22 states that "this land Jershon [that is, inheritance] is the land which we will give unto our brethren for an inheritance." This is an excellent example of wordplay in the Book of Mormon and also makes a statement about the Nephite action of giving the land to the converted Lamanites.[17]

An exacting study of the names can also reveal otherwise unknown influences on Nephite society. One of the better known apostates of the Book of Mormon carried a Jaredite name, *Korihor*.[18] Likewise, one of the most infamous apostate movements in the Book of Mormon also carried a Jaredite name, order of *Nehors*, named after the Nephite, *Nehor*.[19] This name, however, is a Jaredite toponym,[20] appearing as a proper name in the book of Ether. These two examples suggest that some Nephite apostate movements might have been inspired by Jaredite history, either through the twenty-four gold plates found by Limhi's people and translated by Mosiah or through contact with survivors of the Jaredite culture.

Methodology

Requisite to any study of the Book of Mormon onomasticon is primary and accurate control of philologic possibilities. In the example *Jershon* given above, a recently discontinued manual of the Church, quoting a Book of Mormon commentary, states that the name means "land of the exiled, or of the strangers." This false etymology is probably based on the assumption that the root in Hebrew for the Nephite *Jershon* is to be derived from the Hebrew word for stranger, *gēr*. This root begins with a *gimel* (/g/), which normally is transliterated in the King James Bible with a g and not a j. As discussed below, the j in the Hebrew names of the King James Bible usually represents the Hebrew *yod* (/y/). Therefore, if it can be assumed that the normal transliteration techniques employed in the King James Version apply to the Book of Mormon, the meaning "exile" or "stranger" for the word *Jershon* is not possible. In addition, "exile" or "stranger" is unlikely because the sound /š/ in *Jershon* would remain unexplained.[21]

Inseparable from a control of the primary languages is a knowledge of which languages apply to the Book of Mormon onomasticon and to what extent they apply. When considering possible language *Vorlagen* for the Book of Mormon, Hebrew of the biblical period is the first choice. Nearly equal in consideration to Hebrew is Egyptian, followed by the other Semitic languages in use at or before the time of Lehi, including Akkadian, Aramaic, Ugaritic, Phoenician, Moabite, and Ammonite. Semitic languages first attested after the time of Lehi, such as Classical Arabic, the later Aramaic dialects, and Ethiopic dialects, are not as relevant as the earlier languages, but may be used with extreme caution. Other non-Semitic languages with which the Hebrews could have had contact before Lehi's departure, such as Hittite, Greek, Hurrian, and Sumerian, should be a last resort.

Even with these precautions, problems cannot be avoided. A name can have several etymologies based not only on several roots in one language, but it may also be traceable to more than one language. For example, one author has seen in the word *Alma* an Arabic name,[22] while in Hebrew there are at least six theoretical roots: *'lm, ᶜlm, ǵlm, lm', lmᶜ, lmǵ,* though not all of these are necessarily attached to an etymon in West Semitic.

The use of an edition of the received text that also renders all the possible English variants of the names is absolutely necessary for any study of the proper names of the Book of Mormon.[23] For instance, any etymology of the toponym *Cumorah* must be based on an acceptable reading of the received text. The present editions of the Book of Mormon are unanimous in reading *Cumorah*. However, this place name is spelled three different ways in the Printer's Manuscript. Thus, Mormon 6 contains the spelling *Camorah* and *Cumorah* in verse 2, while verse 5 has *Comorah*. In the 1830 edition *Camorah* is standard throughout the

Book of Mormon. *Cumorah* appears in all subsequent editions.[24]

In addition, some variations of the spellings of names have possibly slipped into the present editions seemingly without justification, e.g., *shiblum*. In Alma 11:15-19 *shiblum* is juxtaposed with *shiblon*. In the Printer's Manuscript the *b* is not there, i.e., *shilum*. The *b* could have been inserted inadvertently because of the *b* in *shiblon*.

Second only to the need for a critical edition is the need to posit a theoretical model for the possible transliteration into English of the names as they might have been on the *Vorlage*. Thus, does a *j* in a name in the Book of Mormon represent the phoneme /j/, /y/, /g/, or /h/? The *j* in the transliterated Hebrew names in the King James Bible usually stands for a /y/, the Hebrew letter *yod*. It is notable, however, that the King James renderings are not consistent. The initial Hebrew phonemes of *Jeremiah*, *Isaiah* and *Job* are /y/, /y/, and /h/ respectively. Extrapolating from this example, we might expect relative but not absolute consistency in the transliterations of the Book of Mormon onomasticon.

A further complication involves the commingling of Jaredite and Nephite names. Unless and until it can be determined from which cultural background the Jaredites departed,[25] it will be impossible to do anything but guess about etymologies for Jaredite names. It also appears that Jaredite names surface rather early in the Nephite record[26] and should not be considered together with Lehite and Mulekite language names when etymologies are proposed.

Conclusion

An understanding of the proper names in the language of the *Vorlage* of the Book of Mormon can reveal, via literary nuance, aspects of Nephite/Lamanite culture that remain unrecognized by the reader who is limited to modern languages. However, such results are valid only to the extent that the conclusions are based on sound methodology. This study has proposed an apposite methodology, i.e., control of the posited primary languages, discretion in determining the primary languages, thorough and rigorous examination of all the philological possibilities in the various target languages, and the use of a critical edition that indicates all variations in the various manuscripts and editions.

Needless to say, as the title of this paper indicates, this is only an incipient attempt at defining the relevance of and establishing a methodology for a study of the proper names of the Book of Mormon. Much work still begs attention.

This paper would not be complete without a caveat. Extreme caution both in the tools used and the ways in which they are used must always be the standard. Less is better and conservatism is a virtue. Yet the study of the onomasticon of the Book of Mormon is a must if we are to understand the world of the Nephites and Jaredites. I hope this introductory statement on relevance and methodology will lead to even more significant progress in the study of the proper names of the Book of Mormon.

Notes

1. In making a list of proposed etymologies of Book of Mormon names I have logged over 300 suggestions made over a period of more than 140 years and in more than thirty publications.

2. For example, *LaDell, Shalynn, Sonda,* etc.

3. See Leslie Dunkling and William Gosling, *Everyman's Dictionary of First Names* (London & Melbourne: J. M. Dent, 1983), 290. Cf. also *The Compact Edition of the Oxford English Dictionary* (hereafter *OED*) (Oxford: Oxford University, 1981), 3667-68.

4. E. G. Withycombe, *The Oxford Dictionary of English Christian Names* (Oxford: Clarendon, 1977), 186. See also Dunkling and Gosling, *Everyman's Dictionary,* 148-49.

5. Withycombe, *The Oxford Dictionary,* 28; and Dunkling and Gosling, *Everyman's Dictionary,* 276.

6. Withycombe, *The Oxford Dictionary,* 13; and Dunkling and Gosling, *Everyman's Dictionary,* 251 and 247.

7. The *OED* entries on pp. 3667-68 list the earliest readings for *wayn* (first entry on p. 1250) while the spelling *wain* usually appears several centuries later.

8. See the previous footnote. Though "wagon" was adopted into English around the sixteenth century from Dutch and/or German, see the Early Modern English *wagan* and Old English *wæn*, *wægn* (*OED*, "wagon," p. 3666).

9. That is, (1) when enough is known about a name that it can be traced to its language of origin, and (2) the names can preserve original phonemes and lexemes of the language of origin even though the name originated in a language no longer spoken.

10. Normally the onomasticon (a list of proper names) of the Book of Mormon would not include simple substantives. However, all transliterations of Book of Mormon substantives should be included in any study of the proper names even if there is a question whether or not the substantive is a proper name. For example, *rameumptom* (Alma 31:21) and *irreantum* (1 Nephi 17:5) fall into this category.

11. For instance, see Rivkah Harris, "The *nadītu* Woman," in *Studies Presented to A. Leo Oppenheim* (Chicago: Oriental Institute of the University of Chicago, 1964), 127, who states, in speaking of the names given to *nadītu* priestesses in the Old Babylonian period, "Then as now there were vogues in names."

12. The names, Maher-shalal-hash-baz, "Hurry the spoil, hasten the plunder" (Isaiah 8:3; for the translation, see F. Brown, S. R. Driver, and C. A. Briggs, *A Hebrew and English Lexicon of the Old Testament* [Oxford: Clarendon, 1968], 555), and Shear-jashub, "a remnant shall return" (Isaiah 7:3; for the translation, see ibid., 984), refer to the impending captivity and the subsequent return of a remnant from that captivity. See Isaiah 8:18.

13. In the earlier biblical texts Baal (from the Hebrew root *bʿl*) still carries its original meaning, "lord" or "master." In later biblical texts Baal came to be the proper name of a Canaanite god whose name is otherwise not known.

14. For a recent handling of this topic see A. van Selms, "The Name Nebuchadnezzar," in M. van Voss, Philo Houwink ten Cate, and N. A. van Uchelen, eds., *Travels in the World of the Old Testament*, Studia Semitica Neerlandica 16 (Assen: Van Gorcum, 1974), 223-29.

15. The play on words works best in Akkadian, not at all in Hebrew, and only partially in Aramaic. For this reason it is likely that this dysphemism originated in the cuneiform world and not in Palestine.

16. The root in Hebrew is *yrš. See further in the text for another proposed etymology, albeit undoubtedly false.

17. This was first drawn to my attention by John W. Welch of the BYU Law School faculty.

18. The Jaredite form is with a c, Corihor. The use of a c in the Jaredite name and a k in Nephite poses no phonological problems.

19. For the movement "order of the Nehors," see Alma 21:4 and 24:28. Nehor himself first appears in Alma 1:15.

20. See Ether 7:4 and 9. It is not attested as a Jaredite personal name.

21. For the most likely etymology of the name Jershon see the example given above. With the etymology proposed there, the only unaccounted-for element in the name Jershon is the ending -on, which is probably related to the substantive suffix -ān used in Ugaritic (see 8.58 in C. H. Gordon, Ugaritic Textbook, Analecta Orientalia 38 [Rome: Pontifical Biblical Institute, 1965]), in Hebrew (compare its probable use in the eponym Zebulon [the original pronunciation is preserved in the gentilic in Numbers 26:27 and Judges 12:11]), and in Akkadian (see Wolfram von Soden, Grundriss der akkadischen Grammatik [Rome: Pontifical Biblical Institute, 1969], Analecta Orientalia 33/47, 56r, where it appears to be used only in a narrow sense).

22. Hugh Nibley, An Approach to the Book of Mormon, vol. 6, The Collected Works of Hugh Nibley, 3rd ed. (Salt Lake City: Deseret Book, 1988), 76.

23. Such an edition is now in preparation by Royal Skousen of Brigham Young University. In the meantime, Book of Mormon Critical Text: A Tool for Scholarly Reference (Provo: The Foundation for Ancient Research and Mormon Studies, 1984-87), though not comprehensive, is available.

24. Cumorah appears in Mormon 6:2, 6:4(2x), 6:6(2x) and 8:2; Camorah in 6:2; and Comorah in 6:5 and 6:11; cf. Book of Mormon Critical Text, 3:1086-88.

25. The popular conception in the Church is that the Jaredites departed from Mesopotamia. Hugh Nibley has written that the Jaredites departed from somewhere around Lake Van. See his treatment in Lehi in the Desert, The World of the Jaredites, There Were Jaredites, vol. 5, The Collected Works of Hugh Nibley (Salt Lake City: Deseret Book, 1988), 153-282.

26. The Small Plates in the form we now have, 1 Nephi through the Words of Mormon, do not contain any obviously Jaredite names. Beginning at least with the book of Alma, Jaredite names begin to appear among the Nephite personal names, e.g., Korihor (= Jaredite Corihor in Ether 13:17) in Alma 30. See also Coriantumr in Helaman 1:15-32 and Ether 12-15.

6

The Brass Plates Version of Genesis

Noel B. Reynolds
Brigham Young University, Provo, Utah

When Lehi and his followers left Jerusalem, they took with them an unnamed book of scripture (known simply by its description—"the plates of brass"), which provided their cultural and religious groundings over a thousand-year period. Many Book of Mormon references to this record indicate that it was most likely a Josephite version of the Old Testament (e.g., 1 Nephi 5:10-16). It contained the writings of Isaiah substantially as they have come down in our textual tradition, and it reports many experiences of Moses and Israel as we know them from the Bible. But several intriguing references indicate that it contained materials that are not familiar to students of the Bible: Joseph of Egypt is cited at some length, and on subjects not mentioned in Genesis; otherwise unknown prophets, such as Zenos and Zenock, are important to Lehi's descendants; and David seems to play little or no role in the Book of Mormon understanding of the covenant between Israel and God.[1] The question raised in this paper is whether there are indirect evidences of further distinctive contents of the plates of brass. Can we learn anything else about those plates and their contents through an examination of indirect textual evidence in the Book of Mormon?

The Logic of This Inquiry

This paper reports a simple exercise in which a number of key phrases and concepts occurring in Joseph Smith's

136

book of Moses in the Pearl of Great Price and in the Joseph Smith Translation of the Bible are checked against both the Book of Mormon and the King James Bible.[2] My original impression that a number of these which show up prominently in the Nephite record are absent from the Bible was dramatically vindicated. Whereas most previous comparisons of the Book of Mormon with the Old Testament have emphasized their similarities, I wish here to call attention to some instructive differences. My hypothesis is that the brass plates version of Genesis used by generations of Nephite prophets may have been much more like the version we have received from Joseph Smith as a result of his inspired revision of the Bible published as the book of Moses in the Pearl of Great Price than the Genesis version handed down in our traditional Bible.[3] This in turn has other possible implications, some of which will be discussed. For reasons that will be spelled out below, it is not plausible to conclude that the Book of Mormon is the source for the book of Moses, or that Joseph Smith is the source of both, as some of his critics might want to believe.

It seemed most appropriate to compare the Book of Mormon text with the Old Testament since these two are roughly contemporary in their initial composition and because those who wrote the Book of Mormon saw themselves as belonging to that culture which we would identify with the Old Testament. The Hebrew scriptures available to the Nephites were all in existence by 600 B.C. All the examples presented below are correlations between Moses and Book of Mormon language that do *not* occur in the Old Testament. My approach is built on an initial list of terms, phrases, and concepts common to both the Book of Mormon and the book of Moses. This list was then checked against the Old Testament, and any elements clearly present in that text were eliminated. For a variety of reasons, other sets of parallel references were found unconvincing and were also dropped. The final list contained thirty-three key book of Moses references that show up notably in 145 Book of Mormon passages (see the table in the appendix).

The second stage of my study was to assess the evidence for and against the hypothesis that these texts are independent of one another. The seven criteria of dependence used are listed briefly below and in more detail (along with their assessments) in the appendix:

1. The greater the number of significant terms repeated in parallel phrasings in two texts, the less likely they are to be independent. (F)
2. The more precise the similarities between parallel phrasings in two texts, the less likely they are to be independent. (G)
3. The more deliberately shaped the repetition in parallel phrasings in two texts, the less likely they are to be independent. (H)
4. The more similar the contexts in which parallel phrasings occur, the less likely they are to be independent. (I)
5. Author awareness of a brass plates source reduces the likelihood of independence. (J)
6. The more distinctive the terminology repeated in parallel phrasings in two texts, the less likely they are to be independent. (K)
7. Presence of weak or strong versions of the parallel terminology in the New Testament, and even more so, in the Old Testament, increases the possibility that the book of Moses and Book of Mormon passages are independent. Although clear Old Testament parallels do not prove independence, their existence was considered sufficient reason to drop the occurrence altogether as evidence of dependence. (L)

For each of these seven criteria, two or more levels of persuasiveness are suggested and linked to features of the particular occurrence (see the appendix for these explanations). In all cases, the issue is the likelihood that the particular textual parallel listed could occur independently of any connection between the two texts. The listing in the table of the appendix also includes a linearized calculation performed as a rough means of combining the relative values of the seven categories into a common score to indicate approproximate importance for showing dependency between the two texts. The result indicates greater or lesser probability of dependence, but is not intended as a rigorous measure of distances between probabilities or of confidence levels.

By selecting the highest scores for dependence, I was able to identify a group of parallels between these two texts, each of which is highly persuasive on the basis of criteria ordinarily used by scholars evaluating possible sources of texts. Given the uniqueness of some of these individual parallels and the brevity of the source text, the hypothesis that the texts are independent should be rejected. This conclusion is further illuminated and substantiated by reference to a second and larger group of passages that also fit the pattern, but with less persuasiveness. Textual dependence between the two texts could logically run in either direction. Examination of this question reveals the implausibility of the view that the book of Moses could be derived from the Book of Mormon, even though the latter was published first by Joseph Smith.

Correlations of Words, Phrases, and Concepts

Newcomers to studies of textual sources are often surprised at the small amount of shared material that must generally be demonstrated before scholars will agree that there is some connection between two culturally associated texts. I will first discuss a group of twenty Book of Mormon passages (Group 1 in the table) that present strong parallels with book of Moses materials. This first group is distinguished from the second in that none of these parallels finds expression in the Bible (with the noted exception of Moses 6:52 being found in Acts 4:12).

Moses records "*by reason* of *transgression* cometh the *fall*, which *fall* bringeth *death*" (Moses 6:59). This source cannot be missed in Jacob's sermon which, emphasizing resurrection as the answer to death, explains: "*resurrection* must needs come unto man *by reason* of the *fall*; and the *fall* came *by reason* of *transgression*" (2 Nephi 9:6). Here we have double intensification of an implicit reference to the source—first by substituting "resurrection" for "death," and second by reversing the order of the four terms. This reversing is a technique of biblical writers noticed by M. Zeidel. It is referred to as Zeidel's law or as "inverted quotation," and is particularly characteristic of quotations.[4] Jacob also emphasizes his own adaptation of the distinctive verbal construction "to come *by reason* of" by doubling it.

The book of Moses account of Adam's baptism is followed by the bestowal of the *priesthood* on Adam with the following words: "And thou art *after the order of him* who was *without beginning of days or end of years, from all eternity to all eternity*" (Moses 6:67). This phrasing is reproduced in whole by Alma in his discourse on the priesthood when he said, "This *high priesthood* being *after the order of his Son*, which order was from the foundation of the world; or in other words, being *without beginning of days or end of years*, being prepared *from eternity to all eternity*" (Alma 13:7; cf. Alma 13:9). In slightly altered contexts, both Enoch and two additional Book of Mormon writers use the latter half of this expression to describe the Lord, saying of him that he "is *from all eternity to all eternity*."[5] Although a version of the first half of the larger formula appears in the New Testament (Hebrews 7:3), the second half, and therefore the combination, are both unique to book of Moses and Book of Mormon passages. John W. Welch has identified seven or eight other similarities between Alma 13 and JST Genesis 14, further indicating that Alma possessed an expanded text of the early history of the patriarchs similar to that now found in Joseph Smith's works.[6]

Some of the best examples of connections between these two texts are more complex, involving teachings and ways of thinking about something without exact replication of words or phrases. The doctrine of divinely given free *agency* is implicit in all of scripture, but is only taught explicitly as a fundamental concept in the book of Moses and the Book of Mormon. In Moses we learn that "Satan . . . sought to destroy the agency of man" (Moses 4:3), that God "gave unto man his agency" (Moses 7:32; 4:3), and that men are therefore "agents unto themselves" (Moses 6:56). Lehi picks up these same themes in a major discourse on freedom of choice or agency and teaches that "God gave unto man that he should act for himself" (2 Nephi 2:16); that by the redemption "they have become free forever, knowing good from evil; to act for themselves and not to be acted upon" (2 Nephi 2:26); and that men "are free to choose liberty and eternal life, . . . or to choose captivity and death, according to the captivity and power of the devil" (2 Nephi 2:27).

Moses points out to Satan that because the Lord's *"spirit hath not altogether withdrawn"* from him he can distinguish between God and Satan (Moses 1:15). The Book of Mormon writers frequently used this same language when warning people not to sin lest the Lord's Spirit be withdrawn from them, too. Alma specifically cites this explanation to show why the devil has successfully gained power over certain people (Alma 34:35). Mormon borrows Alma's language several times to explain the weakness of the Nephites, saying that "the *Spirit of the Lord* did no more preserve them; yea, it *had withdrawn from them* because the Spirit of the Lord doth not dwell in unholy temples" (Helaman 5:24).[7] Here we see a string of passages in which the Book of Mormon writers follow one another in a particular application of a phrase from Moses' account, using it to explain a withdrawal of the Lord's Spirit and a corresponding expansion of Satan's power (which Moses had successfully resisted). There is some complexity introduced in this variation, but the concept remains the same and takes on an independent life in the tradition of the Nephites.

Centuries of Christian theology testify to the lack of direct biblical teaching on the salvation of little children. But the book of Moses states simply that because of the atonement, "*children . . . are whole from the foundation* of the world" (Moses 6:54). Two Book of Mormon prophets provide a clear and ringing statement of the doctrine that little children are saved by the atonement of Christ. King Benjamin stated this clearly in his famous discourse (cf. Mosiah 3:16, 21), and Mormon wrote a long epistle on the subject at the end of Nephite history. In particular, Mormon said that "little *children* are *whole*," and that they are "alive in Christ, even *from the foundation* of the world" (Moroni 8:8, 12). An additional persuasive link between these two texts is that both King Benjamin's and Moses' teachings are in the immediate context of a statement that beside the name of Christ there will be "no other name given nor any other way nor means whereby salvation can come" (Mosiah 3:17).[8]

One sentence from Moses seems to have spawned a whole family of formulaic references in the Book of Mormon: "And he became Satan, yea, even the *devil, the father of all lies*, to *deceive* and to *blind* men, and to *lead* them *captive at his will*, even as many as would not hearken unto my voice" (Moses 4:4). This language is echoed precisely by both Lehi and Moroni, who, when mentioning the devil, add the stock qualification: "who is *the father of all lies*" (cf. 2 Nephi 2:18; Ether 8:25), while Jacob says the same thing in similar terms (2 Nephi 9:9). Incidentally, the descriptive term *devil*, which is used frequently to refer to Satan in both Moses and the Book of Mormon, does not occur at all in the Old Testament. New Testament occurrences do not reflect this context.

The Book of Mormon sometimes separates and sometimes combines the elements of this description of the devil from Moses and portrays Satan as one deliberately engaged in *"deceiving* the hearts of the people" and in *"blinding their eyes"* that he might *"lead them away"* (3 Nephi 2:2).[9] Particularly striking is the repeated statement that the devil *will lead* those who do not hearken to the Lord's voice *"captive at his will"* (Moses 4:4). In Alma we find that those who harden their hearts will receive "the lesser portion of the word until they know nothing concerning his mysteries; and then they are *taken captive by the devil,* and *led by his will* down to destruction" (Alma 12:11). Much later, Alma invokes the same phrasing to warn his son Corianton of the plight of the wicked who, "because of their own iniquity," are *"led captive by the will* of the devil" (Alma 40:13). In the passage discussed above, Lehi taught his son Jacob that men "are free to choose liberty and eternal life, . . . or to choose *captivity* and death, according to the *captivity and power of the devil;* for he seeketh that men might be miserable" (2 Nephi 2:27).

A remarkable passage in the first part of the Book of Mormon pulls all these book of Moses themes about Satan together — to describe someone else. The implication is unmistakable when Laman characterizes his brother Nephi as one who *lies* and who *deceives our eyes,* thinking to *lead us away* for the purpose of making himself *"a king and a ruler over us,* that he may do with us *according to his will and pleasure"* (1 Nephi 16:38). Laman insinuates that Nephi, who chastises his wayward brothers, is himself like the devil. And resistance against him is not only righteous, but required. This account has the added complexity that it is a speech of Laman, who is quoted here in a record written by the very brother he attacks. If we accept the possibility that this text is dependent on a passage in the ancient book of Moses, we then recognize a major new dimension of meaning, not only in Laman's speech, but in Nephi's decision to preserve the speech, thus showing his descendants, and any other readers familiar with the Moses text, the full nature of the confrontation between the brothers, as well as the injustice of the attacks he suffered. The full irony is revealed when we reflect on the facts reported in Nephi's record and realize that Laman's false accusation against Nephi is an accurate self-description.

Tracing the Direction of Dependence

The foregoing discussion of Book of Mormon parallels to a number of book of Moses passages constitutes substantial evidence that the two texts are in some way dependent on one another or some common source. The question that follows next concerns the direction of influence. The first of the two major possibilities is that the book of Moses (received by Joseph Smith in June and December of 1830) was based on the Book of Mormon (translated mainly from April to June of 1829), which theory, of course, will be most attractive to those who believe Joseph Smith invented both. Several reasons showing why such a view does not explain the connections between these two texts are advanced below. This leaves only the other hypothesis as the leading explanation — namely, that the writers of the Book of Mormon had access to the book of Moses text.

The Book of Mormon authors explicitly identify their version of the Hebrew scriptures as a lineage history handed down through the descendants of Joseph (1 Nephi 5:10-16). The fact that there are some differences between the record on the brass plates and the Old Testament we have today is evident in the Book of Mormon text. The argument of this essay is that the brass plates account of the creation and the founding generations of the human race might include the material restored in Joseph Smith's book of Moses. This suggests the possibility that by checking the Book of Mormon text against other noncanonical manuscripts we might identify further texts that seem to have been available to the Nephite prophets through the brass plates. That such other manuscripts were once in existence seems clear from some of the New Testament parallels, and particularly the concentration of such usages in the writings of John and Paul.

The idea that the brass plates contained a different Moses account than now survives in Genesis or the Jewish tradition may be consistent with David Noel Freedman's theory that our present Genesis through Kings is a relatively recent edition or compilation designed to shift the emphasis from history to law.[10] The Book of Mormon itself reports a prophecy to the effect that the Bible which would come down to us in the latter days would have had many "plain and precious truths" removed from the original texts (see 1 Nephi 13:26-29, 32, 34-40; 14:23). These observations jointly suggest that the brass plates could contain earlier versions of several books. We might also want to test the hypothesis that our Old Testament version was rewritten for political reasons, as Freedman suggests.[11] Does it justify one particular competing tradition of Jewish origins? If so, it might constitute an early example of the textual corruptions described in the Book of Mormon.

Some people may be tempted to use these findings to argue that Joseph Smith was the common author of Moses and the Book of Mormon. But carefully considered, the evidence runs the other way. First, there is the matter of chronology. We can historically document the fact that Joseph began the Moses translation after the Book of Mormon was published. But it is clearly Moses that provides the unity and coherence to a host of scattered Book of Mormon references. It is the story of creation and subsequent events that supplies meaning to Book of Mormon language connecting (1) the transgression, fall, and death; (2) explaining the origins of human agency; (3) describing the character and modus operandi of Satan; (4) explaining the origins and character of secret combinations and the works of darkness—to mention only a few of the most obvious examples. The Book of Mormon is the derivative document. It shows a number of different authors borrowing from a common source as suited their particular needs—Lehi, Nephi, Benjamin, and Alma all used it frequently, drawing on its context to give added meaning to their own writings.

Perhaps most significantly, we have at hand a control document against which to check this hypothesis. A few years after receiving Moses, Joseph Smith translated an Abrahamic text. In spite of the fact that this new document contained versions of some of the same chapters of Genesis that are paralleled in the book of Moses, and in spite of the fact that the Book of Mormon has a large number of direct references to the Abraham, the person, detailed textual comparison demonstrates that this second document does not feature any of the phrases and concepts that have been reported above linking Moses to the Book of Mormon textual tradition. Nor does the distinctive, non-Old Testament phraseology of the book of Abraham show up in the Book of Mormon. The logic that would lead skeptics to conclude that these common concepts and expressions provide evidence that Joseph Smith wrote the Book of Mormon and the book of Moses runs aground on Abraham, as the skeptical hypothesis would seem to require a similar pattern there. But such a pattern is not even faintly detectable.

It is also impressive that most of the influence from the book of Moses in the Book of Mormon shows up early in the small plates and the writings of the first generation of Book of Mormon prophets—significantly, those who had custody and long-term, firsthand access to the brass plates. Many of the later passages that use book of Moses terminology and concepts tend to repeat earlier Nephite adaptations of the original materials.

When there is evidence of interdependence between two texts, and one of these contains passages which play on parallel passages in the other in ways that assume the reader's familiarity with the other, the first one can be considered to be dependent on the second. The parallel passages discussed above, and some that will be discussed below, contain several examples, in all of which the Book of Mormon writer appears to leave unarticulated much of the meaning he wants to convey, assuming the reader will make the connection with the book of Moses material in his own mind, make a comparison, and draw inferences from both the changes and the similarities that he finds. This is trivially true of inverted quotations (1 Nephi 19:12; 2 Nephi 9:6). But in this latter passage, Jacob substitutes a word to make a point about death and resurrection, depending on our knowledge of the original to help us see his point. Similarly, and perhaps most dramatically, Laman's speech discussed above is significantly more meaningful once we see how it draws on the book of Moses descriptions of the devil to identify Nephi implicitly with the devil. Seeing the dependence of Laman's speech on the book of Moses text transforms a rather routine complaint into the most aggressive indictment possible, and helps explain the life-and-death struggle that eventually grew out of it. However, I could not identify any passages in Moses which depended on the Book of Mormon's context for meaning. These are not the kinds of subtle dependence that could reasonably have been reconstructed by Joseph Smith in 1830 as he produced the book of Moses. There is no reason to believe they are the kinds of things he would ever have noticed himself under any circumstances. His interests, knowledge, and background did not extend to this kind of textual analysis.

Other Book of Mormon Parallels

The above two sections of this paper set out and support the hypothesis that the Book of Mormon writers had access in the brass plates to a document substantially the same as the book of Moses given to Joseph Smith by inspiration in 1830. That hypothesis in turn illuminates a large number of additional parallel passages, which in and of themselves may not constitute the strong kind of evidence given above for dependence of one text on the other. However, this second group of passages corroborates the hypothesis in a cumulative way. These additional passages are treated in groupings below. There are quite a number of less powerful correlations which in and of themselves would not compel us to accept a historical connection between the book of Moses and the Book of Mormon. Some of these may have occurred by chance, and others have recognizable New Testament parallels, but read in light of the much stronger examples listed above, they too seem to add some additional weight to my thesis.

Both the book of Moses and the Book of Mormon are remarkable for their claims to a full revelation of Christ to ancient prophets before New Testament times. While the presence of New Testament teachings and phraseology in these books might be made to fit the view that these books are Joseph Smith's nineteenth-century creations, that approach ignores a number of other significant factors, as indicated in the preceding section of this paper. For those who accept or are even willing to consider the ancient origins of the texts produced by Joseph Smith, correlations between them that include New Testament terminology will be of interest, and will contribute additional evidence for the evaluation of the thesis of dependence between these texts.

The first example shows how a statement from the book of Moses account can permeate the Book of Mormon, providing the stock terminology that will be used at widely separated times to describe the same prophesied event. As reported in Joseph Smith's Moses, Enoch the prophet is shown in vision the future crucifixion of the Lord, at which point he reports that "the *earth groaned*; and the *rocks* were *rent*" (Moses 7:56). Nephi chose nearly the same language to report what he saw in his great vision of what occurred immediately after the crucifixion, for he heard "thunderings and earthquakes, and all manner of *tumultuous noises*," and he saw "the *earth* and the *rocks*, that they *rent*" (1 Nephi 12:4). This passage is recognizably derived from the Moses passage, especially given that it is used as a description of the same future event. But later, Nephi quotes Zenos's description of the same events, saying "the *rocks* of the *earth* must *rend*; and because of the *groanings* of the *earth*, many of the kings of the isles of the sea shall be wrought upon by the Spirit of God to exclaim: The God of nature suffers" (1 Nephi 19:12). Not only does this passage report the exact four terms of the Moses cluster and in the same context, but it nearly reverses them, again following Zeidel's law.

Here we have a complex but exact parallel in a context which indicates the author is consciously quoting, that he has reformulated the material to play on his readers' awareness of the original source, and a stated claim that the brass plates provide the source. We cannot tell whether it is Nephi who reverses the order of terms from the Zenos version (presumably quoted from Moses), or whether Nephi reports straight the reversal written by Zenos. Hundreds of years later the Nephite record described the actual events using the same language of the prophecy, again referring to Zenos: "The *earth* did cease to tremble, and the *rocks* did cease to *rend*, and the dreadful *groanings* did cease, and all the *tumultuous noises* did pass away" (3 Nephi 10:9; cf. also 3 Nephi 10:16; Helaman 14:21; 3 Nephi 8:18-19).

Although the Old Testament does not contain any version of these descriptions, the case for dependence is weakened by the occurrence of a relatively close parallel in one New Testament account of these events where it is reported that "the earth did quake, and the rocks rent" (Matthew 27:51).[12] Still, the character of the parallels outlined above would suggest direct Book of Mormon dependence on the book of Moses source, and a possible distant connection of Matthew with a similar text.

Several examples of idiosyncratic phrases from Moses which are simply repeated by Book of Mormon writers (but not by any biblical authors) seem to indicate a special relationship between these texts. The Moses account introduces a novel phrase to describe the redemptive mission of the Savior of mankind. According to Enoch, the Lord told Adam: "This is the *plan of salvation* unto all men" (Moses 6:62). In his brief writings, Jarom reminds his people of "the *plan of salvation*," which has been revealed (Jarom 1:2). Alma also speaks of angels making "the *plan of salvation*" known to men (Alma 24:14; cf. also Alma 42:5).[13]

One of these recurring phrases in Joseph Smith's Moses is "*eternal life*." In a sweeping verse, now familiar to all Latter-day Saints, the Lord explains to Moses that his work and glory is "to bring to pass the immortality and *eternal life* of man" (Moses 1:39). In other Moses passages the same concept is restated in the same terms (Moses 5:11; 6:59; 7:45). Although this language does not occur in Old Testament texts, the Book of Mormon, like the New Testament, is full of it from beginning to end. It begins in 2 Nephi 2, the chapter that reminds us most strongly of the Moses texts, and is echoed thirty times by Nephi and every major writer of the book.[14] The companion concept of immortality or immortal glory shows up three times in Moses, twice in conjunction with "*eternal life*" (Moses 1:39; 6:59, 61). It is not clearly present in the Old Testament, but occurs in similarly clear passages throughout the Book of Mormon.[15]

Enoch appealed to the language of Adam to show that "*no unclean thing can dwell* there, or dwell *in his presence*" (Moses 6:57). Nephi made exactly the same point in urging people to repent because "*no unclean thing can dwell with God*" (1 Nephi 10:21; cf. also 1 Nephi 15:33; Alma 7:21; Mormon 9:4). This one also shows up in the New Testament (Ephesians 5:5), and even faintly in the Old Testament (cf. Leviticus 22:3; Psalm 140:13).

In this same vein, Enoch records that Adam and his sons, as preachers of righteousness, "*called upon all men, everywhere, to repent*" (Moses 6:23, 5:14, and 6:57 all use similar phrasing). This universal call to repentance is duplicated in key sermons of Lehi and Alma (2 Nephi 2:21; Alma 12:33; see also how the Savior used it at 3 Nephi 11:32). And the concept is used twice by Moroni (Moroni 7:31; 8:8) and occurs in the New Testament (Acts 17:30).

These same passages are sometimes characterized by the additional stipulation that unless men do repent, they "*can in nowise inherit the kingdom of God*" (Moses 6:57). According to Enoch, Adam was commanded to teach this to his children (Moses 6:58). The exact phrase is used in similar contexts in five Book of Mormon speeches (cf. Mosiah 27:26; Alma 5:51; 9:12; 39:9; 3 Nephi 11:38). There are a handful of similar statements in the New Testament, with Galatians 5:21 being the closest.

In the Enoch passages the Lord draws a distinction between "*things which are temporal* and *things which are spiritual*" (Moses 6:63). The Book of Mormon invokes the same distinction in precisely the same words on several occasions. In the small plates Nephi twice explicates visions or scriptures by saying that they refer to "*things* both *temporal and spiritual*" (1 Nephi 15:32; 22:3). King Benjamin reminded his people that those who keep the commandments "are blessed *in all things*, both *temporal and spiritual*"

(Mosiah 2:41). Alma encouraged people to pray for whatsoever *things* they needed, "both *spiritual and temporal*" (Alma 7:23). And he also distinguished between the *spiritual* death and the *temporal* death (Alma 12:16), and between the *temporal and spiritual things* the Lord provides for our benefit (Alma 37:43).[16] This concept of spiritual things shows up in the New Testament, but not paired with references to temporal things (1 Corinthians 2:10-14). Other New Testament passages vary even more as the equation of things temporal and eternal with things seen and not seen (2 Corinthians 4:18; cf. Romans 15:27; 1 Corinthians 9:11).

Speaking first of the city of Enoch, and later of the millennial period, the Moses text says that the Lord's people will *"dwell in righteousness"* (Moses 7:16, 65). Nephi also used the phrase in the same context to describe what would happen in the Millennium. Nephi's usage illuminates the meaning of the phrase even more by suggesting that it is because the people *"dwell in righteousness"* that Satan will be bound and have no power over their hearts during this period (1 Nephi 22:26). A somewhat similar phrase does occur in the New Testament where it also refers to the Millennium. Peter looked forward to "a new earth, wherein dwelleth righteousness" (2 Peter 3:13).

The Moses account also differs sharply from the Old Testament versions in its clear references to the Savior. Moses reports that God instructed Adam to be baptized "in the name of *mine Only Begotten Son*" (Moses 6:52), and informed him that he would receive the Holy Ghost. Numerous other passages in Moses refer to *"mine only begotten."*[17] Whereas this phrase occurs six times in the New Testament (John 1:14, 18; 3:16, 18; Hebrews 11:17; 1 John 4:9), it occurs even more frequently in the teachings of the Book of Mormon prophets. Jacob explains the point in some detail (cf. Jacob 4:5, 11), and Alma raises it again in his preaching (Alma 12:33-34). This is all in addition to the multitude of direct references to Jesus Christ which distinguish both of these texts.

Describing the infernal conspiracies hatched by Cain and his associates, Enoch said that "their *works* were in the *dark*, and they knew every man his brother" (Moses 5:51). From that time, he observed that "the *works of darkness* began to prevail among all the sons of men" (Moses 5:55). Nephi spoke repeatedly of those whose works were "*works of darkness*," using the precise phrasing of the Moses text.[18] His younger brother Jacob and a later Nephi also complained of the "*secret works of darkness*" (2 Nephi 9:9; 10:15; Helaman 8:4; 10:3). Enoch also refers to these conspiracies as "*secret works*" (Moses 6:15). This phrase is also used repeatedly in the Book of Mormon to refer to the same kind of conspiracies[19] and has New Testament parallels (Romans 13:12; Ephesians 5:11).

The other phrase used in Moses to refer to these conspiracies is "*secret combinations*," for "from the days of Cain, there was a *secret combination*" (Moses 5:51). The phrase occurs throughout the Book of Mormon[20] in exactly the same contexts as "secret works" and always carries the much richer and fuller connotations of Enoch's descriptions than do the Old Testament accounts of murderous conspiracies.

Enoch's history twice indicates that the wickedness of men invariably produces "*wars and bloodshed*" (Moses 6:15; 7:16). This is the general term used throughout the Book of Mormon as well,[21] with some occasional variations which reinforce the prominence of the stereotype. Mormon described the opposite condition as "*peace . . . [and] no bloodshed*" (Mormon 1:12).

Moses reports that for their sins Adam and Eve (and later Cain) were "*shut out from [the Lord's] presence*" (Moses 5:4, 41). Enoch later reports that as men are tempted by Satan, they "become carnal, sensual, and devilish, and are *shut out from the presence of God*" (Moses 6:49). In this same general context Jacob taught the early Nephites that without an atonement "our spirits must have become like unto [the devil], and we become devils, angels to a devil, to be *shut out from the presence of our God*" (2 Nephi 9:9).

Joseph Smith's Moses reports the sins of Cain and his descendants in much greater detail than the biblical account. Of particular interest is the evil conspiracy hatched by Cain to murder for gain: "And Cain said: Truly I am Mahan, the master of this great secret, that I may *murder* and *get gain*" (Moses 5:31). The Book of Mormon describes several similar conspiracies. Helaman reports the nefarious band led by Kishkumen and how "it was the object of all those who belonged to his band to *murder*, and to *rob*, and to *gain power*" (Helaman 2:8). From a much earlier period, Moroni reports a group that also administered secret oaths "to keep them in darkness, to help such as sought to *gain power*, and to *murder*, and to *plunder*, and to lie, and to commit all manner of wickedness and whoredoms" (Ether 8:16).

It is characteristic of the Book of Mormon account of evil conspiracies that they are "*seeking for power*." When the lower judges became corrupted, and when the king-men revolted, they were all "*seeking for power*" (Alma 46:4; 60:17). Alma reports an interesting variation where the wicked were "*seeking* to put down all *power* and authority which cometh from God" (Moroni 8:28). Enoch uses the same phrase in the Moses account to describe horrible conspiracies of earlier times in which men fought against their own brothers "*seeking for power*" (Moses 6:15).

Many commentators on the Book of Mormon have noted the unique phrase describing the condition of fallen men as "*carnal, sensual, and devilish*." The phrase is not known in the Bible,[22] but occurs twice in the Book of Mormon, both times in this precise formulaic way. Synonyms are never used, and the three words always occur in the same order (Mosiah 16:3; Alma 42:10; cf. Alma 41:13).

Such usage demands a source in a prominent text or ritual. The book of Moses provides both. For it is here in this key ritual text that we learn how Satan came among the children of Adam and Eve and commanded them not to believe the teachings of their parents. "And they believed it not, and they loved Satan more than God. And men began from that time forth to be *carnal, sensual, and devilish*" (Moses 5:13). The point is exactly restated later when it says "Satan hath come among the children of men, and tempteth them to worship him; and men have become *carnal, sensual, and devilish*, and are shut out from the presence of God" (Moses 6:49).

One phrase that occurs only once in each text still seems quite distinctive. Speaking of an apostate group, the Moses text reports simply that "their *hearts have waxed hard*" (Moses 6:27). When Alma saw "that the *hearts* of the people began to *wax hard*, . . . his *heart* was exceedingly *sorrowful*" (Alma 35:15).[23] This text expands on the phrase by illustrating its opposite in Alma's righteous response.

In a similar vein, the Moses account characterizes the wicked of Noah's day, who defended their ways, as "*lifted up in the imagination of the thoughts of [their] heart*" (Moses 8:22). This is invoked holistically as an implicit comparison when Alma reports the defensive speech of the apostate Nehor who was "*lifted up in the pride of his heart*" (Alma 1:6).[24] This is another case similar to 1 Nephi 16:38, where much of the meaning of the parallel is signalled more by the similarity of context than by the words that are repeated.

The Book of Mormon is notable for what would appear as a unique invention, the cursing of half of Lehi's family and their descendants, and the marking of the cursed group with a dark skin that produced a social isolation between them and their relatives who did not have the curse. But in Moses we see the same thing happening to Cain and his descendants (Moses 5:25; 40-41; 7:22). These passages go far beyond the information available in Genesis, particularly concerning the effect of the skin color upon Cain's descendants (Genesis 4:11, 15).

Describing his encounters with Deity and with the devil, Moses remarks that he was able to look upon Satan "*in the natural man*" (Moses 1:14). The Book of Mormon prophets picked up this same term to distinguish men who did and did not have the Spirit of God upon them. Benjamin explained that "*the natural man* is an enemy to God" and that men can become Saints only by "[putting] off *the natural man*" (Mosiah 3:19). Alma carries the theme forward by inquiring "what *natural man* is there that knoweth these things?" (Alma 26:21). A similar usage crops up in the New Testament once (1 Corinthians 2:14).[25]

In addition to phrase correlations, we have one unique name correlation between Moses and the Book of Mormon. *Omner* was a name of one of the four sons of Mosiah.[26] But in Moses it is the name of a city, and in the Book of Mormon the name of a land (Moses 7:9; Alma 51:26). (The term *shum* also occurs uniquely in these two sources, though it is a name in Moses and a unit of measure for gold in the Book of Mormon.)[27]

Finally, an important form of linguistic punctuation which is used by several Book of Mormon writers and which does not obviously appear in the Old Testament, is used in Moses in the same way. Moses ends an important segment of text with the statement: "And thus it is. Amen."[28] It can be shown that Nephi used this same phrase to mark significant structural junctures in the text.[29] Allusions to final judgment and testimony of the gospel provide additional contextual parallels for some of these passages.

Conclusion

Some final caveats are in order. Any project like this is unavoidably handicapped by the fact that none of the texts being compared is available in the original languages. For those who do not believe that Joseph Smith was a prophet, this point alone would make this entire exercise quite uninteresting. But those of us who do recognize Joseph as an inspired restorer of ancient texts need not be precluded from thoughtful investigation of this matter. It should be sufficient for us to see that neither Joseph's language, nor the language of the Old Testament that was familiar to him, accounts for the correlations we have observed in the foregoing comparisons. New Testament influence is also largely excluded for the primary cases of the first group on which the conclusions of this study rest. Furthermore, there has been no effort made to identify appearances of the key phrases in this study in either the Doctrine and Covenants or Joseph Smith's own writings. Their presence or absence in those texts is equally compatible with the hypothesis developed in this paper. A casual survey suggests that some show up there, and others do not.

Reliance on computerized text comparisons has both advantages and dangers. Many phrases were included only because the computer picked up what was otherwise unnoticed. On the other hand, the computer cannot make judgments of relevance or significance. Computer analyses must always be supplemented by a careful reading and rereading of the text, as the machine cannot pick up more subtle parallels of meaning and context. And because the King James Version is the only biblical text used, there remains a significant likelihood that some of the parallels assembled in this study will eventually be found to have some kind of Old Testament counterparts, thus reducing their contribution to the conclusions drawn here. Unless, however, such future discoveries include most of what is identified here, the textual evidence will continue to favor the thesis that the brass plates version of Genesis had contents similar to the book of Moses and that phrases found in the book of Moses/brass plates would also appropriately be found in the Book of Mormon.

Appendix: Analytical Chart of Book of Moses References That Appear in the Book of Mormon

I am grateful to John W. Welch for giving me the extra encouragement I needed to undertake the following exercise. The point of the chart provided below is twofold. The first purpose is merely to list the passages included in the paper. The second is to attempt a crude computation of statistical probability of dependence between the texts. This is not the kind of thing that scholars have done much with. I offer this analysis only because I think it does produce some useful information, if not clear and precise measures of probability. A key to the chart precedes the specific data, and following the table is a discussion of the assumptions that underlie it.

Column	Description
A.	Cluster number (1-33)
B.	List of key terms in cluster in original order
C.	Book of Moses key reference (multiple references not listed)
D.	Book of Mormon reference
E.	Cluster type (a, b, c) a. single word b. phrase c. synonymous term or phrase
F.	Number of significant repeated terms
G.	Precision of reference (same terms, same order) 1. possible variant, recognizable similarities 2. variant, but recognizably the same 3. minor variation only 4. no variation

H.   Deliberate reshaping or manipulation of source
    1. casual or even accidental reference
    2. paraphrase or other loose reference
    3. adaptation of source to context
    4. exact repetition
    5. play on original terms or word order such that present formulation requires knowledge of original to convey full meaning (including inverted quotations)

I.   Similarity of context
    1. Weak similarity of context
    2. Definite similarity of context
    3. Exact context evident or evoked by repetition of contextual language

J.   Author's awareness of a brass plates source
    1. consciousness of source not implied or meaning not precisely the same and access to brass plates unclear
    2. aware of either book of Moses or intermediary Book of Mormon sources and meaning close to source
    3. stated use or awareness of brass plates as source

K.   Distinctiveness of the concept or the terms (in American discourse)
    1. English terminology common to nineteenth-century Americans
    2. somewhat distinctive terminology
    3. unique or distinctive terminology

L. Other occurrences (clear Old Testament references disqualify items from this study)
1. strong New Testament parallel and/or weak Old Testament parallel
2. weak New Testament parallel and no Old Testament
3. no biblical parallels found, strong or weak

M. Score. This number is calculated in the following manner: The seven criteria (G through L) are weighted modestly to ensure that the more important ones have a larger effect. The values in columns G, H, I, and K are doubled, and the values in L are tripled. All seven values are then multiplied in a linearized calculation that combines them roughly into a common score designed to indicate relative degrees of dependence between the two texts. For convenience, the score is reduced by a factor of .001 and rounded to the nearest whole number to arrive at the score listed in column M.[30] The only object in presenting the results of these calculations is to emphasize differences and not to claim any numerical or quantifiable relationship or to ascribe any particular meaning to the distance between scores.

Table
Group 1

A	B	C	D	E Type	F Terms	G Precision	H Intention	I Context	J Awareness	K Distinctiveness	L Biblical	M Score
1	transgression-fall, fall-death	Moses 6:59	2 Nephi 9:6	b	4	4	5	3	3	2	3	207
2	order-days-years-eternity	Moses 6:67	Alma 13:7	b	6	3	3	3	3	3	2	140
3	Lord-from all eternity-to	Moses 7:29	Mosiah 3:5	b	3	4	4	2	2	3	3	83
3	Lord-from all eternity-to	Moses 7:29	Moroni 8:18	b	3	3	4	2	2	3	3	62
4	God-gave-man-agency	Moses 7:32	2 Nephi 2:16	d	4	3	5	3	3	3	3	233
5	Lord's Spirit-withdraws-from-man	Moses 1:15	Alma 34:35	b	3	4	3	2	2	3	3	62
5	Lord's Spirit-withdraws-from-man	Moses 1:15	Helaman 4:24	b	3	4	5	2	2	3	3	104
5	Lord's Spirit-withdraws-from-man	Moses 1:15	Helaman 6:35	b	3	3	5	2	2	3	3	78
5	Lord's Spirit-withdraws-from-man	Moses 1:15	Helaman 13:8	b	3	3	5	2	2	3	3	78
5	Lord's Spirit-withdraws-from-man	Moses 1:15	Mosiah 2:36	b	3	3	3	2	2	3	3	47
6	children-whole-from foundation	Moses 6:54	Moroni 8:8, 12	b	3	4	3	3	3	3	3	140
7	only name-given-salvation*	Moses 6:52	Mosiah 3:17	b	3	3	5	3	2	3	1	39
8	devil-father-of all lies	Moses 4:4	2 Nephi 2:18	b	3	3	5	3	3	3	3	175
8	devil-father-of all lies	Moses 4:4	Ether 8:25	b	3	3	4	3	2	3	3	93
8	devil-father-of all lies	Moses 4:4	2 Nephi 9:9	b	3	3	3	3	3	3	3	105
9	devil-lead-captive-his will	Moses 4:4	Alma 12:11	c	4	4	3	2	3	3	3	124

* This Group 2 item is listed here because it is linked to the preceding item in the text.

Group 1 (continued)

A	B	C	D	E Type	F Terms	G Precision	H Intention	I Context	J Awareness	K Distinctiveness	L Biblical	M Score
9	devil-lead-captive-his will	Moses 4:4	Alma 40:13	c	4	3	3	3	2	3	3	93
9	devil-lead-captive-his will	Moses 4:4	2 Nephi 2:27	c	4	2	3	3	3	3	3	93
10	devil-deceive-blind-lead	Moses 4:4	3 Nephi 2:2	c	4	4	3	2	2	3	3	83
11	lies-lead-will-deceive-eyes	Moses 4:4	1 Nephi 16:38	c	5	3	5	1	2	3	3	65

Group 2

A	B	C	D	E Type	F Terms	G Precision	H Intention	I Context	J Awareness	K Distinctiveness	L Biblical	M Score
12	earth-groans; rocks-rend	Moses 7:56	1 Nephi 12:4	b	4	3	3	3	2	3	1	31
12	earth-groans; rocks-rend	Moses 7:56	1 Nephi 19:12	b	4	4	4	3	3	3	1	83
12	earth-groans; rocks-rend	Moses 7:56	3 Nephi 10:9	b	4	3	3	3	3	3	1	47
13	plan of salvation	Moses 6:62	Jarom 1:2	b	2	4	4	1	2	3	3	28
13	plan of salvation	Moses 6:62	Alma 24:14	b	2	4	4	2	2	3	3	55
13	plan of salvation	Moses 6:62	Alma 42:5	b	2	4	4	3	3	3	3	124
14	eternal life	Moses 1:39	2 Nephi 2:27	b	2	4	4	2	3	2	1	18
14	eternal life	Moses 1:39	2 Nephi 2:28	b	2	4	4	2	3	2	1	18
14	eternal life	Moses 1:39	2 Nephi 10:23	b	2	4	4	2	3	2	1	18

Group 2 (continued)

A	B	C	D	E Type	F Terms	G Precision	H Intention	I Context	J Awareness	K Distinctiveness	L Biblical	M Score
14	eternal life	Moses 1:39	2 Nephi 31:18	b	2	4	4	2	2	2	1	12
14	eternal life	Moses 1:39	2 Nephi 31:20	b	2	4	4	2	2	2	1	12
14	eternal life	Moses 1:39	Jacob 6:11	b	2	4	4	2	2	2	1	12
14	eternal life	Moses 1:39	Enos 1:3	b	2	4	4	2	1	2	1	6
14	eternal life	Moses 1:39	Mosiah 5:15	b	2	4	4	2	2	2	1	12
14	eternal life	Moses 1:39	Mosiah 15:23	b	2	4	4	2	2	2	1	12
14	eternal life	Moses 1:39	Mosiah 15:24	b	2	4	4	2	2	2	1	12
14	eternal life	Moses 1:39	Mosiah 15:25	b	2	4	4	2	2	2	1	12
14	eternal life	Moses 1:39	Mosiah 18:9	b	2	4	4	2	2	2	1	12
14	eternal life	Moses 1:39	Mosiah 18:13	b	2	4	4	2	2	2	1	12
14	eternal life	Moses 1:39	Mosiah 26:20	b	2	4	4	2	2	2	1	12
14	eternal life	Moses 1:39	Mosiah 28:7	b	2	4	4	2	2	2	1	12
14	eternal life	Moses 1:39	Alma 1:4	b	2	4	4	2	2	2	1	12
14	eternal life	Moses 1:39	Alma 5:28	b	2	4	4	2	2	2	1	12
14	eternal life	Moses 1:39	Alma 7:16	b	2	4	4	2	2	2	1	12
14	eternal life	Moses 1:39	Alma 11:40	b	2	4	4	2	2	2	1	12
14	eternal life	Moses 1:39	Alma 13:29	b	2	4	4	2	2	2	1	12

Group 2 (continued)

A	B	C	D	E Type	F Terms	G Precision	H Intention	I Context	J Awareness	K Distinctiveness	L Biblical	M Score
14	eternal life	Moses 1:39	Alma 22:15	b	2	4	4	2	2	2	1	12
14	eternal life	Moses 1:39	Helaman 5:8	b	2	4	4	2	2	2	1	12
14	eternal life	Moses 1:39	3 Nephi 9:14	b	2	4	4	2	2	2	1	12
14	eternal life	Moses 1:39	3 Nephi 15:9	b	2	4	4	2	2	2	1	12
14	eternal life	Moses 1:39	Moroni 9:25	b	2	4	4	2	2	2	1	12
15	unclean-dwell-presence-God	Moses 6:57	1 Nephi 10:21	b	4	3	3	2	2	2	2	28
15	unclean-dwell-presence-God	Moses 6:57	1 Nephi 15:34	b	4	3	3	3	2	2	2	41
15	unclean-dwell-presence-God	Moses 6:57	Alma 7:21	b	4	2	3	2	2	2	2	18
16	call on-all men-to repent	Moses 6:23	2 Nephi 2:21	b	3	3	3	3	3	1	1	12
16	call on-all men-to repent	Moses 6:23	Alma 12:33	b	3	4	3	3	3	1	1	12
16	call on-all men-to repent	Moses 6:23	3 Nephi 11:32	b	3	3	3	2	2	1	1	7
16	call on-all men-to repent	Moses 6:23	Moroni 7:31	b	3	3	3	1	2	1	1	3
17	nowise-inherit-kingdom of God	Moses 6:57	Mosiah 27:26	b	3	4	4	3	1	1	1	7
17	nowise-inherit-kingdom of God	Moses 6:57	Alma 5:51	b	3	4	4	2	2	1	1	9
17	nowise-inherit-kingdom of God	Moses 6:57	Alma 9:12	b	3	4	4	2	2	1	1	9
17	nowise-inherit-kingdom of God	Moses 6:57	Alma 39:9	b	3	4	4	2	2	1	1	9
17	nowise-inherit-kingdom of God	Moses 6:57	3 Nephi 11:38	b	3	4	4	2	1	1	1	5

Group 2 (continued)

A	B	C	D	Type	Terms	Precision	Intention	Context	Awareness	Distinctiveness	Biblical	Score
				E	F	G	H	I	J	K	L	M
18	things-temporal-spiritual	Moses 6:63	1 Nephi 15:32	b	3	4	3	2	2	2	3	41
18	things-temporal-spiritual	Moses 6:63	1 Nephi 22:3	b	3	4	3	2	2	2	2	14
18	things-temporal-spiritual	Moses 6:63	Mosiah 2:41	b	3	4	3	1	2	2	2	41
18	things-temporal-spiritual	Moses 6:63	Alma 7:23	b	3	4	3	3	2	2	2	28
18	things-temporal-spiritual	Moses 6:63	Alma 12:16	b	3	2	2	2	2	2	2	5
18	things-temporal-spiritual	Moses 6:63	Alma 37:43	b	3	4	3	1	2	2	2	14
18	things-temporal-spiritual	Moses 6:63	Helaman 14:16	b	3	4	3	3	2	2	2	41
19	people-dwell-in righteousness	Moses 7:16	1 Nephi 22:26	b	3	4	4	3	3	2	2	83
20	mine Only Begotten Son	Moses 6:52	Jacob 4:5	b	4	3	2	2	3	2	1	14
20	mine Only Begotten Son	Moses 6:52	Jacob 4:11	b	4	3	2	2	3	2	1	14
20	mine Only Begotten Son	Moses 6:52	Alma 12:33	b	4	3	4	3	3	2	1	41
21	works of darkness	Moses 5:55	2 Nephi 25:2	b	2	4	4	1	2	2	1	6
21	works of darkness	Moses 5:55	2 Nephi 26:10	b	2	4	4	1	2	2	1	6
21	works of darkness	Moses 5:55	2 Nephi 26:22	b	2	4	4	3	2	2	1	18
21	works of darkness	Moses 5:55	2 Nephi 9:9	b	2	4	4	3	2	2	1	18
21	works of darkness	Moses 5:55	2 Nephi 10:15	b	2	4	4	2	2	2	1	12
21	works of darkness	Moses 5:55	Alma 37:21	b	2	4	4	3	2	2	1	18

Group 2 (continued)

A	B	C	D	E Type	F Terms	G Precision	H Intention	I Context	J Awareness	K Distinctiveness	L Biblical	M Score
21	works of darkness	Moses 5:55	Alma 37:23	b	2	4	4	3	2	2	1	18
21	works of darkness	Moses 5:55	Alma 45:12	b	2	4	4	2	2	2	1	12
21	works of darkness	Moses 5:55	Helaman 6:28	b	2	4	4	3	2	2	1	18
21	works of darkness	Moses 5:55	Helaman 6:30	b	2	4	4	3	2	2	1	18
21	works of darkness	Moses 5:55	Helaman 8:4	b	2	4	4	3	2	2	1	18
21	works of darkness	Moses 5:55	Helaman 10:3	b	2	4	4	3	2	2	1	18
21	works of darkness	Moses 5:55	Mormon 8:27	b	2	4	4	3	2	2	1	18
22	secret combination(s)	Moses 5:51	2 Nephi 26:22	b	2	4	4	3	2	3	3	83
22	secret combination(s)	Moses 5:51	Alma 37:30	b	2	4	4	3	2	3	3	83
22	secret combination(s)	Moses 5:51	Alma 37:31	b	2	4	4	3	2	3	3	83
22	secret combination(s)	Moses 5:51	Helaman 2:8	b	2	4	4	3	2	3	3	83
22	secret combination(s)	Moses 5:51	Helaman 3:23	b	2	4	4	3	2	3	3	83
22	secret combination(s)	Moses 5:51	Helaman 6:38	b	2	4	4	3	2	3	3	83
22	secret combination(s)	Moses 5:51	3 Nephi 4:29	b	2	4	4	3	2	3	3	83
22	secret combination(s)	Moses 5:51	3 Nephi 5:6	b	2	4	4	3	2	3	3	83
22	secret combination(s)	Moses 5:51	3 Nephi 7:6	b	2	4	4	3	2	3	3	83
22	secret combination(s)	Moses 5:51	3 Nephi 7:9	b	2	4	4	3	2	3	3	83

Group 2 (continued)

A	B	C	D	E Type	F Terms	G Precision	H Intention	I Context	J Awareness	K Distinctiveness	L Biblical	M Score
22	secret combination(s)	Moses 5:51	3 Nephi 9:9	b	2	4	4	3	2	3	3	83
22	secret combination(s)	Moses 5:51	4 Nephi 1:42	b	2	4	4	3	2	3	3	83
22	secret combination(s)	Moses 5:51	Mormon 8:27	b	2	4	4	3	2	3	3	83
22	secret combination(s)	Moses 5:51	Ether 8:18	b	2	4	4	3	2	3	3	83
22	secret combination(s)	Moses 5:51	Ether 8:19	b	2	4	4	3	2	3	3	83
22	secret combination(s)	Moses 5:51	Ether 8:22	b	2	4	4	3	2	3	3	83
22	secret combination(s)	Moses 5:51	Ether 8:24	b	2	4	4	3	2	3	3	83
22	secret combination(s)	Moses 5:51	Ether 8:27	b	2	4	4	3	2	3	3	83
22	secret combination(s)	Moses 5:51	Ether 9:1	b	2	4	4	3	2	3	3	83
22	secret combination(s)	Moses 5:51	Ether 11:15	b	2	4	4	3	2	3	3	83
22	secret combination(s)	Moses 5:51	Ether 13:18	b	2	4	4	3	2	3	3	83
22	secret combination(s)	Moses 5:51	Ether 14:8	b	2	4	4	3	2	3	3	83
22	secret combination(s)	Moses 5:51	Ether 14:10	b	2	4	4	3	2	3	3	83
23	wars and bloodshed	Moses 6:15	Jacob 7:24	b	2	4	4	2	2	2	3	37
23	war(s) and bloodshed	Moses 6:15	Omni 1:3	b	2	4	3	1	1	2	3	7
23	wars and bloodshed	Moses 6:15	Omni 1:24	b	2	3	3	1	1	2	3	5
23	wars and bloodshed	Moses 6:15	Alma 35:15	b	2	3	3	2	2	2	3	21

Group 2 (continued)

A	B	C	D	Type (E)	Terms (F)	Precision (G)	Intention (H)	Context (I)	Awareness (J)	Distinctiveness (K)	Biblical (L)	Score (M)
23	wars and bloodshed	Moses 6:15	Alma 62:35	b	2	4	4	2	2	2	3	37
23	wars and bloodshed	Moses 6:15	Alma 62:39	b	2	4	4	2	2	2	3	37
23	wars and bloodshed	Moses 6:15	Mormon 1:12	b	2	2	5	1	2	2	3	12
23	wars and bloodshed	Moses 6:15	Mosiah 29:36	b	2	2	2	2	2	2	3	9
23	wars and bloodshed	Moses 6:15	Alma 45:11	b	2	2	2	2	2	2	3	9
23	wars and bloodshed	Moses 6:15	Alma 60:16	b	2	2	2	2	2	2	3	9
23	wars and bloodshed	Moses 6:15	Helaman 6:17	b	2	2	5	3	2	2	3	35
23	wars and bloodshed	Moses 6:15	Mormon 8:8	b	2	2	2	2	2	2	3	9
23	wars and bloodshed	Moses 6:15	Ether 14:21	b	2	2	5	3	2	2	3	35
24	shut out-from presence-God	Moses 6:49	2 Nephi 9:9	b	3	4	4	3	3	3	1	62
25	murder-get gain	Moses 5:31	Helaman 2:8	c	2	3	3	3	2	3	3	47
25	murder-get gain	Moses 5:31	Helaman 7:21	c	2	3	3	2	2	3	3	31
25	murder-get gain	Moses 5:31	Ether 8:16	c	2	3	3	3	2	3	3	31
26	seeking for power	Moses 6:15	Alma 46:4	b	2	4	4	2	2	1	3	18
26	seeking for power	Moses 6:15	Alma 60:17	b	2	4	4	2	2	1	3	18
26	seeking for power	Moses 6:15	Moroni 8:28	b	2	2	2	1	2	1	3	2
27	carnal, sensual, devilish	Moses 5:13	Alma 42:10	b	3	4	4	3	3	3	1	62

Group 2 (continued)

A	B	C	D	Type	Terms	Precision	Intention	Context	Awareness	Distinctiveness	Biblical	Score
27	carnal, sensual, devilish	Moses 5:13	Mosiah 16:3	b	3	4	4	3	3	3	1	62
27	carnal, sensual, devilish	Moses 5:13	Alma 41:13	b	3	2	5	2	2	3	1	17
28	hearts-wax-hard	Moses 6:27	Alma 35:15	b	3	4	3	2	2	3	1	14
29	lifted up-imagination-his heart	Moses 8:22	Alma 1:6	c	3	3	3	3	2	3	1	23
30	natural man	Moses 1:14	Mosiah 3:19	b	2	4	4	1	1	2	3	9
30	natural man	Moses 1:14	Mosiah 3:19	b	2	4	4	1	1	2	3	9
30	natural man	Moses 1:14	Alma 26:21	b	2	4	4	2	1	2	3	18
31	Omner	Moses 7:9	Mosiah 27:34	a	1	4	4	2	2	3	3	28
32	shum	Moses 7:5	Alma 11:5	a	1	4	4	1	2	3	3	14
33	and thus-it was (is)-Amen	Moses 5:59	1 Nephi 9:6	b	4	4	5	1	2	2	3	46
33	and thus-it was (is)-Amen	Moses 5:59	1 Nephi 14:30	b	4	4	5	1	2	2	3	46
33	and thus-it was (is)-Amen	Moses 5:59	1 Nephi 22:31	b	4	4	5	3	2	2	3	138
33	and thus-it was (is)-Amen	Moses 5:59	Alma 13:9	b	4	4	5	3	2	2	3	138
33	and thus-it was (is)-Amen	Moses 5:59	Helaman 12:26	b	4	4	5	2	2	2	3	92

Assumptions of This Model

1. The model assumes a linear relationship between the seven items used in each score calculation. This assumes that each of the seven criteria adds plausibility independently of each of the others. This assumption would be compromised to the extent that any of the seven criteria were interdependent.

2. The model mainly attempts to give greater value to intuitively less likely features of references. A rough effort is made to weight actual differences used to calculate probabilities. Scores indicate greater or lesser probability but not magnitudes.

3. Probability assumptions for categories F through L:

F. *Number of Terms*. The greater the number of significant terms repeated in parallel phrasings in two texts, the less likely they are to be independent.

G. *Precision of reference*. The more precise the similarities between parallel phrasings in two texts, the less likely they are to be independent.

H. *Deliberate reshaping or manipulation of source*. The more deliberately shaped the repetition in parallel phrasings in two texts, the less likely they are to be independent. Intentionality is inferred from contextual adaptation, exact repetition, or intentional manipulation (including inverted quotations) that creates additional meaning for those who recognize the intended reference to the source text. The latter category is deemed least likely to be independent because the intended meaning of the passage is only communicable to a reader who shares the author's awareness of the source. The author not only is influenced by the source, he uses it in new ways to communicate his intentions.

I. *Context*. The more similar the contexts in which parallel phrasings occur, the less likely they are to be independent. The evidence for dependence between two passages where the same concepts or terms occur is stronger when there are additional similarities in the two contexts. Context similarity can take different forms. For example, the two passages might refer to similar situations, feature the same accompanying statement, or be located in similar doctrinal discourses or historical explanations.

J. *Author's awareness of a brass plates source*. Author awareness of a brass plates source reduces the likelihood of independence. This awareness must be inferred contextually with explicit references to brass plates writings as the strongest evidence.

K. *Distinctiveness of the concept or the terms (in American discourse)*. The more distinctive the terminology repeated in parallel phrasings in two texts, the less likely they are to be independent.

L. *Other occurrences (biblical)*, Presence of weak or strong versions of the parallel terminology in the New Testament, and even more so, in the Old Testament, increases the possibility that the book of Moses and Book of Mormon passages are independent. But if these parallel expressions are not found in the Bible, this readily available text is removed as a possible source for Joseph Smith's translation language, thus increasing the probability that Book of Mormon writers are reflecting a source known to them from the brass plates. As already explained, clear Old Testament parallels were considered sufficient reason to drop the occurrence altogether as evidence of dependence.

Notes

1. See John L. Sorenson, "The 'Brass Plates' and Biblical Scholarship," *Dialogue* 10 (Autumn 1977): 35–36.

2. This study is limited to the translation in the King James Version. I assume that checking the following study against original texts may lead to some modification of my list of correlations.

3. Nephi explicitly records that he read to his brothers out of the brass plates, including the books of Moses and Isaiah (1 Nephi 19:21–23).

4. See P. C. Beentjes, "Inverted Quotations in the Bible," *Biblica* 63 (1982): 506-23.

5. Cf. Moses 7:29, 31, with Mosiah 3:5 and Moroni 8:18.

6. See John W. Welch, "The Melchizedek Material in Alma 13:13-19," in this volume.

7. Cf. also Helaman 6:35 and 13:8. King Benjamin gives the same phrase an interesting turn by accusing the wicked of *withdrawing themselves from the Spirit of the Lord* through disobedience (Mosiah 2:36).

8. Cf. Moses 6:52. Acts 4:12 contains nearly the same formula. Because of this New Testament parallel, this passage belongs in Group 2, but is listed in the appendix table in the order it appears in the text with the Group 1 statement to which it is linked contextually.

9. Compare Lehi's account of the devil's efforts to lead the children of men into captivity in 2 Nephi 2:17-29.

10. See David Noel Freedman, "The Formation of the Canon of the Old Testament: The Selection and Identification of the Torah as the Supreme Authority of the Post-Exilic Community," E. Firmage, B. Weiss, and J. Welch, eds., *Religion and Law: Biblical-Judaic and Islamic Perspectives* (Winona Lake, IN: Eisenbrauns, 1989), 315-32. Freedman, who is a prominent American biblical scholar, developed his thesis independently of any of the materials used in the present study.

11. Ibid.

12. Cf. also Romans 8:22: "For we know that the whole creation groaneth and travaileth in pain together until now." Clearly Paul means something altogether different in this passage.

13. See also Jacob 6:8; Alma 12:25-26, 30, 32-33; 17:16; 18:39; 22:13; 29:2; 34:16, 31; 39:18; 42:11, 13, which refer to "the plan of redemption," an idiosyncratic Book of Mormon variant on "plan of salvation."

14. See 2 Nephi 2:27-28; 10:23; 31:18, 20; Jacob 6:11; Enos 1:3; Mosiah 5:15; 15:23-25; 18:9, 13; 26:20; 28:7; Alma 1:4; 5:28; 7:16; 11:40; 13:29; 22:15; Helaman 5:8; 3 Nephi 9:14; 15:9; Moroni 9:25. For sample New Testament parallels see John 6:54; 6:68.

15. The terms "immortal" or "immortality" occur in the following passages: 2 Nephi 9:13, 15; Enos 1:27; Mosiah 2:28, 38; 16:10; Alma 5:15; 11:45; 12:12, 20; 40:2; 41:4; Helaman 3:30; 3 Nephi 28:8, 15, 17, 36; Mormon 6:21.

16. Samuel the Lamanite was able to combine all of these uses of the distinction in one statement. See Helaman 14:16.

17. Cf. Moses 1:6, 16-17, 32-33; 2:1, 26-27; 3:18; 4:1, 3, 28; 6:52, 59, 62; 7:62. Cf. further Moses 7:50, 59.

18. 2 Nephi 25:2; 26:10, 22. See also Alma 37:21, 23; Helaman 6:30; Mormon 8:27.

19. See 2 Nephi 9:9; 10:15; Alma 37:21, 23, 25; Helaman 8:4; 10:3; 3 Nephi 3:7.

20. 2 Nephi 9:9; 26:22; Alma 37:30-31; Helaman 2:8; 3:23; 6:38; 3 Nephi 4:29; 5:6; 7:6, 9; 9:9; 4 Nephi 1:42; Mormon 8:27; Ether 8:18-19, 22, 24; 9:1; 11:15; 13:18; 14:8, 10. Cf. Helaman 6:30; 11:10, 26; Ether 8:9; 9:26; 13:15.

21. Jacob 7:24; Omni 1:3, 24; Alma 35:15; 62:35, 39. Cf. also Mosiah 29:36; Alma 45:11; 60:16; Helaman 6:17; Mormon 8:8; Ether 14:21.

22. See James 3:15, where a similar phrase occurs: "This wisdom descendeth not from above, but is earthly, sensual, devilish."

23. Cf. Matthew 13:15; Acts 28:27; Jacob 1:15; Alma 21:3.

24. Cf. Daniel 5:20; 1 Timothy 3:6; Jacob 2:13; Mosiah 11:5, 19; Alma 6:3; 7:6; 31:25; 45:24; 3 Nephi 16:10; Mormon 8:28, 36.

25. Cf. Mosiah 16:5; Alma 41:11-12; 42:10.

26. Cf. Mosiah 27:34 and numerous other references to this great missionary.

27. Enoch refers once to the valley of Shum (Moses 7:5) and twice to the people of Shum (Moses 7:5, 7). Alma mentions a "shum of gold" twice (Alma 11:5, 9).

28. Cf. Moses 5:59 with 1 Nephi 9:6; 14:30; 22:31; Alma 13:9; Helaman 12:26. Cf. also 1 Nephi 15:36; 2 Nephi 33:15; Mosiah 3:27; Alma 6:8; 7:27; Moses 6:68.

29. See Noel B. Reynolds, "Nephi's Outline," *BYU Studies* 20 (Winter 1980): 134; reprinted in Noel B. Reynolds, ed., *Book of Mormon Authorship: New Light on Ancient Origins* (Provo, UT: BYU Religious Studies Center, 1982), 58.

30. I am grateful to John L. Hilton for reviewing and contributing to the statistical reasoning presented here.

7

The Composition
of Lehi's Family

John L. Sorenson
Brigham Young University, Provo, Utah

A characteristic of Hugh Nibley's study of the Book of Mormon, which he has urged others to emulate, is close study of the scriptural text to reveal information which myopia had previously led readers to ignore. In that spirit, this article reports my microanthropological examination of what the text reveals regarding the composition and demography of Lehi's party from the beginning of their sojourn in the Arabian wilderness to their arrival in the promised land.

The family members most often referred to were the father Lehi and three sons—Nephi, Laman, and Lemuel. In most discussions of the events reported in 1 Nephi, Latter-day Saints have generally acted as though these four men were the only significant actors. Others specifically mentioned as being in the traveling party—but apparently of little consequence to the history—were the mother Sariah; sons Sam, Jacob, and Joseph; Zoram; Ishmael and his unnamed family members (at least a wife, two sons, and five daughters); and Nephi's belatedly mentioned "sisters" (1 Nephi 7:6; 16:7, 2 Nephi 5:6). We shall see, however, that others surely were along.

A first order of priority must be to establish the ages of the *dramatis personae*. The oldest four sons of Lehi were, from eldest to youngest, Laman, Lemuel, Sam, and Nephi (see heading to 1 Nephi). The four were with their parents when they departed Jerusalem. Jacob and Joseph were later born in the Arabian wilderness. The four oldest sons were of marriageable age at the time of departure, for each "took . . . to wife" a daughter of Ishmael soon after the latter arrived at Lehi's camp (1 Nephi 16:7). Furthermore, Ishmael's two sons evidently married daughters of Lehi. Nephi's cryptic mention of his sisters going with him when the colonists split into two factions in the land of promise (2 Nephi 5:6) implied to Sidney B. Sperry that they had left their husbands, sons of Ishmael.[1] I agree. Professor Sperry supported this idea by citing a statement made by Erastus Snow in an address printed in the *Journal of Discourses*.[2] Apostle Snow said, "The Prophet Joseph Smith informed us that the record of Lehi was contained on the 116 pages that were first translated and subsequently stolen . . . [and] that Ishmael['s] sons married into Lehi's family, and Lehi's sons married Ishmael's daughters."

The composition of the party begins to look complex. Rather than to pursue it discursively, I shall sort out the tangled strands of social relationships and ages by initially considering all the personnel more or less in an order determined by the amount of information given about them.

1. Nephi

Nephi describes himself as being "exceeding young, nevertheless . . . large in stature" (1 Nephi 2:16). In 1 Nephi 4:31 he says again that he was "a man large in stature," in the context of seizing a much older Zoram to keep him from fleeing. Both his use of the expression "a man" and his ability to act like one in handling Zoram allow us to suppose that he was already taller than most men of his society and probably as heavy as the average person despite his chronological youth. Again, when he donned Laban's gear (1 Nephi 4:19) and successfully impersonated him, we get a picture of a fully grown male. In manner too, he was socially and linguistically sophisticated enough that he could act in Jerusalem with confidence. Taking into account his own characterization ("exceeding young"), a reasonable guess is that he was coming up on his seventeenth birthday when his account starts.

2. Lehi

The indicators of Lehi's age are paradoxical. By the time the story begins he already has had what we might term a "successful career" managing the "land of his inheritance" (1 Nephi 2:4, 3:16, 22-25). It has been suggested that he was a merchant,[3] and indeed he may have been engaged as such at times, trading on his capital. Others think he was a metalsmith.[4] However, the linkage Nephi makes between his father's wealth and the "land of his inheritance" suggests that his primary economic activity probably was husbandry, chiefly in the sense of being a landlord. As for metalworking, it would be highly unlikely that a man who had inherited land and was considered very wealthy (1 Nephi 3:25) would have been a metalworker, for the men in that role tended to be of lower social status and were usually landless.[5]

With a son aged twenty-two or twenty-three at the time he departed from Jerusalem in 597 B.C., he would have married Sariah around 621 B.C. As we shall see, the sequence of her births requires that she was young—perhaps still sixteen—at her marriage. Lehi probably was a little older, though coming from a family of substance, Lehi would not have had to delay his marriage for economic reasons. I would guess that he was eighteen. If so, then he was born around 639 B.C., although he could have been a few years more. Thus, at the beginning of the Book of Mormon record, Lehi was approximately forty-two or perhaps a bit older.[6] (Latter-day Saint illustrators who depict him only as an aged patriarch should, rather, show him in the early chapters of 1 Nephi at mature middle age.)

He would still sire two sons, plausibly born around his

ages forty-five and forty-seven (1 Nephi 18:7; see the discussion below about Sariah's births). On board ship, he, at age fifty-four, and Sariah are both characterized by Nephi as "stricken in years," having "grey hairs," and about to enter a "watery grave." Still Nephi indicates that this was because of grief brought upon them by their children more than because of age per se (1 Nephi 18:17-18).

Lehi survived the voyage, of course. First Nephi 18:23-19:2 reports the group's initial pioneering in the new land, which need not have consumed more than a single year (the activities are less comprehensive and time-extensive than those reported by Nephi when his party settled in the land of Nephi — 2 Nephi 5:11, 13). Second Nephi opens with Lehi teaching his family. His historical resumé in 2 Nephi 1:1-5 sounds like only a short time had passed since the landing, for he speaks entirely about what had transpired en route. His valedictory continues through chapter 3. In 2 Nephi 4:12, the record abruptly states that after Lehi had spoken those things to his household, "he waxed old" and died. My impression is that Lehi lived no more than a couple of years in America and perhaps less than one. In that case his age at death could have been as early as fifty-seven. Considering the arduous circumstances he faced in the last dozen years of his life and especially the intimation in 1 Nephi 18:17-18 that he was viewed as being somewhat sickly, this seemingly premature death is not really surprising.

3. Laman

We may ponder why this eldest son was not married. Being a number of years older than Nephi, he would normally have had a wife by the time they left Jerusalem. Lehi was a man of wealth, so the family's socioeconomic position should not have hindered his obtaining a wife but likely enhanced the options. One wonders why, if Ishmael and his family became willing to marry into Lehi's family under the difficult circumstances they did, no marriage had been contracted between members of the two families *before* their departure.

But perhaps Laman had been married, the wife having died (the death rate was relatively high, after all, in the ancient world). If so, the deceased spouse could have been a daughter of Ishmael (sororatic marriage, in which a man took as second wife the sister of his first, was a known practice in Israel). Or, possible disorder(s) in Laman's personality, of which there is considerable evidence in Nephi's descriptions of his older brother's behavior, had made it impossible for the family to persuade any father to give him a daughter for his wife.

Nothing is said directly about Laman's physical characteristics, but the fact that the two eldest brothers could "smite [Nephi and Sam] . . . with a rod" and that later they "did lay their hands upon [Nephi]" and "bind [him] with cords" (1 Nephi 3:28, 7:16) could suggest that the older pair were of about the same stature as Nephi. As the eldest son, and a proud and self-centered one at that, Laman comes through in the record as being somewhat haughty and probably pushy among his lessers but, as in dealing with Laban, lacking confidence, being frustrated and unstable in the face of determined opposition (cf. 1 Nephi 2:9; 17:55).

Inasmuch as Nephi appears to have been near seventeen, his eldest brother very likely was not younger than twenty-two. I should think twenty-three more likely. It might be suggested that he was considerably older, but that would only make more difficult accounting for the already long period of fertility of his mother, so that seems highly unlikely.

4. Lemuel

Lemuel seems to have been thoroughly dominated by Laman while possessing many of the same personality characteristics (see their pairing in Lehi's lament, 1 Nephi 2:9-14). Little is said about him as an individual, and never is there an indication that he stood up to or disagreed with Laman (cf. 1 Nephi 3:28, "for he hearkened unto the words of Laman"). His age must have been about twenty-one.

5. Sariah

In the sixth century B.C. (as throughout most of human history), the timing of births was considerably different than what prevails today. Philip Houghton has conveniently summarized scientific findings on fertility and survival as a result of many studies of both skeletons and living humans in Pre-Modern societies.[7] For one thing, diet was usually less nutritional and a good deal less consistent than we enjoy. Both minor and major illnesses were common. As one result of such conditions, women typically did not become fertile until around age nineteen, even though they might marry younger than that. The same biological problems decreased the likelihood that a wife would become pregnant. Miscarriages and stillbirths were not uncommon, and even after a successful birth, infants had much smaller chances of survival in their first few years. Obviously most women nursed their babies, and lack of alternative foods meant that each child would (must) be nursed for two years or more, which further limited fertility. Houghton suggests that women in "tribal societies" (which would surely cover at least the eight years in the wilderness for Lehi's women) "bore children at perhaps four-year intervals." And of those, probably every mother in her lifetime had lost one or more to early death.[8]

In the case of Sariah, numerous questions arise about her birth history. This is so because two sets of facts press credibility toward its limit when they are compared: (1) on the one hand, the oldest four sons were all of marriageable age at the time of the family's departure from Jerusalem, which means that the eldest, Laman, could not plausibly be less than twenty-two or twenty-three; yet, (2) Jacob and Joseph were born "in the wilderness," and the probable timing would make Joseph approximately twenty-four to twenty-eight years younger than Laman. For one woman to have had such a long birth career is sufficiently unlikely that we should examine whether Sariah was the sole mother of all Lehi's mentioned offspring.

Hypothetically some of the four brothers might have been born to an earlier, deceased wife. But there is really no question that Sariah was the mother of all four. The heading to 1 Nephi begins "An account of Lehi and his wife Sariah, and his four sons, being called, (beginning at the eldest) Laman, Lemuel, Sam, and Nephi." (We may think it odd that Nephi did not write this statement as "and *their* four sons," but in an Israelite cultural context, the reference is not strange.) The mention of "his wife" as well as the continuity in the naming of parents and sons strongly imply that Sariah was the only mother. The words of 1 Nephi 5:2, 8, pretty much put the issue to rest, as Sariah expresses fear that Lehi's visionary notions have caused the deaths of "my sons" who had gone up to Jerusalem; and when they return safely, she rejoices that the Lord has protected "my sons."

We cannot be immediately certain that Sariah was the mother of Jacob and Joseph. Nephi says that "my father had begat two sons in the wilderness" (1 Nephi 18:7) but does not mention the mother. Ten verses later, Nephi, during his brothers' rebellion on board ship, refers to "*my* parents being stricken in years" and down on their sickbeds; 1 Nephi 18:19 then mentions that young Jacob and Joseph were "grieved because of the afflictions of *their* mother." This phrasing removes almost all doubt that Sariah was the mother of the last two of Lehi's sons and also assures us that she lived until they were on the boat (she likely died before Nephi left his brothers, for 2 Nephi 5:6 makes no mention of her going with him). Any uncertainty remaining seems to me eliminated at Jacob 2:23-34 where Jacob makes clear that Lehi was opposed in principle to plural marriage, except under very exceptional circumstances, thus the possibility of his having a second wife seems nil.

So we can be confident that Sariah bore six sons. Then, as mentioned above, she also had at least two daughters, based upon Nephi's reference in 2 Nephi 5:6 to "my sisters," although there is no other mention of them. While Sperry held out the possibility of as many as four daughters, there were at least two, to account for Nephi's plural reference. Thus we can be quite certain that Sariah was the mother of at least eight children who survived to adulthood. In addition, it would be likely that she had unmentioned, unsuccessful pregnancies. While this may not be an unprecedented record of fertility and survival in the ancient world, it is highly unusual. (In the Old Testament, a notable fertility record drawing particular mention is that of Leah, wife of Jacob, who bore six sons and one daughter in less than twenty years—Genesis 30:19-20; 31:41.)

It is not the number of these births as much as their spacing that poses the problem under discussion. We are faced here with a sufficiently improbable situation that we should consider whether Sariah's record is reasonable in terms of nature and culture or whether divine intervention must be appealed to.

The dire picture of childbirth and survival in simpler societies that Houghton has painted should alert us to the fact that, unlike in modern times, anciently it was not birth *prevention* that occupied couples' minds but anxiety *for* the bearing and rearing of children. Statistically, conception, pregnancy, birth, and the nurturing of children were all fraught with uncertainty and danger, and a large surviving posterity was exceptional. Still, statistics do not tell us about individuals. In the first place, the Israelites might not have been "typical" of the peoples Houghton was talking about. We do not have enough specific demographic information on them in ancient times to know for sure how they might compare. And then I suppose that the Lord could have picked out of Israel a particular family (Lehi's) to take to the promised land who had biological and spiritual qualities substantially different than "average." So in Sariah's case Houghton's "typical" age of nineteen for the beginning of fertility might not be correct.

The text implies that Sariah lived her first quarter century of married life in circumstances of wealth (1 Nephi 3:24-25) and that she was also likely to have been born into a social situation considerably better than average. She thus could have enjoyed a more favorable dietary and health regime than in "tribal societies." Certainly she held up well physically in the wilderness, all things considered (1 Nephi 17:2), although eventually the hardships and stress caught up with her, seemingly before she was chronologically "old" (1 Nephi 18:17). Finally, the relatively advantaged circumstances under which Lehi's family lived in the land of Jerusalem likely reduced the mortality dangers to the children once they were born.

Divine intervention could have extended her period of fertility, but nothing in Nephi's record supports that idea. Nephi credits the Lord with strengthening "our women" in the difficult wilderness years through unusual metabolism, but not in regard to fertility (cf. 1 Nephi 17:1-3). Still, in Lehi's record, the translation of which was lost by Martin Harris, perhaps there was an indication that Lehi and Sariah considered something miraculous about her final births. Her name, Sariah, hints of a possible typological linkage to Abraham's wife, Sarai/Sarah, who bore Isaac at age ninety. A number of studies have recently shown that Nephi construed his family's life-saving "exodus" to a "promised land" as symbolically parallel to the original exodus of Israel from Egypt. Other studies have shown that the meaning of names of certain Book of Mormon characters seem to tie to events in their lives or to their characteristics.[9] That Lehi and Sariah named their last two sons after their ancestral patriarchs Jacob and Joseph may tell us that they had patriarchal parallels in mind and may have considered Sariah's late pregnancies somehow comparable to Sarai's exceptional bearing of Isaac.

Let us suppose for now that Sariah's first birth occurred when she was seventeen. This seems not likely but possible. Is it plausible for her to have had eight births[10] in an interval of under thirty years? The answer is yes. A tabulation will be presented later that demonstrates that possibility. But first, relevant facts about other family members need to be laid out.

6. Jacob and Joseph

Earlier discussion established with high probability that Sariah, not another wife, was the mother of Jacob and Joseph, and I assume that here. The only substantive clue about when these two sons were born comes from 1 Nephi 18:19. On board ship, when Laman and those who sided with him rebelled against Nephi's leadership, the statement is made that Jacob and Joseph, "being young, having need of much nourishment, were grieved because of the afflictions of their mother." What ages for the boys may we infer from this way of speaking?

What is said about "nourishment" might be thought to refer to being nursed by their mother, but that makes no sense when the expression is applied equally to both, as it is. But the boys were likely far from infancy, so the "nourishment" may refer primarily to fixing appropriate food (no doubt a difficult task at best on the ship). Their aunts or sisters might have taken up the slack for their mother/mother-in-law, but life probably was hard for all of them. (Particularly if there were pregnant women on board the tossing ship, which is likely, there could have been a considerable sharing of child care quite apart from the case of Sariah.) But "nourishment" refers to more than food. While on forty-three occasions in the Book of Mormon "nourish" or a variant term primarily denotes a physical process, two other uses are metaphorical. Probably two senses were intertwined in Nephi's usage—a combination of providing food and emotional nurturance. The boys may have been "delicate" as a result of wilderness malnutrition, or they may have been seasick prone. They may have been particularly dependent psychologically on their mother and distressed by her evident weakness. We do not know of any of those matters. But regardless of what the boys felt about their mother as an individual, a child's life on a smallish, probably crowded, ship with little room to move about and a host of other youngsters always present would have been stressful and demanding of a mother's direct attention. Given the many possibilities, we cannot determine the ages of Jacob and Joseph from the statement on nourishment.

From another angle, however, we note that the younger brothers were born "in the wilderness" (1 Nephi 18:7; cf. 17:1), which presumably means prior to their arrival at Bountiful. That tells us a bit, but the biggest piece of information in this particular puzzle has to be Sariah's age. Her two births make most sense coming early in the trek, when she was in her best health. I can imagine that Jacob's birth came within two years of the departure from Jerusalem and Joseph's two years thereafter. In that case they would have been respectively eight and six on boarding ship. The "nourishment" statement need not contradict those ages.

That the late-born sons married and had offspring after their arrival in the promised land is established by a later reference to Jacobites and Josephites as tribes affiliated with the Nephites (e.g., Jacob 1:13). Whom the men might have wed is not indicated, but the close relations of Nephi with Jacob and Joseph—the older brother no doubt became a foster father to the two boys after the death of Lehi (2 Nephi 5:26; Jacob 1:18) — suggest that they married daughters of Nephi, or perhaps of Sam. (They could not have married Lamanite, Lemuelite, or Ishmaelite cousins because the boys would have separated from them before reaching marriageable age, as a result of moving to the land of Nephi.)

7. Ishmael and His Wife

Ishmael was the first of the trekking party to die, according to the record. Presumably he was older than Lehi. That is supported by the fact that his eldest daughter was too old to marry any of Lehi's sons (she ended up marrying Zoram, the former servant, 1 Nephi 16:7; this was definitely a second-class marriage, though better than none).

Ishmael also had four younger daughters, none of whom was married. No hint is given that the father had mentionable wealth, only a "house" (1 Nephi 7:4). Nibley suggested that Ishmael was "connected with the desert."[11] But a desert man settled into a "house" was usually of somewhat marginal social status in the Near East. In the course of normal events, the prospects for a man of modest means and well along in life to arrange marriages for so many daughters would have been limited. So the appearance of four known young suitors at the door, even if they had not previously made any courtship moves, must have stirred interest in the family even before "the Lord did soften the heart of Ishmael, and also his household" (1 Nephi 7:5). Had the family been prosperous, likely they would not have been so willing to head off into the desert; as it was, they could see advantages.

Still, we must recognize Ishmael as a man of considerable courage and faith to agree to go off into the wilderness when his own chance for arriving at and enjoying the "land of promise" in the flesh was questionable. Surely it was blessing his posterity that concerned him the most.

Once he had made the commitment, he held to it. Only a few days from home (the distance was not great; cf. 1 Nephi 2:4, 6), his resolve was tested by the first rebellion of his two sons and two of his daughters (1 Nephi 7:6), but Ishmael and his wife supported Nephi and were willing to press ahead.

Nibley observed that Lehi and Ishmael were probably related, "since it has ever been the custom among the desert people for a man to marry the daughter of his paternal uncle."[12] That Lehi and Ishmael were somehow kin indeed seems likely, but what that relationship was is not clear. Had they been brothers, as would have been the case for the cited custom to prevail, something might well have been said about that fact. Furthermore, had the brother-brother ("parallel cousin") relationship been as obvious and patterned as Nibley supposed, we would be hard put to explain why marriages had not previously been contracted under normal instead of these urgent conditions. In any case, socioeconomic distinctions between the families probably played a part.

Age differences could also have been a hindrance to contracting marriages under preflight conditions, for it is evident that the eldest daughter was too old to marry any of Lehi's sons, and perhaps it was still customary for the eldest to be married before the younger ones could be betrothed (cf. Genesis 29:26). With Zoram on the scene, however, the matchup may have made more sense.

If, as I suspect, Ishmael's daughters were not quite good enough a catch to interest Lehi's menfolk while they were at home, in extremity the fact that the numbers of Ishmael's daughters and the eligible men in Lehi's party worked out exactly right perhaps made the alliance suddenly both feasible and desirable. We have no warrant, however, for supposing that "love" played much of a role in the arrangements; the relationships were practical, at least in the beginning.

When we consider the interrelations between Ishmael's and Lehi's families, the age distribution of the former's offspring probably was about like this:

Child	Age on Leaving Jerusalem
Daughter 1 (married Zoram)	31
Son 1	29
Son 2	26
Daughter 2 (married Laman)	24
Daughter 3 (married Lemuel)	21
Daughter 4 (married Sam)	19
Daughter 5 (married Nephi)	16

(The order and ages of Daughter 1 and Son 1 might be reversed.)

In the absence of any evidence that Ishmael had inherited social and economic advantages, we may suppose that his own marriage had been at a later age than for Lehi, say about age twenty-one, when his wife was about nineteen. Ishmael might then have been fifty-three or fifty-four when his family departed from the Jerusalem area; his wife would have been between fifty-one and fifty-three. In the absence of definite statements about how long it took the party to move down the Red Sea margin to Shazer and then to Nahom, we cannot be sure of Ishmael's age at the time of his death in Nahom (1 Nephi 16:33-36), but it could have been some five years into the journey. If he died under sixty years of age, this would explain some of the anger of his daughters about what they considered his early demise caused by following Lehi's difficult wilderness agenda. (Incidentally, did the "daughters" who "did mourn exceedingly" include the wives of Nephi, Sam, and Zoram, or only those married to Laman and Lemuel? And since there is no mention of his wife's mourning, was she already dead?)

8. The Sons of Ishmael

These two were probably older than Lehi's sons. Yet their willingness to be led by Laman and Lemuel in re-

bellion indicates that they were still on the younger side
of adulthood, for married men of, say, more than thirty
would be unlikely to follow readily much younger single
men of twenty-three and twenty-one as Laman and Lemuel
were. Both Ishmael's sons had "families" (1 Nephi 7:6)
who accompanied them. The term "families" implies a wife
and at least one child each, but there likely were more
children, considering the fathers' ages. (Had one or both
of the wives been childless, the expression "and their
wives/his wife" would likely have been used instead of
"and their families.") As noted above, it may be that at
some point the daughters of Lehi became wives of the sons
of Ishmael (see also below).

In later Book of Mormon history, the descendants of
both men were incorporated into a single tribe (Jacob 1:13)
for reasons not apparent now. Since Lamoni, local king
over "the land of Ishmael" in Lamanite country in the
second century B.C. was a descendant of Ishmael (Alma
17:21), his father, who was king over all the Lamanite
lands, presumably also counted his lineage to Ishmael.
Thus the Ishmaelite tribe came to play a prominent part
among "the Lamanites."

9. Sam

Sam was the shy and retiring one of the four brothers,
it appears. Though older than Nephi, he followed him
consistently (1 Nephi 2:17). He may not have been very
assertive; at least one would have thought that when Laman and Lemuel "did smite us [two] even with a rod" (1
Nephi 3:28-29) that he could have combined efforts with
Nephi (who was "large in stature") to prevent the beating.
Furthermore, Sam was as frightened as Laman and Lemuel
when Nephi, dressed in Laban's clothes and accompanied
by Zoram, approached them at night (1 Nephi 4:28). Perhaps his retiring if not passive nature is why his father in
his final blessing (2 Nephi 4:11), while saluting Sam's good

heart and behavior, could see that his descendants would not survive as a distinct entity but would be incorporated into Nephi's tribe.

10. Zoram

Zoram had been Laban's servant. At the time when he promised to accompany the party and be granted nominal equal status with the brothers, he must have weighed in his instantaneous calculation of the costs and benefits the fact that as a servant of Laban in Jerusalem, he would always be a third-class citizen and bound to an unadmirable master. (Of course, had he not agreed to go with them, they would have killed him, a rather decisive determinant in his decision!) A man as trusted as he was, with access to Laban's treasury, would have been of some maturity, for he would have had to prove faithful to Laban over a period of years before being given such trust by his master. That he was in his thirties would be reasonable, and such an age agrees with his marrying the daughter whom Ishmael's family may have considered by then their "old maid." Later he had his own tribal descendants (1 Nephi 18:6; Jacob 1:13), so his wife apparently had fertile years remaining after their marriage.

We learn nothing about his nature, physique, or bearing, although he was probably a thorough-going city fellow. Since Laban seems to have played some military role at Jerusalem (1 Nephi 3:31), Zoram likely was also part of the Jewish military apparatus, which may in part account for the military role his descendants later played (Alma 48:5). He aligned himself with the Nephi faction in subsequent disputes (2 Nephi 1:30; 5:6), and a generation or more later his descendants formed one of the small tribes within the broad Nephite category (Jacob 1:13). (Still, a tradition among part of his descendants centuries later [Alma 54:23] suggests that he had been "pressed and brought out of Jerusalem" against his will by Nephi. Perhaps in weak moments, he confessed privately to his children that, like the Mormon pioneers from Nauvoo, he "went willingly, because he had to.") Nothing is said about Zoram's ancestry, but it seems statistically likely, given his bureaucratic/military role in Jerusalem, that he was a Jew, while both Lehi and Ishmael counted descent from Joseph.

11. Others

As we have seen, there were minor characters in the drama who were considered by Nephi insignificant enough not to mention by name. Let us consider each in turn, presenting what we know and can infer about their ages and social positions.

"My sisters." The two (or more) daughters of Lehi and Sariah I presume, on the basis of Erastus Snow's statement, to have become wives of Ishmael's sons. They were minors at the beginning of the account, otherwise there would be no way to place them in Sariah's birth history. I suppose that one was around twelve and the other around nine. When they arrived in Bountiful they would have been twenty and seventeen.

It is logical that in the intimate circumstances of the camp, youths approaching sexual maturity would be in a socially awkward position. Likely, the adult role of wife would be arranged for the two daughters as soon as feasible, say around age sixteen for each in turn, but whom would they marry? The sons of Ishmael alone seem of an age to be possible husbands. Lehi's first daughter may then have become the second wife of Ishmael's first son at about the time they were in Nahom. The second daughter could have become the second wife to Ishmael's second son no later than the time the party reached Bountiful.

This scenario takes the Erastus Snow statement at face value. I realize that to suppose that the daughters became second wives appears to contradict Jacob 2:34; 3:5, where it is said that Lehi was commanded that there should be no plural wives. But perhaps Lehi received that commandment only in the promised land after, and partially because of, bitter experience with the second wifehood of his two daughters, which had led to their separation from Ishmael's sons. Or, these cases may have been covered under the "escape clause" of Jacob 2:30 ("For if I will . . . raise up seed unto me, I will command my people" to make polygamous unions), the daughters having no other prospect of marriage within their party.

Still another possibility is that the arduous wilderness experience had caused the (unmentioned) death of the original wives of the sons of Ishmael, whereupon Lehi's daughters were taken as replacement spouses. A final possibility is that the Snow statement was in error in the recollection of the detail about the daughters and that they never married at all due to lack of partners of a suitable age. Obviously, we cannot settle these details on the basis of so few bits of information given us by Nephi in his record. We may wonder about such matters but ought to restrict our guesses to those with some basis in the text, not simply out-of-the-blue speculations.

Wives of Ishmael's sons. Our recognition of the existence of these wives depends completely on the phrasing of 1 Nephi 7:6: "the two sons of Ishmael and their families." No clue is provided about the age or origin of the women. Given patterns of marriage in preexilic Israel, it would be likely that they were kin to their husbands through their fathers, but that was only an Israelite preference, not an absolute rule. As to their ages, we can only suppose that they were slightly younger than their respective husbands, that is, about twenty-eight and twenty-five at the one time when their existence is implied (1 Nephi 7:6).

Original children of Ishmael's sons. As noted earlier, since both sons had "families," we must suppose that children were involved. Given the probable ages of the parents, two or three each would be plausible, for a total of five Ishmaelite grandchildren as the story opens.

Children born during the trip through the wilderness. Nephi says in 1 Nephi 17:1, "our women did bear children in the wilderness." No numbers are included, nor are any exclusions mentioned. (Two of these births, Jacob and Joseph, have already been discussed.) If we presume that all the younger married women bore children during the eight years, the median number would likely be two, given the rigors of the circumstances—some may have had but one, others three. During the two or more years in Bountiful while they were building the boat, there could have been an additional three born within the group. A distribution like this would be reasonable:

Sariah (Jacob and Joseph)	2
Laman's wife	2
Lemuel's wife	2
Sam's wife	2
Nephi's wife	2
Zoram's wife	2
Wife of Son 1 of Ishmael	2
Wife of Son 2 of Ishmael	2
Total of those born in the wilderness	16
Plus those born in Bountiful	3

Were there servants? No mention is made of male or female servants, yet it is possible that there were some. At first glance, 1 Nephi 2:4 would seem to rule that out, since reference is made only to Lehi's taking "his family." Yet Near Eastern usage would not rule out including servants under that heading without specifically distinguishing them. Lehi's "great wealth" would seem to have called for at least female servants in the household. Nephi's hesitancy about even adding Zoram to their party would not apply in the case of family retainers, who would have known no other life than service to Lehi and Sariah and had no alternative place in society in the land of Jerusalem even if they dreamed of defecting. I do not consider it likely that there were such people along, but the door should not be shut on the possibility, for they might account for some genetic variety in the colony as well as providing additional hands for the construction of the ship when they reached Bountiful.

Finally, I note that Lynn M. Hilton has proposed in an unpublished paper that Laman and Lemuel took dark-skinned South Arabian women as second wives during the sojourn in Bountiful, thus accounting for the skin color attributed to the Lamanites in the promised land in America. This is an interesting idea, however, I am not persuaded by his arguments. That the party had social interaction with local inhabitants in Bountiful on the south Arabian coast does seem likely, in fact inevitable. Among other things, Nephi claims "neither did I build the ship after the manner of men" (1 Nephi 18:2), strongly implying that he had knowledge of other ships which almost certainly would have existed on that coast and had been examined by him. However, Jacob 3:5, which credits the Lamanites with a tradition of strict monogamy, goes against the Hilton suggestion.

Summary

Now that we have recapped the possible personnel, let us see how Sariah's birth history plausibly went. It does seem possible, barely, to accommodate all her children in an atypical but feasible birth sequence.

Child	Age on Leaving Jerusalem	Sariah's Age at the Birth
Laman	23*	17
Lemuel	21	(early) 20
Sam	19	22
Nephi	(late) 16	25
Daughter 1	12	29
Daughter 2	9	32

(Departure from Jerusalem)   (41)
Jacob   -   43*
Joseph   -   45*
(Arrival in Bountiful)   (49)

* By supposing Laman was twenty-two instead of twenty-three and that Jacob was eight and Joseph six at the time of the shipboard need for "nourishment" — and these are the believable extremes — Sariah's age at Joseph's birth could have been forty-four.

One Implication of the Composition of the Group

Assuming the correctness of these calculations, there would have been some seven vigorous adult males, perhaps supplemented by three of the adult females on any given workday, available for the tasks of gathering materials, constructing the ship, and outfitting and testing it. Assume further that other necessary tasks such as obtaining food and camp maintenance consumed a third of the working days of those eleven souls. If the ship took about two years to build and get ready to sail, then a maximum of around 5,000 person-days of (inexperienced) labor were available. Half that much labor might today construct a house of moderate size, but of limited quality, in perhaps a year. Since, however, Nephi's crew had no lumberyard nor hardware store to draw on, about as much time would be consumed in preparing materials as in actual construction of the vessel. Obviously the only ship they could construct within these constraints would be quite small. Perhaps some servants were available as a supplement to the labor force, or perhaps some local inhabitants might have been used (which raises the question of how they might have been paid).

Recasting the demographic information, we see that the group who boarded the vessel would have been distributed something like this (excluding any possible servants):

Age Group	Male	Female	Total
Aged adults	1	2?*	3?

Vigorous adults	8**	7	15
Children	12	13	25
Totals	21	22?	43?

* We have no idea how long Ishmael's wife lived.
** One of the children of Ishmael's first son may have been as old as eighteen by now so is arbitrarily counted here.

These observations may strike some readers as trivial, but I disagree. We have two choices in regard to context or setting as we read the scriptures (or any ancient document): (1) We can impose our own historical and cultural preconceptions on the text (there is no such thing as simply reading a text "literally," in a cultural vacuum); or (2) we we can read it in the best light available to us about the actual, realistic setting. If we do the first, we run the risk of misconstruing the words and subverting the intent of possessing written scripture at all. Truth-lovers will take the latter course every time, in my opinion.

Notes

1. Sidney B. Sperry, "Did Father Lehi Have Daughters Who Married the Sons of Ishmael?" *Improvement Era* 55 (1952): 642.

2. *JD* 23:184.

3. Hugh Nibley, *Lehi in the Desert, The World of the Jaredites, There Were Jaredites*, vol. 5, The Collected Works of Hugh Nibley, John W. Welch, ed. (Salt Lake City: Deseret Book, 1988), 34-35. The arguments presented favoring the merchant role are insufficiently persuasive precisely because they do not follow the text closely nor exhaustively enough.

4. Samuel E. Shepley, "Old World Metal Workers," paper given at Annual Symposium, Society for Early Historic Archaeology, Provo, Utah, 22 October 1983; John A. Tvedtnes, "Was Lehi a Caravaneer?" F.A.R.M.S. Preliminary Report, 1984.

5. As I observed in "Transoceanic Crossings," in Monte S. Nyman and Charles D. Tate, Jr., eds., *The Book of Mormon: First Nephi, The Doctrinal Foundation* (Provo, UT: Brigham Young University Religious Studies Center, 1988), 259, had Lehi been a skilled metalworker, Nephi would hardly have worked up ore into tools by himself when he prepared to build the ship; he could more economically have relied on Lehi's skills (1 Nephi 9:11). However, Nephi might well have observed metalworking repeatedly back on

his father's estate, where itinerant smiths probably stopped periodically to construct or repair tools, and thus have been familiar in general with the required steps and paraphernalia.

6. John W. Welch, "Longevity of Book of Mormon People and the 'Age of Man,' " *Journal of Collegium Aesculapium* (1985): 35-45, and "They Came from Jerusalem," *Ensign* 6 (1976): 28-29, both available as F.A.R.M.S. Reprints, argues for the birth of Lehi around 655 B.C. His assumption that Nephi was Lehi's sixth child (two sisters being older than he) is highly unlikely, for that would stretch out Sariah's fertility history to an unbelievable and unnecessary length. As I show below, even by making Nephi the fourth child, the problem of Sariah's births is barely manageable in natural terms. Moreover, Welch supposes that Lehi must have been of a certain adult age in order to have been affected by King Josiah's reforms and that this fact requires an age for him older than Sariah. But Lehi only had to be aware of those reforms subsequent to their imposition, not to have been an active observer of their application, in order for them to have influenced his own views about the law, the scriptures, and ritual. Contrary arguments about Lehi's age are evident to me, e.g., both Lehi and Sariah show the effects of age simultaneously (1 Nephi 18:17), which suggests that they were nearly the same age.

7. Philip Houghton, *The First New Zealanders* (Auckland: Hodder and Stoughton, 1980), 96-100.

8. The original pioneer cemetery in downtown Salt Lake City excavated by Brigham Young University's Office of Public Archaeology in 1986 revealed a substantial number of infant burials for whom there was no historical record of either birth or death. The evidence strongly indicated malnutrition as a major cause of the deaths.

9. Cf. George S. Tate, "The Typology of the Exodus Pattern in the Book of Mormon," in Neal E. Lambert, ed., *Literature of Belief* (Provo: BYU Religious Studies Center, 1981), 245-62. Still unpublished studies are by S. Kent Brown, Alan Goff, and Terrence L. Szink.

10. As already mentioned, Lehi and Sariah may have had more than two daughters, but lacking any hint of the actual number, I have assumed from this point on the minimum textually satisfactory number—two.

11. Nibley, *Lehi in the Desert*, 260-61.

12. Ibid., 40.

8

King Benjamin and the Feast of Tabernacles[1]

John A. Tvedtnes
West Valley City, Utah

A portion of the brass plates brought by Lehi to the New World contained the books of Moses (1 Nephi 5:10-13). Nephi and other Book of Mormon writers stressed that they obeyed the laws given therein: "And we did observe to keep the judgments, and the statutes, and the commandments of the Lord in all things according to the law of Moses" (2 Nephi 5:10).

But aside from sacrifice[2] and the Ten Commandments,[3] we have few explicit details regarding the Nephite observance of the Mosaic code. One would expect, for example, some mention of the festivals which played such an important role in the religious observances of ancient Israel. Though the Book of Mormon mentions no religious festivals by name, it does detail many significant Nephite assemblies.

One of the more noteworthy of the Nephite ceremonies was the coronation of the second Mosiah by his father, Benjamin.[4] Some years ago, Professor Hugh Nibley outlined the similarities between this Book of Mormon account and ancient Middle Eastern coronation rites.[5] He pointed

---

The first draft of the major portion of this article was prepared in Jerusalem in March 1973. This essay originally appeared in a slightly different form under the title "The Nephite Feast of Tabernacles" in the unpublished "Tinkling Cymbals: Essays in Honor of Hugh Nibley," John W. Welch, ed., 1978, and was later issued as F.A.R.M.S. Preliminary Report TVE-78 in 1983.

197

out that these rites took place at the annual New Year festival, when the people were placed under covenant of obedience to the monarch. My own research further explores the Israelite coronation/New Year rites, and aims to complement other scholarly studies of the ceremonial context of Benjamin's speech.

THE SABBATICAL FEASTS

In the sacred calendar, the Israelite new year began with the month of Abib (later called Nisan), in the spring (end March/beginning April).[6] This month encompassed the feasts of Passover (beginning at sundown on the fourteenth day) and Unleavened Bread (fourteenth through twenty-first days), and included "holy convocations," analogous to the Latter-day Saint April general conference (Leviticus 23:4-8). In the Holy Land, this is the early harvest following the rainy season, and hence is associated with joy and thanksgiving to God. It also commemorates the Exodus from Egypt.[7]

The other festivals in the sacred year also followed the sabbatical system.[8] Every seventh day was a Sabbath, or day of rest, commemorative of the creation and perhaps also the Exodus from Egypt.[9] From the gathering of the first fruits at Passover, the Israelites counted a "sabbath of weeks" to the fiftieth day, called Shavuᶜot ("weeks") in the Old Testament[10] and Pentecost ("count of fifty") in Acts 2:1.

The most sacred month was the seventh, Ethanim (1 Kings 8:2), later called Tishri, which fell at the end of September/beginning of October.[11] The first day of the month, now called Rosh ha-Shanah ("beginning of the year"), was marked by the blowing of trumpets.[12] The tenth day, Yom Kippur ("day of atonement"), was the most sacred of all days, devoted to fasting, repentance, prayer, and sacrifice.[13] Finally, the week of the fifteenth to the twenty-second of the seventh month was the Feast of Ingathering, or of Sukkot ("booths" or "tabernacles").[14] At this time, the Israelites were to construct rough temporary living quarters, called *sukkôt* (singular *sukkāh*), or "booths," in order "that your generations may know that I made the children of Israel to dwell in booths, when I brought them out of the land of Egypt" (Leviticus 23:43).

In addition to these annual feasts, every seventh year was a sabbatical year, during which time it was forbidden to engage in agricultural pursuits.[15] At the end of seven sabbatical years came the fiftieth year, called the jubilee,[16] a year of renewal wherein Hebrew slaves were freed and ownership of the land was returned to the families originally in possession thereof.[17] Both the sabbatical year and the jubilee were proclaimed in the seventh month, rather than the first,[18] since the seventh month begins a new agricultural cycle with the first rainfall, which usually occurs within a month after the Feast of Tabernacles.[19]

SUKKOT

The Feast of Tabernacles (Sukkot), like the Feast of Unleavened Bread/Passover, began and ended with a day of rest, including a "holy convocation" (Heb. *miqrā' qôdeš*, "holy reading," or "holy calling") and a "solemn assembly" (Heb. *ʿaṣeret*, "council").[20] During the week of the feast, the Israelites would gather together and build for each family a booth or tabernacle.[21] Special sacrifices were also ordained (Numbers 29:12-38).

According to Jewish tradition, the first Sukkot was celebrated at the foot of Mount Sinai, six months after the Exodus from Egypt.[22] The last day of the feast has come to be known as Simhat Torah ("joy of the Torah"), in commemoration of the revelation of the Pentateuch or Law (Heb. *Tôrāh*, lit., "teaching") at Sinai.[23] In a sense, Sukkot symbolizes the creation of the world. As God made a covenant with Adam, renewed with Noah after the flood,[24] so, too, he covenanted with Israel at Sinai.

Because they reappear in connection with other known Sukkot assemblies, we shall examine the elements of the first Sukkot, found in Exodus 24:

1. Moses recited *God's commandments,* which he wrote in a book (vss. 3-4).

2. "All the people answered *with one voice,* and said, All the words which the Lord hath said will we do" (vs. 3).[25]

3. An *altar* was constructed, along with "twelve *pillars,*" in token of the covenant (vs. 4).[26]

4. Sacrifices of *burnt and peace offerings* followed (vs. 5).

5. The *blood* of the sacrificial animals was sprinkled on the *altar* (vs. 6).

6. Moses *read to the people from the book of the covenant* (vs. 7).

7. The people repeated their *covenant of obedience* (vs. 7).

8. The *blood of the covenant* was sprinkled on the people, sealing the bargain (vs. 8).

9. The Israelite leaders went up on the mount, where they saw God, *ate and drank* (vss. 9-11).

10. The Lord called Moses up to give him the law and the commandments, *written on stone tables* (vss. 12-13).

11. A cloud and the *glory* of the Lord (described as fire) covered Mount Sinai for six days (vss. 15-17).

12. On the *seventh day,* the Lord called to Moses from the cloud (vs. 16).

About forty years later, as the Israelites were preparing to enter the land of Canaan,

Moses wrote this law, and delivered it unto the priests . . . and unto all the elders of Israel. And Moses commanded them, saying, At the end of every seven years, in the solemnity of the year of release, in the feast of tabernacles, When all Israel is come to appear before the Lord thy God in the place which he shall choose

[i.e., the temple in Jerusalem], thou shalt read this law
before all Israel in their hearing. Gather the people together, men, and women, and children, and thy stranger
that is within thy gates, that they may hear, and that
they may learn, and fear the Lord your God, and observe
to do all the words of this law: And that their children,
which have not known any thing, may hear, and learn
to fear the Lord your God (Deuteronomy 31:9-13).

The book of Deuteronomy was evidently used anciently
as the basis for the liturgy of the Feast of Tabernacles, as
we shall see below.

The gathering together of the people at the Feast of
Tabernacles provided the backdrop for several special ceremonies in ancient Israel, including (a) thanksgiving for
the fall harvest, (b) prayers for rain to begin the new agricultural year, (c) a rehearsal of the law of God and a
public commitment to obey his commandments, (d) coronation of a new king or a renewal of the kingship, (e)
celebration of the end of the season of war (due to rainy
weather) and the establishment of peace, and (f) dedication
of the temple. In the third year, tithes of farm produce
were collected for the Levites and the poor (Deuteronomy
14:27-29; 26:11-14; Amos 4:4), with a call for special help
to the poor during the seventh year (Deuteronomy 15:7-
11).

DEDICATION OF THE TEMPLE

Perhaps the most notable celebration of Sukkot was
when Solomon assembled the people at the dedication of
the newly completed temple (1 Kings 8:1-3; 2 Chronicles
5:2-4). The ark of the covenant was brought by the priests
and placed in the temple, along with sacred vessels borne
by the Levites (1 Kings 8:1, 3-9; 2 Chronicles 5:2, 4-10; 6:11).
Sacrifices and burnt offerings were then made by the
priests (1 Kings 8:5; 2 Chronicles 5:6), while some of the
Levites played music, praised the Lord, and spoke of his

mercy (2 Chronicles 5:12-13). When the priests left the holy place, a cloud filled the temple (1 Kings 8:10-11; 2 Chronicles 5:11, 13-14; cf. 6:1). The presence of the cloud may have been the symbol of God's promise of rain.[27]

Solomon, standing atop a brazen scaffold (2 Chronicles 6:13), then blessed the congregation, who stood to receive him (1 Kings 8:14-21; 2 Chronicles 6:3-11). He spoke of the Exodus from Egypt (1 Kings 8:16, 21; 2 Chronicles 6:5) and emphasized that both he and his father David had been chosen by the Lord (1 Kings 8:15-20; 2 Chronicles 6:4-10). The king then knelt at the altar, spread forth his hands, and offered the dedicatory prayer (1 Kings 8:22-54; 2 Chronicles 6:12-42). The elements of his prayer are found in other Sukkot observances:

> Addressing God, he mentioned the *covenant* and God's *mercy* toward the obedient (1 Kings 8:23; 2 Chronicles 6:14).
>
> He spoke of God's promise of kingship to David's posterity (1 Kings 8:24-26; 2 Chronicles 6:15-17). God had told David that his children should "take heed to their way, that they walk before me as thou hast walked before me" (1 Kings 8:25; cf. 2 Chronicles 6:16).
>
> He asked God to answer the prayers of the faithful addressed toward the temple (1 Kings 8:28-30, 33-39; 2 Chronicles 6:19-21, 24-30, 37-40) and mentioned that *oaths* were to be offered at the temple altar (1 Kings 8:31-32; 2 Chronicles 6:22-23).
>
> He asked the Lord to help the people in their *wars* (1 Kings 8:33, 37, 44-50; 2 Chronicles 6:24, 28, 34-35) and, should they be removed from their land by the enemy, to bring them back to their land (1 Kings 8:34; 2 Chronicles 6:25).
>
> He asked the Lord to answer prayers for *rain* (1 Kings 8:35-36; 2 Chronicles 6:26-27) and to save the people from *famine, pestilence,* and insect infestations (1 Kings 8:37-39; 2 Chronicles 6:28-30).
>
> He noted that the people were to *fear God* (1 Kings

8:40; 2 Chronicles 6:31), that *strangers* were to be blessed (1 Kings 8:41-43; 2 Chronicles 6:32-33), and that repentant sinners would be forgiven (1 Kings 8:33-36, 39, 46-48, 50; 2 Chronicles 6:24-27, 30, 36-39).

The *Exodus* from Egypt was again mentioned briefly (1 Kings 8:53).

Several Sukkot elements were combined in references to priestly clothing, salvation, and rejoicing: "Let thy priests, O Lord God, be *clothed* with *salvation*, and let thy saints *rejoice* in goodness" (2 Chronicles 6:41).

He asked the Lord to remember the king, "thine anointed" (2 Chronicles 6:42).

Following the prayer, Solomon again blessed the congregation (1 Kings 8:55), expressing the hope that the Lord would deal with Israel as with their fathers (1 Kings 8:56-57) and that the people would be obedient to his commandments (1 Kings 8:58, 61). This was followed by more burnt offerings and peace offerings (1 Kings 8:62-64; 2 Chronicles 7:4-5, 7), to musical accompaniment by the Levites, who praised the Lord and spoke of his mercy, while priests sounded trumpets (2 Chronicles 7:6). Fire fell from heaven and consumed the sacrifice and the glory of the Lord filled the house (2 Chronicles 7:1-2). Upon seeing this, the people bowed down with their faces to the ground and praised the Lord, saying, "He is good; for his *mercy* endureth for ever" (2 Chronicles 7:3).

There is no mention that a covenant was made, and the Law was not written as a testimony, probably because the two tables of the Law were already present in the ark (1 Kings 8:9; 2 Chronicles 5:10). Solomon had been seven years in building his temple (1 Kings 6:37-38), which may mean that it was begun and dedicated in sabbatical years. The temple dedication took place during seven or fourteen days,[28] with a solemn assembly on the eighth (1 Kings 8:65-66; 2 Chronicles 7:8-9).[29] On the eighth day of the festival (1 Kings 8:66), the twenty-third day of the month (2 Chronicles 7:10), the people were sent away to their tents, after blessing the king. Shortly thereafter, the Lord appeared to Solomon in a dream and charged him to keep the commandments, lest there come curses and no rain (1 Kings 9:2-9; 2 Chronicles 7:12-22).

David's Role

It was David, Solomon's father, who had laid the plans for the Jerusalem temple (2 Samuel 7:1-17; 1 Chronicles 17:1-15). He gathered together the building materials (1 Chronicles 22). He also organized the priests and Levites for temple service (1 Chronicles 6:31; 9:22; 16:1-7) and wrote some of its liturgy in the form of psalms.

Even before the temple site had been revealed to him,[30] David had brought the ark of the covenant to Jerusalem, in what may have been the renewal of the kingdom at Sukkot. His first attempt was unsuccessful, and the ark was left in the care of villagers not far from the Holy City (2 Samuel 6:1-11). On the second attempt, David and the Israelites brought the ark with great joy to Jerusalem, accompanied by singing, dancing, shouting, and the sound of trumpets.[31] There were also sacrifices along the way (2 Samuel 6:13; 1 Chronicles 15:26), and burnt and peace offerings in Jerusalem (2 Samuel 6:17-18; 1 Chronicles 16:2). The king then blessed the people and distributed food for the feast (2 Samuel 6:18-19; 1 Chronicles 16:2-3). David's divine kingship is mentioned explicitly, thus giving reason to believe this may have been a renewal ceremony (2 Samuel 6:21). In his speech to the assembly, David cited a number of psalms dealing with God's covenant.[32] "And all the people said, Amen, and praised the Lord" (1 Chronicles 16:36). After the people departed for home (1 Chronicles 16:43), the Lord commanded David to build him a house (1 Chronicles 17). The activities described in connection with this celebration suggest that the events occurred at Sukkot.

A ROYAL FESTIVAL

Of special significance is the fact that it was the king, Solomon, who dedicated the temple, and not the high priest or one of the prophets. Indeed, the site had been purchased by his father, David, and it was David who had organized the priests and Levites and who laid plans for building the temple. It is therefore not surprising that, in ancient Israel, it was the king who presided at the Feast of Tabernacles.[33]

The Sukkot assembly of the seventh year was a renewal of the Law given at Sinai. It was, in another sense, the reenactment of Yahweh's enthronement as king of the universe and controller of the elements, with the people entering into a covenant to obey him.[34] In later years, it was the king who stood in the place of God to accept the homage of the people.[35] Various points of the Law were read publicly in the Temple court. The rite as practiced by the exiled Jews in Babylon in the tenth century A.D. was described by Rabbi Nathan the Babylonian, in a letter which was appended to the *Seder Olam*.[36]

In the days of Rabbi Nathan, the Jewish community of Babylon was led by a descendant of David, the exilarch. During the Feast of Tabernacles, he performed the functions formerly assigned to the kings of Israel, then Judah. On one occasion described by Rabbi Nathan, a new exilarch had just been approved by the Jewish community. A ceremonial procession set out on the Sabbath from the house of one of the prominent Babylonian Jews, a court banker, and made its way to the synagogue in Baghdad. Every detail of the ceremony which followed had been laid out in advance. A choir was concealed beneath a wooden tower, with a multicolored cover. The exilarch hid beneath the tower, from which he made his entrance during the recitation of a prayer.

When the exilarch made his appearance, all the people

rose to their feet. The exilarch sat in a seat placed in the middle atop the tower. Then the heads of the Sura Yeshiva and the Pumbedita Yeshiva followed behind and took their seats on his right and left hands, respectively, after bowing to the ruler, who acknowledged them by the same token. The people then took their seats and the reading from the Torah or Law of Moses began. The cantor then chanted the blessings for the exilarch in a low voice, so that they could be heard only by those seated around the tower and the youths concealed beneath it. The youths responded by shouting "Amen."

In the Mishnah, we have a partial description of the Sukkot celebration of Second Temple times:

> After what manner was the paragraph of the king? After the close of the first Festival-day of the Feast [of Tabernacles], in the eighth year, after the going forth of the Seventh Year,[37] they used to prepare for him in the Temple Court a wooden platform on which he sat, for it is written, *At the end of every seven years in the set time. . . .* [38] The minister of the synagogue used to take a scroll of the Law and give it to the chief of the synagogue, and the chief of the synagogue gave it to the Prefect, and the Prefect gave it to the High Priest, and the High Priest gave it to the king, and the king received it standing and read it sitting. King Agrippa received it standing and read it standing, and for this the Sages praised him. And when he reached *Thou mayest not put a foreigner over thee which is not thy brother,*[39] his eyes flowed with tears; but they called to him, 'Our brother art thou! our brother art thou! our brother art thou!' He read from the beginning of Deuteronomy to *Hear, [O Israel]*; and the paragraphs *Hear, [O Israel]* . . . [40] and *And it shall come to pass if ye shall hearken* . . . [41] and *Thou shalt surely tithe*[42] . . . and *When thou hast made an end of tithing*[43] and the paragraph of the king,[44] and the Blessings and the Cursings,[45] until the end. With the same blessings with which the High Priest blesses them, the king blesses

them, save that he pronounces the blessing for the Feasts instead of the blessing for the forgiveness of sin.[46]

Royal Sukkot Liturgy

The choice of the Deuteronomic passages for the liturgy of the festival was most deliberate. The book of Deuteronomy is a unitary reiteration of the Law. It has the fluency and eloquence of a ceremonial speech and, as such, is appropriate for recitation by the king during the festival. The king would first read Deuteronomy 1:1-6:10. Some of the principal elements of this passage are:

1. A recital of *God's dealings with Israel* during the Exodus (Deuteronomy 1:6-3:29; 5:6).

2. *Reading from the Law* (Deuteronomy 4:1-9, 11-25; 5:6-21).

3. An exhortation to *teach the Law to subsequent generations* (Deuteronomy 4:9-10).

4. Recalling the *covenant and assembly* at Sinai (Deuteronomy 4:10-13, 36; 5:1-5, 22-31), including (a) *a recitation of the law* (Deuteronomy 4:14-19), (b) a reminder of the Exodus from Egypt (Deuteronomy 4:20, 34, 37-38), (c) a threat that if the people break the covenant, they will be *driven from the promised land* (Deuteronomy 4:25-27), while if they keep the commandments *their days will be prolonged therein* (Deuteronomy 4:40; 5:31-33), and (d) mention of the *law being written on tablets of stone* (Deuteronomy 5:22). Many of these features are repeated in Moses' exhortation.

5. Heaven and earth called to witness the pronouncing of *curses for disobedience* (Deuteronomy 4:26-39).

6. A promise of *prosperity and long life* for obedience to the Law (Deuteronomy 4:40; 5:32-6:3).

7. The people being sent back to their *tents* (Deuteronomy 5:30).

8. The conclusion, or *Shemaᶜ* (Deuteronomy 6:4-10), which teaches that (a) *God must be loved and honored* (Deuteronomy 6:5), (b) *children should be taught* the Law (6:7),

(c) the law should be *written down*, and (d) that God will reward obedience by *prosperity* (Deuteronomy 6:10-11).[47]

In the subsequent verses, which were not included in the ritual reading according to the Mishnah, further mention is made of oaths (Deuteronomy 6:13), obedience (Deuteronomy 6:17), God's promise of assistance against Israel's enemies (Deuteronomy 6:17-18), the Exodus from Egypt (Deuteronomy 6:20-22), and the promise of life through obedience (Deuteronomy 6:24-25). These elements are found in other examples of Sukkot assemblies.

Next, the king would read from the eleventh chapter of Deuteronomy, which begins with a transitional exhortation to *love and obey God* (Deuteronomy 11:1) and notes that the speech is directed to the adults, *not the children* (Deuteronomy 11:2).[48] The text then proceeds: one must *love and serve God* (Deuteronomy 11:13), after which he will send *rain and prosperity* (Deuteronomy 11:14-15, 17). The Law must be *taught to the children* who are too young to understand (Deuteronomy 11:19), and, for this purpose, *it must be written down* (Deuteronomy 11:20). God will give *long life* to the covenanters (Deuteronomy 11:21), and by obedience they will *defeat their enemies* (Deuteronomy 11:22-25). Finally, the king placed before them *a blessing and a curse*, to be effective upon renewal of the covenant (Deuteronomy 11:26-32). Deuteronomy 27:15-26, also cited by the king, gives instructions for the covenant. Deuteronomy 17:14-20, the "Paragraph of the King," outlined the monarch's responsibilities:

> When thou art come unto the land which the Lord thy God giveth thee, and shalt possess it, and shalt dwell therein, and shalt say, I will set a king over me, like as all the nations that are about me; Thou shalt in any wise set him king over thee, *whom the Lord thy God shall choose*: one from among *thy brethren* shalt thou set king over thee: thou mayest not set a stranger over thee, which is not thy brother.[49] But he shall not *multiply horses to him-*

self, nor cause the people to *return to Egypt*, to the end
that he should multiply horses: forasmuch as the Lord
hath said unto you, Ye shall henceforth return no more
that way. Neither shall he *multiply wives to himself*, that
his heart turn not away: neither shall he greatly *multiply*
to himself silver and gold. And it shall be, when he sitteth
upon the throne of his kingdom, that he shall *write him*
a copy of this law in a book out of that which is before the
priests the Levites: And it shall be with him, and he *shall*
read therein all the days of his life: that he may learn to
fear the Lord his God, to *keep all the words of this law and*
these statutes, to do them: That his heart *be not lifted up*
above his brethren, and that he turn not aside from *the*
commandment, to *the right hand*, or to *the left*: to the end
that he may *prolong his days* in his kingdom, he, and his
children, in the midst of Israel (Deuteronomy 17:14-20).

The remaining passages cited by the king (Deuteronomy 14:22-29; 26:12-19) deal with tithing, collected in the
third and seventh years at the time of the harvest in order
to provide for the Levites and the poor. In his concluding
remarks, the king would bless the people, just as Moses
had blessed each of the tribes prior to the ordination of
Joshua, as recorded in Deuteronomy 33.

BIBLICAL CORONATION CEREMONIES

In ancient Israel, Sukkot was an occasion for anointing
a new king or for renewing the covenant between God,
the king, and the people. And while it may be that not all
biblical coronations took place at this festival, it is instructive to examine the various accounts for Sukkot imagery.

Saul

In 1 Samuel 10, we read of Saul's ascension to the
throne of Israel. He was designated by the prophet Samuel,
upon the insistent petition of the Israelite community for
a king. Samuel and the Lord opposed this move, because
it detracted from God as the true King of Israel (1 Samuel

8:7; 10:19; 12:12). Saul was first met privately by Samuel, who anointed him (1 Samuel 10:1) and then gave him certain instructions, which included a forthcoming meeting at Gilgal after Saul's waiting period of seven days, at the end of which Samuel would sacrifice burnt and peace offerings (1 Samuel 10:2-9). Saul followed most of the prophet's instructions, but impatiently offered sacrifice before Samuel arrived (1 Samuel 10:10-16). Finally, Samuel assembled the tribes at Mizpeh before the Lord (1 Samuel 10:17), where he recited God's dealings with Israel (1 Samuel 10:18-19) and designated Saul as king, amidst cries of "God save the king" (1 Samuel 10:20-24, KJV wording; Hebrew means "may the king live"). The "manner of the kingdom" (1 Samuel 10:25), likely a covenant of some sort (cf. 1 Samuel 8:9), was then written in a book, and the people were sent home (1 Samuel 10:25-26).

A short time later, Samuel convened an assembly to "renew the kingdom" before the Lord, at Gilgal (1 Samuel 11:14-15), a cultic center where Joshua had erected twelve large stones after crossing the Jordan (Joshua 4:9, 17-22). The event took place at the wheat harvest, prior to the onset of the rains (1 Samuel 12:16-19); this would ordinarily place the event in early summer, between April and June, and hence may have taken place at Shavuᶜot. Samuel, in asking God for rain as a sign that the people had sinned in asking for a king, reflects the close tie between the coronation of the king and the prayers for rain which usually took place at Sukkot.[50]

Peace offerings were sacrificed with great rejoicing (1 Samuel 11:15), after which Samuel arose to speak in a manner quite reminiscent of King Benjamin's speech when proclaiming his successor. Samuel was now old, and the king was to replace him (1 Samuel 12:1-2). He wanted to remind the people (as did Benjamin, apparently in keeping with the Paragraph of the King) that he had not taken from them anything which was not his due, and called them to witness (again, like Benjamin) on this point (1 Samuel 12:3-5). He then recited God's dealings with Israel (1 Samuel 12:6-12) and stressed that, while Saul had been chosen by both God and the people (1 Samuel 12:13), nevertheless, it was God who was the true king (1 Samuel 12:12). Finally, he exhorted obedience to the Lord and to the king (cf. Mosiah 2:31), pronouncing the blessings and curses found in the Law (1 Samuel 12:14-15, 20-25).

David

The coronation ceremony took on new meaning with the rise of the Davidic line to replace Saul. David's first anointing as king was performed by Samuel in a small assembly at Bethlehem, accompanied by sacrifices (1 Samuel 16:1-13). At the death of Saul, the elders of Judah anointed David king of their tribe at Hebron (2 Samuel 2:4). After reigning seven years at Hebron,[51] David was anointed king of all Israel by an assembly representing all the tribes (2 Samuel 5:1-5; 1 Chronicles 11:1-3). We cannot know for certain that this took place at Sukkot, but it is interesting that it was seven years after his earlier anointing at Hebron, which suggests that these ceremonies may have occurred during sabbatical years. David soon moved his capital to Jerusalem, which he took from the Jebusites, and began a series of moves which would make it the cultic center of all Israel, complete with temple and priesthood. On the threshing floor of a certain Ornan or Araunah (fitting for a harvest festival), he built an altar and offered burnt and peace offerings (2 Samuel 24:16-25; 1 Chronicles 21:15-28). If this seventh year of David's reign was the sabbatical year, the threshing-floor incident may have been a ritual marking the first harvest of the following season.

Solomon

In his old age, David seems to have lost control of affairs. His son Adonijah enlisted the help of David's cou-

sin Joab and the priest Abiathar to help Adonijah become
king (1 Kings 1:5-7). The party repaired to a nearby spring,
En-Rogel, where they offered sacrifices and feasted amid
cries of "God save king Adonijah" (1 Kings 1:9, 19, 25).
When word of the coronation ceremony reached the
prophet Nathan, the priest Zadok, and the chief captain
Benaiah, they went to David in company with the king's
wife, Bathsheba, to express their concerns and to remind
David that he had promised that Solomon would succeed
him (1 Kings 1:10-32).

David instructed the company to have Solomon ride
on the king's mule to the spring Gihon, where Nathan and
Zadok were to anoint him amid sounding trumpets and
cries of "God save king Solomon" (1 Kings 1:32-37). Oil
was brought from the nearby tabernacle, and the ceremony
proceeded. After following these instructions, the multitude who had followed Solomon celebrated with music
from pipes (1 Kings 1:38-46). With this turn of events,
Adonijah had to renounce his claims to the throne (1 Kings
1:50-52).

In all this, we note that it was King David who was
expected to name his successor (1 Kings 1:20, 30, 35). Nevertheless, after Solomon's coronation, David expressed joy
that *the Lord* had made Solomon king (1 Kings 1:48).

Like Saul, Solomon was renewed in the kingdom. The
account is found in 1 Chronicles 28-29. We read that David
assembled the officers and stood to speak to them (1 Chronicles 28:1-2). He reminded them that God had chosen him
to be king of Israel (1 Chronicles 28:4), and noted that
Solomon, too, had been chosen by God (1 Chronicles 28:5-
6; 29:1). He then gave a charge that Solomon and all Israel
should keep the Lord's commandments, whereupon they
would be blessed to possess the land (1 Chronicles 28:7-
8; 29:23-24). But disobedience would bring curses (1 Chronicles 28:9). The old king then instructed Solomon to build
the temple he had planned (1 Chronicles 28:6, 10-21). The

temple was to be a palace for God, who is the true king of Israel (1 Chronicles 29:10-11) and the source of all possessions (1 Chronicles 29:12).

Following David's speech, the congregation "worshipped the Lord, and the king" (1 Chronicles 29:20). The following day, burnt offerings were made (1 Chronicles 29:21), and a meal was consumed (1 Chronicles 29:22). Solomon was then anointed (1 Chronicles 29:22). As in other accounts of Sukkot celebrations, we read that Solomon and all those who obeyed him prospered (1 Chronicles 29:23-24).

This account is evidently an expanded version of the one given in 1 Kings 2, where we read that David, about to go the way of the earth, gave a charge to Solomon (1 Kings 2:2). He promised his son that if he obeyed God's commandments, he would prosper (1 Kings 2:3-4).

The Divided Kingdom

After Solomon's death, his son Rehoboam went to Shechem for all Israel to make him king (1 Kings 12:1; 2 Chronicles 10:1). He was rejected, however, by the northern tribes, whose representatives returned to their tents (1 Kings 12:16; 2 Chronicles 10:16). As a consequence, Rehoboam became king of Judah, while Jeroboam, of the tribe of Ephraim, became king of Israel.[52] In order to differentiate between the two royal houses, Jeroboam substituted the eighth month for the celebration of Sukkot (1 Kings 12:32-33).

About a century after the split in the kingdom, Omri became king of Israel. He made political marriages for his children. Ahab, his son and successor, married Jezebel, daughter of the Phoenician (Canaanite) king Ethbaal. Athaliah, Omri's daughter, married Jehoram (Joram), king of Judah (2 Kings 8:26-27). When another Jehoram (Joram), Ahab's son, became king, he waged war against the Syrians and was wounded at Ramoth-gilead. Returning to Jezreel to recover, he was visited by his cousin, Ahaziah, son of Jehoram, king of Judah (2 Kings 8:28-29).

It was at this time that the prophet Elisha sent one of the other prophets to Ramoth-gilead with oil to anoint Jehu, captain of the host, as new king of Israel, and to give him a commission to destroy the house of Ahab (2 Kings 9:1-10). After the anointing, Jehu's men put their garments "under him on the top of the *stairs,* and blew with *trumpets,* saying, Jehu is king" (2 Kings 9:11-13). Jehu proceeded to Jezreel, where he slew Jehoram, Ahaziah, and Jezebel (2 Kings 9:14-37). Shortly thereafter, he slew the rest of Ahab's sons (2 Kings 10:1-17). He then called for sacrifice and a *"solemn assembly* for Baal,"* during which he provided Baal's priests with *new clothing,* then slew them (2 Kings 10:18-25).

Meanwhile, in Judah, Athaliah took advantage of her son's death by slaying "all of the seed royal" and usurping the throne. It may be that both Jehu and Athaliah took advantage of the forthcoming renewal rite of Sukkot in the sabbatical year to usurp their respective thrones. This is evidenced by the various acts of Jehu which resemble later Sukkot practices. Further evidence may be adduced from the fact that Athaliah herself was overthrown and replaced by Joash, the rightful king of Judah, seven years later, perhaps indicating that we are dealing with sabbatical years.

Jehosheba, daughter of Jehoram and sister of the slain king Ahaziah, had hidden Joash (Jehoash), the king's infant son, in the temple for six years, thus preserving his life (2 Kings 11:2-3). His coronation as king of Judah in the seventh year is one of the more striking examples of a royal festival. The wicked queen Athaliah had slain all the males of the royal family except the newborn Joash, who was preserved by his brother-in-law, the high priest Jehoiada, and hidden away for seven years (2 Kings 11:11; 2 Chronicles 23:1). Joash's coronation corresponded with the seventh year of the reign of Jehu, king of Israel (2 Kings 12:1), when Joash was seven years old (2 Kings 11:21). If, as we have suggested, Jehu overthrew the house of Ahab in a sabbatical year, then Joash's coronation also took place in a sabbatical year.

The high priest Jehoiada assembled the rulers of Judah at the temple, where they made a covenant (2 Kings 11:4; 2 Chronicles 23:1-3). The king was crowned and anointed, and the "testimony" of the Law placed in his hands, while the people clapped their hands (2 Kings 11:12; 2 Chronicles 23:11). Joash stood by a "pillar" (covenant altar) as trumpets sounded and music played, amidst rejoicing (2 Kings 11:14; 2 Chronicles 23:13). A covenant was concluded between the Lord and the king and the people.[53]

In a similar ceremony, King Josiah later gathered the leaders of Judah to the temple (2 Kings 23:1-2; 2 Chronicles 34:29), where they read from the book of the covenant (2 Kings 23:2; 2 Chronicles 34:30). The king stood by a "pillar" as he covenanted to obey the law, and the people likewise made a covenant (2 Kings 23:3; 2 Chronicles 34:31-32).

The Hasmoneans

When next the Jews had rulers with authority equal to kings, they were under a dynasty quite foreign to David — the Hasmoneans or Maccabees, a priestly clan. The earlier Hasmoneans did not claim royal prerogatives.[54] However, as early as 153 B.C., the Hasmonean high priest, Jonathan, presided at the Feast of Tabernacles, clad in a purple robe and wearing a gold crown (1 Maccabees 10:20-21). The description of an assembly conducted by the Hasmonean Simon (who refortified the Temple) is revealing. We read, in part:

> And finishing the service at the altar, that he might adorn the *offering* of the most high Almighty, he stretched out his hand to the cup, and poured of the *blood of the grape*, he poured out at the foot of the altar

a sweet-smelling savour unto the most high *King of all*.[55]
Then shouted the sons of Aaron, and sounded the *silver
trumpets*, and made a great noise to be heard, for a
remembrance before the most High. Then all the people
together hasted, and *fell down to the earth* upon their faces
to worship their Lord God Almighty, the most High.
The singers also *sang praises* with their voices, with great
variety of sounds was there made sweet melody. And
the people besought the Lord, the most High, by prayer
before him that is merciful, till the solemnity of the Lord
was ended, and they had finished his service. Then he
[Simon] went down, and lifted up his hands over the
whole congregation of the children of Israel, to give the
blessing of the Lord with his lips, and to rejoice in his
name. And they bowed themselves down to worship
the second time, that they might receive a *blessing* from
the most High [Wisdom of Ben Sira (Ecclesiasticus) 50:14-
21; cf. 3 Nephi 19:16-17; 20:1-7].

PRIESTLY ORDINATIONS

Two of the ordination ceremonies described in the Bible
resemble the coronation ceremonies and may have taken
place during the Feast of Tabernacles.

Ordination of Aaron

The ordination of Aaron and his sons to the priesthood
is described in Leviticus 8-9. The ordination is, in a very
real sense, like a coronation, complete with anointing, investiture, sacrifices, exhortations, and, in the case of Aaron
himself, crowning. Moses gathered the congregation to
the door of the tabernacle (Leviticus 8:3-4), where he
washed Aaron and his sons (8:5-6). Aaron was then
dressed like a priestly king, including a miter or crown
(Leviticus 8:7-9). The tabernacle, its altar and vessels, were
then anointed (Leviticus 8:10-11), as was Aaron (Leviticus
8:12).

Aaron's sons were then dressed, with bonnets replacing the miters (Leviticus 8:13). This was followed by the sacrifice of several animals, whose blood was put on the altar (Leviticus 8:14-21). A special "ram of consecration" was then sacrificed and its blood sprinkled on Aaron and his sons (Leviticus 8:22-29). Moses then sprinkled oil on them (Leviticus 8:30-31). The newly consecrated priests were to remain in the tabernacle for seven days (Leviticus 8:33-36), which is the period of time allotted to the Feast of Tabernacles and to the Feast of Unleavened Bread, associated with Passover.

On the eighth day, Moses assembled the new priests and the elders of Israel (Leviticus 9:1), and several more sacrifices were offered and the blood placed on the altar (Leviticus 9:2-21). Moses and Aaron then blessed the people (Leviticus 9:22-23), after which fire came down on the altar and consumed the sacrifices (Leviticus 9:24). This was followed by instructions similar to those repeated at Sukkot. Aaron was to teach the Israelites the statutes of the Lord (Leviticus 10:11), and various commandments were given by the Lord to Moses and Aaron (Leviticus 11-15).[56]

Among the items discussed in subsequent chapters that are also found in the Sukkot observance are: (1) Atonement is available through the shedding of blood (Leviticus 17:11). (2) Israel should not do as Egyptians did (Leviticus 18:1-3), for the Lord had brought them out from Egypt (Leviticus 26:13). (3) God ordained the observance of various festivals (Leviticus 23), the sabbatical year and the jubilee (Leviticus 25). (4) The Lord promised that obedience would bring rain and the defeat of Israel's enemies (Leviticus 26:2-12). On the other hand, if they disobeyed, their enemies would reign over them, and the land would not yield (Leviticus 26:14-20).

Ordination of Joshua

In Deuteronomy 33, we read that Moses blessed the tribes of Israel, then ordained Joshua to be his successor.

The details of Joshua's ordination are given in Numbers 22. It may be that Moses' final speech and the ordination of Joshua as his successor occurred simultaneously at the Feast of Tabernacles. Indeed, this "priestly coronation"[57] has some resemblance to subsequent coronation ceremonies in Israel. It began with God designating, through the prophet, Joshua to succeed Moses (Numbers 27:15-18). Joshua was then brought before the high priest and the congregation for approval (Numbers 27:19, 21-22). Moses gave him a charge and ordained him (Numbers 27:18-20, 23). Other details are lacking, but it is noteworthy that the ordination of the successor appears in the midst of texts commanding the observance of sacrifices, Passover, and Pentecost (Numbers 28), and the sacrifices of the seventh month (Numbers 28-29), and, finally, of vows and oaths made before God during the sacred month (Numbers 30).

Subsequent to the invasion of Canaan, and following instructions from Moses (Deuteronomy 27), Joshua gathered the tribes to Shechem (where God had covenanted with Abraham, Genesis 12:6-7) to renew the covenant of the Law. A stone altar was constructed on Mt. Ebal, and the Law written upon it (Joshua 8:30-32; Deuteronomy 27:2-8). On this, burnt and peace offerings were made (Joshua 8:31; Deuteronomy 27:6-7). The people were divided into two companies, one on Mount Gerizim, one on the adjacent Mount Ebal (Joshua 8:33; Deuteronomy 27:11-13), perhaps symbolic of the separation of righteous and wicked onto the right and left hands of God, as alluded to in Mosiah 5:9-12. That this was intended is evidenced by the fact that the mount of blessing (Gerizim) is on the south and the mount of cursing (Ebal) on the north, and that the Hebrew words yāmîn ("right hand") and śəmô'l ("left hand") also mean "south" and "north," respectively. The blessings and curses of the Law were then read, while the people placed themselves under covenant of obedience by saying, "Amen" (Joshua 8:34-35; Deuteronomy 27:14-26). The assembly included all Israel plus strangers (Joshua 8:35). It took place after Israel's first major battles, at Jericho and Ai, which may be evidence that it took place in the fall, when warfare typically ceased because of the rains.

In the forty-fifth year following the Exodus (Joshua 13:1; 14:7, 10), Joshua again assembled the tribes at Shiloh, where the Tabernacle was erected (Joshua 18:1; 19:51). The land was divided by lot at this time. He praised those of the trans-Jordanian tribes who kept the commandments, promising them divine rewards for continuance, promising them prosperity and victory over their enemies, then sent them "unto their tents" (Joshua 22:1-8). Soon thereafter these tribes constructed a special covenant altar (Joshua 22:10, 16, 19, 22-24, 26-29).

As Joshua's death neared (he was "going the way of all the earth" [Joshua 23:14], as was also the case with Benjamin in Mosiah 1:9), he assembled the elders (Joshua 24:1-2) to make arrangements for the continuation of the covenant (Joshua 23:1). He exhorted them to love and obey God (Joshua 23:6-8, 11), who would then assist them against their enemies (Joshua 23:3-5, 9-10). He also spoke of the curses which followed disobedience to the Law (Joshua 23:12-13, 15-16). Following these preliminary arrangements, the tribes of Israel were assembled together before God at Shechem (Joshua 24:1), where Joshua recounted to them the history of God's dealings with their forefathers (Joshua 24:2-13). He admonished them to fear God and serve Him (Joshua 24:14-15), and the people promised obedience (Joshua 24:16-18, 21). Joshua again recalled the curses which would come upon the ungodly (Joshua 24:19-20). He added, "Ye are witnesses" (cf. Mosiah 2:14), to which the people assented (Joshua 24:22). A covenant was made and written on a great stone at the sanctuary (Joshua 24:24-27), after which the people were dismissed (Joshua 24:28).

THE SUKKOT ASSEMBLY

From the descriptions we have reviewed, we may reconstruct the celebration of the Feast of Tabernacles as observed in the sabbatical and jubilee years, as follows:

1. The people were (a) assembled, most often at the cult site ("before God"), where (b) they were sometimes divided into two companies. (c) Strangers were also invited to attend. (d) At the conclusion of the festival, the assembly was formally dismissed and sent home.

2. The leader (king, where applicable) delivered an address in which (a) he read from the Law of Moses and cited the blessings and curses contained therein, (b) exhorted the people to love and fear God and serve him, (c) recounted God's dealings with the fathers (especially the Exodus from Egypt), (d) designated God as creator and the source of all we have, (e) called upon the people to assist the needy,[58] (f) read (where appropriate) the "Paragraph of the King," (g) blessed the people, and (h) added such other items as necessary (notably, comments on the plan of salvation).

3. God covenanted with his people that, if they would obey his commandments, he would (a) give them prosperity in the land and longevity, (b) defeat their enemies (through the king, who was commander-in-chief),[59] and (c) send rain for the crops.[60]

4. The people (a) covenanted with God to be his servants and to obey his Law. (b) To this they were called to witness. (c) The covenant (or, sometimes, the Law or the ruler's speech) was written down. (d) A "pillar" was erected as a symbol of the covenant.[61]

5. For purposes of sacrifice (a) an altar was constructed and (b) burnt and peace offerings were made upon it.

6. The joy of the people was expressed by praising God, music, and sometimes dance.[62]

7. Trumpets were blown, as was usual for the seventh month.[63]

8. The coronation ceremony stressed (a) that God

was the real King of Israel, (b) that it was God who chose the earthly king—his viceroy—through a prophet,[64] with (c) the approval of the people (who use the formula "God save the king" in KJV) and the previous king. The king was then (d) anointed and (e) given a charge.

9. There were sometimes other elements, such as a communal meal. In addition, there were the features already discussed above (e.g., the presence of tents or booths, the building of a wooden platform, and the presence of strangers or foreigners).

SUKKOT IN ZARAHEMLA

The biblical Sukkot celebration is closely paralleled by the account of King Benjamin's assembly recorded in Mosiah 1:1-6:6. Benjamin began by calling his son Mosiah to discuss with him an assembly that he wished to convene "on the morrow,"[65] and to give him a charge (Mosiah 1:2-17; 6:3).[66] The purpose of the assembly is given in these words: "I shall proclaim unto this my people . . . that thou art a king and a ruler over this people" (Mosiah 1:10-11). But it is evident, from the actual text of Benjamin's discourse, that religious instruction far outweighed the coronation ceremony itself.[67] In fact, only three verses of his speech (Mosiah 2:29-31) are devoted to the succession of the new king, and only a portion of a single verse (Mosiah 6:3) is given to Mosiah's consecration. The account begins:

> And it came to pass that after Mosiah had done as his father had commanded him, and had made a proclamation throughout all the land, that the people gathered themselves together throughout all the land, that they might go up to the temple to hear the words which king Benjamin should speak unto them. And there were a great number, even so many that they did not number them; for they had multiplied exceedingly and waxed great in the land. And they also took of the firstlings of their flocks, that they might offer sacrifice and burnt offerings according to the law of Moses (Mosiah 2:1-3).

Several elements here are characteristic of Sukkot. The gathering of the Nephites "up to the temple"[68] indicates the sanctity of the occasion. Regarding their sacrifices "according to the law of Moses," it is significant to note that there are more sacrifices prescribed for Sukkot than for any of the other festivals. Likewise, the tower which King Benjamin caused to be erected corresponds to the wooden pulpit traditionally constructed for the king on the occasion of the Feast of Tabernacles. Another Sukkot feature is the mention of the blood of Christ (Mosiah 3:11), reminiscent of the blood of the covenant sprinkled on the people by Moses at the first Sukkot (Exodus 24:8).

Furthermore, the Nephite assembly parallels the assembly of the Jews conducted in Jerusalem by Ezra upon the return from Babylon.[69] The temple had been rebuilt, and the Jews sought to recommit themselves to the Law of Moses. For this purpose, they sanctified the seventh month.[70] On the first day of that month, Ezra began reading the Law to the congregation at the Water Gate (Nehemiah 8:1-3, 5). The following day, "they found written in the law which the Lord had commanded by Moses, that the children of Israel should dwell in booths in the feast of the seventh month" (Nehemiah 8:13-14). They therefore set about to construct the booths and kept the feast of Sukkot.

Benjamin's people, too, engaged in a renewal of their observance of Sukkot. Benjamin had studied the scriptures with renewed emphasis on language and, as with Ezra, Benjamin may have felt that this observance of the feast was the first proper one which had been held for some time in the Nephite culture. The Nephites also set up their "tents round about the temple, every man having his tent with the door thereof towards the temple, that thereby they might remain in their tents and hear the words which king Benjamin should speak unto them."[71] These "booths" represented the temporary dwellings used by the Israelites after leaving Egypt,[72] and the practice of pitching tents "with the door thereof towards the temple" finds its antecedent in the camp of Israel (Exodus 33:8-10).

The parallel extends further. As King Benjamin had spoken from a tower, so too Ezra "stood upon a pulpit of wood, which they had made for the purpose."[73] Both Benjamin and Ezra spoke of God as Creator,[74] King Benjamin adding that since God gave us all we have (Mosiah 2:21, 23; 4:19-20), we have a moral obligation to be liberal toward others (Mosiah 2:16-19; 4:15-19, 22-26). Most of Benjamin's address was concerned with exhorting his people to obey the commandments of God (Mosiah 2:22). He spoke of the curses and blessings of the Law,[75] and called upon the testimony of the written word against the people at the last day.[76] In addition, he discussed the atonement as it relates to the Law of Moses.[77] Ezra, too, read to his people from the Law of Moses, exhorting them to repentance (Nehemiah 8:1-3, 5-9, 13, 18; 9:3). Finally, Ezra's words were addressed to "those that could understand" (Nehemiah 8:3), and "every one having knowledge, and having understanding" took the oath (Nehemiah 10:28-29). King Benjamin likewise spoke only to those "who [could] understand [his] words."[78]

King Benjamin's people, hearing his words, and feeling the spirit of the occasion, fell to the ground, repented of their sins, and asked that the atonement be applied to them (Mosiah 4:1-2, 6-7), as all Israelites were expected to do for the Day of Atonement in the seventh month.[79] They then declared their willingness "to enter into a covenant with our God to do his will, and to be obedient to his commandments in all things" (Mosiah 5:5; see vss. 2-6). Following this, King Benjamin recorded "the names of all those who had entered into a covenant with God to keep his commandments" (Mosiah 6:1-3), as he had recorded the text of his speech.

The Jews in Jerusalem, similarly moved by the words of Ezra, "were assembled with fasting, and with sack-clothes, and earth upon them. . . . And they stood up in their place, and read in the book of the law of the Lord their God one fourth part of the day; and another fourth part they confessed, and worshipped the Lord their God" (Nehemiah 9:1, 3). They "entered into a curse, and into an oath, to walk in God's law, which was given by Moses the servant of God, and to observe and do all the commandments of the Lord our Lord, and his judgments and his statutes" (Nehemiah 10:29; compare JST). Here, also, they fell to the ground (Nehemiah 8:6), and names were recorded: "because of all this we make a sure covenant, and write it; and our princes, Levites, and priests, seal unto it" (Nehemiah 9:38). Ezra's congregation also committed their new covenant to writing (Nehemiah 9:34-38).

There are, of course, some points regarding the seventh month celebration under Ezra that cannot be fully demonstrated in the Nephite record. For example, the Jerusalem assembly also participated in a meal (Nehemiah 8:10, 12), and there were strangers present (Nehemiah 9:2). Foreigners among the Mulekites may also have been present in Zarahemla. There are some indications that the Nephite assembly may have taken place in the sabbatical or jubilee year. The sabbatical year is mentioned in Nehemiah 10:31, but there is no direct evidence that the assembly in Jerusalem took place in such a year.

As previously discussed, the Jewish Sukkot liturgy was comprised of readings from Deuteronomy and the Psalms. There are a number of parallels between the Jewish Sukkot liturgy and the speech given by King Benjamin.

Paragraph of the King

One of the primary passages read by the Israelite king at the autumn feast was the "paragraph of the King" (Deuteronomy 17:14-20), that portion of the Mosaic code relating to the king's duties. The ideas contained in this biblical passage were fundamental to King Benjamin's thoughts.

Regarding kingship, where Deuteronomy 17:15 requires that only "one from among thy brethren" may become king, Benjamin addressed his Nephite audience as "my brethren" (Mosiah 2:9, 15, 20, 31, 36; 3:1; 4:4). He also stressed, "I have been chosen by this people, and consecrated by my father, and was suffered by the hand of the Lord that I should be a ruler and a king over this people,"[80] in conformity with Deuteronomy 17:15. He further ascribed to God the choice of Mosiah as his successor (Mosiah 2:29-30).

Concerning the abuse of office, Deuteronomy 17:16-17 warned of the tendency of monarchs to use their power to gain wealth and satisfy their own lusts.[81] King Benjamin, in like manner, stressed that he had not "sought gold nor silver nor any manner of riches" (Mosiah 2:12) nor had he permitted slavery (Mosiah 2:13).[82] It is possible that the commandment regarding "multiplying" horses and wives also lies behind his statements that one should not keep his neighbor's ass (Mosiah 5:14) and that one should not commit adultery (Mosiah 1:13; 2:13).[83]

The king was also humble. Deuteronomy 17:20 requires "that his heart be not lifted up above his brethren." Benjamin said: "I have not commanded you to come up hither that ye should fear me, or that ye should think that I of myself am more than a mortal man. But I am like as yourselves."[84]

Deuteronomy 17:18-19 specifies that the king should keep a copy of the Law with him, that he might always remember the commandments of God. Accordingly, King Benjamin kept the brass plates of Laban, on which was written the Law of Moses.[85] The importance of the Law is reaffirmed in Deuteronomy 17:20: "that he turn not aside from the commandment, to the right hand, or to the left: to the end that he may prolong his days in his kingdom." This is the central theme of the book of Deuteronomy: obedience to God's law will bring prosperity in the land

and long life.[86] This is also a main point of King Benjamin's speech.[87] Benjamin's summary of this principle (Mosiah 2:22) seems to have been directly inspired by Deuteronomy 6:2 or Deuteronomy 17:20.[88] A secondary theme found in both texts, and a feature associated with Sukkot is the exhortation to assist the needy.[89]

Benjamin and Jubilee

A comparative study by John W. Welch[90] has related certain sections of Benjamin's speech to Leviticus 25-26, suggesting the possibility that the coronation of Mosiah occurred during a jubilee year.[91] Parallels between the passages in Leviticus and Mosiah are outlined as follows:[92]

	Leviticus	Mosiah
Return possessions	25:10	4:28
Not to injure one another	25:14, 17	4:13
Render according to due	25:15-16, 50	4:13, 28
Prosperity in the land follows obedience	25:18-19	2:22
Aid the poor	25:35	4:16, 26
Use of riches	25:35-37	4:21
Peace in the land	26:6	2:31
Covenant with God	26:9	5:5-6
Lord's dwelling	26:11	2:37
Lord to be with his people	26:11-12	2:36
Curses for disobedience, including burning	26:14-33	2:38; 3:25-27
"Walk/go contrary . . . "	26:21, 27	2:33, 36

We consistently find that Sukkot and the beginning of the jubilee year (which is announced in the same seventh month) go hand in hand. Nothing in either the attempt to identify sections in the speech that manifest affinity to jubilee, in the thesis of this article regarding tabernacles, or in Hugh Nibley's study of Benjamin's speech as a royal coronation for that matter is exclusive of the other. While some passages in Leviticus 25-26 are similar to Deuteronomic passages already considered (for example, the promise that rain will be sent if Israel keeps God's commandments [Leviticus 26:3-5], and that God will defeat the nation's enemies and establish peace [26:6-8]), the parallels between the passages in Leviticus and Mosiah have independent significance: The fact that the jubilee references are largely concentrated in two portions of the speech makes it very attractive to conclude that Benjamin chose not only Sukkot as the time for the coronation of his son but a jubilee or sabbatical year as well.

CONCLUSION

This study is not intended to be conclusive. Rather, it is just one more probe into the Old World origins of the Book of Mormon civilization and culture. While a few questions have been at least partially answered here, many more still present themselves. How would the Nephites have coped with a new climate in the celebration of a prepluvial festival? (The word "rain" does not occur in King Benjamin's speech, though he speaks of prosperity.) Were all of the elements of the Nephite assembly based on Israelite counterparts, or did some stem from other Middle Eastern civilizations, as suggested by Dr. Nibley? Was there a Nephite Sukkot liturgy? Did Laban's brass plates contain all of the Psalms? Can we use the Book of Mormon material to date the beginnings of the Jewish Sukkot liturgy of the Second Temple period? Although these and other questions must remain unanswered, we can now respond to the question which prompted this study: To what extent did the Nephites keep the rites of the Law of Moses? The preponderance of our evidence certainly verifies the words of Nephi: "And we did observe to keep the judgments, and the statutes, and the commandments of the Lord in all things, according to the law of Moses" (2 Nephi 5:10).

Notes

1. My original article sparked considerable interest among Latter-day Saint scholars, several of whom began to search for further evidences of the observance of Jewish feasts in the Book of Mormon text. Several workshops on Nephite religious festivals were held by F.A.R.M.S., and some preliminary reports resulted. Some additional information is included here. However, a more exhaustive study is under way. Italics are my own unless otherwise noted.

2. For example, 1 Nephi 5:9; 7:22; Mosiah 2:3; Alma 34:13-14; 3 Nephi 9:17-20; 15:2-10.

3. For example, Sabbath observance in Jarom 1:5; Mosiah 13:16-19; 18:23.

4. Mosiah 1-6. Other Nephite assemblies — some perhaps of the same nature — are found in Jacob 1:17-6:13; Mosiah 7:17; 22:1-9; 25:1-18; Alma 2:5-9; 18:9; 20:9-12; 3 Nephi 3:13-14; 4:4. Note also Nephi's speech from the tower in Helaman 7, where he outlines God's dealings with men. Further, compare the comments on the justice of kings in Mosiah 23:8 and especially in Mosiah 29:12-14, where Mosiah is seeking a successor from among his sons.

5. Hugh Nibley, *An Approach to the Book of Mormon*, vol. 6, *The Collected Works of Hugh Nibley* (Salt Lake City: Deseret Book and F.A.R.M.S., 1988), 295-310; and *Since Cumorah*, vol. 7, *The Collected Works of Hugh Nibley* (Salt Lake City: Deseret Book and F.A.R.M.S., 1988), 247-51. See also Hugh Nibley, "The Arrow, the Hunter, and the State," *Western Political Quarterly* 2/3 (1949): 328-44; and "The Hierocentric State," *Western Political Quarterly* 4/2 (1951): 225-53.

6. The Israelite calendar was lunar, with each month beginning at the new moon. The year comprised twelve months of alternating twenty-nine or thirty days. This gave 354 days, or eleven days short of the solar year. Periodically, an intercalary month ("Second Adar") was added to bring the calendar into line with the seasons. In this manner, the month of Abib always encompassed the spring equinox. The system is still followed in today's sacred Jewish calendar. It is reflected in the dating of Easter in the Western churches, which is defined by the Catholic Church as the Sunday closest to the full moon nearest the spring equinox. Passover, of course, falls on the full moon closest to the spring equinox, since it is halfway through the month of Abib.

7. Exodus 12-13. The Prophet Joseph Smith connected the date of April 6 with the birth and death of Christ, Passover, the Creation, and the Restoration of the Church (*HC* 1:337). The first of Abib is the day on which Noah saw that the face of the land was dry (Genesis

8:13), and Moses set up the Tabernacle (Exodus 40:2, 17). There is an obvious symbolism in beginning the year with the spring equinox, when the ground is again alive with greenery.

8. The notable exception was the New Moon, which marked the beginning of each new month (Numbers 10:10; Psalm 81:3).

9. Genesis 2:2-3; Exodus 16:26-30; 20:10-11; 31:13-17; 34:21; 35:2-3; Leviticus 23:3; Deuteronomy 5:12-15. Regarding seven-day periods, note also the cleansing rites for those touching dead bodies (Numbers 19:11-22; 31:19-24), Nazarites (Numbers 6:6-12), and lepers (Leviticus 13; 14:1-9), as also for plagues (Leviticus 14:33-42).

10. Exodus 34:22; Leviticus 23:15-21; Deuteronomy 16:9-10. According to Jewish tradition, the Law was received at Sinai on Shavuʿot; see A. Chill, *The Mitzvot* (Jerusalem: Keter, 1974), 281.

11. Just as the first month includes the spring equinox, the seventh includes the autumn equinox. The Feast of Weeks falls just short of the summer solstice, however, and the winter solstice had no known significance in Old Testament Israel.

12. Leviticus 23:23-25; Numbers 29:1-6. Traditionally Adam's creation; Chill, *The Mitzvot*, 285.

13. Leviticus 16:29-34; 23:26-32; Numbers 29:7-11. According to tradition, this day is the anniversary of Adam's repentance of his sin, of Abraham's circumcision, and of Moses' second descent from the Mount, with the new tablets of the Law; Chill, *The Mitzvot*, 288.

14. Exodus 23:16; Leviticus 23:33-43; Numbers 29:12-39; Deuteronomy 16:13-15; Ezekiel 45:25.

15. Exodus 23:10-11 (note the weekly Sabbath in vs. 12); Leviticus 25:1-7, 18-22; 26:34-35; 2 Chronicles 36:21. Note Deuteronomy 15:1-8, where we find a release of debts to Hebrews, a release of Hebrew slaves, and assistance rendered to the needy.

16. From Hebrew *yôbēl*, "ram's horn," used as a trumpet.

17. Exodus 21:2; Leviticus 25:8-17, 23-34; Deuteronomy 15:1-18. For Leviticus 25:23, cf. the response of Naboth to Ahab in 1 Kings 21:1-3.

18. The jubilee was announced by the blowing of trumpets on Yom Kippur (Leviticus 25:9).

19. In fact, the original purpose of the feast was probably to pray for rain (Deuteronomy 28:12). Once, during the author's eight-year stay in Israel, there was a rainstorm before Sukkot. The chief rabbis issued an official declaration that it was "*not* rain," since rain cannot come before the prayers are offered. (With the same reasoning, just prior to the Feast of Unleavened Bread, after ridding the house of yeast and searching under the furniture with a candle, an Orthodox

Jew will declare that "if there remains any leaven in this house, it is not *my* leaven!")

20. The eighth day, with its special assembly, was originally not counted with the seven. A sukkah was not required for this last day. In 1972, I mentioned to President and Sister Harold B. Lee (then on visit to Jerusalem) that our April and October conferences corresponded with the timing of the ancient festivals of Passover and Tabernacles. Sister Lee noted that she recalled, as a little girl, that the Salt Lake Tabernacle was always decorated with tree branches during October Conference. I have been yet unable to confirm this from other sources.

21. These temporary dwellings have long-standing use in the harvest season of the Middle East, when families spend several days at a time in the fields, rather than commuting daily from the villages. In addition to providing shade for the workers during mealtime, the rough shelters keep the harvested produce out of direct sunlight.

22. The Bible does not provide this information. The Israelites arrived in the wilderness of Sinai during the third month (Exodus 19:1), and the Tabernacle was completed and set up on the first day of the first month of the second year (Exodus 40:1, 17). The law was revealed some time between these two fixed dates. Josephus noted that when Moses ascended the mount to receive the Law, the Israelites pitched their tents about the mountain and were caught in a rain storm; *Antiquities of the Jews* III, 5, 1-2.

23. Today, the annual reading cycle of the Torah ends (and begins anew) at Simhat Torah. This practice of reading assigned portions of the Law each week during each year is traditionally dated to the time of Ezra the Scribe, who renewed the celebration of Sukkot after the Babylonian Captivity (discussed below).

24. The ark landed atop the mountain on the seventeenth day of the seventh month, during Sukkot (Genesis 8:4). Note the covenant in Genesis 8:20-9:17, containing the Sukkot elements of burnt offerings and a promise of "seedtime and harvest" and the rainbow, in addition to a covenant of peace. Professor Nibley has previously intimated that the great autumnal festivals, representing renewal of the earth, were perhaps patterned after the heavenly council convened to plan the creation of the earth; *An Approach to the Book of Mormon*, 309.

25. It is, of course, unlikely (unless unitedly moved upon by the Spirit) that the people all said the same thing simultaneously without a script. Regarding this ritual choral recitation, see Nibley, *An Approach to the Book of Mormon*, 303, 305.

26. The Hebrew altar (*mizbēaḥ*, "place of slaughter/sacrifice") was used for cooking and burning of sacrificial meat. The word is also used for incense altars, which are likewise used for offerings to God. The word generally translated "pillar" in KJV is the Hebrew *maṣṣēbāh* (lit., "something erected"). It is always constructed as the sign of a covenant (e.g., Genesis 28:10-22; 31:44-52), and hence could be termed a "covenant altar."

27. 1 Kings 8:10-12; 2 Chronicles 5:13-14. Compare the cloud at Sinai (Exodus 24:16-18) and during the wanderings in the wilderness (Exodus 13:21-22; 40:34-38), as also the cloud on the Mount of Transfiguration (Matthew 17:1-6), and at Jesus' ascension (Acts 1:8-9). Regarding the Transfiguration, note the presence of Moses (who instituted Sukkot), of Elijah (or Elias, who had power over the rains), and of other elements (e.g., the desire of the three Apostles to build "tabernacles"). Cf. the Transfiguration and D&C 110.

28. 1 Kings 8:65 says "seven days and seven days, even *fourteen* days," though the text notes that on the *eighth* day Solomon sent the people away.

29. Note the mention of tents (1 Kings 8:66; 2 Chronicles 7:10) and of strangers (1 Kings 8:41-43; 2 Chronicles 6:32-33), as also of the brazen scaffold (*kiyyôr nǝḥôšet*) on which Solomon stood (2 Chronicles 6:13).

30. 2 Samuel 24:18-25; 1 Chronicles 21:18-22:1; cf. 2 Chronicles 3:1.

31. 2 Samuel 6:12, 14-16; 1 Chronicles 15:25, 27-29; 16:1.

32. 1 Chronicles 16:7-36. The Psalms cited by David on this occasion were 105:1-15, speaking of God's covenant and his dealings with the people; 96:1-13 (96:13 = 1 Chronicles 16:33), that the Lord is to judge the earth (cf. Mosiah 3:10); and 106:47-48, which is similar to Psalm 118, which later became part of the Sukkot liturgy. Some of the Sukkot elements found in David's recitation in 1 Chronicles 16 include: (a) an exhortation to remember the Lord's dealings with Israel (vss. 8, 12, 24), (b) to praise the Lord (vss. 9-11, 25), (c) to "be ye mindful of his covenant" (vs. 15), (d) sacrifice (vs. 29), (e) the Lord's role as King (vs. 31), and (f) recitation of the Sukkot formula, "Save us, O God of our salvation" (vs. 35, cf. 23). After David's recitation, "all the people said, Amen, and praised the Lord" (vs. 36).

33. In Ezekiel's vision of the future, it is the prince of Israel (i.e., the king) who supervised the activities of both Passover and Sukkot (Ezekiel 45: 22-25).

34. For example, H. L. Jansen, "The Consecration in the Eighth

Chapter of Testamentum Levi," in *The Sacral Worship*, Contributions to the Central Theme of the VIIIth International Congress for the History of Religions, Rome, April 1955 (Leiden: Brill, 1959), 361-62.

35. See Hugh Nibley, *An Approach to the Book of Mormon*, 300-306. Though Sukkot was the main royal festival, note also the royal covenant of the third month in 2 Chronicles 15:10-15 (cf. vss. 12-13 with Mosiah 6:2). Note also the Passovers celebrated by Hezekiah (2 Chronicles 30) and Josiah (2 Kings 23:21-23; 2 Chronicles 35). M *Bikkurim* 3:4 informs us that it was the King who led the firstfruits procession (Deuteronomy 26), which, like Sukkot, featured the playing of pipes (flutes).

36. *Seder Olam Zuta Chronicle,* in A. Neubauer, ed., *Mediaeval Jewish Chronicles and Chronicle Notes,* 2 vols. (Oxford: Clarendon, 1887-95), 2:83; cited by H. H. Ben-Sasson, *A History of the Jewish People* (Cambridge, MA: Harvard University Press, 1976), 422.

37. By the days of King Agrippa (d. 44 A.D.), the seventh month was counted as the first, as today.

38. Deuteronomy 31:10-12.

39. Deuteronomy 17:15. Agrippa's ancestors were Idumeans (Edomites), descendants of Esau. By religion, he was Jewish, by citizenship a Roman.

40. Deuteronomy 6:4-10. This is the *Shema^c* (imperative "Hear!"), most important of the Jewish prayers. It is cited by Jesus in Mark 12:29.

41. Deuteronomy 11:13-22.

42. Deuteronomy 14:22-28.

43. Deuteronomy 26:12-19.

44. Deuteronomy 17:14-20.

45. Deuteronomy 27:15-28:68.

46. M *Sotah* 7:8.

47. One of the principal themes of the Book of Mormon is the Lord's promise that if the people keep his commandments, they shall prosper in the land, while if they disobey him, they shall not prosper (1 Nephi 2:20; 4:14; 2 Nephi 1:9, 20; 4:4; Jarom 1:9; Omni 1:6; Alma 9:13; 36:1, 30; 37:13; 38:1; 48:15, 25; 50:20; Helaman 3:20; 3 Nephi 5:22). The promise was mentioned by King Benjamin in his speech (Mosiah 1:7; 2:22, 31). The promise had also been made to such Israelite leaders as Joshua (Joshua 1:7) and Solomon (1 Kings 2:3; 1 Chronicles 29:23), and is repeated elsewhere in the Old Testament (2 Chronicles 24:20; 31:21; Ezra 6:14; Job 36:11; Jeremiah 22:21) and in our day (D&C 9:13).

48. Compare Mosiah 2:34, 40; 3:21; 6:2.

49. The double emphasis is perhaps because strangers were invited to attend the Sukkot festivities (in the hopes they would be converted, hearing the Law read).

50. In ancient Egypt, it was believed that the king was responsible for the onset of the Nile floods so necessary to that country's agricultural economy. Just prior to the coming of the waters (in September), the king would offer prayers to Hapi, the river god. In actual fact, of course, the king had advance information of the Nile's rising, based on special measuring marks cut into the limestone cataracts upstream.

51. 2 Chronicles 29:27. Seven and a half years according to 2 Samuel 2:11; 5:5; 1 Chronicles 3:4.

52. 1 Kings 12:19-24. Already in the time of Solomon, Jeroboam had been told by the prophet Ahijah that if he kept the commandments, Israel would be his (1 Kings 11:38).

53. 2 Kings 11:17; 2 Chronicles 23:16. The repetition of the words "and between the king also and the people" in 2 Kings 11:17 is a dittographic error committed by a later scribe.

54. In 1 Maccabees 14:41 we read: "Also that the Jews and priests were well pleased that Simon should be their governor and high priest for ever, until there should arise a faithful priest," evidently to reestablish (in proper order), the Davidic line.

55. In later times, it was water from the Spring of Gihon (site of Solomon's coronation) the high priest poured out upon the altar during Sukkot. Water, representing expected rains, was appropriate for the festival. However, wine is also appropriate to Sukkot, which takes place just after the grape harvest.

56. Leviticus 16:1 has reference to 10:1-2 and shows that all of these chapters refer to events which occurred during the consecration ceremony. The rest of chapter 16 speaks of how Aaron was to offer the sacrifice of the day of atonement (vs. 29).

57. The true anointing is to be both a king and a priest to God. In the Bible, both the king and the high priest were called by the title Messiah (Heb. *māšîaḥ*, "anointed one"). See also Jansen, "The Consecration in the Eighth Chapter of Testamentum Levi," 356-65, where he compares Levi's priestly anointing, washing, investiture, and ordination with the enthronement of God as King. He speaks both of the new name (cf. Mosiah 1:11-12; 5:7-13; D&C 130:111; 133:18; Revelation 2:17, 3:12) and notes the implications of *Testament of Levi* 19:2-3 in comparison with biblical Sukkot and coronation rites. The relevant verses read: "And his sons replied, 'Before the Lord we will live according to his Law.' And their father said to

them, 'The Lord is my witness and his angels are witnesses, and you are witnesses, and I am witness concerning the word from your mouth.' And his sons said, '(We are) witnesses.' " James H. Charlesworth, *The Old Testament Pseudepigrapha*, 2 vols. (Garden City, NY: Doubleday, 1983-85), 1:795.

58. Based on Deuteronomy 16:14. The produce of the sabbatical year was left to the poor among the people (Exodus 23:11; Leviticus 25:6).

59. Saul, Israel's first universally acknowledged king, is called, in the earlier parts of Samuel, by the term *nâgîd*, "commander" (KJV "captain"), indicating his role as leader of the army (1 Samuel 10:1; cf. 1 Samuel 11). David's troubles began when he neglected personally to lead the army of Israel in battle (2 Samuel 11, esp. vs. 1). From Egyptian, Assyrian, and Babylonian records, we learn that it was typical for kings to accompany their armies into the field. In the Book of Mormon, Nephi personally wielded the sword of Laban in the defense of his people (Jacob 1:10), as did his successors on the throne (Jarom 1:7, 14; Omni 1:24; Words of Mormon 1:13).

60. To symbolize this, each day of the festival a priest would bring water from the Spring of Gihon and pour it in a basin on the altar, mixing some of it with wine (in the Mishnah, see *Shekalim* 6:30; *Sukkah* 4:1, 9; *Zebahim* 6:2; *Middot* 2:6.)

61. See n. 26.

62. Regarding the "pipes" (KJV) or flutes played at Sukkot, see M *Sukkah* 5:1. The dancing before the Tabernacle at Shiloh (Judges 21:19-23) apparently is for Sukkot. Compare also the Lamanite girls in Mosiah 20:1-5.

63. Probably reminiscent of the "voice of the trumpet" which announced God's appearance on Mt. Sinai (Exodus 19:16-20). Trumpets also announced each New Moon (Numbers 10:10; Psalm 81:3), and were used to assemble the congregation in the wilderness (Numbers 10:7-8).

64. Compare Saul's rejection as king by God. See also 2 Chronicles 24:20-21; cf. Mosiah 2:18-19.

65. Mosiah 1:10. One wonders how King Benjamin could have assembled all of his people "on the morrow." While it is possible that the Nephites lived in a very small area, over which messages could be sent one day and an assembly held the next, it is likewise possible that the assembly was calendared by the annual clock and that the people were already planning to come to Zarahemla from whatever distance to participate in the Feast of Tabernacles. The "proclamation" need not imply that it was an unscheduled event.

In ancient Israel, the King also issued a proclamation for the Passover, though it was a set festival (2 Chronicles 30:1-11; cf. Exodus 32:5).

66. Compare David's charge to Solomon in 1 Kings 2:1-9. Several ancient Egyptian documents comprise admonitions to kings and princes.

67. The royal nature of the Sukkot celebration makes it unnecessary to minimize Mosiah's coronation. The Mishnaic reference to Sukkot as a royal festival, and the nature of Israelite assemblies generally, substantiates the heavily religious nature of coronation rites in Israel.

68. See Mosiah 1:10, 18; 2:1-3, 5.

69. Nehemiah 8-10; see esp. 7:73-8:1, 13. Regular provision for sacrifice was also made at that time (10:34-36).

70. This assembly was represented as the first proper observance of the festival since Joshua (Nehemiah 8:17). Actually, the first company of Jews returning from Babylon had celebrated Sukkot by building an altar and making burnt offerings (Ezra 3:1-6). But enemies hindered the rebuilding of the Temple. About 520 B.C., encouraged by the prophecies of Haggai and Zechariah, the Jews resumed work on the Temple (Ezra 4:24-5:1). One of Haggai's prophecies was given on the first day of Sukkot (Haggai 2:1-9), evidently in memory of Solomon's Temple. Much of the prophecy of Zechariah deals with the future restoration of the monarchy at the time of Sukkot. These are, in effect, messianic prophecies, some of which were fulfilled by Jesus at his first coming, while others will be fulfilled when he returns to Jerusalem. For example, coming seated on an ass (9:9), the blood of the covenant (9:11), the blowing of the trumpet (9:14), and the new wine (9:15-16). In Zechariah 9:16, we read that "in that day" the Lord shall save. There is mention of clouds and of rains (10:1) and a threat to smite horses (9:10; 12:4; 14:15), reminiscent of the Paragraph of the King. There is also mention of the tents of Judah (12:7; 14:15). Each family is apart (12:12-14). A new fountain, to accompany the rains, is to come forth from the Temple (13:1; 14:8). A covenant will be made with the Lord's people (13:9), and Jerusalem will then be cut in half by the enemy (14:2; the two bodies of people at Sukkot? — cf. Mosiah 25:1-4). But the Lord will defeat Israel's enemies (14:3). At the critical moment, he will appear to reign on earth as King (14:9, 16-17; cf. the crown in 9:16). The Feast of Tabernacles will be celebrated (14:16, 18-19), along with sacrifices (14:20-21). Those who do not come to celebrate the feast and make covenant with God will not receive the promised rains (14:17).

Jesus' hesitation to attend the Sukkot festival in Jerusalem (John 7:1-13) was perhaps because the time for his coming in glory was not yet (John 7:6). His first coming in triumph was just before Passover (on what has come to be known as "Palm Sunday"), and his second will be at Sukkot. When, at length, he did attend the Sukkot festival, Jesus spoke of the "living water" (John 7:37-38), probably an allusion to the water poured on the altar during the festival (cf. Zechariah 13:1; 14:8; Ezekiel 47:1-12). There are other allusions to Sukkot in statements made by Jesus at that time.

71. Mosiah 2:5-6. Each tent contained one family. Israel also pitched tents by families in the wilderness (Numbers 2:34). They dwelt in tents at the time they covenanted with God at Sinai (Deuteronomy 5:27-31).

72. The Hebrew '*ōhel*, "tent," has a semantic range including "dwelling, habitation" (Genesis 9:27; 1 Kings 8:66; Job 8:22; Psalm 84:10; Jeremiah 10:20; 30:18).

73. Nehemiah 8:4. The Hebrew word is *migdāl*, generally translated "tower," rather than "pulpit" as here in KJV. Compare the "brazen scaffold" of Solomon and the "stairs" (*mǎʿaleh*, "ascent") in Nehemiah 9:4, from which, in Second Temple times, the Levites sang the "Psalms of Degrees" (Hebrew "ascents") and the priests sounded their trumpets on the last day of Sukkot. Many aspects of the "Psalms of Degrees" and the "Hallel Psalms" sung during Sukkot are also reflected in King Benjamin's speech.

74. Mosiah 2:20-21, 23, 25; 4:9, 21; Nehemiah 9:5-6.

75. Mosiah 1:13-14; 2:22, 24, 33, 36-41; 3:14-15, 25-27; 5:14-15.

76. Mosiah 3:24. Moses, Joshua, and Ezra had likewise made records as testimonies or witnesses, as discussed below.

77. Mosiah 2:34-35; 3:1-16. Regarding the atoning blood, see Mosiah 4:2.

78. Mosiah 2:40. Compare Mosiah 2:34; 3:21; 6:2. Moses also excluded the children (Deuteronomy 11:2).

79. This is still practiced in Judaism. Indeed, Yom Kippur is the only time when Jews prostrate themselves on the ground for prayers. The normal practice is to pray standing or sometimes sitting, but not kneeling.

80. Mosiah 2:11; cf. 1:10.

81. Similarly, when prevailed upon by Israel to anoint the first king, the prophet Samuel was told by the Lord that the king would use his position to his own advantage, taking from the people their children, their riches, and their properties (1 Samuel 8:4-22). This did, in fact, come to pass in the days of Solomon and thereafter (e.g., 1 Kings 4:7, 22-23, 26-28; 10:23-29; 11:1-8).

82. He also called the people to witness (Mosiah 2:14), as had Samuel and Joshua. He had a clear conscience (Mosiah 2:15, 27).

83. In any case, these ideas are part of the Law of Moses. See the jubilee, below.

84. Mosiah 2:10-11. Compare Hugh Nibley, *An Approach to the Book of Mormon*, 301-3.

85. Mosiah 1:2-7. These plates were passed on to Mosiah at the time of the ceremony, and later to the judges. The large plates of Nephi had apparently always been in the hands of the kings (Omni 1:11).

86. For example, Deuteronomy 4:1, 5, 26, 40; 5:33; 10:12-13; 11:21-22.

87. For example, Mosiah 1:7; 2:31, 36; 4:15; 6:6.

88. In the former passage, it refers to the people as a whole, while in the latter it refers to the king only. Both Deuteronomy passages were part of the Sukkot liturgy.

89. Deuteronomy 10:18-19; 14:29; 26:12-13, 17-19; Mosiah 4:16-19. I have cited only passages known to have been read by the king at Sukkot.

90. John W. Welch, "Benjamin's Speech (Mosiah 2:9-5:15): A Textual Analysis with Commentary," unpublished manuscript, 1 January 1973, 52-53, and John W. Welch, compiler, "King Benjamin's Speech in the Context of Ancient Israelite Festivals," F.A.R.M.S. preliminary report, 1985, 58-63.

91. It is sometimes difficult to distinguish between the sabbatical and jubilee years. Both are marked by the release of debts (Deuteronomy 15:1-3; Leviticus 25:33-37) and by the prohibition against agricultural pursuits (Leviticus 25:2-8, 11-12, 20-22). Only in the jubilee does land return to its original owners (Leviticus 25:8-10, 13-16, 23-34; 27:17-24; Numbers 36:4). The procedure for the release of Hebrew slaves is troublesome. Contrast Exodus 21:1-11 with Deuteronomy 15:1, 12-18 and Leviticus 25:39-55.

92. I follow Welch here with a few additions.

9

The Melchizedek Material
in Alma 13:13-19

John W. Welch
Brigham Young University, Provo, Utah

Alma's discourse on how man comes to know and participate in the plan of redemption (Alma 12:9-13:30) contains a noteworthy use of the material about Melchizedek in Genesis 14:17-24 and in other sources available to him. For Alma, the story of Melchizedek is a commanding illustration of how a person can obtain knowledge of the mysteries of the gospel and attain the blessings of sacred priesthood ordinances through faith, repentance, and righteousness (cf. Alma 12:30; 13:3, 10). Drawing these specific illustrations and teachings out of the Genesis and other accounts is unparalleled in a vast array of literature, which treats Melchizedek in a variety of ways.[1]

Alma found his basic information about Melchizedek in the books of Moses and from the ancient history of the Jews written on the plates of brass (1 Nephi 5:11-12) that were in his possession (Alma 37:1-3). In exploring his use of that material, this article approaches Alma's text from several directions. First, I examine Alma's discourse, focusing in particular on his comments about Melchizedek. Second, I consider Alma's possible sources. He may have had a text similar to the short and puzzling text of Genesis 14:17-24, yet more than likely his scriptures contained a

---

This essay originally appeared in a slightly different form in the unpublished "Tinkling Cymbals: Essays in Honor of Hugh Nibley," John W. Welch, ed., 1978.

longer account similar to JST, Genesis 14:17-40. In conjunction with my discussion of the traditional biblical material, I also consider the major interpretations which subsequent Jews and Christians have imposed upon that material through the ages. Those diverse interpretations provide an interesting comparison to the rich messages of Alma 13:13-19.

The Melchizedek Text in Alma 13

Alma turned to Melchizedek to illustrate the doctrine that all people may obtain knowledge of the mysteries of God through humility, righteousness, and the ordinances of the priesthood. It is not the historical details about Melchizedek himself that are important to Alma, but rather the symbolic priesthood ordinances associated with him. Melchizedek was a man of God and peace because he had obtained the spiritual powers and knowledge necessary to lead his people into the rest of the Lord through the order of the Son.

Alma's text is of particular interest for several reasons. First it is unique—*sui generis*. No other known sermon has imputed such a practical religious and ceremonial meaning to Melchizedek, although in certain respects the sacerdotal approach of 2 *Enoch* and the account in the Joseph Smith Translation (discussed below) come close.

Second, on its face it is one of the earliest extant expositions of the significance of Melchizedek. Working in the early first century B.C., Alma acknowledged that ancient scriptures stood behind his interpretation (Alma 13:20). Unless Alma was radically interpolating his sources (which seems unlikely in light of his own warning in Alma 13:20 that readers of the scriptures should not "wrest them"), his text is based upon a preexilic version of Genesis 14 (and perhaps other sources), known to him from the plates of brass.

Third, it gives us a rare opportunity to see one of the

most fertile minds and sensitive spirits among the Book of Mormon prophets at work on a passage of ancient scripture. Where other Jewish and Christian interpreters have seen only remote abstractions, precedents, or shadows, Alma brings forth powerful lessons on humility, repentance, priesthood, ordinances, and revelation.

Alma's sermon in chapters 12 and 13 teaches the principle that God will provide men access to certain mysteries of God (Alma 12:9-11). The first verse of this sermon sets the theme for the entire discourse. Alma says that many know these mysteries as priests (Alma 13:1), but they are laid under a strict condition of secrecy (Alma 12:9) that can be lifted only by the diligence and repentance of the children of men (Alma 12:9-11; 13:18; cf. Alma 26:22). The plan provides all mankind a chance to know the mysteries in full (Alma 12:10), by humility (Alma 12:10-11; 13:13-14) and through the ministrations of properly ordained priests (Alma 13:16; cf. Mosiah 2:9; Alma 26:22).

The substantive portion of the sermon (Alma 12:12-27) describes the judgment of God and tells how man can avert a second death through obedience to a new set of commandments. According to Alma's exposition, the fall of mankind was prefigured by Adam violating a first set of commandments (Alma 12:22); thus men must die in order to come to judgment (Alma 12:24). Messengers (i.e., "angels," Alma 12:29) were then sent, and God conversed with men, making known the plan of mercy through the Son (Alma 12:29). Man was then given a second set of commandments (Alma 12:32) accompanied by an oath that whoever broke those commandments should not enter into the rest or presence of the Lord (Alma 12:35) but would die the ultimate or last death (Alma 12:36).

Following this introductory explanation, Alma expounds upon the Nephite procedure through which the ordinances of the priesthood were received (see Alma 13:16) and how men might choose between obeying the

Lord's commandments and thereby "enter[ing] into the rest of the Lord" (Alma 13:16), or rebelliously disobeying him and suffering death. The Nephite ordination was a symbolic ritual, since it was performed "in a manner that thereby the people might know in what manner to look forward to his Son for redemption" (Alma 13:2). That manner is discussed by Alma only in veiled terms.[2] Candidates were "called and prepared from the foundation of the world" (Alma 13:3) with a "holy calling" (Alma 13:3, 5, 8).[3] This calling was according to a "preparatory redemption" from before the creation of the world (Alma 13:3), and it was patterned after, in, and through the preparation of the Son (Alma 13:5). Then they were "ordained with a holy ordinance" (Alma 13:8), "taking upon them the high priesthood of the holy order" (Alma 13:6, 8-9). Thereby the candidates became "high priests forever, after the order of the Son" (Alma 13:9). Following these preparations, and after making a choice to work righteousness rather than to perish (Alma 13:10), the candidate was sanctified by the Holy Ghost, his garments were washed white, and he "entered into the rest of the Lord" (Alma 13:12).

Having thus discussed this ordination procedure, Alma discusses Melchizedek as the archetype of high priests after this order of the Son. He gives the following account:

The Need for Humility and Signs of Repentance:

> And now, my brethren, I would that ye should humble yourselves before God, and bring forth fruit meet for repentance, that ye may also enter into that rest. Yea, humble yourselves even as the people in the days of Melchizedek, who was also a high priest after this same order which I have spoken, who also took upon him the high priesthood forever. And it was this same Melchizedek to whom Abraham paid tithes; yea even our father Abraham paid tithes of one-tenth part of all he possessed (Alma 13:13-15).

The Need for Symbolic Ordinances:

Now these ordinances were given after this manner, that thereby the people might look forward on the Son of God, it being a type of his order, or it being his order, and this that they might look forward to him for a remission of their sins, that they might enter into the rest of the Lord (Alma 13:16).

Melchizedek as a Leader to Peace through Repentance:

Now this Melchizedek was a king over the land of Salem; and his people had waxed strong in iniquity and abomination; yea, they had all gone astray; they were full of all manner of wickedness. But Melchizedek having exercised mighty faith, and received the office of the high priesthood according to the holy order of God, did preach repentance unto his people. And behold, they did repent; and Melchizedek did establish peace in the land in his days; therefore he was called the prince of peace, for he was the king of Salem; and he did reign under his father (Alma 13:17-18).

The Greatness of Melchizedek among Many:

Now, there were many before him, and also there were many afterwards, but none were greater; therefore, of him they have more particularly made mention (Alma 13:19).

For Alma, Melchizedek was a great high priest who took upon him the high priesthood forever after the order of the Son that Alma has described. Melchizedek's people were wicked, but through repentance, they became humble and were taught by certain ordinances how to look forward on the Son of God for a remission of sins. In this way, Melchizedek established peace in the land of Salem, where he ruled under his father.

In order to compare this information about Melchizedek with that in the Bible, I now turn to examine the biblical narrative and how it has been interpreted.

Genesis 14:17-24 in the Old Testament

Alma's material is fundamentally related to the text of Genesis 14, which contains some of the most ancient history in the Old Testament.[4] Although any quest for a conclusive picture of the historical Melchizedek may ultimately be stifled by our lack of contemporaneous information about the man and his period, an examination of the ancient literature pertaining to him yields valuable insights into the theological treatment of this religious figure through the ages.

Genesis 14:17-24 is the fountainhead of many ideas about Melchizedek. This text recounts the following events:

The Meeting:

And the king of Sodom went out to meet him [Abraham] after his return from the slaughter of Chedorlaomer, and of the kings that were with him, at the valley of Shaveh, which is the king's dale (Genesis 14:17).

Melchizedek's Appearance:

And Melchizedek king of Salem brought forth bread and wine: and he was the priest of the most high God (*El Elyon*) (Genesis 14:18).

Melchizedek's Blessing:

And he blessed him, and said, Blessed be Abram of the most high God, possessor of heaven and earth: And blessed be the most high God, which hath delivered thine enemies into thy hand (Genesis 14:19-20).

The Payment of Tithes:

And he gave him tithes of all (Genesis 14:20).

Division of the Spoils:

And the king of Sodom said unto Abram, Give me the persons, and take the goods to thyself. And Abram

said to the king of Sodom, I have lift up mine hand unto
the Lord, the most high God, the possessor of heaven
and earth, That I will not take from a thread even to a
shoelatchet, and that I will not take any thing that is
thine, lest thou shouldest say, I have made Abram rich:
[I will take] only that which the young men have eaten,
and the portion of the men which went with me, Aner,
Eshcol, and Mamre; let them take their portion (Genesis
14:21-24).

In his brief encounter with Abraham described in this
account, Melchizedek appears as a moderator of peace
serving a dual political and religious role, probably in sanc-
tioning Abraham's disposition of the spoils of war. In the
battle, Abraham had freed his nephew Lot, a resident of
Sodom, who had been taken captive when Sodom fell to
Chedorlaomer and his allies. Upon Abraham's return, the
king of Sodom came out to meet him. At this point, Melchizedek, king of Salem and priest of El the Most High,
brought forth bread (or "food") and wine, and blessed
Abraham with a hymn of beatification, extolling God's
deliverance of the enemy into Abraham's hands. Tithes
were then paid, although Abraham refused to accept any
spoils of war taken from Sodom, lest it should ever be
thought that the king of Sodom, rather than God, had
enriched Abraham.

In general, the organizational dependence of Alma's
words on Genesis 14 is apparent. Similar in length, the
lines of these two passages concerning the payment of
tithes (Genesis 14:20; Alma 13:15), Melchizedek's priesthood (Genesis 14:19; Alma 13:14), and the designation of
Melchizedek as the king over the land of Salem (Genesis
14:18; Alma 13:18) are closely related. Nevertheless, Alma's
text is interpretively independent. His perspective provides unique meanings: Where Genesis begins by simply
describing powerful earthly kings meeting humbly before
this righteous man of God (Genesis 14:17), Alma goes on

to draw an express lesson on humility (Alma 13:13-14); where the Genesis text next speaks of Melchizedek blessing Abraham (Genesis 14:19), Alma next speaks of the ordinances whereby all people might be blessed (Alma 13:16); and where Genesis finally discusses the division of spoils and Abraham's forbearance (14:21-24), Alma concludes by expounding upon the wickedness of the people and their repentance led by Melchizedek's influence (Alma 13:17-18).

When we turn to specifics, however, the Hebrew text leaves many questions unanswered. Out of this account has arisen a multitude of intractable questions over which scholars have puzzled. Consider the Hebrew name *Malkî-ṣedeq*. Does it hold some hidden meaning? It may be translated in many ways, including, "the King is Righteous," or "the King is Legitimate," or perhaps "Righteousness is King,"[5] or "My Lord is Sedeq (a Canaanite deity)."[6] The intrinsic meanings in these roots themselves have led some to claim that Melchizedek is not a personal name in Genesis 14:18 at all. The words may simply refer epithetically to "the just king"[7] (the king of Sodom?),[8] or, as Albright suggests, they may be a corruption of a line once reading "the king who was allied with [Abraham]."[9]

The questions proliferate. What was Melchizedek's political position? What city or land did he rule? Was it Jerusalem, or another town, or is this reference to "Salem" merely figurative?[10] What was his lineage and priesthood, and what was the effect of his blessing upon Abraham? What relations had he previously had with Abraham? Had a political treaty or a religious covenant regarding the campaign against Chedorlaomer been entered into between Abraham and Melchizedek before the war? Why would Melchizedek meet Abraham in the field outside any city walls, especially if the meeting had religious significance? What significance did the offering of bread and wine have?[11] Who paid tithes to whom,[12] and were the tithes

religious contributions or political tribute?[13] Who was Melchizedek's God, El Elyon, the Most High God?[14] My purpose is not to belabor the obfuscated. The point is simply
that the Hebrew text and all archaeological efforts to clarify
it offer little in the way of answers. Aside from the perspectives given by additional scripture or inspiration such
as that offered by Alma, only theology generates avenues
for dealing with these uncertainties.

The only other Old Testament passage in which Melchizedek appears is Psalm 110.[15] It has been read in two
general ways.[16] The standard reading, found in the King
James Version, follows the Septuagint, where the theme
of the psalm is political victory over enemies (Psalms 110:1-
2) through the strength of the Lord (Psalms 110:5-7), with
a central affirmation of the righteous reign of the Davidic
monarch over a willing people Israel (Psalms 110:3-4): "Thy
people shall be willing in the day of thy power. . . . Thou
art a priest forever after the order of (ᶜal dibrātî) Melchizedek." A relationship between the political blessing conveyed in this rendition and the literary image of Melchizedek's blessing of Abraham's military victory in Genesis
14 is readily discernible.

A second reading of the Psalm, however, is suggested
by Mitchell Dahood, who has recently proposed a reconstruction of the text in which malkî-ṣedeq in Psalms 110:4 is
not treated as the proper name "Melchizedek," but as a
construct chain of malk (king) and ṣedeq (legitimate) with a
possessive third-person singular suffix -î (his) interposed,
meaning "his legitimate king."[17] Under this reconstruction,
the psalm is understood to emphasize the king's legitimate
succession to the throne through covenants with God and
has nothing to do with the man Melchizedek, except
through a possible play on words: "You are a priest of the
Eternal according to his pact: His legitimate King, my lord,
according to your right hand."[18] While Dahood's translation is novel and subject to disagreement, both it and the

traditional reading of the psalm may be compared favorably with Alma's text, for Alma refers both to the willingness of the people of Melchizedek to submit to his righteous reign (as in the standard translation) and also to the ordinances or pacts associated with Melchizedek's divine kingship under his Father (as in Dahood's rendition).

If one prefers the traditional approach to Psalm 110, one must also deal with the very difficult Hebrew phrase, ʿal dibrātî malkî-ṣedeq, which is loosely rendered in the Greek as kata tēn taxin Melchisedek.[19] Whether this should be translated "because of Melchizedek," "in the manner of Melchizedek," or "after the order or arrangement or office of Melchizedek," as conventional renditions have suggested,[20] or simply "according to his pact," as Dahood prefers, is quite unsettled. One can concur, however, with Joseph Fitzmyer that the phrase cannot be understood in terms of hereditary succession: "The priesthood of the king is due to something else."[21] Alma's text certainly agrees.

Subsequent Jewish and Christian Interpretations of Melchizedek

From these traditional biblical texts, there have come about as many interpretations of Melchizedek as there have been heresies and orthodoxies, for few systematic biblical commentators have passed over this intriguing figure without accommodating him in one way or another. The importance ascribed to him varies with the system in which each interpretation stands. In some views he is regarded merely as a political figure who established certain legal precedents, while in others he becomes a central eschatological figure who will lead the war against Satan in the final battle against evil. Elsewhere he is raised to membership in the Godhead by one early Christian sect, while he is defamed as a bastard by Jewish apologists who found his unpedigreed preeminence in the Pentateuch disquieting. Gnostics and Christian mystics have ascribed cosmological powers to him, whereas Protestants have dismissed any notion that he was anything more than a feudal Canaanite king. Exactly what is made of the man Melchizedek in The Church of Jesus Christ of Latter-day Saints today is not entirely clear,[22] but Alma's text has been underutilized in this connection.

There is no evidence that Jewish theology took much cognizance of Melchizedek until between 110 B.C. and A.D. 132, when several Jewish writers undertook to present Judaism in various Hellenistic contexts. To this end, Melchizedek readily served as a bridge for them to the Gentile world. Around this time, Melchizedek began to figure importantly in early Christian writings as well.

To the writer of the book of Jubilees,[23] who was sympathetic toward the establishment of a Maccabean royal priesthood over Palestine, Melchizedek provided a convenient precedent for the Maccabean desire to bestow the offices of king and priest upon a single person—and a non-Levite at that. In addition, the Maccabean priests apparently appropriated to themselves for political uses the Melchizedekian epithet, "a priest of the Most High God,"[24] probably because Melchizedek is one of the few non-Levites in the Old Testament acceptably bearing the title of priest. Furthermore, Melchizedek was used to justify the all-important political right of the Maccabean king-priests to receive and personally enjoy the tithes of the people as political tribute and as "an ordinance for ever . . . to [which] law there is no limit of days."[25]

Far more inscrutable and intriguing is the Melchizedek legend in 2 Enoch 71-72, whose date and provenance cannot even be approximated. "All attempts to locate the intellectual background of 2 Enoch have failed. The most remarkable token of continued puzzlement over this work is the failure of scholars to decide whether it came from Jewish or Christian circles. It hardly stands in the mainstream of either religion."[26] It appears, however, that "there was a sect which accepted the Enoch writings as sacred scripture in the highest sense, but who they might have been we cannot now discern."[27] To such people, Melchizedek was sacerdotal.[28] He was miraculously born to the wife of Noah's brother out of her corpse after she had died.[29] His sacred mission was to be sequestered in Paradise and preserved from the Flood, so that he could pass the priesthood on to postdiluvian peoples, becoming "the priest to all holy priests, the head of the priests of the future, and the head of the thirteen priests who existed before."[30] He will be sanctified and changed "into a great people who will sanctify [God],"[31] serving as "the head of priests reigning over a royal people who serve you, O Lord."[32] "Afterward there will be a planting from his tribe, and there will be other people, and there will be another Melkisedek, the head of priests reigning over the people, and performing the liturgy for the Lord."[33] Ultimately for the people who used this text, this Melchizedek prefigured another, who was expected to perform greater miracles than ever before: "In the last generation, there would be another Melkisedek, the first of 12 priests. And the last will be the head of all, a great archpriest, the Word and Power of God."[34]

For the community at Qumran, whose writings in the first century B.C. are largely concerned with apocalyptic events, Melchizedek took on significance as a heavenly warlord. He will wage the last war against evil to free the spirits held captive by Belial and to "restore their captives to them and will proclaim release to them, to set them free and . . . atone . . . in the year of the last jubilee . . . for all the sons of light and men of the lot of Melchizedek."[35] This interpretation is dependent upon Genesis, where Melchizedek was involved in setting free the captives and disposing of the spoils of Abraham's war. Yet the adaptation of this material to an apocalyptic setting is innovative. Melchizedek was also expected by the people at Qumran to "exact the vengeance of the judgments of God [El] . . . with the help of all the eternal gods [*ēlē ʿōlām*],"[36] and by means of some heady textual substitutions he was identified with the royal being (*elohim*) who takes his stand in the solemn assembly of the highest god (*El*).[37] Thus, in this picture of the end of times, Melchizedek serves both priestly and kingly functions, not in an earthly sense but by driving away the wicked and bringing the righteous into their inheritance by his atonement while standing at the side of the magistrate to execute his commands and wage his battles.

For Philo, whose philosophical system intellectualized most of sacred history, Melchizedek was seen as a particular manifestation of the unseen powers of the realm of pure thought. "He is a priestly manifestation of reason (*hiereus logos*) whose possession is reality, for around him circulate high, illustrious and timely thoughts."[38] Like all divine (philosophical) creations for Philo, Melchizedek was created by God with a royal nature "before a single deed of Melchizedek had been performed."[39] He was the king of intellectuality (*basileus nous*) whose peaceful persuasion brought the souls of men into the knowledge of Neoplatonic reality.[40] Interestingly, Philo also latched onto the idea that because Melchizedek was not a product of the patriarchal traditions he, like the philosopher, must have been without teacher, self-taught (*autodidakton*), and intuitively perceptive (*automathē*), making his thoughts products of higher spheres.[41]

Roughly contemporary with the Qumran writings and Philo is the New Testament interpretation of Melchizedek. The author of the epistle to the Hebrews saw in Melchizedek a prototype of Jesus—one without father, without mother, without genealogy, "*having neither beginning of days, nor end of life*; but made *like* unto the Son of God" (Hebrews 7:3).[42] Hebrews 7, arguing on four grounds for the superiority of Jesus the eternal High Priest over the

Levitical priests, uses Melchizedek to substantiate this point. Not all of the arguments are strictly logical. First, the argument runs, because Abraham paid tithes to Melchizedek, Levi (who was then in the loins of Abraham) was less than Melchizedek, because Melchizedek must have been greater than Abraham since the greater allegedly always blesses the lesser (Hebrews 7:4-10). Second, Psalm 110 indicates that a priest *in Judah* must arise "after the similitude of Melchizedek," a priest *forever*, "not after the law of a carnal commandment, but after the power of an endless life" (Hebrews 7:11-19). The psalm itself, however, does not literally make such a prophecy. Third, it is argued that to the Levites no oath was given that their priesthood should remain for ever; but Jesus, like Melchizedek, makes a "surety of a better testament," for the Lord has sworn an oath to this type of being in saying, "Thou art a priest for ever" (Hebrews 7:20-22). This argument presupposes a "likeness" between Jesus and Melchizedek and in order to make this point bends the phrase "after the *order* (*kata tēn taxin*) of Melchizedek" to read "after the *similitude* (*kata tēn homoioteta*) to Melchizedek" (Hebrews 7:15). Fourth, Levitical priests all die and so do their sacrifices, which must be constantly renewed for the benefit of themselves, as well as for the benefit of the people; but in Jesus' case this is not so, for he lives eternally to make intercession for those who come to God by him (Hebrews 7:23-28).[43] Without diminishing the greatness of Melchizedek, it seems that these polemic arguments are somewhat tendentious and not rationally compelling.

In the ensuing centuries, Christian Fathers expanded the typology initiated in Hebrews 7 in a manner which reflected the later Christian liturgy and doctrine. Practically every Father comments on the formulaic ways in which Melchizedek can be said to have foreshadowed Christ: Both Jesus and Melchizedek were seen as kings of justice and of peace (*salem, shalom*).[44] Both were seen as true, non-

Levitical priests.[45] Melchizedek had no biblical genealogy, while Christ was said to be without father in his human generation and without mother in his divine generation.[46] Melchizedek was perceived as being without beginning of days, without natural beginning, just as Christ existed *in principio* ("in the beginning") and will exist forever.[47] Both lived by faith, as Melchizedek was said to have obtained his knowledge of the sacrament of bread and wine by revelation and not by the letter of law;[48] and both offered a sacrifice of bread and wine instead of an animal sacrifice.[49] In many ways, particularly in relationship to the symbols of the eucharist, Melchizedek was simply seen by these Fathers as a Christian before his time.

For the Gnostics, Melchizedek became a subject for even wider speculation, although it is difficult to reconstruct their ideas with confidence. In the spiritual cosmology of certain Gnostics, the "order (*taxis*) of Melchizedek" is the ordering arrangement of the cosmos.[50] He is the great repossessor, purifier, and preparer of the elements of the universe.[51] He himself is the power of the true mystical universe.[52] His powers make men mystics, revealing to them the all.[53] He is the archon of righteousness, of whom Christ is a shadow.[54] Under the name Zorokothora in the Pistis Sophia, he is the Great Receiver of Light who comes mysteriously from the pure light of the fifth tree, but he only appears periodically when his constellation or number comes up.[55] When he is gone, darkness prevails; as he returns, light is victorious.[56] "In the place of those of the right hand," he seals souls to be taken to the Treasury of Light.[57] Melchizedek worship probably reached its zenith in the Gnostic Melchizedekian sect of the third century A.D. To them, Christ himself was subordinate to Melchizedek, for Christ had been said to be of *his* order.[58] They even went so far as to claim that because Melchizedek had no father, he was the father of all, including the father of Jesus.[59] He was also called the virtue or strength of God (*virtutem dei*),[60] an angel with supernatural powers,[61] the Holy Ghost,[62] and sometimes he was given an independent place in the Godhead.[63]

The Jewish rabbinical response to the Christian, Essene, Gnostic, and philosophical aggrandizement of Melchizedek was predictable: Where the challengers of Judaism elevated Melchizedek, the rabbis debased him. Where the innovators cultivated the mysterious or esoteric intrigue of Melchizedek's supernatural powers and origins, the Jewish apologists invented down-to-earth explanations to defuse such doctrines.[64] The basic Jewish attitude, not yet reacting to the Christian, can be observed in Josephus, who simply viewed Melchizedek as a righteous Canaanite, a paragon of hospitality, who gave Jerusalem a noble beginning (as Aeneas had done for Rome).[65] But soon after the time of Josephus, when the Christian challenge to Judaism had become more intense, the focus of rabbinic writing on Melchizedek shifted from his goodness and sought to explain him away. By writing the name as two words, *malkî ṣedeq*, and identifying *ṣedeq* (righteousness) with the city of Jerusalem itself, the *Midrash Rabbah* could speak simply of the "king (*malkî*) of Jerusalem (*ṣedeq*)" and thereby removed the proper name "Melchizedek" from the picture of Genesis 14.[66] In time, the Jewish response to the Christian challenges grew quite pointed. Where the Christians argued against the need to be circumcised on the ground that Abraham had paid tithes to the uncircumcised Melchizedek,[67] the Jews asserted that Melchizedek had been born circumcised.[68] Where it was argued that Melchizedek had a superior priesthood, the Jews retorted that he had lost his powers, which passed to Abraham, when Melchizedek blundered by blessing Abraham before recognizing God.[69] Where it was asserted that the offering of bread and wine foreshadowed the Christian eucharist, the Jews either dismissed this as a mere act of hospitality,[70] or responded in kind, claiming that Melchizedek was instructing Abraham in the shewbread and ritual libations of the Torah.[71] The absence of genealogy was cured by giving him a genealogy—and not always a flattering one. The easiest solution was to call him Shem,[72] but other theories about his parentage, usually attributed to the Jews, also claimed that he was a descendant of Sidon,[73] or of Sidus an Egyptian,[74] Heraklas,[75] Melchi or Malakh,[76] Ham,[77] or a heathen named Melchi.[78] His mother was Astaroth, Astoriane, or Saltiel, or alternatively some argued that his genealogy was not mentioned because he was the son of a prostitute.[79]

And so we have run the gamut. Melchizedek is treated both favorably and unfavorably in these texts. This is a world of diverse theological contrasts.[80] From this brief sampling of the literature, it is clear that people have said of Melchizedek primarily what their theologies required. Whether a text treats him historically, politically, sacerdotally, apocalyptically, philosophically, polemically, typologically, cosmologically, or defensively, the orientation is dictated by the theological framework within which each interpretation of the basic Old Testament texts was made. Such interpretations tend to reveal far more about the interpreters than they do about Melchizedek.

JST, Genesis 14:17-40

Another text that sheds light on Alma 13:13-19 is found in the Joseph Smith Translation of Genesis 14. It reads as follows:

The Meeting:

And the king of Sodom went out to meet him [Abraham] after his return from the slaughter of Chedorlaomer, and of the kings that were with him, at the valley of Shaveh, which is the king's dale (JST, Genesis 14:17).

Melchizedek's Appearance:

And Melchizedek king of Salem brought forth bread and wine: and he brake bread and blest it; and he blest the wine, he being the priest of the most high God (JST, Genesis 14:18).

Melchizedek's First Blessing:

And he blessed him, and said: Blessed be Abram of the most high God, possessor of heaven and earth: And blessed be the most high God, which hath delivered thine enemies into thy hand (JST, Genesis 14:19-20).

The Payment of Tithes:

And he gave him tithes of all (JST, Genesis 14:20).

Division of the Spoils:

And the king of Sodom said unto Abram, Give me the persons, and take the goods to thyself. And Abram said to the king of Sodom, I have lifted up mine hand unto the Lord, the most high God, the possessor of heaven and earth, That I will not take from a thread even to a shoelatchet, and that I will not take any thing that is thine, lest thou shouldest say, I have made Abram rich: [I will take] only that which the young men have eaten, and the portion of the men which went with me, Aner, Eshcol, and Mamre; let them take their portion (JST, Genesis 14:21-24).

Melchizedek's Second Blessing:

And Melchizedek lifted up his voice and blessed Abram (JST, Genesis 14:25).

How Melchizedek Obtained His Priesthood:

Now Melchizedek was a man of faith, who wrought righteousness; and when a child he feared God, and stopped the mouths of lions, and quenched the violence of fire. And thus, having been approved of God, he was ordained an high priest after the order of the covenant which God made with Enoch, It being after the order of the Son of God; which order came, not by man, nor the will of man; neither by father nor mother; neither by beginning of days nor end of years; but of God; And it was delivered unto men by the calling of his own voice, according to his own will, unto as many as believed on his name (JST, Genesis 14:26-29).

The Powers of This Order:
For God having sworn unto Enoch and unto his seed with an oath by himself; that every one being ordained after this order and calling should have power, by faith, to break mountains, to divide the seas, to dry up waters, to turn them out of their course; To put at defiance the armies of nations, to divide the earth, to break every band, to stand in the presence of God; to do all things according to his will, according to his command, subdue principalities and powers; and this by the will of the Son of God which was from before the foundation of the world. And men having this faith, coming up unto this order of God, were translated and taken up into heaven (JST, Genesis 14:30-32).

Melchizedek's Use of These Powers:
And now, Melchizedek was a priest of this order; therefore he obtained peace in Salem, and was called the Prince of peace. And his people wrought righteousness, and obtained heaven, and sought for the city of Enoch which God had before taken, separating it from the earth, having reserved it unto the latter days, or the end of the world; And hath said, and sworn with an oath, that the heavens and the earth should come together; and the sons of God should be tried so as by fire. And this Melchizedek, having thus established righteousness, was called the king of heaven by his people, or, in other words, the King of peace (JST, Genesis 14:33-36).

Melchizedek's Third Blessing:
And he lifted up his voice, and he blessed Abram (JST, Genesis 14:37).

Melchizedek, Keeper of the Storehouse for the Poor:
Being the high priest, and the keeper of the storehouse of God; Him whom God had appointed to receive

tithes for the poor. Wherefore, Abram paid unto him tithes of all that he had, of all the riches which he possessed, which God had given him more than that which he had need (JST, Genesis 14:37-39).

God Fulfills Melchizedek's Blessings:

And it came to pass, that God blessed Abram, and gave unto him riches, and honor, and lands for an everlasting possession; according to the covenant which he had made, and according to the blessing wherewith Melchizedek had blessed him (JST, Genesis 14:40).

This text supplies much information about Melchizedek. Some of its details are interestingly consistent with points reflected in other Jewish and Christian texts discussed above. For example, in the JST, Melchizedek's bread and wine is evidently seen as a form of sacrament (JST, Genesis 14:18), and, somewhat like the remarkable paragraphs in 2 *Enoch* 71-72, the JST reports miraculous events associated with Melchizedek's childhood (stopping the mouths of lions and quenching the violence of fire), leading to his receipt of the priesthood and being translated into heaven, to guide an especially righteous group of followers. Certain aspects of the JST account are also echoed in Alma's text. Thus, both report Melchizedek as a man of extraordinary faith, a worker of righteousness among his people, called and ordained a high priest after the order of the Son of God (JST, Genesis 14:27-30; Alma 13:2-10, 18). Alma, however, indicates no awareness of the idea that such people were translated to heaven, that the order of Melchizedek was pertinent to the covenant made by God with Enoch, that an oath was connected with this priesthood (Genesis 14:30, 35), that Melchizedek was called the king of heaven by his people (JST, Genesis 14:36), or several other such details.

Nevertheless, although one cannot say for certain, several key factors would point toward the conclusion that

Alma's version of Genesis 14 on the plates of brass was similar to the text in the Joseph Smith Translation of the Bible.

Synthesis and Conclusion

Having set the stage, we are now prepared to examine more specifically Alma's use of his Melchizedek sources. As the following eight points show, Alma works the Melchizedek material into his sermon with great perceptiveness.

First, in Genesis, Melchizedek is called a priest of the most high God (*El Elyon*). For Alma, however, he is a *high priest* after the order of the Son of God (Alma 13:14). This is rather singular. Besides the book of Alma and the JST, no other text calls him a high priest (although 2 *Enoch* 71:29 calls him "the priest to all holy priests"). Perhaps the word "high" (*ᶜelyon*) has shifted position in the texts between "high God" and "high priest." The word *ᶜelyon* generally means exalted, or comparatively high. It is a quite distinctive word, most often used to describe the Lord as the Most High God (e.g., Numbers 24:16; Deuteronomy 32:8; 2 Samuel 22:14; Isaiah 14:14; and repeatedly in the Psalms); but sacred things and people can also be called *ᶜelyon*: The temple is called *ᶜelyon* by the Lord (1 Kings 9:8), and his peculiar people are likewise said to be exalted and blessed because of the covenant: "Thy God will set thee on high (*ᶜelyon*) above all nations" (Deuteronomy 28:1), "to make thee high (*ᶜelyon*) above all" (Deuteronomy 26:18-19; cf. 1 Peter 2:9, "a royal priesthood, a peculiar people"). Thus, the term "high priest" in Alma's text is particularly apt and meaningful in describing priests who receive the ordination of which he speaks. Nevertheless, one should also observe that Alma in no way polemicizes against the Levitical priesthood, as does the author of Hebrews. Rather, Melchizedek stands as a precedent for a priesthood composed of all the righteous who receive the ordinances through their faith and good works. Moreover, besides distinguishing Alma's priests favorably from the high (gā-dôl) priest and other priests of the hereditary priesthood at Jerusalem, to which the Nephites (like the Maccabeans) had no claim, Alma's application of the word "high" to these priests "after the order of [God's] Son," rather than to God, may reflect the Nephite understanding that their Lord was not the highest God, but a son of God (e.g., Alma 36:17), who in turn does the will of the Father.

Second, Melchizedek was associated in Alma's mind with the idea of "priests forever after the order of the Son." He could have found such words in Psalm 110, containing the words "priest forever" and the cryptic remark about an "order" or "pact" (cf. Alma 13:14). In Alma 13:2 and 13:14, however, it is clear that this order is not Melchizedek's order (as it is at Qumran, in Psalm 110, in Hebrews 7, and among the Gnostics), but that of the son of God. In this regard, Alma's text is close to the Genesis account in the JST, where the order was "after the order of the covenant which God made with Enoch, it being after the order of the Son of God" (JST, Genesis 14:27-28). The "order" for Alma, however, in its primary sense was understood as a *manner of* ordination rather than an *order* of hierarchy or structured body of priesthood bearers. This would suggest that the phrase ʿal dibrātî could best be understood modally,[81] yielding the sense of "a priest *ordained like* Melchizedek was," i.e., in that manner which looks forward to the Son for redemption (Alma 13:2). Being a priest after the order of Melchizedek ultimately refers to obtaining such ordinances (Alma 13:9), something that only Alma makes explicit.

In an additional sense, however, Alma also uses the term "order" to refer to a specific commission to preach repentance (Alma 5:49) and to teach certain commandments leading into God's rest (Alma 13:6). Indeed, one of the great messages of Melchizedek for Alma (and he is the only commentator to draw such a conclusion) was the success of Melchizedek as a teacher of righteousness. For Alma, such teaching was the paramount responsibility and calling of the priesthood (Alma 5:49; cf. Mosiah 6:3). Little significance appears to be ascribed by Alma to the bureaucratic, authoritarian, official, or sacrificial powers or functions of the priesthood.

Third, the Book of Mormon text portrays Abraham paying tithes to Melchizedek, but unlike other ancient texts in which this tithe is either taken to establish the right of some priestly class to collect revenues or in which it is seen as a religious contribution, a disbursement, or a hospitable gift of the spoils of war,[82] it appears that for Alma the tithe of Abraham illustrates the injunction, "Bring forth fruit meet for repentance" (Alma 13:13), which is a condition for receiving the priesthood ordinances. For Alma, the tithe of Abraham is not just on the spoils of war (as it is in Hebrews and many other texts), but is full and complete, on *all he possessed*, just as the required repentance would have to be total and complete. This interpretation of Genesis 14:20 commends itself in light of the fact that Abraham renounced all interest in the spoils; he would have had no reason to pay a tithe on property in which he claimed no interest, as would be the case if he only tithed on the spoils. It is also consistent with JST, Genesis 14:39: "Abram paid unto him tithes of all that he had, of all the riches which he possessed, which God had given him more than that which he had need," to care for the poor.

Fourth, in the early Christian writings Melchizedek typifies Christ,[83] but in Alma the typology is not found in Melchizedek, his name, his station, or his actions, but in the manner of the priesthood's ordinance, "*it* being a type of God's order" (Alma 13:16). The most prominent touchstone of the Christian typology (the offering of bread and wine) is therefore not used by Alma, although it may stand behind part of Alma's manner of looking forward to the Son of God for redemption.

Fifth, Melchizedek, king of Salem and priest of the most high God, is understood in most traditions primarily in his role as a priest, not as a king.[84] This is carried so far that he is most often depicted by medieval artists in priestly vestments officiating at an altar under a canopy. But in the Book of Mormon, the image of Melchizedek is equally that of a royal leader and a priest: a king who establishes peace in the land among his people through righteousness (Alma 13:17-18). The fascinating account in 2 Enoch 71 comes close to Alma in this regard, reporting that God would change Melchizedek "into a great people who will sanctify [him]" and make him "the head of priests reigning over a royal people."[85] Likewise the JST reports that Melchizedek ruled over his people as a priest and king of heaven and of peace, with power to "subdue principalities" and "to put at defiance the armies of nations" (JST, Genesis 14:31), although in both of these cases the emphasis is more on Melchizedek's role as priest than king. Alma's dual understanding of Melchizedek as king and priest is consistent with local Nephite politics, since the Nephite ruler (i.e., king or chief judge prior to Alma's day) shouldered the highest responsibilities for both church and state.[86]

Sixth, most commentators have been content to speculate about the sources of Melchizedek's knowledge of the priesthood. Some suggest that he received it from Noah, Abraham, the Patriarchs, angels, or philosophical reflection, as well as from a number of fictitious individuals. One tradition holds that he acquired his priesthood from Noah when he was bitten and defiled by a lion as he was disembarking from the ark.[87] It is rare, however, for writers to dwell on how such knowledge is acquired. In Philo's thought, the contemplative man was typified by Melchizedek, but even there he does not become actively involved in any religious process. Alma gives the most information of any text, including the JST, about how such knowledge is acquired from God (Alma 12:29): through the mysteries (Alma 12:9-10), calling upon God's name (Alma 12:30), obedience (Alma 12:32), and after exercising mighty faith, humility, charity, and repentance (Alma 13:14-15, 18).

Seventh, Melchizedek's genealogy or lack thereof raises questions practically everywhere. Nothing in Alma 13, however, hints at the churning conflict which divided the Old World over the question of his birth. There is no inclination toward the later hypothesis that Melchizedek was Shem, and there is no reference to the phrase first found in Hebrews 7:3, "without father, without mother, without descent." In Alma's text, only God and the priesthood order are called eternal: "This high priesthood . . . without beginning of days and end of years" (Alma 13:7; cf. also JST, Hebrews 7:1); "the Only Begotten of the Father, who is without beginning of days or end of years" (Alma 13:9). Alma's perspective here runs parallel to an extent with that of the JST: "Which order came, not by man, nor the will of man; neither by father nor mother; neither by beginning of days nor end of years; but of God" (JST, Genesis 14:28). But if Alma's statement, "and he did reign under his father" (Alma 13:18), refers to a political reign under his mortal father (rather than to a spiritual reign under God) or to a combination of the two (as King Benjamin described his own reign in Mosiah 2:31), we have here a singular and significant reference to Melchizedek's royal parentage and vassalage.

Eighth, perhaps because of the Nephite conviction of the wickedness of Jerusalem (1 Nephi 7:13-14), Alma also makes no attempt to equate Salem with Jerusalem. Indeed, for Alma, Melchizedek was not the king of a city, but of a land of Salem. Alma also feels no need for pendantry over etymologies either regarding the name Salem or the name Melchizedek.

In conclusion, the Melchizedek text of Alma 13 is quite

remarkable. It reveals a profound understanding of Melchizedek. The text is unique and complex, yet internally
coherent and concise. Alma has a clear concept of what
Melchizedek means to him and he relates that meaning
powerfully to the message of his sermon.

Alma's text bears the hallmarks of an early record. In
my opinion, Alma's use of the Melchizedek material from
Genesis is conceptually and textually superior to later interpretations in which the meaning of Melchizedek turns
upon ideological notions and etymological devices. Alma
13:13-19 conveys far more than the usual historical or etiol-
ogical interpretations of the puzzling Genesis account; it
is conceptually prior to the polarization of Jewish and
Christian thought, and it is free from the apocalyptic, philosophical, and metaphysical tendencies that have molded
much of Western thought since Hellenistic times. For
Alma, Melchizedek is not a transcendent or intuitive being,
but an example of the fact that all men can receive the
same knowledge and authority that made Melchizedek
great. He is not a priest who will conduct some cosmic
atonement for man's benefit, but was the teacher of a sacred course that showed men how to benefit from the
atonement of Christ and the manner in which they should
look forward to redemption (Alma 13:2). He is not the
extension of a preexistent form of royal or priestly *logos*,
but he epitomizes a practical realization of each individual's
preexistent potential which was prepared from the foundation of the world (Alma 13:3). He does not typify or
epitomize any other reality.

Alma 13:13-19 also bears characteristics of dependence
on earlier sources. While one can see how Alma may have
derived its key words and phrases from the traditional Old
Testament materials, it appears that his sources were closer
in content to the Genesis text in the JST than to the cryptic
statements in the King James Version.

Moreover, this material was relevant to Alma's own

day and age. His text is integrally bound up with Nephite sacred ritual and practical religion. In addition, many aspects of the traditional Genesis material and the wordings of Psalm 110 harmonize with Nephite religion and politics in Alma's day, for example, in placing emphasis on a joint office of a righteous priest and king under his father, in being silent on the victorious military context of Abraham's encounter with Melchizedek, and in supporting the non-hereditary posture of the Nephite priesthood.

There is no dearth of commentators who have suspected the significance of Melchizedek, but none offers the insights of Alma 13. This chapter of the Book of Mormon is among the best regarding Melchizedek.

Notes

1. Thorough bibliographies of the sources are accumulated by Gottfried Wuttke, *Melchisedech der Priesterkönig von Salem*, Beiheft zur Zeitschrift für die neutestamentliche Wissenschaft und Kund der älteren Kirche, 5 (Giessen: Topelmann, 1927), and Paul J. Kobelski, *Melchizedek and Melchiresha*, Catholic Biblical Quarterly Monograph Series, 10 (Washington: Catholic Biblical Assocation of America, 1981). See also Gerald T. Kennedy, *St. Paul's Conception of the Priesthood of Melchisedech* (Washington: Catholic University of America Press, 1951); and Fred L. Horton, *Melchizedek Tradition through the First Five Centuries C.E.*, SNTSMS 30 (Cambridge: Cambridge University Press, 1976).

2. This is as one would expect, given the accompanying "strict command" of secrecy (Alma 12:9). Although little is known of the Nephite mysteries, it seems clear that they had certain sacred teachings that were not discussed publicly.

3. Was the "calling" a new name, a job assignment, or a ritualistic summons? Mosiah 5:10-12 supports the idea that they were called by a new name in Christ. In Alma's text, however, the people are not only called *with* that holy calling (Alma 13:3) and *by* it (Alma 13:6), but also *to* the calling (Alma 13:4), which would seem to make the calling more like a post or office rather than a new appellation. The ambiguity may be intentional, however, since the important thing is being able to recognize the voice of the Lord when he calls, and that is learned only by serving him (Mosiah 5:12-14); cf. JST,

Genesis 14:29, "it was delivered unto men by the calling of his own voice, according to his will."

4. See generally, Paul Winter, "Note on Salem-Jerusalem," *Novum Testamentum* 2 (1957): 151-52; William F. Albright, "Abram the Hebrew: A New Archaeological Interpretation," *Bulletin of the American School of Oriental Research* 163 (1961): 36-54; Loren R. Fischer, "Abraham and His Priest-King," *Journal of Biblical Literature* 81 (1962): 264-70; Robert H. Smith, "Abraham and Melchizedek," *Zeitschrift für die alttestamentliche Wissenschaft* 77 (1965): 129-53. Discoveries at Ebla seem to confirm the general historicity of materials in Genesis 14.

5. See Joseph A. Fitzmyer, " 'Now this Melchizedek . . . ' (Heb 7,1)," *Catholic Biblical Quarterly* 25 (1963): 305-21. Cf. Adonizedek, the name of an early king of Jerusalem mentioned in Joshua 10:1-3. That name would mean "Ṣedeq [Righteous] is my lord." *Ammi-Ṣeduqa* was the Amorite name of a Babylonian king in the sixteenth century B.C.; ibid., 312.

6. *Ṣedeq* is known to have been the name of a Canaanite deity at Mari, Ugarit, and in South Arabia. Compound names incorporating the name of a god were not uncommon; witness Adonizedek in Joshua 10:1-3; Malchiel (El is my King) in Genesis 46:17; Malchiah (Yahweh is my king) in Ezra 10:31 and Jeremiah 38:6. This is thought to suggest that Canaanite kings had priestly functions and that *Ṣedeq* was part of a local cult. John Gray, *History of Jerusalem* (New York: Prager, 1969), 67.

7. This view is represented as early as the second century of the Christian Era in Targum Neofiti. A. Dies Macho, *Neophyti I: Targum Palestinense I: Genesis* (Madrid: Confejo Superior de investigaciones cientificas, 1969).

8. This has been suggested by H. E. del Medico, "Melchisedech," *Zeitschrift für die alttestamentliche Wissenschaft* 69 (1957): 160-70, since "upright king" and "peaceful king" are epithets of the king of Sodom, mentioned in the previous verse.

9. Albright, "Abram the Hebrew," 52.

10. The Jews, naturally, have preferred the equation of Salem with Jerusalem. See Psalm 75:3; Josephus, *Antiquities* I, 10, 2 (Solyma is later called Jerusalem); Genesis Apocryphon 22:13 ("Salem, that is Jerusalem"). But W. F. Albright is among those who resist the geographical identity between Salem and Jerusalem, in "Abram the Hebrew," 52.

11. To the Christians, seeing a foreshadowing of the sacrament was irresistible here. The Jews figured this constituted instruction

in the laws of the priesthood by alluding to shewbread and libations. H. Freedman and Maurice Simon, trs., *Midrash Rabbah*, 10 vols. (London: Soncino, 1961), 1:356. It has been argued, however, that wine was not used for libations during the time of Abraham. Edward Busse, *Der Wein im Kult des alten Testaments* (Freiburger Theologische Studien 29).

12. The Hebrew text is wholly ambiguous here. Alfred Jeremias, *Old Testament in the Light of the Ancient East* (London: Williams, 1911), 1:29, states that Melchizedek paid tithing to Abraham.

13. A tithe was a political tax often taken as tribute in antiquity; see, e.g., Herodotus, *Historia* II, 135; IV, 152.

14. Is it Yahweh, as in Genesis 14:22, or was Yahweh added there by gloss, since it is absent in the Septuagint, Peshitta, and Genesis Apocryphon? Or are these Canaanite deities? Cf. Numbers 24:16; Isaiah 14:14; Daniel 3:26; see G. Della Vida, "El Elyon in Genesis 14:18-20," *Journal of Biblical Literature* 63 (1944): 2.

15. In addition, some rabbinic speculation on the Song of Songs involves Melchizedek as one of the four craftsmen of Zechariah 2:3. TB *Sukkah* 52b lists the four as: Messiah ben David, Messiah ben Joseph, Elijah, and the priest of Righteousness (*Kohen Sedeq*).

16. Psalm 110 is a royal psalm in which a Davidic king is addressed as a hero and probably associated with the past as a successor of Melchizedek. J. W. Bowker, "Psalm CX," *Vetus Testamentum* 17 (1967): 31-41. Alexander F. Kirkpatrick, *The Book of Psalms* (Cambridge: Cambridge University Press, 1910), 663.

17. Mitchell Dahood, *Psalms*, 3 vols. (Garden City: Doubleday, 1966), 3:117.

18. Ibid.

19. The problems involved in using *taxis* to translate the semitic concepts here are shown by T. Nöldeke, "Taxis im Semitischen," *Zeitschrift für Assyriologie* 23 (1909): 145-49.

20. For a discussion of these translations, see Fitzmyer, "Now This Melchizedek," 305-21.

21. Ibid., 308.

22. The idea, for example, that Melchizedek was Shem has been found in Church literature since John Taylor qualifiedly volunteered it in *Times and Seasons* 5 (December 15, 1844): 745-46, as "not allowing it to be revelation but history." That history, however, is suspect, and some Church writers have prudently declined to follow it. See John A. Widtsoe, *Evidences and Reconciliations*, ed. G. Homer Durham (Salt Lake City: Bookcraft, 1960), 232; Charles E. Haggerty, "Melchizedek . . . King of Salem," *Improvement Era* 55 (1952): 512. Bruce

R. McConkie, *Mormon Doctrine* (Salt Lake City: Bookcraft, 1960) refers to the idea that Shem was Melchizedek as an unconfirmed
Hebrew tradition. But others have gone to extraordinary lengths to
preserve that connection, see Hyrum Andrus, *Principles of Perfection*
(Salt Lake City: Bookcraft, 1970), 422, even in the face of D&C 84:14:
"Abraham received the priesthood from Melchizedek, who received
it through the lineage of his fathers, even till Noah." For a more
tentative approach, see Alma E. Gygi, "Is It Possible That Shem
and Melchizedek Are the Same Person?" *Ensign* 3 (November 1973):
15-16. D&C 138:41 only speaks of Shem as "the great high priest."
The Joseph Smith Translation of the Bible, while silent on any connection between Melchizedek and Shem, adds many other relevant
details to the Genesis account, mentioned further below. For other
information about the power of the Melchizedek priesthood as "the
power of 'endless lives,' " and about Melchizedek giving the priesthood to Abraham, see *TPJS*, 322-23.

    23. *Jubilees* 13:25-29; 32:1. R. H. Charles, *The Book of Jubilees* (Ox-
ford: Oxford University Press, 1976), dates this work around 110
B.C. Unfortunately, however, *Jubilees* 13 has a lacuna in the text
where Melchizedek was probably mentioned, and *Jubilees* 32:1 contains only an allusion to Melchizedek in the expression "priest of
the most high God."

    24. This title is used consistently by Maccabees and elsewhere
to describe them; see 1 Maccabees 14:41; Josephus, *Antiquities* XVI,
6, 2; *Assumption of Moses* 6:1; *Testament of Levi* 8:14-15. The *Testament
of Levi* does not refer to Melchizedek by name, but in a passage
which appears to be free from interpolation, the *Testament* speaks
of a new priesthood called by a new name to be established after
the fashion of the Gentiles. The priesthood of Levi, however, remains the greatest of the three mentioned. *Testament of Levi* 8:13.

    25. *Jubilees* 13:25-27. Note that where *Jubilees* has the *law* of tithing
being without limit of days, and where Hebrews 7:3 has Melchizedek's *genealogy* without beginning of days or end of years, Alma
13:7 denotes the high *order* as being without temporal bounds or,
in other words, arising from the foundation of the world.

    26. *OTP* 1:95.

    27. Ibid., 1:97.

    28. Compare, in several respects, JST, Genesis 14:26-36.

    29. *OTP* 1:206-7; see also A. Vaillant, *Le Livre des Secrets d'Henoch*
(Paris: Institut D'Etudes Slaves, 1952), 77; Rubenstein, "Observation
on the Slavonic Book of Enoch," *Journal of Theological Studies* 13 (1962):
1-21.

30. *2 Enoch* 71:29, 33, in *OTP* 1:208.

31. *2 Enoch* 71:29, in *OTP* 1:209.

32. *2 Enoch* 71:37, in *OTP* 1:211.

33. *2 Enoch* 71:37, in *OTP* 1:209-10.

34. *2 Enoch* 71:33-34, in *OTP* 1:208.

35. *11QMelch* 6-8. See Joseph A. Fitzmyer, "Further Light on Melchizedek from Qumran Cave 11," *Journal of Biblical Literature* 86 (1967): 25-41; J. T. Milik, "Milki-sedeq et Milkiresa dans les anciens escrits juifs et chretiens," *Journal of Theological Studies* 23 (1972): 95-144; James A. Sanders, "The Old Testament in 11Q Melchizedek," *Journal of Near Eastern Studies* 5 (1973): 373-82; Paul J. Kobelski, *Melchizedek and Melchiresha*, Catholic Biblical Quarterly Monograph Series, Number 10 (Washington: Catholic Biblical Assocation of America, 1981).

36. *11QMelch* 13-14.

37. *11QMelch* 15-21 is apparently commenting on Psalm 82:1 and also Isaiah 52:7. The latter was also a cryptic passage to Nephites; see Mosiah 12:20-21.

38. Philo, *Allegorical Interpretation of Genesis II*, III, 82.

39. Ibid., III, 79.

40. Ibid., III, 80-81. See also, Philo, *On Abraham* 235.

41. Philo, *On the Preliminary Studies* 99. For Philo, the adjectives *automathe* and *autodidakton* are attributes of wisdom (*sophia*) and the wise man, and mean that he has not been improved by investigation, drill, and labor, but from his birth he has discovered ready-prepared *sophia* from above showered down from heaven.

42. See generally V. Hamp, "Melchisedek als Typus," *Pro Mundi Vita: Festschrift zum eucharistischen Weltkongress* (Munich, 1960); J. Derambure, "Melchisedech, Type due Messi," *Revue Augustinienne* 12 (1908): 37-62.

43. Cf. *11QMelch* 6-9. The relationship between Hebrews and the writings at Qumran is the strongest on this point, with the exalted status of Melchizedek as eternal priest reflecting the christology of the Epistle to the Hebrews. See M. de Jonge and A. S. van der Woude, "11Q Melchizedek and the New Testament," *New Testament Studies* 12 (1965-66): 301-26.

44. Ambrose, *De Sacramentis* IV, 3, 10 and 12, in *PL* 16:457-58; John Chrysostom, *Homilia XII in Epistolam ad Hebraeos* 7, in *PG* 63:97; Clement of Alexandria, *Stromata* IV, 25, in *PG* 8:1369-71.

45. Athanasius, *De Titulis Psalmorum* CIX, 9, in *PG* 27:1145; see also Ambrose, *De Sacramentis* IV, 3, 10, in *PL* 16:457-58; Augustine, *De diversis Quaestionibus* I, 83, 2, in *PL* 40:49; Cyprian, *Epistolae* LXIII, 4, in *PL* 4:387-88; Isidore, *De Ecclesiasticis Officiis* I, 18, 1, in *PL* 83:754.

46. Alcuin, *Interrogationes et Responsiones in Genesin* 164, in *PL* 100:536; Ambrose, *De Mysteriis* VIII, 45-46, in *PL* 16:421; Bruno, *Expositio in Psalmos* 109, in *PL* 152:1227-28; John Chrysostom, *Homilia de Melchisedeco*, in *PG* 56:259-60; Gregorius Nazianzenus, *Oratorio* XXX, 21, in *PG* 36:132-33; Isidore, *Quaestiones in Vetus Testamentum in Genesin* XI, 4, in *PL* 83:239-40. Theodoret, *Interpretatio Epistolae ad Hebraeos* VII, 3, in *PG* 82:724-25.

47. Fulgentius, *Ad Trasimumdum Regem Vandalorum* II, 6, in *PL* 65:250-51; see also Jerome, *Epistola* 73, in *PL* 22:676-81; Eusebius, *Historia Ecclesiastica* I, 3, in *PG* 20:73-76; Leo the Great, *Sermo* V, 3, in *PL* 54:154; cf. Ambrose, *Hexaemeron* I, 3, 9, in *PL* 14:137-38 ("Deus est enim Melchisedech . . . qui est sine initio.")

48. Chrysostom, *Homilia de Melchisedeco* 3, in *PG* 56:260-62; cf. Ambrose, *Expositio in Lucam* III, 21, in *PL* 15:1680. Cf. JST, Genesis 14:18.

49. Arnobius, *Commentarii in Psalmas* 109, in *PL* 53:496; Bede, *Expositio in Lucae Evangelium* VI, 22, in *PL* 92:596; Bruno, *Expositio in Psalmos* 109, in *PL* 164:1127; Claudius of Turin, *In Hebraeos*, in *PL* 104:926; Isidore, *Allegoriae quaedem Sacrae Scripturae*, in *PL* 83:104; Leo the Great, *Sermo* V, 3, in *PL* 54:154.

50. Epiphanius, *Adversus Haereses* LV, 1, in *PG* 41:972-73.

51. *Pistis Sophia* I, 25-26. See Hugh W. Nibley, "Treasures in the Heavens, Some Early Christian Insights into the Organizing of the Worlds," in *Old Testament and Related Studies*, vol. 1, *Collected Works of Hugh Nibley* (Salt Lake City: Deseret Book and F.A.R.M.S., 1986), 182.

52. Epiphanius, *Adversus Haereses* LV, 1-3, in *PG* 41:972-77.

53. *Melchizedek*, in James M. Robinson, *The Nag Hammadi Library in English* (San Francisco: Harper & Row, 1977), 399-403. Cf. Isidorus of Pelus, *Epistolae* III, 152, in *PG* 78:844.

54. Epiphanius, *Adversus Haereses* LV, 4-5, in *PG* 41:980-81; Origen, *Contra Haereses* VII, 36, in *PG* 16:3343.

55. *Pistis Sophia* 360:13-361:4.

56. Ibid., 34:7-35:24.

57. Ibid., 324:20-325:1.

58. Epiphanius, *Adversus Haereses* LV, 4, in *PG* 41:980-81; Theodoret, *Haereticarum Fabularum Compendium* II, 6, in *PG* 83:392-93.

59. Ibid., LV, 9-13.

60. Pseudo-Augustine, *Quaestiones Veteres et Novi Testamenti* (Vienna: Souter, 1908), 268, question 109; Arnobius, *Praedestinatorum Haeresis* I, 34, in *PL* 53:598.

61. Jerome, *Epistolae* 73, in *PL* 22:681. Melchizedek also enters as

a candidate for being the archangel Michael in Jewish speculation. Such angelology is refuted by Ambrose, *De Fide* III, 11, in *PL* 16:632.

62. This was the reported opinion of Hierax in Epiphanius, *Adversus Haereses* LXVII, 3, in *PG* 42:172-84. See also Jerome, *Epistolae* LXXIII, 1, in *PL* 22:676-77. He is also associated with the baptism of fire in *2 Jeu* 45.

63. Hippolytus, *Refutatio* VII, 24.

64. Gerald T. Kennedy, *St. Paul's Conception of the Priesthood of Melchisedech* (Washington: Catholic University of American Press, 1951), 130, concludes: "The talmudic interpretation of the figure and role of the priest-king of Salem were often the result of wishful thinking or false conclusion from an erroneous apologetic designed to counteract the New Testament clarification of the person and function of Melchizedech."

65. Josephus, *Antiquities* I, 179-81; *Jewish Wars* VI, 438.

66. *Midrash Rabbah Genesis (Lekh Lekha)* 43:6, tr. Freedman and Simon (London: Soncino, 1961), 356. "Jerusalem is called Zedek (righteousness), as it is written, *Zedek* (righteousness) lodged in her (Isaiah 1:21)." The name is also written as two words in Psalm 110:4.

67. Justin Martyr, *Dialogue with Trypho* 19, in *PG* 6:516-17; Tertullian, *Adversus Judaeos* 3, in *PL* 2:640-44. One may quite confidently date the the formulation of the Jewish theories about Melchizedek by the fact that the Jewish arguments were still unknown to Justin in A.D. 165 and Tertullian in A.D. 220.

68. *Genesis Rabbah* 43:6, Jacob Neusner, ed., 3 vols. (Atlanta: Scholars, 1985), 3:119. Rabbi Isaac the Babylonian inferred from the title King of Salem (*Shalem*) that Melchizedek was born circumcised. *Midrash Rabbah Genesis (Lekh Lekha)* 43.

69. TB *Nedarim* 32b. Note that the Jewish explanation of *kata tēn taxin* (after the order of) Melchizedek is to paraphrase it as "according to the blundering utterance of Melchizedek," for thus Abraham became his successor in the priesthood.

70. R. Jizchak, *Bereshit Rabbah* 43 on Genesis 14:19 (third century A.D.).

71. *Midrash Rabbah Genesis (Lekh Lekha)* 43:6, tr. Freedman and Simon, 356, explicating Proverbs 9:5, "come, eat of my bread, and drink of my wine."

72. This is common, beginning with the second-century Targums Neophiti I, Targum Pseudo-Jonathan, Fragmententargum (but not Onqelos). It is assumed without question in most rabbinic writing. See *Bemidbar Rabbah* on Numbers 3:45, *Der Midrasch Bemidbar* (Leipzig, 1885); R. Jizchak, *Bereshit Rabbah* 43 on Genesis 14:19; *Sefer*

Eliahu Rabbah 25; Nachmanides, *Perush ha-Ramban ʿal ha-Torah* 14:18; *Wajikra Rabbah* 25 on Leviticus 19:23; *Pirke de Rabbi Eliezer* 27. The same tradition is reported in Christian writings after the fifth-century: Jerome, *Hebraicae Quaestiones in Genesim* 14, in *PL* 23:1010; Isidore, *De Ortu et Obitu Patrum* 10 in *PL* 83:132; Rupert, *Dialogus Inter Christianum et Judaeum* II, in *PL* 170:583; Jerome, *Epistola* 73, in *PL* 22:679.

73. Epiphanius, *Adversus Haereses* LXVII, 7, in *PG* 42:181.

74. John Malalas, *Chronographa* III, in *PG* 97:134.

75. Epiphanius, *Adversus Haereses* LV, 2, in *PG* 41:973.

76. Georgios Monachos, *Chronikon* I, 10, in *PG* 110:145-48. *The Book of the Cave of Treasures*, E. A. W. Budge, ed. (London, 1927), 152.

77. *Chronikon Paschale*, Dindorf, ed. (Bonn), 90, listed in Wuttke, *Melchisedech der Priesterkönig von Salem*, 48.

78. Athanasius (dubia), *Historia de Melchisedech*, in *PG* 28:525.

79. Eustathius of Antioch, *Nicephoros Cat*. I, 198 (*hyios pornes*), in Wuttke, *Melchisedech der Priesterkönig von Salem*, 48.

80. Numerous other accounts cast Melchizedek in even further roles. One depicts him as a guard over the treasure cave where the body of Adam was buried. He was "set apart all the days of his life. He shall not take a wife, he shall not shed blood, he shall not offer up the offerings of wild animals and feathered fowl; but he shall offer unto God bread and wine, for by these redemption shall be made for Adam and all his posterity. . . . He shall wear a garment of skin, he shall not shave his head, and he shall not cut his nails, but shall remain alone natural because he is the priest of God the most High." *Book of the Cave of Treasures*, Budge, ed., 105-6. There is also a legend that Melchizedek fell asleep in a cave along with Ham and Japheth and awoke at the time of the nativity of Christ to travel to Bethlehem as one of the Magi. Sabine Baring-Gould, *Legends of the Patriarchs and Prophets and Other Old Testament Characters* (New York: Alden, 1885), 141.

81. Cf. Fitzmyer, "Now This Melchizedek," 308-9. See text accompanying nn. 17-21 above.

82. See, for example, Josephus, *Antiquities* I, 181; Hebrews 7:4; *Genesis Apocryphon* 22:12-20.

83. This extends to more recent religious writings as well. See John Lewis, *Melchizedech's Antitype* (London: Okes & Whitakers, 1624); George C. Currie, "Melchisedec," *Virginia Seminary Magazine* (July 1892), in the Duke University Collected Monographs, vol. 288. Luther, however, rejected the typology in his "Predigt über Genesis

14" (1527), in *Martin Luthers Werke: Kritische Gesammtausgabe* (Weiner: Hermann Böhlaus, 1900), 24:277-86; see also *Martin Luthers sämtliche Schriften*, J. Walch, ed. (Gross Oesingen: Lutherische Buchhandlung, 1987), 5:1021, 19:1208. See also *2 Enoch 71*, in *OTP* 1:208.

84. Josephus is an understandable exception, since he wrote in the court of a Roman emperor.

85. *2 Enoch 71*:30, 37, in *OTP* 1:209, 211.

86. This conjunction of kingship and priesthood may also reflect an ancient attribution of divine commission of the king (cf. Mosiah 2:18-19), and it is consistent with ordaining people to become kings and priests. As Joseph Smith taught, the Melchizedek "Priesthood is a perfect law of theocracy." *TPJS*, 322.

87. Baring-Gould, *Legends of the Patriarchs and Prophets*, 141. Cf. JST, Genesis 14:26, "he stopped the mouths of lions."

10

Ancient Burials of Metal Documents in Stone Boxes

H. Curtis Wright
Brigham Young University, Provo, Utah

This paper is an expanded version of a paper presented earlier at the Library History Seminar VI in March 1980. It deals with the persistence, for something like three thousand years, of a strange documentary custom of the Mesopotamian kings, which was distinct and separate from the scribal tradition of clay-tablet writing associated with Assurbanipal. This custom led to numerous regal burials of metallic documents (often encased in stone boxes or other special containers), which were concealed in the foundations or other inaccessible recesses of temples and palaces. The discovery of metal documents beneath the foundations of the Serapis Temple, which housed the Serapeum Library at Alexandria, has also established an archaeological connection between the building practices of the Ptolemies and the Mesopotamian kings.

Introduction

A farmer in the western Peloponnesus was digging a well. Twenty feet down he came upon a stone box. He smashed in its lid. Inside there was a big object "like a bundle," dark in color and crumbly in texture. He

This article originally appeared under the title "Ancient Burials of Metallic Foundation Documents in Stone Boxes," in Occasional Papers, *University of Illinois Graduate School of Library and Information Science 157 (1982): 1-42.*

thought he saw letters written on it. He informed the police, who informed the local director of antiquities; but for some time they could not get out to the farm.

It was 1944-45, and Communist squads were trying to control the roads. When at last the director was able to reach the farm, the object was gone. The farmer had thrown it on the dunghill "because it was not a treasure: it looked like dung and it fell to pieces quite soon." Others, however, had seen "many letters" on it and said that, although fragile, it held together on the dunghill for some days. Clearly it was a book roll . . . ; clearly it was precious to the man who buried it in a stone casket; certainly it would have been precious to us. But it was of no use to the farmer, and it is gone.[1]

On the Ancient Preservation of Writing

Throughout antiquity, records of all kinds were intentionally buried for one reason or another. The Qumran literature, for instance, was not driven underground by the ravages of war. It was deliberately laid to rest in the "solemn communal interment" of a documentary funeral,[2] which served as the "final concealment" of a whole community library.[3]

> This could only have taken place when the community was on the point of dying out. When that happened, however, we do not know. . . . But we know for certain that . . . when Josephus wrote his *Antiquities* . . . , the religious order [of the Essenes] was in a vigorous condition and could have had no reason to store its books carefully in a hidden and inaccessible place.[4]

The Qumran documents were apparently "embalmed" before they were buried. "The careful way in which the MSS were deposited" suggests, more than anything else, "the intention of preserving them as long as possible."[5] There are some intriguing instructions for preserving library materials in the *Assumption of Moses*, where the aging prophet says to Joshua:

> Receive thou this writing [about the preservation of documents] that thou mayest know how to preserve the books [of the Pentateuch] which I shall deliver unto thee: and thou shalt set these [books] in order and anoint them with oil of cedar and put them away in earthen vessels.[6]

These instructions, or something similar, were also behind the creation and preservation of written legal deeds for the transfer of real estate in Jeremiah 32:6-15. The documents, which were duly certified by witnesses, had been drawn up in duplicate (with both a sealed and an open copy) by Jeremiah, who then directed his scribe to "put them in an earthen vessel, that they may continue many days" (Jeremiah 32:14).[7] The documentary methods of Moses and Jeremiah, furthermore, have been attested all over the ancient world. They occur in the Talmud, to be sure, but they are also "fully described in Greek sources" and found in the literatures of both Mesopotamia and Rome.[8] Their presence in the West is implicit in a persistent legend about the books of King Numa, the traditional founder of Roman legal and religious institutions. Refusing cremation, he ordered his followers to make two "stone coffins" (*lithinas sorous*) in order to "bury his books along with his body." When he died, therefore, they sealed the coffins with lead, "the one holding his remains, the other containing the holy books he had written with his own hand," and buried them as directed at the foot of Janus Hill on the west bank of the Tiber.[9] Four or five centuries later,[10] the coffins were accidentally discovered intact.[11] When the lids were removed by breaking their leaden seals, Numa's body had wasted away to nothing,[12] whereas all of his books had been preserved, not merely well, but "in mint condition."[13] The contrast was impressive: the books, written on papyrus scrolls, had been buried with their regal author in a hole in the ground,[14] but they outlasted him hands down because the West, which learned to preserve its documents by procedures derived from the embalming and entombment of corpses, never deigned to mummify its dead.[15] Pliny, following Hemina (who deviates somewhat from other accounts of the burial and retrieval of Numa's books), describes the process in part:

> How these books were able to last so long was amazing to many. But the man who found them had this explanation: a stone cube placed in the center of the coffin had been bound up with waxed cords running in every which direction. On [or in] the top of this stone [or stone box?] three books had been placed [or inserted]; and that probably explains why they had not decayed. Besides, the books themselves had been treated with citrus oil; and that doubtless explains why the moths [or gnawing worms] had not touched them.[16]

Numa's books (three, twelve, or fourteen) survived for half a millennium, if only to be burned by the Romans who found them,[17] because deliberate measures were taken to ensure their survival. They were chemically treated for protection against moth and rust, sealed in a special stone container, and buried deep in the bowels of the earth. Citrus oil, waxed swaddling cords, hewn stone containers, leaden seals—all of this smacks of the cedar oil, waxed linen wrappings, unique earthenware jars, and tightly sealed lids used for preserving the Dead Sea Scrolls.[18] The parallel is too close to be accidental. If using these things at Qumran "proves that the scrolls were hidden in the cave for safe preservation,"[19] if "everything was done to preserve the scrolls as long as possible,"[20] can we say anything less of Numa's books? The Dead Sea Scrolls survived for more than 2000 years to be read in our own day.[21] Why, then, couldn't the scrolls of King Numa survive in good condition for less than one-fourth as long?

Other buried libraries have survived for many centuries in both the Far and Middle East. About A.D. 1035, for example, the Buddhist monks of Chinese Turkestan, who were "under the threat of invasion," walled up their entire collection of books in the cave of Tun-Huang. In A.D. 1900, almost nine centuries later, "the hiding-place was accidentally discovered by a Tibetan monk." Orientalists subsequently explored the cave, "where they found 20,000 scrolls preserved, dating from the sixth and seventh centuries, in Chinese, Tibetan, Sanskrit, and other languages."[22] A second Buddhist library, discovered in the ruins of a tower at Gilgit, "also contained a great number of manuscripts, some dating perhaps from the fourth century."[23] The Nag Hammadi library, a Gnostic "Qumran" of Christian documents, was retrieved through an "earthenware 'time capsule' discovered in the sands of Egypt" when peasants, hunting for fertilizer in 1945, dug up "a large jar filled with leaves of papyrus, bound together like books."[24] The library, "well buried in a tomb very far away from all the monasteries," was virtually intact after more than 15 centuries.[25] It has been described as "the most remarkable ancient library we possess."[26] Its early codex-volumes, whose beautiful leather bindings "are among the oldest ever to survive,"[27] were preserved by the same techniques employed at Qumran.[28] Eusebius even mentions Ksisouthros, better known as Noah, who was commanded before the Deluge "to bury his books (which discussed the beginnings, middles, and endings of all things) in the sunlit city of Sippar." When the flood subsided, therefore, Noah took his family "back to Babylon as commanded, in order to retrieve the buried documents from Sippar and transmit them unto men." Accordingly, they "dug up the documents and began founding cities, setting up temples, and rebuilding Babylon."[29] These records were preserved temporarily, through extremely hazardous circumstances, by special techniques unknown to us. The clay tablet libraries have also survived through documentary techniques differing in significant ways from those which preserved their papyrus cousins.[30]

There are no Qumrans or Nag Hammadis in the West,

for classical literature "is like a city which has been bombed and partially burned"; most of its streets and buildings are in ruins, although many have remained partially (and some wholly) intact.[31] The literature we have is largely from the discard. The tablets from Crete and Mycenae, for example, "were not even fired: they became permanent only when the palaces were burned down."[32] Virtually all of the Greek and Latin papyri, furthermore, "were found quite literally in rubbish dumps or in the ruins of abandoned houses."[33] A few manuscripts have nevertheless survived "because they were deliberately buried." These include two retrieved from coffins, one from a stone box found twenty feet below ground, and several from the wrappings of "cheap mummy cases";[34] some have even come from the "mouths 'and other cavities' " of embalmed sacred crocodiles![35] But many of the writings buried in the West, as in the East, have been metallic documents clearly meant "to survive as long as possible."[36] Lillian Jeffery mentions the use of various metals for writing in the ancient Near East and among the Greeks, who "apparently passed on the practice to the Latin and Etruscan people,"[37] as the Roman use of bronze is firmly established.

> The bronze plaque (pinax or deltos) was widely used. . . . The Greeks themselves appear to have had a tradition that texts of really pre-historic antiquity were (or should be) inscribed on bronze. Thus Agesilaos of Sparta, on opening a tomb at Haliartos . . . , found there . . . a pinax chalkous [bronze tablet] covered with barbaric characters which resembled Egyptian. . . . Akousilaos the Argive historian was said to have compiled his genealogies from deltoi chalkai [bronze tablets] which his father found while digging on his premises. . . . When Lucian's Alexandros went to Kalchedon to stage an elaborate piece of deception, he . . . arranged to excavate deltoi chalkai of incredible age from the old temple of Apollo there, containing alleged statements by Asklepios and Apollo his father.[38]

We have no gold tablets from archaic Greece, although "a fifth-century inscription at Selinous appears to mention one."[39] The nine golden plates of Orphism, however, had been carefully interred in coffins as guidebooks for the dead; they have helped explain the strange Near Eastern overtones of platonism because "Plato and the buried plates were drawing on the same eschatological literature."[40] And the metal tablets from Pyrgi, found "some thirty miles north of Rome" in 1964, were "buried by pious hands" after the smaller of two temples, the sanctuary of Thefarie Velianas, had been reduced to ruins.[41] Rubble from the sanctuary was found "in a rectangular niche between the two temples, carefully and piously disposed" to protect its most valuable records. "There, between large blocks of tufa" salvaged from its walls "and three slabs of its terminal tiles," lying beneath "a heap of terracotta fragments, three sheets of gold leaf, with inscriptions on the outer face, had been hidden."

> Together with these gold leaves, there was a mysterious fourth inscribed sheet of bronze, in very poor condition. . . . The inscription on the bronze sheet with the three others on gold sheets suggests that the niche between the two temples had been made to preserve . . . a part of its archives, which contained different documents established on various occasions.[42]

The Pyrgi tablets recall many ancient burials of metal documents, which include: (1) the legal agreements of a town in Spain with both its guests and its Roman overlords—two bronze tablets, "one placed exactly over the other with their written sides down," discovered beneath "two roofing tiles carefully laid against each other and covered with debris";[43] and (2) the golden "Torah" of Pali Buddhism found "in the brick chamber of an old mound"[44] at Hmawza—"a manuscript in every way similar to the palmleaf manuscript so common in India and Burma but with [twenty] leaves of gold" and two gold covers,[45] which contains "the Law or Dharma Preached by the Buddha."[46]

There is, finally, an interesting burial from the Bertiz Valley near the Turkish province of Maras, where some small silver plates "completely covered with Semitic characters" were discovered in the late 1940s. They had apparently been "unearthed in a badly dilapidated *Bronzekugel*," a brazen sphere "disregarded by the farmers who emptied it because of its beat-up condition."[47] Unusual burials like this are often dismissed as one of a kind. But there is nothing unique in this account: it resembles the Assyrian reburial, probably by Shalmaneser III (858-824 B.C.), of a small silver plate and two small gold plates from the reigns of Shalmaneser I (1274-1245 B.C.) and Tukulti-Ninurta I (1244-1208 B.C.).

> The three tablets had been imbedded in sand in a small bowl. A second, similar bowl was inverted over the top and the two were apparently laced together through holes in their rims. This little "capsule" was half-sunk into the ground, a larger bowl was inverted over it, and the whole thing was buried.[48]

These remarkable burials — of special documents carefully placed in peculiar containers designed specifically to preserve them — may actually be related to the long history of incantation bowl inscriptions which were interred well into the Christian era.[49] They introduce quite naturally the ultimate attempt of the ancients to immortalize their records — the gold and silver plates from Persepolis.[50]

Before and after Persepolis

Old Persian studies got a new lease on life in 1926, "when an inscription of Darius was found at Hamadan, in duplicate on gold and silver tablets."[51] The inscription, wrongly thought to be "wholly novel as to its form and content," was discovered in an old foundation "between

Figure 1. Buried stone box with gold and silver foundation plates, Persepolis, Iran (photo courtesy of the Oriental Institute, University of Chicago)

two square hewn stones that had been carefully prepared to receive it."[52] The find, which established the exact location of ancient Ecbatana, also elicited Herzfeld's prediction that "we may expect with certainty the discovery of similar documents in the excavations at . . . Persepolis" and elsewhere.[53] This prophecy was fulfilled in September 1933, when Herzfeld discovered that "two shallow, neatly made stone boxes with [sealed] lids, each containing two square plates of gold and silver, had been sunk into the bedrock beneath the walls at the corners of . . . the apadana"[54] (the multicolumned audience hall of the Palace at Persepolis). (See figure 1.) The plates, which bore the same inscription as their counterparts from Hamadan, "were laid down, probably in the presence of Darius, in 516-515 B.C."; they were retrieved 2,500 years later in perfect condition, "the metal shining as the day it was incised."[55] There were now six metallic copies of the same inscription, three complete sets of duplicates proclaiming the majesty of Darius and the vast extent of his kingdom.

All these tablets—one gold and one silver from Hamadan, two gold and two silver from Persepolis—were
discovered in situ. . . . The texts of the gold tablets from
Hamadan and Persepolis vary only in the line arrangements imposed by different formats. The Persepolis tablets underlie the issuance of this "edition," whose un-
conventional writing [of a particular word] . . . shows
that all of its copies were created from one and the same
Urtext in a central office. Darius had undertaken simultaneous building projects in Persepolis, Susa, and
Ecbatana, and the administration of these buildings was
a unified thing.[56]

Four more gold tablets found at Hamadan bear inscriptions issued by Ariaramnes, Arsames, Artaxerxes III, and
Darius II.[57] Of the six inscriptions from Hamadan, a full
two-thirds—the silver tablet and three of the five gold tablets—were rescued from looters who had cut them into
pieces for the purpose of melting them down.[58] One shud-
ders to think of the many similar documents which have
not escaped the cutters and melters. The Persepolis plates
constitute the high point in a long tradition of concealed
metallic documents which extend from Sumer to Alexandria. The stone boxes found in holes cut into rock foundations prove conclusively that the plates were building
deposits. The Darius inscription on gold and silver tablets
is therefore "of the same type as the foundation inscriptions on metal tablets of Warad Sin of Larsa [1843-1823
B.C.], of . . . the wife of Rim Sin [1822-1763 B.C.] . . . , of
Tukulti-Ninurta I [1244-1208 B.C.], and of Sargon II [721-
705 B.C.]."[59] Metallic foundation texts are older than that,
however, possibly reaching as far back as Early Dynastic
II (ca. 2700-2500 B.C.).[60] The stone chest may be older still,
if an object dated ca. 2900 B.C. or earlier, which was found
in a temple at Tell Brak, is actually an "early dynastic
foundation box."[61] The metallic foundation tradition,
though frequently interrupted,[62] lived on until the crash

of the Late Assyrian Empire (ca. 626-609 B.C.), when it perished because the Neo-Babylonians instituted other documentary procedures. It was briefly resurrected from the Late Assyrian period by the Achaemenid dynasty of Persia (539-331 B.C.),[63] only to die once more, at least to all appearances, when Alexander the Great fired the palace at Persepolis. But the metallic foundation inscription surfaced yet again at Alexandria in the excavations of (1) a granite box for holding the writings of a late Greek author,[64] and (2) dozens of small metallic plates from the foundations of the Serapis Temple, which housed the Serapeum Library.[65]

The "flames of Persepolis" symbolize in every way the significance of Persia as a major "turning-point in history."[66] She was the mystic counter of Greek naturalism, who created a comprehensive "synthesis of Near Eastern cultures" by combining all of the influences from the Fertile Crescent, "including those of Persia itself, Mesopotamia, Asia Minor, the Syria-Palestine coast, and Egypt."[67] Her material wealth in gold alone was staggering. Antiochus I minted more than $7,250,000 in coins from the golden roofing tiles of one Ecbatana palace;[68] and Alexander the Great systematically looted the palace at Persepolis for "a treasure estimated . . . at over $150,000,000" before putting it to the torch, plus virtually all of the valuable objects "which Persian art had made or Persian conquest gathered."[69] The figures are revealing, even without correction for inflation. The culture of ancient Persia, which "reached one of the high peaks of human experience," also produced the carefully hewn stone boxes of Darius with their magnificent cargo of gold and silver plates. The Darius inscriptions thus mark the "culmination of a metal art which had been at least 2000 years maturing, gathering inspiration from a variety of cultures."[70]

It remains, then, only to review the history of metallic foundation inscriptions before and after the Darius plates, and to summarize its significance for library history. Before doing that, however, we must ask an intriguing question. Only two stone boxes were discovered by Herzfeld, who retrieved them from the northeast and southeast corners of the apadana. But "the cavity meant to hold a third such box was [also] found at the destroyed northwest corner."[71] Who destroyed the northwest corner before the excavators got to it? Could it be that Alexander the Great and his men actually found the missing limestone box with its fabulous treasure of gold and silver plates?

Before Persepolis

The history of metallic foundation inscriptions provides too many boxes and documents to discuss each one separately. This paper therefore reviews that history only in relation to (1) three Neo-Sumerian kings, whose peg deposits probably led to the later burials of metal documents in stone boxes; and (2) nine subsequent rulers, including one Kassite, one Chaldean, two Amorite, and five Assyrian kings, who ruled from the nineteenth through the seventh centuries B.C. The paper thus ignores a mass of material, which includes the numerous metal tablets from Early Dynastic peg deposits,[72] the Akkadian bronze tablet from Samarra,[73] four deposits with uninscribed bronze plates from the Isin Larsa period,[74] the mysterious stone and metal tablets from Old and Middle Assyro-Babylonian times,[75] the vague references to metals deposited in foundations by Shamshi-Adad I (1813-1781 B.C.) and Esarhaddon (699-680 B.C.),[76] the built-up brick boxes from Lagash,[77] the many brick boxes from the Neo-Sumerian and later periods,[78] the door pivot boxes,[79] and the trinkets (beads, amulets, etc.) found embedded in bricks.[80] Hundreds of documents like the Elamitic inscription on a bronze plate (ca. 600 B.C.) found in the treasury of the Persepolis palace, are also ignored because they are not associated with building deposits.[81]

The stone box loaded with metal documents is probably derived from the peg deposits of the Neo-Sumerian Renaissance at Mari in the Ur III period (ca. 2100-2000 B.C.).[82] Parrot uncovered "six foundation deposits" of Niwar-Mer, which had been embedded in the materials used to construct an ancient building. Four of these deposits, "placed very precisely at its corners, identified the building as the Ninhursag Temple, thanks to the inscribed bronze plates,"[83] which they included.

> In each case a bronze plate, about 15 cm. square, was placed directly on the mud bricks. Each plate had a short inscription in one corner. In the center of each was a round hole through which was thrust vertically a bronze peg 12 to 14 cm. long. A slab of wood about the same size as the metal plate was put on top, and a miscellaneous collection of small objects—a spindle whorl, beads, small plaques, a pendant—was placed beside it.[84]

Three of the corners in the temple of Dagan have also produced the foundation deposits of Ishtup-Ilum. More complex than the previous deposits, they definitely suggest a development toward the stone box of Darius. They were found "inside the wall a little above the footing at the base of the temple in a rectangular space"[85] that had been carefully prepared to receive them.

> In one corner of this rectangle was placed a box made of two square stone slabs. The lower slab had a square depression in which a bronze plaque about 13 cm. square was placed. A bronze spike about 27.5 cm. long was thrust through holes in the bronze plaque and the stone slab, and into the mud brickwork beneath. A second stone slab, of the same size as the first but without the depression or hole, was placed over the first. The rest of the . . . rectangle reserved in the brickwork was covered with a layer of round pebbles, among which were numerous small objects. . . . Next to the stone box, bur-

ied among the pebbles, were a tablet of white limestone and one of schist. The tablets and the bronze plaque bore identical inscriptions.[86]

The several deposits of Apil-kin, one of Mari's early governors, were concealed in the boxlike cavities of false bricks built directly into or beneath the foundations themselves. The governor had found "a real hiding place" beneath the inner doors of the *sahuru*, a small entrance hall leading to the "Lions' Temple," which he had built behind the Temple of Ninhursag. This *cachette* was "arranged with much more care" than his predecessors had bestowed on theirs. He had actually "made a box by hollowing out one of the rough bricks in the footings beneath the foundation."

> In this box a bronze plate had been deposited without being nailed down. It was encased in wood, as the cavity was larger than the metal plate. A [wooden] plank, cut to the exact dimensions of the cachette, covered both the plate and its framework. A mat was then placed over the whole thing, the hiding place with its hollow brick was concealed, the brick foundation was laid atop all this as though nothing had happened and construction continued.[87]

The foundation deposits of Niwar-Mer, Ishtup-Ilum and Apil-kin are also related to the elaborate boxes made up of baked bricks "laid flat in bitumen, in courses measuring 3 x 2 1/2 bricks."[88] All of these deposits with their various containers point to the long development which culminates in the rock holes, stone boxes, and metal documents of Darius.

Of more than a dozen rulers listed by Oppenheim, Warad-Sin (1834-1823 B.C.) and Rim-Sin (1822-1763 B.C.) are "the only Larsa kings who used peg deposits";[89] but both of these rulers were involved with either the boxes or the documents of the metallic foundation deposit. While clearing a small temple site in southeastern Ur of its superimposed ruins from the Ur III and Isin-Larsa periods, Woolley dug into the remains of an old wall. He quickly found, in the rubble beside the wall, some "clay foundation cones . . . from its destroyed upper courses." Then about six inches below the wall's highest remaining surface, he uncovered "a box of burnt brick contrived in the mud-brick core of the wall." The box contained "an intact foundation-deposit consisting of the copper figure of the king" and a "brick-shaped inscribed steatite tablet." The cones, the statuette, and the tablet all bore the same inscription, which stated that "the temple was dedicated to En-ki, the water god of Eridu, . . . by Rim Sin king of Larsa," in the ninth year of his reign. The building and its deposit "can therefore be accurately dated to the year 1990 B.C."[90] The excavation disclosed no metal tablets, however, and none are known from Rim-Sin; but Simat-Inanna, "one of the wives of Rim-Sin," did deposit inscribed limestone and copper tablets in the foundations of a Larsa temple, which she dedicated to the goddess Belit-ekallim "during part of the reign of Hammurabi at Babylon [ca. 1792-1750 B.C.]."[91] No deposits actually made by Warad-Sin have ever been recovered, and the same is true of Kurigalzu II (1345-1324 B.C.). But excavation of the later Ningal Temple, built by "the Assyrian governor of Ur in about 650 B.C.,"[92] has produced a pair of steatite and copper tablets from each of those rulers. "The temple had been restored by Nabonidus [555-539 B.C.],"[93] the last Neo-Babylonian king, who also restored its foundation deposits. This reburial of tablets from the Amorite and Kassite dynasties not only proves that Warad-Sin and Kurigalzu II deposited foundation inscriptions in their buildings, but also demonstrates the astonishing antiquity and vitality of this vigorous metallic tradition.

> Under the floor [of room three] there was found loose
> in the soil a [white] limestone foundation-tablet of Kuri-

Galzu and close to this two copper tablets and one of
black steatite; one copper tablet was a duplicate of that
in limestone and recorded the restoration of an ancient
temple . . . , the other two also formed a pair and recorded the building by Warad-sin of "a great wall which
like a tall mountain cannot be undermined" . . . ; neither
of the two texts can have any reference to the site in
which they were found; they must have been unearthed
in the Neo-Babylonian period and given pious reburial
under the new temple that was in course of construction.[94]

After Kurigalzu II, the Assyrian kings more or less
monopolized the metallic foundation deposit until the
breakup of their empire (ca. 600 B.C.) by the Neo-Babylonians. The elaborate reburial by Shalmaneser III of a
Schalenkapsel containing gold and silver plates from Shalmaneser I and Tukulti-Ninurta I has already been discussed.[95] The only other building documents from Shal-
manesers I and III are an inscription of the former stating
that he "placed stones, silver, gold, iron, copper, tin, and
aromatic plants" in foundations,[96] and a lone gold tablet
of unknown provenance from the latter.[97] It is nevertheless
known that "small tablets of precious metal were used from
the time of Shalmaneser I onwards."[98] The most complicated foundation deposits of Mesopotamia, on the other
hand, come from the later Ishtar Temple of Tukulti-Ninurta
I (1244-1208 B.C.), who dedicated its twin shrines to Ishtar
Asshuritu and to Dinitu. The deposits from this temple to
Assur constitute "a very elaborate combination of [in-
scribed] slabs and tablets, large and small, of various materials," installed with "a lavish use of beads and non-
descript fragments of stone."[99] The slabs, which include
seven made of lead (averaging about 5" x 15" x 30" in size
and 880 pounds in weight) and two of limestone (one
almost 9' x 5' x 16", the other about 4' x 6' x 12"), constitute
"the most massive [deposits] so far discovered in Meso-

potamia."[100] The tablets include thirteen made of gold or silver and seven each of lead and alabaster.[101] The complex arrangements of these twenty-seven documents defy verbal description, but they were partially disposed as follows:

> First three lead blocks were placed upon the mud brick sub-foundation; two small inscribed tablets of gold and silver and a tiny square of sheet copper were placed on the middle block. A few baked bricks were laid along the wall face to make a level bed for the stone slab. Glass beads, fragments of stones, and . . . twigs or bits of wood were strewn over these objects, and the limestone slab was placed over them. . . . Mats were laid over the block, and . . . [near] its rear edge were placed more valuable trifles, including beads and . . . bits of ivory. On this "cushion" of beads and mortar went two more gold and silver tablets, and a square of sheet gold. Then the fourth lead block was laid over the lot and the construction of the wall continued in mud brick.[102]

Additional gold and silver tablets were positioned, "together with beads and stone chips, on the cella pavement beneath the dais." Another complex deposit of similar foundation inscriptions was also discovered "beneath and behind the Dinitu shrine."[103]

An important pair of gold and silver plaquettes has survived from Assurnasirpal II (883-859 B.C.).[104] "The actual provenance of these two inscriptions is unknown,"[105] but they were very probably found at Nineveh in the Temple of Nabu, the god of learning, writing, scribes, and secretaries.[106] The possible linkage of Nabu with the tablets is interesting for they present Assurnasirpal II as saying explicitly: "I laid the foundation of the palace at the city of X, the foundations of my royal residence, on tablets of silver and gold."[107] The actual wording of the tablets, as a matter of fact, means "to establish the foundation on documents."[108] In all of cuneiform literature, Bottéro knows specifically of "only one other formula somewhat like this one." It occurs "in the Prism [text] describing the 30th year of Assurbanipal," the librarian-king from Nineveh. In this inscription, which deals with the Temple of Nergal at Kutha, Assurbanipal says: "In a favorable month, on a propitious day, I established its subfoundation on GULA oil, that fine oil, and upon tables of silver and gold." This statement, Bottéro notes, incorporates "the same verb (*addi*), the same preposition (*ina*), and the same mention of gold and silver tablets as in our text."[109] It suggests that foundation documents are not merely inscriptions discovered in foundations. They are basic documents bearing witness to the founding of important royal and religious buildings on *writing*, which was known anciently as "the King's Secret" — a mysterious something giving him both the right and the power to rule.[110] The regal habit of building upon inscriptions, furthermore, probably symbolizes the original founding of the temple, the palace, and the city-state upon the written document,[111] and possibly upon the metallic document. At any rate, the practice was firmly established in ancient Mesopotamia.

> Archaeological digs have amply documented this custom, observed by the Mesopotamian kings, of burying among the substructures of the temples or palaces they built or restored such things as clay nails; cones, barrel cylinders, and stone or metal tablets, on which they inscribed a permanent record of their labors.[112]

The utter seriousness of the kings who made these foundation deposits is exemplified by the solemn curse of Assurnasirpal: "If anyone should efface my name which I have written here, or misuse this document for his own pleasures or purposes, may Assur, the Great Lord, destroy his army, ravage his throne, and cut off from the land his name and all of his descendants!"[113]

The inscribed stone box "appeared for the first time in the reign of Assurnasirpal II [883-859 B.C.],"[114] the last of the Middle Assyrian kings. All previous examples of boxes, including the possible instance from Tell Brak and the box-like cachette of Apil-kin,[115] were either uninscribed or directly incorporated into the structure of some building. In 1929, however, "a damaged stone box bearing an inscription" by Assurnasirpal II showed up in Philadelphia.[116] The box came from the ancient city of Apqu, also known as Bumariyah or Tell Abu-Maria, "some twenty miles west of Mosul, near Telefar," in Iraq.[117] It was pieced together by E. A. Speiser, who "identified it as a foundation box, and deciphered the [long] cuneiform inscription" on its sides and lid.[118] It was probably taken from a foundation hole, although "there is no means of knowing the [actual] conditions under which it was found."[119] Moreover, since the gold and silver tablets of Assurnasirpal II may also have come from Apqu, "it is possible that they were [originally] enclosed in the foundation box."[120]

Another inscribed stone box inscribed by Assurnasirpal II was retrieved from "a mound called Balawat," supposedly the ancient Imgur-Bel near Nineveh, "about fifteen miles to the east of Mossul."[121] It was found while Rassam was in Mossul by the local foreman of the dig, who described it as "a stone coffer with a lid, containing two tablets of stone covered with inscriptions."[122] The foreman, who may or may not have removed the box from its find-spot, did rebury it for protection until Rassam returned to the site. It was apparently taken from the entrance to a burnt-out temple chamber, where Rassam also found, lying on a marble altar, "an inscribed marble tablet of the same size and shape as the other two."[123] Because the stone box had exactly enough room for this third tablet, he concluded that it "belonged to the same set" of documents, that it had been removed from the box and placed on the altar for reading, and "that before the priests had time to deposit it back in the coffer, the temple was burnt down, either by accident or by an enemy."[124] The cavity of the stone

box was something like 8" x 9", large enough to hold three
tablets "twelve-and-a-half inches long, eight wide and two-
and-a-half thick."[125] As that is less than half the length and
width of the box and perhaps three-fourths its depth, the
box itself probably measured about 12" x 18" x 28". It was
a massive marble chest, whose great weight, though un-
specified, was sufficient to tax Rassam's ingenuity in trans-
porting it to Mossul.[126] There is yet another ninth-century
example of this kind from the son of Assurnasirpal II, the
first Neo-Assyrian king. What little is known of the box,
which is engraved on three sides, has been stated by Ellis.

> A similar stone box of Shalmaneser III [858-824 B.C.]
> was found on the ruins of the west gate of the outer
> wall of Assur. Unfortunately it was empty, and it had
> evidently rolled down from some other position to its
> find-spot. In spite of its evidently secondary position,
> the box lay on some agate beads, which may have been
> inside when it rolled to its final position.[127]

These boxes seem to break with the conventional understanding of foundation inscriptions as documents about
buildings. The box from Tell Bumariyah, for example,
"does not include a building text" of any kind, and was
probably "used for some other purpose."[128] The gold and
silver tablets it may have housed also make it clear that
Assurnasirpal II was founding buildings upon documents,
not depositing documents about buildings.[129] The Balawat
box, on the other hand, mentions the building or rebuilding
of both a city and a temple, but "did not appear to have
been buried," and "does not seem to have been a building
deposit."[130] There is not much to say about the stone box
of Shalmaneser III, as its find conditions are unknown: the
king mentions rebuilding the city wall at Assur and urges
its future rebuilder to "restore its ruins" and "to return
my inscription to its place."[131] But where was its place? It
is possible, certainly, that foundation documents served a

double purpose, and that at least some copies "of building inscriptions were kept in the temples, for safekeeping or in order to keep the record . . . permanently before the god,"[132] or even for reading. Marinatos thought a similar marble chest from Mesenia "could have been a library-box."[133] If such a box "was considered a container suitable for stone tablets" or other documents, as at Balawat, "it may be that the stone boxes of Assurnasirpal II and Shal-maneser III served a similar purpose, and were not meant to be deposited in structures."[134] Their inscriptions, which deal mostly with the Great King and his domains, would seem to bear this out. Excavations at Nimrud and Arslan Tash in northern Syria have also disclosed six or seven inscribed "Assyrian statues of deities holding square boxes" in their arms.[135] Their inscriptions state explicitly that "they were set up for . . . Nabu," the learned god of the written word who was also known as "the perfect scribe."[136] All these statues, and especially those from Nim-rud, "are close chronologically to the boxes of Assurna-sirpal II and Shalmaneser III," and it is difficult to deny a connection between them. Mallowan, at any rate, has sug-gested that the statue boxes "might have been meant to hold tablets, in view of Nabu's association with writing and scholarship.[137]

Sargon II (721-705 B.C.) indicates that he deposited in-scribed materials of four to nine different kinds in foun-dations.[138] The fact is that building deposits from the late Assyro-Babylonian kings (858-539 B.C.) often include such inscriptions, a documentary custom actually "mentioned in texts from Sargon's time down to Nabonidus's reign [555-539 B.C.]."[139] The metallic foundation inscription flour-ished under the Neo-Assyrian kings, and it is therefore no surprise that "the depositing of inscribed documents was greatly elaborated in Sargon II's palace at Khorsabad."[140] The excavator of this palace, Victor Place, "was intrigued by the unusual thickness (nearly 26 feet), of one of its

dividing walls." On digging into the wall he found "two
inscribed barrel cylinders" and "an alabaster block which
he carefully unearthed." The block turned out to be "a
stone box (whose lid had been broken by the weight of
the wall), which measured about 11 x 15 x 17 inches; and
in it he discovered five foundation tablets" on which Sargon II had "described the building of Khorsabad" from
scratch.[141] "These epigraphical documents have a high
value for their texts themselves"; but in addition to that,
"the material on which they were engraved increases, if
possible, their extreme rarity," because "one of the tablets
was made of gold, another of silver, the third of bronze,
a fourth of lead, and the last" of a mysterious "white
material," perhaps alabaster or magnesite, which has
proven harder to identify.[142] Of the three metallic inscriptions, the bronze tablet is the largest, the gold tablet the
smallest, and the silver tablet somewhere in between.[143]
The lead tablet and the inscribed stone box,[144] which completed this series of foundation documents from Khorsabad, disappeared in the infamous *naufrage des collections* of
23 May 1855, "in which so many of the archaeological
materials gathered by the French were lost."[145] Here again,
"the box with its tablets was not actually [discovered] in
the foundations," but in a wall "above the level of the
floor."[146] This proves that foundation inscriptions were not
deposited solely in foundations. It does not prove that the
tablets of Sargon II were something other than foundation
inscriptions, for they state repeatedly that he founded the
city of Dur-Sharrukin (Khorsabad) and built its wall, the
various shrines for its gods, and its several palaces; and
they also say—again repeatedly—that he inscribed his
name on those same tablets and deposited them in the
"foundation walls" of the palaces.[147] For what they are
worth, there are also some Urartean deposits from the
Haldis Temple at Toprakkale near Lake Van in Asia Minor,
which are probably contemporary with Sargon II.[148]

> At each corner of the square shrine a square depres-
> sion, about 20 cm. on a side and 3-4 cm. deep, had been
> sunk into the bedrock. In two of these depressions were
> found deposits, each consisting of a square bronze plate
> and two tiny scraps, one of sheet gold, the other of sheet
> silver. None of these objects was inscribed.[149]

The metallic foundation inscription came to an end with
the fall of the Neo-Assyrian Empire ca. 626-609 B.C. "It
was not adopted by the Neo-Babylonian rulers," who preferred "clay cylinders, the only type of inscribed building
deposit used in their time."[150] A clay box[151] and a brick
box[152] are associated with the first and the last Chaldean
kings, and there may be others; but there were few if any
stone or metal inscriptions. The years between 626-609 B.C.
thus mark a chronological datum before which foundation
documents were inscribed on metals but not after. "The
custom was briefly revived by the Achaemenids," who
intentionally resurrected it from the Neo-Assyrian or Urartean past.[153] It died for the second time in 331 B.C. when
the Persian Empire was toppled by Alexander the Great,
but it also underwent a second resurrection, this time in
the great city of Alexandria.

The Alexandrian Echo of Persepolis

Archeology is problematic at Alexandria, where "excavation has yielded, and can yield, but little material for
its reconstruction at any period."[154] There are many reasons
for this, but the major causes are two:

> The first is a general subsidence, probably of about
> four meters, which has taken much of the coastal region
> of the ancient city beneath sea level. . . . This subsidence
> is complicated by a second, man-made difficulty. . . .
> Intense building activity [since ca. 1850] has created a
> new and wholly artificial coastline, to a depth of some
> three hundred meters [900 feet] at its widest extent, in

the area . . . where the Corniche was completed in 1906.[155]

The stratigraphy and ceramic sequences of Alexandria have thus been largely disrupted, as most of the "fill" for the modern city was taken from the ancient city, sherds and all.[156] These artificial conditions of her coastline unfortunately "exclude any possibility of accurate determination of the contours of the most important part of the city."[157] Excavators have therefore been forced to concentrate on the east and west sides of Alexandria, the former containing her ancient cemeteries and the latter her famous Temple of Serapis.[158] "The Serapeum," as a matter of fact, "is the only excavated temple" in the city; and its foundation deposits "may reasonably be described as the most important archaeological find of the Ptolemaic period [ever] made in Alexandria."[159] It is very disconcerting, therefore, to learn that "not only Parsons, *The Alexandrian Library* . . . , but also serious works like the *Handbuch der Bibliothekswissenchaft* . . . or the *Geschichte der Textüberlieferung* . . . [have] failed to take notice of the excavations."[160] The failure is understandable, however, as the archaeological and literary evidence for this temple is so confusing that virtually nobody can make sense of it.[161]

> The Serapeum has been unfortunate in its principal excavators, Botti and Rowe. In the reports of the former it is frequently not clear what structures he is discussing, while the latter had little understanding of the historical problems connected with the site, and was unable to interpret satisfactorily his discoveries, important though some of these were. . . . Detailed interpretation of their plans and descriptions is [therefore] a task of considerable uncertainty.[162]

On 23 August 1943, Alan Rowe discovered "a set of ten foundation plaques bearing bilingual inscriptions in hieroglyphs and Greek stating that Ptolemy III had built

the Temple and the Sacred Enclosure for Serapis." They
were found in a hole sunk into a rock foundation beneath
the southeast corner of the Serapeum at Alexandria. The
set included (1) three metal plates of gold, silver, and
bronze; (2) five opaque glass plates; (3) a tablet made of
faience; and (4) a mud tablet, apparently uninscribed.[163]
The find was repeated on 31 December 1944, when a "similar set of ten plaques of Ptolemy III" were taken from
another deposit hole in the foundation trench under the
southwest corner of the same temple.[164] The inscriptions,
materials, and arrangements of the plaques were essentially the same as before, as was the actual find-spot.[165]
"The holes themselves were filled with sand after the
plaques had been laid at the bottom and then covered over
with limestone foundation blocks which were later removed by unknown persons" who dug up the foundations
without disturbing the foundation trenches.[166] Rowe also
announced "part of a foundation deposit in a small hole
cut in the rock discovered on 30th October, 1945," from
which "the gold, silver, bronze and . . . [some] opaque
glass plaques had been removed in ancient times."[167] The
remaining glass plaques bore "two black ink inscriptions . . . , Greek on one side and hieroglyphic on the
other." As these inscriptions were identical to those previously found, and since the early finds were uniformly
alike, Rowe concluded that the deposit originally contained
"ten plaques as in the temenos corners."[168] This find led
to the discovery of ten more deposit holes, which enabled
the Greco-Roman Museum to distinguish three separate
structures in the same general area of the Serapeum, the
early "Ptolemaic and [later] Roman temples of Serapis and
a [small] Ptolemaic-Shrine of Harpocrates."[169] There were
no less than eight deposit holes in the Shrine of Harpocrates alone, each meant to hold "ten plaques, which were
placed in pairs of two [deposits] in every corner."[170] The
museum also discovered north of these deposit holes "the

rock-cut holes for two other deposits," which may belong to the Harpocrates Shrine or to "the southern part of an adjacent ptolemaic shrine."[171] These holes, like their deposits, were fairly uniform, measuring about 11" x 7" x 3";[172] they were so skillfully hidden that they could not be detected unless the surface of the foundation trench was brushed.[173] The inscription on one of the gold plates, and presumably on the other plaques, "indicates that the shrine was made by Ptolemy IV (221-203 B.C.) and dedicated to Harpocrates, the son of Serapis and Isis."[174] Rowe thus found thirteen rock-cut holes in all, from which he actually retrieved forty-three foundation tablets made of glass, metal, and clay.[175] If these were all foundation holes, and if their deposits were indeed uniform, they should have contained originally 130 tablets—65 of glass and 13 each of gold, silver, bronze, faience, and mud. Other deposits doubtless remain in the northern foundation trenches of the Serapeum Enclosure and of its temples, where they cannot be excavated because they lie beneath the modern Bab Sidra Cemetery.[176] Similar foundation documents are also known from clandestine excavations in Alexandria and from various other sources.[177] Evidence for the Serapeum remains confusing, to say the least;[178] but thanks to Alan Rowe and the foundation plaques, five definite conclusions can now be drawn from it: (1) the buildings and grounds of the Serapeum, known as its temenos, were located on the west side of Alexandria where Pompey's Pillar now stands;[179] (2) the Temple of Serapis was built within the Serapeum Enclosure at its north end;[180] (3) the Shrine of Harpocrates, also inside the Enclosure, was a later adjunct to the southwest corner of the Serapis Temple;[181] (4) Ptolemy III Euergetes (246-221 B.C.) built the Serapeum Enclosure and its Temple of Serapis;[182] and (5) the Shrine of Harpocrates was built by Ptolemy IV Philopator (221-203 B.C.).[183]

There are some hints about the presence of stone boxes

in Alexandria. The third deposit from the Harpocrates
Shrine, for example, "was once enclosed in a kind of plaster
box," whose remains were found by Rowe.[184] He also alludes to rectangular limestone coffers kept in niches in the
long underground passages beneath the Roman Serapeum, "which Botti thought might be Ptolemaic in origin."[185] But the best evidence of stone boxes is the discovery
in 1847 of a granite box bearing the inscription DIOS-
KOURIDES G TOMOI, "For Three Volumes by Dioscurides."[186] Discovered "in the garden of the Consulate General of Prussia," it was wrongly interpreted at first as
"confirming the location of the great library in the same
place."[187]

> Recently, while digging for some stones to use as
> building materials, someone discovered a small block of
> granite 17 1/2 inches (438 mm.) long, by 15 1/2 inches
> (394 mm.) wide and high. A cavity had been hewn in
> this block for holding papyrus rolls. . . . This cavity is
> 10 inches (254 mm.) long by 8 inches (203 mm.) wide
> and 3 inches deep. . . . Thus there would have been
> room for three rolls.[188]

This granite box, which weighed over 380 pounds, was
"already lost in 1848."[189] The grounds where it was found
had been purchased by the Prussian Consul General to
Alexandria, Antonio de Laurin of Austria, "who apparently conducted some [amateur] excavations there. . . .
[But] no one knows what became of the artifacts from these
digs. Unfortunately, they could have fallen into the hands
of Cassavetti," an unscrupulous character who may have
made a killing from the box on the antiquities market.[190]
Whatever its fortunes, however, the whereabouts of the
granite box remains completely unknown.[191] Partly for that
reason it was long thought to be an out-and-out hoax; an
uncritical account of the box was the only one ever published, as it was subsequently ignored by serious scholars.[192] Breccia, for example, repudiated the stories that he

had discovered the box, that it was made to hold ten rolls
instead of three, and so forth.[193] It had been noticed briefly
in 1848 by J. A. Letronne, who was quoting an excerpt
from the letter written by Sir Anthony Charles Harris to
Samuel Birch on 28 December 1847.[194] But this notice was
ignored by virtually everyone until the daughter of Sir
Anthony Harris, almost three decades after his death, delivered some of his notebooks to the Greco-Roman Museum in 1896.[195] Botti, who was then Director of the Museum, was thus able "to find the note which, as the files
of Sir Antonio de Laurin had been scattered and his papers
destroyed by a fire in 1892, takes on the value of an original
source."[196] The description and drawing of a heavy granite
box by the scholarly Harris was impressive. "Although his
note cannot be given the authority of a meticulous epi-
graphic copy . . . , no one familiar with the usual exacti-
tude of his notebooks" could flippantly dismiss the box or
"doubt that the inscription was faithfully reproduced by
him."[197] So, some of the scholars began to reassess the box.
Reinach, for example, wrote about it in a spirit of atonement for his previous skepticism.[198] The box itself, however, which was too cumbersome to be typical,[199] must
have been created for some special purpose, such as containing the *éditions de luxe* of the wealthy, immortalizing
the famous or their works, controlling the humidity, preventing thefts, housing rare books, or protecting illuminated manuscripts.[200] There is also a question about the
actual shape of the box, because the visual proportions of
the drawing by Harris do not fit the measurements he
provides for it.[201]

The inscription of the granite box is dated, on rather
tenuous paleographical evidence, between 220 B.C.-A.D.
140.[202] The most difficult problem with the inscription,
however, is probably its referent: Which Dioscurides is
meant? There are eight or nine possibilities and no sure
method of selecting the right one, although the choices

can be narrowed somewhat if Reinach's dates are accepted.[203] His favorite is Dioscurides *Pedanius*, the one-book author of the *De Materia Medica*, for whom he argues somewhat speciously at great length.[204] My own choice would be Dioscurides *Epigrammaticus*, the brilliant student of Callimachus, for whom I can present no better evidence, perhaps, than wishful thinking; but he certainly cannot be disqualified by the ultimate in scholarly "objectivity" — Reinach's assertion that "light poetry would be out of place in such a heavy chest!"[205] If "the box of Dioscurides raises more questions than it resolves,"[206] it is mostly because Reinach insists on regarding it as unique.[207] It was nothing of the sort: the inscribed granite box had plenty of ancestors in Mesopotamia, and probably also in Egypt.

Conclusion: The Significance of All This for Library History

The antecedents of the foundation inscriptions from Alexandria must be Macedonian, Greek, Roman, Mesopotamian, Egyptian, or some combination thereof. Greco-Roman influence may be ruled out immediately, however, as foundation deposits of this kind have never been attested for any Greek or Roman building,[208] and the influence of Egypt, which is unquestionably at work in the Serapeum, must be evaluated by others.[209] But we are badly mistaken, I think, if we insist on deriving the accomplishments of the Ptolemies from their Greek or Egyptian subjugates. It is above all else the cultural force of Macedon and her long-standing openness to the peoples and influences of Mesopotamia which best account for those accomplishments. "The Ptolemies traced their descent from Dionysus,"[210] who was regarded as the father of Serapis himself.[211] Dionysus, be it remembered, was known as the interloper god of Asian supernaturalism who forced his way into the mainland of Greek naturalistic thought by way of Thrace and Macedonia.[212] When the aging Euripides

left Attica in a huff, disgusted with the smart-alec intellectuals of Athens, he withdrew to Macedonia in the rustic
mountain country of hillbilly Greece; and there, in the
northern backlands of the wild, wild West, he wrote the
Bacchae, a play about the fundamentally irreconcilable conflict of the Apollonian and Dionysiac "gospels" in ancient
Greece.[213] The awesome issues raised here by Euripides
have not been resolved to this day; but the Macedonians,
although fascinated with the sophic traditions of Apollonian Greece, never swerved from their fierce devotion to
the mantic Dionysus. And that, I think, is the basic fact
which must always be remembered in evaluating the influences of Macedon, Mesopotamia, and Egypt upon the
Ptolemies. It is difficult for the modern mentality to comprehend the sacral outlook of the ancient mentality. When
a king runs a foundation trench, lays down a permanent
record of his authority and domains inscribed on stone
tablets or metal plates, and erects a building on top if it,
what is he really doing? He is saying in the sacral language
of a dramatized ritual enactment that every aspect of human civilized culture — the civilizing tendency itself, which
gives birth to the temple, the palace, the city-state, his
entire kingdom, and even to his own powers — is built upon
the written document. Could there possibly be a better
way to say it? The foundation inscription was not used for
communicating in any ordinary sense of the word,[214] but
it was by no means insignificant. It was rather the backbone
of the whole documentary system of Mesopotamia. The
royal inscriptions, written either by the kings or under their
direct supervision, included both the foundation tablets or
other forms of building inscriptions and their historical
elaborations, which were known as "annals" or "chronicles."[215] The inscription was a secondary element in "Early
Dynastic foundation deposits." Its use increased with the
decline of the peg, however, and "the inscription began
to take on more importance." As time wore on, these

"building deposit inscriptions became both longer and more numerous," thus leading to the historical document and "in Assyria [to] the literary prism."[216] The documents derived from building inscriptions, moreover, "must be taken to reflect literary patterns."[217] The royal inscriptions of Assyria, for example, include such things as chronicles, long-winded invocations, paeans, triumphal hymns, poetic language, and episodic narratives. It is "only when the royal inscriptions are linked with their literary background," therefore, that "their diversification and . . . stylistic changes can be explained."[218] Nabonidus even "enlivens inscriptions with dialogs" in which gods, kings, priests, and common laborers participate. He also "quotes in scholarly fashion the texts of the documents his workmen had excavated from the ruins of temples," just as Assurbanipal repeatedly includes "descriptions of his training and . . . achievements as a scholar and a soldier." All of this demonstrates "the continuity and tenacity of a living literary tradition" — distinct from the scribal tradition "preserved in the royal library of Nineveh" — which makes it necessary for the would-be writer of Mesopotamian literary history "to consult these living, changing royal inscriptions."[219] These two literary traditions, the regal and the scribal, were for the most part intertwined in Mesopotamia. They may have shared a common origin; and if they did, it was probably the stereotyped inclusions of the ancient foundation inscription: an invocation of the god, the names and accomplishments of the king, mention of something (like a temple or kingdom) built upon the civilizing functions of writing, a curse on anyone desecrating the foundation document, and blessings for those who honor it.[220]

> The most important development in Assyrian literature is to be found in the royal inscriptions. These were modelled on the old Babylonian building inscription. . . . From this fixed form the Assyrians developed

the long historical inscriptions on which our knowledge
of . . . Mesopotamia is largely based. By elaborating the
title of the king, and giving a more discursive account . . . of the dedication, the scribes were able to give
general accounts of the principal events of their
time. . . . Thus arose the general account of a king's
exploits. The next step was to arrange the events in their
chronological sequence. . . . Finally . . . each year or
each campaign was elaborately and separately described,
and then a complete history of the reign . . . [was] recorded on clay or stone with all the literary art of which
the writer was capable. . . . The building inscription remains, [but] the annalistic element is entirely
new. . . . The annals of the Assyrian kings from Sargon
onwards deserve to be classed with the most important
literary works in cuneiform.[221]

If the history of librarianship is reduced to library history, the substance of this paper has little relevance to it.
There is more to carpentry than the history of boards and
shingles. Why, then, must librarianship be regarded as so
much bibliographic lumber? The history of books and libraries is the history of instruments, like the history of
hammers, nails, saws, tool cribs, and lumberyards. It can
therefore have only instrumental relevance to librarianship, which must use communicative instruments of one
kind or another in order to do its job. But the history of
librarianship is not the history of its instruments; it is the
history of societal information systems in which ideas are
expressed and recognized by means of communicative instruments — such as bard traditions, marked arrows, cattle
brands, metal plates, stone tablets, clay cylinders, palm
leaves, papyrus rolls, waxed boards, parchment codices,
paper books, microforms, magnetic tapes, data banks,
print-outs, computer terminals, and who knows what all.
The information systems of the ancient Near East are thus
an integral part of the history of librarianship. They were

based on "the marvelous function of writing as the great synthesizer," for the old Egyptians and Mesopotamians knew instinctively that "to write is to synthesize."[222] We have forgotten all that in our insane commitment to the scientific analysis of everything. There is therefore no critical librarianship today, no comprehensive synthesis of knowledge in which anything that is known can be located and correlated with everything else that is known. We have pushed Humpty Dumpty off the wall and watched him shatter into thousands of little bits and pieces; and we have descended on the pieces and broken them down into progressively smaller bits and pieces. But we cannot put him together again because we find it much easier to analyze than to synthesize. The modern age has no House of Life, no temple where its knowledge records can be copied and discussed and studied as a whole.

> Ancient records come to us not in single books but in whole libraries. These are not mere collections but organic entities . . . representing every department of human knowledge. . . . There is no aspect of our civilization that does not have its rise in the temple, thanks to the power of the written word. In the all-embracing relationship of the Divine Book everything is relevant. Nothing is really dead or forgotten; every detail belongs in the picture, which would be incomplete without it. Lacking such a synthesizing principle, our present-day knowledge becomes ever more fragmented, and our universities and libraries crumble and disintegrate as they expand. Where the temple that gave it birth is missing, civilization itself becomes a hollow shell.[223]

Notes

1. Gilbert Highet, "The Wondrous Survival of Records," *Horizon* 5 (November 1962): 93.

2. Matthew Black, *The Scrolls and Christian Origins* (New York: Scribner's Sons, 1961), 12. Black notes that "such a burial of the books may have been among the last solemn duties of the remnant Essenes at Qumran, when the sect had either been swallowed up

in Palestinian forms of Christianity or was disappearing owing to the constant pressure and hostility of rabbinical Judaism."

3. Paul E. Kahle, *The Cairo Geniza*, 2nd ed. (Oxford: Blackwell, 1959), 15, cited in Black, *The Scrolls and Christian Origins*, 12, n.1.

4. Ibid.

5. Ibid.

6. *Assumption of Moses* 1:16-18. For an English translation of the text, with critical notes, see R. H. Charles, *The Apocrypha and Pseudepigrapha of the Old Testament*, 2 vols. (Oxford: Clarendon, 1976), 2:415.

7. The expression "earthen vessel" here translates the Hebrew *kəli hāres* and the Greek *aggeion ostrakinon*, both describing a ceramic container of some kind.

8. L. Fischer, "Die Urkunden in Jer. 32:11-14 nach den Ausgrabungen und dem Talmud," *Zeitschrift für die alttestamentliche Wissenschaft* 30 (1910): 139: "Diese Art der Ausstellung eines Dokumentes, wie wir sie bei den erwähnten Papyri, die sämtlich in griechischer Sprache abgeffast und nicht jüdisch sind, gesehen haben, finden wir ebenso in der talmudischen Literatur beschrieben." The Greek sources mentioned here are the Elephantine and the Hibeh papyri. On the Mesopotamian practice of making legal duplicates, see A. Leo Oppenheim, *Ancient Mesopotamia: Portrait of a Dead Civilization* (Chicago: University of Chicago Press, 1972), 282.

9. Plutarch, *Numa* XXII, 2-3. Stone coffins were more common in antiquity than one might think; "for an unburned body a coffin would normally be used, while later the stone sarcophagus, often elaborately carved, became very popular with those who could afford it." See Herbert J. Rose, "Dead, Disposal of," in *Oxford Classical Dictionary*, 2nd ed. (Oxford: Clarendon, 1970). For two examples, see Theophrastus, *De Igne* XLVI, and Dioscorides Medicus I, 124. For the leaden seals see Livy, *Ab Urbe Condita* XL, 29, 3. The ancient custom of writing "on lead and linen scrolls" (*in plumbeis linteisque voluminibus*) is also noted by Pliny, *Historia Naturalis* XIII, 27, 8. See also Augustine, *De Civitate Dei* XXXIV, 26-29. He states that Numa had his books buried "where he thought they were safe" (*obruit ubi tutum putavit*).

10. Plutarch, *Numa* XXII, 4, says "about four hundred years later." Pliny, *Historia Naturalis* XIII, 27, 85 places the discovery of the stone coffins "535 years after Numa's accession" (*ad quos [libros repertos] a regno Numae colliguntur anni DXXXV*). The dates are problematic, but a common guess is that the coffins were buried ca. 672 B.C. and discovered in 181 B.C.

11. They were unearthed by a flood from heavy rains, according to Plutarch, *Numa* XXII, 4; but they were dug up by ploughmen according to Livy, *Ab Urbe Condita* XL, 29, 3; Lactantius, *Divinae Institutiones* I, 22, 5; Valerius Maximus, *Factorum et Dictorum Memorabilia* I, 1, 12; Pliny, *Historia Naturalis* XIII, 27, 84; Augustine, *De Civitate Dei* VII, 34, 7-11, and *De Viris Illustribus Urbis Romae* III, 3.

12. There was nothing left of the body, not even a trace, according to Plutarch, *Numa* XXII, 5. Livy, *Ab Urbe Condita* XL, 29, 5, adds that "the wasting action of so many years had destroyed everything." These statements may be intentionally overdrawn as a way of emphasizing the very different states of preservation observable in the contents of the two coffins. At any rate, there was a body, however decomposed, in Numa's coffin, according to Lactantius, *Divinae Institutiones* I, 22, 5. ("Arcae duae lapideae sunt repertae a fossoribus, quarum in altera corpus Numae fuit, in altera . . . libri," and so forth).

13. Livy, *Ab Urbe Condita* XL, 29, 6. H. Bettenson's translation of *recentissima*. *Non integros modo sed recentissima specie*, might also be translated "not only *in toto* but looking almost new."

14. Pliny, *Historia Naturalis* XIII, 27, 85. ("Hos fuisse e charta, maiore etiamnum miraculo, quod infossi duraverint.")

15. Rose, "Dead," in *Oxford Classical Dictionary*. This article on disposing of the dead, for example, does not mention mummification. The body of Alexander the Great was embalmed in honey following Mesopotamian rather than Egyptian practices. For many sources, see Alan Rowe, "A Contribution to the Archaeology of the Western Desert: III," *Bulletin of the John Rylands Library* 38 (1955-56): 160-61. The preservation techniques of Mesopotamia, on the other hand, are probably themselves derived from Egypt, as those of Moses certainly were. Whatever their ultimate origin, however, the point is that all of these techniques have a common source somewhere in the ancient Near Orient.

16. Pliny, *Historia Naturalis* XIII, 27, 86. The stone cube (*lapidem quadratum circiter*) was quite literally "a stone hewn to the square on every side" — whether hollowed out or not. The text is a bit unstable: the crucial statement is *in eo lapide insuper libros III sitos fuisse*, which would ordinarily mean "three books had been placed on the top of this stone"; but a swarm of variant readings for *sitos* muddies the water. If we read "inserted" (*insitos*) for "placed" (*sitos*), we should probably also read the ambiguous *in* as "in" rather than "on," suggesting that the "stone cube" was a "stone container" of

some sort. But there are other variants (*inse positos, sepositos, impositos, situm,* and so forth), and it will take a better textual critic than I to figure out what is going on here.

17. The ancient sources disagree on the number of books and other particulars. I know of no way to reconcile all of their statements, but the consensus, for what it is worth, seems to be that two sets of seven books each were found in a separate coffin (one set in Latin treating Roman law, the other in Greek discussing sacral matters), not three books on or in a stone container or platform found in Numa's books. See also C. A. Forbes, "Books for the Burning," *Transactions of the American Philological Association* 67 (1936): 118. There exists scholarly skepticism about the whole story of Numa's books, and about everything else related to Numa: see R. M. Ogilvie, *A Commentary on Livy, Books 1-5* (Oxford: Clarendon, 1965), 88-95. See also Leon Herrmann, "Ennius et les Livres de Numa," *Latomus* 5 (January/June 1946): 87-90, for most of the sources dealing with this whole legend in antiquity.

18. C. T. Lewis and C. S. Short, "Citrus," in *A Latin Dictionary* (Oxford: Oxford University Press, 1975). The citrus and cedar trees are closely (even etymologically) related, both producing preservative oils which are poisonous to worms and insects. See also ibid., s.v. "candela." The wax covering a cord "preserved it from decay." Cf. Livy, *Ab Urbe Condita* XL, 29, 6, "Two bundles of seven books each wrapped up in waxed cords" (*duo fasces candelis involuti septenos habuere libros*) with A. Dupont-Sommer, *The Dead Sea Scrolls; a Preliminary Survey* (New York: Macmillan, 1952), 14, who described the linen swaths at Qumran that "were coated with wax or pitch or asphalt." See also Kahle, *The Cairo Geniza,* 14: "The scrolls had originally been wrapped carefully in linen and deposited in the earthenware jars the lids of which were tightly closed"; and Dupont-Sommer, *The Dead Sea Scrolls,* 15: "The shape of the jars," moreover, "is without parallel."

19. Dupont-Sommer, *The Dead Sea Scrolls,* 15.

20. Kahle, *The Cairo Geniza,* 14.

21. Cf. Roland de Vaux, "La Grotte des Manuscrits Hébreux," *Revue Biblique* 56 (1949): 596. He dates the ceramic jars which held the Dead Sea scrolls: "de la fin de l'époque hellénistique, elle est du IIe siècle avant notre ère, á la rigueur du début du Ier siècle, certainement antérieure à l'époque romaine." See also Highet, "Wondrous Survival of Records," 82. The papyrus Book of the Dead was unrolled "in excellent condition" in 1960 "three thousand years after it was buried in the tomb of an Egyptian high priest."

22. Dupont-Sommer, *The Dead Sea Scrolls*, 17. Also cf. Jean Doresse, *The Secret Books of the Egyptian Gnostics* (New York: Viking, 1960), 120-21.

23. Ibid., 121, n. 7.

24. John Dart, *The Laughing Savior: The Discovery and Significance of the Nag Hammadi Gnostic Library* (New York: Harper & Row, 1976), 36, 24, and cf. 49, 51; and Doresse, *Secret Books of Egyptian Gnostics*, 128, 133. For the best account of this discovery, see J. M. Robinson "The Jung Codex: The Rise and Fall of a Monopoly," *Religious Studies Review* 3 (1977): 17-30.

25. Doresse, *Secret Books of Egyptian Gnostics*, 134; and Dart, *The Laughing Savior*, 15. "The manuscripts were probably bound into book form about 350 and may have been hidden in the jar in 367, or as late as 400" (Dart, *The Laughing Savior*, 24). Cf. Doresse, *Secret Books of Egyptian Gnostics*, 135: "This library was hidden, at the latest, about the beginning of the fifth century [A.D. 400]." It has turned out to be "nothing less than the sacred library of an ancient [Christian] sect, to all appearances complete" (120).

26. Jean Doresse, "A Gnostic Library from Upper Egypt," *Archaeology* 3 (Summer 1950): 69-73. Cited in Dart, *The Laughing Savior*, 26. Cf. Doresse, *Secret Books of Egyptian Gnostics*, 136.

27. Dart, *The Laughing Savior*, 26. For a picture of the leather-bound papyrus codices, see 14.

28. Ibid., 22, 24; and Doresse, *Secret Books of Egyptian Gnostics*, 134, n. 35. Doresse also notes the wider application of these techniques: "It was in such receptacles [as jars] . . . that people usually stored their books and many other things" (ibid., 134). According to K. Preisendanz, *Papyrusfunde und Papyrusforschung* (Leipzig: Hiersemann, 1934), 113, "Manuscripts of the pharaonic age as well as the Roman epoch in Egypt have fairly often been found in jars."

29. Eusebius, *Chronicon* I, 3, in *PG* 19:114-16. A tall tale, perhaps; but maybe not, as important historical truths often lurk beneath stories such as this.

30. So many cuneiform libraries have survived from the ancient Near East that one example, the collection from Tell El Amarna, must suffice. See for examples: William F. Albright, "The Amarna Letters from Palestine," in I. E. S. Edwards et al., eds., *The Cambridge Ancient History*, 3rd ed., 12 vols. (Cambridge: Cambridge University Press, 1975), 2:2:98-116; and A. H. Sayce, "The Cuneiform Tablets," in William M. F. Petrie, ed., *Tell el Amarna* (Wiltshire, England: Aris & Phillips, 1974), 34-37. In the West there were two good examples — the palace libraries of Knossus and Pylos; see John A. Chadwick,

The Decipherment of Linear B, 2nd ed. (Cambridge: Cambridge University Press, 1967). The discoveries of both collections—over three thousand tablets found in 1900 by Sir Arthur Evans, and six hundred in 1939 by Carl Blegen—are discussed for nonspecialists in Chadwick's monograph, 5-39.

31. Highet, "Wondrous Survival of Records," 76. Cf. Dart, *The Laughing Savior,* 26: "There does not exist, even in Greek papyri, anything comparable [to the Nag Hammadi library]." Dart is here quoting Doresse, who overstates the case because the full significance of Qumran had not yet become apparent; but Doresse is certainly correct in relation to Greco-Roman literature.

32. Highet, "Wondrous Survival of Records," 90.

33. Ibid., 93, "In one day's work at Oxyrhynchus . . . Bernard P. Grenfell and A. S. Hunt got thirty-six basketfulls of papyrus rolls out of one mound alone. These had apparently been discarded as worthless."

34. Ibid. One of the very earliest Greek manuscripts, which contains our only text of a poem by Timotheus, "was discovered in a leather pouch, laid carefully in the coffin of a dead Greek soldier buried in Egypt." The second book of the *Iliad* "was set in a coffin as a pillow beneath the head of a young woman." The text of a lost play by Euripides, the *Antiope,* was partially restored from a mummy case wrapping; and the scroll from a stone box, which survived for who knows how long, was discarded in a manure pile by the farmer who found it, ibid.

35. Ibid., "At Tebtunis, . . . Grenfell and Hunt came on a cemetery of sacred crocodiles. One dead sacred crocodile is very like another, and the job of excavating these saurian mummies soon palled. Eventually a workman lost his temper and smashed one of them to pieces. Then it appeared that the crocodiles . . . were encased in molded papyri, and some even had rolls stuffed into their mouths 'and other cavities.' From such absurd hiding places do we recover the records of the past."

36. Ibid., 90, "If you wish information to survive for many centuries, however, cut it on stone or bake it on clay. . . . Do not try casting it in metal, for someone will almost certainly melt it down." The lowly clay tablet, which has no intrinsic value, is the all-time winner at the survival game, whereas metals like gold and silver have always been a prime target for looters. Metal documents have nevertheless managed to survive all over the ancient world. See H. Curtis Wright, "Metallic Documents of Antiquity," *BYU Studies* 10 (1970): 457-77. Many hundreds, and perhaps thousands, of exemplars are cited.

37. Lillian H. Jeffery, *The Local Scripts of Archaic Greece* (Oxford: Clarendon, 1963), 55-56. Writings on gold, silver, lead, tin, and other metals are known in the West, which nevertheless seemed to prefer bronze. "The most famous instance [from Italy] is that of the Twelve Tables [of Roman law], c. 450 (*tabulae, deltoi*), but earlier instances are recorded, beginning with Ancus Marcius." Greek examples, "in addition to the large number of Elean and other [bronze] plaques which have survived at Olympia, . . . have been found in Athens, Megara, Ozolian Lokris, Arkadia, Achaia, Sikyon, Lakonia, Argos, Hermion, Mycenae, in Sicily near Leontinoi, and in the Achaian colonies round Kroton," 55.

38. Ibid., 55-56.

39. Ibid., 56: "Lead was used in scroll form in the late Hittite Empire, and this usage may possibly have spread to the Greeks, for Pausanias saw what he thought was a very old text of Hesiod inscribed on lead at Helikon . . . ; but the earliest surviving examples are of curses (*defixiones*) of the fifth and fourth centuries B.C. Silver is used for a plaque dedicated at Ephesus . . . , and [for] a smaller one found at Poseidonia in Italy."

40. William K. C. Guthrie, *Orpheus and Greek Religion: A Study of the Orphic Movement* (New York: Norton, 1966), 176, and pls. 8-10. The Orphic gold plates, found in different parts of the Mediterranean world and dating from the fifth century B.C. to the second or third centuries A.D. constitute the basic sources of Orphic doctrine, 171-87. See also Wright, "Metallic Documents of Antiquity," 465-66, 474-75. Pythagoreanism, which was associated with Numa's books, also helps explain the Near Eastern impact on Plato's thought.

41. Giovanni Colonna, "The Sanctuary at Pyrgi in Etruria," *Archaeology* 19 (January 1966): 11, 23.

42. J. Heurgon, "The Inscriptions of Pyrgi," *Journal of Roman Studies* 56 (1966): 5-6. The bronze inscription "is a little earlier than the three other inscriptions," 6. See Colonna, "The Sanctuary at Pyrgi," 21: The gold inscriptions "go back to ca. 500 B.C., or a little later." The dating of these plates varies somewhat in other scholarly accounts.

43. H. Nesselhauf, "Zwei Bronzeurkunden aus Minigua," *Mitteilungen des deutschen archäologischen Instituts (Madrid)* 1 (1960): 142. These Gast- und Patronatsverträge fall "between the years 27 B.C. and 40 A.D.," although their dates "cannot be determined exactly," 147-48. They were discovered in 1958. "As with all legal agreements, the guest and patron agreements were drawn up on bronze tablets," 147.

44. C. Duroiselle, "Excavations at Hmawza," *Annual Report of the Archaeological Survey of India* (1926-27): 171.

45. Ibid., 179. Cf. "The Gold-leaf Pali Manuscript of Old Prome," *Report of the Superintendent, Archaeological Survey of Burma* (1938-39): 12. "These [twenty] leaves, within their two gold covers, were found bound together by a thick gold wire with its ends fastened to the covers by sealing wax and small glass beads. There are two holes in each leaf and cover, through which the gold wire was passed, to keep the whole in position and proper order. It was necessary to cut this wire in order to free the leaves," Duroiselle, "Excavations at Hmawza," 179, pl. 42g.

46. Ibid., 180. Duroiselle adds that "this is the reason why, in some cases . . . in the absence of other relics, manuscripts are enshrined in pagodas. This custom is responsible for the discovery of our manuscript," which was regarded "as embodying the Dharma." Cf. two other inscribed gold plates from the same region, which were found in a brick in an old pagoda; Maung Tun Nyein, "Maunggun Gold Plates," *Epigraphia Indica* 5 (1898-99): 101-2.

47. M. Anstock-Darga, "Semitische Inschriften auf Silbertafelchen aus dem 'Bertiz'-Tal (Umgebung von 'Maras')," *Jahrbuch für kleinasiatische Forschung* 1 (1950): 199-200. The texts from two of these plates were published by Anstock-Darga in a different journal with a similar title. See *Jahrbuch für kleinasiatische Forschungen* 1 (1949): 75ff. The plates are thought to date from late Hittite times, probably in the late seventh century B.C. The actual details of their discovery are obscure.

48. Richard E. Ellis, *Foundation Deposits in Ancient Mesopotamia* (New Haven, CT: Yale University Press, 1968), 98. The burial of this Schalenkapsel (with pictures of the three bowls, a technical description of the plates, and a sectional drawing of the whole package) is discussed in W. Andrae, *Die jüngeren Ischtar-Tempel in Assur* (Leipzig: Hinrich, 1935), 51-54.

49. See Ellis, *Foundation Deposits*, 124-25, 161; and J. A. Montgomery, *Aramaic Incantation Texts from Nippur*, "Publications of the Babylonian Section," vol. 3 (Philadelphia, PA: The University Museum, 1913), 26-41. The Aramaic incantation bowls, for example, "are roughly hemispherical; the writing is usually on the inside, though sometimes the outside was also inscribed. . . . Most of them have been found buried in the ground upside down; sometimes two bowls are found together, one inverted over the other" (Ellis, *Foundation Deposits*, 124-25).

50. I call these metal tablets "plates" because another set of

seven *stone* tablets, also found at Persepolis, is constantly confused with them. I spent a hectic couple of days, for example, searching the *New York Times* for "Herzfeld's translation into English of two inscriptions": See Roland G. Kent, "The Present Status of Old Persian Studies," *Journal of the American Oriental Society* 56 (1936): 211-12. It finally became clear that the Oriental Institute of Chicago had released only the story of the stone tablets of Xerxes to the *Times* ("Tablets Reveal Deeds of Xerxes," *New York Times*, 9 February 1936, sec. 2, p. 9). But it published both that story and an account of the Darius plates in J. P. Barden, "Xerxes a Doughty Warrior until He Met the Greeks," *University of Chicago Magazine* (February 1936): 23-25. The stone tablets were discovered in 1936 by E. F. Schmidt, the metal plates by Ernst E. Herzfeld in 1933.

51. Kent, "Present Status of Old Persian Studies," 209.

52. Ernst E. Herzfeld, "Eine neue Darius-Inschrift aus Hamadan," *Deutsche Literaturzeitung* 47 (1926): 2105. He adds that the inscription "was thus found in its original position and would have been preserved in perfect condition had it not been subsequently cut up into about twenty small pieces for the purpose of melting it down. As luck would have it, the document was spared this fate." Throughout this article Herzfeld speaks in the singular of "the inscription," which was actually recorded in duplicate on both a gold and a silver plate.

53. Ibid. These plates, which launched a new era of old Persian studies, were much discussed. For further discussion see Carl D. Buck, "A New Darius Inscription," *Language* 3 (1927): 1-5; S. Smith, "Inscription of Darius on Gold Tablet," *Journal of the Royal Asiatic Society* (1926): 433-34; Roland G. Kent, "The Recently Published Old Persian Inscriptions," *Journal of the American Oriental Society* 51 (1931): 229-31; F. H. Weissbach, "Zu der Goldinschrift des Dareios I," *Zeitschrift für Assyrologie und verwandte Gebiete* 37 (1937): 291-94; Ernst E. Herzfeld, "A New Inscription of Darius from Hamadan," *Memoirs of the Archaeological Survey of India* 34 (1928): 1-7.

54. Ellis, *Foundation Deposits*, 104. The lids had been so tightly fitted to the boxes that they were opened only with the greatest of difficulty. The sides of the first box had already been broken before being excavated, but the second box was retrieved intact. They are described as "carefully" and "beautifully" cut limestone boxes by Kent, "Present Status of Old Persian Studies," 212; and Barden, "Xerxes a Doughty Warrior," 25.

55. Barden, "Xerxes a Doughty Warrior," 25.

56. Ernst E. Herzfeld, *Altpersische Inschriften*, Erster Ergänzungs-

band zu den archaeologischen Mitteilungen aus Iran (Berlin: Reimer, 1938), 18-19. See Herzfeld for the photograph of one of the duplicate sets of the Darius plates from Persepolis (pl. VI). The plates from Hamadan were 19 cm square, whereas the Persepolis plates measure 33 cm by 33 cm. This accounts for the different line arrangements of the tablets. Each tablet was trilingual, incidentally, repeating the same information in Old Persian, Elamite, and Babylonian.

57. For Ariaramnes, see Roland G. Kent, "The Oldest Old Persian Inscriptions," *Journal of the American Oriental Society* 66 (1946): 206-12. For Arsames and Artaxerxes II, see A. V. Pope, "Recently Found Treasures: Achaemenid Gold Objects," *Illustrated London News*, 17 July 1946, 58-59; and H. H. Paper, "An Old Persian Text of Darius II (D2Ha)," *Journal of the American Oriental Society* 72 (1953): 169-70, illus. opp. 169. Additional sources on Ariaramnes, Arsames, and Artaxerxes are found in Roland G. Kent, *Old Persian: Grammar, Texts, Lexicon*, 2nd ed. rev. (New Haven, CT: American Oriental Society, 1953), 107, 111-12. Some scholars, but not all by any means, regard the first two plates as forgeries.

58. The gold tablets of Darius I, Ariaramnes, and Arsames were cut into twenty, five, and three pieces respectively. See note 52 above; Kent, "Recently Published Old Persian Inscriptions," 229-30; Kent, "Oldest Old Persian Inscriptions," 207; Pope, "Recently Found Treasures," 58, illus. 5; and Kent, *Old Persian*, 107.

59. Smith, "Inscription of Darius," 433.

60. See the graphic summary of foundation documents on clay, metal, and stone in Ellis, *Foundation Deposits*, illus. 36. Metal foundation inscriptions probably derived from the early Mesopotamian peg deposits, which are "first attested from EDII [2700-2500 B.C.]. The use of the peg was . . . varied in form during EDIII [2500-2300 B.C.]. An important innovation during this period was the inclusion of inscribed objects with building deposits. Inscribed ovoids and cones of stone and metal, which may have been the prototypes of later clay cylinders, were apparently used as building deposits, both alone and together with peg figures, from the time of Eannatum of Lagas," 154.

61. M. E. L. Mallowan, "Excavations at Brak and Chagar Bazar," *Iraq* 9 (1947): 87a, pl. 48, no. 6. The object is called "an alabaster foundation box," 54. It is further described as a "foundation box, white limestone, measuring 51 x 23 x 17 cm. This box, which had been pulled to pieces by plunderers, was reconstituted and photographed on the spot where it was found. . . . It consisted of eight blocks and originally contained two, or possibly four, compart-

ments. The separate blocks were riveted together and stuck with white lime mortar. . . . There is, indeed, no proof that this was a foundation box, since it was not found in its original position, but the fact that it had been torn to pieces suggests that it had originally contained treasure, and there are later analogies for the construction of brick foundation boxes. . . . If the Brak foundation box belonged to the Eye-Temple of the Jamdat Nasr [or late protoliterate] period [3100-2900 B.C.], it is the earliest object of its type, and the absence of its contents is a grievous loss," 195-96.

62. It was interrupted, that is, by the different informational practices of the Akkadians, Neo-Sumerians, and Old Assyrians. The Neo-Babylonians, of course, completely disrupted the tradition, Ellis, *Foundation Deposits*, illus. 36.

63. Ellis, *Foundation Deposits*, 104, 161.

64. Discussed by Adolph J. Reinach, "Dioskourides g tomoi," *Bulletin de la Société Royale d'Archéologie d'Alexandrie* 11 (1909): 350-70.

65. See Alan Rowe, *Discovery of the Famous Temple and Enclosure of Serapis at Alexandria*, Supplement aux Annales du Service des Antiquites de l'Egypt, Cahiere 2 (Le Caire, France: Institut Francais d'Archéologie Orientale, 1946).

66. Cf. Mortimer Wheeler, *Flames over Persepolis, Turning-Point in History* (London: Weidenfeld and Nicolson, 1968), 127: "The end of Persepolis was the end of the Persian Empire."

67. Edward M. Burns and Philip L. Ralph, *World Civilizations: Their History and Their Culture*, 5th ed. (New York: Norton, 1974), 71. "The culture of the Persians . . . was largely derived from that of previous civilizations. Much of it came from Mesopotamia, but a great deal of it from Egypt, and some from Lydia and northern Palestine," 72. The combined influence of this cultural synthesis had been enormous. Mitigated somewhat in Hellenistic times, it nevertheless affected Alexandrian civilization, overwhelmed the Greco-Roman tradition in late antiquity, and sustained the Middle Ages for nearly a thousand years. It has also created the ambivalence of modern thought by confronting humanism with theological presuppositions. After the Egyptian capitulation to Persia in 525 B.C., "the ancient civilization [of Egypt] was never again revived," 32.

68. Ernst E. Herzfeld, *Archaeological History of Iran* (London: Oxford University Press, 1935), 22. "The palaces [at Ecbatana] had columns and roofs of cedar and cypresses . . . covered with metal; the roofs had tiles of silver and gold. . . . This display of wealth . . . is proved to be true by the discovery of similar gold

coverings at Persepolis. These were taken off and folded when Alexander's soldiers plundered the palace. In the same way Alexander and Seleucus I treated Agbatana. And still Antiochus coined 1 1/4 million sterling worth of money out of the tiles of the Anahit temple," 44. Anahit was later identified with Athena.

69. Robert W. Rogers, *A History of Ancient Persia* (New York: Scribner's Sons, 1929), 335-36. The loot from the palace at Persepolis "was conveyed to Susa temporarily and thence later to Ecbatana, whither it was carried, so the story goes, in 10,000 two-mule carts, and upon the backs of 5,000 camels." Cf. Ulrich Wilcken, *Alexander the Great* (New York: Norton, 1967), 337: "That Persepolis was deliberately looted and fired is certain." See also A. T. Olmstead, *History of the Persian Empire* (Chicago: University of Chicago Press, 1948), 520-22: "Their loot was enormous. . . . Had Persepolis been taken by sack and not freely surrendered . . . , it could not have received worse treatment. . . . So thorough was the search for loot that only a handful of coins have been unearthed by the excavators. A few more scraps of gold leaf are all of this precious metal that have rewarded their labors."

70. Pope, "Recently Found Treasures," 58-59.

71. Ellis, *Foundation Deposits*, 104. Cf. Erich F. Schmidt, *Persepolis*, 3 vols. (Chicago: University of Chicago Press, 1970), 1:79: "A square depression in the exposed bedrock at the destroyed northwest corner . . . induced [Fritz] Krefter," Herzfeld's architect, "to calculate the positions of the . . . northeast and southeast corners of the hall," where he discovered the limestone boxes laden with gold and silver plates. "Apparently both foundation boxes had been set into depressions just below the level of the lowest courses of the walls."

72. See André Parrot, *Le Temple d'Ishtar* (Paris: Geuthner, 1956), 55-57, fig. 38, pls. 23-24; André Parrot, "Les Fouilles de Mari: Première Campagne (Hiver 1933-34)," *Syria* 16 (1935): 117-40, fig. 11; André Parrot, "Les Fouilles de Mari: Quatrième Campagne (Hiver 1936-37)," *Syria* 19 (1938): 1-29, pl. 1, 3; and André Parrot, "Les Fouilles de Mari: Septième Campagne (Hiver 1951-52)," *Syria* 29 (1952): 183-203, pl. 18. See also E. J. Banks, *Bismya, or the Lost City of Adab* (New York: Knickerbocker, 1912), 200, 275; Daniel D. Luckenbill, *Inscriptions from Adab* (Chicago: University of Chicago Press, 1930), nos. 19-22; and Ellis, *Foundation Deposits*, 76-77, 154.

73. F. Thureau-Dangin, "Tablette de Samarra," *Revue d'Assyriologie et d'Archéologie Orientale* 9 (1912): 1-4, pl. 1.

74. André Parrot, "Les Fouilles de Mari: Neuvime Campagne (Automne 1953)," *Syria* 31 (1954): 161-62, fig. 5.

75. Ellis, *Foundation Deposits*, 95, 160.

76. Ibid., 146, 151, 173-174, 177-78.

77. E. de Sarzec and L. Herzey, *Decouvertes en Chaldee* (Paris: E. Leroux, 1884-1912), 2:71-72.

78. Ellis, *Foundation Deposits*, 63-64, 66-68, 142-43, 161.

79. Ibid., 130, 143-44.

80. Mallowan, "Excavations at Brak and Chagar Bazar," 33, 36-37, 50-51.

81. For the Elamite inscription, see Schmidt, *Persepolis*, 2:64-65, pls. 27-28. For myriads of similar inscriptions, see also Wright, "Metallic Documents of Antiquity," 457-77.

82. According to Hallo's revision of Porada, the Neo-Sumerian period (2300-2000 B.C.) includes both of the periods known as Post Akkadian (2300-2100 B.C.) and Ur III (2100-2000 B.C.). See William W. Hallo and William K. Simpson, *The Ancient Near East: A History* (New York: Harcourt, Brace, Jovanovich, 1971), 36-37, n. 16, 77. For the history of peg deposits, see Ellis, *Foundation Deposits*, 46-93.

83. André Parrot, "Les Fouilles de Mari: Sixième Campagne (Automne 1938)," *Syria* 21 (1940): 1-28. He added that "heretofore only the temple of Ishtar had yielded foundation deposits, all uninscribed," 5, n. 2. For a diagram of the six find-spots, cf. 6, fig. 4.

84. Ellis, *Foundation Deposits*, 58. For diagrams and photographs, see illus. 11; and Parrot, "Les Fouilles de Mari: Sixième," 7, pl. 2. Cf. G. Dossin, "Inscriptions de Fondation Provenant de Mari," *Syria* 21 (1940): 152-53: "Parrot . . . has explicitly noted that each [of the six deposits] included one or more inscriptions engraven on bronze plates or on stone tablets. The total of these inscriptions has risen to fifteen: four bronze plates from the Ninhursag Temple, two bronze plates from the building known as the shahuru, nine inscriptions from the 'Temple of Lions' (one bronze plate and two stone tablets from each of the three recently cleared deposits). . . . Each of the four bronze plates, in the form of a square, carries the identical inscription in six lines."

85. Parrot, "Les fouilles de Mari: Sixième," 20.

86. Ellis, *Foundation Deposits*, 59. For sketches and photographs, see illus. 12; and Parrot; "Les Fouilles de Mari: Sixième," 19-22, fig. 15, pls. 9-10.

87. Parrot, "Les Fouilles de Mari: Sixième," 6-7. For illustrations see Parrot, fig. 5 and pl. 2; and Ellis, *Foundation Deposits*, illus. 13. "The bronze plate bore a short text in Akkadian stating that Apil-kin had built the sahuru" (Ellis, *Foundation Deposits*, 60). The deposits of Apil-kin also suggest the three brick-lined cavities in the floor of

the palace at Mari, and the twenty-two cavities found at Telloh (Ellis, *Foundation Deposits*, 127-28, 142-43).

88. Ellis, *Foundation Deposits*, 66. He adds that "most of the Ur III deposits . . . were enclosed in capsules or boxes made of square baked bricks. . . . A cavity measuring 1 [brick] by 1/2 brick was reserved in the center of each course. The cavities . . . were [usually] six courses deep. . . . [They] were coated inside with bitumen," 66. For a sketch of the typical Ur III box, see Ellis, *Foundation Deposits*, illus. 21. Pegs and cylinders have also been found in brick boxes from the Isin-Larsa or later periods, 72, 114-15.

89. Ibid., 150. For a list of Amorite rulers in the Larsa Dynasty, see Oppenheim, *Ancient Mesopotamia*, 336-37.

90. Leonard C. Woolley, "Excavations at Ur, 1929-30," *Antiquaries Journal* 10 (1930): 323, fig. 1, pl. 38. Woolley here follows the older high chronology still accepted by some scholars. The date would be ca. 1831 B.C. according to Oppenheim, *Ancient Mesopotamia*, 337, who follows the middle chronology accepted by most scholars today.

91. Cyril J. Gadd, "Babylonian Foundation Texts: 1. Limestone and Copper Tablets of a Wife of Rim-Sin," *Journal of the Royal Asiatic Society* (1926): 679. The limestone and copper tablets, numbered 116662 and 116663 respectively, are now in the British Museum. The tablets are translated, with critical commentary and drawings, 679-84.

92. Leonard C. Woolley, "Excavations at Ur, 1924-1925," *Antiquaries Journal* 5 (1925): 368.

93. Ibid.

94. Leonard C. Woolley, *The Ziggurat and Its Surroundings* (New York: British Museum, 1939), 63. Cf. Woolley's other account of this find in Woolley, "Excavations at Ur, 1924-1925," 370, fig. 3, pl. 36, no. 1; and the account in Ellis, *Foundation Deposits*, 95. Also, "a couple tablets of stone and copper of Kurigalzu II," from the Middle Babylonian Period (ca. 1571-985 B.C.), "were found in secondary context at Ur, while cavities in the sides of a well in the same city probably once held tablets of the same king" (Ellis, *Foundation Deposits*, 160).

95. Ellis, *Foundation Deposits*, 6-7.

96. Ibid., 143, 174.

97. Ibid., 101; and Andrae, *Die jüngeren Ischtar-Tempel in Assur*, 54, n. 2. The tablet bears a Festungsmauerinschrift "that had to come from Assyria" (ibid.). It is translated in Daniel D. Luckenbill, *Ancient Records of Assyria and Babylonia*, 2 vols. (Chicago: University of Chicago Press, 1926-27), 1:251, item 706.

98. Ellis, *Foundation Deposits*, 160. This despite the fact that "the stone tablet was the most common form of building deposit" in the Middle Assyrian Period. Many of the building inscriptions from this period, whether on stone or metal, "were buried in foundations or built into walls," 60.

99. Ibid., 138. For the whole story of these deposits, see Andrae, *Die jüngeren Ischtar-Tempel in Assur*, 37-51, figs. 14-17, pls. 1-3, 17-25.

100. Ellis, *Foundation Deposits*, 99. See also the excellent photographs in Andrae, *Die jüngeren Ischtar-Tempel in Assur*, pls. 18, 21, 23.

101. Ellis, *Foundation Deposits*, 99: "The [alabaster] tablets of Adad-nirari I [1307-1275 B.C.] were buried in Tukulti-Ninurta's time."

102. Ibid., 98. He adds that "all of the inscribed objects, of stone, lead, and precious metals, were placed with the beginnings of their inscriptions up and toward the rear of the cella." Cf. illus. 28 for an informative drawing of these complicated arrangements. See also Andrae, *Die jüngeren Ischtar-Tempel in Assur*, figs. 14-17, pls. 1-3, 17-25.

103. Ellis, *Foundation Deposits*, 99. He adds that the only difference between the two sets of deposits was that "the three lead blocks beneath the stone slab were omitted in the Dinitu shrine."

104. These little "platelets" are described: Jean Bottéro, "Deux tablettes de fondation, en or et en argent, d'Assurnasirpal II," *Semitica* 1 (1948): 25-32. The gold plate measures approximately 1 5/8" by 5/8" by 1/12", the silver plate about 2 1/2" by 1 1/2" by 1/7", 25. "The gold plaquette . . . has suffered a bit, especially on the back side, where it is hammered in spots. Each bears eighteen lines of writing, nine per side," 25.

105. Ibid.

106. R. Campbell Thompson and Richard W. Hutchinson, "The Excavations on the Temple of Nabu at Nineveh," *Archaeologia* 79 (1929): 108, 109, n. 1. The excavators of the Nabu Temple, after listing their "chief finds during 1927-8," were also shown "two small plaques—one in gold, the other in lead—inscribed with a text of Assurnasirpal, indicating that he had decorated the palace of the city Apki for his abode." But they declined to discuss the plaques further, "as it would trench too far on the possessor's rights." See also Ferris J. Stephens, "The Provenience of the Gold and Silver Tablets of Ashurnasirpal," *Journal of Cuneiform Studies* 7 (1953): 73. According to Stephens, "it seems probable that these were our gold

and silver tablets. The silver piece might easily be mistaken for lead since it has indentations on the reverse giving the appearance of softness in the metal. It is of course possible that there was also a lead copy of the inscription. . . . The note of Thompson and Hutchinson is included in the report of finds in 1927-8. This may be taken as the date of the discovery of the pieces," 73.

107. Bottéro, "Deux tablettes de fondation" translated and transliterated by Bottéro. See also Ellis, *Foundation Deposits*, 100: "This is one of the few instances in which we can be certain that a term actually used in a building deposit text refers to the objects on which it is written."

108. Bottéro, "Deux tablettes de fondation," 30: "Établir les fondations sur des documents."

109. Ibid. He adds that "*temmenu* is also basically the synonym of *ussu*." The cuneiform sentence under discussion is *ina arhi tabi umemeseme ina samni GULA samni tabi kaspi hurasi addi temmen-su*. This statement is fully discussed by E. Nassouhi, "Prism d'Assurbanipal daté de se Trentième Année, Provenant du Temple da Gula à Babylone," *Archiv für Keilschriftforschung* 2 (1924-25): 97-106.

110. Hugh Nibley, "Genesis of the Written Word," in Truman G. Madsen, ed., *Nibley on the Timely and the Timeless: Classic Essays of Hugh W. Nibley* (Salt Lake City, UT: Publishers, 1978), 120. See also Ellis, *Foundation Deposits*, 163. "Building deposits are found in both religious and secular buildings," i.e., in temples and palaces, but "private houses did not have them."

111. See H. Curtis Wright, *The Oral Antecedents of Greek Librarianship* (Provo, UT: Brigham Young University Press, 1978). I have discussed this occurrence in the first half of the fourth millennium B.C. in the chapter, "Before and After the Permanent Temple," 43-64. For its recurrence *mutatis mutandis* in the West, see also, "The Age of Revolution," 94-107. The consequences of these two occurrences for civilization are not to be underestimated. The symbolism of foundation documents may also extend to the empires established by the various "fathers" of different peoples, and even to the foundation of the universe by God. See Lord Raglan, *The Origins of Religion* (London: Watts, 1949), 58-69; and Sigmund Mowinckel, *Religion und Kultus* (Göttingen: Vandenhoeck, 1953), 76, 94.

112. Bottéro, "Deux tablettes de fondation," 29. He adds that "it is enough to cite . . . the nine foundation deposits found by Parrot at Mari," and "the tablets of gold, silver, bronze, lead, alabaster, and marble exhumed from the foundations of the palace of Sargon at Nineveh," 10-12. Bottéro also cites as evidence the inscribed gold

and silver plates of Tukulti-Ninurta I, which were "recovered from a bed of pearls," and the gold inscription of Shalmaneser I (Bottéro, "Deux tablettes de fondation, 29, n. 1).

113. Ibid., 26. He adds a blessing if his deposit is respected by a subsequent monarch: "May the Prince who comes after me not efface my name which I have written here! May Assur, the Great Lord, attend his prayer," 26.

114. Ellis, *Foundation Deposits*, 100.

115. See text accompanying n. 61 and 87.

116. "A Foundation-Box from Tell Abu-Maria in Iraq," *Art and Archaeology* 30 (1930): 190.

117. Ephraim A. Speiser, "Translations of the Foundation-Box from Tell Abu-Maria," *Art and Archaeology* 30 (1930): 191.

118. Ibid., 190 (for the decipherment, see 190-91). Inscriptions on the outsides of stone boxes recall the incantation bowl inscriptions on both the insides and outsides of bowls (n. 49).

119. Ibid., 191. The box was given to someone in Philadelphia by friends in Iraq, and no one has been able to determine its exact provenance or find-conditions.

120. Stephens, "Provenience of Gold and Silver Tablets," 74. This article recapitulates the scholarly attempt to locate ancient Apqu (including the original clue provided by Thompson and Hutchinson, the "incorrect interpretation of the name of the city" [p. 74] by Bottéro, and its correct identification by Lewy), and offers this reconstruction: "The first builder of a palace in Apqu was Ashur-resh-ishi I (1132-1115 B.C.), whose grandson Ashur-belkala (1073-1056 B.C.) completed his work. . . . When Adad-nirari II (911-891 B.C.) came to the throne he found the city of Apqu completely ruined. He . . . rebuilt it entirely . . . [and] built a royal palace there. . . . This palace was still standing in the time of Ashur-nasirpal II (883-859 B.C.), the grandson of Adad-nirari II," 73. The discovery at Bumariyah of "a baked brick with an inscription of Ashur-resh-ishi," together with the foundation-box inscription of Assurnasirpal II, makes it very probable "that Bumariyah was ancient Apqu, and that our gold and silver tablets came from there," 74.

121. H. Rassam, "Excavations and Discoveries in Assyria," *Transactions of the Society of Biblical Archaeology* 7 (1882): 45. The identification of Balawat with Imgur-Bel, also known as Imgur-Enlil, is rejected by others. See E. A. Wallis Budge and L. W. King, eds., *Annals of the Kings of Assyria* (London: British Museum), 167-68, n. 2. But it is accepted by Luckenbill, *Ancient Records of Assyria and Babylonia*, 1:194; and regarded as putative by Ekhard Unger, "Imgun-

Enlin," in Max Ebert, ed., *Reallexikon der Vorgeschichte* (Berlin: Verlag W. de Gruyter, 1924-82), 6:50. Only "the upper side of the box was inscribed" (Ellis, *Foundation Deposits*, 101). For the inscription, see E. A. Wallis Budge, "On a Recently Discovered Text of Assur-natsir-pal, B.C. 885," *Transactions of the Society of Biblical Archaeology* 7 (1882): 59-82; Budge and King, *Annals of the Kings of Assyria*, 1:167-73; and Luckenbill, *Ancient Records of Assyria and Babylonia*, 1:194, 96.

122. Rassam, "Excavations and Discoveries in Assyria," 53.

123. Ibid., 54-55. The chamber turned out to be part of the Temple of Machir.

124. Ibid., 55. He adds that "in this chamber a large quantity of human remains were found."

125. Budge, "Recently Discovered Text of Assur-natsir-pal," 59.

126. Rassam, "Excavations and Discoveries in Assyria," 54. "I was meditating about the removal of the coffer to Mossul . . . ; but how to remove this huge block of marble for a distance of about fifteen miles without a cart was more than my wits and engineering could at once accomplish. . . . I was at my wits' end how to accomplish the immediate removal of the marble coffer into Mossul." The box is variously referred to as a "stone coffer," a "marble chest," a "marble coffer," and a "huge block of marble" by Rassam and others, 53-55; as a "limestone coffer" by Budge and King, *Annals of the Kings of Assyria* 1:167, n. 2; and even as "ein Koffer aus Gipsstein mit zwei Steintafeln aus demselben Material" by Unger, "Imgun-Enlin," 6:50. It may have been made of alabaster, as implied by Budge, "Recently Discovered Text of Assur-natsir-pal," 59. Ellis, *Foundation Deposits*, 100-101, is silent as to its material. H. Rassam, *Asshur and the Land of Nimrod* (Cincinnati: Curts & Jennings, 1897), 216-17, merely repeats the above account.

127. Ellis, *Foundation Deposits*, 101. For the text from this box, see O. Schroeder, *Keilschrifttexte aus Assur Historischen Inhalts* (Wissenschaftliche Veröffentlichung der deutschen Orient-Gesselschaft, 16, 37), 2 vols. (Leipzig: Hinrich, 1911-22), 2:66; and W. Andrae, *Die Festungswerke von Assur: Textband* (Ausgrabungen der deutschen Orient Gesselschaft in Assur, A: Baudenkmaler aus assyrischer Zeit, 2; Wissenschaftliche Veröffentlichung der deutschen Orient-Gesellschaft, 23 (Leipzig: Hinrichs, 1913), 175. For its transliteration with a German translation, a drawing, and a photograph see, ibid., 174-75, and pl. 104. For its English translation, see Luckenbill, *Ancient Records of Assyria and Babylonia*, 1:251, items 703-5 (where the box is called an "alabaster slab"!). This box is also discussed in *Die Welt des Orients* 1 (1947-52): 387-88, which I have not seen.

128. Ellis, *Foundation Deposits*, 100.

129. Ibid., 14-15.

130. Ibid., 101, 104-5. Ellis adds that "there is evidently no question of the box having been buried in the structure of the building," 101.

131. Luckenbill, *Ancient Records of Assyria and Babylonia*, 1:251. This common formula is also included in the inscription on the Balawat box. See Budge, "Recently Discovered Text of Assur-natsir-pal," 77.

132. Ellis, *Foundation Deposits*, 105. He adds that "a parallel practice would be the preservation in temples of tablet-shaped kudurru's [boundary stones], which are generally assumed to be 'Tempelurkunden' rather than 'Feldurkunden' " (ibid.).

133. "Es könnte eine Bibliothekskiste gewesen sein," S. Marinatos, "Verlust einer Handschrift in Messenien," *Gnomon* 33 (1961): 233.

134. Ellis, *Foundation Deposits*, 105. He adds that "it would have been simple enough to adopt the box later for tablet-shaped building deposits" or vice versa, I should think.

135. Ibid. "Three such statues have been found in Adad-nirari III's Nabu Temple at Nimrud. Three others, and a fragment that probably belongs to a fourth, turned up at Arslan Tash and nearby sites," 105-6.

136. M. E. L. Mallowan, *Nimrud and Its Remains*, 3 vols. (London: Collins, 1966), 1:260-61, 351-52, n. 48.

137. Ellis, *Foundation Deposits*, 106. Cf. M. E. L. Mallowan, "The Excavations at Nimrud (Kalhu), 1955," *Iraq* 18 (1956): 7 and pl. 2. These statues were each carrying "a box for the god. What was the box supposed to contain? Perhaps it was the tablets, the tablets of destiny or the like, appropriate to the god of learning and the scribal arts, in whose precincts many learned documents, particularly of a religious character, were once housed." See also Mallowan, *Nimrud and Its Remains*, 1:260-61.

138. Ellis, *Foundation Deposits*, 102-3, 134, 152, 176.

139. Ibid., 135.

140. Ibid., 101. Khorsabad, also known as Dur-Sharrukin, was the "capital of Assyria, founded by Sargon II (721-705 B.C.), twelve miles northeast of Nineveh. . . . The city had been built toward the end of the reign of Sargon and seems to have been maintained as seat of a governor for nearly a century thereafter" (Oppenheim, *Ancient Mesopotamia*, 393).

141. Maurice Pillet, *Khorsabad: Les Découvertes de V. Place en As-*

syrie (Paris: Éditions E. Leroux, 1918), 84. I have not seen the basic account of this discovery by Victor Place, *Ninive et l'Assyrie*, 3 vols. (Paris: Imprimerie Imperiale, 1867-70), 1:61-63; 2:267, 303-7; 3: pls. 4, 77. This source should by all means be consulted, if possible. A second account by J. Oppert, who did not witness the discovery, is also presented (Place, *Ninive et l'Assyrie*, 2:303), where seven inscribed materials are listed. Oppert was mistaken here, as he apparently followed Sargon's list of seven epigraphical substances deposited in various foundations instead of reporting what Place actually found (Pillet, *Khorsabad*, 84-85). The mistake has persisted to this day despite its correction; see Jules Oppert, *Expédition Scientifique en Mésopotamie*, 2 vols. (Paris: Imprimerie Imperiale, 1868-69), 2:343. The resulting confusion of the Assyriological literature on this point is discussed; see Ellis, *Foundation Deposits*, 102, n. 2.

142. Pillet, *Khorsabad*, 84. On the identification of the "white material" of the fifth tablet, see B. Landsberger, "Tin and Lead: The Adventures of Two Vocables," *Journal of Near Eastern Studies* 24 (1965): 285-86, and n. 7; and R. Campbell Thompson, *A Dictionary of Assyrian Chemistry and Geology* (Oxford: Clarendon, 1936), 116-17. The material of the fifth tablet was "properly alabaster (carbonate of lime), equated sometimes with parutu, marble," 117, and Landsberger would more or less agree. However, "no inscriptions on marble or alabaster were discovered by the digs of Botta or Place" (Pillet, *Khorsabad*, 85). The material of the fifth tablet is identified as magnesite (Ellis, *Foundation Deposits*, 102). On the "extreme rarity" of metallic documents like Sargon's, I can only say that they are not as scarce as Pillet thinks, for virtually everybody underestimates the relatively large number of gold, silver, bronze, lead, and other metal epigraphs created by the ancients.

143. The measurements of the bronze, silver, and gold tablets in inches are about 8" x 5" x 1/6", and 3" x 1 1/2" x 1/5" respectively; and the tablet of "white material" measures about 4" x 2 1/2" x 2/5" inches: David G. Lyon, *Keilschrifttexte Sargons Könige von Assyrien (722-705 v. Chr.)* (Leipzig: Hinrich, 1883), xii-xiii.

144. Ellis, *Foundation Deposits*, 102. The box "had a lid with a cuneiform inscription."

145. Pillet, *Khorsabad*, 87; and Luckenbill, *Ancient Records of Assyria and Babylonia*, 2:56. The first four tablets, which were brought out of Assyria by Place himself, are presently in the Louvre Museum. As the box and the leaden tablets were too heavy for inclusion in his personal luggage, however, Place decided to load them on the rafts which were supposed to bring the products of his digs down

the Tigris River to Bassora. But the rafts capsized at Qurnah and everything was lost, including the leaden tablet and the stone box with its broken lid-inscription; see Pillet, *Khorsabad*, 85; Pillet, *Expédition Scientifique*, 2:343; Ellis, *Foundation Deposits*, 102; François Lenormant, "Les Norms de l'Airain et du Cuivre," *Transactions of the Society of Biblical Archaeology* 6 (1878): 337; and Lyon, *Keilschrifttexte Sargons*, xii. This may be the most tragic loss of archaeological artifacts in the history of archaeology.

146. Ellis, *Foundation Deposits*, 103.

147. Luckenbill, *Ancient Records of Assyria and Babylonia*, 2:57-59, items 107-15. For the cuneiform texts together with various transliterations, translations, and commentaries, see Oppert, *Expédition Scientifique*, 2:343-50; Lyon, *Keilschrifttexte Sargons*, 20-21, 47-57, 82; and Hugo Winckler, *Die Keilschrifttexte Sargons*, 2 vols. (Leipzig: Pfeiffer, 1889), 2:43-45.

148. Ellis, *Foundation Deposits*, 103. "The date of the founding of the temple is not known, but the city was founded by Rusas I (733-714 B.C.)."

149. Ibid. Ellis adds that "it is impossible to say whether the Urartean practices derived from Mesopotamia, from the Hittites, or were a native development," 103). Urartia was an Iron Age kingdom in central Turkey which paralleled the Neo-Assyrian dynasty (858-609 B.C.).

150. Ibid., 104, 157. The empire started falling to pieces during the reign of Assurbanipal (668-626 B.C.), and he was followed by four minor-league kings who could do nothing to arrest the sudden decline of Assyria or prevent the frightful vengeance taken on her by her enemies. "Building deposits in this [Neo-Babylonian] period were limited almost entirely to clay cylinders," 157.

151. Ellis, *Foundation Deposits*, 105. A clay box "was made in Nabopolassar's reign (625-605 B.C.) to hold an ancient tablet recording a temple endowment by Nabu-apla-iddina, a younger contemporary of Assurnasirpal II (883-859 B.C.). Rassam found the box beneath the bitumen floor of an otherwise undescribed room near the ziggurat of Sippar. What exactly it contained is now difficult to establish; certainly there was a stone tablet with a relief picture and an inscription and two baked clay impressions of the relief on that tablet. The box and the back of one of the [clay] impressions bore inscriptions of Nabopolassar. This box is of course no building deposit but it represents a pious disposal of valued, though useless, antiques."

152. S. M. A. As-Siwani, "A Prism from Ur," *Sumer* 20 (1964):

69. In 1960-61 at Ur, a "barrel-shaped prism in buff clay" was discovered. "It is covered with a cuneiform inscription belonging to Nabuna'id [Nabonidus] (555-539 B.C.), the last Chaldean King of Babylon. . . . It had been built into the wall in a box of burnt bricks lined with bitumen."

153. Ellis, *Foundation Deposits*, 104, 161. Evidence for the disruption of this practice by the Neo-Babylonians is also provided by the Achaemenid jewelers, who deliberately followed Neo-Assyrian rather than Neo-Babylonian customs: See John B. Bury et al., eds., *The Assyrian Empire* (Cambridge: Cambridge University Press, 1929), 109.

154. Peter M. Fraser, *Ptolemaic Alexandria*, 3 vols. (Oxford: Clarendon, 1972), 1:8.

155. Ibid., 8-9. "It is to be noted that the Corniche only completed or elaborated a process which had begun in 1882. . . . 'Much material (often from the ancient city) has been tipped into the sea . . . to secure the site of the new homes built since the events of 1882.' " See also D. G. Hogarth, "Report of Prospects of Research in Alexandria," *Report of the Egypt Exploration Society* (1894-95): 9. (Cited in Fraser, *Ptolemaic Alexandria*, 2:20, n. 34.) A similar subsidence has complicated excavations from the Old Babylonian period at Babylon (Ellis, *Foundation Deposits*, 159).

156. Fraser, *Ptolemaic Alexandria*, 1:9. "When the Corniche was built, and subsequently when 'fill' has been required . . . , the soil necessary for this task was largely taken from . . . the neighbourhood of Lake Mairut and from the mounds . . . between Chatby and the Jewish and Christian cemeteries to the South. The ancient sherds in the soil . . . were emptied along with it in the sea. . . . Consequently, when soil . . . is dug, early Ptolemaic sherds . . . may be found among or above Roman and Byzantine sherds. . . . Soil from modern foundations full of ancient sherds had . . . formed new elevations subsequently built upon. True stratification is thus limited to individual sections of undisturbed building structure and the associated finds, if any." "The built-up pseudo-coastal belt of the harbour area also creates insoluble stratigraphical problems."

157. Ibid., 10.

158. Ibid., 9. The cemetery excavations are also complicated by "the gradual growth of deposits . . . ejected on the sands," as deep as thirty feet at times, which contain "remains of all periods in complete disorder, beneath which the Ptolemaic and Roman graves lie largely undisturbed." The cemeteries have nevertheless yielded

important "tombs of different types and dates" and played "a key role in the determination of the chronology of early Alexandria."

159. Ibid., 1:27-28.

160. Rudolf Pfeiffer, *History of Classical Scholarship* (Oxford: Clarendon, 1968), 102, n. 2.

161. Fraser, *Ptolemaic Alexandria*, 1:36, 37. The result is that "the development of Alexandria as a city largely escapes us" and that "we are still a long way from being able to follow, and shall indeed never be able to follow, the development of the city as a historical process."

162. Ibid., 2:91, n. 191. "The ultimate in confusion is . . . Botti's attempt to explain and identify the statues [described by Letronne]. . . . Rowe . . . also gets into deep waters, where we may leave him" (2:89, n. 190).

163. Rowe, *Discovery of the Famous Temple*, 1. For a tabular description of the plaques and a drawing and photograph of the foundation hole, see ibid., 4-7, and pl. 1.

164. Ibid., 3.

165. "It was . . . in a hole in the rock below the junction of the east and south outer walls that the first set of plaques was discovered; the second set came from a similar position under the outer walls at the south-west angle" (Rowe, *Discovery of the Famous Temple*, 5).

166. Ibid.

167. Ibid., 51, n. 2. He adds that "the deposit hole was not covered by a stone when found."

168. Ibid. The deposit included only a mud plaque and three glass plaques, which meant on the assumption of uniformity that the gold, silver, and bronze plaques, two glass plaques, and faience tablet were missing.

169. Ibid., 51.

170. Ibid., 54, and pl. 16. He adds that "no plaques were found in [the inner] holes Nos. 8, 9, 10, 11 . . . , which had been completely plundered in ancient days."

171. Ibid., 59, and pl. 16. Rowe adds that "No. 5 had been completely robbed in ancient days while No. 7, also robbed, consisted at the time of discovery of a small piece of blackish opaque glass."

172. Rowe, *Discovery of the Famous Temple*, 54, n. 3. "All of the deposit holes . . . [in plate 16, numbers 1-11) are numbered according to the order of their discovery" (59, n. 1). The particular hole described here "was covered by a rectangular block of limestone measuring" 38" x 26 1/2" x 20", p. 55.

173. Rowe, "A Contribution to the Archaeology: III," 160. Rowe adds that brushing was the means by which he discovered the foundation deposits of the Serapeum.

174. Rowe, *Discovery of the Famous Temple*, 55.

175. Rowe, "A Contribution to the Archaeology: III," 160; Alan Rowe, "A Contribution to the Archaeology of the Western Desert: IV," *Bulletin of the John Rylands Library* 39 (1956-57): 489. I have not been able to determine the distribution of these materials among the forty-three plaques, as Rowe tends to discuss them in clusters.

176. Rowe, "A Contribution to the Archaeology: IV," 505, and map opp. p. 492; and Rowe, *Discovery of the Famous Temple*, 54, n. 1, pl. 17.

177. These include the inscribed gold plates from Canopus and from the Old Bourse excavations, which are discussed in W. M. F. Petrie, *Naukratis, Part I: 1884-85* ("Third Memoir of the Egypt Exploration Fund") (London: Trubner, 1886), 32; M. N. Tod, "A Bilingual Dedication from Alexandria," *Journal of Egyptian Archaeology* 28 (1942): 53-56, and pl. 6; H. G. Walters, *A Guide to the Department of Greek and Roman Antiquities in the British Museum*, 6th ed. (London: British Museum), 108-9; and Rowe, *Discovery of the Famous Temple*, 10-13. Several others are described in J. J. Clère, "Deux Nouvelles Plaques de Fondation Bilingues de Ptolémée IV Philopator," *Zeitschrift für Ägyptische Sprache und Altertumskunde* 90 (1963): 16-22. Clère generalizes about Alexandrian foundation deposits: they are usually "bilingual foundation plaques made of different materials, notably of gold or silver or bronze, and of opaque glass or pottery. The plaques made of the last two materials are usually found in clusters of several exemplars, whereas each deposit has only one exemplar of the plates made from each of the different metals," 16.

178. Since "the debris in the Serapeum area has generally been turned over and over again," for example, "no reliable evidence for dating levels is to be obtained from it in most cases" (Rowe, *Discovery of the Famous Temple*, 42).

179. Alan J. Wace, "Recent Ptolemaic Finds in Egypt," *Journal of Hellenic Studies* 65 (1945): 106: "This area has at last been definitely proved to be the site of the famous Serapeum of Alexandria." Also cf. p. 108: "The temenos of Sarapis has now been identified beyond question." Pompey's Pillar, incidentally, is actually the Column of Diocletian.

180. Deposit hole no. 6, discovered by Rowe and Wace, marks "the south-east corner of the Temple of Sarapis, and solves one of the long-standing problems of archaeology. The site of the great

temple of Serapis is now at last fixed," although part of it "presumably lies beneath the Bab Sidra Cemetery" (Wace, "Recent Ptolemaic Finds in Egypt," 108).

181. The foundation documents of this little adjunct bear inscriptions "indicating that here has stood a shrine of Harpocrates" (Wace, "Recent Ptolemaic Finds in Egypt," 108).

182. Ibid., 106, 108. Cf. Pfeiffer, *History of Classical Scholarship*, 102. "Ptolemy III . . . called Euergetes . . . is now attested as founder of the new temple."

183. Ibid., 108. Wace indicates that the Shrine of Harpocrates was "erected by Ptolemy IV Philopator."

184. Rowe, *Discovery of the Famous Temple*, 56.

185. Ibid., 34-35, and 36, fig. 7. Botti felt, however, that these limestone coffers were for holding human or animal remains, not for holding documents, 35. Rowe also refers to one of the sons of Cheops who retrieved an inscription "from a hidden chest in the temple of Hermopolis"; but he does not specify the material of the chest. (Petrie, *Naukratis, Part I: 1884-5*, 32, cited in Rowe, *Discovery of the Famous Temple*, 15, n. 15). This raises the whole issue — which I am not prepared to investigate — of Egyptian foundation deposits.

186. This inscribed granite box is discussed in detail by Reinach, "Dioskourides g tomoi," 350-70.

187. Ibid., 351. Reinach cites Mahmoud Pacha El Falaki's account of his researches in 1865-66. The discovery of a granite box in the garden of the Prussian Consulate proves only that a granite box was discovered in the garden of the Prussian Consulate, nothing more. On this topographical controversy, see Reinach, "Dioskourides g tomoi," 350-52, 354-58, 369; and Fraser, *Ptolemaic Alexandria*, 2:31, n. 77. "Reinach . . . showed that this chance find had no significance for the history or the site of the Library." This topographical fallacy has nevertheless been advocated by André Bernand, *Alexandrie la Grande* (Paris: Arthaud, 1966), 116: "Il est donc parfaitement possible que ce monument indique l'emplacement de l'ancienne bibliothèque, partie du Musée." Serious objections remain to such a view.

188. Reinach, "Dioskourides g tomoi," 355-56. On the dimensions of the box, see also p. 353; and Giuseppe Botti, *Plan de la Ville d'Alexandrie a l'Epoque Ptolémaïque* (Alexandria, Egypt: L. Carrire, 1898), 65.

189. Fraser, *Ptolemaic Alexandria*, 2:31, n. 77. The box weighed 173 kilograms, or 380.6 lbs. Reinach, "Dioskourides g tomoi," 357, 367.

190. Reinach, "Dioskourides g tomoi," 354. Reinach adds that de Laurin was the Austrian Consul General until 1852. "Mrs. Penelope de Laurin remembers, writes Botti, some digs by her late husband on these grounds. Roughly speaking, he could have found there such things as sphinxes, inscriptions, marble busts, and mummies."

191. Cf. ibid. "One regrets . . . that nothing is known of the fortunes of the granite block found on these premises in 1847."

192. Ibid., 350-51. "A published account appeared only in the passage following Mahmoud Pacha El Falaki's explanation of his researches in 1865-66 for the records of Napoleon III." "There is not the slightest hint of the discovery discussed by Brugsch with Mahmoud El Falaki in writers like Puchstein, Dziatzko, Susemihl, or even in Brugsch himself," 352. For the published account, see Bey Mahmud, *Mémoire sur l'Antique Alexandrie, ses Faubourgs et Environs Découverts par les Fouilles* (Copenhagen: B. Luni, 1873), 53. This work, despite its French appearance, is in Arabic.

193. See Reinach, "Dioskourides g tomoi," 350. See also the two notices by Evarsito Breccia, "Monsieur le Directeur," *Bulletin de la Société Archéologique d'Alexandrie* 10 (1908): 250-52; and Breccia, "Dioskourides g tomoi," *Bulletin de la Société Archéologique* 18 (1921): 62-64.

194. See J. A. Letronne, *Revue Archéologique* 5 (1848): 758. I have not been able to lay hands on this article. The portions of the letter cited by Letronne appear in Reinach, "Dioskourides g tomoi," 355-56. See also Botti, *Plan de la Ville d'Alexandrie*, 64.

195. Reinach, "Dioskourides g tomoi," 353, n. 1. "Harris' notebooks were acquired in 1896 by Botti from the daughter of the English Consul," that is, from the daughter of Anthony C. Harris, who was "the British Consul to Alexandria (1846-1872)."

196. Ibid., 352-53. This note, found on page 39 of his Cahier XI, was "discovered precisely as copied into his notebooks" by Harris, 253.

197. Ibid., 360, and 350 for the drawing. The scholarly reputation of A. C. Harris was apparently beyond reproach, although I have been unable to find out very much about him. "His name remains attached to the famous hieratic papyri and to the discourse of Hyperides against Demosthenes, both of which he discovered," 353. Also cf. 368. For a bibliography of over seventy scholarly articles about the Harris Papyri, see Dieter Jankuhn, *Bibliographie der hieratischen und hieroglyphischen Papyri*, Göttinger Orientforschungen, vol. 4 (Wiesbaden, Germany: Harrassowitz, 1974), 48-51.

198. Cf. Reinach, "Dioskourides g tomoi," 369-70. "Is it . . . brash to think that the granite box, brought to light in 1847, will one day take its rightful place in front of the door to the New Museum Library at Alexandria? Can these few pages at least draw attention to such a precious monument and dissipate the doubts and legends surrounding it? I have personally contributed too much to the propagation of these legends and shared too many of these doubts not to hope, by way of reparation, that I have established the reality and demonstrated the importance of the granite box which contained the work of Dioscurides"; cf. also p. 350.

199. See ibid., 357. "Such an inconvenient arrangement, where three rolls would have required a granite box weighing at least 380 pounds, could not have been adopted in a library of 700,000 volumes or so." That would have required well over 200,000 of these "boxes", 355. "Granite is not only the heaviest material anyone could choose but also the most difficult to engrave and the most expensive. It is difficult to imagine the organizers of temple librar- ies . . . bringing . . . the thousands of blocks . . . necessary for even the smallest libraries where each work required such a box. . . . No one could invoke the furnace in order to explain the disappearance of so many tons of granite; and you would be pressed even harder to explain their presence, for granite was apparently used at Alexandria only for very prestigious monuments," 363. Cf. Evaristo Breccia, *Alexandria ad Aegyptum* (Bergamo, Italy: Instituto Italiano d'Arti Grafiche, 1922), 94. "We have only to think of the enormous weight and of the great difficulty of working granite to persuade ourselves that it is impossible for such book-cases to have been used in the Library of the Ptolemies, which possessed hundreds of thousands of rolls."

200. See Reinach, "Dioskourides g tomoi," 364, 366-69.

201. Ibid., 350; 370, n. 1. Reinach removes this difficulty by dou- bling the measurements given by Harris and providing another sketch of his own. The sketch by Harris also appears in Botti, *Plan de la Ville d'Alexandrie*, 65.

202. Reinach, "Dioskourides g tomoi," 359-61. The dating is mostly based on Harris's rendering of sigma by its lineal rather than its round form—the former being common before, the latter after, the Roman annexation of Alexandria. This study needs redoing, I think, by someone competent to judge the scanty available evidence.

203. Ibid., 361. "Those who admit these epigraphical limitations are . . . justified in rejecting the identification of our Dioscurides with three other writers of the same name." Reinach also eliminates

two more candidates whose written works, if they existed at all, were never popular (Reinach, "Dioskourides g tomoi," 361-62). But even that leaves three or four writers with the same name, any one of which could be associated with the granite box.

204. Ibid., 357-63. See Reinach's argument, which is essentially that Pedanius was the only Dioscurides famous enough to be recognized by his name alone, without reference to his works. This long argument may reflect nothing more than a preference for the Dioscurides associated with the famous magical papyri discovered by A. C. Harris. It may, in fact, be ultimately traceable to Harris himself.

205. The Alexandrian selection of poetry from this Dioscurides, which includes only his best, amounts to "about forty epigrams in the Greek Anthology, some based on the work of his predecessors Asclepiades, Callimachus, and Leonidas. Eight deal with famous poets; many are paradoxical anecdotes. The rest—save one hate poem—are lively poems in the sharpest epigrammatic style," Gilbert Highet, "Dioscorides," in *Oxford Classical Dictionary*. For this poetry, see A. S. F. Gow, and D. L. Page, eds., *The Greek Anthology: Hellenistic Epigrams*, 2 vols. (Cambridge: Cambridge University Press, 1965), 1:81-96, lines 1463-772, and 2:235-70.

206. Reinach, "Dioskourides g tomoi," 369.

207. See ibid., 369. "Did not Pharaonic Egypt have to make granite boxes like this for her most venerated papyri? And would not the box of Dioscurides thus be a unique specimen of these boxes created by the Alexandrian enthusiasts for their precious volumes? . . . Does it not become a document, unique in its kind, for the history of the book in antiquity?" Cf. the reference to this box as a "chance find" by Fraser, *Ptolemaic Alexandria*, 2:31, n. 77.

208. I was told this in 1966 by the late Donald W. Bradeen, Professor of Ancient History in the Classics Department of the University of Cincinnati. Cf. the cautious statement of Alan J. Wace cited in Rowe, *Discovery of the Famous Temple*, 18: "At present the evidence about foundation deposits made when a Greek temple was built is unsatisfactory. No certain case is known and as a rule it has not been the practice of excavators of Greek sites to look for foundation deposits in connection with Greek temples." (This statement is also cited in Rowe, "A Contribution to Archaeology: III," 160, n. 1.) Architecturally speaking, furthermore, the Serapeum "follows the Egyptian rather than the Greek custom," as only one instance of "a Ptolemaic sanctuary with buildings constructed in the Greek style has been found in Egypt," namely, the sanctuary discovered

beneath the ruins of the great Basilica at Hermopolis Magna. "Nothing like this has yet been found at Alexandria" (Wace, "Recent Ptolemaic Finds in Egypt," 108-9).

209. I have been remarkably unsuccessful in trying to find my way around in things Egyptian. This is, I think, no place for amateurs unless expert guidance is available. There are, I understand, foundation deposits, metallic documents, and stone boxes in Egypt, although I have never been able to get a solid line on them. See Wright, "Metallic Documents of Antiquity," 473; and Rowe, *Discovery of the Famous Temple*, 13-15. Rowe derives everything from the Egyptian past because he apparently knows nothing of Mesopotamia, as in his discussion of Palestine (ibid., 18-19).

210. Nicholas G. L. Hammond and Guy T. Griffith, *A History of Macedonia*, 3 vols. (Oxford: Clarendon, 1979), 2:17. The new Satyrus fragment (Oxyrhynchus Papyrus no. 2465) "is concerned with the names of the demes in Ptolemaic Alexandria. There the Bacchiad genealogy is traced backwards from Bacchis, king of Corinth, . . . to Antiochus. . . . The mother of Antiochus was Deianeira, who was the daughter of Dionysus and Althaea." It was because of this lineage that two demes of Alexandria were named Deianeiris and Althaeis. The Bacchiadae of Macedon "traced their line back to Heracles and so to Dionysus. . . . Thus Dionysus was the founder of the Bacchiad family" (p. 17), from whom the Ptolemies were descended.

211. For the marble inscription discovered by Botti, which identified Serapis (Serapeion) as the son of Dionysus, see Rowe, "A Contribution to the Archaeology: IV," 499.

212. For a good introduction to Dionysus see Lewis R. Farnell, *The Cults of the Greek States*, 5 vols. (Chicago: Aegaian, 1971), 5:85-324. "The first chorus of the Bacchae is full of names recalling the Asiatic cult of Dionysis," according to Guthrie, *Orpheus and Greek Religion*, 147, n. 40.

213. Much of this is discussed by E. M. Blaiklock, "The Natural Man," *Greece and Rome* 16 (1947): 49-66. See also Guthrie, *Orpheus and Greek Religion*, 114: "Euripides himself makes no secret of the fact that he is fascinated by the thrilling service of the Thracian god, so much so that his play the Bacchae is our richest source of information on the cult. . . . If the orgiastic worship of the Thracians was received with opposition, as in many parts of Greece it was, this opposition was largely fed by feelings of contempt for the Thracians themselves, who to Greek eyes were barbarians and beyond the pale." That goes for the Macedonians, too, who were more or less one with the Thracians in Greek eyes.

214. See Ellis, *Foundation Deposits*, 166-67; and Oppenheim, *Ancient Mesopotamia*, 26: "Only a small fraction of these documents was written for the purpose of recording and conveying information to be read; on the contrary, they were buried carefully in the foundations of temples and palaces or engraved in other inaccessible places." Cf. Oppenheim, *Ancient Mesopotamia*, 146-48.

215. On the identification of annals and chronicles in Assyria, see Carl Roebuck, *The World of Ancient Times* (New York: Scribner's Sons, 1966), 143-44.

216. Ellis, *Foundation Deposits*, 120. Other evidence for this development is the discovery of two tablets (one with a building inscription, the other bearing Shalmaneser's annals) from the same foundation deposit in the city wall of Assur, and the Achaemenid deposits, which follow the Mesopotamian pattern but include no building inscriptions at all, 101, 104, 162. The literary prism often presents massive amounts of historical information, as in the clay prism of Assurbanipal, which contains the annals of his reign (668-626 B.C.). The original has ten sides, is 19 1/2 inches high, and contains 1,303 lines of writing; see Rassam, *Asshur and the Land of Nimrod*, opp. p. 218.

217. Oppenheim, *Ancient Mesopotamia*, 148.

218. Ibid., 148-49.

219. Ibid., 149-50. Assurbanipal "succeeded in assembling in Nineveh what has every right to be called the first systematically collected library in the ancient Near East. . . . [This] collection is representative of the main body, if not the entire content, of the scribal tradition," 15.

220. These fixed ingredients of the recipe for creating foundation inscriptions are listed in Bury, *The Assyrian Empire*, 111.

221. Ibid., 111-12.

222. Nibley, "Genesis of the Written Word," 114.

223. Ibid., 114-16.

11

Cultural Pluralism
or Assimilation?
A Dilemma of Our Times

Genevieve De Hoyos
Brigham Young University, Provo, Utah

> God . . . hath made of one blood all nations of men
> for to dwell on all the face of the earth (Acts 17:26).

Through the ages, relations between ethnic and racial groups have been at best, fragile, at worst, violent and devastating. Men have forgotten they are brothers. To deal with their conflict in the world, they have tried everything from integration, to pluralism, to separatism, even to extermination.

In our own century, we have seen all of these attempts. In the United States, we have witnessed various degrees of assimilation, Civil Rights, the separatist movement, and the enthusiastic adoption of a popular compromise: cultural pluralism. Worldwide, we may know of the relatively successful adjustment of a tripartite Switzerland, but our awareness is drawn more readily to the violent outcomes of attempted separatism: the forced expulsion of thousands of Asians from Uganda, the periodic violence between Moslems and Hindus in India, and the unending civil wars between Catholics and Protestants in Ireland, and between Christians and Moslems in Beirut. We have been horrified by the genocide of the Armenians by the Turks, of the Jews by Nazi Germany, of the Hutu by the Tutsi in Burundi,[1] and of the Tutsi by the Hutu in Rwanda.[2]

The purpose of this paper is to shed some light on the complex problems related to ethnic and racial relations. Thus, we will first focus on the United States as a case study, to identify the basic issues involved in the traditional goal of assimilation. Then we will show that the new policy of cultural pluralism (an obvious compromise brought about by a sense of failure around assimilation) is not a viable goal, since it does not promote structural participation. Therefore, it can only realistically be viewed as a means to an end, or as a rather unstable point between two possible outcomes: assimilation and separatism.

A POLICY OF ASSIMILATION

American society has moved from the policy of Americanization to the melting pot approach, and (as a reaction to minorities' demand for power and separatism) to the cultural pluralism approach. Actually, all three of these approaches represent some degree, some version of assimilation. That is, the American brand of cultural pluralism does not seek separatism in the economic, political, and educational systems. It simply allows greater freedom of choice in more intimate aspects of life such as family, religion, and recreation.[3]

Yet, assimilation is an extremely problematic process which, in order to be achieved, requires: (1) the complete, unqualified acceptance of the minority by the dominant group, as well as (2) the complete, unqualified desire, on the part of the minority, to give up their deepest cultural commitments.[4] Apparently, in the United States, both requirements have often failed to materialize.

A. Relative Assimilation of European Immigrants

The integration of Europeans into American institutions has, for a long time, been taken for granted. A closer look, however, indicates that not all of them have become totally Americanized.

1. Americanization. From the beginning, people from Europe were invited to come to this country and integrate into the five existing institutions—family, economy, government, education, and religion—already established in England. Consequently, a nation of immigrants was to be quickly transformed into a nation of equals, with liberty for all. In fact, as some writers suggest today, all this really meant was that conformity to Anglo-American norms would be expected. This is indicated by the following equation:[5]

$$\text{American assimilation: } A + B + C = A$$

Most Northwest European and Scandinavian immigrants apparently did not mind very much surrendering their distinctive cultural characteristics. These Anglo-Saxon Protestant groups had given up on Europe and resolved to make a future for themselves in America. The frontier was wide open and they were welcomed by the settlers anxious to develop the nation. They were immediately given the right to vote and encouraged to send their children to school.[6] Soon, their sense of identity was drawn solely from American society, their roots were forgotten, and they were indistinguishable from those who had come before them.[7]

This was the quick mutual acceptance that can more easily take place between two groups of equals, with very similar physique, customs, values, ethos, and so forth, at a time when the in-coming group can be viewed not as a rival for social rewards, but as a partner to achieve common goals.[8]

The next settlers, however, were not as amenable to integration. German refugees chose to remain isolated from their American neighbors in the Midwest, establishing their own schools and maintaining their culture and language. Then the Irish came, escaping in large numbers from the potato famine. They settled in the eastern cities, establishing their "Popish" churches and becoming visible as a group.[9]

When the next wave of Europeans came, at the turn of the century, they were even more different. From Central and Southern Europe, they brought with them a diversity of languages, religions, manners, and values. They remained in eastern ghettos. Older Americans felt uneasy about them and invoked thoughts of cultural inferiority to justify their prejudice, discrimination, and the resulting unrepresentative immigration quota of the 1920s.[10]

2. *The Melting Pot.* Interestingly, out of this disillusionment emerged a more lenient and open-minded version of Americanization: the Melting Pot doctrine, often represented as follows:

$$\text{Melting Pot: A + B + C = D}$$

This approach theoretically required the fusion of the minority and majority groups, as they combined to form a new group, a new culture, unlike any of the original groups.[11] It reflected (at a time when prejudice was high) an unexpectedly lenient view of the immigrants, and may have been the unrepresentative product of a few, because by then the well-entrenched American institutions were not going to be modified just to please the newcomers. This unrealistic movement enjoyed surprising popularity during the first few decades of this century. In the end, however, the movement was criticized by both the immigrants and the WASPs. Its death blow came at the onset of the First World War when it was discovered that millions in the United States could not communicate in English, had never obtained citizenship, and were influenced by their foreign governments through newspapers published in their native languages.[12] Thus, World War I reintroduced Americanization as a goal.[13]

Through the depression, through World War II and later, prejudice against European minorities abated, and these continued the assimilation process. At that time, however, researchers found that assimilation is always somewhat selective and perhaps never complete. For example, in the 1950s, a large percentage of Catholics of European origin were found to have acquired a central aspect of the Protestant Ethic—deferred gratification— along with middle-class education and occupations. They had become middle class without becoming WASPs.[14] But on the other hand, social scientists also found that three "religiously defined melting pots" had developed in the United States: one within which the Protestants intra-marry, one for all Catholics, and one for Jews, with few (but slowly increasing) intermarriages in between.[15] Thus, in spite of the dominant society's acceptance of European groups, these have been willing and able to give up some, but not all their expressive culture, their deeper values.[16]

Additional research has shown that, the more different immigrants are from the dominant group, the more their assimilation is opposed by the group in power and resisted by the immigrants. More specifically, differences in phys-ical appearance tend to bring opposition and discrimina-tion on the part of the dominant group, and become the greatest obstacle to assimilation. Differences in religion, on the other hand, tend to prevent the minority group from wanting complete assimilation.[17] This is why assim-ilation is easiest for those who come voluntarily at a time when they are needed by the host society, who are few in numbers or dispersed, and who tend to be culturally and physically similar to the dominant group.[18]

3. *Renewed Ethnic Pluralism*. More recently, a "new trib-alism" seems to have emerged among European ethnic groups. This renewed identification is expressed through a greater interest in native food, dance, and costumes, in folk culture, and in religious traditions. It is also demon-strated through visits to ancestral homes, through the in-creased use of ethnic names, through the establishment of

fraternal organizations, museums, and native-language newspapers, and through the current resurgence in the use of hyphenated nationality terms such as Italian-American or Polish-American.[19] All these efforts to preserve one's heritage appear to confirm one study which claims that third-generation Irish and Italians are expressing a greater sense of being deprived from their roots than their migrant grandparents themselves had.[20]

This rising white ethnic assertiveness is an unexpected and interesting phenomenon occurring among people who have generally been thought to be well accepted and integrated into American society. It may simply be part of the national trend championing individualism. Or it may be defensive pluralism, motivated by the competition presented by other organized groups who are making claims for special treatment.[21] But it certainly tells us that while it is easy to change one's manners, material culture, and superficial beliefs and attitudes, it is much harder to abandon one's identification with the values of one's original culture.[22]

Yet at this time, there is no doubt that European ethnic groups have generally been integrated into American society. To the extent that they are not, it has been due more to their resisting complete assimilation than to rejection by the dominant group.[23] On the other hand, the people of color in the United States have had a different experience.

B. Problematic Adjustment of Racial Groups in the United States

Today, four major groups make up the people of color in this country: the Native Americans who, after the Indian wars, ended up mostly on reservations; the Afro-Americans, most of whom were brought as slaves two centuries ago; the Orientals who started immigrating well over a century ago, and a large and varied Hispanic population. Obviously, each of these groups represent widely different ethnic backgrounds, national origins, reasons for being in the United States, lengths of stay here, and discriminatory experiences. Yet, for the purpose of this paper, we are mainly focusing on the Black movement because of their greater involvement in protest.

1. *The Nature of Race and Racism.* Most scientists agree that the concept of race is extremely unclear: all races overlap widely, and biologists have been unable to separate one race from another on the basis of relevant and visible physical characteristics.[24] This lack of a concrete definition, however, has not stopped many from adopting some social definition of race which is then related to specific (and generally negative) behaviors, abilities, and character traits. These traits often become stereotypes which reinforce prejudice and discrimination, and may open the way to institutional racism, or the establishment of norms, laws, and legal structures regulating relationships of the dominant group to given racial groups, i.e., apartheid in South Africa or Jim Crow legislation in the Southern United States. Then comes segregation, the policy of "separate but equal," which makes minority achievement within the dominant group virtually impossible.[25]

Such developments stand in deep contradiction with the ideals of the American dream, and therefore have been identified as the American dilemma.[26] Through the years, social scientists have tried to explain the existence of racism in the United States in terms of personality maladjustment, economic competition, a desire to exploit, the need to have a scapegoat, and existing racial norms.[27] But the dilemma is complex and resists easy solutions.

2. *Racial Militancy and the Emergence of Cultural Pluralism.* Since World War II, a number of Black movements have emerged, making different (and often uncoordinated) demands on the United States government. During the war, Black leaders obtained both the establishment of the FEPC (the Fair Employment Practices Committee) and the

desegregation of the armed forces. In 1955, Martin Luther King, through his nonviolent movement, made great gains against arbitrary segregation rules in the South.[28] But for some the movement was too slow. Rioting in the streets of some of our large cities made it clear that the Blacks no longer believed that change could be obtained through peaceful protest.[29] Simultaneously, the Black Muslims organized to demand land for a separate Black nation,[30] while the Black Panther Party threateningly demanded equal treatment.[31] These and other militant groups became part of the Black Power movement which created a great sense of Black pride. Other alienated groups followed suit, forming Brown Power, Red Power, and Yellow Power organizations.

The problems are not over. People of color keep coming to the United States. Cubans, Puerto Ricans, Mexicans, and a number of Central Americans have come to escape economic and political problems. A contingent of Haitians unexpectedly came to escape their poverty. The Southeast Asian political refugees are forming one of the newest racial and ethnic groups. And all along, Samoans, Filipinos, Taiwanese, and people from Hong Kong have continued coming in. In addition, research tells us that, in spite of many government programs, the Black ghettos are still extremely depressed,[32] the Native American reservations still have a limited economic base,[33] and too few Hispanics attend college.[34] In addition, some backlash has occurred, raising the cry of "reverse discrimination."

Yet, much has been done. It all started with racial militancy which brought pride to minority groups for their racial and cultural origins. And it continued with the subsequent involvement of the mass media in a campaign to break down racial and ethnic stereotyping. Now it is no longer considered good form to openly express prejudice and discrimination against racial and ethnic groups. And Affirmative Action, along with various educational programs, provided greater chances for upward mobility among all minorities, greatly enlarging the middle class in all groups.[35]

Simultaneously, the goal of minority assimilation has fallen into disrepute. It was first challenged in the 1960s and 1970s by minority leaders and by minority people in the streets. More recently its viability is being challenged by the general public, supported by a few social scientists. The dominant group no longer feels it can insist that Anglo ways are the best. And minority group members derisively challenge: "What do you want me to do, become a white man?" All these new attitudes reflect cultural pluralism, the new and more permissive approach to minorities which has become popular in our country. This new approach is being enthusiastically adopted by politicians and professionals in their policy statements and is supported by many ethnic groups who express a desire for a qualified assimilation.

Notwithstanding the intense popularity of cultural pluralism, the evidence suggests that cultural pluralism, with its relativistic values and ethics and its enormously attractive appeal for tolerance and normative flexibility, actually may just turn out to be a brand new way of ignoring and isolating minorities.

A RATIONAL ARGUMENT AGAINST THE POLICY OF CULTURAL PLURALISM

Most supporters of cultural pluralism appear to interpret this concept as mutual appreciation of cultural differences, along with a resolve to protect each group's right to maintain their own way of life.[36] As such, it is difficult to quarrel with it because tolerance of cultural differences immediately sounds like a beautiful, obvious, and instant solution to intergroup conflict. Yet the notion is rather simplistic and fails to take into consideration basic principles of human interaction.

In an attempt to identify the core issues in racial and ethnic relations, we will argue, first, that minorities would rather participate in American institutions than being "kindly" tolerated, and second, that tolerance, as a goal, may often interfere with institutional participation. Finally, it will be suggested that institutional participation can only be achieved through either assimilation or separatism, with the warning that separatism often leads to violence. In the process, the point will be made that cultural pluralism is not a viable goal, although it is indispensable as a means to achieving assimilation.

Argument No. 1. Cultural Pluralism or Institutional Participation?

What is it that minority group members really want — tolerance of their differences, that is, cultural pluralism, or full participation in the mainstream of America? Some writers indicate that they want and need both — tolerance and participation.[37] But could this not be somewhat contradictory?

The central problem in ethnic and racial relations is the fact that minorities are not fully participating in the mainstream of America and therefore feel deprived economically and socially. In fact, this deprivation is the central aspect of the most accepted definition of a minority group which is described as any group which, because of its members' ethnic or racial characteristics, has limited access to societal rewards.

Thus, participation in the social structure of the five basic social institutions is absolutely indispensable to members of a society, because occupying basic roles in an institution is the only way to receive social rewards. For example, as family members, we can receive love, acceptance, support, loyalty, security, stability, and roots. As

members of a community, as citizens, as voters, we get
some measure of respect, some feeling that we make a
difference, some pride, some security. As students, we get
opportunities to gain recognition in scholastic and extra-
curricular activities as well as a potential status based on
the hope of our future achievement. And as church members, we may get a sense of moral commitment, a sense
of oneness with others, a sense of eternity.

But above all, in the United States, it is through an
occupational role that self-validation comes, because it is
through it that clear, immediate, and consistent community and societal rewards are obtained. That is, with a job
we are given space to work in, as well as an opportunity
to prove our ability and to gain appreciation and recognition from those we work for and those we work with.
We are given a chance to gain new knowledge and experience, and we are given some degree of financial security. More importantly, we are given some title, a social
status, a sense of who we are vis-à-vis our fellowmen.[38]

Thus, because a job in the United States today is the
greatest and most automatic source of social rewards, what
is not needed is the type of tolerance which encourages
the very patterns which ensure inequality. What we need,
on the contrary, is tolerance as a means, tolerance which
facilitates full social participation and unavoidably brings
cultural assimilation.

Argument No. 2. Structural Participation Demands and Facilitates Cultural Assimilation

Social roles always imply behavioral expectations.
Therefore, social roles are always conditionally rewarding.
That is, generally speaking, social rewards are given when
members of a group conform to their role expectations,
and rewards are withdrawn when they do not.[39] Thus,
well-integrated members of our society know that, in most
jobs, they must come to work every day, on time, and

work until it is time to go home. And while on the job, they must clearly show that they are performing to the best of their ability. Some leeway is allowed but if deviations from expectations are frequent, obvious, and visible, the opportunity to work may be withdrawn.

Because of cultural pluralism, job expectations are not always understood by members of subcultural groups. For example, a young Native American obtained a university degree. Armed with it, he got a job off the reservation as a white collar worker in an industry. When asked about his job, he explained that every morning he found on his desk a pile of papers to process. He typically completed such tasks by noon. In the afternoon, with nothing to do, he would sit at his desk and read magazines. This lack of awareness of job expectations can be understood if we know that in his family, his father only worked sporadically as a farm laborer, and that he himself had never before held a job. Of course it did not take long for him to lose his position. Now he is back on his reservation.

This true story illustrates the fact that, typically, cultural confrontations take place at the structural level. They occur when an Anglo boss is faced with the problem of compensating for the absence of a Chicano employee who did not show up because his cousins from El Paso came to visit him that day. They take place when an Indian student, in the last semester of her training, decides to go home with no degree, rather than tell her divorced sister (who is visiting with her four children) that she cannot afford to take care of her. They happen when an Anglo-Saxon employee from Appalachia decides, from one day to the next, to quit his job to avoid being bothered by his many creditors.

The fact is that cultural definitions often clash. For instance, in our American society, self-validation comes through a job, while in many other societies, it does not come that way at all. It may come from having servants and not having to work, as in Spain. It may come from being a leader within the extended family, from being someone on whom everyone can depend, as among many Latin Americans; or being a successful hustler in the inner city; or being a strong fighter and protector among the Mongols; or seeing visions among some Native American tribes of old; or owning cattle among some tribes of Africa; or giving up one's money and social position among Hindus.

But if representatives of these diverse cultures come to settle in our industrial society, wanting to share of our abundance, they will have to act, as a matter of survival, as if they believed that work is their greatest source of satisfaction. And it is in the process of learning this crucial American pattern that they should be given all the patience and tolerance their Anglo middle-class employers can give them, until job responsibility becomes second nature to them. Thus, cultural pluralism may be viable as a means to the end of assimilation, but cannot realistically be seen as an end in itself.

This is because participation not only demands some level of acculturation, but it inexorably brings further acculturation. First it brings external acculturation, the adoption of the more superficial aspects of the new culture (the material things, the language, the manners, the basic norms). Then it introduces the slower process of internal acculturation, the point when social rewards become so emotionally rewarding that identification starts shifting to the dominant group.[40]

Thus, cultural pluralism, as a means to an end, allows minority group members to establish some degree of compartmentalization, that is, working like a dominant group member, but living at home according to minority expectations. Eventually, however, secure in the acceptance of the dominant group, family members can venture into other institutions, perhaps first the PTA, then the banking system, and then into the health facilities. Then they may decide to seek housing among Anglos and to participate in neighborhood and community affairs. They may even attend a church attended by their neighbors. And as they participate in all basic institutions, they become increasingly like their neighbors, increasingly aware of dominant expectations, and share increasingly in dominant social rewards. Because the dominant group is accepting, they do all this without being pushed into a marginal position, rejected by both groups.

To summarize, because cultural pluralism tends to lead to structural inequality, it cannot stand as a viable goal. On the other hand, participation by minorities in dominant social structures eventually brings assimilation, particularly if the dominant group uses tolerance of differences (or cultural pluralism) as a means to the eventual goal of assimilation.

Argument No. 3. Assimilation or Separatism?

If full institutional participation (and assimilation) is not facilitated by the dominant group, eventually the minorities will rebel. When they do, one choice they may demand is separatism, that is, their own land to establish their own separate basic institutions, their own society.

From the very beginning, as the young country welcomed new immigrants, the United States chose assimilation as the preferred approach to cross-cultural relations. This accommodating policy is rather rare worldwide, since most other countries have more typically established some version of separatism. But cases of successful separatism are rare, and most eventually end up in violence.

About the only existing case of lasting stability seems to be Switzerland, which has been tremendously successful in maintaining peace between three "separated" cultural groups under one government. For centuries, that country has existed as a peaceful federation uniting three basic geographical and cultural groups (Germans, French, and Italians), and four languages (German, French, Italian, and Romansh). To survive as a nation, the Swiss had to exercise great rationality in organizing a tripartite government, with clearly delineated rules which permit each group to be fully represented in the central government. To preserve this fragile balance of power, however, the country had to establish stringent laws, such as prohibitive rules against migration. And in spite of their impressive record, in the 1970s a violent separatist movement emerged indicating that not even such workable, rational arrangements can totally eliminate conflict.[41]

In Canada, the French Canadians have attempted to maintain some degree of separatism which has yielded a rather fragile coalition, with the status of the French depending entirely on their current political power. Lebanon established a political arrangement similar to that of the Swiss, but it did not last. When they allowed their tenuous balance of power to be disturbed by the incoming Palestinian refugees, civil war came. And in Africa, many tribes, after a repressed but relatively peaceful coexistence under their colonial masters, are now facing one another sometimes in avoidance, and sometimes in fratricide.

Thus, separatism is not an easy solution. Typically, any type of pluralism brings conflict.[42] But separatism, in addition, carries with it the message that the differences involved are irreconcilable, that assimilation is out, and that compromise is no longer an option. And with this comes the depersonalization, the dehumanization of the enemy, which so often leads to violence in confrontation, and occasionally in extermination.[43]

Such confrontation is well described in a prophecy of war:

> After many days, slaves shall rise up against their masters, who shall be marshaled and disciplined for

war. . . . And thus, with the sword and by bloodshed
the inhabitants of the earth shall mourn (D&C 87:4, 6).

As a conclusion, it must be admitted that it is not easy
to achieve peace amid differences among human beings.
When we compare separatism with assimilation, we can
only conclude that separatism is rather risky and that assimilation probably is, in the long run, a more functional
goal. Yet, assimilation is not easily achieved. In the United
States, the policy of assimilation has worked only when
the groups involved were relatively similar racially as well
as culturally. And recently, even the assimilation of white
Europeans has been questioned. Now, with a sense of
failure, the goal of cultural assimilation has been replaced
with a new goal: that of cultural pluralism, a nonviable
goal because it tends to work against the institutional participation of minorities. No nation can afford to have large
segments of its population excluded from occupying conditionally rewarding roles, because only through roles do
we share in the societal rewards. When demands for institutional assimilation are not met, minorities have only
one other alternative: separatism. But the successful cases
of separatism are few, and only for groups who have some
land autonomy and similar cultures. Peace, for those who
have ambiguous territorial claims and basic cultural differences, is fragile, tenuous, and often turns to violence.

Notes

1. Leo Kruper, *The Pity of It All: Polarization of Racial and Ethnic
Relations* (Minneapolis: University of Minnesota Press, 1977), 197-
208.

2. Ibid., 170-97.

3. J. Ross Eshleman and Barbara G. Cashion, *Sociology* (Boston:
Little, Brown, 1983), 235.

4. Ibid., 233; Richard T. Schaefer, *Racial and Ethnic Groups*, 2nd
ed. (Boston: Little, Brown, 1984), 39.

5. Eshleman and Cashion, *Sociology*, 233.

6. Russell R. Dynes, Alfred C. Clarke, Simon Dinitz, and Iwao

Ishino, *Social Problems: Dissensus and Deviation in an Industrial Society* (New York: Oxford University Press, 1964), 312.

7. Rodney Stark, *Sociology* (Belmont, CA: Wadsworth Publishing, 1985), 248; David B. Brinkerhoff and Lynn K. White, *Sociology* (St. Paul, MN: West Publishing, 1985), 233.

8. Gordon W. Allport, *The Nature of Prejudice* (Garden City, NY: Doubleday-Anchor Books, 1958), 250-68.

9. Dynes, Clarke, Dinitz, and Ishino, *Social Problems,* 312; Schaefer, *Racial and Ethnic Groups,* 115-16.

10. Dynes, Clarke, Dinitz, and Ishino, *Social Problems,* 315-18.

11. Eshleman and Cashion, *Sociology,* 233; Schaefer, *Racial and Ethnic Groups,* 36.

12. Dynes, Clarke, Dinitz, and Ishino, *Social Problems,* 318-21.

13. Ibid., 320.

14. Liston Pope, "Religion and the Class Structure," in Reinhard Bendix and Seymour M. Lipset, eds., *Class Status and Power: A Reader in Social Stratification* (Glencoe, IL: Free Press of Glencoe, 1953), 316-23.

15. Reba Jo R. Kennedy, "Single or Triple Melting Pot? Intermarriage Trends in New Haven, 1870-1940," *American Journal of Sociology* 49/4 (January 1944): 331-39; Martin N. Marger, *Race and Ethnic Relations: American and Global Perspectives* (Belmont, CA: Wadsworth, 1985), 114. Brinkerhoff and White, *Sociology,* 240. Schaefer, *Racial and Ethnic Groups,* 38-39.

16. Eshleman and Cashion, *Sociology,* 235.

17. Elbert W. Stewart, *The Troubled Land,* 2nd ed. (New York: McGraw-Hill, 1976), 148.

18. Marger, *Race and Ethnic Relations,* 76-78.

19. Eshleman and Cashion, *Sociology,* 220-22, 235; Schaefer, *Racial and Ethnic Groups,* 48-49.

20. Eshleman and Cashion, *Sociology,* 221.

21. Brinkerhoff and White, *Sociology,* 254-55; Schaefer, *Racial and Ethnic Groups,* 48-49.

22. Marger, *Race and Ethnic Relations,* 73-74.

23. Eshleman and Cashion, *Sociology,* 233.

24. Ibid., 211-12; Brinkerhoff and White, *Sociology,* 230-31.

25. Eshleman and Cashion, *Sociology,* 212-33; Brinkerhoff and White, *Sociology,* 231; Stark, *Sociology,* 246-47; Charles F. Marden and Gladys Meyer, *Minorities in American Society,* 5th ed. (New York: Van Nostrand, 1978), 28-33.

26. R. Fred Wacker, *Ethnicity, Pluralism, and Race: Race Relations Theory in America before Nyrdal* (Westport, CT: Greenwood Press, 1983), 80-83.

27. Eshleman and Cashion, *Sociology,* 223-24; Stark, *Sociology,* 248-49.

28. James A. Geschwender, *Racial Stratification in America* (Dubuque, IA: Wm. C. Brown, 1789), 220-22.

29. Ibid., 222-25.

30. Ibid., 226-31.

31. Ibid., 231-32.

32. J. Wallace Jackson, "The Afro-American Experience: Five Sociological Perspectives," in Anthony G. Dworkin and Rosalind J. Dworkin, *The Minority Report* (New York: Praeger, 1976), 149-51; Brinkerhoff and White, *Sociology,* 244.

33. Joseph Strauss, Bruce A. Chadwick, and Howard M. Bahr, "Indian Americans: The First Is Last," in Dworkin and Dworkin, *The Minority Report,* 226-52; Brinkerhoff and White, *Sociology,* 248-50.

34. Stewart, *The Troubled Land,* 161.

35. Eshleman and Cashion, *Sociology,* 233.

36. Hubert M. Blalock, Jr., *Race and Ethnic Relations* (Englewood Cliffs, NJ: Prentice-Hall, 1982), 124; Dynes, Clarke, Dinitz, and Ishino, *Social Problems,* 321; Colin Clarke, David Ley, Ceri Peach, eds., *Geography and Ethnic Pluralism* (London: George Allen & Unwin, 1984), 2-3.

37. Eshleman and Cashion, *Sociology,* 235.

38. Richard T. LaPiere, *A Theory of Social Control* (New York: McGraw-Hill, 1954), 80-91.

39. Ibid.

40. Marger, *Race and Ethnic Relations,* 73-74.

41. Ibid., 81-82; Blalock, *Race and Ethnic Relations,* 124-25; Schaefer, *Racial and Ethnic Groups,* 47.

42. Marger, *Race and Ethnic Relations,* 82.

43. Kruper, *The Pity of It All,* 122-24.

12

Twelve Diatribes
of Modern Israel

Avraham Gileadi
Woodland Hills, Utah

This essay serves as a testimony to modern Israel — the Latter-day Saints — that we are beginning to resemble God's ancient covenant people in ways that conflict with our high ideals. Some parallels between the two peoples provide a yardstick by which we can judge ourselves. Unfortunately, these parallels paint a dismal picture of where we are headed and what is in store.

If the type or pattern we draw from the parallels holds true,[1] then by following the parallels through to their conclusion we will know what to expect in our generation. Next to actual prophecy, scriptural types provide the most reliable guide to the future, particularly to the last days. Indeed, all true prophets prophesy, more or less, using types and shadows from Israel's ancient past to predict the future. By familiarizing ourselves with the ancient types, we will know both a sickness and its cure; we will recognize our present condition and know what its outcome must be.

Because biblical parallels do not directly threaten us, we could keep ourselves aloof from their message. Such aloofness, I would point out, is out of character with the man whom I salute in this essay: Hugh Nibley exemplifies one who comes to terms with hidden errors, who searches out the truth, who speaks the unspeakable. He frankly criticizes the Saints, warning and admonishing as well as

353

teaching and instructing them. He serves as a perfect example of the Lord sending "prophets, *and* wise men, and
scribes" to his people (Matthew 23:34; emphasis added).
Many times he has laid his reputation on the line, with
strong reactions, both positive and negative, to his scrip-
turally based arguments. He has served as conscience of
his people, a role that has borne much good fruit in the
lives of Latter-day Saints.

In seeking to apply the parallels of biblical history explicitly to ourselves, I have chosen the term *diatribe* to
express their message. Some may think that in so doing I
am even more severe than Brother Nibley. One has but to
recall his "How Firm a Foundation?" and "Forty Variations
on an Unpopular Theme," however, to recognize that this
essay falls firmly within the Nibley tradition. If all is not
well in Zion, then what is not well? An answer to this
question is idolatry.

I therefore discuss in these pages twelve kinds of idolatry that have become as prevalent among ourselves as
among so-called Gentiles. (Of course, by adopting the customs of the Gentiles, Israel always jeopardized her status
as a chosen people. When ancient Israel did not repent of
the idolatrous practices she learned from the Gentiles, the
Lord cut the people off from his presence and destroyed
them. In one instance, he removed the gospel from a certain group of people and gave it to another.) By choosing
these twelve categories of idolatry, I do not mean to limit
the parallels to them. There exist other forms as well as
subforms of idol worship, but I point to these twelve as
some of the more obvious or pernicious.

When speaking of idolatry, we often think of people
venerating statues, bowing down before "dumb idols," or
perhaps participating in processions with icons raised on
portable pedestals. People still perpetuate these ancient
kinds of idolatry, though not the Latter-day Saints. Idolatry
nonetheless assumes many forms besides these, less tan-

gible than statue worship perhaps, but just as virulent. All idolatry diverts the attention from the true God and his law to a counterfeit. Much of such idolatry is a corruption of what is sacred. The final test in the scriptures of whether a god is true or false is whether he saves his people in the Lord's day of judgment.[2] The ancient prophets made sport of those who, having rejected the Lord God, clung to false gods for deliverance in the time of trouble.[3]

The first of the Ten Commandments acknowledges the existence of other gods by saying, "Thou shalt have none other gods before me" (Deuteronomy 5:7). It then qualifies idolatry as anything less than loving the Lord God "with all thine heart, and with all thy soul, and with all thy might" (Deuteronomy 6:5; compare 5:10). Israel's earliest history is full of admonitions to refrain from "going after the gods of the peoples round about" (Deuteronomy 6:14; 13:1-18; Joshua 23:6-8). These ground rules let everyone know that true worship exists within an extremely narrow compass. Idolatry thus becomes identical with the broad way, the way of the world and nations who surround Israel. God's covenant people maintain their special status so long as they worship God alone.[4] In the biblical pattern of the conquest of Canaan, God will ultimately destroy and dispossess those who indulge in idol worship.[5]

Speaking of Latter-day Saints as idolaters may seem contradictory. Surely, of all peoples on the earth we know best "how to worship, and . . . what [we] worship" (D&C 93:19). Yet it was necessary for the Lord to restore the pure knowledge of God in all dispensations of the gospel. And every dispensation entered on its pathway to apostasy when the people compromised the worship of God with the conventions of men. To love and serve God—to worship him alone—at all times meant keeping his commandments,[6] not in isolation from the world, but in puritanical contrast to universal and prevailing custom.[7] The scriptures from the beginning mark the Gentiles—all nations except Israel—as idolaters.[8] Among the Gentiles, worship of the true God was either nonexistent or perverted, rendering it ineffectual.[9]

The practices of the world deceive the heart (Deuteronomy 11:16). The whole heart must be preoccupied with the things of God and must constantly "remember" his commandments in order to maintain true worship (Numbers 15:39-41). When the Lord's people experience a change of heart because of idolatry, they alienate themselves from the Lord so that they will not hear (Deuteronomy 30:17). They allow themselves to believe that the scriptures, particularly in addressing the wicked deeds of the Lord's people, do not apply to them (cf. Alma 21:6). We feel that prophecies having negative connotations must refer to the Jews or to the Gentiles, surely not to us. In short, idolatry forms an inductive practice: once we get caught up in it, the habit carries its own momentum and supplies its own rationale.

The Lord gave Israel a special charge, therefore, never to depart from his commandments "to the right hand or to the left" (Deuteronomy 5:32). In observing these commandments, Israel should "not add thereto, nor diminish from [them]" (Deuteronomy 12:32). The worship of God must not merely encompass everything, but must retain its purity to be acceptable. It leaves no gray areas of life unaccounted for by divine law. Worship does not function when customs alien to the law of God sully it. Every dispensation of the gospel, whether it taught a higher or a lesser law, demonstrates this kind of apostasy. Israel's righteousness has ever been synonymous with observing to "do all these commandments before the Lord our God, as he hath commanded" (Deuteronomy 6:25). Given such a charge, there is no room for saying, "All is done" (2 Nephi 31:19), "It is enough" (cf. 2 Nephi 28:30), or "All is well" (2 Nephi 28:25).

In pointing to parallels of idolatry between the Lord's

people anciently and today, we must not presume that people worship false gods exclusively. Among the Lord's people, worship of the true God is rarely done away with. Rather, as a rule people worship the true God alongside the false gods. They maintain a careful equilibrium in order to preserve an identity with the national God, the God of Israel or the fathers. At the same time, the people follow their own gods as they please. This happy medium enables people to satisfy both their carnal instincts and their spiritual aspirations. It causes the Lord's prophets to cry in anguished tones, "Choose you this day whom ye will serve" (Joshua 24:15), and "How long will ye halt between two opinions?" (1 Kings 18:21).

In some instances of idolatry, worship of the true God and the false becomes fused. Then the concept of the true God gets distorted, while the false gods assume the authenticity and endorsement that belong to the true God. Of all idolatry, the Lord finds such syncretism or fusion most intolerable. It epitomizes the idea of "philosophies of men mingled with scripture." Things incongruous with true worship thereby acquire an aura of sanctity. For the Lord's people, syncretism lies but one step away from severing spiritual roots. It forms the final stage of apostasy before the Lord brings on judgment.

Ironically, appearances of true worship persist in every stage of apostasy. A symptom of all phases of alienation is the stress that people lay on outward observance. Since false gods are the order of the day, people must scrupulously nurture the exterior of true worship, or all is lost. When people reach this point, they confuse righteousness with actively congregating and religiously performing ecclesiastical duties. In such worship, institutional convention soon becomes the enemy of spontaneity, resulting in dead, stereotypical devotion.

The writings of Isaiah, pertinent to our day,[10] commence with his indictment of those who actively attend religious meetings, who multiply sacrifices at the temple.[11] Because the outward form of worship remained strong in Jerusalem, Laman and Lemuel, in the hour of Judah's exile, asserted, "We know that the people who were in the land of Jerusalem were a righteous people; for they kept the statutes and judgments of the Lord, and all his commandments" (1 Nephi 17:22). Laban was an elder of the church (1 Nephi 4:22, 26), but his heart lusted after riches (1 Nephi 3:25). In actuality, the people of Jerusalem had "changed their gods" (Jeremiah 2:11). Their land was desolated because they were committing abominations, whoring after their idols (Ezekiel 6:9).

In biblical history, each experience of idol worship precedes a divine judgment, such as cataclysm, plague, famine, war, destitution, and desolation. In the last days, therefore, when all biblical types repeat themselves,[12] we may expect "the great day of the Lord" (D&C 43:17-22) — a period of judgment upon all nations of the earth — to commence when these ancient forms of idolatry reappear among the Lord's people. There exists no biblical type or precedent of the Lord bringing on a universal judgment until his own people wallow in apostasy. Their righteousness can stay such a judgment from the earth, but their wickedness constitutes its catalyst when the balance tips in favor of wickedness.[13] Hence the scripture, "upon my house shall it begin" (D&C 112:25).

1. Images

The first of the Ten Commandments prohibits the Lord's people from having "other gods before me" (Exodus 20:3). The expression, "before me" (Hebrew ʿal pānāy), however, literally means "before my face" or "in my presence." It signifies that idolatry cuts us off from the presence of the Lord; an idolater cannot behold his face.

But the first commandment specifies a particular kind of idolatry: the making of "graven images" and "likenesses" (Exodus 20:4). The Hebrew words for these terms (*pesel*; *təmûnāh*) possess the additional connotations of "statue" and "picture." Israel must not make for herself graven images or statues, nor make likenesses or pictures of anything in the heavens above or on the earth beneath, or in the waters below the earth (Exodus 20:4). The scope of the prohibited imagery Moses defines as "any figure . . . male or female," including the likeness of any beast, bird, reptile, or fish (Deuteronomy 4:16-18). The purpose of this prohibition is that no one's heart "turn away" from the Lord to images (Deuteronomy 29:18), that the Lord's people do not bend down to them nor serve them (Exodus 20:5; 23:24).

Despite the great miracles of deliverance Israel's God wrought for his people, they quickly turned to other gods. The Old Testament is full of examples of the Lord's people making images for themselves after they inherited the promised land. They made images of the god Baal and set them up in a house of Baal (1 Kings 16:32; 2 Kings 10:26-27). They set up images in their own houses (Judges 17:4; 18:30) as well as in the houses of their gods (Nahum 1:14). They made images of men and "committed whoredoms" with them (Ezekiel 16:17). They "doted" upon images of the elite of Babylonian society, images in color, images of people in splendid attire (Ezekiel 23:14-16). In homage, as it were, to a urim and thummim, Gideon made an image of an ephod, and "all Israel went whoring after it" (Judges 8:27). The worship of cleverly fashioned images became a way of life, preoccupying the craftsman and patron alike (Hosea 13:2).

Common to all this sort of idol worship was an infatuation with the *image* of a thing rather than its reality. Images require time, energy, and materials to conceive and produce. When made, images represent the fruits of men's labors, something to admire and "dote" over. Meanwhile, people get distracted from what is real. God no longer forms the center of their thoughts, and they have taken the thing they emphasize out of context. Even if they realize their error, however, people still want a return on their investment. They cannot simply discard the idol. Once they make it, it is hard to get rid of. Throughout this preoccupation, people "bend down" toward their idols — away from the Most High God. The word "serve" in Hebrew (ʿābad)[14] also means "work." Whatever people *work* at — spend time and resources on, set their hearts upon — that they *serve*.

In effect, an obsession with unreality of one kind or another forms the crux of idolatry. For those on a low spiritual plane, something tangible or corporeal, such as an image, possesses more appeal than something intangible and incorporeal. Even the golden calf supposedly represented the Lord himself.[15] Aaron called the orgy that attended the calf's dedication a "feast unto the Lord" (Exodus 32:4-5).

When we neither see nor experience God, an image which *represents* him makes him much more real to us. The image brings him down to our level, limits him to our notion of him. God becomes something we can comfortably deal with, something we can sketch, sculpt, or paint, and mass produce. We can thus manipulate him according to our own image of him, until the idea of God no longer threatens us. Moreover, now that we have created a false god, our void is filled. Our "minds" or "hearts" (Hebrew lēbāb) are diverted, and we can the more easily leave off pursuing the real God.

Those who alienate themselves from the Creator find a ready diversion in images of the creature. They exchange the glory of the immortal God for images resembling mortal man, birds, and beasts (Romans 1:23). They change the truth of God into a lie, worshiping the creature rather than the Creator (Romans 1:25). Such substitution leads directly to all kinds of lusts and wickedness (Romans 1:24, 26-32).

When we deviate from God's way to the right or to the left, we render ourselves vulnerable to sin, cut off from God's saving grace. Thus we find every form of moral perversity, from fornication to homosexuality, associated with idol worship.[16]

Because a deference to images leads to these abominations, the images themselves are "abominations" (Deuteronomy 27:15).[17] Their substance of silver or gold—now polluted—also constitutes an "abomination," something that must be burned with fire (Deuteronomy 7:25) or ground to powder (Exodus 32:20; 2 Kings 23:6, 16). By the Lord's standard, even the idolaters themselves become "abominations" (Isaiah 41:24) and "pollutions" (Mormon 8:38). The end result of their life-style is to "perish quickly from off the good land" the Lord gave them (Joshua 23:16).[18]

Those who worship images thus participate in a grand subterfuge, one that endangers not only themselves but an entire people. As many biblical examples show, idolatry is contagious. Once an individual or group gets caught up with it, others tend to follow.[19] Then, within a short time, everyone is doing it. But the idolaters do not recognize what happens to them. They become spiritual imbeciles and mindless without being aware of it (Jeremiah 51:17). Before they become aware, calamitous judgments fall upon them.[20] In the end, people deem the images to which they ascribe power to shape the course of history (Isaiah 48:5) as worthless, mere objects of mockery (Jeremiah 10:15).

Meanwhile, no one expects such a drastic result. Among idol worshipers no clear perception exists of impending calamity (Isaiah 57:1). Of God's hand in the affairs of men, idolaters are "unaware and insensible; their eyes are glazed so they cannot see, their minds are incapable of discernment" (Isaiah 44:18).[21] Nor, in the end, can idolaters free themselves from the sudden catastrophe that overtakes them (Isaiah 47:11-14). They have long ceased to deal spontaneously with spiritual verities (Isaiah 57:11-13). Their behavior when all was well conditions their behavior in the time of crisis (Isaiah 45:16, 20). They are not prepared for the bizarre reward of being unprofitable servants of the Lord (Isaiah 42:17-25).

Not much imagination is required to see parallels of image worship in the modern gentile culture, and thus among the Latter-day Saints. While statues and pictures of deity play their part, "images of the creature" appear much more prolifically. The greater part of today's entertainment industry comes to us in the form of images via television, movies, and videos. These comprise images of people, of birds and beasts, images in color, of male and female.

We put up the graven and molten apparatuses which transmit these images in our own houses as well as in houses set apart for that purpose. Upon these images we dote, preoccupied for hours at a time with our telestial urim and thummim. In order for the images to entertain us, we must bend ourselves down toward them. Preferably, we worship in the dark, like imbeciles mindless of one another. When a social need arises, we resent its intrusion. Our behavior toward one another is colored by what our images dictate. Their power, somehow, diverts our whole attention.

Moreover, to acquire an apparatus that transmits these images, we must spend precious resources, laboring for "what is not bread" (Isaiah 55:2). We set our hearts on the privilege of possessing such an apparatus as we would on a worthy goal. In this, too, there exists an element of competition with, and thus alienation from, others. Those of us who invest more resources than our neighbor will enjoy bigger and better images. Of course, we justify this investment on the basis of personal enjoyment. Make no mistake, the images are there for our self-gratification. When we invite others to view them with us, it palliates our soul to know that they share the same interests. It normalizes an abnormal pastime.

Recent studies, for example, amply document the abnormal effects of watching television. The images our eyes see are stored permanently in our minds. There they mingle with images of the real world, confusing our perception of reality and affecting behavior. Watching television accustoms people to the sensational, the artificial, the novel, so that they begin to require a regular diet of these things to maintain their interest.[22]

The answer to this need lies in watching more television, until its addictive and narcotic effect on people enslaves them. Because their minds and hearts dull toward quiet, normal, everyday happenings, reality appears drab and uninteresting.[23] Television advertising in part compensates for this by creating unnatural wants or needs in people. People satisfy these wants by selfishly indulging in consumer goods.[24]

But more than this, television teaches a false social code, enculturating people, especially children, into norms of divorce, disrupted family life, the supremacy of the peer group, affluence, unisex, alcohol consumption, fast food or junk food habits, coercive health practices, and so forth. Closely linked to this chaotic social structure is television's false morality. While television defines no clear-cut standard of right and wrong and denies the concept of sin, it accepts immorality as normal. Because the finer human emotions are not portrayed well on this medium, television inculcates a national taste for what is depraved, coarse, and unintelligent.[25] It not only vulgarizes the use of language, but stunts its development, discouraging reading and intellectual growth.[26]

That the effects of television, to name but one medium of modern imagery, parallel exactly those of ancient image worship—turning men's minds and hearts away from God, alienating people through a diet of permissiveness, carnality, and servility to a false moral code — we cannot deny. The prophet Micah foretells that images would prevail among the Lord's people in the last days. Micah uses the common rhetoric of "graven images" and "standing images" in predicting that men will worship the works of their hands (Micah 5:13). Jesus affirms that Micah's prophecy relates to the last days when he says that those who will not repent in that day will be cut off from the house of Israel (3 Nephi 21:17, 20).

John the Beloved saw that the ultimate human image will be that of the Antichrist, a tyrannical world-ruler who rises up in the last days.[27] John prophesies that all except a very few will worship the Antichrist's image, an image that will "speak" and command worship (Revelation 13:4, 14-15). For this, the Lord will severely punish people (Revelation 14:9-11; 16:2). Only those who resist worshiping the image, on pain of death, will merit salvation (Revelation 15:2; 20:4). Of course, in order to worship the Antichrist, those now worshiping images will not switch to anything really new. His worship will merely climax a saga that even now is in full play.

2. Violence and Sex

The Lord, on many salient occasions, warned the Israelites through his prophets about their carelessness in letting their neighbors' Baalism influence them.[28] Baalism itself, however, we have not understood well. The cult centers around a myth or fictional account of a life-and-death struggle between the gods. In this story, Baal, the hero, overpowers several rivals. He celebrates his prowess by having intercourse with Anath, his female partner.

The fullest available account of the myth comes from the Baal-Anath Epic of Ugaritic literature.[29] Its alternating scenes of violence and sex — reenacted in real-life dramas that took their cue from the Baal myth — become explicit in their descriptive detail. Pornographic and violent im-

agery, carved or painted, accompanied reenactments of
the story. The myth so incited Israelites who exposed themselves to the Baal cult that forthwith they "played the
harlot" with non-Israelite women, losing all awareness of
their chosen status (Numbers 25:1, 6).

In the Ugaritic myth, Baal obtains permission from a
higher authority, El, to command the gods Yamm (Sea)
and Mot (Death) to comply with Baal's rule or face him in
a confrontation. Yamm and Mot represent forces of chaos
or disorder that will make trouble for Baal and for the world
if Baal does not subdue them. They resist Baal's authority
and each fights him to the death.

Sundry emissaries and cohorts assist Baal and his rivals
in their life-and-death struggle. The versatile craftsman
Koshar fashions the weapons Baal uses against his enemies. These weapons can kill, injure, or maim from a distance. As the central figure of the drama, Baal himself
literally kicks up a storm, he being the "lord"[30] of thunder
and lightning. Baal nonetheless suffers reverses and at one
time appears dead. But with the timely aid of his violent
consort, Anath, he escapes the clutches of death and wins
the victory at the last. The myth thus credits Baal with
restoring order in the world, everyone profiting from his
extraordinary prowess. Sexual relations between him and
Anath, hitherto hampered by adversity, now receive full
expression in a lustful orgy.

In comparing the Baal myth with anything in today's
culture, we recognize readily the basic plot that inspires
so many movies and dramas in our media. Their very
success lies in the amount of violence and sex they contain.
The hero and his cohorts get authorization to kill and do
anything they please, so long as they subdue the enemy
and restore order. They do battle using weapons that kill
and injure from a distance, weapons that strike swiftly like
lightning, that clap aloud like thunder.

In fulfilling his bizarre task, the hero nonetheless experiences setbacks, receives the wounds of battle, stares death in the face. But help always arrives in the nick of time, often by a woman driven to violence. In these stories, sexual aberrations abound—as they do in the Baal myth. Their scenes of sex and violence appear both subtle and explicit—as they do in the Baal myth. The many variations of their crude plots match ancient counterparts. In the biblical narrative we thus find Baal-Peor, Baal-Berith, Baal-Zebub, and other Baals.

The spilling over of violence and sex from fictitious dramas into real life is as well attested today as it was among the Canaanites.[31] By making carnality legitimate in their culture, the Canaanites— and later the Israelites who conquered them—marked themselves ripe for destruction. Through the media that constitute an everyday part of our lives, we let characters enter our homes and minds to perform acts we abhor in real life.

The pornographic images our media depict—the licentious manner of the characters, their distorted standard of values, their predisposition to murder and violence—all subvert and pollute our minds and hearts. Once there, they become a part of us and we of them. By indulging such images we do the contrary of "stopping our ears at the mention of murder, shutting our eyes at the sight of wickedness" (Isaiah 33:15). Yet this forms the standard— an uncompromising standard—that the Lord makes a prerequisite of salvation.

3. Rock Music

The Lord commanded not just ancient Israel but every covenant people to keep themselves unspotted from the world.[32] This commandment applied as much in the days before the Flood as it does in the latter days. One account of the period leading up to the Flood[33] tells how the people of the covenant, who lived on a high mountain plateau,

lost their chosen status: they let the people of Cain, who
lived on the plain, entice them down the mountain.

From the days of Adam, the first man, the Lord commanded the children of the covenant "not to mingle with
the children of Cain, and not to learn their ways" (2 *Adam
and Eve* 19:4). In the days of Jared—whose name means
"going down"—the children of the covenant nonetheless
mingled with them and soon became as they were. When
the Flood came, it swept away both, the people of Cain
and of the covenant alike. Only Noah and his immediate
family, as a type of things to come,[34] preserved their covenant status and were spared (Genesis 6:17-18).

Whether the account that the books of *Adam and Eve*
give is accurate, or whether it represents but a folk memory, does not matter a great deal.[35] What matters is the
thing it describes, a phenomenon that could occur among
any chosen people.

The scriptures predict that the Flood and the apostasy
that preceded it represent something that will repeat itself
in the last days.[36] The kind of wickedness and corruption
that filled the earth before the Flood (Genesis 6:5, 12)
should therefore serve to forewarn us. We cannot—in the
last days—presume to be on the side of Noah when we
live the law of the people of Cain. Those whom the Lord
preserved through the Flood anciently not only abstained
from wickedness, but actively resisted its influence.[37]
When, at the Flood, the Lord baptized the earth with water,
Noah and his family alone merited deliverance. So also,
in the last days, when the Lord cleanses the earth in a
flood of fire, only those purified "as with fire" will be
delivered.[38]

The books of *Adam and Eve* identify drunkenness, licentiousness, hatred, murder, and secret combinations as
existing among the children of Cain (2 *Adam and Eve* 20:4-
10). With this, all known scriptural accounts of the period
before the Flood concur.[39] Prophecies of the last days tell

us that these same evils will precipitate the Lord's judgments[40]—until "the elements . . . melt with fervent heat" (2 Peter 3:12). In describing the period before the Flood, the books of *Adam and Eve* attempt to spell out what the scriptures say perfunctorily.

In brief, what enticed the people to come down from the Holy Mount and mingle with the children of Cain was the appeal of a certain kind of music. This music possessed the power to ravish people's souls (2 *Adam and Eve* 20:3). Once the people descended from the mount, all manner of lusts overcame them. The music had conditioned them for this (2 *Adam and Eve* 20:20, 30-32). The music transformed people who had kept the divine law, who had regularly prayed and fasted, from children of God into children of the devil (2 *Adam and Eve* 20:15-16, 27, 35).[41] The music robbed people of their self-control, and thus of a measure of their agency (2 *Adam and Eve* 20:3, 9). The music's intensity and momentum, when played at all hours by impassioned musicians, inflamed people's hearts and won them over. A godly habit of life gave way to the abominations that were the commonplace of the Cainites (2 *Adam and Eve* 20:2, 4, 12-13).

The account relates how a man called Genun, whom Satan inspired, made various kinds of trumpets, horns, stringed instruments, cymbals, psalteries, lyres, harps, and flutes and "gathered companies upon companies to play on them" (2 *Adam and Eve* 20:2, 4). When Genun and his companions played the instruments, "Satan came into them, so that [out of] them were heard beautiful and sweet sounds that ravished the heart" (2 *Adam and Eve* 20:3). When the bands played, the children of Cain "burned as with fire" among themselves, and as a consequence Satan "increased lust among them" (2 *Adam and Eve* 20:4).

As the music became a part of everyday life, the bands gathered at the foot of the Holy Mountain for the purpose of letting the covenant people hear it (2 *Adam and Eve* 20:11).

After about a year of exposure to the music, many of the covenant people came regularly to look down at the musicians (2 *Adam and Eve* 20:12). Satan then again entered Genun. Satan "taught him to make dyeing-stuffs for garments of divers patterns, and made him to understand how to dye crimson and purple" (2 *Adam and Eve* 20:13). To those of the covenant people who came to be entertained, the Cainites "shone in beauty and gorgeous apparel, gathered together at the foot of the mountain in splendor, with horns and gorgeous dresses" (2 *Adam and Eve* 20:14).

When Satan revealed to Genun a way down from the Holy Mountain, Jared admonished his people that if they went down, God would not permit them to return (2 *Adam and Eve* 20:26). Over a period of time, however, company after company descended until but few remained (2 *Adam and Eve* 20:30; 21:1). For "when they looked at the daughters of Cain, at their beautiful figures, at their hands and feet dyed with color, tattooed in ornaments on their faces, the fire of sin kindled in them" (2 *Adam and Eve* 20:31). Moreover, "Satan made them look most beautiful," so that the people lusted after each other like ravenous beasts, committing abominations and falling into defilement (2 *Adam and Eve* 20:32-34).

When, in remorse, some tried to return up the mount, they were unable. Having "come down from glory," they had forsaken their purity and innocence (2 *Adam and Eve* 20:33-34). Through transgressing—to which the music incited them—the covenant people estranged themselves from being the people of God (2 *Adam and Eve* 21:4-5).

What strikes us about this story is how it resembles our society today. When we recognize the physical descent from the Holy Mount as symbolizing a spiritual descent, the account reads like a contemporary happening. Today, as then, the younger generation of the covenant people has commenced yielding to the enticement of this music.

If there exists any doubt that rock music ravishes the soul,
inflames the heart, or sets on fire the lusts of the flesh, we
have but to witness a concert by any well-known rock
group. The spectacle they create—its fantasy, frenzy, and
hysteria—appeals to the very basest of human emotions,
and the physical appearance of the musicians—their gaudy
and glittering attire and their lewd and suggestive gestures—parallel in every way the Cainites that the books of
Adam and Eve describe. As Isaiah foresaw, "the look on
their faces betrays them: they flaunt their sin like Sodom;
they cannot hide it" (Isaiah 3:9).

We cannot explain away the fact that rock music today
exemplifies what is "carnal, sensual, and devilish" (cf.
Mosiah 16:3; Moses 5:13). Its origin in primitive jazz and
soul music, and its "maturing" into hard, punk, and porno
rock, mark it as "the way of Cain," as "a corruption" and
"a riot" (cf. Jude 1:11; 2 Peter 2:12-13). Its development
into a modern cult, with its attendant rituals of liquor,
prostitution, and drugs, attests to its satanic nature. In
many instances, the musicians themselves confess to pacts
with Satan, admitting that he inspires their music and
lyrics.[42] Scott Temple, a former hippie, calls the spirit of
the music the "unholy ghost."

Studies show that even milder kinds of rock music are
but stepping stones to hard rock.[43] The principle holds true
that once people wallow in the mire, they become the
"servants of corruption" (2 Peter 2:17-22). Attempts to use
rock music—a telestial medium—to convey the celestial
message of the gospel constitute, at best, an abomination.
Syncretism has ever sought to prostitute what is holy and
sanction what is profane.

Since rock music entered Western culture in the 1950s,
moral decline in Christian nations has reached an unprecedented low. Latter-day Saints who tolerate the cult are
discovering, to their dismay, that their moral level is no
higher than that of other Christians. Latter-day Saints have

perhaps taken longer to make the "descent," but moral problems of equal magnitude now plague Latter-day Saints and sectarian Christians.

As in the Babylon of Daniel and his companions, when we hear the sound of horns, flutes, harps, sackbuts, psalteries, dulcimers, and all kinds of music, we worship at the shrine of its creators (Daniel 3:3-15). If any of us, therefore, like Shadrach, Meshach, and Abednego, would walk through the fire in the day of burning (Daniel 3:25),[44] it will be because, like them, we refuse to yield to an idolatrous music.

4. Organized Sports

A second propitious diversion that the Cainites used to entice the covenant people, mentioned only briefly, however, consists of organized sports (2 *Adam and Eve* 20:14). A much more telling example of organized sports, of a kind that swayed the Lord's people in another age, were the popular Greco-Roman games (cf. 1 Maccabees 1:14; 1 Corinthians 9:24-25). In the intertestamental and New Testament periods, the single greatest cultural seduction of the Lord's people was the influence of Hellenism. Those who immersed themselves in Greek and Roman culture, including the games, were thus called Hellenizers or Hellenists. Among the Jews these principally comprised the Sadducees, an aristocratic priestly class (although Hellenism affected all Jews to some extent).[45] Among the Christians, Hellenists formed the bulk of the Church's members from the second century of its existence.[46]

In Palestine, the only legitimate repudiators of Hellenism, either Jewish or Christian, were the Dead Sea sectaries.[47] These formed an early type of the "church in the wilderness" when they left their urban brethren to dwell apart. Among the Christians, all ended in apostasy, with Hellenism as the chief cause.[48] Both Hellenizers and Jewish sectaries play an important role as types.

Interestingly, the Greco-Roman games appear to have originated in religious ritual associated with the ancient Near Eastern fertility cult.[49] An idolatrous amusement — one that turns men's hearts from the law of God to the law of the brute — organized sports had their heyday among the Romans. Although the early Romans adopted many aspects of Greek culture, including gymnasia, athletics, and rigorous disciplining, the Roman appetite far more than the Greek tended toward the sensational, spectacular, and barbaric. Historians link the very decline of Roman civilization to an inordinate disposition the general populace displayed for brute sports.[50]

Participants nonetheless executed such sports with all the finesse and sophistication civilization could bring to bear. Elaborate stadiums, housing as many as 200,000 spectators, with gladiators disciplined and groomed for contests of skill combined with raw strength, characterized sports Roman style. The distinction between the Greek and Roman games coincided, in the main, with the amateur and professional status of the players. While the Greek games were more subdued, nonprofessional events, the Romans went all out in expenditure, professional training, and fanfare.[51]

The games, professional or nonprofessional, consisted of chariot races, running, discus throwing, spear throwing, boxing, wrestling, swordsmanship, and hunting. Men practiced for their contests in special barracks or athletic compounds, using primitive forms of weight training and exercise. Sports events followed set schedules in the yearly calendar, advertised by posters in every inhabited region. Contests took place in the gymnasia, amphitheaters, and circuses that were common to every city. All classes of society, drawn from both city and neighboring towns, attended the games.[52]

Stadiums typically contained multiple entrances, stairways, tiers, and blocks of seating. Admission was facilitated by prepurchased tickets or, as in the case of officials, by virtue of reserved seats. Spectators not seated in the immediate proximity of a contest used a primitive form of field glasses. Great bands of musicians, organized in festal processions, blared on trumpets before and at intervals during the games.[53]

Individual contestants often grew popular. They became household names, whom people knew by their personal statistics and professional records. Women adored certain gladiators almost as gods. People made predictions on the outcome of the games, betting with one another on the results. Vast, unruly crowds frequented the contests, waving handkerchiefs, shouting advice, approval, and insults, rising up from their seats during moments of suspense. When contests neared their conclusion, the fervor of the crowds often reached a dangerously feverish pitch, accompanied by calls for blood. People debated the results of the games long after the event.[54]

As the decline of Roman civilization set in, the games became the total preoccupation of the elite as well as the masses; people made no pretense at anything higher in life. They devoted exorbitant resources to the games, so much that charitable programs rated a poor second.[55] Of all peoples in the Roman Empire, it seems only pious Jews shunned the games, considering them a heathen pastime.[56]

In our own culture, a widespread and rapidly growing preoccupation with sports—whether football, basketball, baseball, athletics, boxing, wrestling, car racing, horse racing, hunting—must make us ask whether we, too, like the Romans and Hellenists, find ourselves in a state of moral and civil decline. Although our laws prohibit bloodshed, so explicit appear the parallels of human behavior that we cannot say that we are different. The abandon and frenzy of the human spirit at such events, the foul language, anger, and even bloodlust reflect the kind of coarse disposition the Romans displayed.

So all-consuming have today's games become that they
govern people's very thoughts, moods, and actions. In the
cause of sports, men desecrate the Sabbath. Family life
suffers to the point that we hear of "sports widows and
orphans." Upcoming events are no longer victories we
ourselves win in working out our salvation, but the next
game or the one after.

The fanfare and pageantry we impose on the games,
the vast resources of money and man-hours we devote to
organized sports, betray an entrenched cult, a full-blown
diversion from life's real contest. It is of absolutely no
consequence to us, in the eternal perspective, whether so-
and-so wins a match, or whether such and such a team
retains its ranking. Our all-absorbing quest to become
Number One in sports means that we become second-
string players, or perhaps mere bench warmers, in our
quest for Zion. When we love sports with all our might,
mind, and strength, as we do, we are indeed damnable
idolaters. Once we catch its infectious spirit, it will not
leave us alone. We must ever be following the progress of
a team, making that, not the gospel, our daily talk, the
focus of our thoughts. To be a "fan" of, or "faithful" to,
something other than God means that we entertain a substitute for true worship.

The type we outline teaches us that few, if any, in-
volvements with organized sports exist—in their modern
embellished form—that are not idolatrous in nature, that
do not divert the mind and heart from being preeminently
involved with things of the spirit. This, of course, does
not include our individual pursuit of excellence while mag-
nifying our talents. But where sports form an end in themselves, where they become an all-consuming quest for excellence for its own sake—or for the sake of money or
becoming popular with the world, beating the world at its
own game—then we overstep the bounds on the side of
idolatry. The total abstinence by pious Jews from the games

cult that swept away a civilization, and with it the early Church, surely constitutes a type and shadow of a latter-day contest.

5. Human Idols

The idea of human idols flows naturally out of other forms of idolatry. Indeed, many ancient gods of myth and ritual had human beginnings, some claiming divine parentage or ancestry.[57] The Hebrew prophets refer to various individuals as false gods. Jeremiah calls an apostate ruler in Judah "a despised broken idol" (Jeremiah 22:28). The Lord punishes this ruler by "writing" him childless (Jeremiah 22:30) — the covenant curse of having no posterity. Zechariah describes false prophets as idols who speak folly and singles out a certain "idol shepherd" who forsakes the flock (Zechariah 10:2; 11:17). Instead of feeding the flock, this religious leader consumes the flesh of the fattest (Zechariah 11:16). The Lord punishes him by smiting him in the arm and blinding him in one eye (Zechariah 11:17), in mock imitation of a marred statue. This punishment renders him ritually blemished and his ministry illegitimate.

Isaiah, through a subtle play on words, identifies prominent figures in society as "idols." By using terms possessing different levels of meaning, Isaiah implies that the people idolize certain "celebrities" or "bigwigs"; the people are "enchanted" and "captivated" by them, and exhibit "covetous desires," "fawning adulation," and "carnal lust" toward them (Isaiah 1:29-30).[58] The idols, on the other hand, exercise "immunity" from the law on account of wealth, power, or fame; they and their enterprises make up the very spark that sets off a fiery destruction of the Lord's people (Isaiah 1:29-31).

The Hebrew prophets predict, as does John the Revelator, that the ultimate human idol will be the Antichrist of the last days.[59] Biblical types of this archtyrant abound: the king of Babylon, the king of Assyria, the king of Tyre, the king of Greece.[60] To this list we may add later Antichrist types, from Nero to Hitler. As in Isaiah, the latter-day Antichrist forms a composite of all evil world-rulers who precede him. He, like them, commands the worship of men (Revelation 13:4, 8). Satan lends him his own power (Revelation 13:2). His heart, like theirs, is lifted up, and he thinks, "I am a God; I sit in the seat of God, in the midst of the seas" (Ezekiel 28:2).

Like some figure out of *Star Wars*, the Antichrist rises in the heavens like the morning star to set his throne above the stars of God (Isaiah 14:13). He ascends above the altitude of the clouds and makes himself "like the Most High" (Isaiah 14:14). He sets his nest on high, in order to escape calamities on the earth (Habakkuk 2:9). He exalts himself above all gods, defying even the God of Gods (Daniel 11:36).

With divine irony, the Lord does not let the Antichrist arise until the world is full of false gods. Worshiping this human idol consists of but an extension of what is already transpiring. As God's instrument, the Antichrist nonetheless condemns the false gods of all peoples to the fire, including those of the Lord's people (Isaiah 10:11; 37:19). He regards no god other than himself, but "magnifies himself above all" (Daniel 11:37).

Under his tyrannous rule, all human idols now worshiped, exalted, extolled, glorified, revered, idolized, and adored will be things of the past. Rock stars, movie stars, sports stars, superstars, tycoons, barons, and bigwigs will be but "despised broken idols." Through the instrumentality of the Antichrist, the Lord will "make all glorying in excellence a profanity, and the world's celebrities an utter execration" (Isaiah 23:9). Until the Lord displaces the Antichrist as King of Kings and Lord of Lords when he comes in glory, the Antichrist's coercive worship will serve as punishment of our present voluntary worship of man.

6. Imaginations of the Heart

Virtually every instance of the expression "imaginations of the heart" in the Bible equates such imaginations
with idolatry and following other gods.[61] At a covenant
ceremony, Moses warns Israel, "Lest there should be
among you a man, woman, family, or tribe whose heart
turns away this day from the Lord our God to go and serve
the gods of these nations; lest there should be among you
a root that bears gall and wormwood" (Deuteronomy
29:18). Moses goes on to cite a classic kind of self-deception,
at the same time harking back to the curses he has just
enumerated in connection with the covenant: "And it come
to pass, when he hears the words of this curse, that he
bless himself in his heart, saying, I shall have peace [sal-
vation], though I walk in the imagination of my heart, to
add drunkenness to thirst" (Deuteronomy 29:19).

Moses thereby gives us to understand that self-deception or "drunkenness" follows a personal lack of or "thirst"
for the knowledge of God. Paul concurs with this when
he says that imaginations, or reasonings, form a kind of
conceit or pretense that exalts itself "against the knowledge
of God" (2 Corinthians 10:5). Moses thus concludes his
warning by showing how the Lord will not withhold his
anger and jealousy from such but will bring "all the curses
that are written in this book" upon them, separating them
unto evil from his people, blotting out their name from
under heaven (Deuteronomy 29:20-21).

Imaginations of the heart nonetheless constitute something each of us has to live with. They form an integral
part of being mortal, expressing a person's innate disposition to think or do evil. Unavoidably, "the imagination
of man's heart is evil from his youth" (Genesis 8:21). People
possess a natural tendency to be proud, mischievous, and
wicked (Proverbs 6:18; Luke 1:51).[62] But when people let
the imagination of their hearts rule them, when they do

not make captive every thought in obedience to Christ (2 Corinthians 10:5), then they fall. Then, though "they knew God, they glorified him not as God, neither were thankful; but became vain in their imaginations, and their foolish heart was darkened" (Romans 1:21).

When God's prophet calls on the people to repent, they think, "There is no hope" — they continue following their own devices, relying for guidance on the imaginations of their heart (Jeremiah 18:12). Instead of hearkening to the Lord's counsel, they hearken to those who say, "Ye shall have peace. . . . No evil shall come upon you" (Jeremiah 23:17). In the end, the Lord esteems such people as good for nothing and vents his wrath upon them (Jeremiah 13:10-14). Biblical types of falling prey to the imagination of the heart include the people before the Flood, the people at the Tower of Babel, and Israel and Judah before the Exile.[63]

Nephi identifies the large and spacious building he and his father saw in vision as the "vain imaginations and the pride of the children of men" (1 Nephi 12:18). Nephi notes that a great and terrible gulf — the justice of the eternal God — divides those in the building from the godly (1 Nephi 12:18). Those who gather in the building consist not just of non-Israelites but also of the house of Israel, mocking, scorning, and fighting their humble brethren (1 Nephi 8:27, 33; 11:35). What distinguishes the multitude in the building is the exceeding fine manner in which they dress (1 Nephi 8:27). Their sophistication and pointing the finger reflect a preoccupation with unreality, as the building in the air, standing high above the earth, also signifies (1 Nephi 8:26). The building's fall, as Nephi sees, is the destruction of all wicked nations, kindreds, tongues, and people (1 Nephi 11:36) — an event of the last days.[64]

Without identifying everything today that would qualify as imaginations of the heart, it seems self-evident that what is worldly and subject to change — all things "new," novel, fashionable, or in vogue; all trends, fads, crazes, and gimmicks; in short, all that is not of God but concocted in the minds of people[65] — the Lord dooms to destruction along with those who love these things. They make up but a passing parade of phantoms intruding upon our senses, whose purpose is to confuse and to befuddle. Because imaginations of the heart vary constantly, those who follow them know no stability. Every wind of change, as it were, sweeps them away.

God, and what is of God, does not behave so. In God there exists no "shadow of changing" (Mormon 9:9). Unlike man, "God doth not walk in crooked paths, neither doth he turn to the right hand nor to the left, neither doth he vary from that which he hath said" (D&C 3:2). His thoughts do not reflect our thoughts, nor his ways our ways (Isaiah 55:8). As the heavens are higher than the earth, so are his ways higher than our ways and his thoughts higher than our thoughts (Isaiah 55:9). In summary, those of us who seek not the Lord to establish his righteousness, but walk every one in our own way, after the image of our own god — whose image is in the likeness of this world, whose substance is that of an idol — shall perish in Babylon, which shall fall (D&C 1:16).

7. Nature Cults

The prophet Isaiah, in several instances, refers to nature worship prevailing among the Lord's people. Nature worship deviates from true worship in that it furnishes a ready substitute for paradise. To Isaiah, a preoccupation with parks or gardens (Hebrew *gan; gannāh*) spells idolatry (Isaiah 1:29-30).[66] Nature lovers often frequent such places to escape responsibility toward God and humanity. The beauties of nature excite the romantic instinct in people, while nature's seclusion paves the way for licentiousness and sexual abuse. Nature religionists can do pretty much as they please away from the common constraints of society. In addition, various cultic quirks characterize nature enthusiasts. These include a preference for particular sorts of foods, a ritualistic way of preparing them, and their communal consumption in the appropriate surroundings. Naturalists shun and make fun of their puritanical brethren. On the other hand, they look up to and imitate favorite personalities.

Isaiah speaks of those who cherish and choose the nature experience in the act of forsaking the Lord their God (Isaiah 1:28-29). These provoke God to his face by "sacrificing in parks, making smoke upon bricks" (Isaiah 65:3). Their favorite resorts include canyons, ravines, and riverbeds (Isaiah 57:5-6). They frequently spend the night in hideaways, among green trees, and under crags of cliffs and rocks (Isaiah 57:5-6; 65:4). There, they burn with lust and commit fornication with one another (Isaiah 57:5; 66:17). They eat the flesh of animals the Mosaic code prohibits, among them pork, prawn, and rodents (Isaiah 65:4; 66:17). They pour drink libations as a toast to their cult; they consume polluted beverages (Isaiah 57:6; 65:4).

Those not of their life-style they bid keep their distance, considering themselves "holier than thou" (Isaiah 65:5). Often, they amuse themselves over the Lord's true worshipers, though they themselves are the slaves of sin (Isaiah 5:18; 57:4). Heedless and in abrogation of their own agency, they ape the behavior of those on whom they center their attention (Isaiah 66:17). Called the offspring of adulterer and harlot, they are born of sin (Isaiah 57:3-4), the product of an apostate people beset by satanic influences. The summital act of their wickedness consists of abusing and slaying children (Isaiah 57:5). In similar style, the Lord makes an end of them in the day of his burning wrath (Isaiah 66:17, 24).

The various kinds of nature worship that prevail in our culture repeat the ancient pattern. From overemphasizing perfection in home gardens and landscaping (while disregarding the needy who pass by in the street) to spending an inordinate amount of time at the ritualistic gatherings and barbecues that many indulge in — the same self-gratifying imbalance marks the society of the Lord's people then and now. Isaiah could have had the latter-day camper culture in mind when he observed idolaters "hitched to transgression like a trailer" (Isaiah 5:18).

The nature lovers among us for whom nature has become a religion could hardly have been outdone by the primitive cult. The fervid weekenders and their sport, and even backyard enthusiasts, display a sophistication the ancients would not have guessed. Today's proliferation of campers, dirt bikes, dune buggies, four-wheelers, skis, snowmobiles, yachts, speedboats, gliders, and related accoutrements betoken a rampant and costly cult. When recreation becomes an end in itself, when promiscuity seeks out recreation as a means of self-expression, then there results a classic kind of idolatry.

8. Mammon

The scriptures in all ages warn that the "mammon of unrighteousness" (Luke 16:9) — the riches of this world — have been and will be the downfall of countless souls. The Lord himself has told us plainly that we cannot serve God *and* mammon. Each is a "master," to be loved at the expense of hating the other.[67] So many are the scriptural counsels warning about the riches of this world that we must suppose they dulled the ears of those who perished with their riches. Or perhaps the rich did not think of themselves as rich, and so did not apply these warnings to themselves. The scriptures speak of self-deception as a trait frequently afflicting the rich.[68]

From the way the scriptures emphasize equality among the Lord's people,[69] we see that the Lord's idea of the rich draws a contrast between the *haves* and *have-nots*. A rich man from another country we may not consider rich in our own, though he possess a surfeit of what others lack.

Being rich, in the scriptural sense, includes *having* when others do not, creating inequality.

To round out this definition, I will cite the dominant characteristics of the rich that the scriptures give. Those who "hasten to be rich have an evil eye" and are not innocent (Proverbs 28:20, 22). They soon fall into temptations and snares, into foolish and hurtful lusts, which "drown men in destruction and perdition" (1 Timothy 6:9). Trusting in "uncertain riches" (1 Timothy 6:17), people grow wise in their own conceit (Proverbs 28:11) and wax proud (Alma 4:6). They lift up their hearts because of their riches (Ezekiel 28:5), refusing to give heed to the word of God (Alma 45:24), becoming unfruitful (Matthew 13:22).

The rich pass over the deeds of the wicked and do not judge the needy's cause (Jeremiah 5:28). They despise the poor and drag them before the judgment seats (James 2:6). They set their hearts on riches and the vain things of the world, scorning and persecuting those who do not believe according to their will and pleasure (Alma 4:8).[70] The rich defraud and condemn the just and suppose that they are better than they (Jacob 2:13; Mosiah 4:22). In brief, the love of money is the root of every kind of evil, causing men to "err from the faith" (1 Timothy 6:10).

When "their treasure is their god" (2 Nephi 9:30), the rich suffer evil consequences. The rich can hardly enter the kingdom of heaven because they already have their consolation (Matthew 19:23; Luke 6:24).[71] Because they are puffed up, God despises them, thrusting them down to hell (2 Nephi 9:42; 28:15). They lay up treasure for themselves on the earth, only to lose their souls (Luke 12:16-21). They carry nothing of their glory or riches beyond the grave (Psalm 49:17). In the day of burning heat, the rich fade away like withering grass whose flower falls (James 1:11). The riches they have swallowed down, they must vomit up again (Job 20:15). Riches "profit not in the day of wrath" (Proverbs 11:4).

In such a day, the treasures of the rich become slippery, so that the rich cannot retain them (Helaman 13:31). The rich who do not give of their substance to the poor will lament in the day of judgment, crying, "The harvest is past, the summer is ended, and my soul is not saved" (D&C 56:16).[72] In the great day of the Lord, the rich hide themselves in dens, crying to the mountains and rocks, "Fall on us, and hide us from the face of him who sits on the throne, and from the wrath of the Lamb" (Revelation 6:15-17).

Yet there is something redeeming about riches. On those who are industrious, Providence often smiles most pleasantly (Jacob 2:13). If men do not learn how to administer the unrighteous mammon, how can the Lord commit to their trust the true riches? (Luke 16:11). As for the rich, they "do good" if they are ready to distribute their wealth to those in need and are willing to communicate with them (1 Timothy 6:18). The Lord has decreed a way to provide for his Saints, namely, "that the poor shall be exalted, in that the rich are made low" (D&C 104:16). The Lord justified the wealthy Zacchaeus, a hated publican who climbed a tree in order to greet him (Luke 19:2-9). Zacchaeus regularly gave "the half of my goods . . . to the poor; and if I have taken any thing from any man by false accusation, I restore [unto] him fourfold" (Luke 19:8).

Jacob counseled the rich to think of their brethren like unto themselves, to be familiar with all and free with their substance—"that they may be rich like unto you" (Jacob 2:17). Before people seek for riches, he advised, they should seek for the kingdom of God, obtaining first a hope in Christ (Jacob 2:18-19). A hope in Christ means that as we devote our lives to God, we at some point receive a witness by the Holy Ghost that we have obtained a remission of our sins. We can justify pursuing riches, therefore, but only within a narrow compass: "for the intent to do good—to clothe the naked, and to feed the hungry, and to liberate the captive, and administer relief to the sick and the afflicted" (Jacob 2:19). In the scriptures, that constitutes the sole justification of pursuing riches.

Since the selfish pursuit of riches is so widespread today, what do the ancient parallels portend for the future? The Lord warns us, the Latter-day Saints, not to become as the Nephites of old (D&C 38:39). Yet the Nephite prophets foresaw that we would indeed become like them.[73] In another type of the last days, the people of the Church at Laodicea had grown rich and increased in goods, lacking nothing (Revelation 3:17). Spiritually, however, they were wretched, miserable, poor, blind, and naked (Revelation 3:17). Because they were neither hot nor cold but lukewarm toward the gospel, the Lord spewed them out of his mouth (Revelation 3:16).

Hosea describes Ephraim as saying, "I have become rich, I have found me out substance: in all my labours they shall find none iniquity in me" (Hosea 12:8). But the Lord responds that he will yet make them dwell in tents (Hosea 12:9).[74] Likewise, before the Lord came to the Nephites a great inequality existed among them, so that the Church broke up (3 Nephi 6:14). This happened because of the immense wealth of some, while others suffered in the depths of humility (3 Nephi 6:10, 13). Finally, the scriptures warn us that first will come the day of the rich and the learned, the wise and the noble (D&C 58:10). After that will come the day of his power, when "the poor, the lame, and the blind, and the deaf, come in unto the marriage of the Lamb, and partake of the supper of the Lord" (D&C 58:11).[75]

9. Babylon

The name *Babylon* means many things to many people. The Hebrew word (*bābel*) goes back to a kingdom Nimrod founded, where the ancients built the tower of Babel, or Babylon (Genesis 10:9-10; 11:1-9). This kingdom evolved into an idolatrous materialistic civilization that reached a zenith in the powerful neo-Babylonian empire of Nebuchadnezzar (cf. Daniel 2:37-38). The prophet Isaiah identifies Babylon typologically as both a people and a place: the sinners and the wicked; the earth and the world (Isaiah 13:1, 9, 11). He predicts latter-day Babylon will suffer the fate of Sodom and Gomorrah, thus likening the world's desolation to a fiery cataclysm falling upon the wicked (Isaiah 13:4-19).

Jeremiah calls Babylon a "destroying mountain" (*har hammašḥît*), an expression that in Hebrew also means a "corrupting" or "decadent" kingdom (Jeremiah 51:25). Babylon's destiny is to become a burned mountain, desolate forever, because Babylon corrupts—and thus ultimately destroys—all the earth (Jeremiah 51:25-26). Babylon's fall in the last days forms a key event ushering in the Millennium.[76]

Isaiah and Jeremiah single out something about Babylon that corrupts all, including the Lord's people. Those who engage in it become "Babylon" themselves and in the end perish with it. This involves the manufacturing, promoting, and selling of idols—the works of men's hands.

A story I heard in rabbinic school relates how Abraham's father, Terah, in the land of Ur of the Babylonians, at times put young Abraham in charge of his store. When Terah, who made and sold idols, went into the forest to fetch wood for their manufacture, Abraham was to sell the idols in his father's place. Typically Abraham would dissuade buyers, reproving the adults for esteeming statues as gods. One day, fed up with his duty, Abraham smashed all his father's wares except a large idol that stood on a top shelf. When Terah returned from the forest, he flew into a rage, demanding an explanation. Abraham responded, "The big one did it!" implying that these were no gods at all, or they could have saved themselves. After that, Abraham became unpopular in Ur and the people sought his life. A sequel to this story appears in the book of Abraham, which commences with, "I, Abraham, saw that it was needful for me to obtain another place of residence" (Abraham 1:1).

As Hugh Nibley has often pointed out, the essence of this sort of idol worship is not that people really believed the idols to be gods, but that their manufacture, promotion, and sale provided them with a living. It formed a socioeconomic system that afforded urban dwellers a means of sustenance. One problem with this system lay in its false economic base and the instability it bred—it fed on itself.

Economic factors determined social behavior—the law of supply. Manufacturing the works of men's hands yielded income but constituted idolatry, because what so many people worked at, oriented their lives around, was ultimately nonproductive. The work of idols did not sustain itself, but demanded to be sustained. It enslaved to a false idea not merely those directly involved with it, but also those who produced foodstuffs and raw materials. The latter labored additionally to provide for all the rest.

The reverse of this phenomenon also applied: false spiritual values influenced directions the economy would take—the law of demand. Because of their association with deity, idols represented something socially acceptable into which people might pour time and money. The prestige the idols furnished made people protective of the system. Those who prospered from it had found a niche. Their real source of subsistence—farmers and husbandmen—took second place in people's minds. Society measured wealth in terms of money and the idols it could buy, rather than by how much food could be produced.

We can thus liken Babylon's socioeconomic structure to an upside-down pyramid, which, as it grows, ever narrows at its base. In it, the many depend on the few for their support. Babylon's mass of people, engaged in producing and selling idols, remain out of touch with their life source, rendering them vulnerable to catastrophe. The greatest height to which Babylon attains thus also forms her lowest point of stability. For when, through some unforeseen (divine) intervention, a single stone jars loose from the base, the entire structure collapses.

By way of contrast, Zion's economy is not so structured. As Israel's prophets outline, Zion possesses a broad rural base, in which every family works its inheritance of land.[77] This makes Zion a stable, self-sustaining structure. In it abide neither poor nor those who appropriate what belongs to others. Zion's people look to their Head, their cornerstone, to bless them with increase. Old Testament and Book of Mormon examples show that such a structure can weather most storms, endure most attacks, and quickly repair or rebuild itself. The direct means of sustenance — the capacity to produce foodstuffs and raw materials — is ready at hand. Even when a people must flee temporarily into the wilderness, this provides them with the greatest maneuverability.

In short, the works of men's hands on which people set their hearts, on which they spend natural and human resources are, by definition, "idols" (Isaiah 2:8; Jeremiah 10:1-5). As the prophets describe them, these are idols that people invent, design, sketch, carve, forge, molten, cast, weld, plate, fit, hammer, rivet, and mass produce.[78] Manufactured, promoted, and sold for gold and silver (Isaiah 44:9; 46:6), the idols form the fruits of a technology of well-nigh magical dimensions (Isaiah 47:10, 12). They follow trends and engage the whole of society (Isaiah 44:11; 47:13). Depending on the kind of idols, people both carry them about and set them in place in their homes (Isaiah 45:20; 46:7).

The entire production of idols, however, is erroneous and vain (Jeremiah 51:18). It causes people to become like the idols themselves — sightless and mindless to things spiritual, unaware and insensible to impending disaster

(Isaiah 42:17-20; 44:9, 18; 45:16). It constitutes a "wine" that makes people drunk and mad—the wine of Babylon (Jeremiah 51:7).

A law unto herself, Babylon tyrannizes and enslaves; yet people do not discern her for what she is (Isaiah 44:20; 47:6-8, 10). In reality, Babylon suffers from gross defects, open wounds that no one can heal (Jeremiah 51:8-9). At her height, she mounts up to heaven, from whence the Lord suddenly and utterly casts her down (Jeremiah 51:8, 53). On her destruction, those intoxicated with her wine do not so much as wake up from their sleep (Jeremiah 51:39). Since their gods, the works of men's hands, did not save them, they profited them nothing in the end (Isaiah 44:9; 46:7).

Although Jeremiah—at Judah's exile—advised his people to serve the king of Babylon (Jeremiah 27:6-17; 40:9), Jeremiah did not mean, "When in Babylon, do as Babylon does!" Indeed, both Isaiah and Jeremiah looked forward to the time Israel would exit Babylon before the Lord destroyed her (Isaiah 48:20; Jeremiah 51:6). The time would come, as with Abraham, when it would no longer be advisable to remain in Babylon. The more she ripened in wickedness, the less possible it would be to live *in* Babylon but not be *of* Babylon.

Isaiah depicts the coming of the Lord's people out of Babylon as a new exodus, patterned after the ancient exodus out of Egypt (Isaiah 48:20-21; 52:11-12). He likens the gathering of a repentant remnant of Israel from the ends of the earth to Abraham's coming out of Babylonia into the wilderness (Isaiah 41:8-9; 51:1-3). The prophets, therefore, speak both of a literal, spontaneous exodus from Babylon on the eve of her destruction, and of a gradual, premeditated exit before that time.[79] As Lot's wife illustrates, those ensconced in Babylon find it hard to leave at a moment's notice.

Doing "the works of Abraham"—in order to merit an

exaltation that compares to his[80]—thus includes leaving and forsaking Babylon as he did, becoming wholly pure of her abominable idols (cf. Isaiah 51:2; 52:11). Not unexpectedly, the limits of any alternative to Babylon are extremely narrow. In prophetic thought, what is not Zion is Babylon and what is not Babylon is Zion. In effect, only two choices remain for the Lord's people: either build up Zion or build up Babylon. This requires that we gain a clear idea about Zion and Babylon—how the prophets define them, what they stand for, and how to implement Zion.

Isaiah, for example, defines Zion as both a people and a place: those of the Lord's people who repent, and the place to which they gather—a safe place in the wilderness during the Lord's day of judgment.[81] According to Isaiah, the Lord's people must urgently repent of Babylonian idolatry—worshiping the works of men's hands.[82] Scriptural precedents prove the principle that those who leave Babylon under the Lord's direction inherit a promised land.[83] According to Jeremiah, a person leaves Babylon in order to go to Zion, throwing in one's lot with the Lord by an everlasting covenant (Jeremiah 50:1-5). To leave Babylon means to go out from among the wicked to establish Zion somewhere else (D&C 38:42; 133:4-9). All who remain in Babylon do so at the peril of their lives.[84]

As for the works of men's hands in today's Babylon, we need say little more to recapture the ancient scene. Essentially the same materialistic economy that prevailed then prevails in our day. Like the ancient port city of Tyre, Babylon's mercantile arm,[85] latter-day Babylon encompasses every kind of trade and merchandise—whatever the souls of men lust after by way of material possessions (Revelation 18:1-24). The manufacture and promotion of contemporary works of men's hands form virtually an unlimited enterprise. Reduplicating the socioeconomic structure of ancient Babylon is the very stuff of modernization.

Technology of almost magical proportions consumes humanity to the point of enslaving us to it. By orienting our lives around their production, sale, and maintenance, we set material things above the glory of God. Taking care of the works of men's hands and servicing them are terms synonymous with loving and serving idols. And yet, as with her ancient counterpart, men do not discern modern Babylon for what she is. The wine with which all nations of the earth are drunk blinds men to life's divine charge and to Babylon's looming collapse (Revelation 17:2; 18:3). As with many other peoples who have grown up in captivity, we ourselves are not cognizant of, or else take for granted, the fact of our bondage.

The question remains, what will Abraham's children do? Will they continue to imbibe the wine of Babylon, or will they ask the way to Zion?

10. The Arm of Flesh

To Israel's prophets, Pharaoh king of Egypt epitomizes the arm of flesh on which the Lord's people lean in times of national crisis. Ancient Egypt—the type of a great latter-day superpower[86]—exemplifies human industry, wealth, and political stability (Ezekiel 31:2-9). At Israel's judgment, however, Pharaoh proves to be but a "splintered reed which enters and pierces the hand of any man who leans on it" (Isaiah 36:6; Ezekiel 29:6-7). When put to the test, Egypt's ample resources of chariots and horsemen prove no match for the ruthless world power the Lord raises up against his people.[87]

By making treaties and alliances with foreign nations, Israel only adds sin to sin—she rejects the Lord's covenant and relies on the arm of flesh (Isaiah 30:1-2). The very act of the Lord's people turning to human strength for protection causes their hearts to turn away from their true source of strength (Jeremiah 17:5-8). In response to such conduct, the Lord denies his protection and shames his people, causing them and their allies to fall before their enemies.[88] Though the Lord holds out a way of escape for the righteous of his people, by far the majority do not "see when good cometh" because they turn their eyes in the wrong direction (Jeremiah 17:6).

But the arm of flesh assumes other forms besides relying on manpower and weaponry. All such forms constitute idolatry, because they put humanity before deity. They overlook God as the author and creator of all, as he who holds all things in being. God gives life and takes it away, often in ways that seem to men miraculous or untimely. God himself raises up adversaries, personal and national, and God disposes of them.[89]

Even as the Lord promises his people a land of inheritance and an enduring posterity—as a covenant blessing, on condition that they live righteously—so he promises to protect them in the face of a mortal threat. The Hebrew prophets do not predict that the Lord will destroy the righteous in the day of judgment. On the contrary, the Lord grants salvation both temporal and spiritual to those who keep his commandments. In the theology of Israel's prophets, temporal and spiritual salvation go hand in hand.[90] Perhaps some of the Lord's people may get killed in order to fill up the measure of their sacrifice, and as a testimony against the wicked.[91] Nevertheless, personal righteousness, in the last days as anciently, is the only criterion for being delivered from death.[92]

Isaiah, therefore, reduces every kind of dependence on things human to a "covenant with Death" (Isaiah 28:15, 18). That includes looking back on past victories and glory (Isaiah 28:1, 4), believing human predictions of a bright future for humanity (Isaiah 30:10; 47:13), relying on the outward observance of worship (Isaiah 29:1, 13), being guided by anything less than direct, divine revelation (Isaiah 28:7-13), contriving secret schemes and contingency plans (Isaiah 28:15; 29:15; 30:16), plotting machinations and intrigues (Isaiah 30:12; 47:12), and every other way of "taking refuge in deception and hiding behind falsehoods" (Isaiah 28:15).[93] In the Lord's day of judgment, the people's covenant with death proves void: a terrible scourge overruns those who trust in the arm of flesh (Isaiah 28:18).

All means of warding off woe by somehow indemnifying against it will then disastrously default (Isaiah 47:11-15). These will prove to be merely bonds that bind men down to destruction (Isaiah 28:22). At the last, human agreements and alliances will be held in contempt and come to nought (Isaiah 8:9-15; 33:7-8; 47:13-15). The compacts people make are deceitful—no brother can be trusted (Jeremiah 9:4-6). Even as they speak together in peaceable terms, people lie in wait to take advantage of one another (Jeremiah 9:8). In summary, all who trust in human counsel are under a curse and will be broken (2 Nephi 28:31; D&C 1:19).

It is no secret that human pacts pervade Western nations today. At the national level, leaders set up compacts such as UN, NATO, and SEATO, ostensibly for the welfare and protection of all. Leaders nonetheless consider simultaneous arms buildups essential for self-preservation. At the individual level, men set up various kinds of securities, indemnities, and insurance, ostensibly to benefit people and their dependents. By fortifying ourselves through these devices against possible future disasters, however, we in fact turn away from the direction whence good comes.

Such human helps betray a lack of trust in him who governs human affairs. These helps serve as a substitute for the welfare and protection that come from keeping one's covenant with God. Relieving people of personal accountability before God, they seek to forestall his righteous decrees. Keeping a lesser law, people reap the fruits thereof. They reject the blessing of the Lord's covenant of life for the curse of a covenant with death. Being concerned primarily for their temporal well-being, people lose spirituality as a governing principle.

Another consequence of man's trusting in man is that, once made, human bonds can be undone often only with dishonor and loss of face. In the Lord's sight, we cannot simply walk away from our word (Ezekiel 17:15-21). Biblical examples, however, show the worst feature of human bonds to be the mind-set individual parties develop. The very disposition of those who rely on the arm of flesh holds them in its grip like a disease. Though they might acknowledge the Lord God, they cannot bring themselves to believe there exists any other way. Like all idolatry, relying on the arm of flesh blinds people to a divine purpose or providence—that God saves those who trust in him (Isaiah 42:17-21). Such an alternative forms an intangible that scares people to death (Isaiah 51:12-13). Even when the Lord brings upon people all manner of extremities, they remain insensible as to the cause (Isaiah 42:22-25). They cannot relate current woes to their own actions. Though they exercise good intentions after suffering the Lord's chastisements, they remain as prone as ever to trust in man before trusting in God (Jeremiah 42:1-44:30).

But when they exercise mighty faith in him who is the source of all good (Jeremiah 33:6-11), when they do not put the counsel of man before the counsel of God (Isaiah 29:15), when they cease to play God—killing those who should live, keeping alive those who should die (Ezekiel 13:19)—when they truly make the Lord their Judge, their Lawgiver, and their King (Isaiah 33:22), then the Lord extends his promise to them. In the destruction God has decreed upon us and our generation,[94] some he will endow with power from on high as a testimony against those who depend on human strength.[95] In that day, a remnant of Ephraim will find the Lord a sure source of strength to repulse the attack at the gates (Isaiah 28:5-6).

11. Elitism-Pharisaism

Parallels between the ancient types and their modern counterparts have till now seemed easily discernible. The two remaining parallels I leave for the reader to judge. Anciently, both conditions of idolatry immediately preceded the destruction of the Lord's people, the Lord delivering only a remnant. If the types hold true, therefore, the recurring of these forms of idolatry will signal the same result. Conversely, when the calamities of the last days appear at the door, it will be because these and other forms of apostasy have grown prevalent among us. For in the last days all types come together, whether for good, as in the restoration of keys and blessings of former dispensations, or for evil, as in the idolatry of Israel that precipitates the great and dreadful day of the Lord.

In setting out these biblical types, I may seem to assume the role of the devil's advocate. In fact, the types incriminate none but the offenders themselves, those who do not learn the lessons of history. We should remind ourselves, however, that such offenders cannot, nor ever will, constitute grounds for our growing disaffected with the Church. The great paradox, the test the Saints endure in our day, surely consists of remaining true, while all around people indulge in idolatry. Every parallel I mention possesses this as a moral.

Hugh Nibley serves as an inspiring example of such faithfulness to the Church. Although he recognizes the great good and the many evils in the Church, he stands aloof from all disaffection. He scrupulously maintains the fine line between discontent—often voiced openly to inspire us to higher things—and malcontent. Malcontent, the sure path to apostasy, receives not so much as a whisper from him.

On the other hand, should we take ourselves so seriously as to get up our ire or plunge into guilt feelings at the whisper of anything critical? Should we not increase our capacity to see through the problems and even laugh at ourselves? The Jews, having endured a much longer history of spiritual heights and depths than ours, form perhaps the best example of a people exercising collective resilience and resourcefulness. Although the Jews take pains to preserve their religious integrity, they never view themselves so sullenly as to decline to discuss their faults and foibles past or present.

To omit the last two parallels would render this study incomplete and therefore defective. Were we to be selective about types or fail to see their total context, we might as well ignore them all. We then would not learn our lesson but would exemplify the folly of man that they teach. The total effect of the parallels surely does not cause us to point the finger at others. Rather, it helps us take the attitude, "Let him who is without sin cast the first stone" (cf. John 8:7). More than that, aberrations existing within a people's leadership, whether political or religious, tend to be symptomatic of the general condition — our leadership reflects what we ourselves are, both at our best and at our worst.

I call this form of idolatry elitism-Pharisaism, because it simultaneously partakes of social pride and hypocrisy. It constitutes idolatry because it puts the institution or peer group before the individual: a person serves the corporate entity, not vice versa. It involves worship, in effect, of the system or organization to which people belong and thus is a kind of self-worship. Typifying this sort of idolatry are the Pharisees of the New Testament period, a group whose elitist tendencies we know well from Jesus' discourses with them. Book of Mormon examples of the same sort of idolatry (not cited here) include the priests of King Noah and the Zoramites (Mosiah 11:1-12:37; Alma 31:1-32:5).

These persons display a form of godliness lacking the power thereof (2 Timothy 3:5). They harbor a naive presumptuousness about being a chosen and elect people

(Luke 3:8). They consider others — their righteous brethren — a lost and fallen people, worthy to be despised as
lesser mortals (John 7:47-52).

A paradoxical aspect of the elitist-Pharisaic phenomenon is that its pastors and teachers do in fact possess
authority to teach and instruct. The Lord requires, therefore, that his people obey them (Matthew 23:1-3). In reality,
however, they have taken away the key of knowledge and
shut up the kingdom, neither entering it themselves nor
letting others enter (Matthew 23:13; Luke 11:52). As a result, they cannot answer difficult religious questions nor
recognize the signs of the times (Matthew 16:2-3; 22:46).
They are blind leaders of the blind, yet they assume they
see things aright (Matthew 15:14; John 9:41). They confuse
their priorities and what is real (Matthew 23:16-24; Luke
11:42). They cancel the good effect the word of God has
in people's lives, overruling intuitive devotion with conventions (Matthew 15:3; Mark 7:13).

Yet, observant in their religion and esteemed by men,
they consider themselves righteous by their own standards
(Luke 16:15; 18:11-12). But their religion consists of what
appears in public (Matthew 23:5). Their thoughts tell another story (Luke 12:1-3). On the outside they appear righteous, but inwardly they raven like wolves; they yield to
wickedness, oppression, excesses (Matthew 23:25-28; Luke
11:39). Though they believe in Christ, they care more for
men's praise than God's (John 5:44; 12:42-43). Like leaven
in bread, hypocrisy permeates their establishment (Luke
12:1). Their hypocrisy, likewise, inspires their communal
prayers (Matthew 23:14). They love for men to call them
by ecclesiastical titles, to greet them publicly and hold them
in admiration (Matthew 23:7; Luke 11:43). In token of reserved seats in the kingdom of heaven, they take the foremost places at meetinghouses and banquets (Matthew 23:6;
Luke 14:7-8). Yet quickly they find fault with those not

conforming to their exterior of worship (Mark 2:18, 24; 7:2, 5; Luke 6:7).

While they themselves covet the things of the world, they hate those mingling with sinners in attempts to rescue them (Matthew 9:11; Luke 7:33-34; 16:14). Their fear of political repercussions outweighs their love of spiritual obligation (John 11:47-48). In the end, they disfellowship those who love and confess Christ (John 12:42). The converts to their form of religion, whom they go to great lengths to gain, they make twofold more children of hell than themselves (Matthew 23:15). Hypocrisy fills their lives so much that it appears incurable (Matthew 23:31-33).

To assure themselves that their religion is well founded, the elitist-Pharisaic faction makes frequent mention of a key prophet or forebear on whom they base their authority.[96] So far have they departed from the prophet's message, however, that if some came among them who taught as he did, they would seek to kill them as did their forefathers (Matthew 23:30-34; Luke 11:47-49). Were their acclaimed prophet to confront them, he would be the first to assert that neither God's love nor word abides in them (John 5:38, 42, 45). Thus, the most righteous among them — one like their acclaimed prophet — they call a deceiver and make a scapegoat (Matthew 27:63; John 11:50). At that point, the Lord removes the kingdom from them, giving it to a people who will bring forth its fruit (Matthew 21:43).

In summing up this somber biblical type, we see among the ancient elitist Pharisees many forms of priestcraft that Jesus and his apostles predicted would corrupt the church of the last days. Indeed, the things they prophesied that would befall us repeat the Pharisaic phenomenon as nearly as any type. Just as their love had waxed cold because of iniquity among them, so will the love of many in the church of the last days wax cold because of iniquity (Matthew 24:12). As they loved themselves and were covetous and treacherous, so also will many in the church in the last days (2 Timothy 3:1-4). As they were ever learning but never coming to a knowledge of the truth, so will many in the church of the last days (2 Timothy 3:5). As they admired men for personal advantage, so will many in the church of the last days (Jude 1:16). As they failed to believe that enemies would invade and destroy their land because of their iniquity, so will many of the church in the last days be willingly ignorant of their role in precipitating a fiery destruction of the wicked (2 Peter 3:3-10). By their idolatry and hypocrisy, they will pollute the church of God, bringing upon themselves God's judgment (Mormon 8:38).

As a consequence, just as messianic impostors from among the Jews preceded Jesus' first coming (Acts 5:36-37)[97] —with the notable exception of John the Baptist—so false Christs and prophets will precede his second coming (Matthew 24:5, 11, 23-24; Mark 13:6, 21-22). The true prophets they will nonetheless withstand, as the false prophets withstood Moses (2 Timothy 3:8-9) and as the Pharisees withstood Jesus.[98]

The righteous among them they will hate, mock, and betray (Matthew 24:10; Mark 13:12-13; Jude 1:18), just as the Jews hated, mocked, and then betrayed Jesus and his disciples to ecclesiastical and political authorities.[99] They will deliver many to councils to be judged and punished for their testimonies, smiting some and killing them unlawfully (Matthew 24:9, 49; Mark 13:9)—even as they delivered Jesus and his disciples to be persecuted and killed by ecclesiastical and political authorities.[100] In the day of judgment that will then be upon them, they will suffer the fate of all hypocrites. Cutting them off from his people, the Lord will cast them into outer darkness, where there is weeping and gnashing of teeth.[101]

12. Pollution of the Temple

A final kind of idolatry, one that caused the Lord's presence to depart from his people as invading armies advanced on them (Ezekiel 8:6; 9:1-11), concerns the pollution of the temple by idols. Several kinds of idolatry polluted the house of God anciently, including the symbol of envy,[102] a man-made idol situated at the inner entrance and exit (Ezekiel 8:3, 5). Men also viewed all manner of images portrayed against a wall (Ezekiel 8:10-12); elders of Israel made clouds of perfume or sweet odors (Ezekiel 8:11);[103] women at the temple bewailed the death of a popular cult figure (Ezekiel 8:14); and men worshiped the great luminary in the temple's precincts (Ezekiel 8:16).

Because the Lord's people polluted the house of God by setting up *their* abominations in it (Jeremiah 7:30; 23:11), the temple proved no place of protection for them in the time of judgment (Jeremiah 7:4-10). When Israel's enemies entered the land, they went in and destroyed the temple (Jeremiah 52:13), or polluted it yet further by setting up their abominations in it (1 Maccabees 1:54). Beginning at the temple, they slew all except a certain few whom the Lord protected (Ezekiel 9:6-7). The latter sighed and cried continually because of the abominations in their midst (Ezekiel 9:4).

Conclusion

Lest we assume that I have overstated the case of idolatrous types, or that somehow we are better than or different from former generations of the Lord's people, I have drawn ten points from President Spencer W. Kimball's bicentennial address to the Saints, entitled "The False Gods We Worship":[104] (1) an idolater is one who sets his or her heart or trust in something other than the God of Israel; (2) an idolater cannot be saved in the kingdom of heaven; (3) telling parallels exist between ancient forms of idolatry and the behavioral patterns of the Latter-day Saints; (4) we live today in conditions resembling the days of Noah before the Flood; (5) "we are, on the whole, an idolatrous people"; (6) idolatry forms a grave and singular contradiction in the lives of the Saints; (7) we must forthwith leave off our idolatry, or be damned; (8) we must serve the Lord at all costs and prepare for what is to come; (9) our modern life-style, tainted by idols, contrasts the rural ideal of a generation ago; (10) if we live righteously, the Lord will protect us from all our enemies.[105]

I trust that what I have attempted by way of saluting our beloved mentor, Hugh Nibley, will have only a positive effect in the lives of the Saints, will help us eliminate the imbalance that is idolatry and move us to center our souls in God. As it has been Brother Nibley's manner to state his case and disappear in the crowd, so I write these words in the same spirit. The imperative to purify our lives seems self-evident. Whether we can do so in time, not whether we must, is the question that hangs over us all. Although we live in a world that combines the evils of the past, the principle that the Lord gives no commandment unless he prepares a way to keep it (1 Nephi 3:7) surely is true of the first commandment — to love the Lord with our whole heart and soul, and with all our might.

Notes

1. We who are familiar with the Book of Mormon, for example, observe how biblical types repeat themselves consistently among that branch of the Lord's people.

2. See Judges 10:13-14; Isaiah 37:18-20; Jeremiah 11:10-15.

3. See Isaiah 44:9-20; 46:1-7; Jeremiah 2:28.

4. See Deuteronomy 7:1-11; Isaiah 50:1; Hosea 1:2-9.

5. See Deuteronomy 28:15-68; Isaiah 65:1-7, 11-15; Jeremiah 44:2-14.

6. See Deuteronomy 10:12-13; D&C 20:19; 42:29.

7. See Deuteronomy 4:1-9; Matthew 15:7-14; D&C 45:28-32.

8. See Deuteronomy 12:28-30; Jeremiah 10:1-16; Revelation 18:2-3.

9. See Deuteronomy 4:23-28; Isaiah 45:20; D&C 1:16.

10. See 2 Nephi 25:8; 3 Nephi 20:11-13; 23:1-3.

11. See Isaiah 1:11-14; cf. Jeremiah 7:1-15; Amos 8:3.

12. I give an overview of biblical types in Avraham Gileadi, *The*

Book of Isaiah: A New Translation with Interpretive Keys from the Book of Mormon (Salt Lake City: Deseret Book, 1988), 66-76.

13. This occurred in two instances of biblical history: first, when the northern tribes of Israel apostatized, leading to Assyria's conquering and desolating of the ancient world; second, when Judah apostatized and Babylon repeated the scenario. The prophets link both events to Israel's idolatry (cf. Hosea 11:1-7; Isaiah 10:3-11; Jeremiah 25:3-11). By likening wicked Israel to Sodom and Gomorrah (cf. Isaiah 1:10; Jeremiah 23:14; Ezekiel 16:49), the prophets allude both to Israel's fate and to a deficit of righteous people (cf. Genesis 18:23-32; 19:24-29).

14. See Exodus 20:5; 23:24.

15. In the biblical narrative one of the Lord's titles is "Bull" of Jacob (Heb. *'ăbîr ya⁽ăqōb̲*, Genesis 49:24).

16. See Exodus 32:6, 25; Leviticus 18:3-19:4; Numbers 25:1, 8; 1 Kings 14:23-24; 2 Kings 23:4-7; 1 Peter 4:3; 1 Nephi 13:8.

17. Cf. Deuteronomy 30:17; Isaiah 44:19; Ezekiel 20:7-8.

18. Cf. Deuteronomy 30:18; Ether 2:8-10; Moroni 8:29.

19. See Judges 8:27; 17-18; 1 Kings 11:4; 12:28.

20. See 1 Samuel 4-7; Jeremiah 10; Ezekiel 6-7.

21. Translations of Isaiah are taken from Gileadi, *The Book of Isaiah*.

22. Jerry Mander, *Four Arguments for the Elimination of Television* (New York: Quill, 1978), 200-15, 240-60, 299-322.

23. Marie Winn, *The Plug-in Drug* (New York: Viking, 1980), 10, 12-29, 69-70, 96-102; Mander, *Four Arguments*, 195-200.

24. Mander, *Four Arguments*, 126-32.

25. Rose K. Goldsen, *The Show and Tell Machine* (New York: Dial, 1977), 28-47, 248; Gregg A. Lewis, *Telegarbage* (Nashville, TN: Thomas Nelson Publishers, 1977), 104-8; Mander, *Four Arguments*, 267-74.

26. Goldsen, *Show and Tell Machine*, 250-52; Winn, *Plug-in Drug*, 42-47.

27. See types of the latter-day Antichrist in Isaiah 14:4-20; Ezekiel 28:1-9; Daniel 11:36.

28. See Deuteronomy 4:1-4; Judges 2:11-13; 8:33.

29. See "Poems about Baal and Anath," tr. H. L. Ginsberg, in J. B. Pritchard, ed., *Ancient Near Eastern Texts Relating to the Old Testament* (Princeton, NJ: Princeton University Press, 1969), 129-42.

30. Baal means "lord."

31. Lewis, *Telegarbage*, 43-69, 86-94.

32. Cf. James 1:27; Alma 13:12; D&C 59:9.

33. The "Books of Adam and Eve," in *The Lost Books of the Bible and the Forgotten Books of Eden* (New York: New American Library, 1974).

34. See the New Flood imagery Isaiah uses to depict a great latter-day cataclysm, Gileadi, *The Book of Isaiah*, 23-24, 69-70, 77, 86-87.

35. Ancient versions of the books of *Adam and Eve* exist in Arabic, Ethiopic, Aramaic, Hebrew, and Greek, showing its wide dissemination in early literatures.

36. See Matthew 24:37-39; Luke 17:26-27; 2 Peter 3:3-14.

37. See Moses 8:20-24; 2 Peter 2:5; *Jasher* 5:22-24.

38. See Zechariah 13:9; Malachi 3:2; 4:1; 1 Peter 1:7; 4:12-13.

39. See Genesis 6:11-13; Moses 5:51; 7:33; 8:15, 22.

40. See 2 Timothy 3:1-6; 3 Nephi 16:10; Ether 8:23-25.

41. See also Moses 7:37; 8:13.

42. See Jacob Aranza, *Backward Masking Unmasked* (Shreveport, LA: Huntington House, 1983); Dick Donovan, "Rock Music Praises Satan," *Weekly World News*, 2 February 1982, 15; "New Lyrics for the Devil's Music," *Time*, 11 March 1985, 60; Lex de Azevedo, "A Closer Look at Popular Music," *Ensign* 15 (March 1985): 39.

43. Goldsen, *Show and Tell Machine*, 80-93.

44. See Isaiah 43:2; Malachi 4:1-3; 1 Nephi 22:17.

45. See Abram Leon Sachar, *A History of the Jews* (New York: Knopf, 1973), 100; F. F. Bruce, *New Testament History* (Garden City, NY: Anchor, 1972), 55, 217-19.

46. Hugh Nibley, *When the Lights Went Out* (Salt Lake City: Deseret Book, 1976), 20-21.

47. William F. Albright, *From Stone Age to Christianity* (New York: Doubleday, 1957), 348-57; Geza Vermes, *The Dead Sea Scrolls in English* (New York: Penguin, 1975), 34, 62-64.

48. Nibley, *When the Lights Went Out*, 1-32.

49. Hugh Nibley, "The Roman Games as a Survival of an Archaic Year-Cult," Ph.D. diss., University of California at Berkeley, 1957.

50. Joseph Vogt, *The Decline of Rome* (London: Weidenfeld and Nicolson, 1967), 20; T. G. Tucker, *Life in the Roman World of Nero and St. Paul* (New York: Macmillan, 1922), 280; Stewart Perowne, *The End of the Roman World* (London: Hodder and Stoughton, 1966), 12.

51. Vogt, *Decline of Rome*, 20; Tucker, *Life in the Roman World*, 263, 273.

52. Tucker, *Life in the Roman World*, 223, 263-64, 273-74, 285; Vogt, *Decline of Rome*, 19-20.

53. Tucker, *Life in the Roman World*, 274-77, 286; Vogt, *Decline of Rome*, 19-20.

54. Tucker, *Life in the Roman World*, 274, 277-79, 284-85, 287; Vogt, *Decline of Rome*, 20; Perowne, *End of the Roman World*, plate 8.

55. Perowne, *End of the Roman World*, 12; Vogt, *Decline of Rome*, 20; Tucker, *Life in the Roman World*, 263.

56. Tucker, *Life in the Roman World*, 280; Louis Ginzberg, *Legends of the Jews*, 6 vols. (Philadelphia: Jewish Publication Society, 1969), 1:30; 4:32.

57. See Edith Hamilton, *Mythology* (New York: New American Library, 1969); Samuel N. Kramer, ed., *Mythologies of the Ancient World* (New York: Doubleday, 1961).

58. See the multiple meanings of the Hebrew nouns *'ēl, 'ēlāh,* and *ḥāsôn,* and Isaiah's use of the Hebrew verbs *bāḥar* and *ḥāmad* (Isaiah 1:29-31).

59. See Daniel 7:19-25; 11:36; 1 John 2:18; Revelation 13:1-8.

60. See Isaiah 10:5-15; 14:4-20; 37:21-29; Ezekiel 28:2-19; Habakkuk 2:2-10; Daniel 8:19-25.

61. Hebrew *yēser/šĕrîrût lēḇ* also means "inventions/concoctions of the mind" and "stubbornness of the heart."

62. See also Mosiah 3:19: "The natural man is an enemy to God."

63. See Genesis 6:5; 11:6; Jeremiah 11:7-10.

64. See Isaiah 34:2; Zechariah 12:9; 1 Nephi 22:16-19; 3 Nephi 20:20.

65. See n. 61.

66. The same terminology in Hebrew defines "parks," "gardens," and "paradise."

67. See Matthew 6:24; Luke 16:13; 3 Nephi 13:24.

68. See Proverbs 18:11; Jeremiah 5:28; Alma 4:6, 8.

69. See 2 Corinthians 8:12-15; Alma 1:26-27; D&C 70:14; 78:6.

70. See also Micah 6:12; 2 Nephi 9:30; Jacob 2:13.

71. This also forms the moral of the story of Lazarus and the rich man (cf. Luke 16:19-25).

72. See also Revelation 18:1-19; Alma 5:53-56; Helaman 13:38.

73. See 2 Nephi 27:1-2; 30:1-2; 3 Nephi 16:10; 20:15-16.

74. See also the church in the wilderness (Isaiah 48:21; Ezekiel 20:35-38; Hosea 2:14).

75. See also Isaiah 25:6; Luke 14:16-24; Revelation 19:9, 17-18.

76. See Revelation 17:1-19:8; D&C 1:1-16.

77. See also the Prophet Joseph Smith's plot for cities of Zion based on a rural economy, *History of the Church*, 6 vols. (Salt Lake City: Deseret Book, 1973), 1:357-59.

78. See Isaiah 40:19-20; 41:7; 44:10, 12-13; 45:16; Jeremiah 51:17.

79. See D&C 133:1-15. Cf. Isaiah 57:1: "The righteous disappear and no man gives it a thought; the godly are gathered out, but no one perceives that from impending calamity the righteous are withdrawn."

80. See John 8:39; D&C 132:32.

81. See Isaiah 1:27; 4:5-6; 35:10; 59:20.

82. See Isaiah 2:5-8; 17:7-8; 46:3-8.

83. See Jared and his company (Ether 1:40-43), Abraham and his company (Genesis 12:1-7), and Lehi and his company (1 Nephi 2:1-4, 20).

84. See Isaiah 48:17-19; Jeremiah 51:6; D&C 64:24.

85. See Isaiah 23; Ezekiel 26-28.

86. Gileadi, The Book of Isaiah, 72-74.

87. See Isaiah 19:4; Jeremiah 43:10-12; 46:1-26; Ezekiel 29:19-32:32.

88. See Isaiah 30:3-5; 31:2-3; Ezekiel 17:16-21; 30:1-8.

89. See Exodus 22:23-24; 1 Kings 11:14, 23; Isaiah 10:5-17; 54:16-17.

90. See Isaiah 8:9-15; 55:3; Jeremiah 21:8-9; 27:12-17; Ezekiel 18:1-32; 33:1-20; Amos 5:1-15.

91. See Isaiah 51:17-23; Jeremiah 51:49; Ezekiel 9:5-7; 37:1-14; Daniel 11:33-35; Revelation 6:9; 13:7-10.

92. See Isaiah 33:14-16; 65:8-16; Jeremiah 51:45; Ezekiel 9:4, 6; Daniel 7:26-27; Revelation 9:4; 12:1-16.

93. Isaiah 28-31 forms a structural unit in which Isaiah typifies human counsel and schemes as a covenant with death.

94. See Daniel 8:24; 12:7; 2 Nephi 30:1; D&C 38:13.

95. See Daniel 7:27; 1 Nephi 14:14; D&C 1:36.

96. See Matthew 3:9; 19:7; Luke 20:28; John 9:28-29.

97. See also Haim Hillel Ben-Sasson, "Messianic Movements," in Encyclopaedia Judaica, 16 vols. (Jerusalem, Israel: Keter Publishing House, 1972), 11:1420.

98. See Matthew 26:67-68; Luke 20:1-2.

99. See Matthew 26:47-27:31; Acts 6:11-15; 18:12-17.

100. See Luke 22:47-23:24; Acts 7:57-59; 12:1-2.

101. See Matthew 8:12; 13:41-42; 24:51; 25:30.

102. Hebrew sēmel haqqin'āh hammaqneh; also "object of envy [which incites envy]."

103. Hebrew ʿāṭar ʿănan haqqšṭōreṯ; literally, "an odorous cloud of perfume/incense."

104. Spencer W. Kimball, "The False Gods We Worship," *Ensign* 6 (June 1976): 3-6.

105. See, respectively, 4 (par. 7); 5 (par. 12); 4 (par. 8); 4 (par. 1); 6 (par. 2); 4-5 (pars. 9, 12); 6 (pars. 8-9); 6 (pars. 13-15); 3 (pars. 2-3); 6 (par. 6).

13

Repentance Also Means Rethinking

Gary P. Gillum
Brigham Young University, Provo, Utah

Although Latter-day Saints have a knowledge of the process of repentance, they lack a complete understanding of how the scriptures use the term repentance: repentance consists not only of remorse, confession, restitution, and forgiveness, but a literal changing of one's entire perspective on life, so that eventually a Latter-day Saint may "repent of having to repent." In a world where temporal, statistical, commercial, political, and pseudoscientific experiences have taken the place of our God-given eternal, moral, and revelatory rights, it is is easy for any of us to be led astray—if we are not prepared. And I submit that repentance is the most important survival tool the Lord has placed at our disposal. "Say nothing but repentance unto this generation; keep my commandments and assist to bring forth my work, according to my commandments" (D&C 6:9). God's first rule is that all men must repent. All men. Repentance is not only for those who have committed sin—it is for everyone, so that they may come to know the mind of God and his eternal perspective. This process also replaces the natural man with the new man in Christ.

Wanting to find true repentance so that I could really feel that I was forgiven of my sins led me to The Church of Jesus Christ of Latter-day Saints and to the waters of

---

This was given as a Sperry Symposium lecture on 26 January 1985.

baptism twenty years ago. I came from a church whose major theological tenets were faith alone, grace alone, and scriptures alone. As a student of the ministry I don't remember learning anything about repentance except for a brief paragraph in my theology textbook by Alan Richardson, which read, "Repentance is thus a 'sine qua non' of the Christian life, not only in its beginning but at every stage; it involves a constant awareness of the fact that all our faith and all our virtue are God's gift and not our achievement."[1] Most of this quote is mere theological opinion or the commandments of men which ignore free agency and man's potential, relegating us to a life of simple subservience to God. However, in exploring the "rethinking" aspect of repentance, I would like to emphasize two phrases of Richardson's: "constant awareness" and "at every stage."

During the first twenty-four years of my life, repentance was not a remorse for sin followed by proper confession and restitution. It was merely a recognition of original sin and of Martin Luther's principle of *pecca fortiter* — "sin boldly that grace may more fully abound!" Who in his right mind would be too concerned about his sins if he felt that the greater the sin the more Christ's atonement would settle the deficit of purity? We were so thoroughly taught of our sinful nature that we were encouraged not to dwell on it, but simply to ask forgiveness from the Lord and confess our sins with the rest of the congregation on communion Sunday once monthly. But I felt no peace. I wanted to be cleansed thoroughly from my sin but didn't know where to turn. Accordingly, like Enos and Joseph Smith, I began praying more from the heart instead of from a prayerbook—with greater sincerity and a desire to find some answers. The Lord taught me patience first, however, rescuing me only just before I was going to pack my bags and leave for San Francisco's Haight-Ashbury to live the "good life" of sex, drugs, and ultimate freedom that 1968 clamored for. That Friday, the thirteenth of December, showed me that the God whom I thought had forsaken me was really alive and supporting me. My spiritual and emotional frustrations from visiting a different church or two every Sunday trying to find the truth were finally allayed, for the missionaries taught me three things which I had never really learned before: the value of a testimony, the importance of living by the Spirit, and the true nature of repentance.

The Old Testament on Repentance

No theologian, minister, or fellow ministerial student first taught me a glimpse of true repentance: just a prophet of the Lord, Elijah. This happened in a very vicarious manner, through the music of Felix Mendelssohn's great oratorio "Elijah." While in my freshman and sophomore years at St. John's College in Winfield, Kansas, the choirs in this school joined with the choirs at the Methodist college in town, Southwestern College, to sing this soul-searching piece of music. I was intrigued by Elijah's life and the power of God which he had access to. But I was also lifted up by his humility before the Lord and his human frailty, which approached that of Jonah. Consider what he was able to accomplish with the power of the Lord: healing the widow's son, withholding rain from the people of Israel, and finally subduing and slaying the priests of Baal. But when Jezebel and Ahab went after him, Elijah felt like all he had done was in vain and wanted the Lord to remove him from that wicked world: "It is enough; now, O Lord, take away my life; for I am not better than my fathers" (1 Kings 19:4). Here he was implying to the Lord that what had happened to this point had been Elijah's doing—that the conversion of Israel was entirely up to him, and that he was not succeeding. But the Lord strengthened Elijah even more, so that later in the oratorio, before he is translated by means of a chariot of fire, he hints of the repentance that had taken place in his life: "I go on my way in the strength of the Lord." In the words of Paul: "I can do all things through Christ which strengtheneth me" (Philippians 4:13). Elijah had not sinned by being immoral or any such thing. His thinking was merely wrong. He then experienced the change of perspective to the mind of God that all of us need—the kind that guides all of our actions through the help of the gift of the Holy Ghost. We find throughout the Old Testament that it was not only Elijah who needed a boost in self-confidence: Moses, Jeremiah, and Enoch are also good examples of prophets who needed to have their minds and hearts infused with a portion of the mind of God.

Two words are used for repentance in the Old Testament. *The Evangelical Dictionary of Theology*[2] states that the Hebrew word *niham* is used thirty-five times. It is usually used to signify a contemplated change in God's dealings with men for good or ill according to his just judgment. ("It repenteth me that I have made them," Genesis 6:7; 1 Samuel 15:11, 35; Jonah 3:9-10). Only in five places does *niham* refer to human repentance or relenting. *Teshuvah* is the other word referring to repentance: a true turning toward God. It also means "recover," "refresh," "restore," "convert," "return," "reverse," or "turn again." It indicates a return to God and the right path (cf. Hosea 14:2; 2 Kings 17:13; Jeremiah 13:14; and Joel 2:12-13). The Rabbis have a saying for *teshuvah*: "Great is 'teshuvah,' for it brings healing to the world. Great is 'teshuvah,' for it reaches to the throne of God. Great is 'teshuvah,' it brings redemption near. Great is 'teshuvah,' for it lengthens a man's life."[3] This rabbinic saying probably has its roots in Deuteronomy 30:9-10, which gives us the essence of the doctrine of repentance in the Old Testament: "And the Lord thy God will make thee plenteous in every work of thine hand, in the fruit of thy body, and in the fruit of thy cattle, and in the fruit of thy land, for good: for the Lord will again rejoice over thee for good, as he rejoiced over thy fathers: If thou shalt hearken unto the voice of the Lord thy God, to keep his commandments and his statutes which are written in this book of the law, and if thou turn unto the Lord thy God with all thine heart, and with all thy soul." This seems to indicate that God is unfailingly responsive to repentance, thereby indicating the depth of it; for as we become ever closer to the mind of God we not only automatically bless ourselves but are blessed by God who responds to our "change of mind." Otherwise, "my thoughts are not your thoughts, neither are your ways my ways, saith the Lord" (Isaiah 55:8-9). How can we know the ways of the Lord unless we do those things that help us to that end? David the Psalmist also recognizes that repentance is a change of thinking: "Create in me a clean heart, O God; and renew a right spirit within me" (Psalm 51:10-11). Two final examples from the Old Testament: "Keep thy heart with all diligence; for out of it are the issues of life" (Proverb 4:23), and "As a man thinketh in his heart, so is he" (Proverb 23:7).

The New Testament on Repentance

The most common Greek words used in the New Testament for "repentance" are *metanoeo* (the verb), *metanoia* (the noun), and *metamelomai* (the present participle). These Greek words usually mean not merely feeling sorry, or changing one's mind, but a complete alteration of the basic motivation and direction of one's life. This explains why John the Baptist demanded baptism as an expression of this repentance, not just for obvious "sinners," but for the "righteous" Jews as well. *Metanoia* was often used in the Septuagint to translate the Hebrew *niham*. So defined, repentance might seem purely intellectual, but this is not the case, for writers of the Bible seemed to be aware of the unity of human personality. To change one's mind was to change one's attitude, and thus to change the actions and even the whole way of life.[4] *Metanoeo* occurs thirty-four times and is mostly used in a favorable sense to include faith. *Metanoia* is used twenty-three times in the sense of the whole process of change. It can mean an inward change of mind, affections, and convictions as well as a commitment rooted in the fear of God and sorrow for offenses committed against him. When accompanied by faith in Jesus Christ, this repentance results in an outward turning from sin to God and his service in all of life. It is a gift from God, and the repentant person never regrets having repented.[5] The Roman Catholic Douai version of the Bible interprets *metanoia* as penance, the performance of ecclesiastically prescribed acts to make satisfaction for postbaptismal sin. According to *The New International Dictionary of the Christian Church*, this use of the word has no place in New Testament Christianity.[6] *Metamelomai* is used very seldom and means "regretting" or "having remorse."

If the use of repentance is both God's gift and man's responsibility, then the call for repentance on the part of man "is a call for him to return to his creaturely and covenant dependence on God."[7] It should be clear to all of us that it is God's way that is important, not ours. Paul said it best in Romans 8:6: "Set your minds on things which are above, where God and Christ dwell, for to be carnally minded is death, but to be spiritually minded is life eternal." God encouraged the Saints, after they had forgotten or erased undesirable thoughts and attitudes and things which were behind, to plant good thoughts in their place, as in Philippians 3:13-14 (or Article of Faith 13): "But this one thing I do, forgetting those things which are behind, and reaching forth unto those things which are before, I press toward the mark for the prize of the high calling of God in Christ." Paul must have experienced repentance in a big way, for prior to his conversion on the road to Damascus he was sure that he was doing the will of the Lord. However, after the Lord had set him straight, he began to change his mind—and heart—about a lot of things, becoming himself renewed in the spirit of his mind, as he later exhorted the Saints in Ephesians 4:17-24. Or as in Romans 12:2: "And be not conformed to this world: but be ye transformed by the renewing of your mind, that ye may prove what is that good, and acceptable, and perfect, will of God." The exhortation of Jesus Christ to "Be ye therefore perfect" (Matthew 5:48) could only be preceded by a change of mind and understanding opened to the things of the Spirit. Otherwise perfection would be impossible both in this world and the next. As it is, "If any man be in Christ, he is a new creature; old things are passed away; behold all things are become new" (2 Corinthians 5:17).

As I read some of these passages of scripture before my own conversion, I had to ask myself a few questions: Is it true that all things are new for me, too? Do I feel renewed in the mind and spirit? If not, is it perhaps because I feel repentance is only for committed sin, not an act which is calculated to bring me ever closer to the Father? Hence, my own change from human thinking to divine understanding was truly a necessary consequence in "putting on the new man." The act of repentance had always been for me a mere remorse for sin and often a half-hearted promise "never to do it again," even though I suspected that the next chance I got I would sin again—such was the force of "negative" theology in my life. It is important to consider, then, that true conversion is incomplete unless it is preceded not only by a remorse for former sins and future rejection of them, but a total transformation of one's entire thought process—one implying an erasure of thoughts and images foreign to the pure gospel revealed to us by the Holy Ghost.

The Book of Mormon and Doctrine and Covenants on Repentance

The Book of Mormon tells us three very important things about repentance: (1) All people must repent, (2) there must be enough time for all people to repent, and (3) faith must be present in the process. One verse covers the first two well: "And the days of the children of men were prolonged, according to the will of God, that they might repent while in the flesh . . . for . . . all men must repent" (2 Nephi 2:21), and another covers the third: "And behold, ye do know of yourselves, for ye have witnessed it, that as many of them as are brought to the knowledge of the truth, and to know of the wicked and abominable traditions of their fathers, and are led to believe the holy scriptures, yea, the prophecies of the holy prophets, which are written, which leadeth them to faith on the Lord, and unto repentance, which faith and repentance bringeth a change of heart unto them" (Helaman 15:7).

Understanding the meanings of repentance as used in the Book of Mormon or the Doctrine and Covenants is more difficult than in the Bible simply because the English language is not as precise as Hebrew or Greek. We must understand the meanings of these by context, inspiration, and revelation—and only secondarily by language.[8] Mosiah 27:26 elucidates this further: "And thus they become new creatures; and unless they do this, they can in nowise inherit the kingdom of God." If Alma the Younger's teaching is to square with Pauline doctrine in the New Testament, then we must assume that the rethinking type of repentance is also necessary to reach this new state. Finally, there is an excellent example in the Book of Mormon about this change of mind in action after true repentance. When the brother of Jared presented the problem of light in the vessels in which he and his company were to cross the ocean, the Lord did not answer the problem, but threw the question back at him: "What will ye that I should do that ye may have light in your vessels?" (Ether 2:23). The brother of Jared was prepared to answer because he had studied it out in his mind already. If the Lord were to tell us what to do all the time, we would not grow; we would not learn to think as he does (D&C 9:7-8).

Following my conversion, I found that my renewed mind and understanding now freed me from the bondage of not only wrong thinking but wrong actions which had proceeded from human thinking. In my freedom I also discovered that I could now act according to the Spirit instead of being acted upon by the natural desires of the flesh.

The Doctrine and Covenants points out some additional teachings about repentance. Sections 137 and 138 are two very important sections which are too often ignored by Latter-day Saints. To me, however, these are two of the most important passages of scripture, both because they can lead to true repentance by helping us to understand better some of the more ineffable facts about our eternal existence and because they answer the challenge of the Lord: "Let the solemnities of eternity rest upon your minds" (D&C 43:34). Joseph Smith has further added this well-known admonition, "The things of God are of deep import, and time and experience and careful, ponderous and solemn thoughts can only find them out. Thy mind, O man, if thou wilt lead a soul unto salvation, must stretch as high as the utmost heavens, and search into and contemplate the darkest abyss, and the broad expanse of eternity. Thou must commune with God."[9]

Those two revelations, added in 1976 to the Doctrine and Covenants, both talk about death and the life hereafter. Perhaps they are important to me because, like many people throughout the world (Latter-day Saint or not), I had a life-after-death experience in 1963 while trying to recover from a critical automobile accident. The experience was like that of Joseph Smith's learning more by looking into the heavens then by reading many books, but the experience has had advantages and disadvantages: on the one hand a small portion of my faith has been replaced by absolute knowledge of life after death. On the other hand, such a glimpse into the eternities results in an extra measure of discernment which gives me a sorrowful impatience concerning the world. (It's like looking into the hearts and minds of anyone you meet, and although it can be very useful in helping teach a wayward student here at Brigham Young University, it can be frustrating to be out in the world where sin and ignorance of spiritual matters are the measure of the children of man.) Moreover, this type of experience gave me an immediate megadose of repentance, or rethinking—what to many people is a figment of foolish imagination rather than a serious matter of eternal consequences. (A friend once remarked to me that with such knowledge I could almost start my own church. Surprised at his comment, I answered that I would not do such a thing *because* of the experience I had had. That very conversation gives us a further hint into how people behave differently in various stages of repentance.)

Several passages of scripture in the Doctrine and Covenants give us further practical information about repentance as well, and I believe they reveal as much about rethinking as they do about remorse, confession, and restitution. One sobering thought is that "surely every man must repent or suffer, for I, God, am endless" (D&C 19:4). However, the Lord graciously gives us our free agency, for the farther along we are in our repentance, the less we have to suffer. In some cases this is simply a change of our attitude, for our sufferings will work to our eternal betterment if we allow them to be growth experiences. Even so, the more our mind thinks like God's, the less we will suffer. Furthermore, the Lord tells us that our "sorrow shall be great" unless we "speedily repent, yea very speedily" (D&C 136:35). That reminds us how much more God knows about each of us and the direction in which we are headed. Do not just "do it," he is saying, "do it *now*." "And how great is his joy in the soul that repenteth" (D&C 18:13). And what godly parent would not want his children to have the mind and wisdom and knowledge of life he or she has had?

Teachings from General Authorities on Repentance

Spencer W. Kimball is one of the Church's leading experts on the teachings of repentance, especially the practical applications of it. Particularly well-known are his five steps for repentance: (1) sorrow for sin, (2) abandonment of sin, (3) confession of sin, (4) restitution for sin, and (5) doing the will of the Father.[10] Rather than spend a lot of time summarizing his own teachings on repentance, I am going to list them briefly so that you will be able to see how they support repentance as rethinking.

1. Repentance must be as universal as sin.[11]

2. The delay in repentance encourages the continuation of sin.[12]

3. If we are humble and desirous of living the gospel, we will come to think of repentance as applying to everything we do in life, whether it be spiritual or temporal in nature. Repentance is for every soul who has not yet reached perfection.[13]

4. Conscience is a celestial spark which God has put into all people for the purpose of saving their souls. It awakens the soul to consciousness of sin, spurs a person to make up his mind to adjust, to convict himself of the transgression without soft-pedaling or minimizing the error, to be willing to face facts, meet the issue, and pay necessary penalties—and until the person is in this frame of mind [!] he has not begun to repent.[14]

5. Repentance is timeless. The evidence of repentance

is transformation. We certainly must keep our values straight and our evaluations intact.[15]

6. True repentance incorporates within it a washing, a purging, a changing of attitudes, a reappraising, a strengthening toward self-mastery. It is not a simple matter for one to transform his life overnight, nor to change attitudes in a moment, nor to rid himself in a hurry of unworthy companions.[16]

7. In abandoning sin one cannot merely wish for better conditions. He must make them. He needs to come to hate the spotted garments and loathe the sin. He must be certain not only that he has abandoned the sin but that he has changed the situations surrounding the sin. He should avoid the places and conditions and circumstances where the sin occurred, for these could most readily breed it again. He must abandon the people with whom the sin was committed. He may not hate the persons involved, but he must avoid them and everything associated with the sin. He must dispose of all letters, trinkets, and things which will remind him of the "old days" and "old times." He must forget addresses, telephone numbers, people, places, and situations from the sinful past, and build a new life. He must eliminate anything which would stir the old memories.[17]

The last passage would seem to indicate practical acts which would enable not only the sinner but the would-be Saint to acquire a godly perspective which enables one to see the eternal plan more clearly. Moreover, all of the passages seem to support one important result of repentance: the ability to forgive all people.

Church leaders who are contemporary with President Kimball can lend further insight to our study. David O. McKay once said that to repent is "to change one's mind [and one's heart] in regard to past or intended actions or conduct on account of regret or dissatisfaction."[18] By now, however, we can see that it is infinitely better and easier to repent *before* reaching the point of regret or dissatisfaction. In fact, Bruce R. McConkie elucidates this further: "Repentance is easy or difficult of attainment by various people depending upon their own attitude and conduct, and upon the seriousness of the sins they have committed."[19]

Nor can we leave out Church leaders who preceded our own day. According to the Prophet Joseph Smith, "It is the will of God that man should repent and serve Him in health, and in the strength and power of his mind, in order to secure his blessing, and not wait until he is called to die."[20]

Repentance is a thing that cannot be trifled with every day. Daily transgression and daily repentance is not that which is pleasing in the sight of God.[21] (The Prophet is probably speaking of penance here.)

Repent! Repent! Obey the Gospel. Turn to God.[22]

Parley P. Pratt, "Cultivate the mind, renew the spirit, invigorate the body, cheer the heart, ennoble the soul of man."[23] All of these things make up true repentance. Brigham Young, "Train your minds."[24] What a simple definition for repentance! And finally, President Young's reverse definition of repentance, "Sin consists in doing wrong when we know and can do better."[25]

Hugh Nibley on Repentance

If Spencer W. Kimball is the Church's most prolific official spokesman on the meaning of repentance, Hugh Nibley is certainly the most prolific apologist and scholar on repentance. Unfortunately, not enough members of the Church take him seriously when he talks about doctrinal subjects. As I have studied his writings during the past few years, I found that most of his recent addresses have more or less been cries of repentance, or as he calls it, "the eschatological viewpoint." That viewpoint is best exemplified by his parable in the November 1955 issue of the

Improvement Era.[26] It is much too long to share here, but since it is one of his most inspiring writings, I would highly recommend it to you for thorough study. Briefly, it tells of a successful businessman who has been told by his doctor that because he suffers from a serious disease, he has but a short time to live. Facing imminent death, the priorities in his life change considerably, so that his perspective has become "eschatological," or having to do with the last things and last days. His colleagues believe he has gone crazy, because the things of the world no longer mean that much to him anymore — it's the intangible, everlasting things about life that now attract our businessman. But lo and behold, he finds out a few days later with a second series of tests that he may yet live for many years. With this new piece of news you would think that this good man would go back to his old habits, but no, he retains his "eschatological" or "repentant" viewpoint, continuing in this positive and eternal mode for the rest of his long life. And that, Nibley insists, is the true eschatological attitude which all Latter-day Saints would do well to emulate: act as if you knew you were to die in the very near future.

Elsewhere, in an article entitled "The Historicity of the Bible," Brother Nibley defines this viewpoint:

> The eschatological viewpoint is that which sees and judges everything in terms of a great eternal plan. Whether we like it or not, we belong to the eternities: we cannot escape the universe. All our thoughts and deeds must be viewed against an infinite background and against no other. *Eschatos* means ultimate and refers to that which lies beyond all local and limited goals and interests. Limited objectives are very well in their way, but only as contributing to something eternal. Extreme as this doctrine may seem, the only alternative, as the philosophers of old repeatedly observed, is a trip to nowhere, a few seconds of pleasure in an hour of pain, and after that only "the depth of emptiness."[27]

When asked what do we think about in this life, Nibley responded, "That very question."

How so, I wondered? I looked in my Nibley subject index under repentance to find out what else he had written, and found the following juicy tidbits:

1. "Sin is waste. It is doing one thing when you should be doing other and better things for which you have the capacity. Hence, there are no innocent idle thoughts. That is why even the righteous must repent, constantly and progressively, since all fall short of their capacity and calling."[28]

2. "The fatal symptom of our day is not that men do wrong—they always have—and commit crimes, and even recognize their wrongdoing as foolish and unfortunate, but that they have *no intention of repenting*, while God has told us that the first rule that he has given the human race is that all men everywhere must repent."[29]

3. "The gospel of repentance is a constant reminder that the most righteous are still being tested and may yet fall, and that the most wicked are not yet beyond redemption and may still be saved. And that is what God wants: 'Have I any pleasure at all that the wicked should die?' There are poles for all to see, but in this life no one has reached and few have ever approached either pole, and no one has any idea at what point between his neighbors stand. Only God knows that."[30]

4. "Does not one person need repentance more than another? . . . You can always find somebody who is worse than you are to make you feel virtuous. It's a cheap shot: those awful terrorists, perverts, communists—they are the ones who need to repent! Yes, indeed they do, and for them repentance will be a full-time job, exactly as it is for all the rest of us."[31]

5. "You are either repenting or not repenting and that is, according to the scriptures, the whole difference between being righteous or being wicked."[32]

Famous Protestant theologians like Malcolm Mugger-
idge have also spoken out in ways similar to Hugh Nibley,
but William Temple comes the closest: "The world, as we
live in it, is like a shop window into which some mischievous person has got overnight, and shifted all the price-
labels so that the cheap things have the high price-labels
on them, and the really precious things are priced low.
We let ourselves be taken in. Repentance means getting
those price-labels back in the right place."[33]

Further Religious Notions of Repentance

Notwithstanding Judaism is considered a non-Christian religion, it is interesting to note that Mormonism
comes closer to Judaism than either Protestantism or Catholicism in the understanding of some theological subjects. Repentance is one of them. In fact, it is regarded so
fundamental by Judaism that it is enumerated in the Talmud as one of the seven things created by God before he
created the world.[34] According to rabbinic teachings, man
was created with an evil inclination (tendency to sin) to
which repentance is the antidote—as long as it means a
sincere changing of ways and returning to God.[35] To the
Jew, repentance means "to think differently after; to
change one's mind, opinion, moral thought, reflection,
apprehensions, character, conduct; the tendency of personal life as a whole."[36]

Rabbi Joseph Dov Baer Halevi Soloveitchik is an orthodox rabbi who studied the typology of man and of
human society. His teachings on repentance are probably
the most prolific of any religious writer I have run across.
He felt that there were four main types of men: repentant,
halakhic (dutiful or obedient), religious, and rational.[37] To
the Rav, "repentance implies that there are powers in man
which allow him to leap from that sense of sin, which
profoundly oppresses him and casts him far away, to a

different feeling of *hazarty le-fanekha* (I am again in Your presence)."[38]

Repentance means nothing other than (1) retrospective contemplation of the past and the distinction between the living and the dead in it; and (2) the vision of the future and its utilization according to the free determination of man. Man's very existence is contingent upon these two realms of activity: (1) in the memory of those situations and experiences undergone by man in the past and which, in many senses, have not died or been erased, but rather continue to exist in the inner recesses of his heart, and (2) in his expectations of the future, in his plans and hopes for the morrow, and for the day following. In these two realms man responds to the question, "Who am I?" Memory and expectation come together and focus on the character of man and give significance to the whole of his life, above and beyond the flow of meaningless time, whose flux is devoid of significance and purpose.[39]

The Rav defined "repentant man" as follows:

1. He expresses his humanity as a creature created in the divine image.

2. He possesses independent creative powers coupled with a compulsion to draw near to the Creator. This creative power enables him to forgo uprooting the past. Rather, it enables him to take up the past and exalt it, and to shape it so that it can be molded with the future to create the present, himself.

3. He has four characteristic traits: profundity of suffering, a depth of experience, the ability to make decisions in the light of free choice, and the capacity to create.[40] Finally, "repentance not only cleanses the sinner of the filth of iniquity, but it contains a kind of fresh act of covenant-making between the individual and the Almighty. . . . Repentance is not merely the purification of the personality, but a special sanctification of the individ-

ual, making him ready once more to conclude a covenant."[41]

Another Jew represents our own day — Dave Brubeck,
an American composer not only of jazz music but of the
powerful oratorio "The Light in the Wilderness." I had the
opportunity to sing this work as part of the Indianapolis
Symphony Choir in 1969 — with Dave Brubeck at the piano.
During the dress rehearsal, Mr. Brubeck gave each of us
performers a mimeographed sheet which included some
of his feelings concerning the writing of his music and the
two men he described in the wilderness: John the Baptist
and Jesus. His comments were the germ for my consideration of repentance as rethinking, coming as it did while
I was being taught by the missionaries:

> When it was clear to Jesus who he was and what he
> must do, he emerged from the desert wilderness with
> the passionate cry to RETHINK! . . . RETHINKING pre-
> cedes effective learning and obedience and sacri-
> fice. . . . Jesus in the wilderness is only touched upon
> by the synoptic gospels. Whatever went on in his mind
> during his solitary fast, it must have been a soul search-
> ing beyond our imagination; and yet he must have asked
> basically the same question we all ask — Who am I?[42]

Other non-Christian religions also have a contribution
to make to our understanding of the principles of repentance, but only very briefly. In the Qur'an, Sura 47:24, the
question is asked: "What, do they not meditate in the
Qur'an? Or is it that there are locks upon their hearts?" Is
that an unrepentant attitude? In Arabic *metanoia* is usually
rendered by *tawba*, which means "repentance," especially
in the sense of turning away from the world and a change
in perspective and values.[43] According to Sri Ramakrishna,
the Bengali Hindu teacher, "A man cannot see God unless
he gives his whole mind to Him."[44] Hujwiri, a Sufi an-
thologist of Afghanistan (ca. 1070), allows that there are
two types of repentance: of fear and of shame. The former

is caused by the revelation of God's majesty, while the repentance of shame is caused by a vision of God's beauty.[45] And of course the best kind of repentance is that which comes not from fear or shame but because of faith, testimony, and a desire to be obedient to the commandments of God.

Secular Notions: Literature, Music, Art, Philosophy, and Psychology

While growing up, some of the earliest influences we have upon our minds and our style of thinking come from the books that are read to us by our teachers and parents, and later from the reading we do ourselves. As a librarian, I am quite aware of how much reading affects behavior. Those who would assert, for instance, that pornographic literature does not affect the reader's behavior are at the same time negating the influence, positive or negative, of *any* kind of reading material. Speaking for myself, at least, I was so sure that the books I had read before my conversion had been instrumental in my conversion that I compiled an annotated bibliography of those preconversion books, and I came up with some startling conclusions. (You may wonder how I could remember all of the things I read. Easy. One of the most important things I have done in my life is to keep a journal since I was a sophomore in high school. The books are listed there, and I still own most of them.) The most important conclusion was that reading material had as much effect upon my later conversion as any other factor. As I reread portions of those books, I was able to find key passages which I had underlined earlier, and most of these had to do with eternal matters — with the deepest sources of knowledge in my soul, those feelings and thoughts which Plato said we learned in a premortal life. As one passage after another superimposed itself on previous passages, I found myself wondering where I could find the distillation of all these things I was not yet experiencing in my life but which I knew were true. (I did not yet know anything about a "testimony.") This process of rethinking, of taking certain parts of my learning and replacing them with things which were "true," is another phase of repentance—renewing and purifying the mind.

You might think at this point, that the types of literature I am talking about are the theological and doctrinal books which I was required to read for my preministerial classes. And you would be partly right. But I hasten to add that just as much came from reading fiction: Charles Dickens, especially *A Christmas Carol*; for in that perennial favorite of mine the three spirits of Christmas give Scrooge a gift that most people cannot enjoy—some help in rethinking his entire life. Repentance? Conversion? You could call it either one, but the fact is Scrooge had to do some rethinking first. Dickens, Tolstoy, Dostoevski, Shakespeare, and Dante inadvertently, or perhaps on purpose, follow the advice of Alexander Pope's "Essay on Man": "Know then thyself, presume not God to scan; the proper study of mankind is man." But of course the truth is that since God was also once a man, we are not incorrect in studying his life either. And that's why we *ponder* the scriptures. How could I not be affected by Lew Wallace's sentiment that repentance must be more than mere remorse of sins: it comprehends a change of nature befitting the heavens.[46] Or that "sin is . . . a turning of our gaze in the wrong direction?"[47]

Many of us have teenagers, and I think right away you can understand why I would correlate rethinking with music. I do not at this time want to pass judgment on any kind of music, for there is bad classical music, good rock music, lousy jazz, and beautiful country and western. The key for me in judging good music of any genre is what it does to me. Does it merely excite physically? Or does it also affect me spiritually, emotionally, and intellectually?

I have found out that my personal "Top Forty" consists of music which affects all four simultaneously, like Dmitri Shostakovich's Symphony No. 5, Simon and Garfunkel's "Bridge Over Troubled Waters," or John Denver's "Sweet Surrender." While working on this paper I had my radio tuned to KBYU-FM listening to Richard Strauss's "Death and Transfiguration." I had to pause from this paper during parts of it, and especially at the end, because this piece of music, like many of my favorites, was as much a look into the eternities for me as it was for the composer. Thus, music cannot only redirect our thinking towards the goal of the Rav's "Repentant Man" but can also constantly remind us of the good, the true, and the beautiful. For me, music is therapeutic on the physical, emotional, spiritual, and mental level. It is one of the ways toward man's highest goals: inner freedom, purity, perfection.

Art, on the other hand, is a bit more difficult to consider. Like music, one of art's highest purposes is to help us see more clearly: ourselves, society, the common things around us, and the uncommon things we should be enjoying but are not. While teaching the epistles of Paul one semester, I required projects of everyone in the class which reflected either their majors or interests. An art major painted an excellent portrayal of Paul's conversion on the road to Damascus, showing me for the first time that truly spiritual experiences can differ from one individual to the next. The painter showed that one of Paul's companions was frightened by the light, another of the voice, and a third was looking around with a puzzled look on his face, wondering what all the fuss was about. Truly good art, like good music, is never on trial: we are, and usually we do not fully understand either until we immerse ourselves in them. For example, I never really understood art through an appreciation class as I did when I took a drawing class. Only then did I begin to understand the creative mind of the artist and the work and sensitivity involved. It's not at all surprising to me, moreover, that most artists and composers have nothing but disdain for the trivia of the world. They are looking to the stars while many of us grovel in the dust. Oh, for the praise of David: "The heavens declare the glory of God; and the firmament sheweth his handywork" (Psalm 19:1). The very truest music and art is of God: the art of nature and the music of the spheres.

A standard joke in academia as well as in society in general is that philosophy never helped improve society: it's just there so that eggheads can have something to think about. I disagree. Many philosophers think only on important, eternal matters and can help us change our outlook, viewpoint, and perspective — if we take to heart what they are writing. They can give us deeper insight into life and a change of attitude leading to an entirely new life — beyond consensual reality to a new state of consciousness about all life. As your view of the world changes, so your source of motivation changes. In your mind your frame of reference has changed, and your reasons to act have changed. They can effect a complete change of mind consequent upon the apprehension of the true moral nature of things, providing an excellent service. For if one wants to revolutionize the thinking of the world without destroying it, how does one begin? With a reorientation of the fundamental thinking patterns of men into a spiritual, eternal frame of mind. In other words, knowing who we really are and what we are here for. Most of the world lacks this knowledge. Other popular "philosophers" are prescribing their own brands of repentance or rethinking. Fritjof Capra's *The Turning Point,* John Naisbitt's *Megatrends,* and Marilyn Ferguson's *The Aquarian Conspiracy* are examples of this new thinking about society. Other grass-roots philosophers such as Dick Gregory identify more with the poorer classes of people, as well as with his fellow Black race, but ends up with a message strikingly similar to our Latter-day Saint "law of the harvest": "Now I realize that you just go on planting the seeds, and be honest and ethical and regardless of what anybody thinks, there's gonna be harvest time. . . . Once you get clear spiritually, it's gonna clear up everything you're gonna do. . . . Your reasoning gets better. And then a lot of old petty things that you normally get hung up with, you don't. That's the first step. The second step is flushing out the mind."[48]

Psychologists and brain scientists have been working for years in two different areas of what we would call rethinking. The first had to do with why the brain retains some messages and learning and disregards others. Here at Brigham Young University in the seventies I did some research with the Youth-Talk Foundation: The International Institute of Self-Image Research. "Riq-ology," the brainchild of the late Ralph Nance (with help from Maxwell Maltz and his "Psychocybernetics"), sought to help grade school children to rethink by eliminating self-defeating self-talk, hang-ups, and mental blocks. Its theories were used successfully with hundreds of local students to help them to unthink, rethink, and reprogram negative "tapes" in the brain so that life would be more fulfilling and positive for them. According to Bernell L. Christensen, who also worked with the institute, the conscious and subconscious mind has to deal with the whole gamut and spectrum of human error, be it moral sin or social impudence. These all have to be dealt with in the mental processes. Mistaken thoughts can include physical clumsiness; mental preoccupation; pleasure at the expense of others; prejudice to the personality or cultural background of others; indiscretions of speech and social actions; attention-getting traits, jokes and sneers for social attention and approval at the expense of the feelings of others; failure to develop little but significant habits of health; and malicious acts of revenge and hatred. Movies, filmstrips, plays, handbooks, and songs were generated from these studies, and some of the finest researchers on campus were involved with it.

Unfortunately, the program lost impetus when Ralph died from injuries suffered in an automobile accident. Nevertheless, his basic theories are correct: We can change all negative and downgrading thoughts which we have "programmed" into our brain and substitute them with more positive and uplifting ones. It is surprising to me how many Latter-day Saints have self-images which are far beneath the wholesome image we should have of ourselves as literal children of our Father in Heaven. Repentance is therefore a necessity for anyone with a low self-image, for the highest human and divine potential cannot be attained without a healthy self-image. It involves asking ourselves what we think of ourselves and then asking what the Lord thinks of us.

The second area of psychological research is that of brain research — specifically with that involving left- and right-brain styles of thinking. I am now entering deep water, and although Joseph Smith said he was wont to swim in deep water, I am not. I may have read everything that has come out on the research in these theories, but that does not make me as qualified as a trained psychologist in the area. Therefore, let me only briefly outline my theories.

Dr. Roger Sperry, a neurosurgeon, was given the 1981 Nobel Prize for his proof of the split-brain theory. His research shows that problem-solving and decision-making skills, as well as our physical, emotional, and mental abilities, and even our personalities, are strongly influenced by which side of the brain we happen to be using. Further studies in a number of books show that people range anywhere from extreme left-brained to extreme right-brained preferences and anywhere in between, including the ideal "balanced" or "orchestrated." This brain research has yielded vast storehouses of insights and understanding which have so far aided interpersonal communication, improvements in educational testing and teaching methods, and enhanced self-knowledge. Unfortunately, religion has so far been untouched, except for a rare article here and there. This has occurred probably because such insights may have the tendency to devolve into more religious intolerance, narrow dogmas, and strict authoritarian notions as to which preferences may be true for a given faith system.

What does all of this have to do with rethinking? Balance. Consider for a minute the predilections of the two hemispheres. A left-hemisphere-dominant person thinks in a sequential or linear manner. He loves to deal with parts (specialization), numbers, and words. He is very rational and logical. He who is on the "right" thinks in images, patterns, and wholes, preferring to look at the creative and artistic "Big Picture" of life. An orchestrated person lives freely in both spheres, and that is where the rethinking part of repentance comes in.

I was raised in a church which preferred rational theology over revelation, prophecy, and visions, which belong on the right. My initial testimony at conversion was one of reason: The Latter-day Saint Church makes sense. But my reasonable testimony did not keep me from tearing up my baptismal certificate six months later and nearly apostatizing. It was wise home teachers who knew what kind of testimony I needed yet, and that was a spiritual one based on knowing that Joseph Smith experienced what he said he experienced and that the Book of Mormon was truly the word of God. What aided me in rethinking along those lines? Prayer and fasting—exactly what my home teachers prescribed. Apostate Christianity evolved through rational expediency—Artistotelian philosophy and pagan traditions—while the Latter-day Saint Church was founded on prayer, revelation, and visions. Today the Church is run rationally but would mean nothing without the continuing guidance the Lord gives us through a prophet. Having come from the outside, it is no surprise to me that Christians have a difficult time accepting some of our teachings — they were raised on reasonable theology, not the mind and will of the Lord through revelation.

Why do fundamentalist Christian groups tend to lean to the right?

Would it be correct to say that while Lehi was right-brained dominant, Nephi was balanced and Laman was left dominant, not understanding of spiritual things because they were not reasonable?

Would Jesus Christ, Paul, and Joseph Smith be considered "balanced?"

How do these theories enlighten us on the preference of the ancient Jews to seek for a sign while the Greeks considered early Christianity "foolishness?"

How does this research explain the differences between Eastern and Western philosophies?

Is The Church of Jesus Christ of Latter-day Saints a balanced faith system which relies on intuition/inspiration and logic/reason?

How does this research help to explain the secularism and humanism so rampant in all religions?

You may be surprised to know that there are tests you can take to discover where your dominance lies, that there are exercises in books which help you to think more on one side or the other, and which if tailored to the Latter-day Saints could indeed help the left-brained Saint better attain a testimony of right-brained spiritual matters. The possibilities are endless and may release a new age of thinking about thinking: about ourselves, about our Heavenly Father, about the nonmember family we are about to teach, and about our loved ones all around. My colleague and friend Curtis Wright would call this a "restructuring of the Thinkatorium." It can also show how the physical, mental, emotional, and spiritual experiences of our lives will predispose us to certain attitudes and perspectives. This may, for instance, explain why a balanced team effort of Dan (left) and Ron (right) Lafferty would go off the deep end.

Roadblocks and Freeways to Repentance

Little discussion is needed here. Lists of roadblocks and freeways should suffice, for they will sound very familiar to you. Repentance, the rethinking kind, is blocked by many things, but here are the most serious:

1. Excuses.
2. Rationalizations.
3. Justifications (repentance, on the other hand, should never lead to self-justification).
4. Defense mechanisms.
5. Lack of humility.
6. Procrastination.
7. Incorrect doctrines.
    a. Cheap grace (Dietrich Bonhoeffer).
    b. Ecclesiocentrism instead of Christocentrism.
    c. Outward appearances meaning more than the soul. (Some of my fellow theology students were more concerned about bishop's rings, colorful stoles, and clean altar vestments than about saving souls.)
    d. Ambivalence or wanting the best of both worlds at the same time. (In Umberto Eco's excellent novel, *The Name of the Rose*, the narrator insists that there is a midpoint between good and evil, at which place a man could go in either direction. The difference between penitence and repentance is that in the first, man is content to stay in the midpoint, having constantly to decide which way to go. The repentant man, however, makes the decision to stay in the good and is overcome by temptation only rarely or never at all.)
8. The complexity of life (simplicity definitely helps us to keep our perspective better).

9. Centering our lives around "having," "knowing," and "doing" — rather than "being" and "becoming" — who we really are.

Unfortunately, the entire process of repentance can be simulated and phony. Only the Lord and I, the repenter, know the difference, for even though repentance should change the relationship I have with myself, others, and my Father in Heaven, it is still conceivable that I could deceive myself. I have found from experience that without an inward and prayerful change of attitude there really was no conquest over the flesh, and thus no true conversion of internal life, let alone perfection.

What helps us in rethinking?

1. Fasting, which includes not only the physical self, but the emotional, mental, and spiritual self as well.

2. Prayer and meditation.

3. Learning by study and also by faith, especially the scriptures. (Drink deeply, do not simply absorb it.)

4. Forgiveness and patience at all times. (Learn to turn to each person as the most sacred person on earth.)

5. Love and understanding.

6. Humility and teachableness.

7. Crying repentance, but overlooking the sins of others while concentrating on yourself.

8. Reading good books, listening to good music, enjoying nature.

9. Keeping a journal, for by so doing, you keep track of your spiritual progress.

10. Genealogy and temple work (there is much that could be said on how these help rethinking, and I will leave that to your imagination).

11. Asking what Christ would do?

12. Living as if to expect his coming at any moment.

Conclusion

I once asked my Gospel Principles and Practices students on the final exam what one principle of the gospel they found the most difficult to live. Most felt that because of the call of the world repentance was that principle, echoing the good rabbi's earlier comment. I submit, however, that it is not only the tempting call of the world that makes repentance difficult, it is that we do not fully know ourselves. I would challenge us to two things: First, we should not disparage ourselves or underestimate our capabilities. We are much greater than we know. Oh, how different from the way I was raised: that man is totally depraved, not merely corruptible, and that I was therefore a "worm" who could do no good. It's no wonder I've had to work on my own self-image ever since I joined the Church. Secondly, we need to learn what God thinks of us—through meditation, revelation, the scriptures, patriarchal blessings—and how we touch others around us.

By way of a conclusion, I would like to quote the best little dialogue on repentance I have yet seen. It is packed with meaning and insight, and I share it with the hope that it will set something in motion within you like it did within me. It happens to be part of Hugh Nibley's "Intellectual Autobiography," in *Nibley on the Timely and the Timeless*:

> We: Dear Father, whenever the end is scheduled to be, can't you give us an extension of time?
>
> He: Willingly. But tell me first, what will you do with it?
>
> We: Well . . . ah . . . we will go on doing pretty much what we have been doing; after all, isn't that why we are asking for an extension?
>
> He: And isn't that exactly why I want to end it soon—because you show no inclination to change? Why should I reverse the order of nature so that you can go on doing the very things I want to put an end to?
>
> We: But is what we are doing so terribly wrong? The economy seems sound enough. Why shouldn't we go on doing the things which have made this country great?

He: Haven't I made it clear enough to you what kind of greatness I expect of my offspring? Forget the statistics; you are capable of better things—your stirring commercials do not impress me in the least.

We: But why should we repent when all we are doing is what each considers to be for the best good of himself and the nation?

He: Because it is not you but I who decide what that shall be, and I have told you a hundred times what is best for you individually and collectively—and that is repentance, no matter who you are.

We: We find your inference objectionable, Sir—quite objectionable.

He: I know.[49]

In conclusion, I know what it is like to wonder where I came from, what I was doing here, and where I was going. I know what it is like to have been taught the truth of the atonement of Jesus Christ without having a true conception of his Father. I now know the difference between avoiding hell and working for heaven, with the help of the Lord. But most of all, I now know that I am here to learn all I can from the Lord and from his servants, the prophets, who communicate with him through the wonderful gift of revelation. And this is what makes this Church, The Church of Jesus Christ of Latter-day Saints, the most effective instrument on the face of the earth for teaching our Father's children the truths of heaven and earth. It is my prayer for all of us that we may spend our days in renewing our knowledge of the eternities and of our familial friendship with Heavenly Father and his son Jesus Christ.

Notes

1. Alan Richardson, *Biblical Theology of the New Testament* (New York: Harper and Row, 1959), 33.

2. Walter A. Elwell, ed., *Evangelical Dictionary of Theology* (Grand Rapids, MI: Baker, 1984), 936.

3. R. J. Zwi Werblowsky, *The Encyclopedia of the Jewish Religion* (New York: Holt, Rinehart and Winston, 1965), 330.

4. J. D. Douglas, ed., *The New International Dictionary of the Christian Church* (Grand Rapids, MI: Zondervan, 1974), 837.

5. *The Illustrated Bible Dictionary*, 3 vols. (Wheaton, IL: Tyndale, 1980), 3:1327-28.

6. Douglas, *The New International Dictionary of the Christian Church*, 837.

7. *The Illustrated Bible Dictionary*, 3:1327-28.

8. An example of this necessity is found in Alma 26:21-22: "And now behold, my brethren, what natural man is there that knoweth these things? I say unto you, there is none that knoweth these things, save it be the penitent. Yea, he that repenteth and exerciseth faith, and bringeth forth good works, and prayeth continually without ceasing — unto such it is given to know the mysteries of God [Ammon certainly was not intimating that normal repentance after a serious transgression will lead someone to the mysteries! On the contrary, only he who has begun to think like God will come to know the mysteries of God]; yea, unto such it shall be given to reveal things which never have been revealed; yea, and it shall be given unto such to bring thousands of souls to repentance, even as it has been given unto us to bring these our brethren to repentance."

9. *TPJS*, 137.

10. Edward L. Kimball, ed., *The Teachings of Spencer W. Kimball* (Salt Lake City: Bookcraft, 1982), 85-86.

11. Ibid., 81.

12. Ibid., 83.

13. Ibid., 81.

14. Ibid., 86.

15. Ibid., 97.

16. Ibid., 105.

17. Ibid., 90.

18. David O. McKay, *Gospel Ideals* (Salt Lake City: Deseret News Press, 1953), 14.

19. Bruce R. McConkie, *Mormon Doctrine* (Salt Lake City: Bookcraft, 1966), 631.

20. *TPJS*, 197.

21. Ibid., 148.

22. Ibid., 361.

23. Letter of Parley P. Pratt to his brother, August 3, 1848, Brigham Young History, MS, Office of the Church Historian, The Church of Jesus Christ of Latter-day Saints, Salt Lake City, 57.

24. *JD* 10:177.

25. John A. Widtsoe, ed., *The Discourses of Brigham Young* (Salt Lake City: Deseret Book, 1954), 156.

26. See Hugh Nibley, "The Apocalyptic Background, I: The Eschatological Dilemma," 58 (November 1955): 829-31.

27. Hugh Nibley, "Historicity of the Bible," in *Old Testament and Related Studies*, vol. 1, *The Collected Works of Hugh Nibley* (Salt Lake City: Deseret Book and F.A.R.M.S., 1986), 1-2.

28. Hugh Nibley, "Zeal without Knowledge," in Truman G. Madsen, ed., *Nibley on the Timely and the Timeless* (Provo: BYU Religious Studies Center, 1978), 264; in *CWHN* 9:66-67.

29. Hugh Nibley, "Beyond Politics," in *Nibley on the Timely and the Timeless*, 22.

30. Hugh Nibley, "The Prophetic Book of Mormon," in *The Prophetic Book of Mormon*, vol. 8, *The Collected Works of Hugh Nibley* (Salt Lake City: Deseret Book and F.A.R.M.S., 1989), 462.

31. Hugh Nibley, "Great Are the Words of Isaiah," in *Old Testament and Related Studies*, 217.

32. Ibid.

33. Tony Castle, ed., *The New Book of Christian Quotations* (New York: Crossroad, 1983), 205.

34. Werblowsky, *The Encyclopedia of the Jewish Religion*, 330.

35. Ibid.

36. Ibid.

37. Pinchas Hacohen Peli, "Repentant Man—A High Level in Rabbi Soloveitchik's Typology of Man," *Tradition: A Journal of Orthodox Jewish Thought* 18 (Summer 1980): 135.

38. Ibid., 145.

39. Ibid., 149-50.

40. Ibid., 150.

41. Ibid., 156.

42. David Brubeck, mimeographed sheet in possession of the author, March 1969.

43. Whitall N. Perry, ed., *A Treasury of Traditional Wisdom* (New York: Simon and Schuster, 1971), 479.

44. Ibid., 491.

45. Ibid., 492.

46. Castle, *The New Book of Christian Quotations*, 205.

47. Simone Weil, *Waiting for God*, tr. Emma Craufurd (New York: G. P. Putnam's Sons, 1951), 124.

48. Dick Gregory, "Up from Soul Food," *East-West Journal* (July 1981): 35.

49. Hugh Nibley, "Intellectual Autobiography," in *Nibley on the Timely and the Timeless*, 279-80.

14

Is There a Cure
for Authoritarianism
in Science?[1]

Richard F. Haglund, Jr.
Vanderbilt University, Nashville, Tennesee

It is a commonplace that "in our time . . . the sciences, physical and social, will be to an increasing degree the accepted point of reference with respect to which the validity (Truth) of all knowledge is gauged."[2] Yet, as Professor Nibley and others have warned, it would be a grave mistake to accept without reservations the hegemony of the sciences in the house of intellect.[3] The widely held notion that science has delivered us an absolutely authoritative source of knowledge simply cannot withstand close scrutiny.

Nowhere is this more apparent than in the history of novel theories and experiments in science. Scientists with radically new ideas have difficulty getting an audience among their more orthodox brethren. Sometimes they are ignored or rejected because of personal animosities or simple inertia. In other cases, the rejection seems to violate the canons of open-minded scientific inquiry. Through the whole spectrum of the sciences, one can document an astonishing disregard for facts which contradict fashionable theories, stereotyping of acceptable approaches to

This essay originally appeared in a slightly different form in the unpublished "Tinkling Cymbals: Essays in Honor of Hugh Nibley," John W. Welch, ed., 1978.

problems and theories, and the waving of academic credentials and ritual invocation of the specialist's mystique to discourage criticism from "outsiders."[4] In these instances, the intellectual conservatism of the scientific community appears to be *authoritarian* rather than *authoritative* in character.

The occurrence of authoritarian behavior patterns appears at first glance to be completely pathological in view of our idealization of science as an objective inquiry after "stubborn irreducible facts." But the personal vanities and insecurities of individual scientists cannot reasonably be invoked to explain widespread authoritarianism in science. Moreover, since the stigmata of rigidity and dogmatism are observable in physics as well as archaeology, the problem cannot arise simply from the peculiarities of individual disciplines, but must be connected with general features of science.

The difficulty lies with the presumed objectivity of scientific investigation.[5] For *facts* are not normative in science — the *consensus* is. To achieve that consensus, the community of science is often forced to make subjective judgments about the relative weight to be given to data, methodology, theoretical elegance, and the credentials of scientists. This sense of the community may be either imposed in authoritarian fashion, or proposed on defensible scientific — and hence authoritative — grounds. But science will always be torn between loyalty to the discipline as it exists and to the ideal of progress, between the desire to *possess* the truth and the striving to *discover* it. Therefore, even though this fundamental tension may on occasion lead to authoritarian behavior, it cannot be eliminated without destroying an essential mechanism of scientific activity.

Theory as the Source of Facts

Almost any science textbook contains a statement to the effect that "experiment, rather than preconceived ideas, are the ultimate authority in science."[6] Because we have been convinced that "an hypothesis will be rejected if even a single known fact is at variance with it,"[7] we tend to view the subordination of fact to theory as *prima facie* evidence of authoritarian, even antiscientific, attitudes.

Such a naive view grossly oversimplifies matters of fact. For all experimental data are, in N. R. Hansen's felicitous phrase, "theory-laden." Two people may experience the same photochemical reaction at the surface of the retina but *see* entirely different things.[8] Thus, as Einstein said, "It is the theory which decides what we can observe."[9] This is true even in so-called "crucial experiments" — which are supposed unambiguously to reject or falsify a given hypothesis, and thus give an authoritative *denial* of a theory. Philosophers and historians of science disagree sharply about the problems of defining such experiments.[10] But in practice, the results of such an experiment are unlikely to win easy acceptance if they fail to match previous expectations.

The genesis of the special theory of relativity provides an instructive case history. In 1864, in his "Dynamical Theory of the Electromagnetic Field," James Clerk Maxwell proposed that electromagnetic waves were transmitted as "vibrations of an aethereal medium filling space and permeating matter."[11] However, the mechanical properties required of this "lumeniferous ether" were an embarrassment; worse yet, it defied all attempts even to verify its existence.

Finally, the American physicist Michelson devised an experiment which, it was hoped, would settle the issue once and for all. The basic idea was to measure the speed of light in two mutually perpendicular directions — parallel and perpendicular to the trajectory of the earth's orbit. The ether theory predicted that the two measurements would show a slight discrepancy (on the order of one part in a hundred million). By 1887, Michelson had perfected an interferometer capable of measuring the anticipated effect.[12] But a series of extraordinarily careful measurements showed no detectable difference in the speed of light in the two directions.

Now if a crucial experiment were in fact an unambiguously authoritative way to resolve scientific controversy, Michelson and everyone else should have abandoned the ether theory. Instead, his reaction was that "since the result of the original experiment was negative, the problem is still demanding a solution."[13] Most physicists agreed with him. Numerous hypotheses were put forward to explain the null result of the experiment without abandoning the ether, although they were never more than *ad hoc* proposals which could not be connected with more general principles.[14]

Then, in 1905, the most famous patent clerk in history proposed the special theory of relativity, which began with the *postulate* that the speed of light is constant in all frames of reference, thus neatly "explaining" the Michelson result. Furthermore, starting from this and two other similarly general postulates, Einstein was able to remove some mathematical inconsistencies in Maxwell's theory of moving charges and to cast into unified form the transformation equations of particle mechanics and the electromagnetic field.

Nevertheless, Einstein's paper was received skeptically rather than gratefully.[15] And it would be a mistake to label this negative response as simple authoritarianism. On the contrary, it effectively demonstrates the impossibility of settling a scientific controversy by means of a single fact. The ether was only one facet of a theory of mechanics which had successfully explained everything from universal gravitation to the motion of a spinning top. And implicit in the modest form and tone of Einstein's paper was a demand for the drastic revision of the classical concepts of space and time—a great weight to hang on the result of a single experiment.

Once special relativity was accepted as authoritative, however, physicists willingly based its validity solely on the null result of the Michelson-Morley experiments.[16] In fact, when a later experimental test of the ether drift appeared to invalidate special relativity, H. A. Lorentz hastened to assure physicists that the experimental results only "indicate the existence of some unknown cause which it will be very important to discover . . . but I think . . . that relativity will be quite safe."[17] Eventually the results were found to arise from a systematic error—thus confirming Eddington's dictum that "It is also a good rule not to put overmuch confidence in the observational results . . . until they are confirmed by theory."[18]

Problems with Paradigms

During periods of "normal science,"[19] the authoritative standard of scientific truth is not data, but the *paradigm*— a framework of validated theories, concepts, and methods of attacking problems which both guides the course of experiment and embodies the data it produces. But, as with the ether-drift experiment, even when a paradigm fails, it will not be torn down until a new one can be constructed. The new consensus is usually not achieved by gathering more data, or by "multiplying existing hypotheses beyond necessity," but by finding a new way to see *existing* theory and experimental experience. This process of "scientific revolution" is, in Polanyi's words, "the classical case of Poe's *Purloined Letter*, of the momentous document lying casually in front of everybody, and hence overlooked by all."[20]

The difficulties of constructing a new paradigm are illustrated nicely by the quantum theory of light. In 1887, Heinrich Hertz found experimental confirmation for Maxwell's conjecture that light was an electromagnetic wave.

Ironically, he also observed what we now know as one manifestation of the photoelectric effect—in which light rays eject electrons from the surfaces of some materials. Over a period of almost two decades, other experimenters after Hertz reported similar phenomena. But the data could not be explained by Maxwell's theory, nor, it seemed, by any other reasonable scheme, so the experiments were mostly ignored by theorists.[21]

In another of his famous trio of 1905 papers, Einstein proposed an heuristic explanation of the result, assuming for purposes of calculation that light waves behaved as particles when interacting with matter.[22] However, he was not taken seriously, because experiments done early in the nineteenth century by Young, Fresnel, and Foucault had convinced physicists that light consisted of waves, not of particles.[23] Gradually, though, Einstein satisfied himself that the wave or particle character of light is not determined *a priori,* but is contingent upon the way in which the light is observed. And although he showed how the photoelectric effect and related phenomena could be explained by his theory, Einstein's arguments rested primarily on his emerging view of a fundamental duality in Nature—between waves and particles, matter and energy.[24] To Robert A. Millikan, accustomed to thinking of waves and particles as mutually exclusive entities, this duality

> seemed completely unreasonable because it *apparently* ignored and indeed seemed to contradict all the manifold facts of interference and thus to be a straight return to the corpuscular theory of light. . . . I spent ten years of my life testing that 1905 equation of Einstein's, and contrary to all my expectations I was compelled in 1915 to assert its unambiguous experimental verification in spite of its unreasonableness.[25]

However, even "unambiguous experimental verification" was not sufficient to establish the dual nature of light as a new paradigm. In 1916, for instance, Max Planck (who had suggested the concept of energy quanta in 1900) nominated Einstein for membership in the Prussian Academy of Science with the caveat:

> That he may sometimes have missed the mark in his speculations, as for example in his hypothesis of light quanta, cannot really be held too much against him. For it is not possible to introduce fundamentally new ideas, even in the most exact sciences, without occasionally taking a risk.[26]

Not until 1923, when Compton showed that the scattering of x-rays from electrons could be treated simply as a collision between particles, did the wave-particle duality in light begin to find unreserved acceptance by physicists.[27] From there it was a short step to de Broglie's hypothesis of wavelike behavior in particles — and what had been a nicely compartmentalized world of particles and waves dissolved almost overnight into a hash of "wavicles."

The tortuous evolution of the wave-particle paradigm is *not* evidence for authoritarian resistance to the concept. Instead, it shows plainly that neither the content nor the internal logic of paradigms furnishes authoritative standards for judging experimental results of a completely novel type. The photoelectric effect was simply incommensurable with existing concepts of the nature of light. It was not predicted by existing paradigms in advance, and, after Hertz's accidental discovery, there was no way to "save the appearances" by grafting new hypotheses onto Maxwell's theory, even in an *ad hoc* fashion. Thus this work was an authentic case of *premature discovery* — today's anomaly or embarrassment which turns out to be the kernel of tomorrow's paradigm.[28] Unfortunately, one can seldom judge accurately *today* whether the result is humbug or the makings of a Nobel Prize.

Thus, the prototypical controversy about new paradigms appears to be a struggle with *language*. "In the beginning of the investigations," writes Heisenberg, " . . . the words are connected with old concepts; the new ones do not exist yet."[29] Thus, the solution of the controversy cannot come from the rules which relate the paradigms to one another, but from a higher level of thought which comprehends the paradigms as special cases—just as a dispute about grammar cannot be resolved by the rules of spelling.[30]

It is tempting to say that questions about paradigms must be settled by metaphysical arguments, but physicists are more easily swayed by elegance than by metaphysics. "It is more important," wrote Dirac, "to have beauty in one's equations than to have them fit experiment," because whatever discrepancies exist "may well be due to minor features . . . that will get cleared up with further developments of the theory."[31] Certainly, the final acceptance of Einstein's quantum theory of light seems to have resulted as much from the strong aesthetic appeal of his conceptualization as from its explanation of the photoelectric effect.

Community, Certifiability, and Quality Control

If neither the data nor the paradigms of science are absolutely authoritative, we are left in a precarious position. The responsibility for adjudicating conflicting claims rests *ipso facto* on the community of science—but the rules of evidence admit not only objective criteria but also such subjective considerations as the aesthetic qualities of theories.[32]

A set of subjective standards may be internalized by the formation of a "school" of scientific thought, but such enterprises have not enjoyed spectacular success.[33] Hence, one may legitimately wonder if there is some way for the community of science to define itself and its patterns of growth so that controversial theories and experiments will always be examined on intellectual merit alone.

But two contrasting idealizations of scientific identity make this an extraordinarily problematical task. On one hand, there is a view of the community of science traceable to Sir Francis Bacon, which stresses the inductive, experimental character of its work; the formal, public apparatus of consensus — journals, societies, and conferences; lengthy schooling and socialization of scientists during which they acquire loyalties to, and are in turn certified by, the community; team research; the elaboration and extension of existing paradigms; and the progressive vanquishing of ignorance across a broad front. On the other hand, there is a tradition personified by René Descartes, which emphasizes the deductive, theoretical side of science — the informal networks of information which spring up among those of like temperament and interest, individual research, imaginative, unorthodox approaches to problems, and the breakthrough to new discoveries in problematical areas of inquiry.[34]

The temper of the average modern scientist is predominantly Baconian, and he senses an enduring and inescapable conflict between himself and the solitary Cartesian genius who periodically shakes the foundations of science. A classic example comes from the history of thermodynamics, one of the frontiers of physics during the early nineteenth century. In 1845, James Waterston explained some of the thermodynamical properties of gases by assuming a gas to consist of "hard-sphere" molecules, moving in random directions with some distribution of velocities. In terms of his model, for instance, the pressure of a gas on the walls of its container would be caused by the aggregate force of all the molecules colliding with the wall. Although Waterston was not a Fellow of the Royal Society, the Society's rules would have permitted his paper to be read before the Society and to be published in its *Philosophical Transactions*. However, the referees did not like Waterston's work, and though it was read in 1846, it was not published by the Society. Due to a technicality in the Society's rules, however, the only copy was retained in its archives, so that Waterston was unable to publish it elsewhere.[35]

In 1892, Lord Rayleigh discovered the paper in the Royal Society Archives and had it printed. In his preface, he remarked that "highly speculative investigations, especially by an unknown author, are best brought before the world through some other channel than a scientific society," and that someone in Waterston's position should establish a reputation "by work whose scope is limited, and whose value is easily judged, before embarking on higher flights."[36]

Hindsight is always cruel, and particularly so in this case, since James Joule won ready acceptance for essentially the same theory about twenty years later.[37] But one ought not to judge Lord Rayleigh's authoritarian *pronunciamento* too harshly. If one is committed to the search for truth, one must also be wary of being led astray. One must leave no stone unturned, but one must also be careful how much time and energy one spends turning over stones that have only the same beetles underneath. The scientist knows from experience that revolutions are infrequent and genius is rare. He is therefore properly skeptical of the paper which proposes "a general theory of Space, Time, Matter and Radiation — an attempt to outdo Quantum Theory and Relativity, Cosmology and the Theory of Elementary Particles in one splendid stroke."[38] He is also likely to be wary of strangers and young upstarts, and to mistrust work which does not appear in his own literature, which he can usually be sure is competently reviewed before getting into print.[39]

On the frontiers of science, his standards may be relaxed somewhat, as a concession to emotional equilibrium in areas where controversy is rife. Recently, for example, the prestigious *Physical Review Letters* simply quit refereeing papers in high-energy physics — a "hot" field where priority and the chance to publish controversial results are highly esteemed.[40] But as long as the community of science is struggling with the conflicting aims and standards of the Baconian and Cartesian ideals, there will always be people like Waterston who are denied their due.

One can argue, of course, that the danger of rejecting possible new insights outweighs the danger of letting uncertified and possibly incompetent persons into the discussion. But science would thereby lose the strength of consensus, which establishes a body of knowledge upon which all can agree for discussion. Take that away, and one has not science, but a collection of warring factions, busily anathematizing one another. If you prefer that, the Baconian would argue, better that you should form your own scientific society![41]

Prognosis

We began with the question of a cure for authoritarianism in science — implying the existence of an illness in the body scientific. Some believe the illness to be acute, and have called for radical therapy.[42] But such a pessimistic diagnosis is almost certainly unwarranted. "Under small perturbations," as they say in physics, the values of the community of science provide authoritative standards for balancing the competing ideals of scientific practice. These normative structures break down primarily when the data fall far outside expectations, when paradigms are incommensurable with experience, or when new methods, new languages, or infant disciplines are struggling through their early development, a circumstance exacerbated by the specialization of science.[43] Thus one may properly speak of "essential" rather than "acute" authoritarianism: The patient cannot be cured — in fact, the symptoms can be removed only at the cost of his life. But the symptoms can be controlled by making the patient aware of his limitations and moving him to a more salubrious climate. This analysis suggests the following course of treatment.

First, scientists — and those who would like to be — need constant reminding that the intellectual and emotional state of a field of inquiry is a sensitive and complicated function of the quality of available data, the complexity and generality of models, and of the patterns of growth in that area. Hence, they must be prepared to change interests and amphoras as the field matures through successive stages: from collecting and classifying data, through the embedding of heuristic schemes into more comprehensive and elegant theories, and finally to the stage where the foundations and interconnections of theories are of paramount interest.[44] To ignore the question of what activities are fruitful for a field at a given stage in its development is to risk carrying on a mere parody of science.[45]

Second, diligent effort is prescribed both in defining paradigms and in exploring their practical and conceptual limitations, to avoid the situation where theories are dismissed without adequate analysis. For sciences where paradigms are as yet not well established, this means a frank recognition that a discipline cannot be a science until a paradigmatic consensus is achieved, no matter how narrow its boundaries.[46] For the "harder" sciences, this medicine contains, in addition, a liberal dose of pessimism about the durability of paradigms. Physicists have lived to see an astonishingly successful and long-lived paradigm — that of classical mechanics — altered almost beyond recognition by experimental and theoretical developments in the early twentieth century. It may well be time for younger sciences to stop mimicking the outworn mechanistic determinism of nineteenth-century physics and to consider how their own discipline's evolution and their efforts will reshape existing paradigms.[47]

The most important part of the cure is fresh air. If

science is about real problems, there must be solutions which cannot yet be described, and which cannot be discovered in any formally prescribed way. The patient, careful work of the Baconian scientist—deeply specialized, intimately familiar with his paradigm—is absolutely essential to the conduct of science. But precisely because of his faithful adherence to the prevailing consensus, he is unlikely to foresee the outlines of those solutions. The germ of a new paradigm is more likely to be brought into the discussion by the Cartesian doubter, the amateur, or the generalist.[48] The formal approaches of the consensus scientist "are certainly beneficial," wrote Einstein, "when one is trying decisively to formulate an already discovered truth, but they almost always fail as heuristic aids."[49] What is needed for revolutions in science is clear vision, and as Bohr often said, "Clarity is gained through breadth."[50]

The overall goal of this cure is not to change the dependence of science on consensus, but to ensure that it is achieved in a healthy way. Where a scientific consensus is established by certifying some given set of data, methods, or credentials as authoritative, that consensus will be enforced, paradoxically but inevitably, in authoritarian fashion. As Popper observes, the setting up of such standards is based on the false assumption that "knowledge may legitimize itself by its pedigree."[51] But if, instead, a consensus is sought without fixed norms for resolving controversies, but with the stipulation that debate continue as long as the participants show good faith, one can avoid the destructive authoritarianism which vitiates scientific inquiry by preventing the free flow of ideas.

It thus becomes desirable to give up the view of rationality as the search for universal, absolute truth in science by means of some specified (and infinitely debatable) set of logical procedures. In its place, we may adopt "the Socratic idea of rationality as a process of conflict between universality and specificity, . . . to wit, rationality as Socratic dialectic."[52] To do so is to accept the quintessentially tentative nature of scientific inquiry, and to be content, if necessary, with the modest task of finding errors in our knowledge by means of civilized and critical discussion.

Professor Nibley has given an appealing sketch of this ideal of science, not as rational *explanation*, but as rational *dialogue*: The method of science, he writes, is "to talk about the material at hand, hoping that in the course of the discussion every participant will privately and inwardly form, reform, change, or abandon his opinions . . . and thereby move in the direction of greater light and knowledge."[53]

Notes

1. This paper was written for and presented at a symposium in honor of Professor Nibley's sixty-fifth birthday in March 1975 and is thus something of a period piece (though not necessarily dated on that account). Updated citations to recent editions have been added. I am grateful to Professor Dietrich Schroeer of the University of North Carolina for helpful discussions during the first writing.

2. George A. Lundberg, *Can Science Save Us?* 2nd ed. repr. (New York: David McKay, 1971), 43.

3. Hugh Nibley, "A New Look at the Pearl of Great Price," *Improvement Era* 71 (January 1968): 20-22; Nibley, "Archaeology and Our Religion," unpublished manuscript; see also Jacques Barzun, *Science: The Glorious Entertainment* (New York: Harper and Row, 1964), chap. 1.

4. Donald G. Miller, "Ignored Intellect: Pierre Duhem," *Physics Today* 19 (December 1966): 47; Bernard Barber, "Resistance by Scientists to Scientific Discovery," *Science* 134 (1 September 1961): 596. A bitter remark by Max Planck illustrates the distress this situation causes for the individual scientist: "A new scientific truth does not triumph by convincing its opponents and making them see the light, but rather because its opponents eventually die. . . . " Max Planck, *Scientific Autobiography*, tr. F. Gaynor (New York: Philosophical Library, 1949), 33-34.

5. The failure of objectivity at the frontiers of science is conceded by many scientists. But historians of science are now challenging the ideal of objectivity even in "normal science." See Stephen G. Brush, "Should the History of Science be Rated X?" *Science* 183 (22

March 1974): 1164. On the importance of consensus, see J. M. Ziman, *Public Knowledge* (Cambridge: Cambridge University Press, 1968).

6. Robert L. Sproull, *Modern Physics*, 2nd ed. (New York: John Wiley, 1963), 81. A counterexample from the heroic age of physics is Newton's manipulation of data on the velocity of sound to make it fit his theory. See Richard S. Westfall, "Newton and the Fudge Factor," *Science* 179 (1973): 751.

7. Franklin Miller, Jr., *College Physics*, 3rd ed. (New York: Harcourt, Brace, Jovanovich, 1972), 2.

8. Norwood R. Hanson, *Patterns of Discovery* (Cambridge: Cambridge University Press, 1958), chap. 1.

9. As reported by Werner Heisenberg, *Physics and Beyond* (New York: Harper and Row, 1971), 63.

10. Imre Lakatos, "Falsification and the Methodology of Scientific Research Programmes," in *Criticism and the Growth of Scientific Knowledge* (Cambridge: Cambridge University Press, 1970), 91-196.

11. As quoted in R. A. R. Tricker, *The Contributions of Faraday and Maxwell to Electrical Science* (London: Pergamon Press, 1966), 108.

12. The interferometer remains one of the most precise instruments available to the physicist. Its operating principles are simple: by means of half-silvered mirrors, a beam of light is split in two, and then reflected along two perpendicular paths of differing lengths. The split beams are then recombined and the location of the "fringes" produced by the interfering waves is measured. See R. S. Shankland, "The Michelson-Morley Experiment," *Scientific American* 211 (November 1964): 107.

13. As quoted in Gerald Holton, *Thematic Origins of Scientific Thought*, rev. ed. (Cambridge, MA: Harvard University Press, 1988), 284.

14. Ibid., 322-34.

15. Ronald W. Clark, *Einstein: The Life and Times* (New York: World, 1971), 107-10.

16. As Holton points out (*Thematic Origins*, 306-15), scientists have generally assumed that Einstein's main concern was the Michelson experiment. Both direct and indirect evidence suggests the contrary: that his overriding concern was the resolution of what he saw as intolerable formal and physical inconsistencies in the transformation theories of mechanics and electrodynamics. Additional experimental evidence for the theory became available in 1909, with the observation of an increased mass of electrons traveling at velocities comparable to that of light. See Robert M. Eisberg, *Fundamentals of Modern Physics* (New York: John Wiley, 1961), 37-38.

17. H. A. Lorentz, *Collected Papers*, 9 vols. (The Hague: Martinus Nijhoff, 1935), 8:415.

18. As quoted in Brush, "Should the History of Science Be Rated X?" 1171-72, n. 35.

19. The use of the terms "normal science," "scientific revolution," and "paradigm" follows Thomas S. Kuhn, *The Structure of Scientific Revolutions,* 2nd ed., enlarged (Chicago: University of Chicago Press, 1970).

20. Michael Polanyi, *The Tacit Dimension* (New York: Doubleday-Anchor, 1967), 22.

21. Max Jammer, *The Conceptual Development of Quantum Mechanics* (New York: McGraw-Hill, 1966), 33ff.

22. A useful introduction to this work, containing Einstein's first two papers on the topic, with references to the early experimental work, is Armin Hermann, *Die Hypothese der Lichtquanten* (Stuttgart: Ernst Battenberg, 1965).

23. The character of these experiments and the discarding of Newton's corpuscular theory of light is handled at length by Norwood R. Hansen, *The Concept of the Positron* (Cambridge: Cambridge University Press, 1963), chap. 1.

24. Some insight into the significance of symmetry concepts in Einstein's thinking is given by Holton, *Thematic Origins*, 362-67.

25. Robert A. Millikan, "Albert Einstein on His Seventieth Birthday," *Reviews of Modern Physics* 21 (1949): 344-45.

26. Quoted by Jammer, *Conceptual Development of Quantum Mechanics*, 44.

27. The history of this change in attitude is recorded in ibid., 160-65.

28. Gunther S. Stent, "Prematurity and Uniqueness in Scientific Discovery," *Scientific American* 227 (December 1972): 84.

29. Werner Heisenberg, "Tradition in Science," *Bulletin of the Atomic Scientists* 29 (December 1973): 4.

30. Polanyi, *The Tacit Dimension*, 33-37.

31. P. A. M. Dirac, "The Evolution of the Physicist's Picture of Nature," *Scientific American* 208 (May 1963): 45.

32. Jerome R. Ravetz, *Scientific Knowledge and Its Social Problems* (Oxford: Oxford University Press, 1971), 223-33.

33. Joseph Haberer, *Politics and the Community of Science* (New York: Van Nostrand Reinhold, 1969), chaps. 3-4. For further analyses of the character of scientific work, see Ravetz, "Science as Craftsman's Work," *Scientific Knowledge*, chap. 3; and Warren Hagstrom, "Social Control in Science," *The Scientific Community* (New York: Basic Books, 1965), chap. 1.

34. As exemplified by Ziman's remark that "Only the crank—or his cousin the rare genius—decides to find the explanation of Gravitation" (*Public Knowledge*, 60).

35. Stephen G. Brush, *Kinetic Theory*, 3 vols. (London: Pergamon Press, 1968), 1:17-19.

36. Ibid., 1:18

37. Ziman, *Public Knowledge*, 113.

38. Ibid., 114.

39. On the sociology of refereeing in physics, see Harriet Zuckerman and Robert K. Merton, "Sociology of Refereeing," *Physics Today* 24 (July 1971): 28.

40. S. A. Goudsmit, "Editorial: A Drastic Change in Policy," *Physical Review Letters* 13 (20 July 1964): 79; S. A. Goudsmit, "Important Announcement Regarding Papers about Fundamental Theories," *Physical Review* 80 (18 July 1973): 357.

41. That is precisely the origin of the British Association for the Advancement of Science (Brush, *Kinetic Theory*, 1:17-19).

42. Gerald Holton, "On Being Caught between Dionysians and Apollonians," *Daedalus* 103/3 (1974): 65.

43. Hagstrom, *The Scientific Community*, 256ff.

44. See the discussion of stages of science in C. H. Waddington, *Behind Appearances* (Cambridge, MA: M. I. T. Press, 1970), 1-6.

45. The social sciences have a particularly difficult time in this connection. See Dankwart A. Rustow, "Relevance in Social Science, or the Proper Study of Mankind," *American Scholar* 40 (Summer 1971): 487.

46. Ravetz, "Immature and Ineffective Fields of Inquiry," *Scientific Knowledge*, chap. 14.

47. Gunther S. Stent, "Limits of the Scientific Understanding of Man," *Science* 187 (1975): 1052.

48. An instructive example from geophysics is discussed by A. Hallam, "Alfred Wegener and the Hypothesis of Continental Drift," *Scientific American* 232 (February 1975): 91.

49. As quoted in Hermann, *Die Hypothese der Lichtquanten*, 15.

50. As quoted in Heisenberg, *Physics and Beyond*, 276.

51. Karl Popper, *Conjectures and Refutations* (New York: Harper Torchbooks, 1968), 25.

52. Joseph Agassi, "Unity and Diversity in Science," in R. S. Cohen and M. W. Wartofsky, eds., *Boston Studies in the Philosophy of Science,* vol. 80 (Dordrecht: Reidel, 1969), 405.

53. Hugh Nibley, *Since Cumorah*, vol. 7, *The Collected Works of Hugh Nibley*, 2nd ed. (Salt Lake City: Deseret Book and F.A.R.M.S.,

1988), xiv. As this paper goes to press, the development of theories describing the dynamics of complex systems — "chaos theory," in the vernacular — are forcing us to question even the postulated connection between determinism and predictability that lies at the heart of the concept of causality in classical mechanics. As this field has developed, all of the issues of authoritative *vs.* authoritarian criticism of new science have been starkly outlined; readers with interests in the history of science may find James Gleick's bestselling *Chaos: Making a New Science* (New York: Penguin, 1987) especially instructive and entertaining. While the philosophical implications of chaos theory are by no means all worked out, it is clear that we shall be forced to confront the habits and mode of scientific discourse in profound new ways. All so much the better for both science and society, of course.

15

Language, Humour, Character, and Persona in Shakespeare

Arthur Henry King
Brigham Young University, Provo, Utah

The first *Oxford English Dictionary* (hereafter *OED*)[1] use of "character" as "a personality invested with distinctive attributes and qualities by a novelist or dramatist" is in Fielding's *Tom Jones* (1749). *OED* does not list the Theophrastian[2] use reflected in sixteenth- and seventeenth-century character-sketches, for example Ben Jonson's play, *Every Man Out of His Humour*, "the characters of the persons" (1599),[3] those in the then current satires, and in translations and collections.[4]

Another *OED* entry under character, "personal appearance" (entry 10) correctly interprets *Twelfth Night* 1.02.51 "outward character"; but that phrase implies "inward character" too, and *OED* misinterprets *Coriolanus* 5.04.26 as the outward sense; but "I paint him in the character" refers to this description of Coriolanus (16-28):

> He no more remembers his mother now than an eight-year-old horse. The tartness of his face sours ripe grapes. When he walks, he moves like an engine, and the ground shrinks before his treading. He is able to pierce a corslet with his eye, talks like a knell, and his hum is a battery. He sits in his state, as a thing made for Alexander. What he bids be done is finish'd with his bidding. He wants nothing of a god but eternity and a heaven to throne in. . . . I paint him in the character. . . . There is no more mercy in him than there is milk in a male tiger.

Compare *Coriolanus* 2.01.46-65, where Menenius sketches an ironical "character" of himself and makes "character" statements about the tribunes:

> I am known to be a humorous patrician, and one that loves a cup of hot wine with not a drop of allaying Tiber in't; said to be something imperfect in favoring the first complaint, hasty and tinder-like upon too trivial motion; one that converses more with the buttock of the night than with the forehead of the morning. What I think, I utter, and spend my malice in my breath. Meeting two such wealsmen as you are (I cannot call you Lycurguses), if the drink you give me touch my palate adversely, I make a crooked face at it. I cannot say your worships have deliver'd the matter well, when I find the ass in compound with the major part of your syllables; and though I must be content to bear with those that say you are reverend grave men, yet they lie deadly that tell you have good faces. If you see this in the map of my microcosm, follows it that I am known well enough too? What harm can your beesom conspectuities glean out of this character, if I be known well enough too?

So Shakespeare knew this use of "character," just as he was familiar with "humour." But to which, if any, of his own *dramatis personae* would he have applied the terms? Which would have been taken so by his audience? Which could we now agree to be "humour" or "character"? How do the terms affect our view of what we now call "characters" (in the sense in which Fielding used it in *Tom Jones*, 1749, and as it has been used since)?

The character-sketch *genre*, strictly Theophrastian or not, ethical, social, or both, combines typical traits (often "humorous" in at least two senses) with generalizations, and reaches its highest expression in La Bruyère[5] (whose link with Molière is clear). The genre descends through *Spectator, Tatler,*[6] and Fielding to a nineteenth-century situation in which the word "character" could cover Flora

Finching in Dickens' *Little Dorrit* and Eugene Wrayburn in his *Our Mutual Friend*—far too broad a category and one from whose breadth we still suffer. It is what we today would call a caricature or even a cartoon.

Though both derive from Greek physiology and psychology, we can probably agree that the "humour"[7] differs from the "character" by having a dominant trait, whereas the "character" represents a number of traits embodied in a portrait. Though I dare not say that Shakespeare would have found this abstract distinction worth making, I will try to exemplify it as a sketch for some temporary scaffolding that may prove useful.

The dominant trait is normally expressed through a linguistic one. Examples:

> Pistol (bombastic scraps).
> Nym (the word "humour" in possible and impossible senses).
> The Host of the Garter (exclamatory allocution and epanalepsis—compare Juniper in Ben Jonson's play, *The Case is Altered* [ca. 1597-98], Tucca in Jonson's play, *Poetaster* [1601], and in Thomas Dekker's play *Satiromastix* [1602], and Lucio's parody in *Measure for Measure* 3.02.43-85 of "this tune, matter, and method" [48]).
> Slender (the language of a provincial fool); a "la" man—he shares this with only one other male, Pandarus.
> Evans and Fluellen (too busy being Welsh to be much else).
> Caius (being French—cf. Doctor Dodypoll).
> Shallow (senile recollections; epizeuxis and epanalepsis; NB this is Shallow in *Henry IV*, Part 2; his function in *The Merry Wives of Windsor* makes him less senile).
> Dull, Dogberry, and Elbow (malapropisms).
> Osric (periphrastic complement laboured to the absurd).
> Probably Holofernes (as a synonymic pedant) but not Armado.

Probably Thersites (speaking in contemporary prose not unlike Jonson's, and using accumulatory invective with comparisons drawn largely from disease) but not Jacques.

Would it be true to say that we could introduce these into a Jonson play without disturbing the atmosphere?

I cannot imagine Shakespeare's thinking of the following as humours; but, in view of Menenius' remarks, he might well have called them "characters." They have not dominant traits, but are complete portraits in language consistent from beginning to end. They are, in fact, static; they end as they began:

> Nurse, Mrs. Quickly, Casca, Jacques, Belch (but not Falstaff), Sir Andrew (very different from Slender), Malvolio, Polonius (but not Menenius), Lucio (he provides an interesting contrast between "character" and "humour" by the parody of Tucca I have already mentioned above).

Each of these "characters" has determined to be what he presents himself as, which means that there is a touch of caricature in them all.

Armando presents a problem: he apparently repents, but his language does not:

> For mine own part, I breathe free breath. I have seen the day of wrong through the little hole of discretion, and I will right myself like a soldier (*Love's Labour's Lost* 5.02.722-25).

but contrast 882-87:

> I will kiss thy royal finger, and take leave. I am a votary; I have vow'd to Jacquenetta to hold the plough for her sweet love three year. But, most esteemed greatness, will you hear the dialogue that the two learned men have compiled in praise of the owl and the cuckoo?

We may regard his repentance as his final posture.

Parolles' repentance *is* reflected in his language:

> Yet am I thankful. If my heart were great,
> 'Twould burst at this. Captain I'll be no more,
> But I will eat and drink, and sleep as soft
> As captain shall. Simply the thing I am
> Shall make me live. Who knows himself a braggart,
> Let him fear this; for it will come to pass
> That every braggart shall be found an ass.
> Rust sword, cool blushes, and, Parolles, live
> Safest in shame! Being fool'd, by fool'ry thrive!
> There's place and means for every man alive
> (*All's Well That Ends Well* 4.03.330-39).

Cf. also 5.02 and 5.03.238-66; he is not a "character."

To clarify our categories, may we regard Bodadilla as a humour, Armado as a "character," and Parolles as a person?

This brings us to *persona*. We have hitherto been dealing with matters that are major in Jonson and Molière, but minor in Shakespeare. Our consideration of *persona* is the reason for our preliminary consideration of the trivialities of humour and character.

I use the word *persona* to be able to retain the sense "mask," for which "person" has apparently not been used. I remember here Yeats's comment that we can be more ourselves with a mask on than without it. At the same time, the Latin form covers also the main English senses I have in mind: "role," "appearance," and "individual." "Person" also makes a distinction between ourselves and other animals.

The ancient Greeks had "characters" not only by Theophrastus, but before him by Plato in the *Republic*—for example, the stages of the character of the tyrant; and Aristophanes parodied real people (e.g., Cleon, Euripides, Socrates), making fun of their language. Such parts in Aristophanes appear to be static and may well be classed with "characters."

However, Aeschylus and Sophocles put on the stage *personae,* who are not particularly distinguished by their language (any more than are the people in Homer) but appear to live (Oedipus, Orestes) somewhat as Shakespeare's *personae* do. For the distinction that I am trying to make, therefore, I take the word "persona" to be a part for the interpretation of an actor or producer, covering, not a set of trait-dominated speeches, or of speeches "in character," but a sequence of varying stylistic experiences. Shakespeare's major parts are not linguistically consistent and their linguistic inconsistencies set up tensions, ironies, and ambiguities fundamental to their nature. We need to remain open-minded in our interpretations, and not to think of these parts, any more than we think of ourselves, as obviously consistent people. There may be consistency—it may ultimately be felt—but it comes after a full and open consideration of all the uncertainties and inconsistencies, after experiencing and living the part. It can be talked about but not formulated. And beyond each part, there is a relationship of the parts to the play as a whole, a whole which can be talked about, but not formulated. A *persona* and a play are never formulae.

We might think of two examples from artists at Shakespeare's own level of genius and not so distant from him in time: Michelangelo's *Last Judgment* with its inclusion of Charon's boat, a vigorous, beardless Christ, and the artist's own face attached to St. Bartholomew's flayed skin; or of Bernini's *St. Theresa* in coital/mystical ecstasy; or of Bernini putting his own head on the statue of slinging David. We ought to be neither so strong nor so crude as to say "either," "or," but rather to say "both." "Bothness" involves irony, but that is inevitable: where there is more than one set of values there is irony.

Though visual examples are clearer, bearing in mind Michelangelo and Bernini is not enough. We might recollect also the ambivalence of the end of *Faust,* with its juxtaposition of a Roman Catholic mysticism verging on the absurd, Mephistopheles' homosexual enthusiasm for young angels, and the final dubious remark about the influence of the eternal feminine; or the ambivalence of Ibsen's *Brand* and *Peer Gynt* (or for that matter most of his plays). Or which posturings of Beethoven's middle period are self-betraying romantic self-assertion, and which dramatic conveniences to convey a deeper irony than the romantic one.

This brings us to posturing. If we are to consider the *personae* of Shakespeare's own time we have to consider the dramatic posturing of that time. The most important element here is Seneca.[8] We are familiar with the crudities of those Elizabethan translations; we have admired Eliot for getting something out of them, and above all for drawing the line forward to what Marlowe made of Seneca and in particular that element of the grotesque which Eliot exemplified in "Cassandra sprawling in the streets," and "swung her howling in the empty air." Eliot might have gone further and indicated the series of evermore refined and varied effects that Shakespeare, knowing little of Greek tragedy, developed from the Senecan tradition. We may need to recognize that most of Shakespeare's work is "posturing." Is *Titus Andronicus* deliberately absurd? Or at least grotesque? What part has the Player's speech in Hamlet in the development? How much of Shakespeare's greatest parts may be described as super-Senecan rant?

As we bear in mind this unexampled progress of Shakespeare from *Titus Andronicus* to *Coriolanus*, do we not need to remember that Shakespeare's age made no distinction between aesthetic and moral judgments? Bad language is associated with bad conduct, good language with good. "Language most shewes a man: speake that I may see thee."[9]

I have been trying in this long parenthesis quickly to establish some universe of discourse among us before exemplifying the sequencing of styles in the treatment of *personae*. Now let us go back to Menenius. He was wrong about Coriolanus: he painted Coriolanus in the character, but it was not Coriolanus's character, because Coriolanus is not a "character." His vituperative choler is given, as is its occasional incoherence. But they do not prepare us for 2.01.175-79,

> My gracious silence, hail!
> Wouldst thou have laugh'd had I come coffin'd
>   home,
> That weep'st to see me triumph? Ah, my dear,
> Such eyes the widows in Corioles wear,
> And mothers that lack sons,

or the entirely reasonable political statements of 3.01.91-161, which are not opportunist but grimly true to an important political standpoint — and the language in which they are expressed is worthy of their importance. Coriolanus is also an imaginative and reasonable man.

Now consider his two soliloquies in 4.04 at Antium (the only time when he is alone with himself).

> A goodly City is this Antium. City,
> 'Tis I that made thy widows; many an heir
> Of these fair edifices 'fore by wars
> have I heard groan and drop. Then know me not,
> Lest that thy wives with spits and boys with stones
> In puny battle slay me.

There is a grimly self-parodic humour in the last two lines. The second soliloquy,

> O world, thy slippery turns! Friends now fast sworn,
> Whose double bosoms seem to wear one hart,
> Whose hours, whose bed, whose meal and exercise
> Are still together, who twin, as 'twere, in love
> Unseparable, shall within this hour,
> On a dissension of a doit, break out
> To bitterest enmity,

echoes in a *Midsummer Night's Dream's* (3.02.203-8) atmosphere of mechanical treachery.

> We, Hermia, like two artificial gods,
> Have with our needles created both one flower,
> Both on one sampler, sitting on one cushion,
> Both warbling of one song, both in one key,
> As if our hands, our sides, voices, and minds
> Had been incorporate.

And indeed the soliloquy as a whole reflects a simplistic
sense of fate and fortune (probably ironic) which is not at
all the political maturity of *Coriolanus* 3.01.

But most remarkable is the stylistic sequence of *Coriolanus* 5.03: the contradictions of 22-37 with the grotesque
of "as if Olympus to a molehill" should "In supplication
nod" and "such a gozling"; his address to his wife he
himself characterizes as "I prate" (48), if we are to accept
Theobald's conjecture. The climax of his artificial self-pro-
tection comes in the ironic rant of his comment on his
mother's kneeling to him (58-62),

> Your knees to me? to your corrected son?
> Then let the pibbles on the hungry beach
> Fillop the stars; then let the mutinous winds
> Strike the proud cedars 'gainst the fiery sun,
> Murd'ring impossibility to make
> What cannot be, slight work,

and the ironically exaggerated complement of his address
to Valeria (64-67):

> The noble sister of Publicola,
> The moon of Rome, chaste as the icicle
> That's curdied by the frost from purest snow
> And hangs on Dian's temple — dear Valeria!

Note also the contrast between the register of his address to his son (70-75), and the register of the boy's own
later comment on the situation (127-28):

> 70. The god of soldiers,
> With the consent of supreme Jove, inform
> Thy thoughts with nobleness, that thou mayest
>   prove
> To shame unvulnerable, and stick i' th' wars
> Like a great sea-mark, standing every flaw,
> And saving those that eye thee!
> 127. 'A shall not tread on me;
> I'll run away till I am bigger, but then I'll fight.

Coriolanus's self-defense is marked as futile by its artificiality. He collapses into simplicity at 182-89.

> O mother, mother!
> What have you done? Behold, the heavens do ope,
> The gods look down, and this unnatural scene
> They laugh at. O my mother, mother! O!
> You have won a happy victory to Rome;
> But, for your son, believe it—O, believe it—
> Most dangerously you have with him prevail'd,
> If not most mortal to him (cf. *Hamlet* 2.02.122).

We cannot believe after this sequence of very different styles and the development which it connotes that Coriolanus could merely revert to vituperative choler in 5.06.102-29 too. We can only presume that he allows his mechanical rage to take over as a means of inciting the Volscians to kill him: he sets his own mousetrap. This interpretation fulfills the development that Shakespeare's variations of style seem to point to and allows Coriolanus a "successful" death instead of one forced upon him by infantile regression.

A few comments on the stylistic variety that is given to Hamlet. We are all familiar with the way in which he plays the Fool with Polonius, with Rosencrantz and Guildenstern, and with Claudius. Not all of us perhaps would agree on how serious his monologues may be. The exclamatorily confused if not actually anacoluthic syntax of *Hamlet* 1.02.129-59 appears to point to a confused spontaneity, but in that case what are those classical references to Hyperion, to Niobe, and to Hercules doing? And above all why is he making a deliberate joke about himself in "but two months dead, nay, not so much, not two" (138), "within a month" (145), "a little month" (147), and "within a month" (153), particularly since he carried that joke further in 3.02.127: "and my father died within 's two hours." The syntactical confusion is repeated again in "So oft it chances" (1.04.23-38) — all one sentence and probably incomplete at that. What about the reference to "my tables" in 1.05.107? The grotesque interview reported by Ophelia in 2.01.74-97? The deliberately affected letter which fits in with that grotesque appearance (2.02.109-28), a letter which the Queen finds it hard to believe, came from Hamlet (114). There is the player's speech with its kitchen imagery: "Bak'd and impasted" (459), "roasted" (461), and "mincing" (514); its compounding of pedantic and Anglo-Saxon: e.g., "coagulate gore" (462); and "see . . . a silence" (483-85) — compare *A Midsummer Night's Dream* 5.01.192-93:

> I see a voice! Now will I to the chink,
> To spy and I can hear my Thisby's face —

Do these point to an example of Hamlet's taste or may his attitude be regarded as "camp"?

"O that this" (1.02.129-59) and "O all you hosts" (1.05.92-106) are exclamatory and lead to nothing. A third exclamatory monologue, "O what a rogue" (2.02.550-87), apparently leads to an excited decision but one already taken: Hamlet has already considered in some detail what to do with the forthcoming play (540-43).

Three of the monologues are in a reflective rather than an exclamatory style. Two of them seem to be tryings-on-for-size of an attitude ("To be" — 3.01.55-87 and "Now might I do it" — 3.03.73-95). "How all occasions" (4.04.32-66) does lead to a decision on a posture ("from this time forth, My thoughts be bloody, or be nothing worth!")

which Hamlet seemingly for the purpose of contrasting himself with Fortinbras? "Now might I do it" (3.03.75-96), if it was Senecan, might lead to assassination; but instead it is a frivolous piece of reasoning for taking no action. "To be" may be compared with the Duke-Friar's speech in *Measure for Measure* 3.01.1-41, a speech which provides completely unchristian advice and is ineffective (cf. Claudio's reaction, 117-31). The fundamental point about the "To be" speech is not whether he is knowingly doing it in front of Ophelia and possibly other listeners, but whether he is posturing or not; and the answer is that he is posturing—to himself or others, and certainly to the audience.

Hamlet's super-Senecan element (which he shares with his father in 1.05) comes out in 92-106 ("O all you hosts of heaven"), 2.02.550-81 ("O what a rogue and peasant slave am I"), 3.02.388-96 (" 'Tis now the very witching time of night"), a good deal of 3.04 (the interview between mother and son); but not in the final interchanges while he is dying (5.02.331-58). Hamlet reacts vigorously against an earlier stage of Senecanism in Laertes's outburst at the grave of Ophelia (5.01.246-54) by parodying it (254-58, 269-71, 274-83). I think everybody is agreed about this, but they may not be agreed about recognizing the style of this as that of the player's speech Hamlet purports to admire.

Another aspect of Hamlet's stylistic changes which may not sufficiently have been dealt with is the gusto of the passage in 3.02.271-95 ("the strooken deer," etc., shared with Horatio), of the letter about the pirates in 4.06, and above all of the "Up from my cabin" account to Horatio in 5.02.12-70 (which covers not only his intense pleasure in success, but also his parody of his uncle's style, his gloating over the fate of Guildenstern and Rosencrantz, and his need to defend to Horatio what he has done about them). We may well have in these scenes Hamlet's own straightforward style, but it is not one that distinguishes him from others. What distinguishes him as a *persona* is the variation in sequencing of the styles he adopts, though none of these is by itself peculiar to him; for example, his style as a Fool is mostly of the "absolute" kind that links him with Feste, Lear's Fool, and to some extent with Touchstone. As a Fool he has a higher absoluteness paralleled by the lower absoluteness of the First Gravedigger. And his syntactic complexity (at times almost turgidity) he shares with Fincentio, with Claudius, and with Prospero in Prospero's account of his dethronement (though the cause of that complexity may in each case be different).

Complex as Hamlet's series of rhetorical stances is, critics seem more able to accept his lack of dignity than they are willing to admit the dubiety of Othello's rhetoric. On the whole, Othello remains the prisoner of his own rhetoric from 1.02 to his very last speech (the comment on which by Lodovico is "O bloody period," which can hardly not be a quibble). Iago's characterization of Othello's wooing of Desdemona as "fantastical lies" (2.01.223-24) is not incorrect. There appear to be threatening lies in 3.04.55-75, when Othello gives an account of a handkerchief which, in contrast to the grim, witchlike atmosphere that Othello weaves around it, has a strawberry pattern (3.03.435).

There are, however, points in the development of Othello that take him beyond the region of a "Character," a mere superbraggart at the top end of the scale beginning with Bobadilla and passing through Armado and Parolles. There is the unfortunate disclaimer of Desdemona's marital affection (1.03.248-59) by his favorseeking 261-74 ("Vouch with me heaven I therefore beg it not"). The jargon of this is striking: "Comply with heat (the young affects in me defunct)," "serious and great business," "light wing'd toys of feather'd Cupid," "wanton dullness," "speculative and offic'd instruments," "my disports corrupt and taint my business," etc. There is Othello's determination (apparently based on pride and a sense of inferiority) not to

confront Desdemona with the accusations against her in-
fidelity. There is his outburst of intense vicious rage when
Desdemona has been "raised up" (2.03.250-51). There is
the pact between Othello and Iago which mounts from
low-Senecan ("Arise, black vengeance, from the hollow
hell," 3.03.447) to the super-Senecan of "Like to the Pontic
Sea . . . I here engage my words" (453-62). Iago enters the
pact in the same register (463-69), and it is problematic
whether this is to be regarded as parody, or whether Iago
has lost himself with Othello in the enthusiasm of hate.
There is certainly a special bond between Iago and Othello
in the sense that the one is satanically passionate to tempt
and the other infernally eager to be tempted. There is the
inability of Othello to go outside his rhetorical stance except
into chaos. This happens at 4.01.35-43, where it ends in a
fit; and again at 5.02.276-82, where he descends from
super-Senecanism to standard declamation ("O cursed
slave. . . . O Desdemon! Dead"); and declines into mere
rolling exclamation. As for his final speech, we have been
familiar with the alternatives since Eliot wrote about it, but
Eliot's "cheering himself up," though a keen pointer, does
not cover the consonance of this final speech with the
whole of the play.

We are given the revelatory contrast with all this rhetoric in Desdemona's simple final words (5.02.124-25): "Nobody, I myself. Farewell! Commend me to my kind lord.
O, farewell!"

Othello's sequence is thus very different from that of
Coriolanus or Hamlet: he opens up to a potential experience with Desdemona, he can match her simplicity
(4.01.195-96, "but yet the pity of it, Iago! O Iago, the pity
of it, Iago!"); but reverts to his Senecan savagery ("I will
chop her into messes. Cuckold me!" 197) and to the rhetorical carapace by which he conceals himself from others
and from himself.

It is easier to accept the stylistic sequencing in *Lear*. In

Lear himself the super-Senecan rant is shown up by the
Fool's running commentary and by Kent's realism. The
height of this rant is reached in 3.02.59-60: "I am a man
more sinn'd against than sinning," which is a simple statement, but a hardening and not a softening one; followed
immediately by "my wits begin to turn." Before entering
the Fool's world, which is the way to mental health, Lear
shows sympathy with the outcasts (one of whom he now
is), but in the wrong register—his own injustice and that
of the heavens are mixed up in his mind and these are not
the words of a broken heart and a contrite spirit (3.04.28-
36). The Fool's role extends to Edgar's simulated role at
the bottom of the world; but Lear's criticism is still directed
at society and still alternates with self-assertion (4.06.83-
187). However, the posturing ends in 4.07.43-84, a simplicity shared between father and daughter.

There is no more posturing in Lear after this, unless
his endeavor to comfort his daughter in 5.03.8-25 should
be so regarded; but if so, it is a posture of a very different
kind. There is posturing in the rest of 5.03, especially by
Edgar, but that demands treatment on another occasion;
as does the question of the button (5.03.310). I would confine myself here to saying that utter simplicity has its interpretive difficulties as much as extreme complexity. However, rhetorically speaking one would need to take the most
famous epizeuxis in all literature ("Never, never, never,
never, never" 311) as a slow one, and note that the epan-
alepsis and alliteration of 311-12 ("Do you see this? Look
on her! Look her lips. Look there, look there!") express a
quickening and an excitement. The alliteration emphasizes
lips and the question narrows down to "What is to be
looked for on her lips?" My own belief is that the button
is not Lear's but Cordelia's, that its undoing releases some
pent-up breath from the dead lungs, that there is some
movement of the lips in consequence, and that Lear dies
in the belief that Cordelia is alive (a matter that has symbolic

importance for the play). But to dispute about this final passage is unnecessary: the climax of the play is not here, but in 4.07.43-84.

I suggested that the sequencing of Lear's part was exemplary. I say so because the development is carefully monitored, can be made clear dramatically in the part on the stage, and issues in one of the supreme scenes (if not the supreme scene) of all literature: 4.07.

In Lear the sequencing has an upward movement. The movement in Macbeth's part is downward and this may well have been the main reason why Lear has been regarded as the greater play and indeed as Shakespeare's greatest. However, that should not disguise the fact that in many points the sequencing of Macbeth's part is more subtle than that of Lear.

I have hitherto been talking artificially about the sequencing in isolation of a part, in order to simplify what I am trying to show. It was almost impossible to do this in *Lear*, since the sequencing of Cordelia's part needs to be seen in parallel with that of her father; but when we come to *Macbeth*, it is impossible to handle the sequencing of Macbeth's part without dealing with Lady Macbeth also. Here, again, I must confine myself to points that are not usually stressed.

Senecan rising to super-Senecan is dominant for them both, and that is no wonder since Macbeth is introduced to us in 1.02 as a butcher (22, "He unseam'd him from the nave to the chops") and is dismissed as a butcher in 5.09.25 — "this dead butcher and his fiendlike queen." Lady Macbeth's "Come, you spirits" (1.05.40-54), although far more imaginative and linguistically rich than Seneca, nevertheless resembles Seneca's *Medea* and through it the source in Euripides.

About the sensitivity in Macbeth's earlier monologues: a good part of it is fear of being found out and apprehension of public opinion against the dead. "If 'twere done, when 'tis done" (1.07.1-28) moves from an apparently rational consideration of disadvantages into a much-admired chaotic hyperbole; but note the oxymoron of a "naked newborn babe *Striding* the blast," and the grotesque fancy that blowing "the horrid deed in every eye" will produce enough tears to drown the wind (it takes a heavy rainstorm to do that). The oxymoron, the irrelevance of "sightless," the Baroque "blowing," and the hyperbole add up to something grotesque rather than noble: "Pity" is Macbeth's enemy in working up public opinion against the deed. Blake's illustration only succeeds in accentuating the posture. And indeed the tone of the monologue immediately drops to Macbeth's reflection about his own inadequacy as an excuse for not daring to do what he wants to do.

The theatricality of "Is this a dagger" (2.01.33-64) shows Macbeth's imagination helping his resolution rather than detracting from it. Having dismissed the dagger as an illusion, he proceeds to paint a night-picture which fills him full of dramatic importance (the posture is not merely super-Senecan in language but Senecan in implied stage-directions). Thus both monologues emphasize sensitiveness by its suppression. True sensitiveness would have conjured up the image of Duncan on arrival at the castle, at the banquet, and now in sleep.

The sense of pleasure in his own importance which is adumbrated in 2.01.49-64 — "Now o'er the one half world," is carried further and made more clear when he makes his bloody hands bearable by envisioning the crime on a cosmic scale and discovering in so doing that he is beginning to take pleasure in slaughter (2.02.57-60).

> Will all great Neptune's ocean wash this blood
> Clean from my hand? No; this my hand will rather
> The multitudinous seas incarnadine,
> Making the green one red.   ·

"The multitudinous sea incarnadine," with its two neologisms, shows a pleasure in language which denote this deeper pleasure, and enables us to see more than artificiality and suspectness in 2.03.111-15:

> Here lay Duncan,
> His silver skin lac'd with his golden blood,
> And his gash'd stabs look'd like a breach in nature
> For ruin's wasteful entrance; there, the murtherers,
> Steep'd in the colors of their trade, their daggers
> Unmannerly breech'd with gore.

The affectation in this last passage has long been seen as evidence of Macbeth's guilt; all that I maintain now is that the same kind of evidence is present in various kinds of artificiality in Macbeth's language throughout; and that we may extend, by careful rhetorical inspection, this category of artificial language, revealing the buried intent of many speeches in Shakespeare's plays that may in the past have been admired "for themselves."

Macbeth's almost gloating trend is carried still further by the twilight meditation of 3.02.46-56. The language in which he describes the scene enables him to consider the process of nature as assistant to the crime he is having committed. The reaction to Banquo's ghost in 3.04. is not pity for what Banquo has been reduced to, as a mangled piece of flesh, and not repentance at having ordered this transformation, but a combination of fear and anger at being disturbed, an accusation to the ghost for behaving unnaturally, indignation that ghosts should be allowed to do these things, and an attempt to exorcise the phenomenon. All these posturing processes enable him to hide from himself the real horror: not what the ghost of Banquo looks like, not his threat to Macbeth, but the mere fact that Macbeth has had him murdered.

From now on Macbeth's paranoid posture of defiance and destruction is fixed, any compunction unreal nostalgia (5.03.22-28—"I have lived long enough"), combined with self-pity. A posturing self-pity combined with cheap phi-losophizing celebrates his wife's death ("Tomorrow and tomorrow and tomorrow" 5.05.19-28) and leads to the final part of the sequence—the pseudo-heroic man of battle on the field as he was described to us at the beginning of the play.

It remains to bring out more clearly than is usually done the struggle for power between Lady Macbeth and Macbeth. Lady Macbeth appears to be the dominant figure at the beginning, but it was not she who took the initiative in broaching the question, and it is not she who carries out the deed. As soon as Macbeth is ensconced as king he withdraws his confidence from her and proceeds to plot on his own (and from then on she lives in constant fear of their being found out). He apparently has a relapse at the banquet and she has to sustain him; but actually he is in a state of defiance beyond being found out. After the banquet scene, in any case, he keeps himself entirely to himself, and it is the apparently more courageous Lady Macbeth who collapses: she turns out to be more depend-ent on him than he on her. In the sleepwalking scene she uses the simplest of language, but it is not the language of repentance or even remorse; she is concerned in her dream with getting rid of the evidence and that seems to be the main reason for saying, "Yet who would have thought the old man to have had so much blood in him," (5.01.39-40) which is a coarse rather than a pitying remark. In saying "the Thane of Fife had a wife" (42-43) with its kind of rhyming tag, she is more likely to be drawing a parallel between herself and Macduff's wife than pitying her: she may even be apprehensive that Macbeth's next step will be to get rid of herself because she is now more likely to give the game away than he. There is also a touch of narcissistic self-pity in "all the perfumes of Arabia will not sweeten this little hand" (5.01.50-101). Simple though

Lady Macbeth's language is, it does not by any means reveal a simple state of mind.

The complex sequencing of Cleopatra's part is well known to us all, but I would wish to concentrate on two passages where I think this complexity has not been sufficiently brought out, the first of which involves one of Shakespeare's developments of Senecan style.

In 4.15.9-11 she reaches the highest level of super-Senecan declamation

> O Sun,
> Burn the great sphere thou mov'st in! darkling stand
> The varying shore o' th' world!

But levels change quickly in this scene and when Antony asks to "speak a little" Cleopatra interrupts at 43-45, "no, let me speak, and let me rail so high, That the false huswife Fortune break her wheel, Provok'd by my offense." Note "rail" and the Fortune image. Her interruption is a distinctly comic point followed by the comic point of Antony's recommending Proculeius to Cleopatra, whereas he is going to be Cleopatra's betrayer (5.02.9-64). At the death of Antony, Cleopatra has lines which we all agree have the poet's full musical endorsement (4.13.62-68).

> O, see, my women:
> The crown o' th' earth doth melt. My lord!
> O, wither'd is the garland of the war,
> The soldier's pole is fall'n! Young boys and girls
> Are level now with men; the odds is gone,
> And there is nothing left remarkable
> Beneath the visiting moon.

When she recovers from her swoon she continues in the same tone.

> No more but e'en a woman, and commanded
> By such poor passion as the maid that milks

And does the meanest chares (73-75).

But this is immediately followed by a Senecan passage at a much lower level which recurs to railing (75-82).

> It were for me
> To throw my sceptre at the injurious gods,
> To tell them that this world did equal theirs
> Till they had stol'n our jewel. All's but naught:
> patience is sottish, and impatience does
> Become a dog that's mad. Then is it sin
> To rush into the secret house of death
> Ere death dare come to us?

This is again succeeded by a few lines of simple and natural language that in its turn modulates once more into super-Senecanism (86-89):

> and then, what's brave, what's noble,
> Let's do't after the high Roman fashion,
> And make death proud to take us. Come, away,
> This case of that huge spirit now is cold.

The railing is still there in the protest to Proculeius (5.02.49-62),

> Sir, I will eat no meat, I'll not drink sir;
> If idle talk will once be necessary
> I'll not sleep either. This mortal house I'll ruin,
> Do Caesar what he can. Know, sir, that I
> Will not wait pinion'd at your master's court,
> Nor once be chastis'd with the sober eye
> Of dull Octavia. Shall they hoist me up,
> And Show me to the shouting valotry
> Of censuring Rome? Rather a ditch in Egypt
> Be gentle grave unto me! rather on nilus' mud
> Lay me stark-nak'd, and let the water-flies
> Blow me into abhorring! rather make
> My country's high pyramides my gibbet,
> And hang me up in chains!

and in the attack (or pseudo-attack) on Seleucus (154-58).

The second passage is quite different. It has the Senecan hyperbole about it, but it seems to combine Seneca with a touch of Rabelais and one wonders whether Cleopatra is not, for part of this passage at least, trying to bemuse Dolabella.

> His face was at the heav'ns, and therein stuck
> A sun and moon, which kept their course, and
>   lighted
> The little O, th' earth . . .
> His legs bestrid the ocean, his rear'd arm
> Crested the world, his voice was propertied
> As all the tuned spheres, and that to friends;
> But when he meant to quail and shake the orb,
> He was as rattling thunder. For his bounty,
> There was no winter in't; an autumn it was
> That grew the more by reaping. His delights
> Were dolphin-like, they show'd his back above
> The element they liv'd in. In his livery
> Walk'd crowns and crownets; realms and islands
>   were
> As plates dropp'd from his pocket (5.02.79-92).

Note in particular "stuck A sun and moon" which is certainly grotesque as a comparison to two similar eyes. "His legs bestrid the ocean, his rear'd arm Crested the world" is an interesting reminiscence of Cassius' description of Caesar and both seem to have a ring of irony in them. The Rabelaisian touch is rather "in his livery Walk'd crowns and crownets"; realms and islands were "As plates dropp'd from his pocket." But in between we have

> For his bounty,
> There was no winter in't; an autumn it was
> That grew the more by reaping. His delights
> Were dolphin-like, they show'd his back above
> The element they liv'd in.

Here Cleopatra modulates not into super-Senecanism but

a strain of the poet's musical endorsement in praise of generosity, including erotic generosity.

The musical endorsement of Cleopatra's end from the entry of Iras with the robe crown, etc., down to Charmian's last words to the soldier I dare say none of us will deny; but it is worth pointing out two humorous touches of a kind which in his other passages of the highest musical endorsement Shakespeare does not use. One is the humorous eroticism of 312: "Nay, I will take thee too" in the midst of the murmurings by which Cleopatra equates death and coitus; and the other is made by Charmian, who produces an ironical parallel in matching "ass unpolicied" (307-8) with "lass unparallel'd" (316). This is one of Shakespeare's finest effects in his combination of high music with the placing of Octavius definitely in a low world; a placing confirmed immediately afterwards by Octavius' entering and pursuing the cause of death like a less effective Lord Peter.

The syntactically, if not lexically, conversational simplicity of Shakespeare at his highest points does not flourish in solitude. This kind of experience can be had only by sharing—not singly between a *persona* and the audience, but between a *persona* and others on the stage and audience. The height of Cleopatra's death scene could not be reached without Iras, Charmian, and the entry of the guard. Indeed, it may well be that the climax of the whole thing and the best contrast with the Senecanism and the super-Senecanism with which we have had to deal is, "It is well done, and fitting for a princess descended of so many royal kings" (5.02.326-27).

The experience of a shared simplicity is also the essence of the reconciliation scene between Cordelia and Lear, as it is of Prospero's repentance at *The Tempest* 5.01.20: "Mine would, sir, were I human" (Ariel), "And mine shall" (Prospero). The sharing widens in 200-213 when Gonzalo (who, not Prospero, is the moral center of the play) bestows a blessing and praises the ways of providence. His comments lead us readily to the most prolonged of these shared scenes of simplicity, heightened by its being a kind of anagnoresis: the passage 5.03.21-128 in *The Winter's Tale's* final scene. The *Pericles* anagnoresis in 5.01.101-235 is not so convincing except for the passage 190-97 ("O Helicanus, strike me, honored sir"). But it does have a great deal of the simplicity we are talking about, and it is shared between father and daughter on stage and with an audience.

The most important point of this paper is to bring out the stylistic sequencing of a *persona* and consequently we have been concentrating artificially on protagonists. More important than the protagonists, however, is the rhetorical pattern of the play as a whole. This invariably follows the main line of the protagonist's part. It may, for example, as in *King Lear, The Winter's Tale, The Tempest,* be from complexity to simplicity; as in *Othello* and *Macbeth,* never emerge from the rhetorical prison except in contrasting moments ("the pity of it," "nobody; I myself," "He has no children"). Ophelia's madness no more relieves the riddle of *Hamlet* than Lady Macbeth's sleepwalking alleviates *Macbeth*. Horatio's simple "So Guildenstern and Rosencrantz go to't" (5.02.56) presents in a flash the whole problem of Hamlet's eternal future, a problem not solved by "Good night sweet prince, And flights of angels sing thee to thy rest!" (359-60) or by Hamlet's own "Absent thee from felicity a while" (5.02.347). With all that has gone before, Hamlet can hardly mean the felicity of existlessness, nor is Hamlet any more likely than Faust to be snatched up to the highest heaven. Yet there is a touch of musical endorsement about these two lines. *Coriolanus* proceeds, like *King Lear,* to a penultimate simplicity, but its ending, unlike that of *King Lear,* provides a further twist. *Measure for Measure* is written as if to crown us when Isabella kneels for Angelo's life, and her lines on the Atonement (2.02.73-79) with their musical endorsement seem to

promise us that; but instead we are given something rationally perfunctory. *Romeo and Juliet,* with the musical
sweep of the balcony scene and the aubade exchange of
the first eleven lines of 3.05, has to decline upon the super-
Senecan rhetoric of Romeo's final speech. In *Julius Caesar,*
political satire as it is, we have to content ourselves with
a mere few remarks between Brutus and Lucius which do
not reach lyrical height. In *Henry IV, Part 1,* and *Henry IV,
Part 2,* the Prince (not yet Prince Hamlet) moves up from
his shared amusement with Falstaff to the resolution but
not simplicity of kingship; while at the same time Falstaff,
in spite of his insight in Part 1 into the falsity of honour,
declines to greater and greater corruption and less and less
awareness of his impending fate in *Henry IV, Part 2.* The
sequencing of *Richard II* demonstrates how much more
complex and sensitive a play it is than *Edward II.* Shakespeare has not chosen to resolve for us whether *Richard II*
moves out of posturing into simplicity — the monologue of
5.05.1-66 does not make up for everything that has gone
before: sixty lines of two posturings lead to two contradictory reactions to the music he hears; and his final lines
are as much a posture as Caesar's last.

What is required of the highest dramatic solution is "a
condition of utter simplicity, costing not less than everything" — everything, that is except itself. If we are to look
for the cause of this type of dramatic construction where
individual posturing, self-assertion, and self-betrayal are
solved or not solved in a shared simplicity, we need to
look to the societies with which even the greatest were
produced and at odds, and in which hardly anything other
than ironical comment was possible (the introduction of
another world to come, could, once again, make possible
nothing but irony). Other societies have produced different
types of literature. In Homer, the gods may behave like
apotheosized feudal lords, and the relation of Odysseus
with Athene is hardly that of Christ with his Father; but

beyond all that is a sense of order and justice that Homer succeeds in making real and not fictive or fantastic. Vergil, with a deep sense of a peaceable agrarian society, had to reconcile singing for that with celebrating a gross and harsh imperium. Dante, placing his friends and enemies at appropriate points in the hereafter, could not but give Francesca an affectation of speech reminiscent of the discarded Provençal style—he would have found it impossible to use Abelard and Heloise. Goethe, constricted in Weimar but with some hopes of an open America, could finish his ironical *Faust*, but not his *Wilhelm Meister*. Cervantes, ranging the styles almost as variously as Shakespeare himself, produces the final scene of his great book at Don Quixote's deathbed; and Shakespeare himself conforms to the deeper Christianity at the base of his two corrupt contemporary churches by simply making Prospero's epilogue a prayer.

The sequencing of *personae* in the comedies up to *Twelfth Night* requires a separate paper, in which humour and courting would play the largest part, and the stress would lie on the complement derived from Arcadianism instead of on the Senecan strain. In those changed terms, the contrast of affectation with the genuine would remain the same.

Notes

1. *Oxford English Dictionary*, 13 vols. (Oxford: Clarendon, 1933, 1961, repr.), 2:281, entry 17.

2. Theophrastus (372-ca. 287 B.C.), Greek philosopher who wrote *Charakteres*, thirty brief character sketches outlining moral types, for ethical purposes.

3. "The Characters of the Persons" is a brief character summary of the primary "dramatis personae" in Ben Jonson's play *Every Man Out of His Humor*.

4. Theophrastus, *Characteres*, 8 vols. (Lyon: Le Preux, 1592); for other works by him see Mark Pattison, *Isaac Casaubon 1559-1614* (Oxford: Clarendon, 1892); cf. also Joseph Hall, *Meditations and Vows . . . with Characters of Virtues and Vices* (London: Fetherstone, 1621); also his *Virgidemise* ca. 1597, satires and character sketches in

A. Davenport, ed., *The Collected Poems of Joseph Hall* (Liverpool: University Press, 1949), 18-87.

5. Jean de La Bruyère (1645-1696), *Les Caractères* (1699); it accompanied his translation of Theophrastus' *Charakteres* and was written in the Theophrastian style which defined qualities (e.g., jealousy) and depicted them in sketches of actual people. La Bruyère commented on the "characteristics" of the age, attempting to reform behavior and morals.

6. *The Tatler* was a periodical printed in London from 1709-11 and written by essayists Richard Steele and Joseph Addison. It satirized manners, society, and ideals. It was succeeded by *The Spectator* (1711-12), another satirical periodical written by the same authors.

7. "Humour," as a dominant trait, derives from the early definition of "humour" as one of four bodily fluids (*OED* "humour" entry 1.1.2,2b) that determine "mental disposition, . . . constitutional tendency, . . . mood" (*OED* "Humour" entry 2.4,5). Shakespeare's knowledge of these usages is found in *Taming of the Shrew* 4.01.209, and *Richard III* 1.02.227-28.

8. Cf. T. S. Eliot, "Christopher Marlowe" and "Shakespeare and the Stoicism of Seneca," *Elizabethan Essays* (New York: Hasbell, 1964), 21-31, 33-54.

9. Cf. Ben Jonson, *Discoveries*, Maurice Castelain, ed. (Paris: Hachette, 1906), 104. This is the "oratio imago animi," the "language picture of the soul," or "language as a picture of the soul." The sentiment is from Apuleius, *Florida* 2, *The Works of Apuleius* (London: Bell, 1893), 374.

16

Talent and the Individual's Tradition: History as Art, and Art as Moral Response

Arthur Henry King and C. Terry Warner
Brigham Young University, Provo, Utah

For(e)bearance

In his essay, "Tradition and the Individual Talent," T. S. Eliot said that "not only the best, but the most individual parts of [the poet's] work may be those in which the dead poets, his ancestors, assert their immortality most vigorously."[1] The poet's ancestors are those to whom he is indebted for all that he has inherited—his language, his sensibility, his outlook, and his standards of conduct. He acknowledges his debt by letting these forebears speak through his work. Paradoxically, the more freely and fully he allows them to speak—which is to say the less he self-indulgently tries to make his work appear original with him—the more completely his work bears the stamp of his individuality. Tradition provides discipline; out of the discipline springs the unselfconscious and uncontrived quality of all good writing, which in this essay we will call "spontaneity."

Eliot wrote this essay before he was converted to An-

This essay originally appeared in a slightly different form in the unpublished "Tinkling Cymbals: Essays in Honor of Hugh Nibley," John W. Welch, ed., 1978.

glicanism. He thought he was describing a general cultural phenomenon, which is that a cultural tradition (for example, that of Europe) could liberate the artist who assimilated it. We agree with Eliot's thesis, but only if it is taken to its proper conclusion. That conclusion is that tradition will liberate the artist only if he becomes a guileless and self-forgetful individual, and we believe self-forgetfulness is possible only by yielding one's heart to God.

Why are assimilation of the tradition and personal self-forgetfulness indispensable qualities of a genuine artist? Why do we add this to Eliot's thesis? Because the artist's talent is more than flair and ability that he possesses naturally. It is also a sensitivity to the ways and heritage of his people; probably without being aware of it he speaks for them, because he uses the language and images bequeathed to his people by its forebears. So, in significant part, his talent is something entrusted to him by others, and it is just for this reason that using this talent self-servingly is forbidden. If he does (and nonuse, too, is a kind of self-service), what he will produce will be artificial. On the other hand, the tradition is given fresh life in and through artists who magnify their talents without self-regard. Nowhere else does literary tradition live. Nowhere but in such artists can a living past be encountered. Without them, ritual petrifies and folk art becomes sentimental or vulgar.

We have inverted the title of Eliot's essay because we want to express this modification of Eliot's thesis. The inversion expands the usual connotations of the terms "talent" and "tradition." It suggests that there is a strong sense in which talents are fully employed by individuals only when they do not regard them as their own (or simply, do not regard them), and that there is an equally strong sense in which tradition exists only in the form of individuals in whom it is reincarnated. We use this word rather than "transmitted" because it suggests that tradition is not merely transported intact by individuals along the passageway of time, but renewed and revitalized.

Eliot was thinking of the literary tradition in a way that comprehends the whole of that tradition, including the writing of philosophy, criticism, drama, social tracts, psychology, and history. What we have to say about the historian in this essay might be said (with appropriate adjustment of detail) about any practitioner of any literary art, and this is a point that needs to be kept firmly in mind if our thesis is to be intelligible. For our motivation in thinking about the subject is not accusatory. We would do ill to write of other people, present or past, as if their plight were not ours. Indeed, we have keenly felt the moral hazards that beset historians in our own disciplines of philology and philosophy.

The discipline that must be acquired in order to assimilate one's tradition is more than an accumulation of information. In the historian's case this discipline is a matter of care, in every sense of that word: carefulness in studying the random residue which past people have left of themselves and caring for them even though they are no longer with us. Without careful discipline there can be no incarnation of tradition, and without incarnation there is no individuality.

By defining the historian's discipline this way, we want to distinguish it from method. Method can be mastered and misused. For some practicing historians (philosophers, psychologists, and so forth), this is just what happens; their method is not simply the thoroughgoing care with which they set out a story of the past. Instead it is an affectation, a style deliberately adopted with an eye for professional legitimacy and success. In the writing of the disciplined historian who is absorbed in what is to be done rather than in any social advantage that might accrue from doing it, there is unmistakable freshness, individuality. On the other hand, the historian who employs method and style for social recognition's sake cannot duplicate these results. The reason is, in seeking recognition he is withholding part of himself from his work, controlling his response as a whole human being to historical situations in favor of what he thinks is an ideal response of a historian. However he may try to make it "original," his work will be stylistically stereotyped. He will produce less than he understands in order to conform to the accepted canons of historical writing. Method and rigor are necessary for the sort of historical work we want to praise, but not suf-ficient—just as the law is honored by all who live the gospel, but not all who live the law honor the gospel. Our subject, then, is the abuse of method which might be thought of as an academic analogue of self-righteousness. And our thesis is that those who are in the historian's profession primarily for themselves will, like the self-righ-teous, make sounds of brass.

Until recent years, stylistic anonymity among histori-ans for self-promotional purposes masqueraded as "ob-jectivity." But the issue is not an epistemological one about the possibility of telling the past's story *"wie es eigentlich gewesen ist,"* even though historiographers may have thought otherwise for decades. The issue is a psychological one about the quality of the historian's motivation. With the breakdown of philosophical positivism in our century, many historians have disclaimed any profession of objec-tivity, yet even some of these still assess one another's work against (largely tacit) methodological and stylistic norms. It is not the objectivity/subjectivity axis that should command our ultimate historiographical concern, but the purity-of-heart/impurity axis. The question is not whether the historian, like other craftsmen, colors what he makes with his own personality, for inevitably he does. Rather, the question is what sort of colors he gives it. Does he discolor it by harboring self-seeking intentions?

We have no disposition to pick on historians. Philosophers are probably even more self-crippling, because the modes of philosophical thinking are more explicit, canonized, and coercive than the modes of historical thinking. For example, many philosophers assume that, except in its most extreme speculative reaches, contemporary logic defines not only the standard of one type of discourse among others, but the single type of discourse in which certain kinds of truths may be stated. Historically, logic was no such standard; instead, it was considered a branch of rhetoric—and that in fact is what it is. To speak with philosophical precision is to adopt a very narrow register of human speech in which much that human beings experience cannot be expressed or described. Why would anyone speak so artificially? Why would anyone be willing to censor his responses as a whole person in deference to narrow philosophical canons of expression? Recent work in the rhetoric of scientific discourse suggests that at least some of the motives are self-assertion and professional legitimacy, and if there are others, we do not know them. So philosophers and historians alike make myths when they take themselves too seriously: when they promote themselves in their work. (Of course, this means not taking themselves seriously enough as individual human beings—trusting the canons of their discipline more than their own sensibility.)

Believing that a disciplinary method is a mode of knowing rather than a heuristic device for arranging material for specific purposes may not be simply an error. It may be a sin. The historian or philosopher who uses his discipline self-promotionally finds immediate promise of exoneration in the view that the discipline can validate his work independently of his intentions. He clings to the idea that his social purposes are professionally irrelevant. By this means, he provides himself with an alibi if his conscience accuses him of seeking his own interest. How can he be accused of coloring his materials, he insists, when his constant aim is to rid them of coloration? Preoccupation with technique and method fits Plato's definition of sophistry and pinpoints the self-seeking in it: one sends out a highly controlled signal in order to elicit a highly manipulated response. One can sin in scholarship as anywhere else. It is wrong in writing to do anything but write what is in us to be written.

Understanding Past People

The problem of understanding people in the past, including their policies and institutions, is only a form of the problem of understanding people generally. By setting out certain features of our ability to understand our contemporaries, we may illuminate the claims we are making about historical knowledge. Consider the following points:

Knowing *about* people is not knowing *them*; that is, it is not understanding them. One cannot but withdraw from other human beings — and thus render them humanly unreal — if one concentrates on what properties they have, for that construes them as objects. Nietzsche, Heidegger, Buber, Polanyi, and Levinas have all taught us this by numerous cogent insights. When we know a person, we know more than we can tell; and supposing otherwise is a mode of pushing that person away. Understanding people, as opposed to knowing about them, comes in the course of being with them unselfconsciously; it is a residuum of living in a sharing, trusting, and caring community with them. *Hence to observe people in order to know about them rather than to respond unguardedly to them is to withdraw from the conditions which must obtain if they are to be understood.*

Thus, acting as if one is an observing center rather than a person does not mean one is disinterested. Such action is an apparent self-obliteration in the form of a perceptual and stylistic anonymity which is actually an intense preoccupation with guarding, vindicating, and advancing the self. It is an intense form of self-assertion.

A historian can live with and understand past people only if he regards the accoutrements of his profession (the habits, the jargon, the frame of reference, and so forth) as inferior to, and less valuable than, himself as a man and any man as a man. Only then can he enter with unselfconscious empathy into others' situations.

The Historian as Tradition Incarnate

Contrast the self-seeking, depersonalizing writer of history with the guileless one. The former imposes generalizations and theories upon "the data." The latter expresses patterns of selection in his work that go beyond what he can deliberately produce or even completely comprehend. These living patterns of selection taken together are an expression of what he is as one who by historical study has assimilated tradition through his language, in his interaction with his immediate forebears. This tradition then expresses itself in his unselfconscious writing and teaching. And therefore what he produces is right. It is not false to what he transforms. When he speaks or writes it is as if history is finding one expression of its accumulating truth in his responses to that part of the world which has preceded him. The self-serving historian, on the other hand, stylizes what he comprehends of the past and thwarts the flow of tradition through him. He is untrue to the living tradition that has enabled him to become both a person and a historian.

If a historian accepts the gospel, he is adopted; he gains a new ancestry; a fresh heritage becomes active in him. His open, artless, and fresh way of seeing and speaking about the past will be a correlative, an expression, of the new person he has become. If purely motivated, he gives the history he has absorbed a spontaneous — that is, an unguarded and guileless — expression. That kind of expression is wisdom. On the other hand, the self-deceived historian performs something extraneous to the purpose of the history which had made him what he is, and he is thereby unfaithful to himself. And if he knows anything about the gospel, he is unfaithful to the Lord. He does not produce wisdom.

Let us further contrast generalization and wisdom. Generalizations are generally valid for general purposes; they are not valid for specific purposes. We may induce a generalization from a number of specifics, but when we have done so we find that it does not completely apply to any of them. Perhaps in natural science it could (or could it?), but historically it will not. Any generalization to be valid has to be one arising totally from a total specific situation, not a generalization inductively arrived at over many instances.

This is where the word "wisdom" comes in: We read history in order to gain the great historian's wisdom. In him we encounter a unique historical situation alive in a living, interfusing, and blending individual, the historian. And we discover in the nature of that unique totality something of the nature of all other unique totalities — something which cannot be expressed in any list of generalizations, however lengthy. That is why history is an art rather than a science (we are assuming, we suspect incorrectly, that there are in fact sciences, the essence of which can be expressed in a theory, i.e., in an adequate and consistent set of generalizations). It is why a fine history, like a Baucis-and-Philemon pitcher, is inexhaustible (though not unfathomable). There is no essential difference between the way in which Herodotus and Thucydides use their material and the way in which Aeschylus and Sophocles use theirs. The Swedish philosopher, Hans Larsson, said in 1892 (in spite of the shadow of Herbert Spencer) that social scientists should not ignore the fact that literature has given them far more subtle exemplars of human behavior than they themselves describe. (The converse is also true: When social scientists describe behavior well, they write literature; Adler is not literature but Freud is, and that is the only reason why Freud is worth more attention.)

The historian can be true to the history reposited within him only if he endeavors to give it the form that suits the whole of it, and not merely parts of it. In doing this, he is doing the same thing as someone who makes a poem. He should from this point of view recognize himself as an artist and realize that his totality of knowledge should be expressed through a totality of means. The historian who has a style that is true to him will produce history that is also true to him, and because it is true to him in this naive sense it will have truth in it.

This is a patently different sense of "truth" than is current among many social scientists. It is predicated upon the view that contact with history is not contact with the past as such but with the historian who embodies the tradition in his own unique way. The book he writes is only an aspect of what he has achieved in human terms and cannot be understood apart from that achievement. The historian whose style is true to him will be one in whom the tradition will have been truly incarnated; style and what we are calling "incarnation" are but aspects of the same thing. And if the style is wrong, the history written will be wrong. There is no question of the style's varying independently of the "facts" — of the style's being wrong and the "facts" right or of the style being right and the "facts" wrong. To think otherwise is to have a befuddled — an objectivist — view of factuality. In the light of this personifying view of truth Gibbon comes off as a great historian, for his style expresses himself. The same can be said of Thucydides, Herodotus, and Livy; it could not be said of those nineteenth-century historians who were eager to put rational order onto the material; or of those twentieth-century historians who consider it imperative to order the material professionally and impersonally. There is never a more significant result of the study of history than the historian himself.

Historical Uniqueness and Moral Universalizability

These three things happen together if they happen at all: the author is self-forgetful, the historical situation is captured in its uniqueness, and—we have not mentioned this yet—the history written serves as an inexhaustible fund for moral lessons. Yet it is not didactic in any ordinary sense of that term. Only a history that in the first instance tried to abstract out the moral content of a past situation would in the second instance be compelled to try to reimpose it in the form of cautionary conclusions.

A situation captured in its uniqueness has moral relevance because it is a whole situation like our own situation. We are free to see it in any of indefinitely many ways, including those most instructive for us. But when the historical situation is subsumed under a generalization, it is seen in just one way, and we can easily exclude ourselves from it. Many similarities between that situation and our circumstance are artificially suppressed. (This is one of the great lessons of Nietzsche's doctrine that all events, including the propagation of ideas, have multiple genealogies.) We let our preoccupation with discrete personal properties and comparisons become a pseudo-Mosaic alternative to conscience. (Why aren't we led by everything we see to have a broken heart and contrite spirit? Certainly it is not because we don't have ample cause.) But letting the story tell itself in all of the completeness with which we spontaneously apprehend it is tantamount to a repudiation of this pseudo-Mosaic context. The reader is left to face up to the whole of the matter—to be impressed by moral dimensions and standards inherent in the story, dimensions which even the author may not suspect are there.

Take the example of David. David is not just any oriental monarch. He has been chosen by the Lord to be the leader of Israel. He has shown himself obedient in every particular to the Lord. He has not tried to hasten or evade the Lord's plan for him; he has not anticipated the time when he is to take over the kingdom; he has left the shape and direction of his destiny to the Lord. He spares Saul's life more than once. He makes his way faultlessly to the throne. Who else in history ever did that? Only after he has achieved the throne does he fail, and the story of his failure, down to his last bloody deathbed utterance, is told in more detail than the story of his success. Now to make the moral point of the story of David other than the way in which Nathan did would be to hide that point. That is, to impose a superficial moral generalization on the story would be to rob it of its moral applicability to every reader—its moral universalizability. What Nathan did was to set David a trap by presenting a parable, and David fell into the trap. The climax of David's life is Nathan's statement: "Thou art the man." This climax is not set out in detail and the moral point is not put in a proposition: it could not be. We cannot even say that the story shows the moral point (i.e., the punishment for adultery and murder). That is too cut and dried and limited a characterization, for the punishment does not "fit the crime": the crime's consequences are its punishment—to be an adulterer is the punishment for adultery. Instead, the history's moral point pulsates throughout the whole of it, as through a parable, and cannot be abstracted from it. And we in our own individual and different ways—in ways apposite to our individual cases—draw the parable's conclusion—a conclusion which may well differ from what we may discover upon returning to the story later, after further experiences have altered us. We are allowed to experience David's life totally, to sense its emotive tides, to work out the ironical implications of the account. The inspired historian has produced, in a language of the whole man which uses all the devices of rhetoric (including juxtaposition), a better biography, a finer account, than any other anywhere. It is written for a spiritually educated and subtle people. It goes as far as history can go, which is to re-create the story of a past human being in the terms in which it is lived and valued, which is to say, in predominantly moral terms.

The closest a self-deceiving historian can come to morality is this: "There but for the grace of God go I." This effort at self-decontamination is not found in a historian who produces pure history, precisely because his acknowledgment of impurity has been for him a path to purity. The response of the guileless historian is therefore, "Lord, have mercy on me, there go I also." This is what the prophet Nathan, speaking for the Lord, meant when he said, "Thou art the man." And for us, in all of the pages of history, there is implicit in every line the unarticulated reminder: "We are the men."

Thus does the response of the guileless historian place him in community with the past people he encounters in his work. He understands them as people. It is remarkable that only as we become more individual, rather than less, can we live in community with one another. And conversely: Only as we live in and through one another in our individual uniqueness—the historian taking past people to understand and they taking him to be understood by— is it possible for us to partake of each other's strengths and be individually richer for it. Otherwise, our relation to one another is manipulative: we treat ourselves and each other as replicable—indeed, as artifacts which in our social interaction with one another we ourselves are continuously producing. For those of us who insulate ourselves from one another by using each other, even the present is a sort of past, cadaverized, an unbridgeable distance away; whereas for the pure even the past is present, vivified and immediately felt. This is in the spirit not only of the gospel but of thinkers like Heidegger, who have tried to clear away the intellectual debris from our modern mentality so that we might receive the revelation from God if only it were to come.

What Shall It Profit a Man?

It cannot profit a person to *try* to be individualistic in his way of perceiving others' situations or in his way of writing about them. It is as unprofitable as trying to be nonchalant or sincere. One who does not feel exigencies in his present situation is nonchalant; one who tries to be nonchalant is tense. One who is concentrating wholly on something other than himself in what he is doing is sincere; one who is trying to be sincere is concentrating on himself, no matter how hard he pretends he is not. Taking thought to make ourselves or our work *be* some particular way or other is in principle self-defeating.

Another reason why it is profitless to try to be an individual is that taking thought to make ourselves is self-delimiting. Taking thought for the morrow in any way at all means trying to conform to an anticipated pattern of self which in principle is too simple to be a self. The more we conform to that pattern, the more we make of ourselves not an individual but rather a replicable artifact — our own artifact. And the work we produce is also too simple to be the work of the self, for behind it was the motivation to produce that which will reflect a character too simple to be a self.

A third reason why we cannot by taking thought add a cubit to our stature as historians: By trying to conform ourselves to a replicable model of what a historian should be we block our own creativity. How? Taking thought for the morrow means substituting an imagined tomorrow for the one that is really going to be there. And as we do not know the one that is really going to be there, we prepare ourselves for a number of hypothetical tomorrows that will never come. We do this instead of being ready, by merely being ourselves, for any tomorrow that will come. When we wake up in the morning, we don't readily pick up the thread of the day that awaits us, for we have determined in advance where it will be, and therefore we do not see where it really is. Alas for Benjamin Franklin, planning his day at 5:00 A.M., how he will manipulate various Philadelphians! He must compulsively and obsessively try to extrude many threads, to manipulate many clues to the labyrinth in order to convince himself that he is on the right track. And Franklin's kind of planning for the future is simply the mirror image of the self-serving historian's planning for the past. The generalizations the historian has convinced himself are the right guidelines for interpreting history preclude him from discovering new patterns in the history he encounters; he is only able to gather more details.

Here is a fourth reason why writing the kind of history we have suggested is not something a person could possibly set out to do: To try to get for ourselves in any fashion is to be anxious over the treasure we seek, and to be thus anxious is to forfeit the freedom and spontaneity or openness necessary for a total response to a total situation. That is a message of W. H. Auden's poem, "The Bard."

> He was their servant—some say he was blind—
> And moved among their faces and their things;
> Their feeling gathered in him like a wind
> And sang: they cried—'It is a God that sings'—
>
> And worshipped him and set him up apart
> And made him vain till he mistook for song
> The little tremors of his mind and heart
> At each domestic wrong.
>
> Songs came no more: he had to make them.
> With what precision was each strophe planned.
> He hugged his sorrow like a plot of land,

And walked like an assassin through the town,
And looked at men and did not like them,
But trembled if one passed him with a frown.[2]

The moment we start to care about succeeding we forfeit every possibility of it.

Auden's bard was, to begin with, a servant; later, a slave. At first he did not regard himself as being original. He did not repeat himself at all. Instead he expressed what came to him to be expressed and thus passed on an oral tradition. Later, he insisted on his originality and individuality and suffocated his creativity. In the first phase he was a classicist; in the second, a romantic. A Milton landscape is a characteristic landscape — it is a typical landscape; yet at the same time it is Milton's landscape. He did not *try* to make it his: it is his because in looking in another direction than himself he did not obstruct the expression of his personality in and through it. It is only the inferior artist who feels a need to make a highly individual response in order to be able to do something original, new, and different. The result is strained. The result is precious. The result, ironically, is replicable: the original of the piece is already a stereotype. For his part, the classicist is never concerned with individuality for its own sake. He is concerned with tradition. Were we living in 1798 and afflicted with tremors of insecurity about whether what we were writing would be regarded as individual, we might take exception to this statement, because our contemporaries would be interpreting the tradition as a means of throttling individuality. But the truth is that tradition can liberate the person who interacts with it.

Almost any moderately intelligent human being could produce something highly individual and profound if he took no thought for what was in it for him, provided he had assimilated a good deal of the tradition. The old statement that everyone has at least one book in him is relevant here; and, indeed, we have had occasional examples in English literature of a peculiar pellucidity appearing just once. John Woolman's *Journal* is an example. Compare it with Franklin's *Autobiography*. The inadequacy and arrogance of Franklin resemble the explanations of the knights in Eliot's *Murder in the Cathedral*. They are murderers who rationally explain away their act. (Whatever books there may have been in Franklin, he murdered them.) It is not beside the point that in creating the rationalizing knights Eliot was satirizing Shaw. Shaw's plays are appealing to many, for they offer an easy clarity, and (like many psychiatrists and psychotherapists and like Eliot's knights) a facile—a *reasonable*—mode of explaining away personal guilt. The witch doctor, the advertiser, and the politician make similar offers—reasonable offers.

These offers are quackery. An essential feature of this kind of quackery is its respectability. The offers come in the guise of a virtuous practice to be followed, an approved technique or method, with all of the half-suspected quasitheory shared by the people who endorse it. The quacks rail at historicism and point to the history Hitler wrote as a misuse of history. That is a way of establishing *their* respectability by comparison. Their doctrine is almost irresistible when made so respectable—so decently indecent. From that point they can perpetrate immoralities in an atmosphere of legitimacy, as in the contemporary theater where lewdness frolics on the stage without being condemned as such because, besides being immoral, it is also dishonest about what it is. Was not Hitler partly seduced by the wrong kind of history that he read?

For a person to be a historian—a genuine historian—is for him cheerfully to run the risk that he may never be acknowledged as such. He will also have to concede in advance that he himself may discover what he has had to say after, rather than before, he writes his words. He will draw his identity at a source different from the well of his peers' opinions.

Enthusiasm

We have been advocating what used to be called "enthusiasm." Contrary to what some would have us believe, enthusiasm has nothing to do with romanticism; and if they think it historically has nothing to do with classicism, it is because they tend not to consider the classicists, like Milton and Dante, who were enthusiastic Christians.

We acknowledge that nothing could be more alien to the intellectualist ideal of calculated impersonality. It is true that this ideal seems not altogether unwarranted, for historical instances of enthusiasm have been justifiably attacked. There is this danger in enthusiasm, that impure people, like Hitler, will yield to an impure spirit. Our thesis in this paper is that by the same token, there is an equally horrifying danger in the repudiation of enthusiasm— namely, in the protection which some erect against novelty and spontaneity in themselves—a disguised form of demonism in which seizure by the Holy Spirit is precisely what is resisted. The one alternative to being possessed by some sort of devil is to yield to—voluntarily to let ourselves be taken over by—God's Spirit. The depersonalizing "wisdom" of the age, like the so-called wisdom of ages generally, will when unmasked be seen to be only the self-protective smoke screen of a professional clique so fearful of self-revelation through their productions that they have yielded themselves up proudly to the demon of reasonableness.

> What was to be the value of the long looked forward
>   to,
> Long hoped for calm, the autumnal serenity
> And the wisdom of age? Had they deceived us
> Or deceived themselves, the quiet-voiced elders,
> Bequeathing us merely a receipt for deceit?

The serenity only a deliberate hebetude,
The wisdom only the knowledge of dead secrets
Useless in the darkness into which they peered
Or from which they turned their eyes. There is, it
    seems to us,
At best, only a limited value
In the knowledge derived from experience.
The knowledge imposes a pattern, and falsifies,
For the pattern is new in every moment
And every moment is a new and shocking
Valuation of all we have been. We are only
    undeceived
Of that which, deceiving, could no longer harm.
In the middle, not only in the middle of the way
But all the way, in a dark wood, in a bramble,
On the edge of a grimpen, where is no secure
    foothold,
And menaced by monsters, fancy lights,
Risking enchantment. Do not let me hear
Of the wisdom of old men, but rather of their folly,
Their fear of fear and frenzy, their fear of possession,
Of belonging to another, or to others, or to God.
The only wisdom we can hope to acquire
Is the wisdom of humility: humility is endless.
                                        —T. S. Eliot, "East Coker"[3]

If you ask us to point to a historian who represents much of what we say, we can readily do it: Hugh Nibley, of whom we thought as we wrote. Who among us has been more completely absorbed in peoples of the past and less occupied with impressing anyone with his style? Who has expressed his own personality so well, with so little thought for it? Who has better inspired us to care about and learn from the vast population of historical souls who have intrigued and delighted him over the years? And he has done this not by exhortation but by his example of wonder and absorption in his constant learning and his gracious acts of sharing it with us.

Notes

1. T. S. Eliot, *Selected Essays*, new ed. (New York: Harcourt, Brace and World, 1960), 4.

2. W. H. Auden, *A Selection by the Author* (Harmondsworth, Middlesex: Penguin, 1958), 60.

3. T. S. Eliot, *Collected Poems 1909-1962* (New York: Harcourt, Brace and World, 1963), 184-85.

17

The Challenge of Historical Consciousness: Mormon History and the Encounter with Secular Modernity

Louis Midgley
Brigham Young University, Provo, Utah

Martin E. Marty, distinguished Professor of the History of Modern Christianity at the University of Chicago, has made an important contribution to the understanding of "the crisis in Mormon historiography."[1] I will set forth his arguments and examine their soundness. I will also show that on most issues this most esteemed American church historian is close to the position I wish to advance, and that his stance is more refined and better grounded than that taken by historians who fashion naturalistic explanations of the Book of Mormon and Joseph Smith's prophetic claims. Marty's analysis of what is currently being discussed by Mormon historians constitutes both a clarification of key issues upon which there has been some confusion, and a sound starting point for further clarification.

In spite of the narrow focus of Marty's essay, he manages to describe a quandary of faith among Mormon historians that is older than the two decades in which the writing of Mormon history has become professionalized. The crisis which he describes, which he seems to see as rather recent, has actually been unfolding for half a cen-

502

tury. The first signs of an exigency over the Mormon past reached the attention of the Saints with the publication in 1945 of *No Man Knows My History*, Fawn M. Brodie's notorious biography of Joseph Smith,[2] which began as an attack on the Book of Mormon,[3] and eventually constituted a full-scale naturalistic explanation of Joseph Smith's prophetic claims. Set over against such efforts were various essays by Hugh Nibley, who after 1948 became the primary intellectual champion of the truth of the Book of Mormon, including both its message and historical authenticity, and also for the related prophetic claims of Joseph Smith. His understanding of the restored gospel manifests a disdain for secular fundamentalism, an ideology which, by the end of World War II, had decoyed almost an entire generation of Latter-day Saint intellectuals, as well as an aversion to the sentimental sectarian fundamentalism found in much American conservative religiosity.[4]

The current spate of Revisionist accounts,[5] and the ensuing discussion of their implications and coherence, which indicate for Marty a "crisis in Mormon historiography," are not always as forthright or elegant as the work of earlier internal dissenters like Brodie or Dale L. Morgan.[6] Still, in subtle ways these accounts entail the transformation of Latter-day Saint faith by the use of naturalistic terms and categories to interpret the Mormon foundational texts and events. And they spring from a desire to reach an accommodation with modernity, and especially with elements of secular fundamentalism — the naturalistic ideology which has dominated the understanding of divine things in academic circles since the Enlightenment.[7] The historiographical crisis which Marty examines has only recently drawn serious attention from those either inside or outside the Mormon community,[8] even though it is clearly rooted in older struggles, and it somewhat resembles an older debate that has taken place in Christian and Jewish communities. Though the details of those older debates are not immediately relevant to Marty's analysis of "the crisis of Mormon historiography," it seems to me that what is at stake in the current debate is nothing less than the content and even the possibility of faith as Latter-day Saints have known it. I wish to show that the founding events and texts—Joseph Smith's prophetic claims and the Book of Mormon—are now being discussed and debated in an academic arena in which a struggle is being waged for the control of the Mormon past, and that this struggle is central to the faith. To see why this is so and to grasp exactly what is at stake, I will now turn to Marty's analysis.

Scandal, Controversy, and Crisis

Professor Marty understands Mormon faith to be characterized by a "thoroughly historical mode and mold"[9] that opens it to both inquiry and controversy. Joseph Smith told a strange story. Was it the truth? If he was the victim of illusion or charlatanry and his message false, ultimately we have nothing that places us in touch with deity. But if he told the truth, and if the foundational texts like the Book of Mormon are genuine, then we have something. History is therefore the arena in which the truth claims of the restored gospel have been contested. Those who have received the Book of Mormon and the story of Joseph Smith's prophetic gifts have found therein the grounds for faith in God. Others do not receive the message, and, according to Marty, "there have been Mormons who left the faith because their view of the historical events which gave shape to it no longer permitted them to sustain it."[10] The Book of Mormon and Joseph Smith's story are clearly a stumbling block, but they also furnish the grounds for a distinctive community of memory and faith.

As the writing of Mormon history in the last two decades has moved from cottage to academic industry, Marty believes that the discussion of the historical foundations of faith has grown in both intensity and urgency[11] to the point where it has now reached a critical stage. Some of the questions now being debated concern the very core of the faith. "Mormon thought is experiencing a crisis comparable to but more profound than that which Roman Catholicism recognized around the time of the Second Vatican Council (1962-65)."[12] The Catholic crisis was dogmatic; the Mormon agitation is historical in the sense that it involves the understanding of the historical foundations of the faith.[13]

The reason for the crisis of faith among some Mormon historians, according to Marty, is that a "faith attached to or mediated through historical events has always had some dimensions of an 'offense' or 'scandal' to the insider just as it has been *only* that to the outsider who despises."[14] Some find unseemly the account of Joseph Smith's prophetic gifts, visits with angels, the Book of Mormon and other revelations. But why should the ferment now reach inside the community and touch the faith of some intellectuals? It was inevitable, according to Marty, since the Mormon faith is thoroughly historical in "mode and mold,"[15] that this kind of crisis would overtake some Saints as they confront their past under the impact of the assumptions at work behind some elements of secular culture. The primary source of the present crisis of faith is the appropriation by some historians of competing or conflicting ideologies that began to dominate the thinking of educated people beginning with the Enlightenment.[16] The crisis is rooted in conflict between the substance of Mormon faith, especially the prophetic claims upon which it rests, and certain of the dominant ideas found in the secular culture. Prophetic claims appear questionable, if not absurd, from the perspective of secular modernity, which also provides the ideological grounds for both rival explanations of the faith, and competing secular accounts of the meaning of life.

Marty maintains that the current crisis centers on the

attempts of certain Latter-day Saint historians to assess the historical foundations of the faith in the light of categories and assumptions borrowed from the larger culture. Naturalistic or secular explanations may compete with the content of faith and may also provide intellectual justifications for unbelief. The crisis is not generated by the discovery or publication of texts; new texts only complicate or enhance the picture of the Mormon past. The difficulties arise in the way texts are to be understood, and this always involves assumptions brought to the task by the historian. The crisis is, therefore, not a difficulty forced on Latter-day Saint historians by some dramatic discovery that suddenly unravels the truth claims of the faith. Marty describes the difficulty confronting Mormon historians as a crisis of understanding, and hence of faith, and not of history as such.[17]

Marty correctly rejects as "trivial the question of whether the faith is threatened by the revelation of human shortcomings" of the Mormon people or its leaders.[18] This question raises public relations and pedagogical issues, or what he calls "political embarrassments" or merely "borderline religious issues."[19] As important as such issues may appear to be, "intellectually these are not of much interest." Marty attempts to "cut through all the peripheral issues"[20] that plague the discussion of the history of Mormon things in order to address what is really at stake. He shows that the crisis centers on the way the founding events are to be understood—it is not a crisis brought on by the dazzling refutation of something essential to the faith, though it centers on the understanding of Joseph Smith's gifts, special revelations, and the Book of Mormon.

The substance of the current discussion is traced by Marty to the impact on Mormon historians of certain of the dominant ideas of the larger culture. He holds that both the content as well as the possibility of faith are linked to the way the past is understood. He correctly insists that "if the beginning . . . , the First Vision and the Book of Mormon, can survive the crisis, then the rest of the promenade follows and nothing that happens in it can really detract from the miracle of the whole. If the first steps do not survive, there can be only antiquarian, not fateful or faith-full interest in the rest of the story."[21] This is a clear statement of the decisive issue in the current controversy generated by fashioning new naturalistic (or secular) understandings on the crucial foundations of Mormon things.

The Acids of Modernity

Marty grants that there has been no proof that Joseph Smith was a fraud or the victim of an illusion or delusion or that the Book of Mormon is fiction;[22] there is only a crisis of faith. The roots of this crisis he traces to ideologies that began corroding Protestant and Roman Catholic piety with the Enlightenment. According to Marty, the challenges to the historical foundations of the faith of the Saints are analogous to those corroding Christian and Jewish faith. In other essays, he describes the challenges to Christian faith from "modernity,"[23] a term commonly used to describe a cluster of related, though also competing, secular ideologies that distinguish the Modern from the Pre-Modern world.[24] He uses the expression "acids of modernity"[25] to describe "the process of corrosion which affected the vessel of apostolicity."[26] Modernity yields scientism—a new secular religion of science, as well as the ideologies that dislodge God from history and the world generally. Modernity eventually comes to full fruition in the writings of Marx, Nietzsche, Darwin, and Freud—the so-called "God-Killers."[27]

Modernity includes the new understandings of history that challenged the historical foundations of biblical faith, as well as the rise of an historical consciousness which plunged all elements of culture into a sea of relativity. The source of the malaise, instead of being religion within the

limits of reason alone that challenges the claims of historically grounded and mediated faith, becomes the historicist
belief in the relativity of all positions, especially those resting on special revelations, and even of those grounded in
unaided human reason. It is not that the truths of history
cannot be demonstrated; even that understanding of truth,
from the perspective of historicism, is itself only a part of
the perpetual flux of ideas in history.[28]

The "crisis of historical consciousness" that Marty believes has "cut to the marrow in the Protestant body of
thoughtful scholars in Western Europe in the nineteenth
century"[29] continues to trouble the Christian world. The
crisis is analogous to the one which the Saints are now
facing as they emerge from a prereflective naiveté about
their past. One of the chief sources of the crisis is a remnant
of Enlightenment-grounded fear of superstition. The as-
sault on Christian piety also came from ideologies linked
to an historical consciousness which began "to relativize
Christian distinctiveness in the face of other ways."[30] Modernity thus includes the Romantic reaction to the Enlightenment, commonly known as historicism.

Modernity includes other ideologies that have found
their way into the hearts and minds of historians: "In the
nineteenth century," according to Marty, "the age of modern critical history, the crisis of historical consciousness
became intense and drastic. Now no events, experiences,
traces, or texts were exempt from scrutiny by historians
who believed they could be value-free, dispassionate. Today, of course, no one sees them as being successful in
their search. They were tainted by radical Hegelian di-
alectics, neo-Kantian rigorisms, or the biases of a positivism
that thought it could be unbiased."[31] All this now seems
naive, but it was once "highly successful at destroying the
primitive naiveté among those who read them seriously."[32]
Marty traces the crisis among Mormon historians to ideologies with roots going back to the Enlightenment: to con-

fidence in reason and fear of superstition, to naive positivist notions of historical objectivity, to the historicist insistence on the relativity and hence equality of all faith or of all religions. But these ideologies have now fallen on hard times. Should these intellectual fashions of the past serve as the foundation for the understanding of the Mormon past? On that issue he is silent.

Elsewhere, Marty both describes and expresses apprehension about the wanton capitulation of believers to the fashions of modernity. He has made the delicious irony of the various encounters between the faithful and modernity the core of his interpretation of American religiosity. He also argues persuasively that Christian faith, whatever its content and contours, has a legitimate place in the doing of history.[33] The corrosive effects of modernity have an impact on diverse types of religiosity in different ways. The particular "aspect of modernity" that has generated the current crisis of faith among some Mormon historians "has to do with the challenge of modern historical consciousness and criticism," which, he maintains, is rooted in what he calls "the burden of history" that "confronts Mormons most directly."[34]

Christians who confronted the corrosive ideologies of the nineteenth century responded in various ways. Marty describes the range of these responses. "Some lost faith," he explains, as they felt the pull of what was earlier described as a secular fundamentalism. While others, according to Marty, found ways of affirming their faith in some seemingly more satisfactory manner; others transformed the content of faith to accommodate secular ideological pressures, and some turned to "defensive fundamentalisms,"[35] which were earlier labelled sectarian fundamentalism. Yet, when Marty examines the impact of modernity on Mormon historians, he does not acknowledge the same range of responses.[36] His account would have been more balanced and complete — more coherent —

if he had examined the full range of responses to the crisis of faith among Mormon historians. These, as will be shown, have issued as dissent and denial, or loss of faith, or radical alterations to the content of faith to accommodate certain competing ideologies in revisionist accounts. But in some notable cases it has yielded more adequate accounts of the Mormon faith and its history.[37] Unfortunately, Marty neglects to carry through on the range of alternatives set forth in his analogy.

The crisis, Marty realizes, does not involve secondary or peripheral issues[38] like polygamy or the faults of the Saints, or their leaders. His discussion is focused on *"generative* issues."[39] The primary question concerns the veracity of Joseph Smith's "theophanies" and "revelations." Joseph's epiphanies — the prophetic charisms, visits with angels, and the seer stones, are linked to the founding revelation — the Book of Mormon. These work together to constitute "a single base for Mormon history. When historians call into question both the process and the product, they come to or stand on holy ground."[40] If the revelations do not survive "there can be only antiquarian, not fateful or faith-full interest in the rest of the story."[41] The primary issue becomes a combination of two related questions: Was Joseph Smith a genuine seer and prophet, and is the Book of Mormon true? If either one or the other is true, because both are linked, the truth of the other is thereby warranted. Marty insists that the primary questions must be answered in the affirmative for there to be more than antiquarian curiosity concerning the Mormon past. Hence a fateful response to the Mormon past depends upon those founding events being simply true. "To say 'prophet' made one a Saint" and to deny or reject the prophetic claims "is precisely what made one leave Mormonism or never convert in the first place."[42]

Fashioning a More Socially Acceptable Past

The "stark prophet/fraud polarity"[43] troubles Marty. Asking if Joseph Smith was a genuine prophet exerts a chilling effect on discussions between believers and sympathetic unbelievers, and it seems unlikely that it is a question that can be resolved to the satisfaction of everyone. In any case, most historians do not wish to concentrate on that particular question. Perhaps a different way of formulating the fundamental question might facilitate attention to secondary issues with which historians, especially those in the grasp of modernity, would feel somewhat more comfortable. Marty struggles to move outside of or "beyond the prophet/fraud issue addressed to generative Mormon events."[44] But he also explains why Joseph Smith's claims are such that they demand either a prophet or a not-prophet answer. When dealing with the generative events, Marty senses that one cannot have it both ways.

Yet, Marty strives to avoid the old prophet/fraud dialectic, while still addressing Joseph Smith's prophetic claims. He has proposed two ways to do this. First, historians might simply bracket or suspend the question of whether Joseph Smith was a genuine prophet and the Book of Mormon an authentic ancient history. They could do so in order to deal with what Marty calls "a new range of questions," which include: "what sort of people are these people [who believe such things], what sort of faith is this faith, what sort of prophet with what sort of theophany and revelation was Joseph Smith?"[45] The primary question can be bracketed in order to inquire into secondary questions. But whether it is possible to deal with those "other questions" without an implicit answer on the primary issue coming into play has not been discussed, let alone settled.[46]

Marty also holds that it is unlikely that historians are going to disprove Joseph Smith's prophetic claims. They "may find it possible to prove to their own satisfaction that

Smith was a fraud,"[47] but may have difficulty convincing others that they have succeeded. In any case, "the issue of fraud, hoax, or charlatanry simply need not, does not, preoccupy the historical profession most of the time,"[48] but that is not to say that it does not occupy the attention of historians some of the time, or that the opinions historians form on the truth of Joseph Smith's prophetic claims do not wield a subtle influence on answers to the questions that preoccupy them most of the time. Marty admits that those historians who attempt to bracket the question of the truth of Joseph Smith's claims are still "nagged or tantalized"[49] by it. The answer to the question of whether Joseph Smith was a genuine prophet and the Book of Mormon true may influence if not control what they make of the rest.

The second way around the question of the truth of Joseph Smith's prophetic claims has been fashioned by some Latter-day Saint historians who have started asking "more radical questions than before. They had to move through history and interpretation toward a 'second na- iveté' which made possible transformed belief and per- sistent identification with the people. They brought new instruments to their inquiry into Mormon origins."[50] Marty grants that these historians, no doubt, have achieved a "transformed belief" through their "interpretation."[51] The product of such transformations could well be called re- visionist history. For them the historical events which shaped their faith no longer sustain it, and yet some "re- mained with the Mormon people" for various reasons. They have, he feels, "made their own adjustment."[52] Hence some Mormon historians have experienced the cor- rosive power of the ideological acids of modernity, but they still desire "persistent identification with the people" of their own faith.[53]

"They brought new instruments to their inquiry into Mormon origins,"[54] and instead of charging Joseph Smith with fraud, pictured him as a sincere though superstitious rustic with a genius for expressing the religious concerns of his age. He was a mystic, a magician, a myth-maker who eventually managed to found a new religious tradition. The new revised standard version differs from the old standard version in that it does not accuse Joseph Smith of fraud or deceit, as did the line of critics running from Alexander Campbell through Fawn Brodie and Dale Morgan. Instead, the revised standard version sees in Joseph Smith an inventive, conflicted, dissociative, sincerely superstitious scryer or magus. This is, of course, one possible way around the "prophet/fraud dialectic."[55] But the revised standard version ends up denying the historical foundations of the faith, and with them it also compromises Joseph Smith's prophetic claims — there can be no equivocation on that issue. To begin to understand the foundations as essentially mystical,[56] mythical,[57] or magical[58] is to deny that they are simply true. Why is that so?

Abraham Joshua Heschel, from the Hasidic tradition, has examined the range of possible explanations of special revelations. For Heschel, one who confronts the core message of the Bible is presented with certain claims. "The problem concerning us most is whether revelation has ever taken place," and again, "Is revelation a fact? Did it actually take place?"[59] Heschel finds that "there are only three ways of judging the prophets: they [a] told the truth, [b] deliberately invented a tale, or [c] were victims of an illusion. In other words, a revelation is either a fact or the product of insanity, self-delusion, or a pedagogical invention, the product of a mental confusion, or wishful thinking [that is, an outgrowth of 'the spirit of the age'] or a subconscious activity."[60] The so-called "New Mormon History," in its secularist mode,[61] entertains or embraces one or more of these alternatives but without always carefully considering whether they are inimical to a faith-full response to the Mormon past.

Marty describes three approaches to religious history that can be used to explain the Mormon past that go "beyond the prophet/fraud issue [and that can be] addressed to generative Mormon events."[62] The first approach includes what he calls "consciousness" studies or psychological explanations of Joseph Smith that would "make plausible the prophethood and throw light on prophetic character."[63] Both Klaus J. Hansen and Lawrence Foster have turned to psychological explanations *after* flatly rejecting the Book of Mormon and Joseph Smith's prophetic claims.[64] The second approach is most attractively presented by Jan Shipps. She strives to avoid the question of whether Joseph Smith was a genuine prophet. She believes, according to Marty, that the Book of Mormon and Joseph Smith's story are "best understood in the context of his sequential assumptions of positions/roles that allowed the Saints to recover a usable past" by linking the Saints with ancient and true Israel through mythical histories, that is, through what is essentially fiction — the Book of Mormon — which Joseph Smith either knowingly or unknowingly fabricated. "That was his *religious* function and achievement."[65]

Shipps holds that "as far as history is concerned, the question of whether Smith was prophet or fraud is not particularly important."[66] But to make that question seem unimportant, for historians, is not the way to suspend unbelief in order to enter into understanding, or to bracket questions about truth. Obviously it is not important whether Joseph Smith was a genuine prophet in the history that is done by one with only an antiquarian curiosity about Mormon things. Nor does it make a difference whether the Book of Mormon is true or whether Joseph was a genuine prophet from an essentially historicist perspective.[67] Though her recent book is insightful, especially about the place of the Book of Mormon in the faith of the Saints, and she approaches her subject matter with sympathy, Shipps does not manage to suspend unbelief; she merely makes questions of truth seem irrelevant to her questions. Her approach does not genuinely allow the possibility that the Book of Mormon is simply true.

But, of course, from the point of view of the believer or potential believer the question of whether Joseph was a genuine prophet and whether the Book of Mormon is true makes all the difference in the world. Shipps correctly insists that the Saints cannot finally *prove* that the Book of Mormon is true or that Joseph Smith was a prophet. From that she wrongly concludes that the Book of Mormon "has never lent itself to the same process of verification that historians use to verify ordinary accounts of what happened in the past. The historicity of the Book of Mormon has been *asserted* through demonstrations that ancient concepts, practices, doctrines, and rituals are present in the work." However, she claims that "such demonstrations point, finally, only to plausibility. Proof is a different matter."[68] Historians, from her point of view, provide proofs, that is, those who are objective (and not mere apologists for the "myths" of faith) deal in proofs and not just plausibilities; they may seek "intellectual verification" and try to know "what really happened."[69] On this issue she is simply wrong, for plausibility is about as good as one might expect from any historical account or explanation. But from her vantage point, *real* historians tell us what *really* happened in the past by providing *proofs*, while believers are seen as in thrall to a mythical or fictional past which apologists for the faith can render only plausible.[70]

The Question of the Integrity of Faith

Marty does not examine the background assumptions at work behind the history done by Hansen, Hill, Foster and Shipps. Instead, he merely bestows "integrity" on both the radical mythological and psychological accounts of Mormon foundational texts and events. But he also ad-

mits that such accounts have obviously "transformed belief."[71] Both what is believed and the belief itself have been
radically altered when the story of Lehi and his people is
understood as fictional and the messenger with the plates
transformed into merely crude magic,[72] or into a product
of a dream of surcease of a troubled rustic with the urge
to prophesy, or into an expression of mysticism, or when
the message or teachings of the Book of Mormon are seen
as Joseph Smith's own imaginative effort to deal with sectarian controversies in his own time through expansions
on various theological themes in biblical fashion.

Marty's "two integrities" identify first, the integrity of
the faith that a child might have (or an entirely unreflective
adult) and, second, the integrity of one whose faith has
survived an encounter with ideas in the outside world
which compete with the content of faith.[73] This more mature faith—Marty's "second naiveté"—has faced and overcome doubts brought on by the confrontation with the
secular fundamentalism of modernity. The crisis he depicts
is the turning point in which either the desire for faith or
the presence of faith, or both, eventually disappear in a
loss or denial of faith, or are affirmed in a more complete
and mature faith. When the soul of the troubled one is
healed of unbelief by a new and deeper affirmation of faith,
one could speak of a new secondary integrity. But such
an integrity cannot exist if the essential grounds and content of faith are compromised. In such a case there would
be no genuine faith, but only denial or loss of faith or
perhaps what Marty calls a "transformed belief" in which
an alien content has taken the place of faith. This has to
be the reason Marty holds that the "generative events"
(the Book of Mormon and the special revelations flowing
from the prophetic gifts) must survive for there to be a
"fateful or faith-full" response to the Mormon past. "If the
first steps do not survive, there can be only antiquarian,
not fateful or faith-full interest in the rest of the story."[74]

His "two integrities" identify a condition of soundness of faith that stands on either side of the crisis of faith. The crisis is clearly centered in the heart and mind of those charmed as well as troubled by modernity.

A puzzling thing about Marty's essay is the attention he gives to the work of Shipps and Foster. Neither is a Latter-day Saint, and neither entertains the possibility that the Book of Mormon is authentic history. Standing outside the faith, they are at their best when they ask, for example, how the Book of Mormon functions in the life of believers. From their perspective the Book of Mormon is fiction, or what Shipps calls "myth," and not a genuine historical reality. And one would expect no more from even a sympathetic outsider. But why should Marty wish to draw attention to their work? Has either Shipps or Foster really fashioned ways in which troubled Latter-day Saint historians might resolve their own crisis of faith? Presumably, from Marty's perspective, they have. Yet, at the same time, he seems to move beyond, and perhaps even to dismiss, their approaches in favor of another way of understanding and doing history.

Shipps did not invent her account of a "usable Mormon past" — she borrowed the outlines from Marvin S. Hill. She drew upon his opinion that there is a kind of middle ground somewhere between genuine prophet and fraud. Presumably such a stance would somehow avoid the old quarrel over the truth of the Mormon faith. Hill provided Shipps with a seemingly scholarly Latter-day Saint peg upon which to hang her new explanation of "Mormonism." She has, however, moved away from her earlier claim that Joseph Smith was a typical mystic and the Book of Mormon a typical mystical text — the explanations with which she began her own career; she now holds that he began as a magician and, eventually, also became a powerful mythmaker.[75]

Hill has tried to work out an explanation of the story

of the Book of Mormon and an account of Joseph Smith's prophetic claims that would find room somewhere between the prophet or fraud alternatives.[76] His argument runs as follows:

> In attempting a psychological explanation of Smith rather than that of daring deception, the mature Brodie seems to be telling us that her old interpretation was too simple. Perhaps what Brodie may have recognized at last is that her original interpretation perceived Joseph Smith in falacious [sic] terms, as either prophet in the traditional Mormon sense or else as a faker. Her original thesis opens considerable room for speculation because its either-or alternatives were precisely the same as those of the early Mormon apologist and missionary, Orson Pratt.[77]

Fawn Brodie thought that the key to Joseph Smith was the Book of Mormon.[78] Once one determined that the Book of Mormon was fiction, the rest involved working out a plausible explanation of how and why Joseph made it up. Brodie played with a number of different explanations for the Mormon imposture. In 1959, Hill seems to side with an explanation that he labeled the "Smith hypothesis" that comes out against the view that the Book of Mormon is an authentic history. In setting forth the idea that the Book of Mormon was Joseph Smith's romantic fiction, Hill attempted to discredit the work of Hugh Nibley on the Book of Mormon.[79] Hill's version of the "Smith hypothesis" was a sketchy modification of the account already worked out by Fawn Brodie in *No Man Knows My History*. Following a line of explanations that began with Alexander Campbell,[80] she tried to show that Joseph Smith's claims were fraudulent—her "Joseph" began with a tale which only later took on the trappings of religion. Hill has striven to locate what he called in 1974 a "broad, promising middle ground" between the traditional alternatives of genuine prophet or faker-fraud.[81] Hill's account, like that of Shipps, rests on the assumption that Mormon things must be explained in "naturalistic terms."[82] When that is done, prophetic claims are clearly made to fit within the category of delusion or illusion—Morgan and Brodie were at least clear on that issue. Needless to say, such a one may, according to Marty, desire "a personal identification with the people."[83] But such history will necessarily compete at crucial points with both the grounds and categories of faith.

In subsequent essays, Hill has elaborated his thesis in such a way that he could distinguish it from certain details in Brodie's accounts. He stresses Joseph's sincerity as well as his superstitious (or mystical and magical) religiosity. Joseph's "religion" was the product of elements common in his culture, his religiosity was the product of his attempt to provide surcease for stresses in his environment. Hill attributes Joseph Smith's story of visits with heavenly messengers and the resulting revelations (including the Book of Mormon) to superstition, sincere confusions, and later embellishments of youthful half-forgotten dreams; it was all a product of mysticism, magic, and myth rather than gross imposture, deception, or charlatanry. That Joseph was both sincere and "religious" in his illusion or delusion seems to constitute Hill's middle ground between genuine prophet and faker or conscious fraud. Shipps has appropriated some of Hill's position on these issues, but she goes further in the direction of a mythological rather than a psychological-environmental explanation. One can, of course, fashion explanations of the Book of Mormon and of Joseph Smith's prophetic claims that render them false without picturing them as instances of conscious deception and fraud and, in that way, work around the "prophet/fraud dialectic,"[84] as Marty calls it. But the prophetic claims are such that they present the believer and unbeliever alike with either a prophet or not-prophet alternative.

Until recently, the standard "gentile" explanation of the beginnings of Mormonism was that Joseph Smith was a conscious or intentional fraud—his was a "deliberately invented . . . tale," to use Heschel's language. Joseph Smith is pictured in the revised standard version as a sincerely religious victim "of an illusion"[85] that was put upon him by his crude magic-saturated, rustic, and deeply superstitious environment. Perhaps he was confused, caught up in the spirit of his age, even dissociative or some combination of possibilities, all of which tend to render the prophetic claims questionable or false through a kind of inadvertence. These new alternative accounts of Joseph Smith (and the Book of Mormon), logically preclude the possibility of the gospel he preached being true. And, as Marty points out, if the first steps do not survive, all that is possible with these new explanations is antiquarian curiosity, not "fateful or faith-full" response.

Revisionist History—The Great Leap Forward

Some are still insisting that the Church must abandon the traditional understanding of the beginnings of the faith.[86] Why is such a revisionist history, as it is now being called, especially by RLDS historians, either desirable or necessary? Presumably, a competent, honest scrutiny of the historical foundations of the faith, that is, a serious look at the beginnings, discloses what Sterling M. McMurrin labels "a good many unsavory things."[87] McMurrin, for example, charges "that the Church has intentionally distorted its own history by dealing fast and loose with historical data and imposing theological and religious interpretations on those data that are entirely unwarranted."[88]

For McMurrin, the Mormon "faith is so mixed up with so many commitments to historical events—or to events that are purported to be historical—that a competent study of history can be very disillusioning. Mormonism is a historically oriented religion. To a remarkable degree, the Church has concealed much of its history from its people, while at the same time causing them to tie their religious faith to its own controlled interpretations of its history." The problem, as McMurrin sees it, is a "fault of the weakness of the faith" which should not be tied at all to history.[89] He strives to separate faith from history, substituting "naturalistic humanism"[90] for prophetic faith—promoting the enterprise of philosophical theology as a substitute for divine special revelations. McMurrin provides the least sentimental statement of the intellectual grounds for a secular revisionist Mormon history, that is, one done entirely in naturalistic terms. McMurrin sees the Mormon past in what Leonard Arrington once called "human or naturalistic terms."[91]

We should, from McMurrin's perspective, begin with the dogma "that you don't get books from angels and translate them by miracles; it is just that simple."[92] A history resting on that premise would require a fundamental reordering of the faith.[93] His program would retain only fragments of a culture resting on abandoned beliefs. Marty, straying from the core of his argument, eventually introduces "many kinds of integrity. Some of these are appropriate to insiders and others to outsiders, some to church authorities and some to historians."[94] But given what Marty had already shown about the necessity of the decisive generative events surviving the acids of modernity, it is difficult to see how he could defend the integrity of a stance such as McMurrin's. Certainly McMurrin's denials do not permit the survival of the crucial historical foundations. But still, Marty defends the history being done by some of those on the fringes of the Church whose arguments are not as coherent as those of McMurrin, yet whose premises are not unlike certain of his dogmas.[95]

Faith and the Limits of History: Listening to the Text

Marty's final approach to doing religious history rests on a rather different understanding of the method and limits of history[96] than of those historians for whom he offers an apology, or of those who approach Mormon history or the Book of Mormon with naturalistic assumptions. Marty claims a superiority—not merely a distinction—for his approach over that of others. He also claims that his way has been used by some Mormon historians to achieve a "second naiveté," but without citing any instances. Marty, unlike the others, has no illusions about objectivity or about the desirability of avoiding bias.[97] "People used to say," according to Marty, "they should be 'objective,' but," he claims, "objectivity seems to be a dream denied."[98] Ironically, Marvin Hill began his doctoral thesis, which was signed by Marty, with a claim of objectivity or "detachment," as he called it. Hill also appeals to something called "objective evaluation."[99] Recently he has passionately defended "the possibility of an objective history" against what he describes as the view "that historians can never escape their own culture and personal biases."[100] Unfortunately, Hill still seems enthralled by outmoded dogmas about the necessity and possibility of objectivity. Marty describes those historians who "used to say they should be 'objective,' but objectivity seems to be a dream denied,"[101] while Hill seems to cling to such a dream, perhaps because it provides for him the only possible way to avoid what he feels would be a destructive relativism and nihilism, if historians were unable to avoid having biases or preferences.[102] But thoughtful scholars now realize that positivism (or historical objectivism) lacks coherence, and that talk about the necessity of avoiding bias, detachment, and neutrality is confused and even illusory precisely because the historian always brings assumptions, biases, and a viewpoint to the task of interpreting texts and providing explanations. Nor does Marty hold, unlike Jan Shipps,[103] that it is possible to discover what really happened in the past, or that historians provide proofs.

Drawing upon some portions of the current literature

on hermeneutics, Marty maintains that all understanding rests on preunderstandings.[104] Historians strive to understand the texts that provide windows to the past from within the formal and informal preunderstandings with which everyone necessarily must approach texts.[105] The older challenges to the historical foundations of faith were "tainted" by ideologies about which some historians remained naive and uncritical. Historians were then, as some of the Saints are now, enthralled by what Marty calls "the biases of a positivism that thought it could be unbiased."[106] Just such a bias fuels the demand for objectivity, neutrality, or detachment from faith that flows from the new secular revisionist Mormon history.[107]

For Marty, history "is not a reproduction of reality," hence "the historian invents."[108] Since historians are necessarily involved in a "social construction of reality," they cannot discover what really happened. Only faint "traces" of the past remain, and from these only more or less plausible social constructions of a past are open to us, and these are accessible only through texts which are themselves colored by understanding. Even plausibility is dependent upon a network of preunderstandings. And every text or complex set of texts remains open to more or less plausible, though competing, interpretations and explanations. Marty's account of method is unlike that of historians currently enthralled by some variety of historical objectivism.

Marty's description of the method, limits, and situated character of the historian has something to contribute to a resolution or clarification of the current debate over Mormon history. Historians may not even be aware of the assumptions upon which they operate, because these form, for them, a natural horizon. Marty has helped to identify certain of the powerful ideologies that control the way in which cultural Mormons do history. He also sets out a version of historical skepticism which seems to make room for the possibility of faith in the face of scientism, naturalistic humanism, and dogmatic unbelief. A suspension of unbelief is what is needed in order to enter into the categories, norms, and explanations internal to the faith. But the dogmatisms of modernity stand in the way of the suspension of unbelief that is necessary for the truth of the faith to shine through when we encounter prophetic messages. Even genuine historical understanding rests on suspension of unbelief, or a willingness to grant the possibility that things are other than what the dogmatisms of secular modernity demand.

I agree with Marty that proof is not possible in history, and it is neither possible nor necessary in matters of faith.[109] Still, faith, if it is an "historical faith," is one in which texts witness to divine things.[110] The texts upon which the Mormon faith rests confront us with a message that makes claims upon us, and through listening to it we may come to what Marty calls a testimony of the truth of the message. Marty tells us that we can, if so disposed, hear the message contained in texts; we must then judge whether it will be true for us. He calls this, following Paul Ricoeur, the "hermeneutics . . . of testimony."[111]

How then do we come to believe and then justify our faith? What is it that we believe when faith has as part of its object a complex network of events in the past? We are, of course, shielded from direct access to the past and can only encounter a small segment of it already interpreted for us through texts. The historian, like everyone else, is confronted with the question of whether certain of these texts, for example, the crucial Book of Mormon, witnesses to the truth. An "historical faith," like that of the Saints, comes to be believed by hearing and listening, that is, by our seeking the truth found in the witness contained in the sacred texts. The Book of Mormon makes claims upon us concerning a then and there in which the deity acted, which we must judge by hearing the witness and receiving the testimony of the message for our own here and now.

In that way, a text like the Book of Mormon may serve as the bearer of the memory of divine things which we may begin to appropriate through the interpretative enterprise. Marty struggles toward just such a view of the thoroughly historical faith of Latter-day Saints.

The Book of Mormon, when viewed as a fictional or mythical account, and not as reality, no longer can have authority over us or provide genuine hope for the future. To treat the Book of Mormon as a strange theologically motivated brand of fiction, and in that sense as myth, is to alter radically both the form and content of faith and thereby fashion a new "church" in which the texts are told what they can and cannot mean on the basis of some exterior ideology. To reduce the Book of Mormon to mere myth weakens, if not destroys, the possibility of it witnessing to the truth about divine things. A fictional Book of Mormon fabricated by Joseph Smith, even when his inventiveness, genius, or inspiration is celebrated, does not witness to Jesus Christ but to human folly. A true Book of Mormon is a powerful witness; a fictional one is hardly worth reading and pondering.[112] Still, the claims of the text must be scrutinized and tested, then either believed or not believed without a final historical proof.

An historically grounded faith is vulnerable to the potential ravages of historical inquiry, but it is also one that could be true in a way that would make a profound difference. We are left, by God, with a witness to mighty acts, but we must judge, for we are always at the turning point between two ways. And listening to the text, not proving it true — an impossibility if not a presumption — to discover what its truth is for us, both reveals its truth and makes the sacred past plausible and thereby gives meaning to the life and deepest longings of the believer.

The truth of the prophetic message found in the Book of Mormon is linked to both its claim to be an authentic history and to Joseph Smith's story of how we came to have the book. To be a Latter-day Saint is to believe, among other things, that the Book of Mormon is true, that there once was a Lehi who made a covenant with God and was led out of Jerusalem and so forth.

Marty feels that to begin to understand the message of a text like the Book of Mormon frees us so that we are somehow "less burdened by concern over the exact reference to literal historical events."[113] He is correct if he means that a deeper and more profound understanding of the Book of Mormon removes obstacles that seekers may confront in grasping its truths, and thereby assists them in trusting its message. In various ways, the Book of Mormon has provided an anchor for the faith of the Saints; it also offers guidance for those anxious and willing to grasp its truths. But when the Book of Mormon is understood as fiction, and in that sense the material for what is sometimes called "the Mormon myth," we have, at best, one more melancholy instance of human folly and, from that perspective, not the word of God. To begin to suppose that it is even possible that the Book of Mormon is true, requires that the text be taken with genuine seriousness in all its various aspects. Therefore, it is a mistake to argue that a mature faith calls for or yields a lessening of concerns about details in the Book of Mormon, which somehow makes the historical and literary elements in that text less crucial, or allows the faithful to abandon the question of whether there was a Lehi colony with whom God made a covenant, with whether Jesus was resurrected or whether angels visited Joseph Smith. Only when faith is an empty routine or reduced to mere sentimentality, and thereby shorn of its deepest substance and meaning, as well as separated from hope, does it no longer matter if the Book of Mormon is an authentic ancient history and its teachings true. What it means for the Mormon faith to have what Marty describes as a "thoroughly historical mode and mold"[114] includes, among other things, that Joseph Smith's story and the Book of Mormon are known to be a genuine history providing prophetic access to divine things, and not merely entertained in some weak Pickwickian, allegorical, or sentimental sense.

Notes

1. Martin E. Marty, "Two Integrities: An Address to the Crisis in Mormon Historiography," an address given at the meeting of the Mormon History Association on May 7, 1983, in Omaha, Nebraska, and published in the *Journal of Mormon History* 10 (1983): 3-19; reprinted as "History: The Case of the Mormons, a Special People," in his *Religion and Republic: The American Circumstance* (Boston: Beacon Press, 1987), 303-25, 377-78. Pages referring to this reprint will appear in brackets following the page numbers for "Two Integrities." He was responding to "On the Question of Faith and History," a paper I read at the Western History Association meetings in October 1981 in San Antonio, Texas.

2. Fawn M. Brodie, *No Man Knows My History: The Life of Joseph Smith*, 2nd ed. (New York: Knopf, 1971).

3. Fawn M. Brodie, "Fawn McKay Brodie: An Oral Interview," *Dialogue* 14/2 (Summer 1981): 104-5 (a truncated, somewhat modified and garbled version of Shirley E. Stephenson's oral history interview with Brodie called "Biography of Fawn McKay Brodie," California State University, Fullerton, 30 November 1975, taken from 7-10, 22-23 in that text).

4. Nibley's influence among Latter-day Saints has been considerable, but he has not been a favorite of the network of Mormon historians anxious to promote a naturalistic Mormon history. For instances of disagreement with Nibley's method, see Thomas G. Alexander, "Toward the New Mormon History: An Examination of the Literature on the Latter-day Saints in the Far West," in Michael P. Malone, ed., *Historians and the American West* (Lincoln: University of Nebraska Press, 1983), 347-48; Thomas G. Alexander, "The Place of Joseph Smith in the Development of American Religion," *Journal of Mormon History* 5 (1978): 10, n. 9; Marvin S. Hill, "The Historiography of Mormonism," *Church History* 28/4 (1959): 418-19; Marvin S. Hill, "The 'New Mormon History' Reassessed in Light of Recent Books on Joseph Smith and Mormon Origins," *Dialogue* 21/3 (Autumn 1988): 118-19.

5. "Well may we applaud the revisionist historians," according to RLDS Church Historian Richard P. Howard, "for stimulating the document diggers to a new intensity of activity," even though their

undertaking eventually led Mark Hofmann to "actions inimical to the entire historical enterprise. In any case, the revisionist process will continue, for it has a life of its own." Hofmann's forgeries merely "served as catalysts" for revisionist pursuits, but did not initiate such proclivities among Mormon historians. "The process of revisionist history is fully under way. Thanks to [Leonard J.] Arrington and Company, and many others, it has been moving forward for many years" (Richard P. Howard, "Revisionist History and the Document Diggers," *Dialogue* 19/4 [Winter 1986]: 69). But the bulk of post-1950 Mormon history has not been revisionist, for it has either rejected naturalistic explanations, or has not been clearly dependent upon them. But revisionist accounts should not be entirely discounted, for some of them have been influential partly because of the passion with which they are promoted and defended, and they tend to draw inordinate attention.

6. Morgan's contributions to the study of Mormon things were mostly incidental or bibliographical. He worked on a three-volume Mormon history for seventeen years, convincing his admirers that his would be the definitive study; he produced a draft of four chapters, and rough notes for three additional chapters (Dale L. Morgan, *Dale Morgan on Early Mormonism: Correspondence and a New History*, John P. Walker, ed. [Salt Lake City: Signature Press, 1986], 219-319). He also provided extensive assistance to Brodie in the production of her account of Joseph Smith, which he then lavishly praised in an influential review (Dale Morgan, "A Prophet and His Legend," a review of Fawn M. Brodie, *No Man Knows My History*, in *Saturday Review*, November 24, 1945, 7-8). Their naturalistic perspective rested upon the assumption that there is no God, hence claims to divine revelation must be explained as instances of conscious fraud, perhaps eventually mixed with elements of delusion or illusion. According to Davis Bitton and Leonard J. Arrington, if Morgan "had completed a history of the Mormon Church, it would have been a work to reckon with. Such was Morgan's ambition. To judge from the draft chapters he did complete, it would not have pleased believing Mormons any more than Fawn Brodie's biography did, for he too placed stress on the evolving nature of Joseph Smith's own self-understanding" (*Mormons and Their Historians* [Salt Lake City: University of Utah Press, 1988], 118). This is an understatement, for Morgan, like Brodie, began with an ideology that denied the possibility of truth in prophetic claims. With that dogma in place, the task was merely to fashion a plausible and coherent naturalistic account. Bitton and Arrington point out that, "as one would expect,"

Morgan's accounts "provide naturalistic explanations for some of the key events in early Mormon history." Inexplicably, they describe Morgan's failure to complete his "ambitious three-volume history of Mormonism" as "one of the tragedies of the present book." They also opine that, with Morgan's "combination of skills and his established reputation for excellence, there was every reason to expect that he would write the great history of the Church for his generation, although even he would have had difficulty satisfying the incompatible demands of rival audiences" (Bitton and Arrington, *Mormons and Their Historians*, 117).

7. Louis Midgley, "Faith and History," in Robert L. Millet, ed., *"To Be Learned Is Good If . . . "* (Salt Lake City: Bookcraft, 1987), 219-20, 223-25.

8. Marty's recognition that there is a current "crisis in Mormon historiography" contrasts with the views of apologists for revisionist Mormon history. For example, Alexander denies that there is such an exigency; "Historiography and the New Mormon History: A Historian's Perspective," *Dialogue* 19/3 (Fall 1986): 25-49, and also "Toward the New Mormon History," 344, 358-361, 368. For fifteen years, since the label was introduced, it was fashionable to designate as "New Mormon History" naturalistic accounts of the Mormon past. During this period, every fashion in Mormon historiography was pictured as unproblematic—a Great Leap Forward. But the apparent tranquility only masked a fervent discussion seething beneath the surface, which has only recently drawn public attention. M. Gerald Bradford ("The Case for the New Mormon History: Thomas G. Alexander and His Critics," *Dialogue* 21/4 [Winter 1988]: 143-44) has called attention to the ferocity of some of the participants in a fine assessment of one layer of the quarrel. The controversies generated by revisionist history, which were fueled by the Hofmann forgeries as they drew public attention in lurid distortions by the press, have reached an intensity that both rivals and parallels earlier quarrels.

9. Marty, "Two Integrities," 3 [304].

10. Ibid., 8 [309].

11. Ibid., 8, 3-4 [309-10, 304-6].

12. Ibid., 3 [303].

13. Ibid., 3 [303-4].

14. Ibid., 8 [309].

15. Ibid., 3 [304].

16. Ibid., 5-8 [306-9].

17. Marty is on the right track when he maintains that historians

cannot "prove that Smith was a prophet" and it is "improbable that they will prove him a fraud." "Similarly, historians cannot prove that the Book of Mormon was translated from golden plates and have not proven that it was simply a fiction of Joseph Smith"; Marty, "Two Integrities," 18, cf. 11, 12 [324, cf. 314].

18. Ibid., 9 [311].

19. Ibid., 10 [312].

20. Ibid., 9 [311].

21. Ibid.

22. Ibid., 11, 12, 18 [314, 315, 324].

23. Martin E. Marty, *A Short History of Christianity* (New York: Meridian, 1959, 1967), 296.

24. Roman Catholics and Protestants are also faced with "the crisis of faith" that marks our age. Continental Protestants, like French Catholics, "have stared into the face of practical and metaphysical atheism and have seen what modernity has done to the meaning of faith itself." Religious controversies in America are mostly internal to the churches simply because "so many of the battles seem to have to do with matters of faith." The reason for this is that such quarrels have "grown up on the sparse soil of modernity"; Martin E. Marty, "Afterword," in Martin E. Marty, ed., *Where the Spirit Leads: American Denominations Today* (Atlanta: John Knox Press, 1980), 231, 233.

25. Martin E. Marty, *The Public Church: Mainline-Evangelical-Catholic* (New York: Crossroad, 1981), ix; Marty, *A Short History*, 294, 296.

26. Ibid., 296.

27. Ibid., 298-301.

28. Marty, "Two Integrities," 7 [308-9].

29. Ibid., 5 [306].

30. Ibid., 6 [307].

31. Ibid.

32. Ibid.

33. Martin E. Marty, "The Difference in Being a Christian and the Difference It Makes—for History," in C. T. McIntire and Ronald A. Wells, eds., *History and Historical Understanding* (Grand Rapids: Eerdmans, 1984), 41-54.

34. Marty, "History: The Case of the Mormons," 303.

35. Marty, "Two Integrities," 6 [307].

36. Marty has served as apologist for the Mormon history done by his students and associates. He signed Marvin S. Hill's "The Role of Christian Primitivism in the Origin and Development of the

Mormon Kingdom, 1830-1845," Ph.D. diss., University of Chicago, 1968. He provided a "Foreword" to a book by Klaus J. Hansen, *Mormonism and the American Experience* (Chicago/London: University of Chicago Press, 1981), ix-xiv, which he published in the Chicago History of American Religion series. Lawrence Foster refers to him as "major advisor" on a book, *Religion and Sexuality: The Shakers, the Mormons, and the Oneida Community* (Urbana/Chicago: University of Illinois Press, 1984), vii, originally published with the subtitle *Three American Communal Experiments of the Nineteenth Century* (New York: Oxford University Press, 1981). Marty provided a blurb for the jacket of Jan Shipps, *Mormonism: The Story of a New Religious Tradition* (Urbana/Chicago: University of Illinois Press, 1985), and published her essay entitled "The Mormons" in his *Where the Spirit Leads*, 25-40.

    37. For example, Richard L. Bushman, *Joseph Smith and the Beginnings of Mormonism* (Urbana/Chicago: University of Illinois Press, 1984).

    38. Marty, "Two Integrities," 9, 10-11 [311, 313-14].

    39. Ibid., 10 [312].

    40. Ibid., 11 [313].

    41. Ibid., 9 [311].

    42. Ibid., 11 [313].

    43. Ibid., 11 [314].

    44. Ibid., 12 [315].

    45. Ibid., 11 [314].

    46. Those interested in Mormon issues often address secondary questions. For the most part, the issues they deal with stand outside the controversy over whether the Book of Mormon is true and Joseph Smith a genuine prophet. Yet opinions on the truth of the foundations may still control, or be reflected in the way they address secondary issues. Lawrence Foster contends that he is inclined "to grapple with Joseph Smith's formative personal experiences." But, "as a scholar in the field of religious history who has read hundreds of similar visionary experiences [presumably entirely comparable to those claimed by Joseph Smith], I tend (unless I find compelling evidence to the contrary) to try to focus on the naturalistic (including psychological) components which accompanied—and which may or may not 'explain'—such phenomena." Foster ("A Radical Misstatement," *Dialogue* 22/2 [Summer 1988]: 5) seems to believe that by approaching Joseph Smith's prophetic claims in naturalistic terms he will succeed in "reconstructing precisely *what* Joseph Smith actually experienced." When applied to the Book of Mormon, he has,

for example, suggested "some of the sources that could contribute to the development of a comprehensive naturalistic explanation of the Book of Mormon—an explanation which could go beyond the conventional Mormon view that it is a literal history translated by Joseph Smith or the conventional anti-Mormon view that it is a conscious fraud" (Foster, *Religion and Sexuality*, 294). Though he does not refer to his naturalistic explanation as constituting a "middle ground" between the two alternatives, as he set them forth, that would be an appropriate description. Such explicit naturalistic answers to the primary questions may, in addition, color or even control approaches to secondary questions.

47. Marty, "Two Integrities," 12, also 11, 18 [314, also 324].

48. Ibid., 12 [315].

49. Ibid., 11 [314].

50. Ibid.

51. Ibid.

52. Ibid., 8 [309].

53. Ibid., 11 [314].

54. Ibid.

55. Ibid.

56. Efforts to turn Joseph Smith into a mystic may be contrasted with Hugh Nibley, "Prophets and Mystics," in *The World and the Prophets*, vol. 3, *The Collected Works of Hugh Nibley* (Salt Lake City: Deseret Book and F.A.R.M.S., 1987), 98-107, who distinguishes genuine prophets from mystics. Jan Shipps, "Mormons in Politics," Ph.D. diss., University of Colorado, 1965, 31-32, opined that Joseph Smith was a typical mystic and the Book of Mormon a typical mystical text. Her opinion was then promoted by Leonard J. Arrington— see, for example, Leonard J. Arrington and Davis Bitton, *The Mormon Experience: A History of the Latter-day Saints* (New York: Vintage Press, 1979), 5, where Joseph's special revelations are described as mystical theophanies—and taken up by Thomas G. Alexander, "Wilford Woodruff and the Changing Nature of Mormon Religious Experience," *Church History* 45/1 (March 1976): 60-61, 69; cf. Alexander, "The Place of Joseph Smith," 14-15. Paul M. Edwards, "The Secular Smiths," *Journal of Mormon History* 4 (1977): 3-17 (reprinted in Maurice L. Draper and A. Bruce Lindgren, eds., *Restoration Studies II* [Independence, MO: Herald House, 1983], 89-101) turns Joseph Smith into an Eastern mystic. Max Nolan, "Joseph Smith and Mysticism," *Journal of Mormon History* 10 (1983): 105-16, challenged that view. Paul M. Edwards attempts to account for the Book of Mormon as Joseph Smith's "speculative work that gives the story of his

experience," which he understands as mystical. Edwards pictures Joseph Smith as both "mystic and technician. . . . He sought to present his teachings within the bounds of ancient scripture, often reworking the old text to fit his new conceptions. He also gathered his own teaching into the Book of Mormon, a speculative work that gives the story of his experience, and the truths he arrived at from considering the experiences" (*Preface to Faith: A Philosophical Inquiry into RLDS Beliefs* [Midvale, UT: Signature Books, 1984], 31-34, especially 33). Another version of the argument that Joseph Smith was a mystic was advanced in 1983 by Anthony A. Hutchinson, "A Mormon Midrash? LDS Creation Narratives in Redaction-Critical Perspective," a paper presented at the Mormon History Association meetings in Omaha, Nebraska, in May 1983, 10-14, who overtly associated mysticism with fiction-fabrication, myth-production, or parable in Joseph Smith's dissociative personality, in order to explain the book of Moses and Book of Mormon, as well as the story of Moroni. By 1988, he was more cautious with both his claims and his language (Anthony A. Hutchinson, "A Mormon Midrash? LDS Creation Narratives Reconsidered," *Dialogue*, 21/4 [Winter 1988]: 18, n. 5), though he had not entirely abandoned his notion that Joseph Smith was something like a mystic, rather than a prophet as that has been understood by the Saints, and as biblical prophets are understood in much of the critical literature not driven by a narrow theological agenda. Hill, on the other hand, once attempted to link superstition, mysticism, and magic in his naturalistic explanation of Joseph Smith: "Secular or Sectarian History?" *Church History* 43/1 (March 1974): 80, 86, 92; and "Brodie Revisited," *Dialogue* 7/4 (Winter 1972): 75, 76-78.

57. Leonard J. Arrington, "Why I Am a Believer" *Sunstone* 10/1 (1985): 36-38 (an edited version is reprinted in Philip L. Barlow, *A Thoughtful Faith: Essays on Belief by Mormon Scholars* [Centerville, UT: Canon Press, 1986], 225-33); Shipps, *Mormonism*, 46. Klaus J. Hansen, "Jan Shipps and the Mormon Tradition," *Journal of Mormon History* 11 (1984): 138, cf. 144-45, says that Shipps avoids the question of truth with the vague word "myth." In 1984 he maintained that the question of the truth of the Book of Mormon is of decisive importance, though that seems to contradict an earlier opinion. In 1981 (in his *Mormonism*), Hansen essentially took the position now taken by Shipps and also by Lawrence Foster, "New Perspectives on the Mormon Past," *Sunstone* 7/1 (January-February 1982): 41-45.

58. Shipps, *Mormonism*, xii, 6-8, 18, 36, 68. She credits Hill with

fashioning this explanation. Earlier, Dale Morgan and others attempted to link Joseph Smith with magic. The culmination of these efforts is D. Michael Quinn's *Early Mormonism and the Magic World View* (Salt Lake City: Signature Press, 1987). Quinn assembles an elaborate, richly documented, fanciful, and highly exaggerated case for seeing Joseph Smith as a magician. Unfortunately, though Quinn proclaims his piety (xx-xxi), he does not show how some of his more bizarre claims about the alleged involvement of Joseph Smith with certain elements of magic can be made consistent with the content of Mormon faith, nor does he attempt to assess the logical implications of his stance for understanding the Book of Mormon or Joseph Smith's prophetic claims. For a wise assessment of the current enthrallment of Mormon historians with the presumed involvement of Joseph Smith with folk magic, see Richard L. Bushman, "The Book of Mormon in Early Mormon History," in Davis Bitton and Maureen U. Beecher, eds., *New Views of Mormon History: A Collection of Essays in Honor of Leonard J. Arrington* (Salt Lake City: University of Utah Press, 1987), 3-4. Without discounting the magical elements in Joseph's early youth and in the world in which he lived, Bushman sets the whole matter in proper perspective, and thereby allows the prophetic message to have its own integrity apart from the trappings of folk culture.

59. Abraham Heschel, *God in Search of Man* (New York: Meridian and Jewish Publication Society, 1959), 218.

60. Ibid., 223, itemizing letters supplied.

61. Alexander, who had earlier defended all the Mormon history done in the last forty years, now distinguishes between the history written from within the categories of faith and the secular history which explains Mormon things with categories borrowed from secular or sectarian religious studies and the social or behavioral sciences. The essays that show signs of Marty's "crisis in Mormon historiography" are primarily the work of Alexander's "Secularists." The work of most of those he labels "New Mormon Historians" raise few fundamental issues except by inadvertence. Alexander ("Historiography and the New Mormon History," 30, 45-46) now admits that there is a secularized strand of Mormon history that challenges the faith (cf. Bradford, "The Case for the New Mormon History," 143-50, for a searching criticism of Alexander's attack on the critics of naturalistic history). On the other hand, Hill ("The 'New Mormon History' Reassessed," 124-25) denies that a history done in naturalistic terms can challenge the integrity of Mormon faith. He justifies that conclusion by insisting that "mak-

ing concessions where evidence requires merely shifts the way we perceive some things and not the substance of the things themselves" (ibid., 125). He then points to a survey of the readers of *Dialogue*, apparently as an example, indicating that "nearly half" of those few readers who reject the Book of Mormon as an authentic history still claim to "believe in its divine origin" (ibid., 125). He fails to show how such a shift would avoid compromising "the missionary message of the restoration" (ibid., 125) or how it would avoid turning the Book of Mormon into a mere antiquarian curiosity, lacking genuine divine authority, or the power to put the Saints in touch with a real past.

62. Marty, "Two Integrities," 12 [315].

63. Ibid.

64. Foster, *Religion and Sexuality*, 294-97; Hansen, *Mormonism and the American Experience*, 10-16; cf. Hansen, "Jan Shipps," 144-45.

65. Marty, "Two Integrities," 13 [316].

66. Shipps, *Mormonism: The Story of a New Religious Tradition*, 39. Shipps claims that "serious critics" of the Book of Mormon have found it "not only worthless but a fraud." However, she insists that they need to explore the implications of its content and religious function for believers. "Without accepting the work at face value," Shipps claims, "it is nevertheless possible to regard the Book of Mormon as the product of an extraordinary and profound act of the religious imagination" (Shipps, "The Mormons," 29-30). Some have seen her move as legerdemain. According to Hansen, "a major reason for her success is her historicist approach, which allows her to dismiss epithets such as fraud or delusion as utterly irrelevant to the kind of questions she asks." He objects to that ploy because it avoids the question of truth. "Significantly, . . . Fawn Brodie, Sterling McMurrin, and the author of this essay . . . believe that if the Book of Mormon wasn't true, it must be a monumental fraud." For Hansen, Brodie demonstrated that the Book of Mormon is fraudulent (Hansen, "Jan Shipps and the Mormon Tradition," 144-45). Thomas G. Alexander ("An Approach to the Mormon Past," a review of Klaus J. Hansen, *Mormonism and the American Experience*, in *Dialogue* 16/4 [Winter 1983]: 146-48) makes Hansen into a defender of the faith. More recently, he has located Hansen and others in a group he labels "Secularists." Though the bulk of his essay is a denial that any Mormon historians have been influenced by positivism, he admits that those he calls "Secularists" make the mistake of "attempting to move it *more* toward positivism" (Alexander, "His-

toriography and the New Mormon History," 31; cf. 39). Alexander ("The Pursuit of Understanding," *Dialogue* 18/1 [Spring 1985]: 110) acknowledges that secular, naturalistic accounts of the Mormon past, that is, history resting on positivist assumptions, are incompatible with faith. He strives to avoid positivism by insisting that he is an historicist. He disregards the threat posed by historicist relativism. He claims that "contrary to what some of the critics of the New Mormon History have asserted, it is possible—perhaps even necessary—for purposes of analysis to separate the question of authenticity from the question of significance. . . . It may even prove useful to address the latter question and ignore the former" (Alexander, "An Approach," 148). He assumes that neutrality on the prophetic truth claims is compatible with accepting the Latter-day Saints on their own terms.

67. Thomas G. Alexander ("Substantial, Important, and Brilliant," a review of Jan Shipps, *Mormonism: The Story of a New Religious Tradition*, in *Dialogue* 18/4 [Winter 1985]: 186) defends Shipps against Hansen's criticisms of her historicist relativism by claiming that those concerned with truth-claims wrongly "engage in sectarian controversy." Troubled by criticisms directed at Shipps, Alexander states that "Hansen, on the left, has joined forces with critics of the 'New Mormon History' on the right" by arguing that the prophetic claims are such that historians cannot entirely avoid or dismiss the question of whether they involve fraud or delusion, or truth. From Alexander's point of view, both modes of criticism "are unfounded, since they erroneously assume the reification of an abstraction and the equivalence of the model and the actual condition," whatever that may mean (Alexander, "Toward the New Mormon History," 368). On the other hand, Hill opposes relativism. He senses that historicist relativism, if taken seriously, threatens to become a form of nihilism, because it denies that explanations have a relationship to a real past. Hence Hill, "Richard L. Bushman—Scholar and Apologist," *Journal of Mormon History* 11 (1984): 133, inveighs against those who "would abandon themselves to a wreckless [*sic*] historical relativity that would logically sacrifice all history as possible truth." Hill does not aim that criticism at Alexander, who has boldly announced his own relativism in an effort to defend himself from the claim that the illusion of an objective history is blemished by positivism, but at critics of revisionist history. Unlike Alexander, Hill insists on the effort to recover the past in "an objective way." He claims that "the historical relativists may have gone too far. If those who doubt the possibility of an objective history had thought their

position through, they would have perceived that if it is not possible to say anything truthful about the past, the missionary message of the restoration would be included. A position so cynical would destroy all Mormon claims to historical truth" (Hill, "The 'New Mormon History' Reassessed," 125). If anyone has begun to move in that direction, it is those anxious to defend themselves from the claim that their history manifests traces of positivism; cf. Alexander, "Historiography and the New Mormon History."

68. Shipps, *Mormonism: The Story of a New Religious Tradition,* 28.

69. Ibid., 29, 43.

70. But the crucial question is whether accounts of human and divine things, and hence myth in that sense, disclose historical reality. Bushman shows that the strength and "staying power of the Latter-day Saints from 1830 to the present rest on belief in the reality" of certain crucial events, including "that the Book of Mormon was true history" (Bushman, *Joseph Smith and the Beginnings of Mormonism,* 188). Yet he claims that "Shipps's work breaks the deadlock between believers and skeptics" (ibid., 192). Though their positions have some things in common, in the decisive respect Bushman's position differs from that of Shipps, who holds that what the Saints have is myth (understood as fiction), at least when seen from the perspective of history. That implies that faith is not in touch with a genuine historical reality.

71. Marty, "Two Integrities," 11 [314].

72. When asked about the so-called Salamander Letter (one of Mark Hofmann's sensational forgeries), Shipps said that "the church hierarchy and the Mormon in the street [must] confront the fact that the Mormon story as they believe it is not the way it was." She claimed that, instead of the traditional Mormon account of messengers from the heavens, one of whom made available an authentic ancient text, the roots of Mormon faith actually rest on "magic and occult practices" (Richard Ostling and Christine Arrington, "Challenging Mormonism's Roots," *Time,* May 20, 1985, 44). The disclosure of Hofmann's forgeries has not altered her stance on magic providing the explanation for the Book of Mormon and Joseph Smith's prophetic claims. "The future prophet," she asserts, "could very well have been employing the magic arts when he sought treasure in the Hill Cumorah, where he said the plates were found. But since religion and magic were not mutually exclusive . . . , his having been involved in folk magic does not indicate that psychobiographer Fawn M. Brodie was necessarily correct in describing

Joseph Smith as a village scryer who engaged in conscious deception. It is entirely possible that rather than being quite aware that he was creating a work of fiction that he afterward came to accept as true, Smith became convinced as the text of the Book of Mormon started to take shape that the words he dictated" constituted the restoration of an ancient history (Jan Shipps, "The Reality of the Restoration and the Restoration Ideal in the Mormon Tradition," in Richard T. Hughes, ed., *The American Quest for the Primitive Church* [Urbana: University of Illinois Press, 1988], 184).

73. Marty uses Paul Ricoeur's expression "primitive naiveté" to describe the beliefs of the child or isolated tribe or unreflective adult, and uses "secondary naiveté" to describe the faith of one who has faced a crisis of faith by encountering competition to his beliefs and has managed to retain them. Marty makes much of the "primitive naiveté" of the Saints (Marty, "Two Integrities," 5, 9 [306, 312]), or of what he calls "unreflective" Saints (ibid., 10 [312]). The crisis is brought on by threats to naive faith through the recognition of other possibilities. But the Saints have always been involved in controversy over the connection of faith to the Mormon past because their faith is tied to history, and that seems often to have taken them beyond primitive naiveté to reflective understanding.

74. Marty, "Two Integrities," 9 [311].

75. Shipps, "The Mormons in Politics," 31-32.

76. Hill, "Secular or Sectarian History?" 96.

77. Ibid., who is citing Brodie's "Supplement," *No Man Knows My History*, 405-25. Hill does not sense the subtle sophistication of Brodie's position, perhaps because he did not have access to the discussions that took place within the Brodie-Morgan circle. These materials are available in Special Collections at the University of Utah's Marriott Library. Following publication of Bernard DeVoto's review of Brodie's *No Man Knows My History*, "The Case of the Prophet, Joseph Smith," *New York Herald Tribune*, Sunday, December 16, 1945, 7:1, there was a discussion between Morgan, DeVoto, and Brodie over whether it was possible to explain Joseph Smith as other than a conscious fraud, if one began with the assumption or otherwise reached the conclusion that he could not have been a genuine prophet. Morgan held that a Great Divide logically separates the kind of history that can be done by those who believe or bracket their unbelief and those who do not. The problem for those whose *a priori* was that Joseph Smith was not a genuine prophet was to fashion, on that side of the Divide, a coherent and plausible

naturalistic account. Morgan and Brodie realized that there were many scenarios on the unbelieving side of the Great Divide. And, on either side of the Divide, the accounts could be more or less well done. The problem for one attempting to provide a naturalistic account was to figure out a coherent one. Morgan and Brodie argued that, whatever the psychological component of the explanation, the most plausible explanation had to start with and include an element of conscious fraud. For the details of this discussion see *Dale Morgan to Juanita Brooks, 12 April 1942 (for background); *Morgan to Brooks, 15 December 1945; *Morgan to DeVoto, 20 December 1945; *Morgan to Brodie, 22 December 1945; DeVoto to Brodie, 28 December 1945; (DeVoto to Morgan, 28 December 1945); Brodie to DeVoto, 29 December 1945; *Morgan to DeVoto, 2 January 1946; *Morgan to Brodie, 7 January 1946; Morgan to Brodie, 28 January 1946; see Madeline McQuown's notes on the discussion between DeVoto, Morgan, and Brodie, no date, for a summary — these are all available in the Marriott Library Special Collections. Letters marked with an asterisk are in Morgan, *Dale Morgan*, 25-29, 84-119.

78. Brodie, "An Oral Interview," 103-5, 111.

79. Hill, "Historiography of Mormonism," 418-19.

80. Alexander Campbell, *Delusions: An Analysis of the Book of Mormon* (Boston: Benjamin H. Greene, 1832).

81. Hill, "Secular or Sectarian History?" 96. Hill now claims that in 1974 (ibid., 96) he "used the term 'middle ground' to describe a position between those who said Mormonism is untrue and those who insisted on conclusive proof that it is true" (Hill, "The 'New Mormon History' Reassessed," 116, n. 1). That is not an accurate paraphrase of the formula advanced in "Secular or Sectarian History?" Nowhere in that essay does he search for a middle ground between a conservative "right" among Mormon historians insisting on conclusive proof of Joseph Smith's prophetic claims, and an anti-Mormon "left" which claims "that Mormonism is historically untrue" (ibid., 115). The mode of explanation that he called for in 1974 was clearly somewhere between prophet and faker. What he now proffers as a "middle ground" is an agnosticism about the Book of Mormon and Joseph Smith's prophetic claims. Hill's "middle ground historians" do not try to *prove* either that Joseph Smith was a prophet or a fraud (ibid., 117). From his perspective, all attempts to test or examine the truthfulness of the Book of Mormon are misguided, for the question of the historical authenticity of the Book of Mormon (1) is not one that can be examined by professional

historians, and (2) such questions are irrelevant to the truth of the faith, for what might make a religion "true" is merely its "essential social usefulness" (ibid.). After incorrectly charging Noel Reynolds with holding that a final proof of the historical authenticity of the Book of Mormon is a simple matter, Hill wonders "after 150 years of arguments whether it is that easy to finally establish the historicity of the Book of Mormon, or to disprove it" (ibid., 116, cf. a similar remark in Hill, "Brodie Revisited," 72). By denying that the historical authenticity of the Book of Mormon can be tested, Hill skirts the question of whether Joseph Smith's prophetic claims and the Book of Mormon are within the arena of history in such a way that they can be addressed by historians, even if the issue of veracity cannot be settled in that manner. To treat the Mormon faith as anything but firmly rooted in history is to rob it of its essential character, and thereby transform the faith (Midgley, "Faith and History," 220-25). Hill seems to realize that this is true, for he asserts that one of his critics, contrary to what he has written, denies that anything can be said about the past. Hill reasons that to adopt such a relativist position would rob the faith of something essential, which he apparently is not willing to do (Hill, "The 'New Mormon History' Reassessed," 125). Yet, he attacks efforts to test the historical authenticity of the Book of Mormon (ibid., 116, 118-121, where his targets are Nibley, Bushman, Reynolds, John W. Welch, and Truman G. Madsen; cf. "The Historiography of Mormonism," 418, where Hill takes on Nibley).

82. See Marvin S. Hill, "Critical Examination of *No Man Knows My History*, by Fawn M. Brodie," copy of a manuscript in Special Collections, Harold B. Lee Library, Brigham Young University, n.p., n.d., 17. The acceptance of "a deterministic, environmental interpretation of Joseph's history" he called "a naturalistic interpretation of Joseph Smith." This bias can be seen in Hill's recent essay (Hill, "Richard L. Bushman," 126) where he struggles to save "environmentalism," as he now calls his naturalistic *a priori*, from Bushman's account which separates the core of the message of the restored gospel from narrow environmental causation, or from simplistic product-of-culture explanations.

83. Marty, "Two Integrities," 11 [314].

84. Ibid.

85. Heschel, *God in Search of Man*, 218.

86. John Farrell, "The Historian's Dilemma, in "Utah: Inside the Church/State," *Denver Post*, November 21-28, 1982, Special Report, 45; Ostling and Arrington, "Challenging Mormonism's Roots," 44.

87. Sterling M. McMurrin, "An Interview with Sterling Mc-Murrin," *Dialogue* 17/1 (Spring 1984): 23 (a version was also published under the title, "The History of Mormonism and Church Authorities: An Interview with Sterling M. McMurrin," in *Free Inquiry* 4/1 [Winter 1983/84]: 32-34).

88. Ibid., 22.

89. Ibid., 20.

90. Sterling M. McMurrin, *Religion, Reason, and Truth* (Salt Lake City: University of Utah Press, 1982), 279-80, cf. 166-67.

91. Leonard J. Arrington, "Scholarly Studies of Mormonism in the Twentieth Century," *Dialogue* 1/1 (Spring 1966): 28. For additional apologies for naturalistic explanations, see the preface to Leonard J. Arrington's *Great Basin Kingdom* (Lincoln: University of Nebraska Press, 1966), viii-ix; Foster, *Religion and Sexuality*, 294; Sterling M. McMurrin, "A New Climate of Liberation: A Tribute to Fawn McKay Brodie," *Dialogue* 14/1 (Spring 1981): 74; Alexander, "An Approach to the Mormon Past," 146; Marvin S. Hill, "A Note on Joseph Smith's First Vision and Its Import in the Shaping of Early Mormonism," *Dialogue* 12/1 (Spring 1979): 90, 95, 97; and also Hill, "The 'New Mormon History' Reassessed," 115, where he quotes Arrington with approval (see Arrington, "Scholarly Studies of Mormonism," 28) that "Mormon history and culture can be studied in human or naturalistic terms — indeed, must be so studied." Hill does not attribute that statement to Arrington, but, like Alexander ("Historiography and the New Mormon History," 25), he mistakenly attributes it to Moses Rischin, a non-Mormon historian, who in a brief and obscure essay on recent literature on Mormon history, wrote the following: "*Leonard Arrington wrote*: 'Most of those who have promoted both the [Mormon History] Association and *Dialogue* are practicing Latter-day Saints; they share basic agreement that the Mormon religion and its history are subject to discussion, if not to argument, and that any particular feature of Mormon life is fair game for detached examination and clarification. They believe that the details of Mormon history and culture can be studied in human and naturalistic terms — indeed, must be so studied — and thus without rejecting the divinity of the Church's origin and work' " (Moses Rischin, "The New Mormon History," *American West* 6/2 [March 1969], 49, quoting Arrington's "Scholarly Studies of Mormonism," 28). In their recent survey of Mormon historians, Arrington and Bitton call special attention to the naturalistic explanations or assumptions of Morgan, Brodie, and Bernard DeVoto (*Mormons and Their Historians*, 117, 119, 123). They also stress that Arrington "did

not hesitate to give a naturalistic interpretation to certain historical themes sacred to the memories of Latter-day Saints" (ibid., 131-132), as they quote the passage from the preface to *Great Basin Kingdom*, vii-viii, in which Arrington defends his use of naturalistic explanations of divine revelations. Hill recently has quoted, but not entirely accurately and yet with approval, Arrington's original apology for his use of naturalistic explanations of the causes of revelation (Hill, "The 'New Mormon History' Reassessed," 117). Robert B. Flanders, with roots in the RLDS community, in 1974 fastened the label "New Mormon History" on middle-ground revisionist accounts of the Mormon past ("Some Reflections on the New Mormon History," *Dialogue* 9/1 [Spring 1974]: 34-41). "Thirty years ago," according to Flanders, "Leonard Arrington in *Great Basin Kingdom* raised for Mormons a fundamental question of epistemology: can empiricism, the secular method of modern history, stand with or even shoulder aside prophetic insight as a means of describing and understanding the saints' experience with the Kingdom in time and space? The challenge of the question," Flanders claims, "continues its work" (Robert B. Flanders, Review of *New Views of Mormon History: A Collection of Essays in Honor of Leonard J. Arrington*, Davis Bitton and Maureen U. Beecher, eds., *John Whitmer Historical Association Journal* 8 [1988]: 91). Unlike RLDS historians, the LDS historians who have taken up the effort to provide naturalistic accounts "are revisionist primarily in the extent to which they rely on the critical methods of secular historical analysis. But it is a revisionism both gentle and veiled. Generally, they leave church politics and leadership alone, as subjects that are inappropriate, taboo, or likely to prove counterproductive. Products of a subculture that questions leadership but little, perhaps they simply never learn to do it," quite unlike their more radically revisionist counterparts among the RLDS (Flanders, Review of *New Views*, 93).

92. McMurrin, "An Interview," 25.

93. Such a history would dispense, except for sentimental purposes, with the traditional belief that Joseph Smith had access to divine things through special revelations. A seemingly less radical approach would be to begin to treat the historical portions of the foundational texts and events as instances of myth or fiction and not as historical reality. For example, Arrington is prepared to accept Joseph Smith's visions or the Book of Mormon as symbolic, or metaphorical, or mythical, or as actual events (Arrington, "Why I Am a Believer," 37). From his perspective, it does not seem to matter how one understands them. He explains that the religious "truth" he

finds in those accounts is on the same order as one might find in something like Pearl Buck's *The Good Earth*. This may explain John Farrell's having reported that "during the Arrington years, the historians tried to gently nudge the church away from its insistence on literal interpretation" (Farrell, "The Historian's Dilemma, 45). Arrington came to the study of Mormon things already equipped with the notion of "myth" which he learned from reading George Santayana, which allowed him to understand the sacred texts and founding events as myths or symbols, if they were not genuine historical realities. From his point of view, it does not matter whether messengers from heaven visited with Joseph Smith or whether the resurrected Jesus visited Nephites because Santayana held that even fiction could contain "religious truth" (see Arrington, "Why I Am a Believer," 36-37). "Liberal Latter-day Saints," according to Farrell, "would find it easier to stick with their church if only it would treat The Book of Mormon as an allegorical story that teaches righteous behavior but isn't necessarily historic truth—the way the Christian churches treat" the Bible (Farrell, "The Historians Dilemma," 42). Farrell also commented that "it would be easier if the church were willing to treat . . . the Book of Mormon and the Book of Abraham as parables, but the hierarchy won't back down" (ibid., 45).

94. Marty, "Two Integrities," 19, cf. 10 [324, cf. 312].

95. What meaning and authority might the Book of Mormon have, when read as "the casting of theology in story form" (Hutchinson, "A Mormon Midrash? LDS Creation Narratives Reconsidered," 16), or as "*inspired fiction*" (ibid., 15)? He insists that "such a sensitive and crucial subject is too complex and broad to be addressed" in a sixty-four page essay setting forth a revisionist ideology. And yet he affirms that stories, when understood as mere myths, have "in some ways gained a new power because of their newly acquired clarity of meaning," though he also grants that he "suffered a sense of loss," and "experienced a certain disappointment" as he rejected "the claim of many of Joseph Smith's works that they not only have a divine origin but also have an ancient origin" (ibid., 70). He now advances the notion that "imaginative appropriation" (ibid., 12), "imaginative reworking" (ibid., 14), or "creative reworking" of older beliefs, stories or traditions by "inspired" redactors constitutes divine revelation. The product of "imagination" (ibid., 15, 16, 17, 17, n. 3) is "myth," understood as "the casting of theology in story form" (ibid., 16). And yet "one may freely agree that a myth's power in part depends upon the historical reality of events or persons within it" (ibid., 17, n. 3),

perhaps as a result of what he demurely labels "vigorous criticism" (ibid., 11). But historical reality must stand behind the myth "only when this historical reality is somehow directly related to the reality the myth seeks to mediate" (ibid., 17, n. 3; cf. Midgley, "Faith and History," 221-22). When might that be? "The power of a myth about redemption through Christ crucified and resurrected, however, seems directly dependent on whether Jesus in fact died and then bodily reappeared to his disciples" (Hutchinson, "A Mormon Midrash? LDS Creation Narratives Reconsidered," 17, n. 3), but the power of the restored gospel is not dependent upon whether angels visited with Joseph Smith, or whether certain of Joseph Smith's works have a genuine ancient origin. The Book of Mormon, book of Abraham, and book of Moses (including the Enoch materials) are, for him, merely "myths" generated by Joseph Smith's "creative reworking" of biblical and other lore. Those in thrall to naturalistic accounts of the Book of Mormon (and hence of the Mormon past) turn to what McMurrin once denigrated as "sophisticated theories of symbol and myth" (McMurrin, *Religion, Reason, and Truth*, 143), borrowed from Protestant or Catholic theologians or similar sources in an effort to turn prophets into mystics in order to salvage some semblance of "religious" meaning from stories no longer believed to be simply true. The difference between a Hutchinson and a McMurrin is the degree of sentimentality about elements of the faith whose grounds have been rejected or abandoned.

96. Marty, "Two Integrities," 4-5 [305].

97. Cf. Hill, "Richard L. Bushman," 125-33. Hill seemed troubled by the ease with which Bushman was able to tell Joseph Smith's story and defend the Book of Mormon against traditional criticism. He faulted Bushman's book because he saw it as an apology, and, from his perspective, faith necessarily introduces a corrupting bias. Hill has also faulted Richard L. Anderson for manifesting a "pro-Mormon bias of such intensity that it leads too often to overstatement, errors in logic, and misreading of evidence" (Marvin S. Hill, Review of Richard L. Anderson, *Joseph Smith's New England Heritage*, in *The New England Quarterly* 46/1 [March 1973]: 156.) Hill (review of Leonard J. Arrington and Davis Bitton's *The Mormon Experience*, in *American Historical Review* 84/5 [December 1979]: 1487-88) complains that the authors of that book have a "booster spirit" or an "affirmative bias" that causes them to overlook or distort things. They "demonstrate a strong Mormon bias that leads to errors that may not be observed except by specialists." He claims, by way of illustration, that they fail to mention that two of

the three witnesses to the Book of Mormon later denied their testimony, and they are guilty of "ignoring the romantic disposition"
of the plot and characters of the Book of Mormon. Hill's polemic
against Bushman's book also reflects a demand among certain historians, who long for the appearance of neutrality and dispassionate
objectivity, for detachment from belief in the doing of Mormon
history. By clinging to the myth that the historian can and must be
detached from the corrupting bias of faith, Mormon historians may
or may not sense that the naturalistic bias standing behind environmental explanations betrays the faith.

98. Marty, "Two Integrities," 4 [305]. "Subservience to a particular religion is therefore incompatible with honest inquiry,
whether by historians or by anyone else" (James L. Clayton, "Does
History Undermine Faith?" *Sunstone* 7/2 [March-April 1982]: 34).

99. Hill, "Secular or Sectarian History?" 80, 88, 89.

100. Hill, "The 'New Mormon History' Reassessed," 125.

101. Marty, "Two Integrities," 4 [305]; cf. Peter Novick, *That Noble
Dream: The "Objectivity Question" and the American Historical Profession*
(New York: Cambridge University Press, 1988).

102. Hill, "The 'New Mormon History' Reassessed," 125.

103. Shipps, *Mormonism: The Story of a New Religious Tradition*,
28.

104. Marty, "Two Integrities," 14 [318]. Revisionist historians
tend to be uncomfortable with this literature. The following is an
example: "Most of the recent interest in the study of hermeneutics,"
according to Hutchinson, "influenced by New Criticism, the philosophical hermeneutics of the late [Martin] Heiddeger [*sic*], and
French Structuralism, has centered in noematics [thoughts about
texts and their meaning] and the question of intent" (Anthony A.
Hutchinson, "LDS Approaches to the Holy Bible," *Dialogue* 15/1
[Spring 1982]: 119, n. 9). "Although the recent discussion is needed
and somewhat helpful, I think," Hutchinson opines, "that some
basic cautions are needed," though he has not indicated what they
might be. He has been influenced by the discussion of hermeneutical
issues, for he grants that a presuppositionless exegesis of texts is
impossible (ibid., 118, n. 8). His misgivings about philosophical
hermeneutics may betray an uneasiness about a discussion of the
implications of the assumptions upon which his own ideology
rests.

105. Marty turns to the current literature on hermeneutics (Marty
"Two Integrities," 6, 14-18 [307, 317-24]). Martin Heidegger has
shown, according to Marty, "that unprejudiced, objective knowl-

edge was not possible" by identifying the formal and informal preunderstandings that stand behind all interpretations and explanations. Marty assumes that what he calls hermeneutics is a special approach to texts. It is actually the attempt to understand the conditions necessary for understanding any text or text analogue. Hermeneutics is an endeavor to clarify historical method and is not a special technique that can be set over against other techniques. Marty also seems to neglect the function of tradition in making the meaning of texts accessible.

106. Marty, "Two Integrities," 6 [307].

107. Though the bulk of his essay is an effort to show that no one doing so-called "New Mormon History" has been influenced by positivism, Alexander now admits that "the term 'objectivity' has become so weighted with the positivistic connotation of full detachment . . . that it should be abandoned." Furthermore, he admits, "it is clear that some historians, including some of the New Mormon Historians—in the search for objectivity—have tried to detach their personal religious and moral views from their writing" ("Historiography and the New Mormon History," 39). He cites Hill and Melvin T. Smith as examples, but the list could be extended to include others like Michael T. Walton and George D. Smith. The pressure on Mormon historians to leave their own belief out of their history comes at least partly from those who simply do not believe. Both the demand for objectivity in the sense of detachment from faith, and for naturalistic treatments of Mormon history originally came from unbelievers who thought they had somehow avoided the corrupting commitments of those they brushed aside as mere apologists. Morgan and Brodie, both writers with roots in Mormon culture, were flush with that illusion. But both Morgan's work, as well as the recent seemingly more neutral or detached history done by people like Hill and Hansen, suffer in comparison with that done by those who are believers, and who are not embarrassed to have their faith, rather than an absence of faith, play a role in their history. The strength of Morgan's position is that he correctly sensed that it had to be one way or the other—that there is a Great Divide necessarily separating those who write history with naturalistic assumptions from those who allow the possibility that the prophetic claims could be simply true. When Bushman's *Joseph Smith and the Beginnings of Mormonism* is compared with Morgan's efforts—both cover somewhat the same ground—it turns out that Bushman's work is clearly superior in content, style, and plausibility, yet it does not manifest the affectation of seeming detachment or neutrality that

leaves the reader guessing about the controlling biases. Those signals are often placed in the text by writers anxious to make their writing acceptable to what Bitton and Arrington call the *demands* of different audiences.

108. Marty, "Two Integrities," 5 [305].

109. Ibid., 15 [319-20].

110. Bushman, *Joseph Smith and the Beginnings of Mormonism*, 187. The crux of Hill's quarrel with Bushman concerns the Book of Mormon. Hill claims "that Bushman says nothing about the theology of the Book of Mormon" (Hill, "Richard L. Bushman" 127, 129-30), and that "Bushman's conservatism is also manifest in his failure to treat Book of Mormon themes, except to argue that Book of Mormon theocratic tendencies hardly match Republican values in 1820 America" (Hill, "The 'New Mormon History' Reassessed," 120, citing Bushman, *Joseph Smith and the Beginnings of Mormonism*, 132-33). Though Bushman provided a rather full account of its prophetic message (see chap. 4, 115-42, which is entitled "The Book of Mormon," and also Bushman's fine essay entitled "The Book of Mormon in Early Mormon History," 3-18, which Hill overlooks), he did not, as Hill seems to prefer, opine that the Book of Mormon contains a pessimistic Calvinism which Joseph Smith later contradicted and replaced with an optimistic, progressive (or liberal) view of man, and a correspondingly different view of God. Alexander maintains that it is "bad history" to hold that even the central prophetic messages of the restoration—the understanding of God and man—unfold in a coherent manner or "build on each other in a hierarchical fashion." To hold such a view, he feels, "leaves an unwarranted impression of continuity and consistency." Instead, he sees in the teachings of Joseph Smith and others after 1835 a radical shift away from a form of Calvinism (or "basically sensual and devilish man"), as well as an "essentially trinitarian" understanding of God similar to that found in nineteenth-century American Protestantism. He seems anxious that the current interest in the message of the Book of Mormon will replace what he (and others) see as a later optimistic, "progressive theology," which he thinks came on the scene in what he calls the "progressive reconstruction of doctrine" between 1893 and 1925 (Alexander, "The Reconstruction of Mormon Doctrine: From Joseph Smith to Progressive Theology," *Sunstone* 5/4 [July-August 1980]: 24-33; reprinted in *Sunstone* 10/5 [May 1985]: 8-18). Though he denies that the revelations to Joseph Smith constitute a coherent line-upon-line adding to the Mormon understanding of divine things, Alexander still feels that "the Book of Mormon is an

ancient text and that the doctrines explicated in the book are doctrines believed by the Nephites and other ancient peoples whose record the book contains" (Alexander, "Afterwords," *BYU Studies* 29/4 [1989]: 143). That avowal may make his theory of a radical "reconstruction" of the early and presumably pessimistic views on man and God to a later optimistic, "progressive theology" somewhat less attractive to revisionist historians. He is anxious to defend "progressive theology" against the presumably pessimistic Calvinist orthodoxy, moderated with touches of Arminianism, to which he finds parallels in the Book of Mormon and other early revelations. This appears to be an argument against what he and others (for example, McMurrin and O. Kendall White, Jr., *Mormon New-Orthodoxy: A Crisis Theology* [Salt Lake City: Signature Press, 1987]) have labelled "Mormon Neo-Orthodoxy," which they fault for taking the contents of the Book of Mormon and Joseph Smith's prophetic claims seriously. Alexander claims that even the understanding of "the atonement and salvation," which he concludes was originally "similar" to the teaching "that might have been found in many contemporary Protestant denominations," underwent a "transformation" or "reconstruction" in the "doctrinal development" of the Nauvoo period (Thomas G. Alexander, " 'A New and Everlasting Covenant': An Approach to the Theology of Joseph Smith," in Davis Bitton and Maureen U. Beecher, eds., *New Views of Mormon History: A Collection of Essays in Honor of Leonard J. Arrington* [Salt Lake City: University of Utah Press, 1987], 57-58). The King Follett funeral sermon is, for Alexander, the culmination of a radical transformation in "Joseph Smith's theology" ("Reconstruction of Mormon Doctrine," 28; "A New and Everlasting Covenant," 58-59). Hill assumes that "Alexander has demonstrated the negative, Calvinistic view of man in early Mormonism" (Hill, "Richard L. Bushman," 127), and he conjectures that Bushman skirted those troubling conclusions in his treatment of the Book of Mormon. Hill's paraphrase of Alexander's inference, however, is flawed, for Alexander actually maintains that "the Mormon doctrine of man in New York contained elements of both Calvinism and Arminianism, though tending toward the latter" ("Reconstruction of Mormon Doctrine," 25). Alexander's language is ambiguous. For example, a number of his inferences can be read as holding that Joseph Smith drew upon strands of Protestant sectarian theology in fashioning the Book of Mormon and early revelations, a position that Alexander would want to deny. But this leaves unclear the meaning of his claims that the Book of Mormon and early teachings of Joseph Smith are "close" or "similar" to contemporary orthodox Protestant theology. In one place he argues that "biblical interpretation is dependent upon a theological system. . . . The system of interpretation which Mormons adopted in 1830 was drawn from contemporary Protestantism" ("The Reconstruction of Mormon Doctrine," 18, n. 23). These statements seem to entail that the system of theology entertained by Mormons in 1830 was drawn from contemporary Protestantism. But Alexander is very anxious to eschew such an inference. Unfortunately he has remained silent on the crucial issues, as he has maintained that "Mormon theology" underwent a "transformation" or "reconstruction" after 1835, as it became more "optimistic," and "progressive," or what others (McMurrin, White) call "liberal." The evolutionary explanation of Mormon beliefs raises fundamental questions about both the character of revelation and the position of the Book of Mormon. Other than Alexander, the tendency of those who argue that there has been a radical "reconstruction" of "Mormon theology" is to hold that the Book of Mormon has no authentic ties to the ancient world, and is, therefore, simply Joseph Smith's fiction, inspired or otherwise. Alexander has yet to explain how one can both believe that the Book of Mormon is an authentic ancient text and yet contain teachings remarkably similar to contemporary Protestantism or whether such apparent similarities are significant. Others, for example, McMurrin, Hutchinson, and perhaps Ostler, have tried to fashion more explicit and coherent revisionist explanations of the Book of Mormon, but have jettisoned, either in whole or in part, historical components of the text, as well as the account of its coming forth through the agency of an angel.

111. Marty, "Two Integrities," 15 [319]. This portion of Marty's essay (Marty, "Two Integrities," 14-18 [317-24]) is mired in a terminology he borrows from the literature on hermeneutics where he is not particularly at home. But it is also the best part of his essay because he has gotten to the crux of the issues and has separated himself from both the relativistic historicism and historical objectivism of writers like Shipps and Foster.

112. Hutchinson argues that the Book of Mormon is "nineteenth-century fiction," but it is still somehow "inspired" (Anthony A. Hutchinson, "The Word of God Is Enough: The Book of Mormon as Nineteenth-Century Fiction," transcript of a talk delivered at the 1987 Washington Sunstone Symposium, May 15-16, 1987, 1, 7-9.) He insists that it is now necessary for specially enlightened Saints to see that the Book of Mormon is not genuine history in order, among other things, to avoid idolatry (ibid., 7-8), as well as to begin

to conform to the standards of secular fundamentalism that he thinks constitutes the standard of scholarship. His primary target is Hugh Nibley (ibid., 3-4). But he is also critical of Blake Ostler's view (ibid., 5) that, while there may be some reasons for believing that the historical portions of the Book of Mormon are authentic, the teachings found in that text were inventions by Joseph Smith (Blake Ostler, "The Book of Mormon as a Modern Expansion of an Ancient Text," *Dialogue* 10/1 [Spring 1987]: 66, 76-87, 108-15). In order to make his theory of "expansions" palatable, Ostler claims that the absorption and adaptation of dogmas from the sectarian environment by Joseph Smith must now be understood as constituting a kind of "inspiration." Hutchinson correctly senses that one must flatly reject the understanding of revelation contained in the Book of Mormon — an understanding directly linked to "its claims about itself" (Hutchinson, "The Word of God Is Enough," 6), and hence to its claim to be an authentic historical record — in order to put in place the kind of theology which he has in mind and which he has borrowed from Catholic and Protestant theologians. Less thoughtful and less strident versions of the position advanced by Hutchinson are occasionally offered, sometimes where the need to see texts like the Book of Mormon as merely inspired fiction is made to grow out of assessments of the findings of critical historical studies on the Bible. Ostler is less coherent than Hutchinson and hence seemingly less radical. However, he also senses that his "expansion" theory demands fundamental alterations in the understanding of what constitutes divine revelation. He advances what he labels "A Mormon Model of Revelation" (Ostler, "The Book of Mormon as a Modern Expansion," 109-11). His novel theory of revelation feeds his "expansion" theory. And he grants that "some may see [his] expansion theory as compromising the historicity of the Book of Mormon. To a certain extent it does" (ibid., 114). Hutchinson, at this point, complains that Ostler has failed to see that, once one has compromised any of those claims (Hutchinson, "The Word of God Is Enough," 5-7), *all* of the claims made by the Book of Mormon about itself must be rejected. Hutchinson, unlike Ostler, capitulates entirely to secular fundamentalism to avoid what both consider the sectarian fundamentalism inherent in the Latter-day Saint understanding of the Book of Mormon and Joseph Smith's prophetic claims. Quinn seems to have incorporated some version of the Hutchinson-Ostler type of approach to the Book of Mormon (*Early Mormonism and the Magic World View*, 150, where he cites Ostler, "The Book of Mormon as a Modern Expansion," 66-67, 100, 104-

15), but without attempting to show how that position can be reconciled with an acceptance of the Book of Mormon as an authentic ancient text and Joseph Smith as a genuine prophet.

113. Marty, "Two Integrities," 17 [321].
114. Ibid., 3 [304].

18

Why No New Judaisms in the Twentieth Century?

Jacob Neusner
The Institute for Advanced Study, Princeton, New Jersey

Since Professor Hugh Nibley has served the scholarly community as a scholar of religion through the study of his specialty, it is appropriate to speak of religions through the study of another particular specialty. What I wish to explain in his honor is what conditions favor the formation of religious systems. This I do through particular attention to the condition of Judaism in the twentieth century, in which, for a long spell now, there has been no new Judaism. As we face the onset of a new age of *systemopoeia*, of the making of religious systems, in Judaism, with the renaissance of energy and faith so characteristic of contemporary Judaism, it is well to look back on the barren age now ended. I do so as an act of esteem and respect for a scholar of religion who, when he receives his audience, will be seen as one of the fecund intellects of the study of religion in our century.

The middle of the twentieth century—until practically our own time—has produced no important and influential Judaic systems. The well-established Judaisms that flourish today—Reform, Orthodoxy, Conservative Judaism—all took shape in the nineteenth century, and in Germany. From after the beginning of Reform Judaism at the start of

A shorter version of this article appeared as "Can Judaism Survive the Twentieth Century?" Tikkun 4/4 (July-August 1989): 38-42.

the nineteenth century to the later twentieth century we identify three periods of enormous system-building in Judaism, or, to invent a word, Judaic *systemopoeia*. At each of these the manufacture of Judaic systems came into sharp focus: 1850-60 for the systems of Orthodoxy and the positive Historical School; and, for the secular Judaisms, 1890-1900 for Jewish Socialism and Zionism. So all of the Judaic systems came into being in the hundred years from 1800 to 1900: first Reform, then, some decades later, in the middle of the century, Orthodoxy and the Historical School; thereafter, again some decades later, at the end of the century, Zionism and Jewish Socialism. We therefore wonder how it is possible that one period produced a range of Judaic systems of depth and enormous breadth, which attracted mass support and persuaded many of the meaning of their lives, while the next three quarters of a century did not. And, further, what are we now to expect, on the eve of the twenty-first century? For I think we are on the threshold of another great age of *systemopoeia* in Judaism.[1]

POLITICAL CHANGE AND SYSTEMIC INERTIA

Why no new Judaisms for so long? We may eliminate answers deriving from the mere accidents of political change; given the important shifts in the political circumstances of Israel, the Jewish people, we should have anticipated exercises in symbolic redefinition to accommodate the social change at hand. That is to say, the stimulus for system-building surely should have come from the creation of the Jewish state, an enormous event. Take the state of Israel, for example. The creation of the first Jewish state in two thousand years yielded nothing more interesting than a flag and a rather domestic politics, not a worldview and a way of life such as the founders of the American republic, Madison and Hamilton, enunciated, for example, and such as their contemporaries, Washington and Jefferson, for instance, imagined that they constructed. State-building need not yield large visions and revisioning of everyday life and how it should be lived; in most cases it has not done so, though in the American case it did. In the Israeli case, it did not. But no Judaic systems have emerged there, only rehearsals and re-presentations of European ones. The rise of the state of Israel destroyed a system, the Zionist one, but replaced it with nothing pertinent to Jewry at large.

But American Jewry presents the same picture. Wars and dislocations, migration and relocation—these in the past stimulated those large-scale reconsiderations that generated and sustained system-building in Jews' societies. The political changes affecting Jews in America, who became Jewish Americans in ways in which Jews did not become Jewish Germans or Jewish Frenchmen or Englishmen or women, yielded no encompassing system. The Judaic system of Holocaust and Redemption leaves unaffected the larger dimensions of human existence of Jewish Americans—and that is part of its power. When we consider the strength, in the Judaisms of America, of Reform, Orthodoxy, and Historical or Conservative Judaism, each in its German formulation, we see the reality.

The Judaic systems of the nineteenth century have endured in America, none of them—until now—facing significant competition of scale. That means millions of people moved from one world to another, changed in language, occupation, and virtually every other significant social and cultural indicator—and produced nothing more than a set of recapitulations of three Judaic systems serviceable under utterly different circumstances. The failure of Israeli Jewry to generate system-building finds its match in the still more startling unproductivity of American Jewry. Nothing much has happened in either of the two massive communities of Israel in the twentieth century.

Political change should have precipitated fresh thought

and experiment, and Judaic systems should have come forth. So change of an unprecedented order yielded a rehearsal of ideas familiar only from other contexts. Israeli nationalism as a Jewish version of third-world nationalism, American Judaism as a Jewish version of a national cultural malaise on account of a lost war—these set forth a set of stale notions altogether. Let me now recapitulate the question, before proceeding to my answer: why no system-building for seventy-five years or so? And we come, then, to the reason for what is, in my judgment, the simple fact that, beyond World War I, Judaic system-building (with the possible exception of the system of Judaic reversion) has come to an end.

WHY NO NEW JUDAIC SYSTEMS FOR SEVENTY-FIVE YEARS?

I see three pertinent factors to explain why no Judaic systems have come forth since the end of the nineteenth century. I do not claim that these factors are sufficient. But I think they are necessary to answer the question before us.

The Holocaust

The demographic factor comes in two parts. First, the most productive sector of world Jewry perished. Second, the conditions that put forth the great systemic creations vanished with the six million who died. Stated as naked truth, not only too many (one is too many!), but the wrong Jews died. What I mean is that Judaic systems in all their variety emerged in Europe, not in America or in what was then Palestine and is now the state of Israel, and within Europe they came from Central and Eastern European Jewry. We may account for the *systemopoeia* of Central and Eastern European Jews in two ways. First, the Jews in the East, in particular, formed a vast population with enormous learning and diverse interests. Second, the systems of the nineteenth and twentieth centuries arose out of a vast population that lived in self-aware circumstances, not scattered and individual but composed and bonded. The Jews who perished formed enormous and self-conscious communities of vast intellectual riches.

To them, being Jewish constituted a collective enterprise, not an individual predilection. In the West, the prevailing attitude of mind identifies religion with belief to the near-exclusion of behavior, and religion tends to identify itself with faith; so religion is understood as a personal state of mind or an individual's personal and private attitude. So the Judaic systems that took shape beyond 1900 exhibit that same Western bias not for society but self, not for culture and community but conscience and character. Under such circumstances *systemopoeia* hardly flourishes, for systems speak of communities and create worlds of meaning, answer pressing public questions, and produce broadly self-evident answers. This can be seen in the contrast between the circumstance of reversionary systems of Judaisms, which involves individuals "coming home" one by one, with the context of the ideological Judaic systems, all of them, in fact, mass movements and Jewish idiomatic statements of still larger mass movements. The demographic fact, then, speaks for itself. I do not know whether one can specify a particular demographic (and not merely intellectual) base necessary for the foundation of a given Judaic system. As I said, the reversionary systems demand a demographic base of one person, but Zionist and Socialist systems, millions. Yet everyone who has traced the history of Judaic systems in modern and contemporary times has found in the mass populations of Central and Eastern Europe the point of origin of nearly all systems. That fact then highlights our original observation that the period of the preparation for, then the mass murder of, European Jewry from the later 1930s to the mid-1940s, marked the end of Judaic *systemopoeia*. We cannot, then, underestimate the impact of the destruction of European Jewry.

One of the as-yet-untallied costs of the murder of six million Jews in Europe therefore encompasses the matter of system-building. The destruction of European Jewry in Eastern and Central Europe brought to an end for a very long time the great age of Judaic system construction and explains the paralysis of imagination and will that has left the Jews to forage in the detritus of an earlier age: re-hearsing other peoples' answers to other peoples' questions. Indeed, I maintain that until Judaic system-builders come to grips with the full extent of the effects of the "Holocaust," they will do little more than recapitulate a world now done with, for the systems before us answered the questions urgent to European Jewry in its situation in the nineteenth and earlier twentieth centuries—those questions, not others.

Yet the demographic issue by itself cannot suffice. For today's Jewish populations produce massive communities, three hundred thousand here, half a million there, and there are, after all, both American Judaism and Israeli na-tionalism to testify to the possibilities of system-building even beyond the mass murder of European Jewry. When we consider, moreover, the strikingly unproductive char-acter of large populations of Jews, the inert and passive character of ideology (such as it is) in the Jewries of France, Britain, South Africa, and the Soviet Union, for instance, in which, so far as the world knows, no Judaic systems have come forth—no worldviews joined to definitions of a way of life capable of sustaining an Israel, a society—the picture becomes clear. Even where there are populations capable of generating and sustaining distinctive Judaic sys-tems, none is in sight. So we have to point to yet another factor, which, as a matter of fact, proves correlative with the first, the loss of European Jewry.

The Demise of Intellect

What we noticed about the Judaic systems of the twentieth century — their utter indifference to the received writings of the Judaism of the dual Torah (i.e., oral and written Torah) — calls our attention to the second explanation for the end of *systemopoeia*. It is the as-yet-unappreciated factor of sheer ignorance, the profound pathos of Jews' illiteracy in all books but the book of the streets and marketplaces of the day. That second factor, the utter loss of access to that permanent treasury of the human experience of Jewry preserved and handed on in the canonical Torah, has already impressed us: the extant raw materials of system-building now prove barren and leached.

The Judaisms that survive provide ready access to emotional or political encounters, readily available to all — by definition. But they offer none to that confrontation of taste and judgment, intellect and reflection, that takes place in traditional cultures and with tradition: worlds in which words matter. People presently resort mainly to the immediately accessible experiences of emotions and of politics. We recall that the systems of the nineteenth and twentieth centuries made constant reference to the Judaism of the dual Torah, at first intimate, later on merely by way of allusion and rejection. The nineteenth-century systems drew depth and breadth of vision from the received Judaism of the dual Torah, out of which they produced — by their own word — variations and continuations. So the received system and its continuators realized not only the world of perceived experience at hand. They also made accessible the alien but interesting human potentialities of other ages, other encounters altogether with the potentialities of life in society. The repertoire of human experience in the Judaism of the dual Torah presents as human options the opposite of the banal, the one-dimensional, the immediate. Jews received and used the heritage of human experience captured, as in amber, in the words of the dual Torah. So they did not have to make things up fresh every morning or rely only on that small sector of the range of human experience immediately accessible and near at hand.

By contrast, Israeli nationalism and the American Judaism of Holocaust and Redemption—the two most influential systems that move Jews to action in the world today—scarcely concern themselves with that Judaism. They find themselves left only with what is near at hand. They work with the raw materials made available by contemporary experience—emotions on the one side, politics on the other. Access to realms beyond requires learning in literature, the only resource for human experience beyond the immediate. But the Judaic systems of the twentieth century, except for the reversionary Judaisms, do not resort to the reading of books as a principal act of their way of life, in the way in which the Judaism of the dual Torah and its continuators did and do. The consequence is a strikingly abbreviated agenda of issues, a remarkably one-dimensional program of urgent questions.

In this regard the reversionary systems point toward a renewed engagement with the canon and system of the dual Torah, but consequently I think those systems prove (quite properly) transitory and preparatory: ways back to "Sinai." So their very definitive characteristic points toward what has *not* happened: a systematic exploitation, by system-builders working out an original and urgent program of questions and answers, of the received Judaism of the dual Torah. The reason for neglect is the self-evident fact that the Jews of the world today, especially in France and elsewhere in Western Europe, the Soviet Union, and the United States, but also in Canada, Australia, South Africa, Argentina, Brazil, and other areas of sizable demographic consequence, in point of fact have lost all access to the Judaism of the dual Torah that sustained fifteen centuries of Jews before now. The appeal to contemporary experience, whether in emotions or in politics, draws upon not so rich a treasury of reflection and response to the human condition. And the utter failure of imagination, the poverty of contemporary system-building where it takes place at all, shows the result. From a mansion Israel has moved into a hovel. Jews in the European, African, and Australian worlds no longer regard "being Jewish" as a matter of intellect at all, and so far as they frame a world-view for themselves, it bears few points of intersection with the Judaic canon.

One reason that Judaic systems did not emerge in the American Judaic setting derives from the astounding fail-ure of education to transmit to the bulk of Jewry in America the received system in any accessible form. American Jewry denied itself access to the resources on which other Jewish communities had drawn, that is, the canon of the Judaism of the dual Torah, and attempted to create a domestic Judaism resting on experiences no one had undergone or would want to. It has virtually no school system for fully half of its children, and most of the other half receive an education of slight consequence. So Jewish Americans have neither studied Torah nor closely reflected on their own lives in a free society.

They have opted for neither the worst of one world nor the the best of another. That is, they focused such imaginative energies as they generated upon "the Holo-caust," and they centered their eschatological fantasies on "the beginning of our redemption" in the state of Israel. But they had not gone through the one nor chosen to participate in the other. Not having lived through the mass murder of European Jewry, American Jews restated the problem of evil in unanswerable form and then trans-formed that problem into an obsession. Not choosing to settle in the state of Israel, moreover, American Jews fur-ther defined redemption, the resolution of the problem of evil, in terms remote from their world. One need not look far to find the limitations of the system of American Judaism: its stress on a world other than the one in which the devotees in fact were living. As to the reversionary Judaisms of the hour, it is too soon to tell what they will yield or how they will endure. By nature transient; by doctrine alien to the canonical system they allege, they merely recapitulate; and by program of deed separate from the world to which they allegedly propose to gain access, they have yet to show us how, and whether, they will last. That is what I mean by failure of intellect.

The Triumph of Large-Scale Organization

Third and distinct from the other two is the bureaucratization of Jewry in consequence of the tasks it rightly has identified as urgent. To meet the problems Jews find self-evidently urgent, they have had to adopt a way of life of building and maintaining and working through very large organizations and institutions. The contemporary class structure of Jewry therefore places in positions of influence Jews who place slight value on matters of intellect and learning and that same system accords no sustained hearing to Jews who strive to reflect. The tasks, instead, are those that call forth other gifts than those of heart and mind. The exemplary experiences of those who exercise influence derives from politics, through law, from economic activity, through business, from institutional careers, through government, industry, and the like. As the gifts of establishing routine take precedence over the endowments of charisma of an intellectual order, the experiences people know and understand — politics, emotions of ready access — serve, also, for the raw materials of Judaic system-building. Experiences that, in a Judaic context, people scarcely know, do not so serve. This I take to be yet another consequence of the ineluctable tasks of the twentieth century: to build large-scale organizations to solve large-scale problems. Organizations, in the nature of things, require specialization. The difference between the classes that produce systemic change today and those who created systems in the nineteenth and earlier twentieth centuries then proves striking. What brought it about, if not the great war conducted against the Jews, beginning not in 1933 but with the organization of political anti-Semitism joined to economic exclusion, from the 1880s onward. So in a profound sense the type of structure now characteristic of Jewry represents one of the uncounted costs of the Holocaust.

Intellectuals, today no longer needed, create systems. Administrators do not; and when they need ideas, they call for propaganda and hire publicists and journalists. When we remember that all of the Judaic systems of the nineteenth and early twentieth centuries derive from intellectuals, we realize what has changed. Herzl was a journalist, for instance, and those who organized Jewish Socialism and brought Yiddishism all wrote books. The founders of the system of Reform Judaism were mainly scholars, rabbis, writers, and other intellectuals. It is not because they were lawyers that the framers of the positive Historical School produced the historicistic system that they made. The emphases of Hirsch and other creators of Orthodoxy lay on doctrine, and all of them wrote important books and articles of a reflective and even philosophical character. So much for Reform, Orthodox, Conservative, Socialist-Yiddishist, and Zionist systems: the work of intellectuals, one and all.

THE UNCOUNTED COST OF
THE HOLOCAUST

These three factors—demographic, cultural, institutional and bureaucratic—scarcely exhaust the potential explanation for the long span of time in which, it would appear, Jews have brought forth few Judaic systems, relying instead on those formed in a prior and different age and circumstance. But I do think all of them will figure in any rigorous account of what has happened, and has not happened, in the present century. And they point directly or indirectly to the extraordinary price yet to be exacted from Jewry on account of the murder of six million Jews in Europe. The demographic loss requires no comment, and the passage of time from the age in which the Judaism of the dual Torah predominated has already impressed us. Those causes are direct and immediate.

But the correlation between mass murder and an exemplary leadership of lawyers and businessmen and politicians and generals demands explanation. Administrators, not intellectuals, bureaucrats, or charismatic thinkers, formed the cadre of the hour. In an age in which, to survive at all, Jews had to address the issues of politics and economics, build a state (in the state of Israel) and a massive and effective set of organizations capable of collective political action (in the United States), not sages but *politicians* in the deepest sense of the word, namely, those able to do the work of the polity, alone could do what had to be done. And they did come forward. They did their task, as well as one might have hoped. The time therefore demanded gifts other than those prized by intellectuals. And the correlation between mass murder and a culture of organizations proves exact: the war against the Jews called forth from the Jews people capable of building institutions to protect the collectivity of Israel, so far as anyone could be saved. Consequently much was saved. But much was lost.

Celebrating the victory of survival, we should not lose sight of the cost. Determining the full cost of the murder of the six million Jews of Europe will require a long time. The end of the remarkable age of Judaic *systemopoeia* may prove a more serious charge against the future, a more calamitous cost of the destruction of European Jewry, than anyone has yet realized. The gas chambers suffocated not merely Jews, but spirit too.

JUDAIC SYSTEMS: THE CORPORATE MODEL

The banality of survival forms a counterpoint to the banality of evil: in an age of the common, why look for distinction in Jewry? People draw upon only their experience of emotions, inside, and politics, without. They then assign themselves the central position in the paradigm of humanity, seeing what they are as all they can become. But we need not find that surprising. Who does otherwise, except for those with eyes upon a long past, a distant future: a vision? The system-builders, the intellectuals, book-readers, book-writers, truth-tellers—these are the ones who appeal to experience of the ages as precedent for the hour. This characterized all the Judaic systems born in the death of the received one: whether Reform theologians invoked the precedent of change or Orthodox ones of Sinai. Today there are no system-builders, so we can scarcely ask for the rich perspectives, the striking initiatives, that yield compelling systems of life and thought. But whence the nullities that have taken the place of the system-builders? And how come the banality of the Judaic systems of the hour?

The twentieth century presented to Jews the necessity to create large bureaucracies to deal with large problems. In the nature of things, individuals, participants in systems of belief and behavior, had sought explanations for what they themselves did. Now the place for the individual was his or her own place: a part of the task, not the entirety of it. It is no accident that system-building came to an end in the encounter with an age of large Jewish organizations: armies and governments in the state of Israel and enormous instruments of fund-raising and politics in America. The resentment of intellectuals, no longer needed, should not allow ready rejection of their observation. The lawyers and administrators and managers who have succeeded the intellectuals did not build systems, because they built something else, and what they could build was what the hour required — the last, most awful charge exacted by the Holocaust from the survivors.

So let us dwell on this matter of the building by specialists of large organizations. Such specialization in modern times meant that systems required their elite (the specialists) and relegated all others to a life essentially at the fringes of the system. Every Judaist in a Judaic system of the dual Torah said prayers on his own (women were not given the same task). But Zionists who attended meetings did not do the same thing as did the Zionists who built the land, for example. Specialization as part of the construction of a rational system, a calling expressed in a particularity of work — these characterize organization, that is, collective action, in modern times. And all the Judaic systems of the twentieth century conformed to the requirements of organization in that age: all formed, as I said, systems of organization, meaning specialization for all, but then the doing of the distinctive work of the system by only a few. The specialized work of organizations demanded from all their renunciation of a role in the general scheme of the system.

In so stating, of course, I draw upon the image of the iron cage of Max Weber.[2] Weber alludes to the "iron cage" in the following famous passage: "The care for external goods should only lie on the shoulders of the saint like a light cloak, which can be thrown aside at any moment, but fate decreed that the cloak should become an iron cage." What he says — in a justly famous passage of enormous power — about economic action applies equally to the sort of large-scale systemic, existential behavior to which we refer when we speak of a Judaism characterized by the following:

> Where the fulfillment of the calling cannot directly
> be related to the highest spiritual and cultural val-
> ues, . . . the individual generally abandons the attempt
> to justify it at all. . . . No one knows who will live in
> this cage in the future. . . . For of the last stage of this
> cultural development, it might well be truly said: Spe-
> cialists without spirit, sensualists without heart; this
> nullity imagines that it has attained a level of civilization
> never before achieved.[3]

The point of intersection with organizations in the twentieth century I locate at the reference to "specialists without spirit." When we note the division of labor that has rendered a mockery of the category of a way of life joined to a worldview, we understand why we cannot define a distinctive way of life associated with a given worldview.

When I describe the worldview of a movement, in the nineteenth century I allude to an encompassing theory that explains a life of actions in a given and very particular pattern. When I speak of the worldview of a movement of the twentieth century, I refer to the explanation of why people, in a given, distinctive circumstance, should do pretty much what everyone is doing somewhere, under some equivalent circumstance: an army is an army anywhere, but study of the Torah is unique to Israel. Anyone can join a union, and why invoke a Judaic worldview to explain why to join a Jewish union? I know only that Judaic worldviews did offer such an explanation and made a great difference to those to whom that explanation answered an urgent question. What has changed? I find the answer in the history of Western civilization. The processes that shaped the Judaic systems of modern and contemporary times form part of the larger movement of humanity—a distinctive and therefore exemplary part to be sure. Let me specify what I think has made all the difference.

The critical Judaic component of the Christian civilization of the West spoke of God and God's will for humanity, what it meant to live in God's image, after God's likeness. So said the Judaism of the dual Torah, so said Christianity in its worship of God made flesh. So that message of humanity in God's image, of a people seeking to conform to God's will, found resonance in the Christian world as well: both components of the world, the Christian dough, the Judaic yeast, bore a single message about humanity. The first century beyond the Christian formulation of the West, that is, the twentieth century, spoke of class and nation, not one humanity in the image of one God. Calling for heroes, it demanded sacrifice not for God but for state. When asked what it meant to live with irreconcilable difference, the century responded with total war on civilians in their homes, made foxholes. Asked to celebrate the image of humanity, the twentieth century created an improbable likeness of humanity: mountains of corpses, the dead of the Somme of World War I and of Auschwitz of World War II and all the other victims of the state that took the place of church and synagogue, even up to the third of the population of the Khmer killed by their own government, and the half of the world's Armenians by what, alas, was theirs, — and the Jews, and the Jews, and the Jews.

The first century found its enduring memory in one man on a hill, on a cross, the twentieth, six million making up a Golgotha — a hill of skulls — of their own. No wonder then that the Judaisms of the age struggled heroically to frame a Judaic system appropriate to the issues of the age — and failed. Who would want to have succeeded to frame a worldview congruent to such an age, a way of life to be lived in an age of death? And no wonder — if I may pass my opinion — that the Judaisms of the age proved transient and evanescent. For, I like to think no Judaic system could ever have found an enduring fit with an age such as the one that, at the turning of the century, draws to a close.

The age of reversionary Judaisms, dawning at the first light of the century beyond, forms the right, the hopeful epitaph on the Judaisms of the dying century. They had formed Judaisms that, to Israel, the Jewish people, struggled to speak of hope and of life in the valley of the darkest shadows. But they had to fail, and their failure forms their vindication. For the Jews are a people that never could find a home in the twentieth century. That, in the aspect of eternity, may prove the highest tribute God will pay to those whom God among humanity first chose.[4]

THE END OF THE JUDAISMS
OF THE NINETEENTH CENTURY

But I think the impact of the Holocaust has run its course. While the events will never pass from our hearts, the power of those events to form a system is pretty well exhausted by the Judaism of Holocaust and Redemption. And that Judaism, for a variety of reasons, is losing its hold. First, it stresses negative experiences, on which people find they cannot raise their children. Second, it focuses upon the world beyond, not the life within, and people turn to a Judaism to guide their lives together, not their public policy toward the outside world. Third, the Judaism of Holocaust and Redemption appeals, for the redemptive myth, to the creation of the state of Israel. But that event has now lost its power to surprise and enchant. The state of Israel is an important fact of Jewish existence, which most of us celebrate every day. It is not the object of wonder and awe that it was forty years ago, nor should it be. In all, we have outgrown the events of World War II and its aftermath. And that is as it should be: generations do pass.

But among the five great Judaisms of the first third of the twentieth century, none retains vitality, and all have lost nerve. Jewish Socialism cum Yiddishism is a victim of the Holocaust. Zionism achieved fulfillment and has no important message that Israelism within the complex of the Judaism of Holocaust and Redemption fails to present. Conservative, Reform, and Orthodox Judaisms all have lost out, Conservatism because of a failure of purpose, Reform because of a failure of nerve, and Orthodoxy because of a failure of intellect.

Conservative Judaism struggles to find room in the vital center that it created, for everyone wants a place there. Reform Judaism, having sold its soul to the Judaism of Holocaust and Redemption, has lost the source of its energy and power in the prophetic tradition of Judaism. Western Orthodoxy answered questions about living by the Torah in Western society that few seem to wish to ask anymore. Those who want tradition and also a place in an open society — the question that Hirsch answered in nineteenth-century Germany — find it in a variety of Judaisms. The diverse Orthodoxies now concur, with the exception of the minority around Yeshiva University, that to be Orthodox is to live a life of segregation and scarcely veiled hostility to the rest of the world of Judaism, not to mention to goyim. Accordingly, everyone wants a place in the center.

The single most powerful idea in modern and contemporary Judaic life is the ideal we now identify with Conservative Judaism. All but a few extremists on the fringes of far-out Reform and Orthodoxy share that ideal, and, for the Jewish lay people, it is the one thing on which most concur. That ideal is that we wish to be Judaic in an integrated society, and that we want our Judaism to infuse our lives as Americans with meaning. That is a mediating, a healing, a centrist and moderate definition. Clearly, most Jews in America wish to live like other Americans and not in conditions of a ghetto. Equally obviously, most Jews in America wish to remain distinctively Jewish, with traits that join them together and distinguish them from others. And, the third truism, most Jews in America look to the

Judaic religious tradition for guidance on how to be different — but not too different.

And that is the centrist position. It defines the tensions and limits of the vital center. We look to tradition for guidance, but we make up our own minds — that is one way of stating matters. We want to live by something we call "Judaism," but we want to accept the possibility of change and modification where appropriate, where necessary, where desirable (thus, modern Orthodoxy, Conservative, Reform). The alternative positions are those of self-segregation, which requires no change in whatever is perceived to be "the tradition," and total assimilation, which permits no point of difference with "everybody else" (if there is an "everybody else").

Now that I have outlined what I think is the basic conviction of the vital center, readers probably recognize two facts. First of all, in simple terms, I have spelled out the social policy of the Conservative Movement in Judaism. It is what Conservative Judaism represents to us. Second, I also have outlined views that equally well characterize much of Orthodox and most of Reform and Reconstructionist Judaisms as well. And that is my point: Conservative Judaism is only one of the many center-movements in contemporary American Judaism, and while its centrist position enjoys enormous appeal and power (as I believe it should), it is the position that matters, not the institution.

The institutions of Conservative Judaism, as distinct from the ideology of the vital center, are weak. They do not enjoy the financial support of the lay people. Much of the Conservative rabbinate is alienated. Many of the people in charge treat with disdain and scorn the movement "out there" and regard as their private park and personal garden the affairs of the movement and its policies. In consequence many people wonder what is going to happen to the vital center. They ask whether Conservative Judaism has a future at all, or will it disintegrate and divide up among

Orthodoxy and Reform (as, rabbis tell me, people now expect). In institutional terms, I not only do not know the answer to that question, I also do not care, because I do not think it matters.

If the Jewish Theological Seminary of America forms a center for the living Judaism of the vital center, if from that institution and its associated organizations important ideas come forth, inspiration and leadership, energy and imagination — then the future of the institutional Conservative movement matters a great deal. But it is bright and secure (and, by the way, the money will flow). If the Jewish Theological Seminary of America continues its present attitudes and policies toward its constituency near at hand and toward Jewry at large (and many of us hope that the institution will change those attitudes and policies and come back to Jewry at large with humility and hope), then what difference does it make? We can have a new Jewish Theological Seminary of America — if for the twenty-first century that is the best institutional model. Or we can decide to educate our rabbis and teachers and cantors and other religious figures in different ways. The institutional model of a private and isolated institution, doing everything on its own and by itself, certainly competes with alternatives.

No institution can claim a permanent hold, and none has a mortgage on our future. The vital center — that religious attitude and position presently represented (but only partially) by the Jewish Theological Seminary, United Synagogue, Rabbinical Assembly — will flourish, if not in the presently deeply flawed, paralyzed institutions and organizations that today represent the center, then in the many others that now flourish or will come into existence. It is the religious ideal, the Judaic ideal, that will endure: the ideal of free Jews, freely choosing to be Judaic and to build a distinctive Judaic religious life in an integrated and open society. No institution has a monopoly on that ideal:

it is American Judaism for — I would guess — 90 percent of American Jews. So much for the vital center: too crowded for the Judaism that created it. What of Reform Judaism?

If I had to choose two words to characterize the contemporary state of Reform Judaism, they would be sloth and envy. I call Reform Judaism slothful because it has become lazy about developing its own virtues and so deprives all Judaisms of its invaluable gifts, its insights, and its powerful ideas. I call it envious because it sees virtue in others and despises itself. The single greatest and most urgent idea in the Jewish world today is the one idea that Reform Judaism has made its own and developed for us all, and that is the idea that God loves all humanity, not only holy Israel. Today, no single idea is more urgent than that one. Reform Judaism in the temples and in the schools lacks vitality, even while it correctly points to enormous growth. Reform Judaism in the United States is the most numerous Judaism and is growing faster than Conservativism and, in absolute numbers, much faster than Orthodoxy. The reason is that Reform Judaism has accurately taken the measure of the condition of American Jewry and has framed a Judaism that deals with the real and urgent issues of contemporary American Jewish life.

But that success, for which the lay people must take credit, since they are the creators of Reform Judaism, has yet to make its mark on the morale and attitude of the Reform movement. The movement still regards itself as a second-class and somehow less than fully legitimate Judaism. By "the movement" I do not mean a few theologians at Hebrew Union College who have set forth a solid and substantial rationale for Reform Judaism in both history (Michael A. Meyer) and theology (Jakob J. Petuchowski). I mean the vast number of pulpit rabbis and lay persons, who see more observant Jews and think they are somehow inferior, who meet more learned Jews and think they are in some way less.

Without conceding for one minute that less observance or less learning are to be treated as unimportant, I think Reform Judaism has a message to offer to all Jews, including the most Orthodox of the Orthodox and the most nationalistic of the nationalists, and one that in importance outweighs not eating lobster and studying the Talmud. It is that Judaism as Reform Judaism defines Judaism as a religion of respect and love for the other, as much as for the self. Reform Judaism teaches that God loves all people, finds and emphasizes those teachings of the received holy books of the Torah that deliver that message, and rejects bigotry and prejudice when practiced not only by Gentiles but even by Jews.

And there should be no doubt at all that the single most urgent moral crisis facing the communities of Judaisms today is the Jews' self-indulgent hostility toward the other or the outsider. The novelist, Norman Mailer,[5] in language reminiscent of the prophetic tradition stated what I conceive to be the great contribution of Reform Judaism to the life of Jewry everywhere:

> What made us great as a people is that we, of all ethnic groups, were the most concerned with the world's problems. . . . We understood as no other people how the concerns of the world were our concerns. The welfare of all the people of the world came before our own welfare. . . . The imperative to survive at all costs . . . left us smaller, greedier, narrower, preternaturally touchy and self-seeking. We entered the true and essentially hopeless world of the politics of self-interest, "is this good for the Jews?" became, for all too many of us, all of our politics.

Mailer concluded, "The seed of any vital American future must still break through the century-old hard-pack of hate, contempt, corruption, guilt, odium, and horror. . . . I am tired of living in the miasma of our indefinable and ongoing national shame." I find in Mailer's comments that morally vital prophetic tradition that Reform Judaism — alone among contemporary Judaisms — espouses. But today Reform Judaism has lost its nerve, and just when Jewry needs precisely that for which Reform Judaism has always stood, the message is muffled.

The costs to the Jewish people are to be measured by our incapacity to work out our relationships to the world beyond. I refer to an address by Professor Yehoshaphat Harkabi, Hebrew University, to the Council of Reform and Liberal Rabbis at the Liberal Jewish Synagogue in London last year. Harkabi chose his platform well, the only religious Judaic platform for his message, that there is a crisis in our relationships to the Gentiles ("the goyim"). He raised in a stunning public statement the issue of the divisive power of the Jewish religion within the Jewish people itself. Harkabi raised the possibility that "the Jewish religion that hitherto has bolstered Jewish existence may become detrimental to it." Harkabi pointed to manifestations of hostility against Gentiles, formerly repressed, but ascendant in the past decade. In the state of Israel, in particular, that hostility took such forms as the following: The Chief Rabbi Mordekhai Eliahu forbade Jews in the state of Israel to sell apartments to Gentiles. A former Chief Rabbi ruled that a Jew had to burn a copy of the New Testament. A scholar who has received the Israel Prize in Judaic Studies, Rabbi Eliezer Waldenberg, declared that a Gentile should not be permitted to live in Jerusalem. The body of a Gentile woman who lived as a Jew without official conversion was disinterred from a Jewish cemetery.

Explaining these and many other expressions of anti-Gentile prejudice, Harkabi pointed to the belief of what he called "religious radicals" in the imminent coming of the Messiah as explanation for these developments. They are not limited to the state of Israel. Harkabi called for "discarding those elements" of Judaism that instill or express hostility to outsiders. He said, "Demonstrating to

Orthodoxy that some of its rulings are liable to raise general opprobrium may facilitate the achievement of a modus vivendi between it and the other streams in contemporary Judaism."

Where are we to find the corpus of ideas concerning Gentiles to counter these appalling actions and opinions of the pseudomessianic Orthodoxy of the state of Israel? I find them these days mainly in Reform Judaism. And in the state of Israel Reform Judaism has made its mark. But in our own community, it is, as I said, lazy and envious of others, insecure and slothful and conciliatory of views it must reject and abhor. That is not to suggest that only Reform Judaism has a contribution to make to the moral renaissance of the Jewish people, correctly characterized by Mailer as now too self-absorbed for their own good. Hebrew Union College-Jewish Institute of Religion has delivered to Reform Jews a corps of rabbis bearing a moral concern and — more important — an intellectual system and structure that form a monument to the capacity of Israel — the Jewish people — to think both of itself and also of the other, and to love not only itself but also the outsider. Now, when we need Reform Judaism more than ever for the moral renewal of all Israel — the Jewish people — what Reform Jews must find within their hearts are not sloth and envy but the two opposite virtues: energy and conviction.

And what of Orthodoxy? If Reform Judaism exhibits a failure of nerve, all Orthodox Judaisms display a failure of intellect. It is not that they are stupid or wrong or venal, merely that they are irrelevant to the great issues of the world and the age. Except for Yeshiva-University Orthodoxy, all of the Orthodox Judaisms of the day (the "Haredim" in various guises) exhibit the same enormous incapacity to speak to the Jewish condition. In the various formulations claiming to give us true-blue Judaism, all of them sailing under the flag of Orthodoxy (a whole fleet of motley ships, from rowboats to battleships, all of them obsolete), we find the same failure of mind. And the worst thing a religion can do is fall silent before the urgent issues of the age. Khomeini is, at least, relevant, capable of shaping events. Whether in Bnei Braq or among the Lubovitch Hasidim and at all stations inbetween and around, all Orthodox Judaisms pretend there is no there there.

That is not to suggest Orthodox Judaisms are ignorant of the classics of Judaism or misrepresent their content. To the contrary, the representation of Torah-true Judaism by the Haredim is sound on every point. Knowledgeable people can quote chapter and verse in talmudic writings in support of their position on all issues. On issue after issue they represent the Torah — oral and written — precisely as the received, classical sources of the Torah portray matters.

And that is precisely why the policies and program of the Haredim, and therefore of the Judaism of the dual Torah, oral and written, as they accurately represent those policies, offer no meaningful option to Jews in the world today — I do not say to "Orthodox" or "Religious" Jews, but to any Jews. The Haredim appeal, after all, to the fact that they authentically portray "Judaism," or the Torah, more accurately than anyone else, more so than Western or Modern Orthodoxy, more authentically than the Orthodoxy of the Zionist-Religious parties. And that appeal, to the spiritual and the romantic in us all, is very real. It is why the Haredim gain converts to their Judaism from among the Religious-Zionists and the secular alike: there is a very real choice. So there is, and the 95 percent of the Jews who by instinct reject the reading of the Torah, or of Judaism, by the Haredim, make a sound judgment. The claim to authenticity to "the tradition" or "the Torah" requires us to ask whether the Torah in its received or authentic or accurate version, as the Haredim represent it, can serve in the twenty-first century. I think it cannot.

The Torah as the Haredim read it (rightly, as I said) omits all systematic doctrine on the three critical matters of contemporary life: politics, economics, and science. The Torah in its authentic version has nothing at all to say about three matters so fundamental that any Judaism today that authentically realizes the Torah, oral and written, demands that Jews live only a partial life and, in the case of the state of Israel, dismantle the Jewish state. Jews living in the Golah or Exile, for their part, without a position on politics, economics, and science simply will have to retreat into ghettos, having no way to cope with the formative forces in the world today. The Haredim want to make us all into Amish, and the Jews are not going to agree, even though, just now, more than a few would like to walk out on the world as it is.

The three most powerful and formative forces in all of human civilization today are democracy, capitalism, and science, and on those three subjects, the authentic, classical Judaism, accurately represented by the Haredim, either has nothing at all to say, or simply says the wrong things. Authentic Judaism, as the Haredim teach it, is ignorant of the things that matter today. We cannot look to the Haredim for intelligent public policy. The Haredim can make their extravagant claims on the rest of us only by relating to the remainder of the Jewish people essentially as parasites: we do the politics, the economics, and the science, so they can live out their private lives off in a corner. Abandon the Jewish state, for Israelis, and give up all public life, for Jews in the Golah; that is the message of their authentic Judaism, with its stunning silence on democracy, capitalism, and science and technology.

There are three reasons for this silence, because of their very valid claim to authenticity to the tradition. First, we look in vain in the Talmud and related writings for a political theory that fits together with the politics of a democratic state. Israelis need no instruction from the Golah on that awful fact. If the Haredim gain in politics, it will end democracy in the state of Israel, pure and simple. Second, we find nothing in talmudic and related writings that makes possible scientific inquiry, that is, systematic formulation of theory and empirical testing of hypothesis. When philosophy, including science, found a capacious place within Judaism, it was only because modes of thought deriving not from talmudic but from Greek-Muslim philosophical sources had found entry. And they were perceived as alien. The great philosophers and scientists did not come from the circles who studied only the Torah, and the institutions of the Torah did not produce philosophy or science, any more than, today, they study those subjects. The Haredim have nothing to say of interest to, or to learn from, the world of science and technology. But that is where the world is made today.

Third, systematic thought on economics, such as the Mishnah assuredly presupposes, by the end of talmudic times had given way to an essentially magical conception that if one studies Torah, economic questions will be solved by themselves. Rational decision-making, the conception of a market and of a market-economy — these and other givens of economics find no place whatsoever in the (at best) petty entrepreneurial thinking of the Torah in its authentic mode. Consequently, Judaism as the Haredim accurately represent it, falls silent on questions of economics. How can people utterly ignorant of economics pretend to govern a modern state or to lead the Jewish community overseas?

Modern Orthodoxy in the United States of America, the Orthodoxy of Bar Ilan University and Yeshiva University, and of the Israeli Zionist-Religious parties, all have made ample room for science, democracy, and economic theory in the curriculum in the academy and also in its formulation of public policy (though here, the Zionist Religious parties seem to leave such matters to the partners in whatever coalition gives them their annual prohibition of pork or its counterpart). That Western Orthodoxy is losing out, so it seems, to the valid claim of authenticity to the true Torah set forth by the Haredim and by their political instrumentalities. It is pure romanticism or utter fantasy to opt for the authentic merely because it is true about the things of which it speaks. Jewish public life, both in the Golah and in the Jewish state, have also to ask about the ominous silences. The Judaism of the Talmud accurately represented, so far as the sources portray it, by the Haredim, simply cannot and will not work, not because it is wrong or humanly deficient, but because it falls silent when the work of the world has to be done.

No state can work without well-crafted public policy, without economic policy, without access to science and technology. Any lingering appeal of the Haredim to that isolationism that makes us Jews want to turn our backs on the world, any deep impulse in us all to be only Jewish, always Jewish, and, at last, the right way, the way of the true Torah of Sinai—any appeal to that profound and natural sense in us all of our Jewishness as our fate and faith and destiny will have to compete with another appeal. It is the appeal to the simple fact that, if we are going to live in the twenty-first century, we require not only the Torah but also economics, politics, and science and technology, about which the Torah, in the authentic statement of the Haredim, simply has nothing to say, nothing whatsoever. World Jewry has no choice but to turn its back on the Haredim, as they have turned their back on the twenty-first century—and for precisely the same reason. Would that God had made the world so simple as the Haredim wish it to be!

They are right, and therefore all of us have to reject them and their entirely authentic Torah. After all, there were valid reasons for inventing Reform Judaism and the Orthodoxy of Samson Raphael Hirsch, the Religious Zionist parties, the secular Jews, Conservative Judaism, Reconstructionist Judaism, Jewish Socialism, Yiddishism, and all the rest. The opposition to these movements rightly claimed they were not authentic, and the opposition was right. But Reform Judaism and Western Orthodoxy and the Religious Zionists, Yeshiva University and Bar Ilan University — these were still more right, because they were, and remain, relevant. They do address all of life as we now know it, and they have something to say about politics, science, economics, while the Haredim do not.

The Haredim have nothing to say on all the urgent issues of the hour. We do not solve problems by pretending they are not there. So the Haredim and all the Orthodox Judaisms that find a place within that classification do not present an option or a possibility for Jews who do not live in ghettos and do not pretend the twenty-first century can simply be ignored, as though it were not going to happen. When the dream is over, the world will be there, perhaps a nightmare, when we wake up. So, fond farewell to the fantasy that the authentic Torah of Sinai, as the framers of the Bavli read it in the seventh century, is, or can ever be, the authentic Torah of Sinai, as Israel, the Jewish people everywhere, receive and affirm it in the twenty-first century: we shall do and we shall hear, indeed: *today*.

AND YET: TOMORROW

Were the story to end with the creation of the new Judaisms of the nineteenth and early twentieth centuries, we should face an unhappy ending. But the advent of the twenty-first century, in my view, marks the beginning of a new age of Judaic *systemopoeia*. The vital signs appear round about. I point to the formation of a distinctively Judaic politics and another among the intellectuals of the Right as well. These two intellectual formations present two of the three prerequisites of a Judaism: a worldview and a way of life. Both of them join the everyday and the here and now to an ideal in which people can find the meaning and purpose of their life together. Whether these political Judaisms can take root in the social worlds of numbers of Jews and so constitute of themselves not merely theologies and life-patterns but "Israels," that is, social entities, remains to be seen. Reform, Conservatism, and Western Orthodoxy, as well as Zionism and Jewish Socialism-Yiddishism, all formed not merely intellectual positions but social worlds. Their strength lay in transforming organizations into societies, so to speak. So far what we have in *Tikkun* and *Commentary* is more than a viewpoint, but less than a broad social movement, widely diffused.

I point further to the havurah movement, the renewal of Reconstructionism with Arthur Waskow and Arthur Green, the development of an accessible Judaic mysticism by Zalman Schachter, the intense engagement by feminists of Jewish origin in the framing of a what we may call a feminist-Judaism, and the like. Each of these extraordinarily vital religious formations gives promise of establishing a Judaism: a worldview, a way of life, realized within a social entity that calls itself (not necessarily exclusively) "Israel." All of them have identified urgent questions and presented in response answers that, to the framers, prove self-evidently valid. And with these five conditions—a worldview, way of life, attained by an "Israel," that all together identifies an urgent question and answers it in a manner self-evidently valid to the engaged persons—we have a Judaism. So I think the long period in which there were no new Judaisms in formation is coming to an end, though it is much too soon to tell which Judaisms in North America at least will inherit the greater part of Jewry and take over, as Conservative Judaism did in the second and third generations, and as Reform Judaism has been doing in the third, fourth, and fifth generations.

What accounts for the hopeful future? I pointed to three factors in accounting for the barren age: the intense political crisis culminating in the Holocaust with its demographic catastrophe, the demise of intellect, and the (correlative) formation of large-scale organizations that reformed Jewry within the corporate model. The new Judaisms of the acutely contemporary age succeed, I think, because we have pretty well overcome the demographic and cultural catastrophe of the Holocaust. We have in North America a vast Jewish population, capable of sustaining the variety of Judaisms that the vast ocean of Jewry in central and eastern Europe did in the later nineteenth and earlier twentieth centuries. It is perfectly clear from the character of the examples of new Judaisms to which I have pointed that the one source of strength in *systemopoeia* today is intellect. Jewish intellectual life within Judaism flourishes in North America in a way that, I think, would have stirred envy in even the proudest Jews of Germany and Poland between the Wars.

And the corporate model for organized Jewry has shown its limitations. The decay of Bnai Brith, the demise on the local scene of organizations such as the American Jewish Congress, the retreat of Jewish organizational life from the scale of the retail to that of the wholesale, the retreat of the Federations from the ideal of forming "the organized Jewish community" and their transformation into mere fund-raising agencies — these show what is happening. The decline of the powerful national organizations at the center strongly suggests that, in the everyday world at home, Jews no longer find interesting a Judaic existence consisting of going to meetings to talk about something happening somewhere else. Merely giving money, for instance, to help another Jew help a third Jew settle in the state of Israel has lost all credibility. People want hands-on engagement, and the corporate model affords the opposite. Common to all the hopeful signs of nascent Judaic systems is the immediate engagement of the individual in achieving the purposes of the social group. The hallmark of the havurah movement, at least as some of us thought it up thirty years ago,[6] was individual engagement in the ultimate purpose of the group. And that rejection of the corporate model and affirmation of the place of the individual at the center of activity now marks the mode of organization of every important new Judaism today.[7]

To explain why no new Judaisms, I can therefore account also for why we now see many new and vital Judaisms: we no longer live in an iron cage, and the fulfillment of our calling to be Israel comes only through our immediate and complete engagement with our highest spiritual and cultural values—whatever our Judaism tells us these are. We have, in other words, survived the twentieth century.

Notes

1. My thanks to Michael Lerner for insisting that I take account of that fact, on which much more presently.

2. My entire intellectual life has addressed the program of Max Weber, from my dissertation onward. My entire notion of systemic analysis and the comparison of systems within Judaism, worked out most fully and in acute detail in the study of the Judaic systems of late antiquity, simply applies in detail his main perspectives.

3. Max Weber, *The Protestant Ethic and the Spirit of Capitalism*, tr. Talcott Parsons, with a foreword by R. H. Tawney (New York: Charles Scribner's, 1930), 182.

4. I amplify these matters in my *Death and Birth of Judaism* (New York: Basic, 1987).

5. *New York Times*, 18 April 1988.

6. The original idea of the ancient Jewish havurot as a model for social organization is in Jakob J. Petuchowski's article in *The Reconstructionist* in 1957. There followed my articles on the subject, collected in my *Fellowship in Judaism* (London: Vallentine, Mitchell, 1963), where I proposed the idea of regaining access to the havurot of antiquity. Other early writings by those active in the earliest phases of the movement are collected in the book I edited, *Contemporary Judaic Fellowship in Theory and in Practice* (New York: KTAV, 1972).

7. The *Tikkun* conference in New York City is an example of that fact. I see no clear counterpart in the political Judaism of the Right, which seems to me fragmented in social circles, e.g., around *Commentary* for some, around *National Review* and *Chronicles* for others (myself included). Professors of Jewish origin in the new National Association of Scholars, for example, hardly form the counterpart to the social formation attained at the *Tikkun* conference. In this regard the Left has provided the Right with a model of how to do things.

19

Thoughts about Joseph Smith: Upon Reading Donna Hill's *Joseph Smith: The First Mormon*

Thomas F. Rogers
Brigham Young University, Provo, Utah

"Toute vue des choses qui n'est pas étrange est fausse."[1]

Valery

This paper first lists a number of personal experiences which are mentioned but not unduly emphasized in Donna Hill's biography and which, taken together, appear to have been more than coincidental influences on the formulation of Latter-day Saint doctrine and Church practices. Against the seemingly syncretic character of Joseph Smith's activity as a founding prophet who claimed divine authority for his principal pronouncements are then weighed the following considerations, which cannot be easily dismissed or explained away:

1. Joseph Smith's essential innocence, sincerity, unflinching forthrightness, other-directness, and self-effacement;

2. The profound and inspiring explication of otherwise less well understood Christian principles in the scriptures translated and brought forth by his hand and in the ordinances of the temple;

This was presented at the Mormon History Association meetings on 7 May 1982 in Ogden, Utah.

3. The parallels between Joseph Smith's belittlement and persecution and that of acknowledged prophets in past ages;

4. The comprehensiveness of Joseph Smith's ontological vision.

This paper implies our need for respecting and accepting Joseph Smith's claims on empirical grounds, apart from what in his history may prove disturbing and, though open to interpretation, cannot be denied.

Donna Hill's *Joseph Smith: The First Mormon* strikes me as the man's first fully adequate biography[2] — comprehensive, detached, balanced, and fair. Or so it seems. Either what is therein claimed about the Prophet is true or it is not. So far no one has come forth to dispute its assertions. And I am in a state of shock — or was for weeks after I read it. Nothing has so much forced me to reexamine my most cherished preconceptions. I am a middle-aged professor who has for some time dealt with the literary expression of mankind's thorniest dilemmas. I have found the play of ideas a delightful stimulation. Nor have I found it particularly difficult to live with the ambiguity and paradox that seem to abound at life's every turn and which are so attested to in the scriptures — to remain tenuous about so much that seems to "throw" many another believer. At the same time — thanks in part to a number of choice experiences afforded by callings in the Church — my testimony regarding the restored gospel and the reality and divinity of the Savior has never been stronger, my faith never more profound.

If what has only so recently come to my attention about Joseph Smith — much of which in my thinking I had earlier relegated to malicious rumor — can have "thrown" me as it did, at least temporarily, I can well understand how in the past those who "knew better" may have been anxious to keep the Prophet's image so vaguely idealized. By doing so, however, we fail, I believe, to recognize the nature of the revelatory process in almost every dispensation and why prophets have been so universally misunderstood, even detested. In his "King Follett Discourse" the Prophet insisted that no man knew his history. How a reading of Hill's book confirms that statement: the more one ponders the available biographical detail, the more enigmatic the man emerges, and the more puzzling, at least on the surface, appear his motives. Like nothing else, the experience reminds me of that existential trauma we all underwent when first indoctrinated, whether by peers in the back woodshed or by parents, about the birds and the bees. Those who first dissected the human body must have been similarly amazed and, for a time at least, equally dismayed by what they beheld. The facts of life and the reality that is more than skin deep do not generally accord with a child's uninformed suppositions. Why then should the truth about another human being, easily as taxed and torn as we who are less illustrious know ourselves to be, prove to be any less complex?

These are the thoughts which, on balance, have occurred to me, since reading Hill, as I have pondered the man Joseph Smith. What has been perhaps most disconcerting is that practically everything he enunciated and brought forth was so syncretic—appears, that is, to have been suggested by the ideas and the experiences he randomly encountered in his particular social environment. The coincidences, if that is what they are, suggest a consistent pattern of impressionability and truly ingenious adaptation of both the most bizarre and seemingly most mundane sources of inspiration, often secular, even spurious in character. We can no longer deny, for instance, that prior to discovering the Golden Plates and the Urim and Thummim he was several times hired to seek buried treasure by means of a so-called "peep stone," being sought after for his adeptness in its use. Moreover, although there is nothing substantively in common between the Reverend Ethan Smith's *View of the Hebrews* and the Book of Mormon, the earlier work, published in 1823 by a contemporary in a neighboring state, advances a similar thesis, claiming to trace the history of descendants of the lost ten tribes among the American Indians, and could well have been known to the Prophet. One of the Book of Mormon's most significant archetypes—Lehi's vision— bears striking parallels to a dream which—at least according to his mother's 1845 account—Joseph's own father had earlier shared with his family members.[3] Consequent to a dramatic conversion late in life, moreover, Joseph's maternal grandfather had published a book of Christian exhortation and thereupon traveled about, peddling it in the capacity of an itinerant missionary.

Another puzzling "coincidence" occurs with the Book of Mormon's quotation from certain New Testament scriptures. The inclusion of passages from Isaiah in 2 Nephi is, given the plates of Laban, quite understandable. It is also very conceivable that, in visiting the Nephites, the Savior would reiterate, even verbatim, the wisdom of the Sermon on the Mount. But the literal citation in Mormon's teaching of the familiar utterances of both Paul on charity (cf. Moroni 7:45 with 1 Corinthians 13:4-7) and John on divine sonship (cf. Moroni 7:48 with 1 John 3:2-3) can only be reconciled by assuming that such statements are so profound and memorable, which these in fact tend to be, that Christ enunciated them himself and that in both Jerusalem and among the Nephites they were subsequently passed from one generation of disciples to the next. Consistent with the statement in the New Testament that "there are also many other things which Jesus did, the which, if they should be written every one, I suppose that even the world itself could not contain the books that should be written" (John 21:25), Mormon asserts that "there cannot be written in this book even a hundredth part of the things which Jesus did truly teach unto the people" (3 Nephi 26:6). The foregoing seems a plausible explanation, but, without it, credibility would — at least for those who recognize and ponder such matters — be considerably strained.

In addition there is the weird and convoluted history of the Egyptian sarcophagi that Joseph Smith acquired from the descendant of a sideshow entrepreneur and that contained papyri which, when translated, produced one of the Church's four sacred scriptures. And there is Sidney Rigdon's prior experience with communal living among the Campbellites and who, after he became the Church's First Elder, probably urged Joseph to consider instituting the law of consecration and stewardship or the United Order. Finally, the correspondences between the Masonic ritual, to which Joseph Smith was initiated, and both the apparel and symbolic gestures of the endowment ceremony in LDS temples are so strikingly similar that it is hard not to imagine that exposure to the one readily led to the genesis of the other. Now that these circumstances have so fully come to light, it would ill serve the cause of the Church to pretend they are not so. Both those within and without who know otherwise will expect their recognition and further explanation, while those who learn of them from non-Mormon sources will risk even greater disenchantment.

Indeed, to anyone who does not already have a personal appreciation of Joseph Smith's spiritual nature, the cosmic significance of his life and work, and their remarkable consequences in the lives of now millions of human beings, the foregoing circumstances could hardly lead to anything but skepticism and the view that Joseph was a brazen and fairly incautious plagiarizer with one of the most unbridled imaginations that ever found expression among the children of men. Let us, therefore, as we can best discern them, take a reading of the other aspects of Joseph Smith's personality and behavior to determine how well these corroborate the notion that he was or was not

a charlatan, *par excellence*: First, a strong case can be made —
though it does not establish the veracity of his claims —
that Joseph was basically innocent and deeply sincere. As
a fourteen-year-old with, by present-day standards, an extremely limited education and knowledge of the world at
large, he was, upon entering the sacred grove, ideally
suited to become the transparent vessel for receiving and
disseminating astoundingly pristine principles which
those more knowledgeable or steeped in Western theology
were far more prone to qualify and compromise. Such
persons would also have been less inclined to seek answers
from deity than to rely on both already established authority and their own intellectual assumptions.

By contrast, from the moment of his hearing of the
passage in James which prompted his inquiry about the
true church, the pattern emerges — so natural it seems profane — that no revelation, no inspiration would ever come
to Joseph without first being prompted by some immediate
stimulus which in turn impelled the recipient to inquire
about it by next petitioning deity. It is also worth noting
that Joseph Smith did not always appear to have so fully
understood the import of the answers he received as those
who came after him. What he expressly went to the grove
to learn was fully communicated: no existing churches
were authorized by Jesus Christ and God the Father. The
overarching significance of their appearance as separate
personages with glorified anthropomorphic bodies does
not seem to have dawned on him, at least at the time,
nearly so much as on subsequent Latter-day Saints. This
may be another reason why the First Vision was not recorded or even mentioned until some time later. Nor did
Joseph ever emphasize the fact that the nature of his experience in the grove, including his initial encounter with
the Powers of Darkness, was in the archetypal manner of
trial and initiation, always in some isolated natural setting,
which the founders of previous dispensations appear to

have undergone prior to receiving a divine commission to embark on their respective missions. Both the endowment ceremony and the Pearl of Great Price recount comparable incidents in the case of Adam, Enoch, Noah, Abraham, and Moses. The Old Testament suggests something similar for Isaac, Jacob, and Joseph, as does the New Testament for Christ during his forty days in the wilderness. But Joseph Smith never made anything of the parallel in his own instance. It is likely that it did not even occur to him.

All of this tends to suggest that, far from exploiting a number of circumstances which might have served his personal self-aggrandizement, the young Joseph was even naively oblivious to their possible implications. It makes him seem far less a scheming manipulator of other men's minds. Another area in which Joseph Smith seems less than shrewd was in his uncompromising sense of urgency regarding the principles and practices that lost for him the support of so many associates and made him and his movement, in the minds of their gentile neighbors in Missouri and Illinois, so much more suspicious and threatening. His undeviating persistence in such matters led in fact directly to his martyrdom. Chief among these was polygamy. As Hill points out, "Joseph seemed more and more determined that the Saints accept the doctrine of celestial marriage as holy and necessary." Citing Joseph F. Smith, she adds, "as the late President George A. Smith repeatedly said, to me and others, 'The Prophet seemed irresistibly moved by the power of God to establish that principle, not only in theory in the hearts and minds of his brethren, but in practice also, he himself having led the way.' "[4] Hill elsewhere asserts, "It never occurred to Joseph and his followers that their teachings had given gross offense."[5]

One of Joseph's most endearing qualities was his magnanimity and generosity, his deep, impulsive affection for others, particularly those of humble circumstances. T. Edgar Lyon has, for one, recounted a number of anecdotal instances from reminiscences by various members in the early days of the Church.[6] Joseph's failure as a storekeeper in Kirtland because he could not withhold credit from needy Saints is also well established. The accounts of his great distress at the loss of those who died of cholera in Zion's Camp and his joyous weeping on the occasion of his own parents' baptisms also attest to his sublime and expansive personal qualities. It is surely meaningful that, knowing their son as only Joseph, Sr., and Lucy could, they and all his siblings were sufficiently convinced of Joseph's integrity, credibility, and claim to be a prophet. The great love and undeviating lifelong trust in Joseph of such practical and worldly wise men as Heber C. Kimball and Brigham Young are also a strong testimonial to his character; Brigham's last dying words — "Joseph! Joseph!" — a poignant evocation. Hill's sensitive analysis further suggests to what extent the Prophet's insistence on extended kinship and polygamous marriage evinced an uncontainable Christlike love for all his fellowmen:

> If the prophet's teachings and the cohesiveness and comprehensiveness of his message are not ignored, it must be recognized that his drive to establish polygamy was complex. It cannot be dismissed, as some historians have tried to do, simply by the suggestion that he had excessive sexual needs. Neither is it sufficient to say that Emma was worn out and frequently ill from the hard life of pioneering and childbearing. Nor can it merely be called an aspect of his Old Testament orientation, nor be said to have relieved his strict Puritan conscience which would not allow extra-marital sex, nor to have derived from a wish not to dishonor the women he loved, nor to have been advice to cloak his proclivities by making polygamy accepted by his community, although a case might be made to support each of these assumptions. Account must be taken also of his enormous capacity to love, which has been made manifest by scores of his contemporaries of both sexes and all ages, and of

his wish to bind his loved ones to himself forever, in this life, in the millennium and throughout eternity.[7]

Reading Hill's account of the Prophet's life further strengthens the impression that, upon leaving the grove and for the rest of his life, Joseph never again knew a moment's respite from either persecution or misunderstanding on the part of his closest friends, even his wife, Emma. One unwittingly asks how he or anyone could have borne it and still maintained all he did if he did not know with a surety that the cause he pursued was "well pleasing" in God's sight. The severe test of that saving knowledge — mentioned in the sixth Lecture on Faith — without which we must ultimately weary and fall short if we do not willingly sacrifice "all earthly things," including our very lives, is profoundly attested by the faithfulness and eventual martyrdom of the Prophet himself. That he fully knew what he professed is nowhere so plainly, hence forcefully, asserted as in the Doctrine and Covenants 76:22-23: "And now, after the many testimonies which have been given of him, this is the testimony, last of all, which we give of him: That he lives! For we saw him, even on the right hand of God."

It is difficult not to contrast to him certain self-styled prophets who have arisen in our own day — the man named Jones, for instance, who, in *his* final desperate hour, could not succumb without taking with him in Napoleonic or Hitlerian fashion — "*Après moi le déluge*" — his followers. How unlike such men was Joseph, who knew how to roll up his shirt-sleeves and shoulder more than his share of toil and whose life was worth nothing to him if not to his friends.

Despite his claims to be the Lord's vessel, Joseph was, in a number of instances, also remarkably self-effacing and far more willing than most Latter-day Mormons to admit his own personal fallibility. On one occasion, according to a gentile journalist, "he remarked that he had been represented as pretending to be a Savior, a worker of miracles, etc. All this was false. . . . He was but a man, he said; a plain, untutored man; seeking what he should do to be saved. . . . There was no violence, no fury, no denunciation. His religion appears to be a religion of meekness."[8]

According to Hill:

> John D. Lee reported that in 1840 he [Joseph Smith] said publicly that he had his failings, passions and temptations to struggle against, just as had the greatest stranger to God, and that no man was justified in submitting to his sinful nature. He did not want his followers to sanctify him. In a speech of May 21, 1843, he said, "I have not an idea that there has been a great many very good men since Adam. . . . I do not want you to think I am very righteous for I am not very righteous." To keep his actions from being misconstrued, Joseph frequently pointed out the difference between his behavior as a man and as a prophet. On one occasion he told visitors to Nauvoo, "A prophet is only a prophet when he is acting as such."[9]

In addition, there are in the Prophet's teachings and public utterances a number of striking statements that further convey his truly sublime understanding and espousal of the Greatest Commandment:

> If you do not accuse each other, God will not accuse you. If you have no accuser you will enter heaven, and if you will follow the revelations and instructions which God gives you through me, I will take you into heaven as my back load. If you will not accuse me, I will not accuse you. If you will throw a cloak of charity over my sins, I will over yours—for charity covereth a multitude of sins.[10]

> Nothing is so much calculated to lead people to forsake sin as to take them by the hand, and watch over them with tenderness. When persons manifest the least

kindness and love to me, O what power it has over my mind, while the opposite course has a tendency to harrow up all the harsh feelings and depress the human mind.[11]

You must enlarge your souls towards each other. . . . Let your hearts expand, let them be enlarged towards others.[12]

The mind or the intelligence which man possesses is co-equal with God himself. . . . All the minds and spirits that God ever sent into the world are susceptible of enlargement . . . so that they might have one glory upon another.[13]

According to Truman Madsen, the critical and astute B. H. Roberts,

having gone word by word and line by line through the writings of Joseph Smith, and having read everything he could find on his life, . . . found Joseph Smith to be possessed of a deeper and richer comprehension of Christ than anyone he had read in the Christian tradition since the apostles. Through all Roberts's buffetings and his intellectual probings, honing his own mind with the major figures in the history of Western thought, this conviction never diminished. And as his extensive knowledge of the alternatives increased, his conviction deepened: Joseph Smith told the truth, Joseph Smith was a prism of the Lord Jesus Christ.[14]

If, as Paul cogently argued, Christ is the essential cornerstone in the foundation of the church that bears his name, then Joseph Smith is as much the cornerstone of that church's restoration. It follows that, besides the priesthood and authority to which the restored Church makes unique claims; the several volumes of scripture and revelation which came to light through him, particularly the Book of Mormon; and also the ordinances of initiation, endowment, and sealing that take place in Latter-day Saint temples[15] are essential buttresses to the foundation and cornerstone of the restored Church. By way of internal evidence and striking compatibility with its purported cultural matrix, Hugh Nibley's extensive and provocative writings on the Book of Mormon leave much to consider.[16] In addition there are the aphorisms which, according to Madsen,[17] Roberts thought "comparable in their edge and insight not only to Biblical but also to Hindu and Chinese classics" and like them reflecting "the moral wisdom of the ages" which only accumulates throughout millennia of life-and-death human experience. Among such "trenchant sayings," Roberts listed the following:

> • Adam fell that men might be; and men are, that they might have joy (2 Nephi 2:25).
> • It must needs be that there is an opposition in all things (2 Nephi 2:11).
> • When ye are in the service of your fellow beings ye are only in the service of your God (Mosiah 2:17).
> • See that ye bridle all your passions, that ye may be filled with love (Alma 38:12).
> • Wickedness never was happiness (Alma 41:10).
> • I give unto men weakness that they may be humble; . . . for if they humble themselves before me, and have faith in me, then will I make weak things become strong unto them (Ether 12:27).
> • Charity is the pure love of Christ, and it endureth forever (Moroni 7:47).
> • Despair cometh because of iniquity (Moroni 10:22).[18]

I would expand Roberts's list, in terms of a number of remarkable spiritual principles nowhere so fully or clearly expounded as in the Book of Mormon. These include:

> • the purpose and function of scripture (1 Nephi 19:23, 2 Nephi 6:5);
> • an ongoing elucidation of Christ's atonement as the central event in human history, including a powerful

explanation of the need for Christ's passion—that he might learn godly *com*passion for all mankind (Alma 7:12);

• the unequivocal identification of Christ as Jehovah, thus resolving the Jewish challenge to Christians that the Old Testament deity pronounced himself "the Savior, and beside me there is no other" (3 Nephi 15:4-5; cf. also D&C 43:34; 76:1);

• an astoundingly sensible resolution of the faith-works controversy which has for so many centuries divided Protestants and Catholics: both God's grace and men's works are necessary to salvation; they are not mutually exclusive (2 Nephi 25:23);

• the accountability of adult human beings in every generation for their own lives and behavior, with obvious implications for traditional views on Eve's complicity and Adam's Fall: "Adam fell that men might be; and men are that they might have joy" (2 Nephi 2:11-25); on infant baptism (Moroni 8); and on the terms, conditions, and consequences of our earthly probation (Alma 28:13-14);

• the nature of true charity (Mosiah 4);

• the qualifications for true discipleship (Mosiah 18; Alma 5; Alma 38:12);

• the nature and process of developing faith (Alma 32), discerning truth by the light of Christ (Moroni 7), receiving a personal testimony (Moroni 10:3-5), and qualifying for sanctification (Moroni 10:32-33).

How, one asks, could anyone who was either duplicitous or whose mind and heart were not in fact informed by the Spirit presume to understand, let alone formulate, such a profound conception of the gospel?

As they reread the Book of Mormon, moreover, young missionaries readily identify with the personal struggles, the attitudes and feelings of so many young prophets who embarked in great weakness upon comparable proselyting ventures (cf. 2 Nephi 4:16-35; Enos; Alma 36). With its account of their exploits and the conversions that followed those of these young proselyters, the Book of Mormon is, among other things, a great prognosticator of the workings of faith and the attendant feelings experienced by many a latter-day missionary. It is worth noting, however, that the Book of Mormon was translated and published before the latter-day church was ever organized and its first missionaries called. How could Joseph Smith so intimately know what missionary experience was like before he had undertaken it himself? (It seems unlikely that his Grandfather Mack's late tracting, as a traditional Christian among fellow Christians, was nearly so compelling as the accounts of Ammon, Alma, the sons of Mosiah, and others.) The book's contrasting depiction of recalcitrants, the atavistic degeneration of the ungodly, and the mentality of apostates and anti-Christs (cf. Alma 30:12-18) is, in twentieth-century terms, also strikingly realistic. How deprived the world is without these additional role models and object lessons afforded by the Book of Mormon.

With the Dead Sea scrolls, a variety of newly transcribed apocryphal sources, and his own research on the pyramid texts in mind, Nibley argues that

> the staggering *prodigality* of the gifts brought to mankind by Joseph is just beginning to appear as the Scriptures he gave us are held up for comparison with the newly discovered or rediscovered documents of the ancients purporting to come from the times and places he describes in those revelations. He has placed in our hands fragments of writings from the leaders of all the major dispensations; and now, only in very recent times, has the world come into possession of whole libraries of ancient texts against which his purported scriptures can be tested.[19]

As Nibley also knows, these corroborative sources equally support the view that the teachings and ritual symbols of the Latter-day Saint temple have antecedents which long predate Masonry. The endowment ceremony's glorious vision of each mortal's potential for eternal exaltation and its culminating promise of eternal family union are movingly enforced by ordinances which, by contrast with the Catholic Stations of the Cross, suggest wherein Christ's atonement was also a gesture of the truest, most endearing fellowship wherewith Christ can raise us to him with ever more secure handholds as, by covenanting with him, we acknowledge and benefit from his ordeal upon the cross. His passion and our salvation are — or can be — intimately one, culminating one day in his embracing and welcoming us to his eternal kingdom as beloved heirs. Particularly significant among the temple's several ordinances is the initiatory anointing: Bearing in mind what each initiate is individually promised there and that the Savior's title "Christ" itself literally means "the anointed one," it is no exaggeration, I believe, that with this most important anointing we are in turn set apart to be "Saviors on Mount Zion," with all that implies about our consecrating ourselves ever after, consistently blessing others' lives rather than in any way impeding their spiritual progress, and in turn, throughout the eternities as literal joint-heirs, while realizing our individual divine potential, enjoying a kind of existence, a fulness of challenge and self-fulfillment, which mortals could not and never have imagined. What could ever more profoundly commit and motivate us to be his faithful disciples? Such meaning, which is the heart and purpose of all the rest, is quite absent in the mass as in the Masonic rite, by contrast a somehow well-preserved but empty husk. Its occurrence in even more ancient fragments like the aforementioned Egyptian rites; certain forms of Buddhist ritual; the Hopi kiva ceremony; the concept of Kundalini Yoga; the consecration through washing, anointing, and garmenting described in the Hindu Satapatha-Brahmana Veda; an apparent Judaic source for washing and anointing; and the veil motif in various Catholic

churches[20] — none of which were known to Joseph Smith —
further corroborates its pristine origins.

So what was Joseph Smith? A facile or not-so-facile
plagiarist? Or one so in touch with the spiritual essence in
otherwise earthly phenomena that, somehow divinely directed to it in the form of seerstones, sarcophagi, and Masonry, he was also led to interpret and wrest from them
a significance entirely alien to his culture and his times but
of astoundingly universal import — further substantiating
the notion that "all things denote there is a God; yea, even
the earth, and all things that are upon the face of it" (Alma
30:44)?[21] Was Joseph Smith unusually naive and imper-
vious to the ways of men and to respectable, civilized
religious tradition? A megalomaniac who would rework it
all to suit himself, in his own fashion? Or was he, by virtue
of his youth and cultural isolation, still sufficiently pliable
and open to what for almost two thousand years God had
waited to recall to men's attention when their social circumstances would once again allow such a cataclysmic
intrusion in their settled affairs, their rationally ordered
but strictly temporal and self-serving alignments of secular,
economic, ecclesiastical, and domestic forces? Was Joseph
Smith just unusually stubborn? Or was he faithful unto
death, one of God's few true martyrs? Was he merely
sentimental or filled, like few others, with Christlike love
and a seer's vision of mankind's glorious potential as God's
own offspring? For all Hill's sound, instructive investigation into his life — a life not yet 150 years past with roots
and a social context not unlike that of many other English-
speaking Americans — we seem no closer to a satisfying
answer than previously.

The only adequate confirmation must, it would seem,
be a transcendent one. But how appropriate and how needful that, point for point, Joseph's authenticity as a prophet
would elude and battle those who seek to understand spiritual matters by strictly rational means. Was Joseph in this

respect really so very different from the many other prophets, including Christ, who were so often rejected by those
closest to them? In the "man of sorrows" verses—which
figure in the lyrics sung by John Taylor in Carthage Jail—
Isaiah says that the Lord "hath no form nor comeliness;
and when we shall see him, there is no beauty that we
should desire him" (Isaiah 53:2). To his contemporaries,
Jesus' teachings were hardly more popular than those of
Elijah, who cried, "The children of Israel have forsaken
thy covenant, thrown down thine altars, slain thy prophets
with the sword; and I, even I only, am left; and they seek
my life, to take it away" (1 Kings 19:14), or of Jeremiah,
who complained, "The word of the Lord was made a reproach unto me, and a derision, daily" (Jeremiah 20:8).
Christ seemed less than surprised that this was so: "Jesus
knew from the beginning who they were that believed not,
and who should betray him. And he said, Therefore said
I unto you, that no man can come unto me, except it were
given him of my Father" (John 6:64-65). Time and again
he seems, almost deliberately, to provoke those who are
inclined to take offense at his words: "I am the living bread"
(John 6:51), he asserts, insisting that "Except ye eat the
flesh of the Son of man, and drink his blood, ye have no
life in you" (John 6:53). "From that time," we are told,
"many of his disciples went back, and walked no more
with him" (John 6:66).

Is this frustrating circumstance not itself an archetypal
substantiation which every prophet, including Joseph, was
understandably anxious to avoid but could not? The austere, "unnatural" nature of a prophet is again well characterized by Isaiah:

> Then said I, Woe is me! for I am undone; because I
> am a man of unclean lips, and I dwell in the midst of a
> people of unclean lips: for mine eyes have seen the King,
> the Lord of hosts. Then flew one of the seraphims unto
> me, having a live coal in his hand, which he had taken

> with the tongs from off the altar: And he laid it upon
> my mouth, and said, Lo, this hath touched thy lips; and
> thine iniquity is taken away, and thy sin purged. Also
> I heard the voice of the Lord, saying, Whom shall I send,
> and who will go for us? Then said I, Here am I; send
> me. And he said, Go, and tell this people, Hear ye in-
> deed, but understand not; and see ye indeed, but per-
> ceive not. Make the heart of this people fat, and make
> their ears heavy, and shut their eyes; lest they see with
> their eyes, and hear with their ears, and understand with
> their heart, and convert, and be healed. Then said I,
> Lord, how long? And he answered, Until the cities be
> wasted without inhabitant, and the houses without man,
> and the land be utterly desolate (Isaiah 6:5-11).

Persons so commissioned do not put the majority of men
at ease and traditionally are often exiled or stoned. Joseph
was one of these.

Whenever a prophet arises in any given generation,
moreover, he is often least recognized by those who are
most attached to the prophets who preceded him. When
the Pharisees taunted Christ for blasphemy, he reminded
them that in their cherished Torah their revered fathers
had been told, "Ye are gods" (John 10:33-36; Psalm 82:6).
Perhaps we too should make sure that whatever tends to
violate our immediate sense of what is proper and appropriate not preclude our better perception of as yet unap-
prehended, ultimate truth. By analogy with the way we
first reacted to sex and the design of our bodies, we might
well expect other realities to shock us. Carl Sagan vividly
describes with what tenacity and courage Johannes Kepler
finally came to recognize that the orbits of the planets were
elliptical and not, as seemed to everyone till then, indis-
putably circular. Of himself, Kepler said, "The truth of
nature which I had rejected and chased away, returned by
stealth through the back door, disguising itself to be accepted. . . . Oh, what a foolish bird I have been."[22] And

Sagan adds: "The Thirty Years' War obliterated his grave. If a marker were to be erected today, it might read, in homage to his scientific courage: 'He preferred the hard truth to his dearest illusions.' "[23] In this regard one similarly recalls the statement of the renowned historian of Renaissance Italy, Jacob Burkhardt: "The denial of complexity is the essence of tyranny," and the deep moral which underlies the otherwise seemingly frivolous poem by Shakespeare's contemporary, Robert Herrick:

> A sweet disorder in the dress
> Kindles in clothes a wantonness:
> A lawn about the shoulders thrown
> Into a fine distraction:
> An erring lace, which here and there
> Enthralls the crimson stomacher:
> A cuff neglectful, and thereby
> Ribbands to flow confusedly:
> A winning wave (deserving note)
> In the tempestuous petticoat:
> A careless shoe-string, in whose tie
> I see a wild civility
> Do more bewitch me, than when art
> Is too precise in every part.[24]

Life is doubtless so wonderful because it is so much more novel than our limited minds and imaginations would have it be.

Meanwhile, the claims made by and for Joseph Smith are themselves so novel, so distinctive, their implications so universally profound, that no one can afford to be indifferent or avoid their serious, unbiased investigation. Truman Madsen intimates their import as he discusses the sense of limitless multiplicity and ever-expanding, ever more enriching interpersonal relationships and opportunities for self-realization which, in key phrases like the promise of "eternal lives," attended the Prophet's eternal vision.[25] Madsen has acutely perceived wherein Joseph

Smith's teachings resolve a number of otherwise perturb-
ing age-old philosophical questions: the paradox of God's
infinite nature; the egoism-altruism controversy; the relativity versus absolutism of Divine Will; the doctrine of
Adam's "wounding fall" and man's consequently deficient
merit for salvation: "God has to save us though we don't
deserve it"; man's corrupt mortal nature, ostensibly pre-
cluding the possibility of divine potential in human beings;
and so forth.[26] Among the many false dichotomies inherited by Western secular and religious thought since Pla-
tonic idealism reversed the astounding insights of sixth-
century B.C. Ionians are indeed the oppressive notions of
disparity between what is material and spiritual, emotional
and intellectual, human and divine. By contrast, Joseph
Smith's expanding vision restores a sense of true eternity
(including a premortal existence and the coeternality of
intelligences); affords a sense of relevant human spiritual
history which, in terms of priesthood, ordinances, and
revealed doctrine, extends through the dispensations from
Adam, rather than effectively from the meridian of time,
as with most Christianity; similarly accounts for the spiritual history of both Eastern and Western hemispheres;
sacralizes the secular, subjecting all human experience,
including health and marriage, to eternal laws and posi-
tioning the Earth's ultimate transformation into a celestial
sphere; binds the human family in ties of eternal kinship,
literally turning "the heart of the fathers to the children,
and the heart of the children to their fathers" (Malachi 4:6);
links man to God as his literal heir and thus enables man
to know and live for a glorious eternal destiny of divine
promise. Finally, with Joseph Smith's perspective and vision, faith and reason are no longer unalterably opposed,
and the role of Evil as a necessary counterpoint to Good
dispels the dilemma of theodicy, guaranteeing that, as an
always extant intelligence, man is not only fully accountable for his fate but ever free and obligated to choose.

As Nibley puts it, Joseph gave us "a choice between nothing or something—and what a something!"[27] As we ponder that something's seeming strangeness, we might profitably consider the criteria which the Savior suggested in his own behalf: "The same works that I do, bear witness of me, that the Father hath sent me" (John 5:36); "Had ye believed Moses, ye would have believed me: for he wrote of me" (John 5:46); "If any man will do his will, he shall know of the doctrine, whether it be of God, or whether I speak of myself" (John 7:17). John Taylor—Joseph Smith's counselor, witness to his martyrdom, and his eventual successor (after Brigham Young) as prophet, seer, and revelator—declared in 1853, "If there is any truth in heaven, earth, or hell, I want to embrace it. I care not what shape it comes in to me, who brings it, or who believes in it, whether it is popular or unpopular."[28] C. S. Lewis elaborates:

> Another thing I've noticed about reality is that, besides being difficult, it's odd: it isn't neat, it isn't what you expect. . . . Reality, in fact, is always something you could not have guessed. That's one of the reasons I believe in Christianity. It's a religion you could not have guessed. If it offered us just the kind of universe we'd always expected, I'd feel we were making it up. . . . It has just that queer twist about it that real things have. So let's leave behind all these boys' philosophies—these over-simple answers. The problem isn't simple and the answer isn't going to be simple either. . . . Either this man was, and is, the Son of God, or else a madman or something worse. . . . But don't let us come with any patronizing nonsense about his being a great human teacher. He has not left that open to us. . . . I'm trying here to prevent anyone from saying that really silly thing that people often say about Him: 'I'm ready to accept Jesus as a great moral teacher, but I don't accept His claim to be a God.' That is the thing we must not say. A man who was merely a man and said the sort of things

Jesus said, would not be a great moral teacher. He'd be either a lunatic—on the level with the man who says he's a poached egg—or else he'd be the Devil of Hell.[29]

These words apply in a lesser measure to Joseph Smith or any true prophet! "In the vocabulary of any relevant faith there is bound to be the 'word' of desperation, as well as of expectancy."[30] As I, a humanist, address this body of, among others, historians—some, like myself, believers in Joseph Smith's prophetic claims, who sometimes doubt despite their desires; some, skeptics who perhaps at times are overwhelmed and wistful to believe "if it were only true"—what I would now like to say is simply this: to remind you and myself that matters of faith and religion are, by definition, fraught with logical uncertainty and that we can never disprove or prove their claims of authenticity, however absurd or repulsive certain features may strike us on the one hand, or however consistent, comprehensive, and edifying they may seem to us on the other. So we should stop trying. If we are really professional, we will, when addressing such phenomena, dissociate ourselves from whatever prejudices and presuppositions to which we are viscerally inclined. Or we will at least try to. It may also help to remind ourselves that, in whatever we ultimately place our credence, we have, as Hans Küng would say, consciously chosen to do so, and also that choice is unavoidable: Not to choose is itself a choice.[31] Therefore, meaningful conversion to any religious proposition—even its rejection—involves a freely and consciously willed personal choice and a commitment to a particular metaphysical worldview. This is not to say that one's choice and commitment should not rest upon the very best, most conceivably rewarding, and spiritually redeeming grounds. And my purpose here has been to remind us all in the express instance of Joseph Smith just how redeeming are those grounds despite some appearances to the contrary. Nor is this to deny the importance of transcendental witness and spiritual confirmation, or that they are possible. They are, after all, the essential epistemological component of all religion. The Apostle Paul said, "the natural man receiveth not the things of the Spirit of God: for they are foolishness unto him: neither can he know them, because they are spiritually discerned" (1 Corinthians 2:14). The logical man, the scholar, as such, *is* the natural man of whom Paul spoke. No scholar is objectively equipped either to dismiss or to verify the things of the spirit, at least not in this life. No scholar is objectively equipped to call Joseph Smith either "a conscious fraud" *or*, by implication, an unconscious one.

On the other hand, any commitment of faith which fosters reverence for the source of life — affirms life itself and the special significance of the life in every individual, sustains hope, and encourages decency and goodness — is sacred and deserves our respect. Moreover, when we too freely begin to prescribe what we think is best for a given religion, though it be in the light of what we consider most reasonable and just, we are no longer submitting *our* mind and will to that of the Lord but subjecting it to *our own* instead. And that, however enlightened, is no longer religion.

I was recently introduced to the community of Russian Old Believers, five thousand strong, in Oregon's Willamette Valley. Since the seventeenth century these people have maintained a tight-knit community whose every activity and codified gesture is permeated with devotion to the gospel of Christ and whose families are strongly bonded by that devotion. To maintain their identity they have variously migrated from Russia to points as distant as Turkey, mainland China, Brazil, Argentina and, more recently, the United States. But does it lessen any the beauty and the nobility of their way of life to know that it originated during a dispute we would consider downright

silly? In the 1600s their ancestors broke away from the
official Russian Church because, among other things, its
patriarch proclaimed that (as in Greek Orthodoxy from
which Russian Orthodoxy derived its beliefs and customs)
three fingers should be used in crossing oneself instead of
two and not two but three hallelujahs chanted in the liturgy. In terms of this earlier historical precedent, the Old
Believers and all the Russians before them were seemingly
in the wrong and, for their fanatical insistence on Old
Russian ritual, were ever after severely ostracized and persecuted. Yet centuries later and despite their concomitant
sense of superiority and exclusiveness, we can admire,
even envy, the way their religion so profoundly informs,
sustains, and integrates their individual and communal
existence. If Mormons tend to put others off because of a
similar sense of exclusiveness — and they do — it is really
no different. As Kenneth Cragg avers, "With religions comparative, one becomes comparatively religious. Decisive
faith appears unnecessary or intolerant."[32] And insofar as
that goes, I would reiterate Ed Ashment's quite fairly posed
rhetorical question: "Why must the LDS Church stand or
fall on the basis of 'scientific evidence,' while it is not felt
necessary for other denominations to be subjected to such
rigorous testing?"[33] In all fairness the Mormon Church's
both "unprovable" and "undisprovable" origins deserve
the same open-ended recognition by scholars as those of
any other religion — none of which, including the pristine
Christian Church, has a more authoritatively reliable foundation in secular terms.

But all we have considered so far has at least been
couched in a comfortable Christian context. What about
the other world religions in which Christ does not su-
premely figure — those "other guides than ours to life and
meaning" which, as in the case of too many a so-called
Christian, "have not, for the most part, been options freely
chosen . . . but rather denominators of birth and culture,

of language and geography"?[34] How ought we to address them, without feeling threatened, yet without condescension? As Cragg, an Anglican specialist, asserts in his *The Christian and Other Religion*, "The art of loyalty and the art of relationship must be understood and practiced, as complementary. . . . Here . . . we have to do with felt and lived religious meaning, rather than with its abstraction into 'ism.' "[35] Cragg further pleads

> the case of reverence for reverence and the need to penetrate faiths as their insiders know them, if there is to be hope of reciprocal awareness. This does not mean a sentimentality oblivious of the compromises or the crimes of which religions have been guilty. But realism has its positive duties, too, and the first of these is a hospitable mind.[36]

No less should be expected of those who take it upon themselves to study the origins, its founding prophet, or any other aspect of Mormonism. Again, in Cragg's words:

> A particular beginning is as inescapable in any religion, as in any philosophy. One cannot start presuppositionless. What matters is that the point of departure fulfills itself in where it leads. To end authentically is to vindicate one's beginning, and this is what the Christian claims of his Old Testament indebtedness.[37]

But to those who in their turn selectively handle Mormon history and discourage our probing it in a number of areas in order to "gild" the Church's "lily," one needs to say (or at least ask): Haven't we been, if anything, overly cautious, overly mistrustful, overly condescending to a membership and a public who are far more perceptive and discerning than we often give them credit for? Haven't we, in our care not to offend a soul or cause anyone the least misunderstanding, too much deprived such individuals of needful occasions for personal growth and more in-depth life-probing experience? In our neurotic cautiousness, our

fear of venturing, haven't we often settled for an all too
shallow and confining common denominator that insults
the very Intelligence we presume to glorify and is also
dishonest because, deep down, we all know better? Isn't
our intervention often too arbitrary, reflecting the hasty,
uninformed reaction of only one or a couple of influential
objectors? Don't we in the process too severely and need-
lessly test the loyalty and respect of and lose credibility
with many more than we imagine? Isn't there a tendency
among us, bred by the fear of displeasing, to avoid healthy
self-disclosure—public or private—and to pretend about
ourselves to ourselves and others, and doesn't this in turn
breed loneliness and make us, more than it should,
strangers to each other? And when we are too calculating,
too self-conscious, too mistrustful, too prescriptive, and
too regimental about our roots and about one another's
aesthetic, intellectual, and spiritual life, aren't we self-defeating?

Ultimately we only come to understand the things of
greatest worth through Christlike love: The nature of truth
lies not in knowledge, but in love. If we would constantly
keep this in mind we would not fear exposure or what
others could ever say about us. We would have more confidence in the redeeming light we've been given. We would
fearlessly let it shine, and it would convince others—how
many more others?—despite themselves and their own
feeble logic. The rest would not matter. If our *own* faith
were only not so feeble. And *if* we were also that righteous.
But, forgetting, we become extremely wary and reticent to
be fully disclosing, to the point that we are discouraged
from much alluding to even so familiar and fundamental
a feature of the Mormon past as polygamy. It may not be
prudent to disseminate problematic historical facts or freely
allude to every complex and difficult real-life circumstance.
We justly resent the common imputation by so many elsewhere that present-day polygamous cults and their fre-

quently deranged, gangland-style leaders are part and parcel of the mainstream Church. But it is equally ineffective to suppress the ostensible facts or to intimidate those who know of, and are attempting to be reconciled to, them. Suspicion, mistrust, the leveling of intellectual expectations, the condescending slanting of available data will not do. Instead, credibility indeed suffers and the unwarranted idolization of other human beings, even divinely elected persons, prevents us from loving *them* as much as we might if we *knew* them better, together with the traditions we associate with them. That is surely even more the case for those who do not particularly cherish such persons and traditions—in other words, those we would most like to interest in them. It also offers a field day to those who wish to disparage what we hold sacred, the implication being that, the more we deny some things or appear to, the more we must ourselves harbor serious doubts and have something to hide.

If we cannot afford to investigate and face up to the "if only likely" facts, as these come to our attention, and must instead be content with the most favorable and safe, the most stereotypical generalizations, are we not, besides cheating ourselves of a more approximate and more real acquaintance with the persons and events in question, submitting to self-deception—much as have the socialist masses to Marxist theory and propaganda, to an inevitably one-sided explanation which, deep down, no thinking Marxist believes? The dilemmas are not only historical. They abound, as they always have, in the context of our contemporary social and institutional life. What is needed is, in the first order, a willingness to be more open and honest, more self-disclosing about our doubts and fears. The consequence of doing so is not necessarily, as some suspect, the dissolution of faith. And here I fully agree with Professor Foster that it need not "reduce the sense of mystery, awe and power in Mormonism."[38] Indeed all that the Prophet Joseph ever suggested regarding "un-righteous dominion" (e.g., D&C 121:37) seems most applicable here, particularly in terms of our need for, and right to, personal intellectual inquiry. No, life and religion are not so simplistic. God's ways are not ours. Reality (with a capital "R") is indeed paradoxical and full of surprises. Our best attempts to make it seem respectable, predictable, and homogenized in fact avoid and even thwart the necessity to come to know and believe it alone through the witness that transcends and surpasses our natural capacity for comprehension, and that is a very personal undertaking. We cannot, moreover, possibly force ourselves to agree with what we cannot confidently grasp or with what disturbs our conscience. To pretend otherwise is to live a lie.

What, along with our faith, we are intellectually in need of is an essential *empiricism*, which allows for, in fact, prescribes the prudent holding in balance of seemingly contradictory phenomena and the statements made about them. This is an approach which, admittedly, the mainstream members of few, if any, ethnic groups are ever encouraged to consider. But for those confronted by the dilemmas others manage to ignore, it can make a critical difference. Here are the perceptive comments of a returned missionary and graduate student:

> My mission was a glorious experience: I may say, without boasting, that I did some amazing things, rare things, miraculous things, because I realized that no one but me could be the judge and director of my work; yet that realization made me sometimes feel alone, almost existentially "nauseated" with the freedom and ensuing responsibilities I had. When the sky is the limit (and not 60 hours proselyting time), then you realize, not without a great deal of fear and trembling, that you alone determine the success you will have, and not that success automatically follows cheerful, but unthinking, obedi-

ence. In light of all that, then, I think my question is: How do you, in the environment where obedience operates in a causal fashion, try to instill a sense of the awesome freedom and responsibility each individual missionary has? Or perhaps that is a sacred, and therefore ineffable, secret, that only those find out who need to. I suppose many of my companions never felt such an emotion, not to their loss, they are just different. . . . Did I go too far in the mission field to realize that obedience and visible results are not causally connected, that I was horrifically free? Do I go too far now when I realize that though I have the gospel, there are still . . . an awful lot of subtleties I must supply for myself? That I ask these questions suggests I do not think there is a simple answer.

Note these further remarks by a recent convert and returned missionary:

To assume that paradox can be avoided seems naive. There is no question of if, but only of when members of the Church will be confronted and confused by paradox. . . . Is the confusion and insecurity caused by confronting paradox any greater than that caused by confronting family and friends (as a convert) and feeling all their negative social pressure? Is it any greater than the confusion and insecurity produced when the investigator with his shaky new-found faith has to confront his temptations and weaknesses and overcome them to live the commandments? And if paradox is avoided, can a meaningful conversion take place? Confidence and conversion occur after the trials of our faith, and if we avoid certain trials, what does that tell us about our confidence in the Lord and ourselves, as well as the . . . [depth] of our conversion?

If we do not feel called upon to walk such a razor's edge, we may, as certain information even inadvertently comes to our awareness, be called upon to do so. How likely is it, for those who become so exposed but lack sufficient training and sophistication, that coping will be at all successful, let alone easy? For those already exposed (an increasing number), how — without violating their innermost integrity — can such information — even if it is largely secondary and, like all other earthly information, incomplete and subject to further qualification — be ignored and not somehow reconciled? Only weeks ago I received a pamphlet from the ex-Mormons for Jesus which was intended to disturb me with respect to the correspondences between Masonry and the endowment ceremony. How grateful I was that I had already read a transcript of the Masonic rite and was already reconciled to the strong possibility of syncretism in the founding of the Church and of this being revelation nonetheless. But those who dare not entertain that possibility could easily be "thrown" by the surface truth in such assertions.

We have mentioned "exclusiveness," but, however exclusively right for him the true believer must view his particular faith, he has no right to assume that those in other traditions do not have as valid and meaningful an access to transcendent virtue and inspiration. If, with all our soul, we are inclined to witness to what is "virtuous, lovely, or of good report or praiseworthy" (Article of Faith 13) — hence sublimely true — in our own spiritual experience, we should also rejoice when anyone else can so witness for his. This applies both to believer and critic. As Cragg puts it, "only an instinctive courtesy can save him . . . from precipitate judgments where rich issues will be impatiently foreclosed. He must beware the instinct to set simplicity (his) over against evasion (theirs)."[39] I have cited Cragg so extensively because there are lessons here that many of us need. Mormons so rarely see things this way — or their critics.

"Dogma," Cragg insists,

> often thought of as defensive, preservative, even clinical,

ensuring truth, must be seen also as hospitable and inviting. Frontiers that need guards and guardians also enclose areas in which liberties are secured. Faith, as credally defined, is a territory to inhabit, a house to occupy, as well as a fence to maintain and a wall to build. What matters is that habitation should be open to prospectives as well as defensible to inhabitants. Doctrine means invitation to discovery as well as warning against deviation. . . . The deep sense the Christian must surely feel . . . that he is in trust with truth he has no mandate to barter but only to serve and to share, must always be paramount. The question about witness is not Whether? but How? There must be no evasion of issues. . . . But they must be appropriately joined. This means that they must be allowed to emerge *within*, rather than merely against, the intimate meanings and preoccupations of the other man's world. An alert sense of the relevance to us and to our witness, of what otherwise we might be minded to dismiss or to dispute, is truly consistent with the positive and inward loyalties of Christian doctrine. . . . In so far as religions are cultures . . . with legacies of pride and tradition, the lesson is clear. It is when they are allowed their cultural selves that they can best reach beyond themselves. It is when they are consciously under threat that they are suspiciously isolated in temper. It is only when we are allowed our own humanity that we seek an inclusive humanness. Reciprocal courtesy is, therefore, the wisest, as well as the truest, prescript for relationship. . . . Relevance *in* any religion is relevance *for* all. While they may be deliberately separate in their findings, they are common in their human habitation. Perhaps the largest test of their integrity is their integrity about each other. . . . The mystery of evil is not solved but dissolved, if there is no liability to accuse.[40]

Or as Nibley might say to the narrowness on either side, "A plague on both your houses."

The intent of this paper has simply been to point out

those aspects of Joseph Smith's biography which argue in his favor as opposed to those which imply he was a charlatan; to list the remarkable theological concepts which constitute his immensely comprehensive and, at least for his followers, edifying system of thought; to suggest to what extent that system profoundly explicates and interprets the already extant Christian gospel; and finally to observe how his enigmatic character and the common response to it in fact parallel what we know of others whom we have traditionally cast in the prophetic mold. These matters are not intended as testimony, though they may, of course, be witnessed to in a more personal and subjective manner. The enigmas and controversies that invariably arise as, with Donna Hill, we view the prophet's earthly record, nevertheless tend to suggest that few can be totally indifferent or dispassionate toward Joseph Smith and the claims of the restored Church and that where, for whatever reason, people resist them, they also tend to draw their own often unwarranted conclusions—a kind of testimony by default.

"No man knows [his] history"—so why should any historian? We can view Joseph Smith with great confidence, but only when assisted by the Spirit and by thoughtfully weighing all he has given us. As we do so, may we, like Johannes Kepler, always prefer "the hard truth" to "our dearest illusions."

Notes

1. Cited in Robert Carlier, Jean-Louis Lalanne, et al., *Larousse Thematique: Dictionnaire des citations françaises* (Paris: France Loisirs, 1977), 557.

2. Donna Hill, *Joseph Smith: The First Mormon* (Garden City, NY: Doubleday, 1977).

3. Ibid., 44.

4. Ibid., 345.

5. Ibid., 114.

6. T. Edgar Lyon, "Recollections of 'Old Nauvooers': Memories from Oral History," *BYU Studies* 18 (1978): 143-50.

7. Hill, *Joseph Smith: The First Mormon*, 342-43.

8. Ibid., 273.

9. Ibid., 343.

10. *DHC* 4:445.

11. Ibid., 5:23-24.

12. *TPJS*, 228.

13. Ibid., 353-54.

14. Truman G. Madsen, *Defender of the Faith: The B. H. Roberts Story* (Salt Lake City: Bookcraft, 1980), 93.

15. Hill, incidentally, does not discuss the temple or its ordinances.

16. See volumes 5 through 8 in the *Collected Works of Hugh Nibley*.

17. Paraphrases from Truman G. Madsen, "B. H. Roberts and the Book of Mormon," *BYU Studies* 19 (1979): 434.

18. Ibid., 435.

19. Hugh Nibley, "How Firm a Foundation! What Makes It So?" *Dialogue* 12 (1979): 30.

20. Cf. Marcus von Wellnitz, "The Catholic Liturgy and the Mormon Temple," *BYU Studies* 21 (1981): 3-35.

21. This would be in keeping with the peculiar Mormon insistence that all things earthly are indeed spiritual — hence the emphasis on the Word of Wisdom as a spiritual law, marriage as a celestial ordinance, a literal physical resurrection, and the anticipation that the earth itself will be the focus of an eternal celestial kingdom. Carl Sagan suggests how radically this view departs from that generally held in Western culture, and why: "Plato and Aristotle . . . taught that alienation of the body from the mind (a natural enough ideal in a slave society); they separated matter from thought; they divorced the Earth from the heavens — divisions that were to dominate Western thinking for more than twenty centuries. . . . The Platonists and their Christian successors held the peculiar notion that the Earth was tainted and somehow nasty, while the heavens were perfect and divine." Carl Sagan, *Cosmos* (New York: Random House, 1980), 187-88.

22. Ibid., 62.

23. Ibid., 67.

24. Robert Herrick, "Delight in Disorder," in F. W. Moorman, ed., *The Poetical Works of Robert Herrick* (London, Oxford University Press, 1957), 28.

25. Truman G. Madsen, "Is Mormonism a World Religion?" Library Lecture, Brigham Young University, November 1980.

26. Truman G. Madsen, "Joseph Smith and the Problems of Eth-

ics," in Donald Hill, ed., *Perspectives in Mormon Ethics* (Salt Lake City: Publishers, 1983), 29-48.

27. Nibley, "How Firm a Foundation," 30.

28. *JD* 1:155.

29. C. S. Lewis, *The Case for Christianity* (New York: Macmillan, 1968), 36, 45.

30. Kenneth Cragg, *The Christian and Other Religion: The Measure of Christ* (London: Mowbray, 1977), 38.

31. Hans Küng, *Does God Exist? An Answer for Today*, tr. Edward Quinn (Garden City, NY: Doubleday, 1980), 438.

32. Cragg, *The Christian and Other Religion*, 13.

33. Ed Ashment, "A Questionable Enterprise" (review), *The Sunstone Review* 2 (1982): 24.

34. Cragg, *The Christian and Other Religion*, xi.

35. Ibid., xii-xiii.

36. Ibid., xiii.

37. Ibid., 51.

38. Lawrence Foster, "New Perspectives on the Mormon Past," *Sunstone* 7/1 (January-February 1982): 45.

39. Cragg, *The Christian and Other Religion*, 21.

40. Ibid., 25-28, 38.

20

Utopia and Garden: The Relationship of *Candide* to Laxness's *Paradísarheimt*

George S. Tate
Brigham Young University, Provo, Utah

I have heard Hugh Nibley tell how he used to ride his bicycle from Provo to Spanish Fork in order to learn Icelandic and to acquire books from members of the Icelandic community, which was founded in 1855 — the oldest continuous Icelandic settlement in North America. In several of his early articles on political theory, Dr. Nibley cites customs and institutions (e.g., the war arrow, the Althing, and so forth) in Icelandic sagas and historical texts to illustrate his arguments.[1] This fascination has been passed on to his son, Michael, who took two courses in Old Icelandic from me some years ago. Because of these interests and also because Dr. Nibley has at times shown a marvelous capacity for earnest satire, it seemed to me an appropriate contribution to his *Festschrift* to discuss a novel about Mormons by Iceland's Nobel laureate, Halldór Laxness, which is set partly in Spanish Fork and is influenced both by the Icelandic sagas and by Voltaire's satiric masterpiece *Candide*.

*   *   *

Although an author's decision to translate a work by a writer of another age or nationality may not be the surest indication of his own view of the relative importance of the work in the span of world literature, it is at least evidence of serious appreciation — perhaps, even, an acknowledgment of apprenticeship. One thinks, for example, of Baudelaire's translation of Poe, Hofmannsthal's of Molière, Lundkvist's of D. H. Lawrence, and Nabokov's of Pushkin. It is worth noticing, therefore, that except for his Icelandic translations of several Danish novels by his fellow countryman Gunnar Gunnarsson, Halldór Laxness has translated only two major works in over sixty years of literary productivity — both of these in the war years of the early 1940s: Hemingway's *A Farewell to Arms*, which he published as *Vopnin kvödd* in 1941, and Voltaire's *Candide*, which he translated in twelve days late in 1943 and published under the title *Birtíngur* (*Optimist*) in 1945.[2]

Hallberg, Bergsveinsson, and others have examined Hemingway's influence on the development of Laxness's style. In the preface to *Vopnin kvödd*, Laxness himself implies this influence in his discussion of the similarity between Hemingway's terse telegraphic style and the laconic style of the sagas. Hallberg argues that Laxness's translation of Hemingway's novel is the corollary to his contemporaneous editing of several of the sagas, using modern Icelandic spelling. Both of these activities of the early 1940s were, he suggests, preparations for the new terse, objective, nonsentimental style forged in *Íslandsklukkan* (*Bell of Iceland*), which first appeared in 1943.[3]

Little has been written, though, on the possibility of Voltaire's influence on Laxness. Sønderholm identifies as Voltairean the praise of daily labor for one's livelihood with which Laxness concludes his first novel *Barn náttúrunnar* (*Child of Nature*, 1919), but this is his only mention of Voltaire.[4] In his critical study *Skaldens hus*, Peter Hallberg limits his discussion of Voltaire's influence on Laxness to the gestation of *Íslandsklukkan*, noting some similarity between certain military experiences of *Candide* and Laxness's hero Jón Hreggvidsson — forcible induction, drills, attempted desertion, and punishment.[5] Beyond this, Hallberg suggests that "Voltaire's little book may have contributed a detail or two to the milieu description" of Laxness's novel, which is set in roughly the same period, but he does not specify what these details might be.[6]

The scope of the inquiry needs now to be extended, however, for it is not in *Barn náttúrunnar* or in *Íslandsklukkan* but in his Mormon novel *Paradísarheimt*, which appeared five years after his winning of the Nobel Prize, that one finds the greatest influence of Voltaire on Laxness's oeuvre. Indeed, our understanding of this novel is considerably heightened when it is read against *Candide*. Even though over fifteen years elapsed between his translation of *Candide* and the publication of *Paradísarheimt*, Laxness has indicated that he began wrestling with the ideas that led to *Paradísarheimt* as early as 1927, that is, that the novel had begun to take shape in his mind even before he translated *Candide*.[7] René Hilleret, in the preface to the French translation of *Paradísarheimt*, comments in passing on the Voltairean quality of Laxness's irony: "Et il est impossible, tant par le style que par l'ironie souriante, mais au fond féroce, de ne pas comparer Laxness à Voltaire, au Voltaire ennemi acharné de l'intolérance, mère du fanatisme."[8] But no one, to my knowledge, has explored the structural and thematic correspondences between *Paradísarheimt* and *Candide*.

It will be useful to the subsequent discussion to summarize briefly the plot of Laxness's novel and to identify its main source. *Paradísarheimt* tells of a simple Icelandic farmer, Steinar, who dreams of obtaining the Promised Land for his children. Recalling tales of the munificence of Viking kings, from whom he is descended, he first hopes to purchase a promised land in the form of property by giving a wonder-pony, symbol of his children's sense of the marvelous, to the Danish prince when the royalty visit Iceland in 1874 for the millennial celebration of the founding of the country. But for his efforts he is only invited to visit the royal palace in Copenhagen where he receives, rather than a kingdom, autographed photographs, which he later trades for four cobbler's needles. At the assurance of Bishop Thjódrekur, a Mormon missionary whom he had met in Iceland and now in Denmark, that the Promised Land of God has been established in Utah, Steinar sets out on the second part of his quest and remains in Utah, only partly assimilated into the Mormon community in Spanish Fork, awaiting the arrival of his wife and children who, in his absence, have been physically and economically exploited. His wife dies aboard ship; Steinar feels estranged from his children who arrive having long since thought him dead. With unarticulated disappointment, he returns to Iceland as a missionary, eventually making his way back to the old farm whence he began his quest. In the final scene he is laying stone upon stone, mending the broken walls of the derelict farm.

The overall plot of the novel is based on the writings of Eiríkur Ólafsson á Brúnum (1832-1900), a colorful figure and rather well-known writer of naive travel books and other autobiographical pieces, who became a Mormon in 1881. In his first travel book, Eiríkur tells how he sold a horse to the prince of Denmark during the millennial celebration in 1874 and how he went to Denmark and was received by the royalty who gave him autographed photographs. In 1879 Eiríkur, who was born at Hlíd, the setting of Steinar's farm, moved to Mosfellssveit (where Laxness grew up) and there became a Mormon, convinced initially by Thórdur Didriksson's adaptation of Parley P. Pratt's *A Voice of Warning* (which he bought for a bottle of cheap brandy) and finally moved to join the Church by "the unjustified hatred heaped upon the Mormons."[9] He and his family traveled to Utah in 1881 (his wife died in Nebraska on the way); he stayed in Spanish Fork for eight years, filling one mission to Iceland, before leaving the

Church and returning to Iceland for good in 1889. His second travel book and several shorter pieces document these experiences.[10]

Voltaire's influence is less immediately apparent. The first point of correspondence between *Candide* and *Paradísarheimt* concerns genre: both works take their bearings from the picaresque tradition, and both are characterized by a tension between this tradition and other generic norms. Voltaire, as is well known, disliked the novels of sentiment and adventure that flourished in the eighteenth century. He developed his own narrative form, the *conte philosophique*, in a different direction. As Bottiglia defines it, the philosophic tale "is a fictitious prose narrative wherein theme molds all the other component elements (action, character, setting, diction, etc.) into a stylized, two-dimensional, emotionally sublimated demonstration."[11] The form has "a serious purpose of social satire or philosophic truth veiled beneath surface pleasantry and brilliance" and "a pervasive ironical tone pungently flavored with realism of detail."[12] But what is interesting about *Candide*, among the other philosophic tales, is that Voltaire commingles the *conte philosophique* and the picaresque novel, appropriating the latter in order to parody it and turn it against itself through ironic imitation.[13] As Pierre de St. Victor has written, "C'est une destruction de la forme par la forme même."[14]

Generic tension works at several levels in *Paradísarheimt*. In his essay on "The Origins of *Paradise Reclaimed*," Laxness refers to the simple travel accounts of Eiríkur á Brúnum, Steinar's historical prototype, as "a crude picaresque story."[15] Laxness seems not only to have perceived the picaresque quality of Eiríkur's narratives, but also the ironic possibilities of the picaresque in his other model, *Candide*. Sigurdur Magnússon has commented that *Paradísarheimt* "is not constructed like a novel," that it is a kind of "filosofisk lignelse" ("philosophical parable"; cf.

conte philosophique), and that it is closely related to the picaresque novel in that there is a moral developed through irony and humor.[16] The picaresque form is at best a tenuous vehicle for the representation of a quest for a philosophical ideal, but Laxness — ever the ironist whose creative energy thrives on a tension between humor and pathos — playfully undermines the seriousness of Steinar's quest for the Promised Land by drawing upon a further narrative paradigm: the "Lucky Hans" folktale in which a simple-minded peasant sets out to market with a horse, barters for items of increasingly smaller value (for a sheep, a dog, and so forth), is easily persuaded to foolish decisions, and, returning home with only some cobbler's needles for his efforts, loses these as he fords a stream.[17]

Voltaire had parodied the picaresque novel, it is true, but he had also used it to ironize his own philosophical inquiry; Laxness compounds the genres of novel, philosophic parable, picaresque narrative, and naive folktale in a way that at once enhances and undermines the seriousness of his subject.

In specifics of plotting, *Paradísarheimt* and *Candide* differ more than they resemble each other, but in overall design — beginning, middle, and end — they are remarkably similar. Both begin in a garden of childlike innocence; in the course of their peregrinations the protagonists of both — notable for their honest judgment and great simplicity of heart — visit a utopia; and at the end both affirm useful activity in a garden, a garden which stands in some contrastive relationship to the utopia. As long as Candide's early experience is limited to the microcosm of the Castle of Thunder-ten-tronckh, the sententious pronouncement of Pangloss, "the greatest philosopher in the province and consequently in the entire world,"[18] that this is the best of all possible worlds makes perfectly good sense. Candide listens intently and believes implicitly, "with all the good faith of his age" and innocence.[19] Voltaire drives home the point of this protected garden by referring to the castle and its environs as the "paradis terrestre,"[20] out of which Candide is driven when he is found embracing Cunegonde.

Similarly, Steinar's little farm is a garden of innocence. The emphasis falls on a sense of continuity with the historical and legendary past and on the innocent wonder of childhood. Even the adults have "the same expression as children" and "their tribulations [are] as natural to them as the sorrows of childhood."[21] Whereas the optimist Pangloss had urged his position on a receptive audience, here his momentary counterpart, District Magistrate Benediktsson, whom Laxness calls an "idealist," urges Steinar, who has fostered a sense of the marvelous in his children: "Never sell your children's fairy tales."[22] And Steinar himself is heard to say, "The whole point is . . . that when the world ceases to be miraculous in the eyes of our children, then there is very little left."[23]

After a variety of adventures and misadventures dotted here and there by sea travels and a journey across America (South for one and North for the other), both heroes arrive in a utopia — Candide in Eldorado and Steinar in "God's City of Zion" in Utah. There are many points of correspondence between these two utopias: In both, the visitors are given a guided tour of the city; in both, material prosperity is seen as a sign of God's special favor and as substantiation of Truth. In Eldorado, "the countryside was tended for pleasure as well as profit; everywhere the useful was joined to the agreeable."[24] In Zion, Pastor Runólfur tells Steinar: "You forget that every single thing contains a higher concept — good broth no less than a pair of topboots; the Greeks called this the Idea. It is this spiritual and eternal quality in all existence and in every thing that we Mormons live by. If anyone is so incompetent that he has neither broth nor topboots . . . he is not likely to have the Spirit, or eternal life either."[25] In both Eldorado and

Zion, engineers build marvelous structures.[26] In Eldorado, Candide marvels at the many "mathematical and physical instruments";[27] in Zion it is the sewing machine that gives practical evidence of the "cosmic wisdom." Steinar's guide says to him, "The cosmic wisdom . . . does not only manifest itself in enormous truths which can only be contained in the brains of fearfully largeheaded university professors; no, it lives also in the sewing machines." Steinar responds that it cannot be denied "that it needs a great deal of philosophy to match a sewing machine."[28] The old Eldoradian tells Candide that his countrymen have nothing to pray for since everything they need has been granted;[29] in Zion an outsider observes of the inhabitants that "When everyone has become sainted and is in Heaven, it's impossible to do anyone any good."[30] In both Eldorado and Zion, God is praised all day long.[31] Candide learns that in Eldorado everyone is a priest;[32] in Zion, the lay priesthood extends to all men. In both Eldorado and Zion tables of plenty are described.[33] The sheep of Eldorado differ in color, speed, and quality from European sheep;[34] in Zion Runólfur shows Steinar the sheep he looks after in order to let him "admire how beautiful and thick their tails [are] compared with the stumps on Icelandic sheep."[35] Whereas Steinar had thirty sheep in Iceland,[36] it is typical in Zion for a farmer to have ten thousand.[37] Both of these utopias, which are bounded by high mountains containing precious metals, are associated with gold. In Zion, society is "governed by the All-Wisdom according to the Golden Book";[38] Steinar, who like the Eldoradians has never valued gold, says of Zion, "Sometimes I have the feeling that I am dead and have come to the land of eternity . . . [where stands] a wondrous palace on pillars, inlaid with gold and brighter than the sun."[39] In Eldorado the "yellow mud" itself is gold;[40] in Zion the clay of which Steinar makes bricks, in cooperation with the "sun which the Lord of Hosts has given to people of correct opinions,"[41] yields a steady stream of coins on which the sun also shines.[42]

Voltaire scholars disagree whether Eldorado constitutes, as Bottiglia would have it, "a dream of perfection, a philosophic ideal for human aspiration,"[43] "a dynamic perfection,"[44] or, as Kahn suggests, "a place of idle, sterile life" that "does not leave any room for amelioration or for activity, social or otherwise," a "life pleasant, placid, and stagnant rather than ideal."[45] But there is no explicit condemnation of Eldorado in the work; here all indeed seems to be well. It is clear, however, that for all its virtues of Zion—and despite the hymn refrain "All is well, all is well"—the utopia Laxness describes has imperfections in and about its edges, perceived by people at the periphery who have not fully caught its vision. There is some religious intolerance (the broken cross on the Lutheran church testifies of the cosmic wisdom),[46] some class distinction between Mormons and Gentiles (a Lutheran says "The man who has the best doctrine is the one who can prove that he has the most to eat; and good shoes. I have neither, and live in a dugout"),[47] and some social ostracism (people no longer patronize a Josephite seamstress when her daughter has an illegitimate child by a Gentile;[48] and Steinar himself admits in a letter to Bishop Thjódrekur that he has "sometimes noticed a certain coldness towards him from others").[49] But for believers at least, it is a place of abundance, a heaven on earth.

These criticisms of Zion are mild compared with those in Eiríkur á Brúnum's exposé of 1891 or in the books of various other disaffected Scandinavians (like the Norwegian Julie Ingerøe, the Swede Johan Ahmanson, and the Dane Christian Michelsen) who wrote sensationally about their experiences in Utah.[50] Laxness did considerable historical research, both in Utah and elsewhere, in preparation for the writing of the novel. This research led to his publication of several articles on Mormon history and society.[51]

In addition to Mormon scriptures, studies by Mormon historians (including Kate Bearnson Carter's articles on the Icelandic settlement at Spanish Fork),[52] and the writings of Eiríkur á Brúnum and Thórdur Didriksson[53] (on whom Bishop Thjódrekur is modeled), Laxness read many accounts—both positive and negative—by nineteenth-century Scandinavians who experienced the Mormon Zion firsthand. One such account may have strengthened the connection he had begun to see between Voltaire's utopia and Zion. Nels Bourkersson, a Swedish immigrant to Utah who lost his Mormon wife to a polygamist and returned disillusioned to his homeland, published a relatively well-known account of his experiences under the title *Tre år i Mormonlandet* (*Three Years in Mormon Country*) in 1867. Bourkersson, who delights in literary quotation (each chapter has its quaint epigraph), refers disparagingly to the Utah of the Mormons not only as "their 'paradise' " but also as "their Eldorado."[54]

After they have experienced their similar utopias in the course of their journeys, both Candide and Steinar find themselves finally in a garden. Here Pangloss, feeling that his theory requires unceasing demonstration, reminds Candide that when man was put into the Garden of Eden he was put there to work it. He then says:

> All events are linked together in the best of possible worlds; for, after all, if you had not been driven from a fine castle by being kicked in the backside for love of Miss Cunegonde, if you hadn't been sent before the Inquisition, if you hadn't traveled across America on foot [as had the Mormon pioneers] . . . , if you hadn't lost all your sheep from the good land of Eldorado [related to the "Lucky Hans" tale?], you wouldn't be sitting here eating candied citron and pistachios.

That is very well put, said Candide, but we must cultivate our garden.[55]

In the final scene of *Paradísarheimt*, when Steinar, after

returning to Iceland as a missionary and being received
with cordial indifference rather than persecution, wanders
out to the site of his old farm and notices that stones have
rolled down, knocking over the stone fences,

> he laid down his knapsack . . . , slipped off his jacket
> and took off his hat; then he began to gather stones to
> make a few repairs to the wall. There was a lot of work
> waiting for one man here; walls like these, in fact, take
> the man with them if they are to stand.
>
> A passer-by saw that a stranger had started to potter
> with the dykes of this derelict croft. "Who are you?"
> asked the traveller. The other replied, "I am the man
> who reclaimed Paradise after it had been lost and gave
> it to his children."
>
> "What is such a man doing here?" asked the passer-
> by.
>
> "I have found the truth and the land that it lives in,"
> said the wall-builder, correcting himself. "And that is
> assuredly very important. But now the most important
> thing is to build up this wall again."
>
> And with that, Steinar of Hlídar went on just as if
> nothing had happened, laying stone against stone in
> these ancient walls, until the sun went down on Hlídar
> in Steinahlídar.[56]

Although, as Paul Ilie has written, "It would of course
be rash to identify Voltaire fully with Candide," he may
nevertheless be viewed in some sense as his surrogate.[57]
Ilie, Wolper,[58] and others have examined the biographical
matrix of Candide and have concluded that the themes of
disillusionment, renunciation, and disengagement in Voltaire's letters of the period lie at the heart of the work.
Although there is still wide disagreement about the specific
meaning of the ending of the work and about the relationship of the garden to Eldorado, it is clear that the idea
of cultivating one's garden—a phrase that becomes a commonplace formula in the letters—undergoes a develop-

ment and enlargement in Voltaire's thinking. To quote Ilie: "Having begun with the realistic need for protective withdrawal [to his garden-retreat], Voltaire had then idealized the garden as a higher state of perfection. But now he claimed for gardening a superior state of philosophical activity, an all-inclusive and hence self-sufficient philosophizing condition."[59] Disengagement does not mean a withdrawal to idleness; it is a dynamic ideal.

Partly through Laxness's own invitation, interpretation of *Paradísarheimt* also finds a corner in the Icelander's biography. Hallberg finds it tempting to interpret Steinar's journey with his "soul-casket" to Copenhagen as corresponding to Laxness's early immersion in Catholicism, Steinar's quest for a material paradise for his family in Utah as representing Laxness's socialist stage, and the final resignation as characterizing his own present refusal to be identified with any ideology.[60] Sønderholm sees a relationship between the stages represented by Eiríkur's three main works and Laxness's own development: For him Eiríkur's first little travel book on his journey to Denmark, which has no religious interest, corresponds to Laxness's life before his conversion to Catholicism; Eiríkur's second travel book, which tells of his conversion — his discovery of an ideology of salvation — and his eventual difficulty in reconciling this ideology with its social and material manifestation in Utah, corresponds to the two related periods in which Laxness subscribed to salvation ideologies, first to Catholicism in the 1920s and then to the radical socialism that dominated his thinking from the 1930s to the 1950s; and finally, Eiríkur's repudiation of Mormon theology and custom in his last work of any length corresponds to Laxness's own renunciation of all ideologies.[61]

Although such topical equations are, as Hallberg cautions, perhaps too pat, the novel is at once personal and universal. There is something of Laxness's own spiritual and ideological odyssey in Steinar's. From the standpoint of its overall treatment of a quest for truth and utopia, *Paradísarheimt* is perhaps Laxness's most nearly autobiographical novel. Steinar's cultivated habit of never saying yes or no reflects Laxness's own ideological neutrality. Characteristic of his renunciation is his loss of interest in truth per se. In an interview for the newspaper *Morgunbladid* in which he was asked, "Has your consideration of the life of the Mormons brought you closer to the truth yourself?" Laxness responded, "I am not so much concerned with truth as with facts. The truth is to me such a philosophical notion. But those men who have sacrificed the facts for their system and have immersed themselves in their truth obtain a viable position in the world."[62] The favoring of fact over truth is a theme of the novel, as will have been apparent from Steinar's comment that it "takes a great deal of philosophy to match a sewing machine."

In "The Origins of *Paradise Reclaimed*," Laxness discusses his longstanding fascination with the idea of a promised land ever since he stood before the temple and tabernacle in Salt Lake City in 1927 and recalled his childhood reading of Eiríkur á Brúnum's travel books. He tried again and again to treat the topic, but could not get it into focus and gave up for years. He writes:

> The truth is that to write successfully about the Promised Land you must have sought and found it in your own life with all that is implied in the concept. You must have made the pilgrimage yourself; figuratively speaking you must have crossed the ocean holding the rank of cattle, walked across the Big Desert on foot, fought within and outside yourself the continuous battles for your land over the years.
>
> You go groping along through a jungle of ideas, which it would take volumes to describe, sometimes you get into blind alleys, at other times you are stuck in bottomless quicksand and saved by a miracle — until finally you find yourself in a small place, in a little enclo-

sure which, it seems to you, has a sort of familiar look, a place that somehow looks like the old home. Was it the same garden from which you started? It seems so, but it is not. A wise man has said: He who goes away will never come back; it means that when he returns he is a different kind of person. Between the garden from which you set out and the garden to which you return lie not only the many kingdoms, but also the big oceans and the big deserts of the world — and the Promised Land itself as well.[63]

Candide ends in community, *Paradísarheimt* in isolation. The stylized generic mixture of Voltaire's tale precludes sympathy with its characters; the novelistic level of *Paradísarheimt* engages our sympathy. The novel is informed by a deep melancholia at lost innocence and the passage of time — relieved, yet paradoxically augmented, by the puzzling humor that plays through the work. The novel suggests that man's seemingly futile quest for paradise is not, as he so often supposes, a forward journey to a material promised land, a wedding of "a dream to geography and its truth to facts," but an unaware attempt to retrace his steps back to innocence. The mellow tone becomes more poignant as time progresses in the fictive world Laxness creates and as Steinar senses that he left to find what he lost by leaving. As the novel says: only the man who sacrifices everything can obtain the promised land.[64]

But there is also a more affirmative sense of this ending — a sense more in line, perhaps, with the reading of Voltaire's *cultiver notre jardin* as positive action. It represents a homecoming. In Zion, we are told, "Iceland vanished as soon as its name was spoken"; no one remembered its proverbs, no one recognized well-known quotations from the sagas.[65] That too had been sacrificed. As brickmaker in Zion, Steinar had molded his clay before sunrise so that the sun, symbol of the All-Wisdom, could transform these perfect rectangular bricks into the building blocks of

Zion, a harmony of matter and spirit.[66] Although "the stone that tumbles down off the mountains of Steinahlídar on to the home-fields is as froth compared to the hand-made Utah stone sun-baked by the grace of God,"[67] even Steinar's new name, Stone P. (for Peter "rock"?) *Stanford*, affirms his fundamental affinity for the irregular stones of Hlídar. (*Stein-* in Icelandic means "stone", as does Old English *stan*.) Generations had worked the walls of his homefield, indeed their best sections had been built by his forefathers. This human continuity is suggested by his patronym Steinsson and his daughter's name Steinbjörg Steinarsdóttir, just as the rest of his name, Steinar of Hlídar in Steinahlídar (stone of slopes in stone slopes), links him to the land and to the ancient struggle to establish order below the peril of stone slopes. Even though, at the end, it is at sunset rather than sunrise that he begins to repair the old walls of his garden, there is a sense of new beginning, a more fundamental fact than philosophical truth, a more affirmative act than renunciation.

Notes

1. "The Arrow, the Hunter, and the State," *Western Political Quarterly* 2/3 (1949): 328-44; "The Hierocentric State," *Western Political Quarterly* 4/2 (1951): 226-53; and "Tenting, Toll, and Taxing," *Western Political Quarterly* 19/4 (1966): 599-630. These papers are also available as reprints through F.A.R.M.S., Brigham Young University, Provo, Utah.

2. Halldór Laxness, tr., *Vopnin kvödd* (Reykjavík: Mál og menning, 1941) and *Birtíngur* (Reykjavík: Helgafell, 1945; rev. 1975). On Laxness generally see Peter Hallberg, *Halldór Laxness*, tr. Rory McTurk (New York: Twayne Publishers, 1971), and Erik Sønderholm, *Halldór Laxness: En monografi* (Copenhagen: Gyldendal, 1981).

3. Hallberg, *Halldór Laxness*, 153-55; Peter Hallberg, *Skaldens hus: Laxness' diktning från* Salka Valka *till* Gerpla (Stockholm: Rabén & Sjögren, 1956), 436-55. Cf. Sveinn Bergsveinsson, "Sagaen og den haardkogte Roman," *Edda* (1942): 56-62.

4. Sønderholm, *Halldór Laxness*, 95.

5. Hallberg, *Skaldens hus*, 419, 438.

6. Ibid., 438. Translations from the Swedish of Hallberg and

Bourkersson, the Danish of Magnússon and Sønderholm, and the Icelandic of Eiríkur á Brúnum and Laxness (newspaper interview only) are my own. I have left the brief critical statements by French scholars in the original.

7. Halldór Laxness, "The Origins of *Paradise Reclaimed*" (New York: Crowell, 1962), 5; this is a pamphlet issued in conjunction with the publication of the English translation of the novel.

8. René Hilleret, preface to Laxness, *Le Paradis retrouvé*, tr. (from English) René Hilleret (Paris: Gallimard, 1966), 7.

9. Eiríkur Ólafsson á Brúnum, *Eiríkur á Brúnum: Ferdasögur, Sagnathaettir, Mormónarit* (Reykjavík: Ísafold, 1946), 8, 102.

10. According to Hallberg, Eiríkur's writings exerted an influence on Laxness's eighteenth-century novel *Íslandsklukkan* as well. Jón Hreggvidsson, hero of the novel, is to some extent based on Eiríkur as well as on Candide (Peter Hallberg, "Laxness, konstnärskapet, ideologierna: Noget om hans senere diktning," *Nordisk Tidskrift* [1967]: 88). This is further evidence that Laxness saw a relationship between Candide and Eiríkur's naive travel books by the early 1940s.

11. William F. Bottiglia, "Voltaire's *Candide*: Analysis of a Classic," *Studies on Voltaire and the Eighteenth Century* 7 (1959): 59.

12. Ibid., 58; citing (but not quoting) Dorothy McGhee, *Fortunes of a Tale* (Menasha, WI: Banta, 1954), 11-15, 35.

13. Bottiglia, "Voltaire's *Candide*," 134.

14. Pierre de Saint Victor, "*Candide*: De la parodie du roman au conte philosophique" *Kentucky Romance Quarterly* [now *Romance Quarterly*] 15 (1968): 383.

15. Laxness, "Origins," 5.

16. Sigurdur A. Magnússon, "Islandsk skönlitteratur, 1959-61," *Nordisk Tidskrift* (1962): 142.

17. This folktale, "Hans in Luck," Grimm no. 83, Type 1415, is widely attested. I have cited the Icelandic version, see Jón Árnason, ed. *Íslenzkar Thjódsögur og Æventýri*, 2 vols. (Reykjavík: Sögufélag, 1954-61), 2:504-5. Cf. English version in *The Complete Grimm's Fairy Tales* (New York: Pantheon, 1944; repr. 1972), 381-86.

18. *Candide: or Optimism*, tr. Robert M. Adams, Norton Critical Editions (New York: Norton, 1966), 2; Voltaire, *Candide ou l'optimisme*, ed. René Pomeau, *The Complete Works of Voltaire*, 48 (Oxford: Oxford University Press, 1980), 120. I quote throughout from the Adams translation but also give the page reference to the standard Oxford edition by Pomeau.

19. Adams, tr., *Candide*, 1; Pomeau, ed., *Candide*, 119.

20. Adams, tr., *Candide*, 3; Pomeau, ed., *Candide*, 122.

21. Halldór Laxness, *Paradise Reclaimed*, tr. Magnús Magnússon (New York: Crowell, 1962), 27; original Icelandic edition, Halldór Laxness, *Paradísarheimt* (Reykjavík: Helgafell, 1960), 30. I quote from Magnússon's English translation, which I have adjusted silently on occasion when it is clear that Laxness knew the Mormon idiom where his translator did not, but I also give the page reference to the Icelandic edition. On the theme of loss of paradise as the loss of childlike innocence in the novel, see Tryggvi Gíslason, "Paradís í *Paradísarheimt*," *Skírnir* 146 (1972): 48-55. Sønderholm, who writes illuminatingly of the social and ideological matrix of the novel (capitalism, industrialism, renunciation of ideology), argues that in the novel "the paradise of childhood is fantasy and illusion," that it is not the paradise Steinar seeks (*Halldór Laxness*, 295).

22. Magnússon, tr., *Paradise Reclaimed*, 16; Laxness, *Paradísarheimt*, 17.

23. Magnússon, tr., *Paradise Reclaimed*, 17; Laxness, *Paradísarheimt*, 18-19.

24. Adams, tr., *Candide*, 34; Pomeau, ed., *Candide*, 183.

25. Magnússon, tr., *Paradise Reclaimed*, 164; Laxness, *Paradísarheimt*, 191.

26. Adams, tr., *Candide*, 39, 40; Pomeau, ed., *Candide*, 190-91, 193; Magnússon, tr., *Paradise Reclaimed*, 145-46, Laxness, *Paradísarheimt*, 168.

27. Adams, tr., *Candide*, 39; Pomeau, ed., *Candide*, 191.

28. Magnússon, tr., *Paradise Reclaimed*, 141-42; Laxness, *Paradísarheimt*, 163.

29. Adams, tr., *Candide*, 37-38; Pomeau, ed., *Candide*, 189.

30. Magnússon, tr., *Paradise Reclaimed*, 153; Laxness, *Paradísarheimt*, 177.

31. Adams, tr., *Candide*, 37; Pomeau, ed., *Candide*, 188; Magnússon, tr., *Paradise Reclaimed*, 153; Laxness, *Paradísarheimt*, 177.

32. Adams, tr., *Candide*, 38; Pomeau, ed., *Candide*, 189.

33. Adams, tr., *Candide*, 35-36; Pomeau, ed., *Candide*, 185; Magnússon, tr., *Paradise Reclaimed*, 159; Laxness, *Paradísarheimt*, 185.

34. Adams, tr., *Candide*, 35; Pomeau, ed., *Candide*, 183.

35. Magnússon, tr., *Paradise Reclaimed*, 139; Laxness, *Paradísarheimt*, 160.

36. Magnússon, tr., *Paradise Reclaimed*, 60; Laxness, *Paradísarheimt*, 64.

37. Magnússon, tr., *Paradise Reclaimed*, 30; Laxness, *Paradísarheimt*, 33.

38. Magnússon, tr., *Paradise Reclaimed*, 250; Laxness, *Paradísarheimt*, 296.

39. Magnússon, tr., *Paradise Reclaimed*, 151; Laxness, *Paradísarheimt*, 175.

40. Adams, tr., *Candide*, 40; Pomeau, ed., *Candide*, 192.

41. Magnússon, tr., *Paradise Reclaimed*, 148; Laxness, *Paradísarheimt*, 171-73.

42. Magnússon, tr., *Paradise Reclaimed*, 150; Laxness, *Paradísarheimt*, 173.

43. Bottiglia, "Voltaire's *Candide*," 120.

44. Ibid., 116.

45. Ludwig W. Kahn, "Voltaire's 'Candide' and the Problem of Secularization," *Publications of the Modern Language Association of America* 67 (1952): 888. For the continuing debate on the meaning and relationship of Eldorado and the garden, see (in addition to the studies of Bottiglia and Kahn) Donna I. Dalnekoff, "The Meaning of Eldorado: Utopia and Satire in *Candide*," *Studies on Voltaire and the Eighteenth Century* 127 (1974): 41-59; Rita Falke, "Eldorado: Le meilleur des mondes possibles," *Studies on Voltaire and the Eighteenth Century* 2 (1956): 25-41; Dennis Fletcher, "Candide and the Theme of the Happy Husbandman," *Studies on Voltaire and the Eighteenth Century* 161 (1976): 137-47; Jean Goldzink, "Roman et idéologie dans *Candide*: Le jardin," *La Pensée* 155 (1971): 78-91; Patrick Henry, "Sacred and Profane Gardens in *Candide*," *Studies on Voltaire and the Eighteenth Century* 176 (1979): 133-52; Paul Ilie, "The Voices in Candide's Garden 1755-1759: A Methodology for Voltaire's Correspondence," *Studies on Voltaire and the Eighteenth Century* 148 (1976): 37-113; Manfred Kusch, "The River and the Garden: Basic Spatial Models in *Candide* and *La nouvelle Héloise*," *Eighteenth Century Studies* 12 (1978-79): 1-15; Norman L. Torrey, "Candide's Garden and the Lord's Vineyard," *Studies on Voltaire and the Eighteenth Century* 27 (1963): 1657-66; and Roy S. Wolper, "Candide, Gull in the Garden?" *Eighteenth Century Studies* 3 (1969-70): 265-77.

46. Magnússon, tr., *Paradise Reclaimed*, 142; Laxness, *Paradísarheimt*, 163.

47. Magnússon, tr., *Paradise Reclaimed*, 164; Laxness, *Paradísarheimt*, 191.

48. Magnússon, tr., *Paradise Reclaimed*, 170; Laxness, *Paradísarheimt*, 198.

49. Magnússon, tr., *Paradise Reclaimed*, 162; Laxness, *Paradísarheimt*, 189.

50. William Mulder, *Homeward to Zion: The Mormon Migration from Scandinavia* (Minneapolis: University of Minnesota Press, 1957), 96-98.

51. I have discussed Laxness's Mormon interests at length in "Halldór Laxness, the Mormons and the Promised Land," *Dialogue* 11/2 (1978): 25-37 (which also appears in Icelandic as "Halldór Laxness, Mormónarnir, og fyrirheitna Landid," tr. Jóhann S. Hannesson and Halldór Laxness, *Lesbók Morgunbladsins*, 5 May 1979, 1-5, 14-15). This study includes quotations from Laxness's Mormon articles, newspaper interviews, and correspondence with Mormons, and is based in part on my interview with him in 1972.

52. See, for example, her "The First Icelandic Settlement in America" in Kate B. Carter, *Our Pioneer Heritage* (Salt Lake City: Daughters of the Utah Pioneers/Utah State Historical Society, 1964), 7:477-556.

53. Thórdur Didriksson, *Advörunar og sannleiksraust* (Copenhagen: Vilhelmsen, 1879).

54. Nels Bourkersson, *Tre år i Mormonlandet: Berättelser efter egna iakttagelser* (Malmö: Cronholm, 1867), 9. Bourkersson's book is discussed in detail by Richard G. Ellsworth, "The Dilemma of a Pernicious Zion," *BYU Studies* 8/4 (1968): 407-22. See also Mulder, *Homeward to Zion*, 63, 98, 183, 255.

55. Adams, tr., *Candide*, 77; Pomeau, ed., *Candide*, 260.

56. Magnússon, tr., *Paradise Reclaimed*, 254; Laxness, *Paradísarheimt*, 300-301.

57. Ilie, "The Voices in Candide's Garden, 1755-1759," 112-13.

58. Wolper, "Candide, Gull in the Garden?" 265-77.

59. Ilie, "The Voices in Candide's Garden, 1755-1759," 87.

60. Hallberg, "Laxness, konstnärskapet, ideologierna," 96.

61. Erik Sønderholm, *Kongsfærd og bonderejse: En islandsk bonde i København 1876*, Politikens Historiske Bibliotek (Copenhagen: Politiken, 1974), 206-7.

62. Halldór Laxness, as interviewed in *Morgunbladid* (Reykjavík) 23 July 1960, 9; cf. Tate, "Halldór Laxness, the Mormons and the Promised Land," 33-34.

63. Laxness, "Origins," 6-7.

64. Magnússon, tr., *Paradise Reclaimed*, 49; Laxness, *Paradísarheimt*, 55.

65. Magnússon, tr., *Paradise Reclaimed*, 138; Laxness, *Paradísarheimt*, 159.

66. Magnússon, tr., *Paradise Reclaimed*, 148; Laxness, *Paradísarheimt*, 171.

67. Magnússon, tr., *Paradise Reclaimed*, 148; Laxness, *Paradísarheimt*, 171.

Index of Passages

Subject Index